SUMMARY OF FORTRAN 77 STATEMENTS AND FUNCTIONS
USED IN THIS TEXT

STATEMENT	DESCRIPTION (TEXT PAGE)	EXE-CUT-ABLE?	EXAMPLES
END	Defines end of program unit; in main program, terminates execution; in subprogram, returns execution to calling program (35)	Yes	END
END IF	Corresponds to particular block IF statement; its execution has no effect (141)	Yes	END IF
ENDFILE	Places endfile record on sequential-access file (409)	Yes	ENDFILE(UNIT = 10) ENDFILE 10
EQUIVALENCE	Specifies sharing of storage locations by two or more entities in same program unit (351)	No	EQUIVALENCE(A,B,C),(D,ARRAY(5))
FORMAT	Provides format specification (439, 466, 482)	No	90 FORMAT('1',T9,'NAMES'/('0',A20)) 92 FORMAT(2I5,F10.2,E15.6,20X,D20.10)
FUNCTION	Defines beginning of function subprogram (356)	No	FUNCTION MINI(M,N,G) . . . END
GO TO	Transfers control to labeled statement unconditionally, when form is that of *unconditional* GO TO statement (184)	Yes	GO TO 50
GO TO	Transfers control to one of several labeled statements conditional upon value in integer expression, when form is that of *computed* GO TO statement; used to set up CASE structure (188)	Yes	GO TO (100,200,300,400)CODE
IF	Tests logical expression and executes statement to right if result is true, when form is that of *logical* IF statement (186)	Yes	IF (A .GT. B)MAX = A IF (A .LE. B)MAX = B

IF	Tests logical expression and defines IF-block in IF-THEN and IF-THEN-ELSE decision structures, when form is that of *block* IF statement (141)	Yes	IF (A .GT. B) THEN
			  MAX = A
			ELSE
			  MAX = B
			END IF

Applied
FORTRAN 77
featuring
Structured Programming

ROY AGELOFF
University of Rhode Island

RICHARD MOJENA
University of Rhode Island

WADSWORTH PUBLISHING COMPANY
Belmont, California
A division of Wadsworth, Inc.

ISBN 0-534-00961-1

Library of Congress Cataloging in Publication Data

Ageloff, Roy, 1943–
  Applied FORTRAN 77.

  Includes index.
  1. FORTRAN (Computer program language)
2. Structured programming. I. Mojena, Richard,
joint author. II. Title.
QA76.73.F25A33   001.64′24   80-27418
ISBN 0-534-00961-1

Editorial production services by Cobb/Dunlop Publisher Services, Inc.

About the Cover: Cover shows Doppler radar, the latest method for detecting storms in early stages. Colors represent varying wind velocities. Photograph courtesy Severe Storms Laboratory, NOAA, Norman, Oklahoma.

Printed in the United States of America

6 7 8 9 10——85 84 83

To Our Parents

Preface

This textbook is designed for a first course in FORTRAN programming. No prerequisites are required other than a willingness to develop problem-solving skills.

The combination of features described below distinguishes this book from others in the field.

FORTRAN 77 implementation.   FORTRAN 77 is the basis of the FORTRAN material, as established by the document labeled ANSI X3.9-1978. By FORTRAN 77 we mean "full" FORTRAN 77 rather than "subset" FORTRAN 77. Statements and functions used in this book are summarized and illustrated inside the front and back covers.

Evolutionary design.   Following a comprehensive overview of the field in Chapter 1, coverage of programming proceeds from simple to difficult, with the student writing complete programs by the end of Chapter 2 and running programs by the end of Chapter 3.

By design, the pace of Chapters 2–4 builds slowly, to encourage confidence and to develop a sound foundation. This approach necessarily discards the complete treatment of a topic in one place. For example, loop structures are first overviewed in Chapter 4, and a DO-loop implementation is illustrated. General DO-WHILE, DO-UNTIL, and Last-Record-Check loops, however, are not implemented until Chapter 6.

Structured programming.   The structured programming philosophy is presented early in Chapter 4, elaborated upon in Chapters 4–6, and adhered to throughout the book.

Chapter 4 implements the loop structure through DO/CONTINUE statements. The early implementation of the loop structure based on DO/CONTINUE statements has several advantages: it allows the early introduction of realistic problems and the power of repetitive processing; it's "cleaner" than the IF/GO TO approach; and it minimizes breadth of coverage (thereby student confusion) in one chapter by postponing the introduction of IF-type statements.

Program design and style.   Good program design and style are emphasized throughout the book. For example, in Chapter 2 we present a four-step program-writing procedure that includes flowcharts and pseudocode. Other style considerations include documentation (from Chapter 3 on), indentation (from Chapter 4 on), structured programming (Chapters 4–11), the "proper" use of GO TO statements (Chapter 6), top-down design (Module E), and modular programming (Module F).

Additionally, Module G summarizes a number of issues in good program design, including the interrelationships among structured, top-down, and modular programming; the readability versus efficiency tradeoff; the design of general versus specific programs; the use of documentation aids; and considerations regarding debugging, transportability, reliability, and management practices.

Use of Modules. We have attempted to design flexibility into the use of this book by placing certain topics in modules at the book's end. Intrinsic functions (Module A) are first used in Chapter 2; I/O with formats (Modules B–D) is not used specifically until Chapter 7, but can be assigned at any time after Chapter 4; top-down design, including stepwise refinement (Module E), can be assigned either during or after Chapter 5; modular programming (Module F) can be assigned at the end of Chapter 9; and Module G (On Designing Better Programs) can be assigned any time after Chapter 6.

Emphasis on meaningful applications. The word "applied" in the title of the book is used to suggest our emphasis throughout on meaningful applications of the computer. Applications include those relating to *information processing* and those relating to *mathematical modeling*. They are described in a wide variety of contexts, including areas in business, economics, mathematics, statistics, and the sciences, as well as emerging areas in the public sector (such as health care delivery, emergency response systems, and allocation of public resources).

Table A summarizes and references the applications described in the book through examples and exercises. This table clearly illustrates our philosophy that problems should be presented in an *evolutionary* context. As new material is learned, many examples and exercises improve upon previous versions of the same problem. This approach not only is pedagogically sound but also is consistent with (but not identical to) the evolutionary nature of program design in the "real world."

Extensive examples and exercises. The learning of FORTRAN is greatly facilitated by numerous and carefully designed examples and exercises. More than 60 *complete* programs are illustrated in this book; entirely new programs are accompanied by flowcharts and/or pseudocode. Exercises are found both within chapters (Follow-up Exercises) and at the end of chapters (Additional Exercises). The book has 493 exercises, many with multiple parts. The chapters on programming (Chapters 2–11) average better than 40 exercises per chapter.

Follow-up exercises serve to reinforce, integrate, and extend preceding material. This feature gives the book a "programmed learning" flavor without the regimentation of such an approach. Additionally, we have found that such exercises create an excellent basis for planning many classroom lectures. *Answers to selected follow-up exercises are provided at the back of the textbook.* Solutions to those follow-up exercises identified by either a single or double asterisk are given in the *Instructor's Manual.*

The chapter-end exercises offer opportunities for review and the development of new programming problems. All programming problems include test data. Examples

TABLE A   Page References for Applications Programs

Information Processing

student billing 23, 56, 60, 71, 110, 117, 437, 462
form letter 136, 393
sales bonus 143, 153, 166, 186, 203, 206
finding minimum value 151
postal zone fees 155, 161
property tax assessment 176, 276
personnel benefits budget 178
computerized matching—a file search 179, 316, 422
credit billing 180, 422
traffic court fines 191
mailing list 217, 316, 422
telephone company billing 219
checking account report 220
analysis of bank deposits 229
direct access to array element—SAT scores 257
table look-up: life insurance premium 260
sorting 268

crime data summary 276, 316
revenue sharing 277, 423
exam grading 280
stock portfolio valuation 281
income tax 304
projected enrollments 311
interactive airline reservation system 316, 423
personnel salary budget 319
questionnaire analysis 320
electric bill 361, 424
text editing 374, 381, 388, 398
text analysis 386, 394, 395
text processing 395
cryptography 396, 397
personnel file 411, 414
blood bank inventory control system 418, 423
payroll 424
class grades 426
Government Printing Office orders 496

Mathematical Modeling

bank savings 61, 80, 112, 137
area 64, 98, 133
microeconomics 64, 98, 134
temperature conversion 64, 98, 133
blood bank inventory 65, 98, 135
forecasting population growth 65, 98, 216
automobile financing 65, 98, 135
mean exam scores 123, 126, 127
exponential CDF 136
retirement contribution 138
optimal cost per credit 139
factorials 177
quadratic roots 178
police car replacement 182
inflation curse 196, 200
root search algorithm 208

Poisson probability function 218
crew selection—a combination problem 222, 337
Newton's approximation method 223
numerical integration 225
polynomial plot 265
support facility for oil drilling platforms 276
sales forecasts 279
vector representation of a matrix 303
Poisson-distributed electronic failures 318
matrix multiplication 322
combinations 325, 353
mean of one-dimensional array 338
statistical analyses 363
automobile rental decision 508

and exercises are generally framed in a "real world" context that will interest and motivate the student. Exercises are ordered from least difficult to most difficult. The more difficult exercises are designed to challenge the good student, and are identified by a double asterisk. The *Instructor's Manual* gives answers to all chapter-end exercises.

Common errors.   The necessary process of debugging is time consuming, frustrating, and difficult to master by beginning programmers. In our experience, students commit certain programming errors more commonly than others. Accordingly, the book features sections on debugging procedures and common errors at the end of *each* programming chapter, beginning with Chapter 3 and ending with Chapter 11.

I/O with formats.   Our treatment of I/O with formats is carefully designed to give instructors as much flexibility as possible regarding the choice of list-directed I/O versus format-directed I/O. The topic (I/O with formats) is set off in modules (B–D), which can be assigned as early as the end of Chapter 4. Within chapters, the use of format specifications is postponed until Chapter 7; thereafter the use of format specifications is either clearly labeled (and easily skipped) or incidental to the material.

In effect, the book is essentially independent of I/O with formats, but is designed to facilitate timing and integration of the topic. Our own preference is to delay its introduction until after Chapter 6, to provide ample time first for algorithmic design.

Batch and time sharing.   Since the computer systems at institutions of higher education vary, we illustrate both batch and time-sharing approaches to computing. Time sharing is given more than a superficial treatment in keeping with its increased use in universities, governmental agencies, and companies.

To accommodate both batch and time-sharing users, most programs and discussions of FORTRAN are independent of processing environments. For example, we consciously use the term input record instead of card.

Where appropriate (Chapters 3 and 11) we design programs for either batch or time-sharing environments. This allows us to describe features of each system. In general, however, the book can be used without bias by either batch or time-sharing users. Better yet, as in our own treatment of programming, it can be used by courses that require exposure to both processing environments. In particular we favor the growing use of *batch interface*.

A book on programming and problem solving, not a programming manual.   We believe that a FORTRAN course should be much more than just a course that teaches the FORTRAN language. It should teach the process of programming as a creative activity, from conceptualization of the problem to implementation of the computer program.

In keeping with this belief, we sacrifice some scope in the FORTRAN language by devoting more space to pedagogy through patient explanations and extensive examples and exercises. Additionally, we emphasize the development of problem solving by formalizing the writing of programs through a four-step procedure first introduced in Chapter 2, which subsequently is integrated with top-down design and modular programming.

A programming course also should broaden a student's perspective. Accordingly, Chapter 1 presents a more thorough overview of the field than does the typical introductory chapter, and Module G summarizes style issues of keen topical interest.

ACKNOWLEDGMENTS

We wish to express our deep appreciation to many who have contributed to this project: to Jon Thompson, our editor, for unflagging encouragement, support, and expert advice; to Jerry Holloway of Wadsworth and Lila Gardner of Cobb/Dunlop for editorial/production magic and liaison par excellence; to Richard R. Weeks, Dean, University of Rhode Island, for administrative support; to David Wishart, CLUSTAN, and A. Jack Cole, Computational Science Department, University of St. Andrews, Scotland, for their generous and kind support; to the Computer Laboratories at the University of Rhode Island and the University of St. Andrews, for obvious reasons; to our reviewers, Nell Dale, University of Texas, Austin, Donald R. Chand, Georgia State University, Mark Luker, University of Minnesota, Duluth, Dale Grosvenor, Iowa State University, Kenneth Joy, Northern Michigan University, Thomas J. Murray, University of Missouri, St. Louis, and Donald Woods, Texas A & M University who provided invaluable corrections and suggestions for manuscript revisions; to Fred Wild, Andrew Ehrlich, and Susan Rose for "grunt" work on end-of-chapter solutions; to Fran Mojena and Marjorie Nield for their skill, patience, and steadiness in typing the manuscript; to our students, who always teach us something about teaching; and to our immediate families, who are wondering when it will all end.

January, 1981   ROY AGELOFF
Kingston, Rhode Island   RICHARD MOJENA

Contents

CHAPTER 1

Orientation

The electronic computer is one of humankind's foremost technological inventions; for good or for bad, its presence affects each of us, and its future holds even more potential to affect our lives.

This chapter is an orientation to the course you are about to take. We first define the computer and discuss its impact. Thereafter we provide a relatively complete, nontechnical overview of what makes up a computer system and a preview of how to communicate with the computer. Finally, we outline how you will benefit from this course.

If you are warm-blooded and living in the twentieth century, then we suspect that you are curious about the computer. By the time this course is over we hope that we (together with your instructor) will have helped you translate that curiosity into a continuing, productive, and rewarding experience.

1.1
WHAT IS A COMPUTER?

A **computer** can be defined most generally as *a device which is capable of manipulating data to achieve some task.* Given this definition, adding machines, cash registers, gasoline pumps, and electronic calculators all qualify as simple computers. The machine we usually think of as a computer, however, can be identified by four significant characteristics.

1. It's electronic.
2. It's fast.
3. It can store large amounts of data.
4. It can execute stored instructions.

Characteristics of Electronic Computers

The great speed of today's electronic computers is a direct result of miniaturization in solid-state electronics. To give you a rough idea of the speed capabilities of large electronic computers, consider the following estimates. One minute of computer time is equivalent to approximately 6700 hours of skilled labor by a person using a calculator.

1

In other words, a person using a calculator would take one hour to accomplish what a computer can accomplish in less than one hundredth of a second. In fact, the electronic transfers within computers are so fast that computer designers use a basic unit of time equal to one billionth of a second (called a *nanosecond*)—quite a feat when you consider that the basic unit of time for us mortals is one second.

Another significant characteristic of electronic computers is their capacity to store large amounts of data and instructions for later recall. In other words, much like the human brain, the computer has "memory." For example, computers at most universities can store several million characters of data in primary storage and hundreds of millions of characters in secondary storage.

Finally, an electronic computer is differentiated from most other computing devices by its ability to store instructions in memory. By this we mean that the computer can execute a set of instructions without interference from human beings. This characteristic makes the computer efficient: it can carry on automatically while we do something else. Of course, the computer cannot completely do without us, but more about that later.

Computer Classifications

To further narrow the definition of an electronic computer, we make the following distinctions: analog versus digital computers and special-purpose versus general-purpose computers.

The **analog computer** manipulates data representing continuous physical processes such as temperature, pressure, and voltage. The fuel injection system of an automobile, for example, deals with physical processes as it regulates the fuel/air ratio in the carburetor on the basis of engine speed, temperature, and pressure; the gasoline pump converts the flow of fuel into price (dollars and cents) and volume (gallons to the nearest tenth). Not surprisingly, therefore, analog computers are used primarily to control such processes. For example, analog computers now control the production of products such as steel and gasoline, provide on-board guidance for aircraft and spacecraft, regulate the peak energy demands of large office buildings or factories, and monitor the vital life signs of patients in critical condition.

As a strict computational device, however, the analog computer lacks the precision one needs with counting. Place yourself in the role of a computer that has the task of adding the numbers 1 and 2. Your props are a ruler, pencil, paper, and a jar of beads. You might proceed with your task as follows: First, you take one bead from the jar and place it on the paper. Next, you take two beads from the jar and place them on the paper. Finally, you count the number of beads you have on the paper. *Exactly* three, right? Now, be an analog computer. With pencil, paper, and ruler, draw a line 1 inch in length. Next, draw a 2-inch line at the end of the 1-inch line you drew earlier. Now measure the length of this overall line. Is your line exactly 3 inches long? Not really, only *approximately 3*—as the accuracy of your answer depends on the precision of the scale on the ruler, the steadiness of your hand, the acuteness of your eyesight, and the sharpness of your pencil point. When it comes to calculating, the counting approach based on beads is more accurate than the approach based on measurement.

You will be using the **digital computer**, which operates by counting digits. This type of computer manipulates data (numbers in our decimal system, letters in our alphabet, and special characters) by counting binary (two-state or 0–1) digits. **Hybrid computers,** which combine the features of digital and analog computers, have been designed for certain types of applications, such as the analysis of aircraft designs that are tested in wind tunnel experiments.

We have been classifying computers by how they process data, but we can also classify them according to their function. **Special-purpose computers** are designed to accomplish a single task, whereas **general-purpose computers** are designed to accept programs of instruction for carrying out different tasks. For example, one special-purpose computer has been designed strictly to do navigational calculations for ships and aircraft. The instructions for carrying out this task are built into the electronic circuitry of the machine so that the navigator simply keys in data and receives the answer. Other special-purpose computers include those used in color television sets to improve color reception; those used in PBX (Private Branch Exchange) telephones to perform various functions, such as automatic placement of a call at a preset time and simplified dialing of frequently used telephone numbers; and those used in automobiles to calculate such items as "miles of fuel left" and "time of destination," and to monitor and read out instantaneously the status of oil level, gasoline level, engine temperature, brake-lining wear, and other operating conditions.

In contrast, a general-purpose computer used by a corporation might accomplish tasks relating to the preparation of payrolls and production schedules and the analyses of financial, marketing, and engineering data all in one day. Similarly, the academic computer you are about to use might run a management simulation one minute and analyze the results of a psychology experiment the next minute, or it might even accomplish both of these tasks (and more) concurrently.

In general, compared with the special-purpose computer, the general-purpose computer has the flexibility of satisfying the needs of a variety of users, but at the expense of speed and economy. In this textbook, we focus strictly on the *electronic, digital, general-purpose computer.*

1.2
IMPACT OF THE COMPUTER

Since the first sale of an electronic computer by Remington Rand in 1951, the computer industry has grown to such an extent that by the mid-1970s it had generated over $75 billion in sales and provided at least 700,000 jobs. The computer has revolutionized the operations of many governmental agencies, private enterprises, and public institutions, and many experts agree that the computer industry is a "young child," if not still an "infant." In this section we present a brief historical sketch of the development of the computer, provide you with a sample of computer applications, and end with an assessment of the computer's impact.

Historical Sketch

Many conceptions and inventions dating back to the early nineteenth century were necessary precedents to the development of the computer. The first digital general-purpose computer was completed in 1944 when Howard Aiken at Harvard University designed the **Mark I** to generate mathematical tables. Unlike electronic computers, the Mark I was a mechanical computer that operated by a system of telephone relays, mechanized wheels, and tabulating equipment. By current standards, it was *very* large, *very* unreliable, *very* slow, and *very* limited in its scope of applications. In 1946 the team of J. W. Mauchly and J. P. Eckert, Jr., from the University of Pennsylvania, completed the first *electronic* computer. This computer was named **ENIAC,** for the intimidating title <u>E</u>lectronic <u>N</u>umerical <u>I</u>ntegrator <u>A</u>nd <u>C</u>alculator. Essentially, ENIAC was an electronic version of Mark I, in which vacuum tubes replaced the function of telephone relays; this replacement resulted in an increase of computing speed by a factor of nearly 200. Commissioned by the U.S. Army, it did an incomparable job (for the times) of generating artillery trajectory tables, but weighed 30 tons, and filled a 150-square-meter room.

UNIVAC I (<u>U</u>niversal <u>A</u>utomatic <u>C</u>omputer), developed by Remington (now Sperry) Rand in 1951, was the first commercial computer. Unlike its predecessors, it computed using binary arithmetic and allowed the storage of instructions in internal computer memory. During this **first-generation** period computers were developed by RCA, Philco, GE, Burroughs, Honeywell, NCR, and IBM. The first computer to achieve dominance in the industry was the IBM 650, which became the commercial leader during the period 1954–1959. These first-generation machines used vacuum tubes, required air conditioning, had relatively small amounts of internal memory, and were slow by today's standards.

Subsequent generations of computers resulted in dramatic reductions in *size* and relative *cost* and increases in *speed, reliability,* and the capacity for *storage.* **Second-generation** computers during the period 1959–1965 replaced the vacuum tubes of the first-generation computers with transistors. The most widely used second-generation computers were the IBM 1620, the IBM 1401, and the IBM 7094.

The **third-generation** computers (1965–1970) that followed made use of the emerging field of microelectronics (miniaturized circuits), which increased the packing densities of transistorized circuits by a factor of 100. The third-generation computers were more reliable, faster, and more sophisticated than earlier computers. They also had the ability to handle several programs concurrently (multiprogramming), resulting in a more efficient use of the computer. The most prominent family of computers in this generation was the IBM System/360.

During the 1970s, a series of refinements and improvements to third-generation machines were marketed. These computers utilized large-scale integrated circuitry (LSI) and other microminiaturization features, resulting in further reductions in size and power requirements as compared with earlier computers.

Another significant development in the 1970s was the use of small (in physical size and memory capacity), inexpensive, yet powerful computers referred to as **minicomputers** and **microcomputers.** The use of minicomputers is common in small to medium companies, colleges, hospitals, governmental agencies, and other organizations. In the past decade many organizations have decentralized their computer processing activities by implementing what is called **distributed processing,** whereby a network of computers links together geographically remote locations. A typical configuration is a minicomputer at each location for either local processing tasks or communication to a large central computer for major processing tasks.

Microcomputers, which are smaller than minicomputers, currently are marketed by consumer retail outlets such as Radio Shack. Today's desk-top microcomputers are

20 times faster, have larger memory, are thousands of times more reliable, consume the power of a light bulb rather than a locomotive, occupy one 30,000th of the volume and cost one 10,000th ($500 versus $5 million) as much as the massive first-generation machines that filled an entire room. Their use in small organizations and homes is expected to increase dramatically in the next decade.

Applications

The computer represents a revolutionary technological tool for extending our applied capabilities. The diversity of the sample applications listed in Table 1.1 should give you

---

TABLE 1.1   Sample Applications of the Computer

Information Processing

Preparation of payroll and billings
Maintenance of inventory information
Maintenance of customer accounts
Technical processing of reference information by media and public libraries
Calculation of income taxes by the IRS
Maintenance of student records by universities
Maintenance of flight and reservation information by airlines
Cataloguing of blood supplies by regional blood banks
Maintenance of checking accounts by banks
Editing and reproduction of typed manuscripts
Maintenance of criminal records by the FBI
Maintenance of property tax records by a municipality
Budgeting by organizations and individuals
Recording of monetary distributions by state and federal welfare agencies

Mathematical Modeling

Statistical analyses of census data, biological data, engineering data, etc.
Production scheduling and inventory control
Medical diagnosis
Orbital analysis for satellites
Management of financial portfolios
Location of fire stations in an urban area
Simulation of economic decay in a city
Dietary meal planning in institutions
Statistical forecasting
Educational planning and school bus scheduling
Design of airway and highway traffic systems
Chemical analysis
Design of solar energy systems
Planning, scheduling, and controlling of complex projects (such as construction of a submarine, office building, or sports stadium)

an idea of the increasing influence of computers. Users of the computer include all facets of our society: individuals, private organizations such as industrial companies and banks, and public institutions such as hospitals, universities, and governmental agencies.

Basic information processing such as updating customer accounts, preparing payrolls, and generating status reports on personnel, sales, production, and inventories was a common early use of the computer. Although these automated approaches were more effective than hours of "hand-crunching" effort by an "army" of clerks, they failed to integrate adequately the sources and uses of information in complex organizations. Today, users are calling for the design and implementation of *management information systems (MIS)* that can integrate and aggregate timely information for use by management in their decision-making activities.

Engineers, scientists, and mathematicians have used computers since their introduction for extensive mathematical calculations. In recent years, managers and social scientists have increasingly emphasized mathematical modeling in their decision-making activities. For example, disciplines such as *operations research* and *management science* develop and apply quantitative techniques (mathematics, probability, statistics) to help solve problems faced by managers of public and private organizations.

The second part of Table 1.1 gives you an idea of the types of problems that lend themselves to mathematical modeling. In many cases the data required for these quantitative approaches to decision making are best provided by an MIS, which effectively integrates our two broad classes of applications.

Inevitably, the following question is asked: Can computers think? The computer cannot think in the usual sense, for it can accomplish only what people instruct it to accomplish through written programs of instruction. It is best at solving problems that are well structured—that is, problems whose solutions can be determined on a step-by-step basis that is quite explicit. Problems that require ill-defined or spontaneous actions to cope with complex or entirely new situations do not lend themselves as well to computer solution. For example, an executive can reorganize a company better than a computer can; a composer writes music better than does a computer; a chess master plays better chess than a computer does; and an inventor is more capable of inventing than is a computer.

As scientists come to understand better the thinking processes behind creativity, adaptation, and judgment, programs of instruction for solving ill-structured problems will improve. This area of research, called *artificial intelligence,* has made some progress as computers have been programmed to compose music, play chess, prove theorems, and solve puzzles. Success, however, has been limited, and future progress in this area is uncertain.

Assessment

Any task that can be performed by a general-purpose digital computer can also be performed by a human being (given enough time). Of course, when it comes to the amount of data that can be stored and the speed with which these data can be manipulated, the computer is in a class by itself. In effect, therefore, the computer magnifies our own capacities. This results in both advantages and disadvantages, which we now summarize.

ADVANTAGES

1. *Power of analysis and technological advancement.* The computer can accomplish massive amounts of scientific calculation in a short span of time and can control complex processes such as steel making, automatic guidance of spacecraft, and air–ground traffic control.
2. *Career opportunities.* The computer upgrades the skill requirements of jobs and creates new career opportunities both for labor and management; the current (and projected) supply of skilled people in this area is far short of demand.
3. *Information needs.* As the society becomes more complex (and the individuals become more numerous), the computer provides a means to satisfy society's information needs.
4. *Level of service.* The computer provides faster and better quality service to members of society; examples include airline reservation systems, health care delivery systems, bank accounts, and preregistration of classes for university students. To illustrate the scale of service that the computer makes possible, consider this:

> The U.S. Department of Health and Human Services provides round-the-clock services that go directly to 115 million Americans and indirectly touch just about everybody in the nation. It is an empire, moreover, of 1,125,000 bureaucrats augmented by computers. Without its electronic marvels, [its] accomplishments would be unthinkable. While most of the departments programs are administered from its huge Washington headquarters, Social Security data are processed in a building outside Baltimore by the most extensive computer system in the world. Every day an average of 20,000 claims are filed; every night the complete Social Security wage file, contained on 220,000 reels of tape, is run through the computers to provide information on the claimants. Next day off go the forms that bring life-sustaining checks to the nation's aged and disabled.[1]

5. *Cost savings to society.* The computer results in a more efficient delivery of services when used in applications where it is more productive than alternative approaches.

DISADVANTAGES

1. *Mistakes.* A survey of the public showed that 34 percent of those surveyed have had a problem because of the computer,[2] with billing problems accounting for the majority of reported mistakes insofar as the public is concerned. In recent years, however, channels of communication for correcting errors have been improved; *The source of such mistakes is typically traced to computer personnel, rather than to the computer equipment.*
2. *Legalities.* Invasion of privacy and safeguards to programs of instruction and data have become major issues of national concern. The increasing centralization of files that contain information about individuals requires the legal protection of accuracy and confidentiality. Moreover, computer crime has been one of the fastest growing categories of crime; examples of such crimes include the $2 billion Equity Funding

---

[1] "The Beneficient Monster," *Time Magazine*, June 12, 1978, p. 24.
[2] "A National Survey of the Public's Attitude Toward Computers," available from *Time Magazine*, Rockefeller Center, New York, NY.

Corporation swindle of the early 1970s, bank embezzlements that average $500,000 per swindle, and the theft of computer data tapes for ransom.[3]

3. *Regulatory problems.* Federal and state agencies have an increasing problem in regulatory issues relating to computer product pricing policies, protection of copyrights and patents, and quality of data transmission over telephone lines.

4. *Job displacement.* The creation of new jobs by the computer has resulted in the displacement of old jobs, a result that is typical of all new technologies (automobiles, airplanes, electricity, and so on); inevitably this causes psychological trauma, social displacement, and economic deprivation for the affected segment of the population.

5. *Dependence.* Our increasing dependence on the computer raises philosophical and practical issues regarding security—for example, backup systems are needed in airport traffic control should the main computer become disabled; and duplicate copies of critical data files should be maintained in case the original files are destroyed.

On balance, the positive aspects of the computer far outweigh its negative aspects. As with all new technologies, however, those in positions of responsibility must strive toward correcting existing problems and, more important, toward preventing potential problems.

1.3
ORGANIZATION OF A COMPUTER

Figure 1.1 should give you a "feel" for the makeup of a digital general-purpose computer. As you can see, six components have been identified by the nature of their functions. But before describing each of these components, we define two terms that we use often.

An **instruction** represents a specific task for the computer to accomplish. For example, the following represents three instructions.

1. Read and store the name of a student and the grades received for the school term.
2. Calculate and store the grade point average.
3. Print the student's name and grade point average.

Data represent facts or observations that the computer is to input, manipulate, and/or output. In the above example, the student's name, grades, and grade point average all represent data.

As you read through the remainder of this section you might find it useful to look frequently at Figures 1.1 and 1.2. The first illustration relates components functionally, and the second shows specific components.

Input Units

The input function of the computer brings data and instructions from the "outside world" to the computer's memory. To accomplish this transfer process the data and

[3] See, for example, Don Parker, *Crime by Computer*, New York: Scribner's, 1976.

FIGURE 1.1   *Functional Organization of a Digital General-Purpose Computer*

instructions must be converted into a "machine-readable" input medium. The more commonly used **input media** are punched cards, magnetic tapes, magnetic disks, punched paper tape, optical characters, and magnetic ink characters.

These media require **data preparation devices** to convert data from source documents (bills, invoices) to the desired medium. For example, the *keypunch machine* (Figure 1.2B) is a data preparation device for converting data on source documents to punched cards; a *key-to-tape machine* transfers data from source documents to magnetic tapes.

Data, once in machine-readable form, are transferred to the computer through an **input unit.** This device "reads" the coded data on the input medium and converts them into electric impulses, which are transferred to the memory unit of the computer. For example, the holes in a punched card are sensed by a *punched card reader* (Figure 1.2E) and converted to appropriate electric signals, which are submitted to the computer's memory for storage.

Table 1.2 lists some input units which are used with specific input media.

By the way, MICR units are used by banks to process checks, and OCR units are widely used by universities for processing student records and grading exams.

FIGURE 1.2A   Functional Components of a Computer System (IBM 370). Courtesy of IBM.

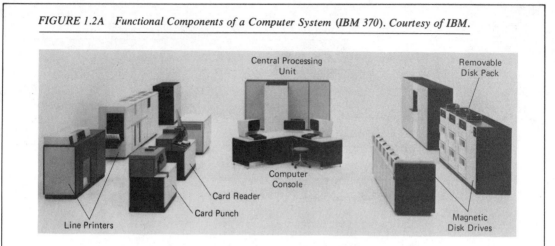

FIGURE 1.2B   IBM 059 Keypunch Machine. Courtesy of IBM.

FIGURE 1.2C   NCR 798-401 Video (CRT) Terminal. Courtesy of NCR.

FIGURE 1.2D   Xerox 1760 Typewriter Terminal. Courtesy of Xerox Corporation.

FIGURE 1.2E   IBM 3505 Card Reader Unit. Courtesy of IBM.

FIGURE 1.2F   IBM 3420 Magnetic Tape Drive. Courtesy of IBM.

FIGURE 1.2G   IBM 3211 Line Printer. Courtesy of IBM.

FIGURE 1.2H   An Integrated Circuit. Courtesy of IBM.

FIGURE 1.2I   Radio Shack TRS-80 Microcomputer System. Courtesy of Tandy Corporation.

Video monitor

Power supply

Cassettes

Keyboard and CPU

Cassette recorder
(for processing secondary
storage on cassettes)

FIGURE 1.2J   HP 300 (left) and HP 3000 Series 33 Minicomputer Systems. Courtesy of Hewlett- Packard Corporation.

TABLE 1.2   *Input Units and Input Media*

MEDIUM	CORRESPONDING INPUT UNIT
Punched card	Punched card reader (Figure 1.2A,E)
Punched paper tape	Paper tape reader
Optical characters	Optical character reader (OCR)
Magnetic ink characters	Magnetic ink character reader (MICR)
Magnetic tape	Tape drive (Figure 1.2F)
Magnetic disk	Disk drive (Figure 1.2A)
Cassette	Cassette recorder (Figure 1.2I)

Data and instructions also may be entered into a computer through **online terminals** (Figure 1.2C,D). The terminals are connected directly to the computer (the meaning of online) by either cable or telephone lines. Terminals have a keyboard for entering data and instructions, and either a visual display (video) screen or teleprinter for output.

In general, a computer system will have more than one input unit. The mix of input units in any one computer system, however, will depend on factors such as cost, the amount of data to be processed, and the method by which data originate.

Central Processing Unit (CPU)

Input and output units are part of the computer system, but they are not generally considered the "computer"; rather they are *peripheral* to the computer. The **central processing unit** (CPU), consisting of primary memory, control unit, and arithmetic-logic unit, is what most professionals think of as *the* computer, as illustrated in Figures 1.1 and 1.2A.

The **primary (internal) memory** unit of the computer stores instructions and data. Sometimes this unit is called *core storage,* because in some computers primary memory is made up of thousands of "doughnut" shaped magnetic cores strung like beads on wire. More recent computer models use *semiconductor memory* where the basic memory component is the microelectronic (silicon) chip, two of which are illustrated in Figure 1.2H. These units are cheaper, faster, and more compact than core memory. Incidentally, in the early 1960s engineers could place eight transistors on a chip; by 1980 they could manage a quarter of a million.

Another recent type of primary memory is called *bubble memory*. This technology creates and manipulates tiny magnetic fields in a crystalline or semiconductor material. These fields appear as little black specks or bubbles under a microscope, hence the name "bubble" memory.

Regardless of the technology used to construct memory units, primary memory consists of storage locations that have numerical designations called addresses. Figure 1.3 represents a means of visualizing the storage locations of primary memory. Each storage location is assigned a number (**address**) that is used to reference the location whenever the item of data stored within that location (**contents**) is to be accessed. For

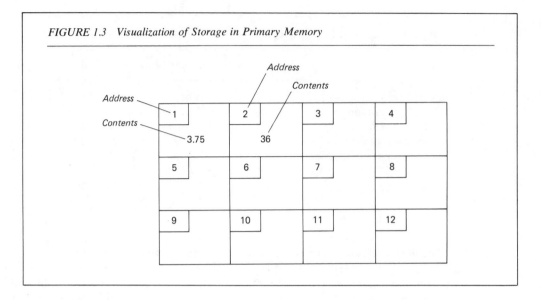

FIGURE 1.3   *Visualization of Storage in Primary Memory*

example, in Figure 1.3 an employee's rate of pay, $3.75, is stored in location 1 and the number of hours worked by that employee, 36, is stored in location 2.

The storage capacity of computer memory may be expressed in terms of the number of characters (bytes) that can be stored. By a **character** or **byte** we mean a letter, numerical digit, comma, plus sign, and so on. Because of the way memory units are constructed, storage capacity is usually expressed as some multiple of 1024, where the number 1024 is represented by the letter K. For example, recent microelectronic chips smaller than the tip of your finger have quoted memory capacities of 64K, which means that each chip can store 65,536 (that is, 64 × 1024) characters of data. Primary memory units usually range in storage capacity from 4K to 8 megabytes (or 8M), where a *megabyte* is one million bytes.

Data stored in primary storage are transferred to the **arithmetic-logic unit** whenever processing of data is required. Basic arithmetic operations such as addition, subtraction, multiplication, and division are performed within the arithmetic-logic unit. Moreover, logical operations such as comparison of values can be made. This capability permits the testing of various conditions, for example, whether an employee is entitled to receive overtime pay.

The **control unit** of a computer directs the operation of all other units associated with the computer, including peripheral devices (input/output units). The control unit obtains instructions from primary memory, interprets these instructions, and then transmits directions to the appropriate computer components. For example, suppose the instruction "read and store student's name and grades" is obtained from memory and interpreted by the control unit; the input unit would be directed to read these data into memory. The next instruction might be "calculate and store the grade point average"; the control unit would direct the memory unit to provide the arithmetic-logic unit with the data; then the arithmetic-logic unit would be directed to perform the calculations and to transmit the result to primary memory.

Interestingly, current technology can place an entire CPU on a single microelectronic chip that is less than one quarter of an inch square. These so-called **microprocessors** are as effective as small second-generation computers in terms of calculating and storage capabilities. In effect, a microprocessor that you can balance on the tip of your finger is equivalent to an early 1960's computer with a CPU as large as an office desk.

Output Units

The function of an **output unit** is exactly opposite that of an input unit; that is, an output unit receives data from the computer in the form of electronic signals and converts these data into a form that can be used by either humans or computers. The list below summarizes output units; of these, most likely you will use line printers and online terminals.

Line Printers.   If output of data is meant for human "consumption," then the line printer may be used. The *line printer* illustrated in Figure 1.2G is capable of printing 2000 lines per minute, each line having up to 132 characters. Picture yourself standing in front of such a printer. At 65 lines per page, you would see approximately 31 pages of printed output whiz by you in the time span of one minute.

Online Terminals.   If you are using either a video or teleprinter terminal as an input unit, then most likely you are using the terminal as an output unit. This is convenient, but compared with a line printer the speed of output is slow. Many computer systems, however, allow input through terminals and output on line printers, a feature which is advantageous if a particular job requires a high volume of printed output on paper.

Other Output Units.   Other output units include *magnetic tape drives,* which have both read (input) and write (output) capabilities using the magnetic tape medium (Figure 1.2F); *paper tape units,* some of which can be attached to remote, online terminals for the purpose of both input from and output to punched paper tape; *magnetic disk drives,* which allow both input from and output to magnetized disks that resemble a stack of LP phonograph records (Figure 1.2A); *card punch units,* which allow output onto punched cards (Figure 1.2A); and *voice response units,* which process verbal output. Voice response units have been used by telephone companies for many years. Without realizing it, you might have listened to the computer give you someone's new telephone number.

Secondary Storage

Secondary storage (**auxiliary** or **external storage**) is memory that is housed outside the central processing unit. Instructions and data not currently in use are kept on secondary storage and read into primary storage when needed. Magnetic tapes, disks, drums, and data cells are used for secondary storage. Compared with primary storage, secondary storage has greater capacity at less cost, but the amount of time it takes to access data is greater.

1.4
COMMUNICATING WITH THE COMPUTER

If we wish to solve a problem using a computer, we must communicate our instructions to the computer through a language. A *language* can be defined as patterns that have meaning. To a computer, these patterns are electronic; to a human being, they are symbolic (letter, numbers, punctuation). Unfortunately, no computer can understand any of the some 4000 languages practiced on Earth. It was necessary, therefore, to invent **computer languages** for the express purpose of person–machine communication. These can be classified into the three categories shown below. The designation **high-level** refers to a computer language that is far removed from the patterns "understood" directly by the computer. A **low-level** language, therefore, deals with patterns that are more nearly compatible with the electronic patterns of the machine.

1.	Procedure- and problem-oriented languages	High-level languages
2.	Assembly languages	⇑
3.	Machine languages	Low-level languages

Procedure- and Problem-Oriented Languages

Any language can be distinguished from any other language by its **syntax,** that is, by the rules for arranging a specified set of symbols into recognizable patterns. You will be communicating your instructions to the computer using a language called **FORTRAN.**[4] This is one of many so-called **procedure-oriented languages.** In general, these computer languages are easily understood by us humans (after some education, of course) and are relatively *machine-independent,* which means that they can be used across a wide variety of computers. FORTRAN is the most popular high-level language used for solving algebraic or scientific-type problems. By this we mean that FORTRAN is an excellent language for solving the types of problems that we described earlier as "mathematical modeling." Moreover, FORTRAN can be used for "information processing" applications as well, although COBOL (COmmon Business Oriented Language) is a more widely used language for such applications. BASIC (Beginners All-purpose Symbolic Instruction Code) is another popular procedure-oriented language that is commonly implemented on microcomputers.

Problem-oriented languages usually refer to a set of high-level languages which have been developed for solving certain special-purpose problems, such as the simulation of traffic flows in a city or the computer editing of newspaper articles.

A **computer program** *is a complete set of instructions written in a computer language for solving a specific problem.* Table 1.3 illustrates and describes a FORTRAN program having exactly five statements. **Statement** is another term for instruction. In the next chapter, we examine this program in detail (so don't be concerned about it, yet).

---

[4] This stands for FORmula TRANslation. It was originally developed by IBM in the 1950s.

TABLE 1.3   *FORTRAN Program for Calculating and Printing the Balance ($) Due a University Based on a Student's Tuition and Fees*

FORTRAN PROGRAM	HOW THE COMPUTER EXECUTES EACH INSTRUCTION (AND WHAT IT MEANS IN ENGLISH)
CREDIT = 15.	Store a value of 15. as the contents of a storage location addressed or identified as CREDIT. (The 15. represents the number of credits taken during the school term.)
TUIT = CREDIT*100.	Multiply the contents of the storage location known as CREDIT by 100. and store this result in the location called TUIT. [In other words, the tuition is the number of credits (15) times the cost per credit ($100), or $1500.]
BALDUE = TUIT + 250.	Take the contents of the address known as TUIT, add 250., and store this result in the address known as BALDUE. (The balance due the university is tuition plus $250 in fees, or $1750.)
PRINT *,BALDUE	Print the contents of the address known as BALDUE. (The number 1750 is printed by either the line printer or the online terminal.)
END	This instruction defines the end of the program.

Assembly and Machine Languages

Each type of computer has associated with it an assembly language and a machine language. An **assembly language** is specifically designed for a particular type of computer; hence it can accomplish more detailed tasks for that computer than could a high-level language. Such a language, however, requires more specialized training for persons who would use it. In other words, it is more difficult for us to learn an assembly language than to learn a high-level language. Another disadvantage of assembly languages is that they vary from one computer type to another. Thus, if we were restricted to programming only in assembly languages, we would need to learn a new assembly language for each computer type we might use—and worse yet, every computer program written for one computer would have to be rewritten for use on another computer.

After all this, you might be surprised to learn that computers do not directly "understand" either high-level or assembly languages! Computers understand only machine language. An instruction in **machine language** is written in binary form as a series of 0s and 1s, as this scheme conforms to the needs of the electronic circuitry in binary computers. Needless to say, programming in machine language is tedious, which is one reason why high-level languages were developed.

The Compiler

How is it possible for the computer to understand the FORTRAN program that you write? Well, each computer manufacturer provides the means for that computer to translate your FORTRAN-language program into an equivalent program in machine language. This translation of a high-level language into its equivalent machine language is accomplished by a computer program called a **compiler.** In other words, the compiler acts as the language interpreter between you and the computer, much as a foreign language interpreter would translate from English into, say, Spanish.

The compiler resides as a separate program in primary memory. It first translates all instructions line by line. If a particular instruction violates syntax, then the compiler does not "understand" the instruction and prints an error message to that effect. When there are no syntax errors, the compilation process generates a separate program in machine language called the **object program.** The instructions in the object program are then *executed,* or carried out, by the computer. In this case, the program written in the high-level language is called the **source program.**

Each manufacturer of a general-purpose computer provides its own FORTRAN compiler. Most FORTRAN compilers conform to a standard form of FORTRAN developed by the American National Standards Institute (ANSI); however, some manufacturers may also provide certain extensions of *ANSI FORTRAN* that differ from the prescribed standard. In 1978 ANSI finalized its latest version of FORTRAN in a document labeled ANSI X3.9-1978. This version of the language, called **FORTRAN 77,** is a significant revision of the 1966 version. *FORTRAN 77 is the basis of the FORTRAN material in this textbook.*

1.5
COMPUTER SYSTEMS

Your interactions with the computer involve much more than a simple communication between you and the CPU. In fact, you will be dealing with a comprehensive computer system.

Hardware and Software

The **computer system** is a collection of related hardware and software. As the name implies, **hardware** refers to the physical equipment: input/output (I/O) units, CPU, secondary storage, and other specialized machinery. The term **software** refers to computer programs, procedures, and specialized aids that contribute to the operation of a computer system. In general, software is classified as either systems software or applications software.

Systems software is a term for programs that are designed to facilitate the use of hardware. The **operating system** of a computer (supplied by the computer manufacturer) is the most important piece of systems software. This software, which is often called the "manager," "monitor," or "supervisor," consists of a number of specialized programs for operating the computer efficiently. Among others, the following important functions are performed by the operating system.

1. Scheduling the sequence of jobs within the computer[5]
2. Supplying the appropriate compiler
3. Allocating storage for programs and data
4. Controlling input and output operations
5. Performing "housekeeping" chores, such as accounting for the amount of CPU time used by each user

Applications software denotes programs that are written in either high-level or assembly languages to solve specific types of problems. These programs are normally developed "in-house" (by the organization's systems analysts and programmers) to process applications such as payroll, inventories, billing, and accounts receivable.

Many computer manufacturers and independent software companies prepare generalized applications packages ("canned" software) for widely used applications. The cost of these packages ranges from a few hundred dollars to amounts in excess of $100,000. For example, the MRP (Materials Requirement Planning) package provided by IBM is designed to assist a manufacturing company in managing its labor force, machines, materials, and money; Information Associates, Inc., has developed a package called "Students Records System" for generating class rosters, grade reports, and student transcripts; and SAS (Statistical Analysis System), SPSS (Statistical Package for the Social Sciences), and BMD (BioMeDical) are three statistical packages widely used by researchers. The types of programs that you will be writing in your computer class are examples of applications programs.

Batch versus Time-Shared Processing

The specific configuration of hardware and software in a computer system is determined by the needs of that organization. For example, many small- to medium-sized organizations use minicomputers for all of their data processing needs. Microcomputers in particular are becoming commonplace in small businesses and in homes. Two of the more common processing environments in academic institutions are batch processing and time-shared processing.

Batch Processing.   Those of you who will be punching programs on cards most likely will be submitting jobs by the "batch" method. After you have punched your program onto cards, you submit your job to the computing center personnel in order to have your program compiled and executed. In this mode of operation, programs are grouped and executed at the computing center according to job priorities established by computing center personnel. In some batch environments, each program is run serially, that is, one program at a time. In more sophisticated systems, with *multiprogramming* capabilities, several programs may be executed "simultaneously" under the control of the operating system. In either case, it may take from a few minutes to several hours before the results of your program are available to you. When you pick up your job at the computing center, errors may exist. These errors must be identified and corrected, and the job must be resubmitted. This cycle continues until you are satisfied with the results.

---

[5] Each computer program which is to be run (executed) is called a "job."

Time-Shared Processing.   Many of you will process jobs in a "time-sharing" environ-ment. In a time-sharing environment many users working at online terminals have "simultaneous" utilization of the computer system. In this mode of processing jobs, you send data and instructions to the computer via terminals, and the computer re-sponds within seconds. This dialogue between you and the computer continues until you complete the task on which you are working. Thus you code, execute, and correct programs at a terminal that is connected directly to the computer. While sitting at a terminal you may believe you have the computer to yourself. Actually, you and others who use terminals are sharing the computer's CPU in rotation under the control of the operating system (thus the term "time sharing").

Many of today's computer systems are hybrid in that they include two or more processing environments. For example, the computer systems in many colleges and universities include both batch and time-shared processing. Many of these same sys-tems also feature *remote batch,* whereby *you* can submit your own jobs to the card reader and receive your results at a line printer in a location which is removed from the computer center; and *batch interface,* whereby you can bypass the use of cards al-together by entering your program at a terminal into the batch "stream" and receiving your output on either the line printer at the computer center or the online terminal.

Which system is best for you depends on many factors, some of which we list here.

1. *Turnaround time* is usually less for time sharing than for batch processing. By turnaround time we mean the time between submission and completion of a job.
2. The *process of correcting programs* is more convenient by time sharing than by batch processing, for two reasons. First, in time sharing, it can all be done in one place. In other words, you submit your job, get results, and make corrections all at the terminal in one sitting. Second, time-sharing systems have powerful *editing* capabilities for making changes in programs. For example, if you have to change the same letter in each of 20 different lines in a program, then you must repunch each of 20 cards in the batch approach. In time sharing, a single command may automatically make the 20 changes in your internally stored program.
3. *Direct interaction* between person and machine is facilitated by time sharing. This is useful for many types of analyses and decision processes that require the user to make a sequence of decisions on the basis of feedback from the computer. For example, a computer program which simulates factors such as levels of world population, pollution, energy consumption, depletion of natural resources, and per capita income can be used interactively by government officials to answer "What if . . . ?" types of questions. (Such programs do exist!)
4. Jobs that require *many computations* are best handled by batch processing. This is so because time-shared jobs must wait their turn for CPU time. For example, a job that requires, say, 60 minutes of CPU time would reside at least 60 minutes within the computer in a batch environment, but may take several hours to complete in a relatively busy time-sharing environment. Incidentally, your jobs will probably use less than 1 second of CPU time.
5. Jobs that require *large amounts of input or output* also are best run in a batch environment. For example, a job that prints 30 pages of output may take 1 minute on a line printer and 120 minutes on a teleprinter terminal that prints 30 characters per second.

1.6
BEFORE YOU LEAP

Before you "leap" into your course in FORTRAN, we offer some objectives for you to ponder, and some advice which we believe is sound.

Objectives

By now we should have convinced you that the computer is used increasingly as an indispensable tool for clerical purposes, to satisfy information needs, and to make decisions. Moreover, according to a survey that is already outdated, 49 percent of the public have had a job that required either direct or indirect contact with a computer, 15 percent feel that their current job requires some knowledge of the computer, and 7 percent state that their job requires working directly with computers.[6] Given current trends, these percentages will increase dramatically in the future. In fact, the job market in computer-related fields looks quite promising for years to come.[7]

What does all of this mean to you? Well, we feel that if you do not accomplish the two objectives stated below, then you are shortchanging what will prove to be a very relevant part of your education.

Objective 1. Achieving a modest level of programming and problem-solving skills
Objective 2. Acquiring a basic knowledge of computer concepts, uses, and limitations

The first objective is intended to develop your ability to access, utilize, and exploit the computer for the purpose of more effectively analyzing problems and making decisions, both in subsequent academic courses and in your career. The second objective should serve to dispel the mystique and misconceptions surrounding computers—and to aid you in feeling "comfortable" and in operating effectively in a computerized environment.

Advice

Some of you have a great aptitude for the material that follows. We hope you will get "turned on" to do fine things in this field. Others of you are less inclined to absorb this type of material readily. If you feel that you are in the latter category, then you should take the following advice seriously.

1. Pay close attention to *written detail*. The computer is not very permissive. For example, if you spell REID instead of READ, the computer will not understand.
2. Pay close attention to *logical detail*. The computer is a machine. Therefore, you must tell it what to do in rather precise detail, which is broken down into logical steps.
3. Develop *good habits*. Work consistently (not constantly!). Try to rely on others as little as possible, in order to sharpen your own inherent problem-solving skills. Try

---

[6] "A National Survey of the Public's Attitude Toward Computers," *op. cit.*
[7] Estimates by the Bureau of Labor Statistics show over 50,000 new openings annually for programmers and systems analysts.

to solve the "Follow-up Exercises"—before looking up answers in the back of the book.

4. Be *patient*. Don't become frustrated by your mistakes. Don't get angry at the computer if it breaks down (after all, it also works hard). Finally, give yourself time. Our years of teaching this course show that many students take about six to eight weeks before the material crystallizes.

EXERCISES

1. Can you define the following terms?

computer	secondary storage
analog computer	computer language
digital computer	high-level language
special-purpose computer	low-level language
general-purpose computer	procedure-oriented language
minicomputer	problem-oriented language
microcomputer	FORTRAN
distributed processing	computer program
instruction	statement
data	assembly language
input media	machine language
data preparation devices	compiler
input unit	object program
online terminal	source program
CPU	FORTRAN 77
primary or internal memory	computer system
address	hardware
contents	software
byte	systems software
character	applications software
arithmetic-logic unit	operating system
control unit	batch processing
microprocessor	time-shared processing
output unit	

2. Identify and briefly discuss the four outstanding characteristics of computers.
3. Identify two broad areas of computer applications. Give a sample application in each area.
4. Cite some advantages and disadvantages of the widespread use of computers. (Don't necessarily restrict yourself to what we said.)
5. Sketch the organization of a digital general-purpose computer. Briefly describe the functions of each component.
6. Briefly describe the functions of the operating system.
7. Briefly describe the functions of the compiler.
8. Compare batch and time-shared processing with respect to various criteria.
9. How are you doing?

CHAPTER 2

Fundamentals of FORTRAN

This chapter shows you how to write a computer program and provides you with some fundamentals of the FORTRAN language. By the end of this chapter, you will be able to write a complete (although simple) FORTRAN program; by the end of the next chapter, you will be able to run such a computer program on either a batch or a time-sharing system.

2.1
STEPS IN WRITING COMPUTER PROGRAMS

As you might recall from Chapter 1, a **computer program** is a complete set of instructions written in a computer language; its purpose is to solve a problem which has been defined by the programmer. This problem is solved when the computer program is executed in a logical sequence by the computer.

Writing a computer program involves the following **four-step procedure.**

1. Problem statement
2. Specification of algorithm (flowchart/pseudocode versions)
3. Specification of code (FORTRAN version)
4. Debugging process

Step 1: Problem Statement

First, we need to state the nature of the problem. A common approach is to specify

a. The data we will provide the computer
b. The output we wish to receive as the solution to the problem
c. The computations and/or logical processes by which the computer converts the provided data to the output data

As an illustration, suppose that State College is in the process of converting its student billing system from a manual to a computerized system. The total student bill or balance due the college is made up of charges for tuition and fees. The tuition charge at the college varies depending on the number of credits for which a student is enrolled. The present charge is $100 per credit. Other fees include an activity fee, a union fee, and a health fee, for a total of $250.

In our problem statement we need to specify clearly three aspects of this problem.

a. *Provided data*
Cost of tuition per credit ($100)
Cost of fees ($250)
Number of credits for which a student is enrolled (15 as a test case)

b. *Output data*
Balance due State College

c. *Computations*
Multiply the number of credits for which the student is enrolled (15) by the cost of tuition per credit ($100) to determine the tuition charge. Add the tuition charge to the fees ($250) to determine the balance due the college.

Step 2: Specification of Algorithm (Flowchart/Pseudocode Versions)

An **algorithm** is the sequence of instructions that solves the problem. Its specification includes the logical sequence by which data are provided, manipulated, and output. In effect it is an elaboration of the problem statement in the preceding step. The manner in which we specify the algorithm, however, is closer to the problem-solving logic of the computer than to the type of prose statement in our preceding step. Throughout this textbook we use flowcharts and pseudocode to specify the algorithm.

A **flowchart** is a drawing of the algorithm. It has two primary uses: to help us write the computer program by serving as a "blueprint" and to document the logic of the computer program for future review.

Flowcharts use specific symbols to represent different activities and a written message within each symbol to explain each activity. Table 2.1 shows the flowcharting symbols we use in this textbook, and Figure 2.1 illustrates the flowchart for the student billing problem.

The flowchart in Figure 2.1 breaks the problem down into several steps.

1. Store the number of credits in a memory location.
2. Calculate tuition.
3. Calculate balance due the college.
4. Print the output.

Note that this flowchart uses only the first four symbols in Table 2.1. The other symbols are introduced in later chapters, as your programming becomes more sophisticated.

In general, a flowchart must indicate a "Start" and must have at least one "Stop." The flow generally runs from top to bottom and from left to right. As an option, you can use arrowheads to indicate the direction of flow, which is our preference.

TABLE 2.1   *Flowcharting Symbols*

SYMBOL	NAME	MEANING
⬭	Terminal	Indicates the start or end of the program.
▱	Input/output	Indicates when an input or output operation is to be performed.
▭	Process	Indicates calculations or data manipulation.
⇄	Flowline	Represents the flow of logic.
◇	Decision	Represents a decision point or question that requires a choice of which logical path to follow.
○	Connector	Connects parts of the flowchart.
⬡	Preparation	Indicates a preparation step as in describing a DO-loop (Chapter 4).
▯	Predefined process	Indicates a predefined process or step where the details are not shown in this flowchart, as in calling a subprogram (Chapter 9).

A flowchart is one way of diagramming the logic of a program. Many professional programmers and systems analysts use them regularly; others do not. One reason for not using flowcharts is the difficulty in revising the flowchart once a program has been modified.

In the past few years, a program design tool called **pseudocode** has been gaining acceptance among professional programmers. Pseudocode expresses the logic required in the solution of a problem using English-like phrases. A key reason for the growing acceptance of pseudocode is its compatibility with the thinking processes of the programmer. Unfortunately, pseudocode has not been standardized; as a result there are many variations. The example that follows, however, should give you some idea of its syntax and structure.

Before writing the student billing program we can map out its structure by using a "false" (pseudo) code, as follows:

```
Number of credits = 15
Tuition = number of credits × $100
Balance due = tuition + $250
PRINT balance due
Stop
```

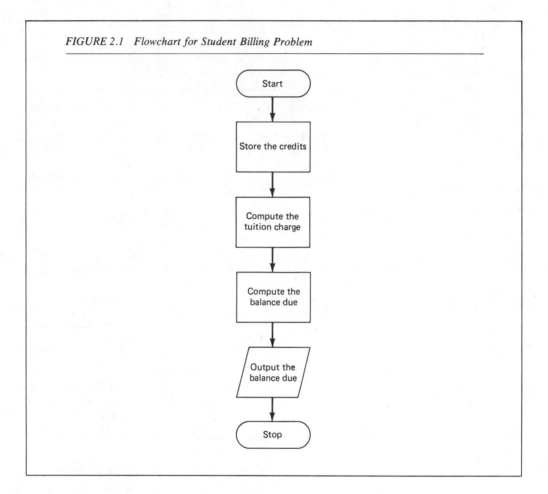

FIGURE 2.1   *Flowchart for Student Billing Problem*

In general, a program written in pseudocode is similar to a program written in a higher-level language such as FORTRAN. The major difference is the emphasis placed on structure versus syntax. Pseudocode primarily concentrates on mapping out the structure of a program, with little regard for the syntax of the actual programming language to be used. Thus we are free to concentrate on the design of the program by expressing its structure using ordinary English, including abbreviations, symbols, and formulas. The word PRINT appears in capital letters in the above pseudocode because this word—called a keyword—is used in the FORTRAN program in the next step.

Either flowcharts or pseudocode can be used to design and document programs. The simplicity and compactness of pseudocode, however, may tip the balance in its favor, particularly for documenting programs that are likely to undergo frequent modification.

We prefer pseudocode to flowcharts in designing and documenting programs, but believe that flowcharts are useful as a pedagogical tool for teaching a programming language. Thus, in this textbook we use both flowcharts and pseudocode to specify algorithms.

Although the above flowchart and pseudocode are rather simple, and you may be tempted not to use them for such a simple problem, *we strongly suggest that you get in the habit of using either pseudocode or flowcharts now.* As programs become more complex, you will find these design tools increasingly helpful.

Step 3: Specification of Code (*FORTRAN Version*)

Coding is the translation of our problem-solving logic from the flowchart or pseudocode into a computer program. In other words, we use the flowchart or pseudocode as a guide for writing instructions to the computer.

The computer language that our instructions are to be written in must be decided by this step in the procedure. (Quite often the same flowchart or pseudocode can be used with any computer language.) Some languages are more suitable than others, depending on the application.

In this textbook, we use FORTRAN 77. The (relative) ease of learning FORTRAN and its excellent mathematical capabilities are two reasons for the widespread use of this language.

FORTRAN code for the student billing program is shown below. Note the correspondence between the program and its flowchart/pseudocode predecessors.

FORTRAN	Comments
CREDIT = 15.	Assign the value 15. to a memory location named CREDIT.
TUIT = CREDIT*100.	Compute the tuition. (The * represents multiplication.)
BALDUE = TUIT + 250.	Compute the balance due.
PRINT *,BALDUE	Print the balance due. (The asterisk does not mean multiplication; we will explain later.)
END	The last FORTRAN instruction in the program. (This instruction also stops execution.)

For simple programs, this correspondence is *almost* one for one; that is, each symbol in the flowchart (except for "Start") or line in the pseudocode will have a corresponding instruction in the program. As problems grow in length and complexity, however, the number of symbols in the flowchart or lines in the pseudocode will be less than the number of instructions in the program, for two reasons.

1. Symbols in the flowchart or lines in the pseudocode can be used to summarize related groups of instructions in a program. For example, "Compute the tuition charge" and "Compute the balance due" in Figure 2.1 can be combined into a single rectangle that reads "Compute the tuition charge and the balance due."

2. Not all instructions need be represented in flowchart/pseudocode versions. We need only represent what we call executable instructions. We take up this topic later in the chapter.

At this point you need not worry about the exact meaning of each instruction in the program, for we will discuss them further throughout the chapter. However, the program should make some sense to you.

Typically, we first write our code on either a regular sheet of paper or on special paper called FORTRAN *coding form*. After we are reasonably sure the program is correct, we place the code on the appropriate input medium for our system. As a beginning programmer you will most likely use either a keypunch for punched cards or a computer terminal. Details on these procedures are presented in Chapter 3.

Step 4: Debugging Process

The next step is to run or execute the program on the computer. By **run** or **execute** we mean that the instructions that make up the program code are processed (carried out) by the computer. Our purpose in this case is to detect and correct errors.

You will often write programs that fail to run or will run improperly. (It happens to all of us.) **Debugging is** the process of locating and correcting errors, or "getting out the bugs." Types of bugs and methods for correcting them are illustrated in the next chapter.

2.2
ELEMENTS OF FORTRAN

Nine elements describe the structure of the FORTRAN language. These are briefly described here for the purpose of perspective and are elaborated upon in the remainder of this chapter and other chapters.

1. Character Set

Forty-nine characters can be used in FORTRAN: 26 alphabetic characters (the letters of the alphabet), 10 numeric characters (the digits 0 through 9), and 13 special characters (plus sign, minus sign, asterisk, slash, equal sign, left parenthesis, right parenthesis, comma, decimal point, apostrophe, dollar sign, colon, and blank space). These characters represent the most fundamental element of the language, since they are used to construct the other eight elements.

2. Data Types

FORTRAN allows the representation of six types of data. We will regularly use the following three types.

a. *Integer type.*   Used to represent exactly an integer (integral or whole-number) value, such as 80 and −705; these can be positive, negative, or zero.

b. *Real type.*   Used to represent approximately a real (decimal) value, such as 250.0, 6.14, and −0.157; these can be positive, negative, or zero.

c. *Character type.*   Used to represent a *string* (sequence) of characters, such as CLARK S. KENT; the *length* of a character datum is the number of characters in the string (13 in the above example), including the two blank characters surrounding the middle initial. Character data can include any of the 49 characters in the character set.

FORTRAN also includes three other data types: *double precision* to increase the number of digits stored in a real value; *logical* to represent the logical values "true" and "false"; and *complex* to represent complex (imaginary) numbers.

3. Constants and Variables

Constants and variables are used to reference arithmetic (integer, real, double precision, and complex), logical, and character data within programs. For example, the real constants 15., 100., and 250., and the real variable names CREDIT, TUIT, and BALDUE are used in the student billing program on page 27. These we discuss fully in the next section.

4. Keywords

Certain words, called **keywords,** are used either to describe an operation which is to be performed by the computer or to communicate certain information to the computer. PRINT and END are keywords in the student billing program. We introduce other keywords throughout the remainder of the book.

5. Function Names

Certain operations can be performed by using what are called function names. For example, we can use SQRT to take square roots and LOG10 to find base 10 logarithms. These and other functions are discussed in Module A.

6. Expressions

Expressions are combinations of variable names, constants, function names, and special characters. They are used to express arithmetic calculations, character data, and logical comparisons. For example, CREDIT*100. is an arithmetic expression in the program on page 27. We introduce arithmetic and character expressions in Section 2.5 and relational/logical expressions in Chapter 5.

7. Statements

A **statement** is an instruction that either directs the computer to perform a specific task or declares certain information that the computer needs. FORTRAN statements are combinations of characters, variables, constants, keywords, function names, and expressions. Thus they utilize the first six elements of FORTRAN. The program on page 27 contains five statements. We introduce the various types of FORTRAN statements in Section 2.4 and discuss them in detail throughout the book.

8. Statement Numbers (Labels)

Individual statements may be labeled by preceding the statement with a statement number. We discuss statement numbers when first used in Chapter 4.

9. Lines

A **line** is a sequence of 72 characters, including blanks. Programs contain three types of lines: initial lines, continuation lines, and comment lines. *Initial lines* are those that initiate a statement. If a particular statement is too long to fit within the initial line, it can be continued on one or more *continuation lines. Comment lines* are used to document programs. The program on page 27 contains five initial lines and no continuation or comment lines. Continuation and comment lines are illustrated later in the book.

2.3
FORTRAN VARIABLES AND CONSTANTS

Programmers use *symbolic names* to reference memory locations in a way that communicates the nature of the contents. For example, BALDUE in the student billing program is a symbolic name that clearly indicates that the balance due the college is stored in this location.

In FORTRAN a symbolic name that represents a storage location is called a **variable name,** or simply a **variable.** A variable name, therefore, identifies a location in memory where a particular item of data is stored (found). The student billing program used three variables: TUIT, which represents "tuition charge"; CREDIT, which represents "number of credits for which the student is enrolled"; and BALDUE, which represents "balance due the college." In choosing a variable name, you can use a combination of letters and/or numbers; however, it is best to choose meaningful names to help you remember what values you are storing in the memory locations.

FORTRAN has three rules for forming a variable name.

1. A variable name must have six characters or fewer.
2. The first character of a variable name must be a letter.
3. The remaining characters can be letters, digits, or a combination of both. No special characters such as plus (+), slash (/), asterisk (*), or comma (,) are permitted. Blanks are ignored by the compiler. For example, TAXDUE and TAX DUE are interpreted as the same memory location.

In the remainder of this section we focus on variables and constants that represent integer, real, and character data types. Later in this chapter we introduce variables and constants for double-precision and logical data types. Throughout we omit and make no further mention of complex data types.

EXAMPLE 2.1

The following list illustrates both acceptable and unacceptable variable names in FORTRAN.

Variable Name	Comment
VELOCITY	Unacceptable. Too many characters.
VEL	Acceptable.
1EXAM	Unacceptable. Does not begin with a letter.
EXAM1	Acceptable.
X + Y	Unacceptable. Special character not allowed.

XPY	Acceptable.
MALESEX.	Unacceptable. Too many characters and use of period.
M SEX	Acceptable, but not recommended.
MSEX	Acceptable.

Follow-up Exercise

1. Tell whether each of the following variable names is acceptable or unacceptable. If a name is unacceptable, indicate why.

   a. X   g. SUM*
   b. IX   h. ACCELERATION
   c. 3Y   i. ACCEL
   d. Y3   j. SET-UPCOST
   e. AGE/35   k. SU COST
   f. AGE35   l. SUCOST

Integer, Real, and Character Variables

Two common types of numeric values that can be stored in memory locations are integer values and real values. *Integer values* are whole numbers with no decimal point, such as 25, 175, −42, or 24; *real values* are numbers with a decimal point, such as 25.3, −7.26, 1234567., or 24.0.

The distinction between real and integer data types is necessary because the computer stores integer values differently from real values. Moreover, this distinction allows certain advantages and efficiencies, which we discuss later.

Because both integer and real values can be stored in a memory location, the computer needs to know which type of value (integer or real) a particular location is going to hold. We indicate which type of value the memory location holds in one of two ways, implicit typing and explicit typing.

Implicit typing determines the data type (integer or real) of a variable by the first letter of the variable name. To tell the computer we wish to store an integer value, we select a variable name beginning with a letter I through N; the variable is referred to as an **integer variable.** For example, INDEX, MONEY, and NUMBER are storage locations in which integers are stored.

If we begin a variable name with the letters A through H or O through Z, we are telling the computer to store real values, and the variable is called a **real variable.** RATE, PAY, and BALDUE are all examples of real variables.

Explicit typing uses certain statements to declare the data type of a variable. We discuss these statements in Section 2.4.

Character variables store character data. These variables are primarily used to store names, addresses, text, and other nonnumeric data. The typing or identification of a character variable is best accomplished by explicit typing, as discussed in the next section.

Integer, Real, and Character Constants

Not all data in a computer program need to be stored in memory locations that are referenced by names. In some situations it is best to use a *constant* (unchanging) value, such as the constant π in the computation πr^2. In this case, we can write the number 3.141593 directly into a FORTRAN program.

In the student billing program the instruction

    BALDUE = TUIT + 250.

consists of two real variables, BALDUE and TUIT, and the constant 250. The values stored in the variable may change whenever the computer executes an instruction, but the value 250. is not subject to change. **A constant,** therefore, represents a fixed, unvarying value that does not change during the execution of a program.

As with variables, FORTRAN makes a distinction between integer and real constants. An **integer constant** represents a whole-number value and does not include a decimal point. For example, in the instruction

    KOUNT = KOUNT + 1

the "1" is an integer constant. An integer constant is written as an optional sign (+ or −), followed by a string of digits. Thus,

    15   −100   6000   123046

are all examples of integer constants.

A **real constant** represents a real value and is generally written as an optional sign (+ or −), an integer part, a decimal point, and an optional fractional part, in that order. For example,

    250.   −1.645   0.7074   650.01

are all real constants.

Very small or very large real constants can be represented by using scientific or **E-notation,** as follows:

Table 2.2 shows several examples of E-notation used in the FORTRAN language and equivalent conventional scientific notation. Thus, E represents "times 10 to the power given by the digits following." In other words, E6 in the constant −0.845E6 says to multiply −0.845 by 10 raised to the power 6, or multiply −0.845 by 10^6, giving −0.845 × 1,000,000 or −845,000. In "plain English," E6 simply denotes move the decimal point 6 places to the right and E−8 says move the decimal point 8 places to the left.

Most likely you will first see E-notation when reading computer output, since systems store and print large numeric values using this convention. In fact, some

TABLE 2.2   *E-Notation Examples*

E-NOTATION	SCIENTIFIC NOTATION	STANDARD NOTATION	COMMENT
7.2E+12 7.2E12 +7.2E12	7.2×10^{12}	7,200,000,000,000.	Move decimal point 12 places to the right (multiply by 10^{12}).
−0.845E06 −0.845E6 −0.845E+06 −0.845E+6	-0.845×10^{6}	−845,000.	Move decimal point 6 places to the right (multiply by 10^{6}).
5E−8 5.E−8	5×10^{-8}	0.00000005	Move decimal point 8 places to the left (divide by 10^{8}).
0.5E−7	0.5×10^{-7}	0.00000005	This constant is identical to the preceding.

systems print all real values in E-notation when certain output statements are used. Thus, an understanding of E-notation facilitates the reading of computer output.

You should be aware of the following issues when using numeric constants.

1. Commas and other special characters are not permissible within a numeric constant. For example, both the constants 6,000 and $54.50 would provoke errors from a FORTRAN compiler.
2. All computers have a limit to the number of digits used to represent a value. This is referred to as the **precision** of the computer. A real number typically can have no more than seven significant digits, although this limit varies from system to system. For example, when the precision is seven digits, the real constant 500.6182 is retained as is; the value 50027.629 is retained as 50027.62 or 50027.63; and the value 98765432.1 is retained as 98765430.
3. The maximum and minimum values (magnitudes) allowed for a number differ from system to system. Integer values on the IBM 370 range from −2,147,483,648 to 2,147,483,647 (-2^{31} to $2^{31} - 1$) while on the CDC CYBER series they range from $-(2^{59} - 1)$ to $2^{59} - 1$. Thus the integer constant 12345678 is within the range of acceptable integer values on both these machines; however, the integer constant 123456789012 is beyond the range (cannot be retained) on the IBM machine but is acceptable on the CDC machine. Real values on the IBM 370 range from 10^{-78} to 10^{75} and on the CDC CYBER from 10^{-293} to 10^{322}. Thus a value such as 2.5E82 is too

large on the IBM machine but acceptable on the CDC machine. *Ask your instructor about the limits on your system.*

A **character constant** is a character datum enclosed in apostrophes—that is, an apostrophe followed by a string of characters followed by an apostrophe. Thus,

'CLARK S. KENT'
'BALANCE DUE IS $'
'JULY 4, 1776'

are all legitimate character constants. Note that character constants can include letters, digits, and special characters such as blanks, commas, and dollar signs.

The maximum length for a character constant varies from system to system. For example, if you are using a Digital Equipment VAX-11 machine, the limit is 255 characters; on a Honeywell Series 60 or 6000 machine, the limit is 511 characters.

We use character constants to store data within character variables (Section 2.5), to print labels, report headings, messages, and other text (Section 2.6), and to effect logical comparisons (Chapter 5).

Follow-up Exercises

2. Identify each of the following as integer constant, real constant, or unacceptable constant.

   a. 5,000   d. −0.05   g. 7.351E03
   b. 5000   e. +0.05   h. 7,351
   c. 5000.   f. 0.050   i. 7351

3. Identify each of the following as an integer variable, real variable, or unacceptable variable.

   a. YEAR   e. AGE
   b. NYEAR   f. JAGE
   c. K   g. 72P
   d. XK   h. P72

4. Express the following constants using E-notation.

   a. -6.142×10^{15}
   b. -6142×10^{12}
   c. 0.0000000007
   d. 7×10^{-10}
   e. 0.167×10^{125}

5. Express the following constants using standard notation.

   a. 123E4
   b. 0.123E7
   c. 456E−8
   d. 0.456E−5

6. Identify what is wrong, if anything, with each of the following character constants.

   a. 'DELTA WING
   b. "ENCOUNTERS OF THE 3RD KIND"
   c. 'YOU'RE OK, I'M OK'

TABLE 2.3   Types of Executable Statements

Type	Activity
1. Assignment	Computes and/or stores data
2. Output	Causes output unit to print stored data
3. Input	Causes input unit to accept data for storage
4. Termination	Causes control unit to stop execution
5. Transfer of control	Alters sequence of execution in the program

2.4 FORTRAN STATEMENTS

The statements in a FORTRAN program can be classified as those that are executable and those that are not executable.

Executable versus Nonexecutable Statements

An **executable statement** is one that causes activity within the CPU *during execution of the program*. Table 2.3 indicates five types of executable statements and the activities they represent.

We discuss termination statements in this section, the assignment statement in the next section, simple versions of input and output statements later in this chapter, and transfer of control in Chapter 4.

A **nonexecutable statement** is used to provide or declare certain information to the computer during compilation of the program. *Nonexecutable statements are ignored during execution of the program.* We introduce six types of nonexecutable statements in this section and others throughout the book.

END and STOP Statements

Look at the student billing program on page 27. The statement

is an *executable* statement that terminates the execution of a program. It also defines the last physical line in a FORTRAN program. It simply tells the compiler that this is the last instruction of the program. Once this instruction is compiled, execution of the program begins, provided that rules of the FORTRAN language have not been violated.

Don't forget to include the END statement in every program you write.[1]

The following executable statement also terminates execution.

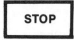

---

[1] More generally, the END statement is a transfer of control statement that also defines the end of a program unit. We discuss this in Chapter 9.

Unlike the END statement, one or more STOP statements can be placed anywhere in the program, as we illustrate later in the book.

INTEGER, REAL, DOUBLE PRECISION, LOGICAL and CHARACTER Statements

In Section 2.3 we illustrated how integer and real variables can be typed implicitly, and altogether glossed over the typing of character variables. A **type statement** is used to *explicitly* type names, which supersedes any implicit typing. In this section we discuss the three type statements that correspond to integer, real, and character names; present a fourth type statement that approximately doubles the precision of real values; and introduce a fifth type statement that declares logical names.

The statement

INTEGER *list of names*

explicitly informs the compiler that the names in the list are to be typed as integers. For example,

```
INTEGER   YEAR, AGE
```

causes the compiler to treat YEAR and AGE as integer variables. This means that YEAR and AGE will store integer numbers and will be treated as integer variables. The fact that they begin with letters other than I through N is ignored in determining data type.

The INTEGER statement improves the description of names. For example, if AGE is to store whole numbers only and is to be used only in integer arithmetic, then it should be treated as an integer variable. The name AGE is more descriptive than, say, JAGE, so we select AGE and use the INTEGER statement to ensure integer type.

As a matter of good programming style, we recommend that you use the INTEGER statement to type all integer names explicitly.[2]

The statement

REAL *list of names*

explicitly informs the compiler that the names in the list are to be typed as real. For example,

```
REAL INC, LOAD, NARC
```

causes the compiler to treat the variables INC, LOAD, and NARC as if they were real variables. In other words, the fact that they begin with letters in the range I through N is

---

[2] Later in the book we make minor exceptions to explicit typing of integer variables when using the variables I, J, K, L, M, and N. We might also note that the list of names in type statements can include not only variable names but also other symbolic names: array names and array declarators (Chapters 7, 8), symbolic names of constants (next subsection), function names (Module A and Chapter 9), and dummy procedure names (not in this book).

not used by the compiler to determine type. Thus, these variables will store real numbers and will be treated by the computer as real variables.

Use the REAL statement to type all real symbolic names in a program, as this improves the selection of names and clearly indicates which names in the program are typed real.

The statement

> **DOUBLE PRECISION** *list of names*

explicitly declares to the compiler that the names in the list are to be typed as double precision. For example,

    DOUBLE PRECISION INC, LOAD, NARC

specifies that the variables INC, LOAD, and NARC are to store real values having approximately double the number of digits as the usual (single) precision of the computer. To illustrate, if LOAD is typed real, then it stores real values with, say, 7 digits; however, if LOAD is typed double precision, then it usually stores slightly more than double the number of digits in real values, say, 15 or 16 digits. Double-precision variables are useful in circumventing certain roundoff error problems, which we discuss at different points later in the book.

The statement

> **LOGICAL** *list of names*

explicitly declares that names in the list are to be typed as logical. For example,

    LOGICAL SWITCH,FINIS

identifies SWITCH and FINIS as **logical variables,** that is, variables that store either the logical value *true* or the logical value *false*. Incidentally, the forms .TRUE. and .FALSE. represent **logical constants.** We illustrate the use of logical values in Chapters 5 and 6.

The statement

> **CHARACTER** *name∗length, name∗length, . . .*

explicitly declares character variables and their respective lengths. By length we mean the number of characters in the string that can be stored within the storage location identified by the character variable. For example,

    CHARACTER NAME∗18,ITEM∗10,ANSWER∗70,CODE

instructs the compiler that character strings of lengths of 18 characters, 10 characters, and 70 characters are to be stored in the respective character variables NAME, ITEM, and ANSWER. Thus the 13-character string CLARK S. KENT would appear within the 18-character storage location NAME as follows:

Variable name

NAME

CLARK $\emptyset$ S $\emptyset$ KENT $\emptyset\emptyset\emptyset\emptyset\emptyset$

Contents
(18 characters)

We use the symbol $\emptyset$ to represent the blank space character (space bar on the keyboard of a keypunch or terminal). Note that the computer pads in five blanks at the end of the data item, since the specified length is 18 and the data item only contains 13 characters. Just how we get the computer to store this string in the character variable is a topic in the next section. *If the length specification is omitted, then a length of 1 is assumed,* as illustrated by the variable CODE in the example.

All type statements are *nonexecutable,* and must appear in the program before all executable statements and DATA statements (Section 4.7).

In designing your programs you will have to decide both the type of each variable and its name. *Decide type on the basis of the data needs of the problem.* For example, if the number of credits in the student billing problem is to include half credits, then the variable that represents credits should be real, and its name should suggest what it represents. Thus we selected the name CREDIT and implicitly typed it as real.

From this point on, *each program in the book will use type statements for all key names in the program.* Although it is not necessary to type explicitly, this practice minimizes confusion with respect to type, thereby improving programming style.

PARAMETER *Statement*

Sometimes it's desirable to reference a constant by using a symbolic name. For instance, we might wish to refer to the constant 3.141593 as PI. Constants referenced by symbolic names are called **symbolic names of constants,** and are defined by using the PARAMETER statement

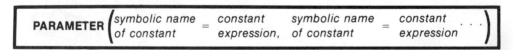

PARAMETER (symbolic name of constant = constant expression, symbolic name of constant = constant expression ...)

For example, given

    REAL PI
    PARAMETER (PI = 3.141593)

the first statement types PI as real and the second statement identifies PI as a symbolic name of a constant with a value of 3.141593. Similarly, the statements

    CHARACTER CODEA*10, CODEB*10
    PARAMETER (CODEA = 'SHAKTI',CODEB = 'SHANTI')

declare CODEA and CODEB as character symbolic names of constants with respective values given by SHAKTI and SHANTI.

Symbolic names of constants are named in the same manner as variable names (maximum of six characters, first character a letter, no special characters) and preferably are typed explicitly. Moreover, symbolic names of constants are used in a manner similar to variable names. Unlike variable names, however, they must not be redefined (assigned another value) within the same program.

The PARAMETER statement is nonexecutable, and must precede all executable and DATA statements. If the symbolic names in the PARAMETER statement are to be explicitly typed, then relevant type statements must precede the PARAMETER statement, as done above.

In our examples, we used constants to the right of equal signs in the PARAMETER statement, but more generally *constant expressions* made up of constants and other symbolic names of constants are permitted. We discuss expressions in the next section.

Follow-up Exercise

7. Indicate what is wrong, if anything, with the following program.

```
PARAMETER (LATHE = 4.178, PRESS = 7042)
CHARACTER 15*FOIL, LEVEL*5
REAL      LATHE,COST,X
:} Series of executable statements
INTEGER I,PRESS
END
```

2.5
ASSIGNMENT STATEMENTS

An **assignment statement** is used (1) to perform and store calculations, (2) to assign a constant to a storage location, or (3) to copy the contents of one storage location to another. In the student billing program, the instruction

    BALDUE = TUIT + 250.

is an example of an assignment statement. This statement adds the value stored in TUIT to the constant 250. and stores the result in the storage location named BALDUE.

Structure

In more general terms, the assignment statement in FORTRAN is structured as follows:

$$\boxed{name = expression}$$

On the left-hand side of the equal sign, a single variable name identifies a storage location in internal computer memory.[3] The right-hand side of the equal sign is a character expression, an arithmetic expression, or a logical expression (Chapter 5).

Character Expression. A **character expression** can include either a character constant or a character variable.[4] For example, if we define the character variables R and S by

---

[3] The only other name permitted to the left of the equal sign is an array element name (Chapters 7, 8).
[4] More generally, a character expression also can take the form of the symbolic name of a character constant, character array element (Chapters 7, 8), character substring (Section 10.2), character function (Section 10.4), and expressions that use character operators and parentheses (Section 10.3).

CHARACTER R*20,S*20

then execution of

R = 'ⱴLOVEⱴFORTRAN'

would store the following in memory.

Unused character positions
filled with blanks

where again the symbol ⱴ is our way of representing the blank space character. In this case the character expression is a character constant of length 14, including the two blanks surrounding LOVE but excluding the apostrophes.

The assignment statement thus tells the computer to "replace the contents of R by the expression to the right of the equal sign."

Note that the length of 14 for the constant is six characters less than the specified length of 20 for R in the CHARACTER statement. As a result, the computer left-justified the character value in storage by filling in the rightmost unused character positions with six blanks. *In general, if the number of characters we attempt to store in the character variable is less than the length specified in the CHARACTER statement, then the computer fills in the remaining (rightmost) character storage positions with blanks. Alternatively, if we attempt to store more characters than the length we have specified in storage, then the computer fills up storage by truncating the rightmost characters.* For example, if we had only specified a length of 6 for R in the CHARACTER statement, then IⱴLOVE would have been stored in R.

If the computer next executes

S = R

then memory for these two character variables would appear as follows:

In this case the character expression to the right of the equal sign is the character variable R. Note that the assignment statement simply copies the contents of R into S, *leaving the contents of R unaffected.*

If the computer next executes

Note the double apostrophe

R = 'I''MⱴNOTⱴSOⱴSURE'

then memory would appear as follows:

Note that the apostrophe in the contraction I'M requires a double apostrophe in the character expression in order for the compiler to distinguish between embedded apostrophes and the apostrophe that ends the constant.

You should clearly realize that *the equal sign in an assignment statement dictates that the storage content of the variable to the left of the equal sign is to be replaced by the value of the expression to the right of the equal sign.*

Follow-up Exercise

8. Write down the necessary statements to store the string CLARK S. KENT within the 20-character memory location called NAME. Draw the memory box and clearly indicate its contents. How would the memory box look if only 15 characters were reserved in NAME? Only 10 characters?

Arithmetic Expressions. An **arithmetic expression** is used to express a numeric computation and can consist of a single numeric constant, a single numeric variable, or a combination of numeric constants and numeric variables separated by parentheses and arithmetic operators.[5] An **arithmetic operator** indicates the type of computation that is desired. Five arithmetic operators are used in the FORTRAN language to indicate the type of arithmetic operation, as described in Table 2.4.

Table 2.5 illustrates three sample uses of assignment statements. In the first illustration the real constant 5000. is placed in the storage location identified by VOL. In the second case, the contents of the storage location called MONEY are copied by the storage location called COST. Note, however, that this transfer is electronic; that is,

---

TABLE 2.4   *Arithmetic Operators*

OPERATOR	ARITHMETIC OPERATION
+	Addition
−	Subtraction
/	Division
*	Multiplication
**	Exponentiation (raise to a power)

---

[5] More generally, arithmetic expressions also can include symbolic names of numeric constants, numeric array elements (Chapters 7, 8), and numeric functions (Module A and Chapter 9).

TABLE 2.5   *Sample Arithmetic Assignment Statements*

variable name = arithmetic expression	
TYPE	ILLUSTRATION
Variable = Constant	VOL = 5000.
Variable = Variable	COST = MONEY
Variable = Combination of constants and variables separated by arithmetic operators	PROF = 7.∗VOL − COST

whatever is in MONEY remains there, but whatever was in COST gets replaced by whatever is in MONEY. Finally, the third illustration places the computational result of 7.∗VOL − COST in the storage location called PROF. This means that the contents of COST will be subtracted from seven times the contents of VOL and the result will be stored in PROF. Note that an asterisk (∗) *must* be used for multiplication; implied multiplication such as 7VOL would give a syntax error since the compiler takes this to be an illegal variable name.

Again you should carefully note the meaning of the equal sign (=) in FORTRAN. It means "place the value indicated by the expression on the right in the storage location indicated by the name on the left." Because of this meaning, an assignment such as

$$I = I + 1$$

makes sense in FORTRAN but not in algebra. Note that each time this statement is executed by the computer, the content (value) of I gets increased by 1. In other words, this statement instructs the computer to "add 1 to the contents of I and place this result in I." This type of statement is used quite often in FORTRAN programs for the purpose of "counting," as you will see in the chapters that follow.

Try to avoid the following two language violations. *Two arithmetic operators must never appear adjacent to one another,* as this would cause a syntax error.[6] *Avoid raising a negative value to a nonintegral power,* as this would cause an error during execution. Negative values may be raised only to whole-number powers (see Exercise 9).

Finally, we should mention that the precision with which arithmetic expressions are evaluated varies somewhat from system to system. Most systems, however, maintain at least seven digits of precision. More on this issue later.

EXAMPLE 2.2

In the student billing program, three assignment statements were used:

```
CREDIT = 15.
TUIT = CREDIT∗100.
BALDUE = TUIT + 250.
```

---

[6] Note that the double asterisk (∗∗) is treated as a single operator for exponentiation.

In the first assignment statement the expression is a single constant; hence the value 15. is simply stored in the memory location named CREDIT, as indicated below.

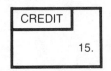

The second statement instructs the computer to multiply the constant 100. by the contents of the memory location named CREDIT, and to store the result in the memory location TUIT. After this calculation, the memory locations appear as follows:

The third instruction tells the computer to add the constant 250. to the contents of the memory location TUIT, and to store the result in the memory location BALDUE. After this calculation, the memory locations appear as follows:

Follow-up Exercises

9. Identify what is wrong with each of the following assignment statements.
   a. $B + C = A$
   b. $D = 4.* - X$
   c. $5. = AGE$
   d. $X = Y = 5.3$
   e. $K = J**3.2$ where J stores a negative value
   f. $K = J**3$ where J stores a negative value
10. Consider the following sequence of instructions
    $A = 37./C$
    $B = A + 1.6$
    $D = B**2$
    and the current contents of the specified storage locations given below.

Indicate the new contents following the execution of the above instructions.

11. Given the instructions

        KOUNT = KOUNT + 1
        SUM = SUM + X

and the current contents

determine the new contents if these instructions are executed three times in sequence.

12. For the sequence of instructions in Table 2.5, indicate the contents of VOL, COST, and PROF if MONEY contains 25000.

Integer and Real Arithmetic Expressions

There are four types of arithmetic expressions, two of which are used routinely: integer and real.[7] An expression is an **integer expression** if *all* of its data type constituents (constants and symbolic names) are of type integer. The right-hand sides of the following assignment statements are examples of integer expressions (assuming implicit typing of variables).

        NUM   = 50
        KOUNT = KOUNT + 1
        INVEST = MATERL + LABOR
        MONEY = NUMSLD*ITMCST + 5000

An integer expression performs *integer arithmetic;* that is, the results will be integer values. Awareness of this is particularly important in *integer division,* where an integer quantity is divided by another integer quantity. In this case, the "whole number" portion of the result is retained and the fractional portion is lost. This procedure is called **truncation;** the result is not rounded, as illustrated next.

EXAMPLE 2.3

As universities become more cost conscious, computer programs that calculate the costs of educating different majors are increasingly common. Such programs might include the assignment statement

        MTCPS = MATHCT/NUMBER

---

[7] The other two types are double precision (see page 46) and complex (not covered in this book).

where MTCPS represents the "cost per student for the Math Department," MATHCT represents the "total cost for the Math Department," and NUMBER represents the "number of majors in the Math Department." Note that each variable is implicity typed as integer because the first letter in the name is in the range I through N.

If 150175 is stored in MATHCT and 100 is stored in NUMBER, then 1501 will be stored in MTCPS. Note that the numerical result is not rounded up to 1502; rather, the fractional value (.75) is truncated, since MATHCT/NUMBER is an integer expression.

An expression is a **real expression** if all of its data type constituents are of type real. The right-hand sides of the following statements are examples of real expressions (assuming implicit typing of variables).

```
BALDUE = TUIT + 250.
CREDIT = 15.
PAY    = HOURS*RATE
WAGE   = PAY
VEL    = DIST/TIME
```

A real expression performs real arithmetic. That is, the result will be a real value.

EXAMPLE 2.4

A student received an 85 and a 94 on two exams. The average can be found by using the following arithmetic statements.

```
SUM = EXAM1 + EXAM2
AVG = SUM/2.
```

If EXAM1 has the value 85. and EXAM2 has the value 94., then SUM has the value 179.0 and AVG the value 89.5. Note that both expressions are real since EXAM1, EXAM2, and SUM are implicitly typed as real and 2. is a real constant.

If numeric data types are combined in an expression, *the exception being a real value raised to an integer power,* then the expression is known as a **mixed-type expression.** The following are examples of mixed-type expressions.

Mixed-Type Expression	Comment
T + 2	T is a real variable and 2 is an integer constant. The result is a real value.
50.5*I	I is an integer variable and 50.5 is a real constant. The result is a real value.
SUM/N	SUM is a real variable and N is an integer variable. The result is a real value.

As a programmer you must pay very close attention to mixed-type expressions for two reasons. First, *integer values in a mixed-type expression are converted to real type during pairwise computations, and the final result will be a real value;* however, the exact value of the final result may differ, depending on the sequence of computations. A "pairwise computation" is one that involves a single arithmetic operator, as illustrated by the evaluation of each of the three mixed-type expressions above.

In general, *it is good programming practice to avoid complicated mixed-type expressions,* since the process of conversion is inefficient and follows complicated rules. We use mixed-type expressions when it is convenient to do so, as illustrated in various examples throughout the book.

A second reason for you to pay close attention to the use of mixed-type expressions is that you may get an incorrect or undesirable result. To illustrate, the cost per student in Example 2.3 is actually $1501.75. If truncation is undesirable for a particular computation, then a real expression should be used.

Finally, we note some other items of interest.

1. In our definitions of integer, real, and mixed-type expressions we omitted one complicating factor. *Any expression (positive or negative) may be raised to a (positive or negative) integer power, but only (positive) real expressions may be raised to real powers. Expressions having negative values can be raised only to integer powers.* Study Example 2.5 to make sure you understand this condition.

2. When truncation is of no concern, integer arithmetic is preferred to real arithmetic because it is faster.

3. In some applications truncation is desirable, as we illustrate later in the book.

4. For many computers, the maximum number of digits retained in integer arithmetic is ten;[8] the maximum number of significant digits in real arithmetic is generally seven, although double-precision declarations approximately double this figure. Thus, for example, a computational result having an actual real value given by 575.45248 is either rounded to 575.4525 or truncated to 575.4524, and one having an actual value of 98765432.1 is retained as 98765430.

5. If greater precision is required, then double-precision variables and constants can be used. An expression is a **double-precision expression** if all of its data type constituents are of type double precision. A **double-precision variable** is declared by using the DOUBLE PRECISION statement and a **double-precision constant** is written in the manner of a real constant in E-notation, except that E is replaced by D. For example, if we declare

    DOUBLE PRECISION RADIUS

    then the expression

    .3141592654D01*RADIUS**2

    is a double-precision expression; that is, its value is retained with greater precision than an equivalent real expression.

6. If an integer or real value exceeds the upper limit allowed by the computer, then

---

[8] More specifically, machines that use 32 *bits* (0 or 1 digit) in a *word* (a single unit of storage that holds data or instructions) can retain integer values in the range -2^{31} to $2^{31} - 1$ or $-2,147,483,648$ to $2,147,483,647$; a 16-bit word machine stores a maximum integer value of $2^{15} - 1$, or 32,767.

overflow has occurred; values smaller than the lower limit cause **underflow.** For example, an actual value such as 0.15E85 would cause overflow on most computers. The computer usually prints an error message whenever overflow or underflow occur during execution, as we illustrate in the next chapter.

7. A vexing problem called **roundoff error** is caused by the computer's *precision* (digit retention limitations). Assuming a computer that stores seven digits in real arithmetic, we can illustrate the problem by evaluating the expression 1./3., which of course has the actual value 0.3333333333. . . . Since the computer stores 0.3333333, the sum 1./3. + 1./3. +1./3. would yield 0.9999999 rather than exactly 1. While this may seem insignificant, roundoff error is a serious problem for many applications, as in the computation of trajectories in space flight. We return to this problem throughout the book as it affects new material.

EXAMPLE 2.5

Expression Raised to a Power	Comment
X**K	Real expression (X) may be raised to integer power (K); X is simply multiplied by itself a total of K times. For example, if 5. is in X and 3 is in K, then the result is 5. × 5. × 5., or 125.
J**8	Integer expression (J) may be raised to integer power (8). J is multiplied by itself eight times.
J**8.	Considered mixed type. J is treated as real for this calculation and the computer evaluates antilog of 8. log (J). Whenever a real power is used, the computer uses logarithms in the evaluation. J**8 is preferred for greater efficiency and precision.
K**X	Considered mixed type. Same treatment as preceding case.
(−4.)**L	Use of parentheses causes treatment of 4. as a negative number. This is permissible since the power is integer. If 2 is in L, then the result is (−4.) × (−4.), or 16. If 3 is in L, then the result is −64.
A**3.	This is permissible if A stores a positive value, but A**3 is preferred.
(−A)**3.	This is not allowed since the expression is negative (assuming A stores a positive value) and the power is real. The computer attempts to evaluate this as the antilog of 3log(−A), but the log of a negative number is undefined.

EXAMPLE 2.6

Consider the sequence of instructions

```
J = X/2.
Y = 2*J
I = .4*Y
```

where the real number (5.) is in the storage location labeled X. After the execution of these statements, the storage locations for J, Y, and I would contain the following values:

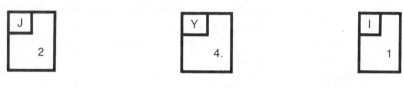

Thus, the computation (X/2.) yields the real number 2.5, but this is truncated to the integer number 2 for storage in the location for integer variable J. (Note that a decimal point does not appear in the storage location for J.) The computation (2∗J) yields the integer number 4, but this is stored as the real number 4. because Y is a real variable. Finally, the computation .4∗Y gives the real number 1.6, which is truncated and stored as the integer number 1 because I is an integer variable.

Finally, note that *it is permissible for the variable to the left of the equal sign to differ in type from the arithmetic expression to the right of the equal sign.* The type of this variable simply determines the type of the value stored. The term "mixed type" refers only to relationships within the arithmetic expression itself.

Follow-up Exercises

13. Fill in the contents for

after the following statements are executed. Assume implicit typing.

        C = L/2
        K = C − 10.2

14. Identify any mixed-type expressions and eliminate them by appropriately modifying the constants. State the type of the rewritten expression. Assume implicit typing.
    a. STRESS − 100
    b. 5.∗K − 1
    c. 7∗∗Q
    d. (−7.)∗∗Q
    e. Y∗∗2

15. For each of the following expressions, identify the type of result and state its value.
    a. I/J where 4 is in I and 10 is in J
    b. A/B where 4. is in A and 10. is in B.
    c. I∗J where 12345678901 is in I and 10987654321 is in J. (Any potential problems here?)

> d. A*B where 2E50 is in A and 4E70 is in B. (Any potential problems here?)
> e. A*B where 2D50 is in A and 4E70 is in B.
>
> **16.** Assuming implicit typing, are the following considered mixed-type expressions?
>
>   CREDIT = 15
>   COST = MONEY
>
> Comment on how you think the computer handles these.

Arithmetic Hierarchy

Computers do arithmetic on only two numbers at a time, called **pairwise arithmetic.** Therefore, an arithmetic expression involving several computations must be computed in a certain sequence.

In FORTRAN the sequence for performing arithmetic operations is

First: All exponentiation is performed.
Second: All multiplication and division is completed.
Third: All addition and subtraction is performed.

We illustrate this so-called **arithmetic hierarchy** through examples.

EXAMPLE 2.7   Student Billing Revisited

The calculation of amount due for tuition and fees in the student billing program can be combined into one assignment statement, as follows:

    BALDUE = 250. + CREDIT*100.

If CREDIT has a value of 15., then 1750. is stored in BALDUE. This value is arrived at through the following steps:

First, CREDIT is multiplied by 100. because multiplication is completed before addition. The result is 1500.

Second, 250. is added to 1500. The result is 1750.

EXAMPLE 2.8   Area Problem

An analyst for Prangles Potato Chips, a competitor of Pringles, wishes to determine the area of the top that would be required of a super-economy-size cylindrical container of radius 5 inches. As you might recall, the area of a circle is computed by using the formula $area = \pi r^2$, where r is the radius. This can be written in FORTRAN as

    AREA = PI*RADIUS**2

If the variable RADIUS has the value 5. and PI is the symbolic name of a constant with a value of 3.141593, then 78.53982 is stored in AREA. This result is achieved as follows.

First, RADIUS is raised to the second power because exponentiation is performed before multiplication. The result is 25.

Second, 3.141593 is multiplied by 25. The result is 78.53982.

EXAMPLE 2.9 Mixed-Type Blues and Intrinsic Functions

Unwanted truncation is a common error in mixed-type expressions. For example, the expression

    1.2 + K/4

is evaluated as 3.2 instead of 3.7 when 10 is stored in K.

First K/4 is evaluated using *integer* arithmetic, which gives 10/4 = 2 instead of 2.5.

Next 1.2 and 2 must be added, but first mixed typing (1.2 is real and 2 is integer) causes the conversion of the integer value 2 to the real value 2.0; now we have the addition of two real values, which gives the real value 3.2.

A simple way to ensure the correct result is to write

    1.2 + K/4.

Now the mixed typing given by K/4. is evaluated using real arithmetic because K is treated as real when divided by a real constant. Of course, we still have a mixed-type expression, but the correct result is guaranteed.

Many programmers prefer to avoid mixed-type expressions altogether since the kind of error illustrated above can "sneak through" if care is not exercised. The foregoing expression can be made real in any of the following three ways.

Version A	Version B	Version C
.		
.		
.	REAL K	
XK = K	.	.
	.	.
	.	.
T = 1.2 + XK/4.	T = 1.2 + K/4.	T = 1.2 + REAL(K)/4.
.	.	.
.	.	.
.	.	.

If fractional values need to be stored in K, then version B is preferred. If K is to store only integer values, then we prefer version C to the others.

Did you accept version C without question? The term **REAL (K)** is called an **intrinsic function,** as described in Module A following the text; it is not the same as the REAL statement in version B. In version B, K is treated as a real variable throughout the program; in version C, the value in K is treated as real only in the computation.

In effect, REAL (K)/4. and K/4. are computationally equivalent since K is converted to real in the mixed-type expression K/4.0.

Note, however, that REAL (K/4) gives the result 2.0, which is incorrect for our purposes. In other words, *the intrinsic function REAL does not affect the way the expression within parentheses is evaluated; it only converts the value of the expression to real type.*

Alternatively, if we wish temporarily to treat a real value as integer, then we can use the intrinsic function **INT,** as described in Module A. For example,

R = 2∗K + INT(X − 1.5)

stores 17. in R when 5 is in K and 8.8 is in X. Without the INT function, the statement

R = 2∗K + X − 1.5

would store 17.3 in R.

Left-to-Right Rule

The exact order of computation when two or more operations are at the same level of arithmetic hierarchy will differ depending on the complexity of the arithmetic expression and the particular computer system. If you avoid intricate mixed-type expressions, however, then *the computational result will be consistent with a left-to-right scan of the arithmetic expression,* as the following examples illustrate.

EXAMPLE 2.10   Percentages

The percentage of engineering students relative to the university enrollment is calculated using the following assignment statement:

PERCT = ENG/UNIV∗100.

If 1000. is stored in ENG and 5000. is stored in UNIV, then 20. is stored in PERCT. The value of 20. is determined by the following sequence:

First, ENG is divided by UNIV because division and multiplication are at the same level, so that operations are from left to right. The result is 0.2.

Second, 0.2 is multiplied by 100. The result is 20.

Note that the left-to-right rule prevents the wrong sequence of first multiplying UNIV by 100. (giving 500000.) and then dividing this result into ENG (giving 0.002 for PERCT).

EXAMPLE 2.11   Microeconomics Problem

The daily cost in dollars (*c*) of operating a small manufacturing firm is described by the equation

$$c = u^3 - 6u^2 + 250$$

where *u* represents the number of units produced by the firm per day. The equivalent assignment statement in FORTRAN is

COST = UNITS**3 − 6.*UNITS**2 + 250.

If UNITS has the value 20., then 5850. will be stored in COST. The value 5850. is determined as follows.

First, UNITS is raised to the third power because exponentiation is the first operation performed, and UNITS**3 appears to the *left* of UNITS**2. The result is 8000.

Second, UNITS is raised to the second power. The result is 400.

Third, 6. is multiplied by 400. because multiplication is performed before addition and subtraction. The result is 2400.

Fourth, 2400. is subtracted from 8000. because the subtraction operation is found to the left of the addition operation. The result is 5600.

Fifth, 250. is added to 5600., giving 5850.

EXAMPLE 2.12   Pairwise Integer to Real Conversions

Let's take a look at mixed-type expressions again to illustrate better the pairwise nature of integer to real conversions. Consider the expression below and the sequence of computational steps, where 2.1 is in A, 6 is in N, 10 is in I, and 3 is in J.

Expression	Computational Steps	Description
A*N + I/J − 5.2	—	
2.1*6 + 10/3 − 5.2	—	
2.1*6.	1	6 converted to 6. since we have mixed type in this pairwise multiplication.
12.6	2	12.6 placed in intermediate storage.
3	3	Integer division truncates this result. Note that this pairwise division is not mixed type, so integer arithmetic is used.
3.	4	3 converted to 3. in preparation for pairwise mixed-type addition.
15.6	5	15.6 placed in intermediate storage.
10.4	6	The value of this mixed-type expression is 10.4.

If integer division is unwanted in this case, then the expression should be written

A*N + REAL(I)/REAL(J) − 5.2

The purist might also convert A*N to A*REAL(N), although this is not necessary.

Note that *type real takes precedence in an integer-real mixed-type pairwise computation;* that is, the integer value is converted to real and the value of the result is real. Similarly, *double-precision data types take precedence over both integer and real data types when pairwise arithmetic is performed.*

Use of Parentheses

The insertion of parentheses within arithmetic expressions changes the order of computation according to the following rules.

1. The operations enclosed within parentheses are computed before operations not included in parentheses.
2. Parentheses may be embedded inside other parentheses in complicated expressions.
3. The innermost set of parentheses contains the computations done first.

We might note that within parentheses themselves the hierarchy and left-to-right rules apply.

EXAMPLE 2.13   Temperature Conversion

Conversion of temperatures from Fahrenheit to Celsius is given by the formula

$$Celsius = \tfrac{5}{9} (Fahrenheit - 32)$$

In FORTRAN the formula is written

    CEL = 5./9.*(FAHREN - 32.)

If 212. is stored in FAHREN, then 100.0000 will be stored in CEL according to the following steps.

First, 32. is subtracted from FAHREN because this operation is enclosed in parentheses. The result is 180.

Second, 5. is divided by 9. because the division operation is found to the left of the multiplication operation. The result is 0.5555556.

Third, 0.5555556 is multiplied by 180. The result is 100.0000.

Note: dividing 5 by 9 actually gives the irrational number 0.555555555 . . . , that is, the 5s never end. We expressed the result to 7 significant digits according to items 4 and 7 on page 46. When this 7-digit number is multiplied by 180, the precise result is 100.000008, which we have expressed to 7 digits as 100.0000.

EXAMPLE 2.14   Potpourri

In the preceding example, *parentheses were used as a means of improving the readability of the arithmetic expression,* since we could have written the mathematically equivalent but less readable

    CEL = 5./9*FAHREN - 5./9.*32.

Similarly, readability plays a role in expressing the algebraic expression $x \cdot (-y)$ as

X*(−Y)

rather than as

−X*Y

Note that we would not express this as

X* − Y

since it violates the rule that two arithmetic operators must not be adjacent.

In many cases, however, parentheses must be used. For example, an expression for a statistic called variance is given by

$$\frac{s^2}{p-1}$$

In FORTRAN we would write this as

S**2/(P − 1.)

The square root of variance, called the standard deviation, is algebraically given by

$$\left(\frac{s^2}{p-1}\right)^{1/2} \quad \text{or} \quad \sqrt{\frac{s^2}{p-1}}$$

In FORTRAN we can write this by *nesting the parentheses* as follows:

(S**2/(P − 1.))**.5

A preferred alternative is to use the *intrinsic function for square roots* (**SQRT** as given in Module A, following the text):

SQRT(S**2/(P − 1.))

The SQRT function is preferred because the expression SQRT (real expression) is more readable, is more computationally efficient, and gives less roundoff error than (real expression) **.5.

One final point: *When nesting parentheses, take care that the number of left parentheses equals the number of right parentheses, as a mismatch in these numbers is a common error.*

Follow-up Exercises

It is very important that you pay close attention to hierarchy, left-to-right, and parentheses rules when you are writing FORTRAN expressions. Inattention to these rules is a leading cause of logic errors. The following exercises emphasize this point. Assume implicit typing throughout.

17. In Example 2.13, what would be stored under CEL if the assignment statement were as follows?

CEL = 5./9.*FAHREN − 32.

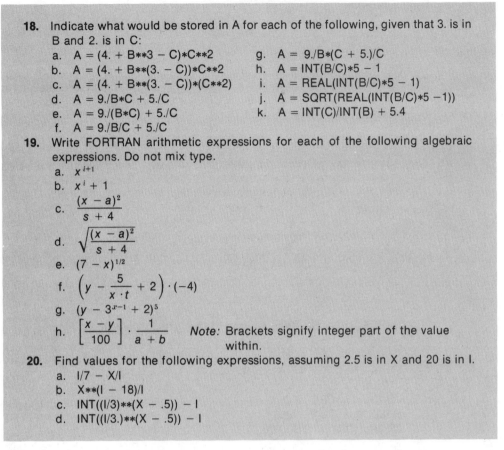

18. Indicate what would be stored in A for each of the following, given that 3. is in B and 2. is in C:

a. A = (4. + B**3 − C)*C**2   g. A = 9./B*(C + 5.)/C

b. A = (4. + B**(3. − C))*C**2   h. A = INT(B/C)*5 − 1

c. A = (4. + B**(3. − C))*(C**2)   i. A = REAL(INT(B/C)*5 − 1)

d. A = 9./B*C + 5./C   j. A = SQRT(REAL(INT(B/C)*5 −1))

e. A = 9./(B*C) + 5./C   k. A = INT(C)/INT(B) + 5.4

f. A = 9./B/C + 5./C

19. Write FORTRAN arithmetic expressions for each of the following algebraic expressions. Do not mix type.

a. x^{i+1}

b. $x^i + 1$

c. $\dfrac{(x - a)^2}{s + 4}$

d. $\sqrt{\dfrac{(x - a)^2}{s + 4}}$

e. $(7 - x)^{1/2}$

f. $\left(y - \dfrac{5}{x \cdot t} + 2\right) \cdot (-4)$

g. $(y - 3^{x-1} + 2)^5$

h. $\left[\dfrac{x - y}{100}\right] \cdot \dfrac{1}{a + b}$ *Note:* Brackets signify integer part of the value within.

20. Find values for the following expressions, assuming 2.5 is in X and 20 is in I.

a. I/7 − X/I

b. X**(I − 18)/I

c. INT((I/3)**(X − .5)) − I

d. INT((I/3.)**(X − .5)) − I

2.6
LIST-DIRECTED INPUT/OUTPUT (I/O)

In this section we complete your introduction to FORTRAN by presenting simplified input and output statements that do not require us to specify formats for exactly how data are to appear on input and output media. This type of I/O is termed *list-directed* because we need only specify the "list" of items that we wish to input or output.[9]

The PRINT Statement

The PRINT statement is used to transmit or output the values of constants, variables, or expressions to an output unit such as a line printer or terminal. PRINT statements enable us to observe the results of programs on media such as printed paper or video screens.

A general form of the **list-directed PRINT statement** is given by

PRINT *, *list*

---

[9] Modules B, C, and D present formatted I/O, whereby the programmer controls the exact placement of data.

where *list* refers to

1. A constant (numeric or string)
2. A variable (numeric or string)
3. An expression (numeric or string)
4. Any combination of constants, variables, and expressions separated by commas

For example, execution of

```
PRINT *,BALDUE
```

in the student billing program on page 27 results in a printed real value of either

```
1750.0
```

or in E-notation

```
0.1750000E 04
```

depending on the system. Some compilers print all list-directed real values in E-notation.

EXAMPLE 2.15 Student Billing With Output Variations

Consider the following version of the student billing program.

```
REAL CREDIT, TUIT, BALDUE
CREDIT  = 15.
TUIT    = CREDIT*100.
BALDUE = TUIT + 250.
PRINT *,CREDIT,TUIT,BALDUE
END
```

When this program is executed the following line is printed.

```
15.0    1500.0    1750.0
```

Note that the output appears on one line; that the sequence of numbers in the output corresponds to the sequence of variables in the list; and that each number contains a decimal point, since each variable in the list is a real variable. Again, some systems will print these values using E-notation.

Now, suppose we replace the PRINT statement by the following sequence of PRINT statements.

```
PRINT *,CREDIT
PRINT *,TUIT
PRINT *,BALDUE
```

In this case the output would appear as follows:

```
15.0    ← Print line 1
1500.0  ← Print line 2
1750.0  ← Print line 3
```

Note that each PRINT statement has one variable in its list; hence each print line has a single value. Further note that *a new print line is printed each time a new PRINT statement is executed.*

Most programs include labels for numeric output in order to improve the readability of output. For example, the three output values above would be meaningless to a person not familiar with the program. From this point forward, *all of our programs will include labeled output.*

To label the student billing output we might use the following PRINT statements.

```
PRINT *,'NUMBER OF CREDITS: ',CREDIT
PRINT *,'TUITION           :$',TUIT
PRINT *,'BALANCE DUE       :$',BALDUE
```

Now the printed output would appear as follows:

NUMBER OF CREDITS :	15.0	
TUITION	: $	1500.0
BALANCE DUE	: $	1750.0

Note: The exact output form and placement of numeric values differ from system to system.

Thus, output can be labeled by using character constants.

Did you notice how nicely we aligned the labels? *Good program design dictates thoughtful design of output to ensure its readability.*

Finally, consider the following version of the program.

```
INTEGER      ID
REAL         CREDIT,TUIT,BALDUE
CHARACTER    NAME*15

NAME       = 'W. MITTY'
ID         = 266612463
CREDIT     = 15.
TUIT       = CREDIT*100.
BALDUE     = TUIT + 250.

PRINT *,'NAME             : ',NAME
PRINT *,'ID NUMBER        : ',ID
PRINT *,'   '
PRINT *,'NUMBER OF CREDITS: ',CREDIT
PRINT *,'TUITION          :$',TUIT
PRINT *,'BALANCE DUE      :$',BALDUE

END
```

Output for this version would appear as follows:

NAME	:	W. MITTY
ID NUMBER	:	266612463
NUMBER OF CREDITS :	15.0	
TUITION	: $	1500.0
BALANCE DUE	: $	1750.0

Notice that we have included the output of character variables. Also note that *we can control vertical spacing by using the null character constant 'ƀ' in the list of a PRINT statement*. Thus the statement

PRINT *,'ƀ'

following the statement that prints ID has the effect of printing a blank line immediately following the print line for ID.[10]

Follow-up Exercises

21. Modify the last program in Example 2.15 so that CREDIT, TUIT, and BALDUE are treated as integer variables. How would the output change? What advantages do you see in using integer variables? Disadvantages?

*22. Modify the last program in Example 2.15 so as to print the following output.

```
NAME                :    W. MITTY
ID NUMBER           :    266-61-2463
NUMBER OF CREDITS :    15.0

                              ←———————— Two blank lines

FEES .............  $      250.0
TUITION  ..........  $     1500.0
BALANCE DUE .....  $     1750.0
```

*23. Create two versions of the *first* program (page 56) in Example 2.15 such that
    a. All assignment statements are eliminated in favor of one PRINT statement that prints the number of credits, the tuition charge, and the balance due.
    b. The cost per credit of $100 is stored in a real variable named CPC and the fee of $250 is stored in a real variable named FEES.
    Can you state advantages and disadvantages of each approach?

24. **Computer as Hand Calculator.** The computer can be used as an expensive hand calculator by writing short programs that include all calculations in the list of PRINT statements. Specify a PRINT statement for each of the following.
    a. $\dfrac{-6.5 + \sqrt{(6.5)^2 - (4) \cdot (-3.4) \cdot (50)}}{(2) \cdot (-3.4)}$
    b. The square, cube, square root, and cube root of the number 100.56
    c. The base 10 logarithm of 100 and 10 raised to the base 10 logarithm of 100 (see Module A)
    d. The quantity $e^{6.21461}$, the base e logarithm of 50, and the base e logarithm of $e^{6.21461}$

25. **WRITE Statement.** The following list-directed WRITE statement is an alternative to the PRINT statement.

---

[10] The number of positions used to output list-directed integer, real, and character values is system dependent. Ask your instructor or consult the manual for your system.

* Answers to exercises marked with a single or double asterisk are not given at the end of the text. Ask your instructor for these answers.

> ### WRITE (*output unit number,* *) *list*
>
> where "output unit number" is an integer number that identifies the output unit for that system. For example, IBM 370 systems use
>
>   WRITE(6,*)list
>
> for output to a line printer or terminal. Find the output unit number for your system and rewrite the first program in Example 2.15 using the WRITE statement.

The READ Statement

You need to make an important distinction between your computer program (that is, the instructions that tell the computer what to do) and your input data (that is, the data that you want processed through an input unit). For example, an employer has data on the number of hours worked and the rate of pay for each employee. The employer has recorded these data on an appropriate input medium such as cards or magnetic tape, and uses these to compute each employee's pay. The hours worked and rate of pay for each employee are considered input data; the FORTRAN instructions to determine each employee's pay represent the computer program.

In the student billing program, three items of data were provided: cost of tuition per credit ($100), cost of fees ($250), and number of credits (15). By definition, these are not input data, since they represent constants in the computer program. For example, the assignment statement

    CREDIT = 15.

was used to store 15. in CREDIT and the 100. and 250. were incorporated in the assignment statements

    TUIT = CREDIT*100.

and

    BALDUE = TUIT + 250.

The READ statement is an alternative approach to storing data in memory locations and *is preferred to the assignment statement whenever data have a high likelihood of changing values each time the program is executed.* The READ statement enables the computer to transfer the data from some source, such as punched card or terminal, to the appropriate storage locations in computer memory.

A common form of the **list-directed READ statement** is

> ### READ *, *list of names*

where the *list of names* contains variable names (separated by commas) in the same sequence as distinct items of data that are to be entered into memory.

EXAMPLE 2.16   Student Billing With Input

The following version of the student billing program treats NAME, ID, and CREDIT as input variables that are to be read in by a single READ statement.

```
INTEGER     ID
REAL        CREDIT,TUIT,BALDUE
CHARACTER NAME*15
READ *,NAME,ID,CREDIT
TUIT    = CREDIT*100.
BALDUE = TUIT + 250.
:} PRINT statements as in Example 2.15
END
```

The only difference between this version and the one in Example 2.15 on page 57 is that the single statement

```
READ *,NAME,ID,CREDIT
```

replaces the three assignment statements

```
NAME   = 'W. MITTY'
ID     = 266612463
CREDIT = 15.
```

For now, assume that the data items W. MITTY for NAME, 266612463 for ID, and 15. for CREDIT are either on a punched card for batch processing or to be typed at the terminal for time-shared processing. (Just how we do this is a topic in the next chapter.) The READ instruction activates the appropriate input unit and transfers the values on the input medium to the memory locations NAME, ID, and CREDIT. After the READ instruction is executed, the memory locations appear as

The use of a READ statement for NAME, ID, and CREDIT is preferred to the use of assignment statements, since the values of NAME, ID, and CREDIT will change for each student who is processed. If a READ statement were not used, then the assignment statements would have to be changed for each student, which is both cumbersome and more costly than the use of input data.

Follow-up Exercises

*26. Change the program in Example 2.16 in each of the following ways.

    a. Treat the "cost of tuition per credit" (CPC) and the "cost of fees" (FEES) as input variables. Use a single READ statement for these two variables, separate from the other READ statement.

b. Instead of defining CPC and FEES as input variables, use assignment statements.

c. Treat CPC and FEES as symbolic names of constants.

Why might it be best to treat the values 100. and 250. as symbolic names rather than constants? Under what conditions might any one of the above approaches be preferred to the others?

27. **Alternative READ Statement.** The following READ statement is an alternative to the READ statement used earlier.

> **READ**(*input unit number,* ∗)*list of names*

where the "input unit number" refers to a specific input unit such as a card reader or a terminal; the asterisk identifies this input statement as list-directed; and the "list" contains variable names separated by commas.

The input unit number varies from system to system. For example, IBM 370 systems use the number 5 for the card reader or terminal, as follows:

READ(5,∗)list of names

Ask your instructor about this number on your system and modify the program in Example 2.16 to use this version of the READ statement.

2.7
BANK SAVINGS PROBLEM

To complete your introduction to fundamentals of FORTRAN we present one more problem scenario for which we write a complete FORTRAN program.

Suppose that we have $1000 to invest in a savings account that yields interest of 0.015 ($1\frac{1}{2}$ percent) per quarter (every three months). If we deposit the $1000 now, then one quarter from now we have our original $1000 plus $15 interest ($1000 \times 0.015$), or a total of $1015. This calculation can be written as follows:

$$1015 = 1000 + 1000 \times (0.015)$$
$$= 1000 \times (1 + 0.015)$$

Now, consider how much we would have two quarters from now: the $1015 at the end of the first quarter plus the new interest of $15.22 on this amount ($1015 \times 0.015$), or a total of $1030.22. In other words,

$$1030.22 = 1015 + 1015 \times (0.015)$$
$$= 1015 \times (1 + 0.015)$$

But we already know that

$$1015 = 1000 \times (1 + 0.015)$$

Thus,

$$1030.22 = 1015 \times (1 + 0.015)$$
$$= 1000 \times (1 + 0.015) \times (1 + 0.015)$$
$$= 1000 \times (1 + 0.015)^2$$

Do you see an emerging pattern? In general, if A represents our accumulated funds, N represents the number of quarters into the future, P represents the principal we start off with, and R represents the quarterly interest rate, then

$$A = P \cdot (1 + R)^N$$

Today's banks have computerized virtually all computational aspects dealing with savings and checking accounts, mortgages, loans, and investments. The following four-step procedure illustrates a simple program for determining accumulated funds in a savings account.

Step 1: Statement

Bank savings account program that determines accumulated funds given the principal, quarterly interest rate, and number of quarters.

a. *Input data*
   Principal
   Quarterly interest rate
   Number of quarters
b. *Output data*
   All input data
   Accumulated funds
c. *Computations*
   Accumulated funds = Principal $\times$ (1 + Rate)$^{\text{Number of quarters}}$

Step 2: Algorithm

Flowchart and pseudocode representations of the algorithm are illustrated in Figure 2.2.

Step 3: Code

Variables in the program below are defined as follows.

```
PRIN   = Principal
RATE   = Quarterly interest rate
ACCUM  = Accumulated funds
NUM    = Number of quarters
```

```
      INTEGER NUM
      REAL    PRIN,RATE,ACCUM

      READ *,PRIN,RATE,NUM

      ACCUM = PRIN*(1. + RATE)**NUM

      PRINT *,'PRINCIPAL = ',PRIN
      PRINT *,'RATE      = ',RATE
      PRINT *,'QUARTERS  = ',NUM
      PRINT *,'AMOUNT    = ',ACCUM

      END
```

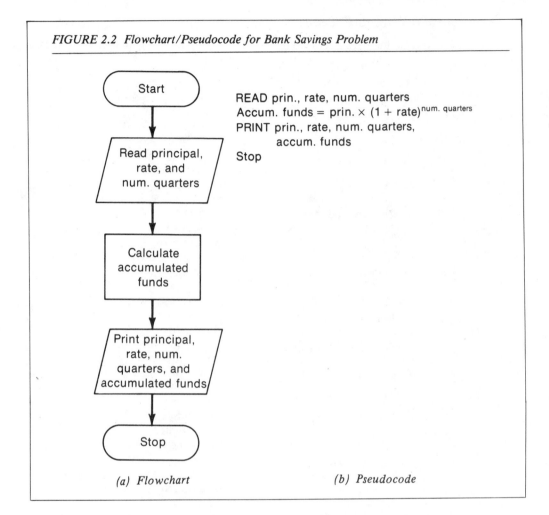

FIGURE 2.2 *Flowchart/Pseudocode for Bank Savings Problem*

READ prin., rate, num. quarters
Accum. funds = prin. $\times$ (1 + rate)$^{\text{num. quarters}}$
PRINT prin., rate, num. quarters,
        accum. funds
Stop

Flowchart boxes:
- Start
- Read principal, rate, and num. quarters
- Calculate accumulated funds
- Print principal, rate, num. quarters, and accumulated funds
- Stop

(a) Flowchart   *(b) Pseudocode*

Step 4: Debugging

We defer this step (and the running of the program) to Section 3.2 in the next chapter.

Follow-up Exercises

28. Why is it best to use a READ statement rather than assignment statements for storing values in PRIN, RATE, and NUM?

29. Write down expected printed output if 1000. is stored in PRIN, 0.015 in RATE, and 2 in NUM. Be specific by showing the print lines.

30. Modify the program to input the customer's name (20 characters), street address (20 characters), and city-state-zip (30 characters). Print these data just before the output of PRIN, making sure that two blank lines separate the print line for city-state-zip from the print line for PRIN.

ADDITIONAL EXERCISES

31. Define the terms below. For each, where appropriate, include FORTRAN rules for its use and state its purpose or function.

computer program	type statement
four-step procedure	INTEGER statement
algorithm	REAL statement
flowchart	DOUBLE PRECISION statement
pseudocode	LOGICAL statement
coding	logical variable
run	logical constant
execute	CHARACTER statement
debugging	PARAMETER statement
FORTRAN character set	symbolic name of constant
data types	assignment statement
keywords	character expression
function names	arithmetic expression
statement	arithmetic operators
line	integer expression
variable name	real expression
integer variable	mixed-type expression
real variable	truncation
character variable	double-precision expression
implicit typing	double-precision variable
explicit typing	double-precision constant
constant	overflow
integer constant	underflow
real constant	roundoff error
E-notation	pairwise arithmetic
precision	arithmetic hierarchy
character constant	intrinsic function
executable statement	list-directed PRINT statement
nonexecutable statement	list-directed READ statement
END statement	input data
STOP statement	

32. **Temperature Conversion.** Write a program that accepts degrees Fahrenheit as input and outputs degrees Celsius. (See Example 2.13 on page 53.) Don't forget to specify the first three steps in the four-step procedure. *Note:* Input data for this problem are provided in Exercise 12 of the next chapter.

33. **Area Problem.** Consider the scenario in Example 2.8 on page 49. Suppose that each top costs C dollars per square inch of surface and X containers are needed. Write a computer program which determines the total cost of X containers. Treat RADIUS, C, and X as input variables. Don't forget to specify the first three steps in the four-step procedure. *Note:* Input data for this problem are provided in Exercise 13 of the next chapter.

34. **Microeconomics Problem.** Consider the scenario in Example 2.11 on page 51. Suppose that all units produced can be sold at a constant price of $100 per unit. Noting that daily revenue is price times the number of units produced and sold in one day and that daily profit is daily revenue less daily cost, write a program that calculates daily profit. Treat UNITS as an input variable, and

print the daily revenue, daily cost, and daily profit. Don't forget to specify the first three steps in the four-step procedure. *Note:* Input data for this problem are provided in Exercise 14 of the next chapter.

35. **Blood Bank Inventory Problem.** Decision making relating to the management of physical inventories is an established area in the management sciences, which, in recent years has been applied increasingly in semiprivate and public organizations.

Suppose that whenever à hospital replenishes its supply of a certain type of blood, it orders from a regional blood bank the amount indicated by the following formula:

$$q = \sqrt{2 \cdot c \cdot d/h}$$

where q is the number of pints of blood to order, c is the administrative and shipping cost (in dollars) of placing the order, d is the average weekly demand (usage) for this type of blood, and h is the cost (dollars per pint per week) of refrigerating the blood.

Also, it can be shown that the cost per week of this inventory policy is given by the formula

$$e = \sqrt{2 \cdot c \cdot h \cdot d}$$

where e is the expected cost (dollars) per week. Write a computer program that inputs values of c, h, and d, and determines how much blood to order and the cost of such a policy. Don't forget to specify the first three steps in the four-step procedure. *Note:* Input data for this problem are provided in Exercise 15 of the next chapter.

36. **Forecasting Population Growth.** In recent years, the prediction of world population levels into the next century has been a concern of many political, environmental, and agricultural planners. The following equation can be used to predict future levels of world population.

$$p = c \cdot (1 + b - d)^n$$

where p is the predicted level of future population, b is the birth rate, c is the current level of population, d is the death rate, and n is the number of years into the future.

Write a program that can be used to predict future population level given the current level, the birth rate, the death rate, and the number of years into the future as input data. Don't forget to specify the first three steps in the four-step procedure. *Note:* Input data for this problem are provided in Exercise 16 of the next chapter.

37. **Automobile Financing Problem.** Many consumer automobile loans require the borrower to pay the same amount of money to the lending institution each month throughout the life of the loan. The monthly payment is based on the amount borrowed (purchase price − trade-in of used car − down payment), the time required for repayment, and the interest rate. A lending institution uses the following formula to determine the car buyer's monthly payment.

$$a = i \cdot (p - d - t) \cdot \left(\frac{(1 + i)^m}{(1 + i)^m - 1} \right)$$

where a = monthly payments

p = purchase price of car

d = down payment

t = trade-in allowance

i = monthly interest rate

m = total number of monthly payments

If the interest rate is expressed on an annual basis, then i in the above formula is replaced by $i/12$. Note that $(p - d - t)$ is the amount to be borrowed.

a. Write a program that determines monthly payments given purchase price, down payment, trade-in allowance, *annual* interest rate, and total number of monthly payments as input data. Include amount borrowed, total number of months, and annual *percent* interest rate in your output, along with the monthly payment. Also include the make and model of the automobile as part of your I/O.

b. Design your program to also calculate and print:

total amount paid over the life of the loan

total interest paid over the life of the loan

the ratio of total interest to total amount paid

Don't forget to specify the first three steps in the four-step procedure. *Note:* Input data for this problem are provided in Exercise 17 of the next chapter.

CHAPTER 3

Running the Complete Computer Program

By now you should have written on paper at least one program from the problems at the end of the last chapter, which, presumably, you are impatient to run on the computer. In this chapter we give you that opportunity by describing and illustrating procedures for running FORTRAN programs in batch and time-sharing environments. *Note:* If you use a terminal to interface with the batch environment, you should study both Section 3.1 and Section 3.2.

3.1
RUNNING A FORTRAN PROGRAM IN A BATCH ENVIRONMENT

If you are using a terminal to interface with the batch environment, then this section still applies to you. In this case, treat lines on the screen or paper as if they were the "image" of a punched card. Your instructor should explain this procedure.

Punched Cards

Computer programs run in a batch environment may use punched cards to transmit both the computer program and the input data to the computer.

The **punched card** illustrated in Figure 3.1 has 80 columns. Each column is capable of holding one character (a digit, a letter, or a special character). Rectangular holes punched in specific positions on the card represent a code of the different characters. Observe that a single hole is used for numbers (0–9), two holes for letters (A–Z), and one, two, or three holes for special characters.

As mentioned in Chapter 1, a *keypunch machine* is used to enter characters onto a punched card. Your instructor should give you a brief introduction to operating the type of keypunch available to you. Then find a keypunch machine and try your hand at it. Really, it's easy.

The Card Deck

To submit a FORTRAN program to a batch environment you need to prepare a **card deck,** which generally consists of four different types of punched cards.

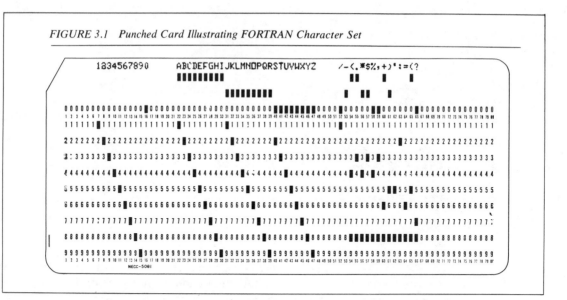

FIGURE 3.1   *Punched Card Illustrating FORTRAN Character Set*

1. Cards for FORTRAN instructions
2. Cards for comments
3. Cards for control
4. Cards for data

Each of these uses the standard 80-column punched card, but differs with respect to subject matter, purpose, and layout.

Instruction Cards.   Each FORTRAN instruction is punched on one or more cards according to a prescribed set of rules that specify how the instruction is to be placed on the punched card. Figure 3.2 summarizes these rules, and Figure 3.3 illustrates the appearance of the FORTRAN *instruction cards* within the card deck for a revised student billing program. Notice that each statement must be punched anywhere between column 7 and column 72 inclusive. At this point, you should begin each statement in column 7, which avoids wasted space and is visually appealing. Later, we will show you how certain indentations further improve the appearance of a program.

The statement number field is used for labeling statements. The instruction cards in Figure 3.3 do not use this field, as we do not have a need for statement numbers until the next chapter.

The continuation field described in Figure 3.2 is not utilized by the instruction cards in Figure 3.3, since no statement is too long for one card. FORTRAN allows up to 19 successive continuation lines (cards).

Finally, in columns 73 through 80 of Figure 3.3 we have identified each instruction card as SB (which is our abbreviation for student billing) and sequenced each card numerically. The use of this identification/sequence field is optional; in most cases, you probably will not use it. Many commercial programs use it, but you should have no need for it.

FIGURE 3.2   *Rules for Placement of FORTRAN Instruction on Punched Card*

Columns On Punched Card	Use	Explanation
1–5	Statement number field	These may contain an unsigned, nonzero, integer constant that serves as a statement number.
6	Continuation field	This is used when a statement is too long to fit on the preceding card. Any character other than a blank or zero in column 6 identifies this card as a continuation of the preceding card.
7–72	Statement field	These contain the FORTRAN statement, except for the statement number.
73–80	Identification/ sequence field	These are used either to identify a particular program or to sequence cards within the program so that if cards are dropped, the deck can be reordered correctly. The contents of this field are ignored by the compiler.

Have you been wondering about the *use of blank spaces in FORTRAN statements?* With the exception of blanks within character constants, the compiler ignores blank spaces. For example, you need not be concerned about the number of blank spaces between NAME, ID, and CREDIT in the READ list, or around equal signs and arithmetic operators in assignment statements. Use blank spaces simply to improve readability. It's even permissible to embed blank spaces within key words, such as RE AD, but we don't recommend it since it detracts from readability.

Comment Cards.   Each card that has a C punched in column 1 is known as a *comment card* or *comment line.* Thus the comment cards in Figure 3.3 identify this program as

FIGURE 3.3   *Complete Card Deck for Running the Revised Student Billing Program*

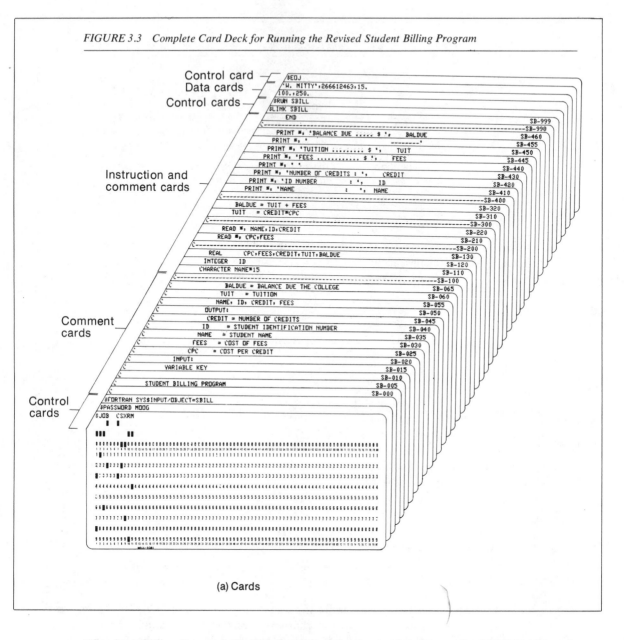

Control card
Data cards
Control cards
Instruction and comment cards
Comment cards
Control cards

```
$EOJ
'W. MITTY',266612463,15.
100.,250.
$RUN SBILL
$LINK SBILL
        END                                              SB-999
C-------------------------------------------------------SB-998
        PRINT *, 'BALANCE DUE ..... $ ',    BALDUE       SB-460
        PRINT *, '                        ----------'    SB-455
        PRINT *, 'TUITION ......... $ ',    TUIT         SB-450
        PRINT *, 'FEES ............ $ ',    FEES         SB-445
        PRINT *, ' '                                     SB-440
        PRINT *, 'NUMBER OF CREDITS : ',    CREDIT       SB-430
        PRINT *, 'ID NUMBER      : ',    ID              SB-420
        PRINT *, 'NAME           : ',    NAME            SB-410
C-------------------------------------------------------SB-400
        BALDUE = TUIT + FEES                             SB-320
        TUIT   = CREDIT*CPC                              SB-310
C-------------------------------------------------------SB-300
        READ *, NAME,ID,CREDIT                           SB-220
        READ *, CPC,FEES                                 SB-210
C-------------------------------------------------------SB-200
        REAL       CPC,FEES,CREDIT,TUIT,BALDUE           SB-130
        INTEGER    ID                                    SB-120
        CHARACTER NAME*15                                SB-110
C-------------------------------------------------------SB-100
C       BALDUE = BALANCE DUE THE COLLEGE                 SB-065
C       TUIT   = TUITION                                 SB-060
C       NAME, ID, CREDIT, FEES                           SB-055
C       OUTPUT:                                          SB-050
C       CREDIT = NUMBER OF CREDITS                       SB-045
C       ID     = STUDENT IDENTIFICATION NUMBER           SB-040
C       NAME   = STUDENT NAME                            SB-035
C       FEES   = COST OF FEES                            SB-030
C       CPC    = COST PER CREDIT                         SB-025
C       INPUT:                                           SB-020
C       VARIABLE KEY                                     SB-015
C                                                        SB-010
C       STUDENT BILLING PROGRAM                          SB-005
C                                                        SB-000
$FORTRAN SYS$INPUT/OBJECT=SBILL
$PASSWORD MOOG
$JOB  CSXRM
```

(a) Cards

"Student Billing Program," describe the variables, and segment the FORTRAN code for better readability. An asterisk in column 1 also identifies a comment line in FORTRAN 77. A completely blank card also passes as a comment line in FORTRAN 77, which is convenient for visually segmenting portions of a program.

Comment lines are useful for program **documentation.** This means that they can be used to describe programs, identify sections of programs, explain logic, and define variables. In fact, the entire description under Step 1 in the four-step procedure and the

```
Control        ⎧ $JOB  CSXRM
cards          ⎨ $PASSWORD MOOG
               ⎩ $FORTRAN SYS$INPUT/OBJECT=SBILL
               ⎧ C                                                              SB-000
               ⎪ C         STUDENT BILLING PROGRAM                              SB-005
               ⎪ C                                                              SB-010
               ⎪ C                                                              SB-015
               ⎪ C         VARIABLE KEY                                         SB-020
               ⎪ C           INPUT:                                             SB-025
Comment        ⎪ C             CPC     = COST PER CREDIT                        SB-030
cards          ⎨ C             FEES    = COST OF FEES                           SB-035
               ⎪ C             NAME    = STUDENT NAME                           SB-040
               ⎪ C             ID      = STUDENT IDENTIFICATION NUMBER          SB-045
               ⎪ C             CREDIT  = NUMBER OF CREDITS                       SB-050
               ⎪ C           OUTPUT:                                            SB-055
               ⎪ C             NAME, ID, CREDIT, FEES                           SB-060
               ⎪ C             TUIT    = TUITION                                SB-065
               ⎩ C             BALDUE  = BALANCE DUE THE COLLEGE                SB-100
               ⎧ C----------------------------------------------------------    SB-110
               ⎪       CHARACTER NAME*15                                        SB-120
               ⎪       INTEGER   ID                                             SB-130
               ⎪       REAL      CPC,FEES,CREDIT,TUIT,BALDUE                    SB-200
               ⎪ C----------------------------------------------------------    SB-210
               ⎪       READ *, CPC,FEES                                         SB-220
               ⎪       READ *, NAME,ID,CREDIT                                   SB-300
               ⎪ C----------------------------------------------------------    SB-310
               ⎪       TUIT   = CREDIT*CPC                                      SB-320
Instruction and⎨       BALDUE = TUIT + FEES                                     SB-400
comment cards  ⎪ C----------------------------------------------------------    SB-410
               ⎪       PRINT *, 'NAME              :  ',    NAME               SB-420
               ⎪       PRINT *, 'ID NUMBER         : ',     ID                 SB-430
               ⎪       PRINT *, 'NUMBER OF CREDITS : ',     CREDIT             SB-440
               ⎪       PRINT *, ' '                                            SB-445
               ⎪       PRINT *, 'FEES ........... $ ',      FEES               SB-450
               ⎪       PRINT *, 'TUITION ........ $ ',      TUIT               SB-455
               ⎪       PRINT *, '            _____'                         SB-460
               ⎪       PRINT *, 'BALANCE DUE ..... $ ',     BALDUE             SB-998
               ⎩ C----------------------------------------------------------    SB-999
                       END
Control cards  ⎧ $LINK SBILL
               ⎨ $RUN  SBILL
Data cards     ⎧ 100.,250.
               ⎨ 'W. MITTY',266612463,15.
Control card   ⎧ $EOJ
```

(b) Listing of card deck (equivalent to "card" deck typed at terminal for processing by batch interface)

pseudocode version in Step 2 can be incorporated in a program by using comment lines. At a minimum, *each program you write should include comment lines that identify the program and describe symbolic names.*

Note that the comment lines made up of dashes effectively segment the program into "blocks" of related instructions. This small effort improves the style of the program, which facilitates readability and any subsequent maintenance (changes). See the listing in Figure 3.3(b) to realize how visually appealing this is, since it's difficult to appreciate this point by looking at a card deck.

You can place comment cards anywhere within the set of instruction cards, as they are ignored by the compiler. Also, *all 80 columns of the comment card can be used.*

Control Cards.   *Control cards* supply information to the operating system regarding user identification number, user name, expected processing time, programming language, and other factors.

Control cards are *not* part of the FORTRAN language: moreover, the specific control cards necessary to run a program vary from computer center to computer center. All computer centers, however, require the use of control cards; otherwise, the essential information they supply would not be available for the operating system to do its job. *Your instructor will provide you with additional information concerning the control cards for your computer center.*

Data Cards.   Typically, computer programs are designed to "read" data from an external source such as punched cards. For example, in the program of Figure 3.3, the data for NAME, ID, and CREDIT are not part of the FORTRAN program. Instead, the program contains a READ instruction to transfer the student data from a punched card to computer memory. In general, cards that contain data for processing by a READ statement are called *data cards.*

The placement of data on a punched card does not follow the rules specified for placing a FORTRAN instruction on a punched card. *Data may be punched in columns 1 through 80.*

Data cards must physically follow the instruction cards that make up the entire FORTRAN program, since the instruction cards must be processed first by the card reader in order for the program to *compile.* If the program compiles without errors, then the computer begins *executing* or "running" the program; that is, it carries out your executable instructions in the same sequence given by the cards. *Each time the computer executes a READ statement, a new data card is processed.*

The first list-directed READ statement in Figure 3.3 has a list of two real variables: CPC and FEES. Hence the *first* data card has two real data items, 100. and 250., separated by a comma. *Besides the comma, one or more blanks or a slash can be used to separate data items that are to be input through a list-directed READ statement.*[1]

The second list-directed READ statement has a list of three variables: the character variable NAME, the integer variable ID, and the real variable CREDIT. Thus the *second* data card has three data items: the character value 'W. MITTY', the integer value 266612463, and the real value 15.0. *Note that character values must be enclosed in apostrophes when input through list-directed READ statements.*

You should carefully note the consistency of sequence and data type between the values in the data cards and the list of variables in the READ statements, as described below.

---

[1] We don't recommend use of the slash to separate data items (unless you know what you're doing), as this causes termination of execution for that READ statement after the assignment of the immediately preceding data item.

Remember that each time the computer executes a READ statement, a new data card is processed. For example, if the READ statements were arranged as

```
READ *,CPC,FEES
READ *,NAME
READ *,ID
READ *,CREDIT
```

then data would have to be arranged as shown here.

Data Card	Values
First	100., 250.
Second	'W. MITTY'
Third	266612463
Fourth	15.

The general setup for a card deck is depicted by Figure 3.4. Once again, however, we remind you that the nature and placement of control cards is specific to each system.

Process of Running the Program

Figure 3.5 describes the process of running a FORTRAN program in a batch environment. Figure 3.6 illustrates **computer printouts** when the card deck of Figure 3.3 is submitted to a VAX-11/780 computer.[2]

[2] Most likely your computer is different. Read on, however, since the general discussion still applies to you.

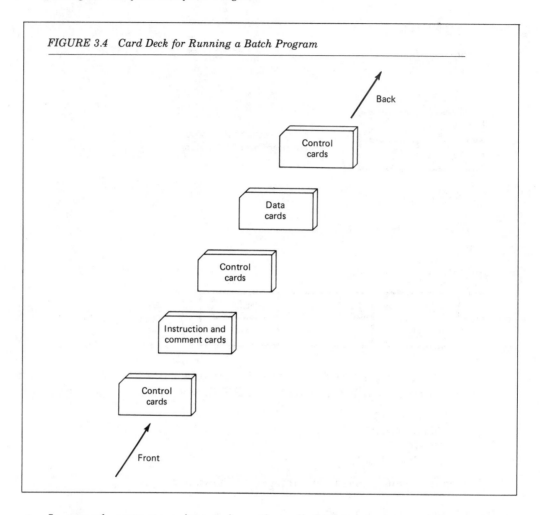

FIGURE 3.4   *Card Deck for Running a Batch Program*

In general, computer printouts have three distinct segments, assuming errors are absent:

1. Listing
2. Output
3. Technical matter

The **listing** is a printed copy of the FORTRAN program. This is simply a convenience which is especially useful when you are debugging or modifying a program. The **output** is printed matter based on the execution of PRINT statements in the program. **Technical matter** includes the technical information on control cards and other information, such as amount of memory and CPU time which has been utilized. For example, the program in Figure 3.6 used 5.12 seconds of CPU time to compile and execute. To simplify Figure 3.6 (and spare you the agony), we have eliminated more than two pages of technical matter between the listing and the output.

FIGURE 3.5   *Process of Running a FORTRAN Program in a Batch Environment*

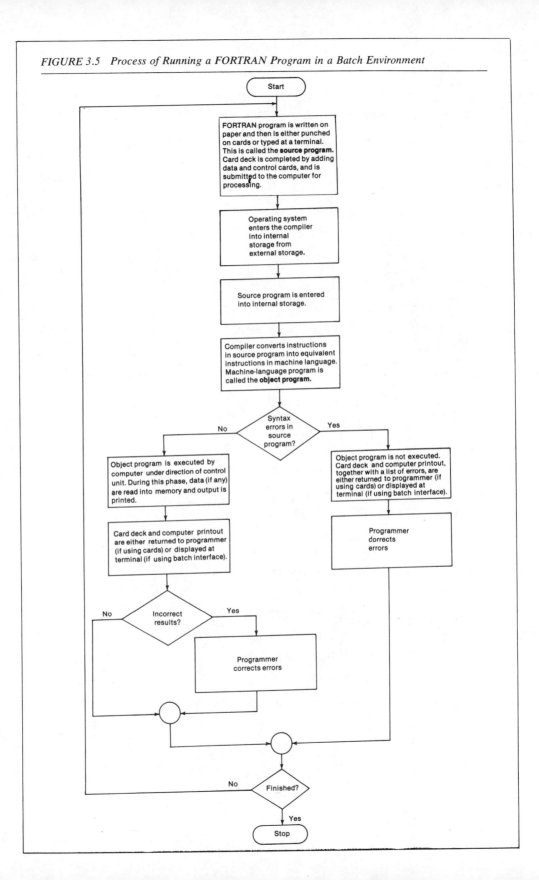

FIGURE 3.6   *Computer Printout for Card Deck of Figure 3.3*

```
      C                                                              SB-000
      C            STUDENT BILLING PROGRAM                           SB-005
      C                                                              SB-010
      C            VARIABLE KEY                                      SB-015
      C              INPUT:                                          SB-020
      C                CPC     = COST PER CREDIT                     SB-025
      C                FEES    = COST OF FEES                        SB-030
      C                NAME    = STUDENT NAME                        SB-035
      C                ID      = STUDENT IDENTIFICATION NUMBER       SB-040
      C                CREDIT  = NUMBER OF CREDITS                   SB-045
      C              OUTPUT:                                         SB-050
      C                NAME, ID, CREDIT, FEES                        SB-055
      C                TUIT    = TUITION                             SB-060
      C                BALDUE  = BALANCE DUE THE COLLEGE             SB-065
      C--------------------------------------------------------------SB-100
0001            CHARACTER NAME*15                                    SB-110
0002            INTEGER    ID                                        SB-120
0003            REAL      CPC,FEES,CREDIT,TUIT,BALDUE                SB-130
      C--------------------------------------------------------------SB-200
0004            READ *, CPC,FEES                                     SB-210
0005            READ *, NAME,ID,CREDIT                               SB-220
      C--------------------------------------------------------------SB-300
0006            TUIT   = CREDIT*CPC                                  SB-310
0007            BALDUE = TUIT + FEES                                 SB-320
      C--------------------------------------------------------------SB-400
0008            PRINT *, 'NAME              :   ',    NAME           SB-410
0009            PRINT *, 'ID NUMBER         : ',      ID             SB-420
0010            PRINT *, 'NUMBER OF CREDITS : ',      CREDIT         SB-430
0011            PRINT *, ' '                                         SB-440
0012            PRINT *, 'FEES ........... $ ',       FEES           SB-445
0013            PRINT *, 'TUITION ........ $ ',       TUIT           SB-450
0014            PRINT *, '                   --------'               SB-455
0015            PRINT *, 'BALANCE DUE ..... $ ',      BALDUE         SB-460
      C--------------------------------------------------------------SB-998
0016            END                                                  SB-999
```
} Listing

⌐— Line numbers are added by this system

(Omitted Technical Matter)

```
NAME              :    W. MITTY
ID NUMBER         :    266612463
NUMBER OF CREDITS :    15.00000
FEES ........... $     250.0000
TUITION ........ $     1500.000
                       --------
BALANCE DUE ..... $    1750.000
```
} Output

```
$EOJ
   CSXRM        JOB TERMINATED AT 12-AUG-1980 15:24:15.64

   ACCOUNTING INFORMATION:
   BUFFERED I/O COUNT:          80      PEAK WORKING SET SIZE:   150
   DIRECT I/O COUNT:            99      PEAK VIRTUAL SIZE:       218
   PAGE FAULTS:                508      MOUNTED VOLUMES:           0
   ELAPSED TIME:      0 00:00:05.12     ELAPSED TIME:      0 00:01:35.18
```
} Technical matter

Note that the value of the integer variable ID is printed without a decimal point whereas the values of the real variables CREDIT, FEES, TUIT, and BALDUE are printed with decimal points. In general, the spacing of list-directed output differs from system to system. You should confirm, however, that all output values are correct.

Finally, note that the input data punched on data cards do not directly appear anywhere on the computer printout. These data can be printed out only through PRINT statements, which is what we did with NAME, ID, CREDIT, and FEES.

Follow-up Exercises

Prepare and submit a card deck on your particular batch system for the exercises below.

1. **Student Billing Program.** First submit the job in part a; then make the necessary changes and submit the job in part b.
   a. Prepare the same program as that in Figure 3.3, but input 18.5 credits and whatever name and id number you wish. Confirm that your output is correct.
   b. Prepare the same program as that in Figure 3.3, but type CREDIT and all other numeric variables as integer. Use the same data input as the example, with one change: Include dashes in the student identification (Social Security) number, that is, 266-61-2463. How must you type ID? What are the advantages of typing the computational variables integer? The disadvantages?

2. **Bank Savings Program.** Prepare and submit the same program as in Section 2.7 on page 62. Use 1000. for PRIN, 0.015 for RATE, and 4 for NUM. Confirm that your output is correct by hand calculation. Repeat for the same PRIN and RATE values but change NUM to 20. Include comment cards at the beginning of the program that identify the program as a BANK SAVINGS PROGRAM and define the variables.

3.2
RUNNING A FORTRAN PROGRAM IN A TIME-SHARING ENVIRONMENT

FORTRAN programs that are run in a time-sharing environment are similar to those run in a batch environment. You should, however, be aware of some differences.

In time sharing you enter your program via a terminal, whereas in batch you might enter the program using punched cards.

In time sharing the output comes back to you at the terminal; in batch your output is usually produced on a line printer.

In time sharing the time between submitting a program and receiving the results is almost instantaneous; in batch this "turnaround time" could run anywhere from a few seconds (if remote job entry is used) to hours.

If you are using a batch interface system (that is, using a terminal to prepare and submit batch jobs), these distinctions become blurred. In this case, you can take advantage of desirable features in each environment.

System Commands

In time sharing you communicate with the computer by entering your program at a terminal, through which information is transmitted over either a telephone line or a cable to the computer. To interact with the operating system when you are at the terminal requires the use of a set of commands called **system commands.**[3] Among other things, system commands allow you to run the program, list the program, and save the program for future recall. Therefore, when you run programs in a time-sharing environment, you will have a set of system commands to learn in addition to the FORTRAN instructions.

Unfortunately, system commands are not universal, which means that they differ from one time-sharing system to another. *Your instructor, therefore, must provide you with the system commands that are specific to your system.*

Work Area versus Secondary Storage Area

The first step in using a time-sharing system is "signing on." This means that you must type your assigned identification (user) code, which is then validated by the operating system. If your identification code is acceptable, the operating system assigns you a portion of memory, which we call the **work area.** In fact, each user currently utilizing the time-sharing system is assigned a separate work area. The purpose of the work area is to store both FORTRAN instructions and values for variable names.

Once you "sign off" a time-sharing system, the program in your work area is "erased." For this reason, each user of a time-sharing system also has an assigned **secondary storage area** (usually magnetic disk), which is often called a **library.** The secondary storage area allows you to save programs that you prepare in your work area for recall at a later date. In other words, your library saves you the trouble of having to retype programs that you previously entered into your work area.

In addition to storing programs, libraries also store data that can be used as input to programs. A set of data stored in this manner is called a **data file.** The creation and processing of data files are different for each time-sharing system, so we omit the topic in this book. Its use, however, is quite important. Ask your instructor if data files will be used in your course.

Illustration

In this section we illustrate a time-sharing run on Honeywell's TSS system. *If you use a different system, your system will not operate exactly as shown in the illustration.* In this case, just pay attention to the principles, since these are universal. *Your instructor will discuss the appropriate modifications for your system.*

The program we use is a modified version of the bank savings program on page 62.

---

[3] These commands are the time-sharing counterpart of the control language on control cards in a batch system.

The following changes were made in the original program.

1. Comment lines and conversational input were added, as discussed shortly. These features improve the design of the program.
2. Each line in the program was numbered in order for the computer to sequence statements and the user to make modifications. This is necessary on all time-sharing systems.

In what follows on page 80, boxed segments indicate the computer run and marginal notes describe the corresponding boxed segment. To point out clearly the interactions between the user and the computer, all information typed by the computer is shaded; information typed by the user is not shaded.

Line Numbers.   Note that, as the FORTRAN program is entered at the terminal, each instruction is preceded by a **line number.** These numbers, which typically run from one to five digits in length, are used to sequence time-shared programs. After a program is entered and before it is executed, the operating system rearranges the instructions in the work area from lowest to highest number. In other words, the instructions can be entered "out of order," but the computer executes in the desired sequence according to the line numbers. This feature makes it convenient to insert instructions into an existing program. For example, suppose we inadvertently omit the REAL statement in the above illustration and realize this once the END statement has been typed. We can simply "insert" the REAL statement by typing it after the END statement and giving it a line number that numerically falls between the line numbers of the INTEGER statement and the next statement (between 300 and 390). Also note that we have incremented line numbers by at least 10, that is, each line number changes by no less than 10. This allows room to insert new instructions at some future time, should it be necessary to do so. Finally, a minimum of one blank space must separate your instruction from your line number.

Comment Lines.   Line 100 in the program is called a **comment line.** Its purpose is to document the name of the program within the program itself. Lines 100–200, 390, 490, 590, and 690 are all comment lines. In general, comment lines are used for program **documentation,** which means that they are meant for human eyes to describe programs, identify sections of programs, explain logic, and define variables. In fact, both the entire description under Step 1 in the four-step procedure and the pseudocode version in Step 2 can be incorporated in a program by using comment lines. At a minimum, *each program you write should include comment lines that identify the program and describe symbolic names.*

Note that lines 200, 390, 490, 590, and 690 are used to segment the program into "blocks" of related instructions. Moreover, each block has a certain range of line numbers (400s, 500s, etc.). These little efforts improve the style of the program, which facilitates readability and any subsequent maintenance (changes).

Comment lines are ignored by the compiler; they are simply listed along with the program. How does the compiler distinguish a comment line from a FORTRAN instruc-

1.

```
USER ID -SAG20
PASSWORD-- ▓▓▓▓▓▓▓▓▓▓▓▓
```

Entry of user identification and password for signing on. Password entry is printed over by the computer for security purposes. *Note:* Each time you finish typing a line, you must depress the carriage return key on the terminal.

2.

```
*NEW BANK
```

The computer types an asterisk to indicate that it is ready for us to do something next. Our response is a system command that clears the work area and indicates that a new program named BANK will be entered.

3.

```
*100C      BANK SAVINGS PROGRAM
*110C
*120C      VARIABLE KEY
*130C      INPUT:
*140C         PRIN  =  PRINCIPAL
*150C         RATE  =  QUARTERLY INTEREST RATE
*160C         NUM   =  NUMBER OF QUARTERS
*170C      OUTPUT:
*180C         ALL INPUT VARIABLES
*190C         ACCUM =  ACCUMULATED FUNDS
*200C      ------------------------------------
*300       INTEGER NUM
*310       REAL    PRIN,RATE,ACCUM
*390C      ------------------------------------
*400       PRINT *,'PLEASE ENTER PRINCIPAL, QUARTERLY'
*410       PRINT *,'INTEREST RATE, AND NUMBER QUARTERS'
*420       READ *,  PRIN,RATE,NUM
*490C      ------------------------------------
*500       ACCUM = PRIN*(1. + RATE)**NUM
*590C      ------------------------------------
*600       PRINT *,'PRINCIPAL = ',PRIN
*610       PRINT *,'RATE      = ',RATE
*620       PRINT *,'QUARTERS  = ',NUM
*630       PRINT *,'AMOUNT    = ',ACCUM
*690C      ------------------------------------
*700       END
```

Entry of program into work area; lines 100–200, 390, 490, 590, and 690 are comment lines.

4.

```
*FRN
```

System command that first compiles and then executes a FORTRAN program.

5.

```
PLEASE ENTER PRINCIPAL, QUARTERLY
INTEREST RATE, AND NUMBER QUARTERS
=1000,.015,4
```

Computer executes lines 400–420. We respond with data input. Computer stores 1000. in PRIN, .015 in RATE, and 4 in NUM.

6.

```
PRINCIPAL =    0.1000000E 04
RATE      =    0.1500000E-01
QUARTERS  =           4
AMOUNT    =    0.1061363E 04
```

Computer executes lines 600–630, and then stops processing when it executes line 700.

7.

```
*SAVE BANK
```

System command for creating in the library a duplicate copy of program in work area; program now has been saved for recall at a later time.

8.

```
*DELETE;*
```

System command for erasing program from the work area; program still remains in the library.

9.

```
*FRN

LOADER DIAGNOSTICS
<F> ENTRY NOT FOUND
```

Attempted run of nonexistent program in the work area; error message confirms that program was not found in the work area.

10.

```
*OLD BANK
```

System command for creating in the work area a duplicate copy of a specific program in the library (program BANK in this case); a copy of the program still remains in the library.

11.

```
*LIST
```

System command to list (at the terminal) program in the work area.

12.

```
100C     BANK SAVINGS PROGRAM
110C
120C     VARIABLE KEY
130C       INPUT:
140C         PRIN  = PRINCIPAL
150C         RATE  = QUARTERLY INTEREST RATE
160C         NUM   = NUMBER OF QUARTERS
170C       OUTPUT:
180C         ALL INPUT VARIABLES
190C         ACCUM = ACCUMULATED FUNDS
200C
300      INTEGER NUM
310      REAL    PRIN,RATE,ACCUM
390C
400      PRINT *,'PLEASE ENTER PRINCIPAL, QUARTERLY'
410      PRINT *,'INTEREST RATE, AND NUMBER QUARTERS'
420      READ *,  PRIN,RATE,NUM
490C
500      ACCUM = PRIN*(1. + RATE)**NUM
590C
600      PRINT *, 'PRINCIPAL =',PRIN
610      PRINT *, 'RATE      =',RATE
620      PRINT *, 'QUARTERS  =',NUM
630      PRINT *, 'AMOUNT    =',ACCUM
690C
700      END
```

Listing of program in the work area; programs need not be listed to be run.

13.

```
*FRN

PLEASE ENTER PRINCIPAL, QUARTERLY
INTEREST RATE, AND NUMBER QUARTERS
=1000.,.015,20

PRINCIPAL =   0.10000000E 04
RATE      =   0.15000000E-01
QUARTERS  =   20
AMOUNT    =   0.13468550E 04
```

Rerun of program in the work area for each new set of data input.

14.

```
*BYE
```

System command for signing off.

15.

```
**COST: $  1.63  TO DATE: .$   811.90=   1%
**ON AT 13.817 - OFF AT 14.009 ON 03/20/80
```

System prints cost usage statistics, time connected to system, and date.

tion? In the above case, we typed a C immediately after the line number. We also could have used an asterisk; both are consistent with the ANSI Standard. *Methods of identifying comment lines, however, can differ from time-sharing system to time-sharing system.* Ask your instructor how comment lines are specified on your time-sharing system.

Other System Commands.   The system commands which we have illustrated represent a small subset of the many commands available for a typical system. For example, powerful commands exist for making either editorial or debugging changes that are far superior to the process of making changes in a batch environment. Also, please note that, unless the time-sharing system you are about to use is a Honeywell TSS system, the system commands for your system will differ from those described here. Your instructor will provide you with the details.

Compilation versus Execution.   As you know from Chapter 1, a high-level language such as FORTRAN first must be translated or compiled into the machine language of the computer. This process is known as **compilation.** If rules of the FORTRAN language have not been violated, the operating system instructs the control unit of the computer to execute or "run" the program. **Execution** means that the computer carries out your executable instructions in the sequence indicated by your line numbers. Thus, in our illustration, line 400 is executed first (since lines 100–390 are nonexecutable), then line 410, and so on through line 700. Boxes 4–6 and 13 illustrate this process.

Conversational Programming.   A good programming practice is to print a "prompting" message reminding the program user of what data are to be entered next. This is accomplished by placing a PRINT statement containing a description of the input data *immediately before* the corresponding READ statement. In our illustration, we implement this idea in lines 400 to 420. The sequence in box 5 illustrates this so-called **conversational** or **interactive programming,** whereby the computer and the user carry out a "dialogue." In this type of program design, each PRINT statement that precedes a READ statement prints "conversation" in the form of a computer request. The READ statement then accepts the user's response.

The first two lines in box 5 are printed when the computer executes lines 400 and 410 in the program. Next, the computer executes the READ statement in line 420 and prints an = sign at the terminal. [Many systems print a question mark (?) instead of an equal sign (=).] At this point we can enter the appropriate data corresponding to the variable list in the READ statement.

The READ statement in line 420 contains a list of three variables: PRIN, RATE, and NUM; hence, following the equal sign, we type the three corresponding data items given by 1000., .015, 4. After typing the last data item, we depress the carriage return key on the terminal. This act completes the execution of the READ statement, which results in the storage of 1000. for PRIN, 0.015 for RATE, and 4 for NUM as illustrated on the next page.

Each time the computer executes a READ statement, a new data line is requested (a new equal sign is printed in our case). For example, if the single READ statement were to be replaced by the statements

```
420 READ *,PRIN
430 READ *,RATE
440 READ *,NUM
```

then data input would appear as

```
= 1000.
= 0.015
= 4
```

Character values should be enclosed in apostrophes in the input line, as illustrated below.

Other methods of data input exist, depending on the system. Again, your instructor will provide the details.

Blank Spaces. The compiler ignores blank spaces within FORTRAN statements, with the exception of character data. For example, you need not be concerned about the number of blank spaces between PRIN, RATE, NUM in the READ list or PRIN, RATE, ACCUM in the REAL list; around equal signs (=) and arithmetic operators in assignment statements; and around commas in READ and PRINT statements. Use blank spaces simply to improve readability. It's even permissible to embed blank spaces within keywords, such as PR INT, but we don't recommend it since it detracts from readability.

---

[4] If you're really on top of things, you will have noticed that we slipped up and forgot the decimal point for 1000 in box 5. It's best to include the decimal point, but if we forget, the computer places the decimal point after the last digit in storage for a real variable.

Continuation Lines.   Occasionally, a FORTRAN instruction will be too long to fit on one line, which means that it must be continued on the next line. The method of accomplishing this differs from one system to another, so ask your instructor.

Follow-up Exercises

3. Answer the following on the basis of the foregoing illustration.
    a. How much money do we end up with after four quarters when we start with $1000 and earn interest at 6 percent per year compounded quarterly?
    b. After five years?
4. For your particular time-sharing system, run the following.
    a. The program of Example 2.16 on page 60. Use 18.5 for CREDIT and whatever name and identification number you wish. Confirm that your output is correct by hand calculation. Repeat for 12 credits. Include comment lines at the beginning of the program. The first comment line states STUDENT BILLING PROGRAM and other comment lines define the variables ID, CREDIT, TUIT, and BALDUE. List your program.
    b. The program in our illustration above. Use 1000. for PRIN and .015 for RATE, but successively change NUM as follows: 4, 8, 12, 16, 20, 40. List your program.

3.3
DEBUGGING PROGRAMS

Debugging is the process of detecting and correcting errors. Much of your time, in fact, will be spent on this process. To help you along, we now define general types of errors, illustrate each in both batch and time-sharing environments, and indicate how you go about debugging such errors.

Error Detection and Correction

Any programming error can be classified into one of the following three categories:

1. Syntax error
2. Execution error
3. Logic error

A **syntax error** occurs when a FORTRAN instruction violates a rule of the FORTRAN language. When you make this type of error, your program will fail to compile, and the compiler will identify the incorrect instruction by an appropriate diagnostic message. Thus syntax errors are detected by the compiler during the compilation of the program. If a syntax error is found, it follows that the program never enters the execution phase.

Common syntax errors at this point in your programming development include the following.

1. Typing error, as when READ is typed as REED.
2. Variable name that exceeds the allowable number of characters (six in the ANSI FORTRAN standard). *Note:* A separate error message will be printed for each statement that contains this variable name.
3. Imbalance between the number of left parentheses and the number of right parentheses in an arithmetic expression.
4. Missing equal sign (=) in an assignment statement.
5. Arithmetic expression to the left of the equal sign in an assignment statement.
6. For those of you using punched cards, a violation of the rules for placing a statement on a card, as when the keyword END is punched within the first six columns of a card.
7. Forgetting to include an END statement.
8. Forgetting to use an asterisk for multiplication. (This one might get by the compiler but will then show up as either an execution or logic error.)
9. Omitting required commas in READ and PRINT statements.

Once you determine the exact nature of your syntax error (with the help of the error message), you simply replace the incorrect instruction with a syntactically correct instruction.

Your program begins executing only after it is free of syntax errors. Unfortunately, a second type of error can occur after the compilation phase: An **execution error** is one that takes place during the execution of your program. Typically, when an execution error is encountered, an error message or code is printed and the computer terminates execution. Common execution errors include the following.

1. Incorrect data input, as when a letter is typed for numeric data input.
2. End-of-file condition, as when the computer attempts to execute a READ statement and a data item is not provided.
3. Improper numeric condition during the evaluation of an arithmetic expression; for example, you might attempt to divide by a variable that has the value zero in its storage location, or you might attempt to raise a negative real number to a real power, or you might attempt to take the square root of a negative value, or the value might exceed the range of values allowed (underflow or overflow). In the last case, some systems continue execution by assigning machine "infinity" (largest possible value) to the value that overflows and machine zero to the value that underflows, whereas other systems stop execution. *Note:* Some systems do not identify integer overflow/underflow. They print a "junk" number, so beware (and solve Exercise 10 at the end of the chapter).
4. Initialization of variables, where **initialization** is a term that refers to the initial value taken on by a variable. Just before execution, some systems assign arbitrary values to all variables, whereas other systems initialize all variables to zero. To illustrate the possible difficulties you might encounter, consider the following statement.

$$N = N + 1$$

Now, suppose that prior to this statement you have not *explicitly* assigned a value to N. One of three things will happen when the system executes this statement.

a. An arbitrary (wrong) value is used for the N to the right of the equal sign.
b. A value of zero is used for the N to the right of the equal sign.
c. The system treats the initial contents of N as undefined and aborts execution. Thus whenever a variable is used in an arithmetic expression it needs to have been previously defined (explicitly assigned a value) either through an assignment statement or through an input statement. For example, if we want N to have an initial value of zero, then earlier in the program we should write

$$N = 0$$

Generally, it is more difficult to determine the exact location and nature of an execution error than of a syntax error, for several reasons: execution errors tend to be system dependent; execution error messages may be more ambiguous than syntax error messages in locating and diagnosing errors; the cause of an execution error may be due to faulty program logic, which is related to the third category of errors.

If your program runs but gives you unexpected, unwanted, or erroneous output, then you may assume that a **logic error** exists. Common logic errors include the following.

1. No output. Did you forget to include PRINT statements?
2. Wrong numeric results.
    a. Are the input data correct?
    b. Are the arithmetic expressions and assignment statements correct? In particular, check the sequence of arithmetic calculations within arithmetic expressions.
    c. Is the program logic correct? For example, are the statements in proper sequence?
    d. Have any statements been omitted?
3. Unintentional, displeasing, or unaligned output. Output from a program should be labeled, easy to read, and visually appealing. Before writing down your PRINT statements, you should map out your output on a sheet of paper. You might be surprised at how much effort will be saved by this practice. By the way, once you're assigned Modules B and D, you will (theoretically) be able to control the placement of output exactly.

Here is some emphatic advice: *Just because your program runs (that is, you get results) it does not mean your program is correct—check your results for logic errors against a set of known results.* We cannot overemphasize the importance of this advice. In Step 4 of the four-step procedure, *always* validate your program under varying conditions using a set of test data for which you already know the correct results.

In your efforts to debug execution and logic errors, you might try the following **classic debugging techniques.**

1. **Roleplaying the computer.** Pretend that you're the computer and begin "executing" your program line by line. As you do this, enter data into boxes that represent

storage locations. You will be surprised at how many errors you can find this way. Really. You should do this with every program you write.

2. **Mirror or echo printing.**   To check your data input for errors, place a PRINT statement immediately after each READ statement. The paired READ and PRINT statements must have identical variable lists. Once you have confirmed that the input data are correct, remove these statements.

3. **Diagnostic PRINT (trace) statements.**   Place temporary PRINT statements at strategic points in your program. These should print the values of important variables as the calculating sequence evolves. In other words, these PRINT statements provide you intermediate results that may be helpful in tracing what, where, and when something went wrong. When the error is corrected, remove these PRINT statements.

4. *Programming technique.*   You will avoid many errors if you carefully develop the first three steps of our four-step procedure. Get in the habit now.

5. *Experience.*   Learn by your mistakes. Experience is a classic teacher.

6. *Attitude.*   Debugging can be fun. Finding errors and correcting them can be a very satisfying experience. Perhaps you will become the greatest debugging sleuth in computer history.

Batch Environment

Figure 3.7 shows a listing for the student billing program that purposely incorporates syntax, execution, and logic errors. The syntax error messages are those given by the VAX 11/780 compiler.[5] The compiler has printed several syntax error messages, each of which begins with a percent (%) sign, although this varies from compiler to compiler. Note that each error message is printed immediately following the incorrect line of instruction.

As you can see, some error messages are helpful, while others are either ambiguous or misleading. You should note that error messages vary from compiler to compiler, and some messages may require you to seek more detailed explanations in manuals for this purpose. The following description should clarify the nature of these errors.

Line	Syntax Error
1–3	No syntax errors
4	READ mispelled as REED
5–6	No syntax errors
7	Arithmetic expression to left of equal sign
8–10	No syntax errors
11	Missing comma following PRINT *
12–15	No syntax errors
16	END punched in columns 1–3 instead of columns 7–9. Note that this last error generated three sets of error messages. If the END statement is simply omitted, then this compiler prints the third error message and automatically inserts the END statement, as described by the message "END is assumed."

[5] It's also possible to make an error in preparing your control cards, in which case your program will not execute. **Control card errors** are specific to the system you're using, so carefully review the instructions you received for preparing control cards.

FIGURE 3.7   Illustration of Syntax Errors

```
      C                                                                    SB-000
      C           STUDENT BILLING PROGRAM                                  SB-005
      C                                                                    SB-010
      C           VARIABLE KEY                                             SB-015
      C             INPUT:                                                 SB-020
      C               CPC    = COST PER CREDIT                             SB-025
      C               FEES   = COST OF FEES                                SB-030
      C               NAME   = STUDENT NAME                                SB-035
      C               ID     = STUDENT IDENTIFICATION NUMBER              SB-040
      C               CREDIT = NUMBER OF CREDITS                           SB-045
      C             OUTPUT:                                                SB-050
      C               NAME, ID, CREDIT, FEES                              SB-055
      C               TUIT   = TUITION                                     SB-060
      C               BALDUE = BALANCE DUE THE COLLEGE                    SB-065
      C----------------------------------------------------------------SB-100
0001          CHARACTER NAME*15                                          SB-110
0002          INTEGER   ID                                               SB-120
0003          REAL      CPC,FEES,CREDIT,TUIT,BALDUE                      SB-130
      C----------------------------------------------------------------SB-200
0004          REED *, CPC,FEES                                           SB-210

%FORT-F-ERROR 22, MISSING VARIABLE OR CONSTANT
      [REED *, ] IN MODULE FOR$MAIN AT LINE 4

0005          READ *, NAME,ID,CREDIT                                     SB-220
      C----------------------------------------------------------------SB-300
0006          TUIT  = CREDIT**CPC                                        SB-310
0007          TUIT - FEES = BALDUE                                       SB-320
      C----------------------------------------------------------------SB-400

%FORT-F-ERROR 56, LEFT SIDE OF ASSIGNMENT MUST BE VARIABLE OR ARRAY ELEMENT
      [TUIT - FEES = ] IN MODULE FOR$MAIN AT LINE 7

0008          PRINT *, 'NAME              :   ',    NAME               SB-410
0009          PRINT *, 'ID NUMBER         : ',      ID                 SB-420
0010          PRINT *, 'NUMBER OF CREDITS : ',      CREDIT             SB-430
0011          PRINT *  ' '                                              SB-440

%FORT-F-ERROR 23, MISSING OPERATOR OR DELIMITER SYMBOL
      [PRINT *  ' '   ] IN MODULE FOR$MAIN AT LINE 11

0012          PRINT *, 'FEES ............ $ ',       FEES              SB-445
0013          PRINT *, 'TUITION ......... $ ',       TUIT              SB-450
0014          PRINT *, '                    --------'                   SB-455
0015          PRINT *, 'BALANCE DUE ..... $ ',       BALDUE            SB-460
      C----------------------------------------------------------------SB-998
0016   END                                                             SB-999

%FORT-W-ERROR 9, INVALID STATEMENT LABEL IGNORED
      IN MODULE FOR$MAIN AT LINE 16

%FORT-F-ERROR 56, LEFT SIDE OF ASSIGNMENT MUST BE VARIABLE OR ARRAY ELEMENT
      [                 ] IN MODULE FOR$MAIN AT LINE 16

%FORT-E-ERROR 65, MISSING END STATEMENT, END IS ASSUMED
      IN MODULE FOR$MAIN AT LINE 17
```

The above syntax errors were corrected by repunching a new card for each statement in error and then resubmitting the job.[6] This time the program compiled without syntax errors; however, an execution error was encountered, as illustrated in Figure 3.8. The message "floating overflow" indicates that the computation of a real value exceeds the maximum value permitted by this computer. Line 6 in the listing illustrates the problem: we have mistakenly used exponentiation instead of multiplication. This error was corrected and the job was resubmitted once again.

FIGURE 3.8   Illustration of Execution Error

```
        C                                                          SB-000
        C           STUDENT BILLING PROGRAM                        SB-005
        C                                                          SB-010
        C           VARIABLE KEY                                   SB-015
        C             INPUT:                                       SB-020
        C               CPC     = COST PER CREDIT                  SB-025
        C               FEES    = COST OF FEES                     SB-030
        C               NAME    = STUDENT NAME                     SB-035
        C               ID      = STUDENT IDENTIFICATION NUMBER    SB-040
        C               CREDIT  = NUMBER OF CREDITS                SB-045
        C             OUTPUT:                                      SB-050
        C               NAME, ID, CREDIT, FEES                     SB-055
        C               TUIT    = TUITION                          SB-060
        C               BALDUE  = BALANCE DUE THE COLLEGE          SB-065
        C-------------------------------------------------------SB-100
                                                                   SB-110
0001            CHARACTER NAME*15                                  SB-120
0002            INTEGER   ID                                       SB-130
0003            REAL      CPC,FEES,CREDIT,TUIT,BALDUE              SB-200
        C-------------------------------------------------------SB-200
0004            READ *, CPC,FEES                                   SB-210
0005            READ *, NAME,ID,CREDIT ──Cause of execution error  SB-220
        C-------------------------------------------------------SB-300
0006            TUIT   = CREDIT**CPC                               SB-310
0007            BALDUE = TUIT - FEES                               SB-320
        C-------------------------------------------------------SB-400
0008            PRINT *, 'NAME               :   ',   NAME         SB-410
0009            PRINT *, 'ID NUMBER          : ',     ID           SB-420
0010            PRINT *, 'NUMBER OF CREDITS : ',      CREDIT       SB-430
0011            PRINT *, ' '                                       SB-440
0012            PRINT *, 'FEES ............ $ ',      FEES         SB-445
0013            PRINT *, 'TUITION ......... $ ',      TUIT         SB-450
0014            PRINT *, '              --------- '                SB-455
0015            PRINT *, 'BALANCE DUE ..... $ ',      BALDUE       SB-460
        C-------------------------------------------------------SB-998
0016            END                                                SB-999
```

(Omitted Technical Matter)

```
%MTH-F-FLOOVEMAT, FLOATING OVERFLOW IN MATH LIBRARY  ⎫ Execution
   USER PC 00000669                                  ⎬ Error
%TRACE-F-TRACEBACK, SYMBOLIC STACK DUMP FOLLOWS      ⎭ Message
```

(Omitted Technical Matter)

---

[6] If you're using a terminal to submit batch jobs (as we actually are), then errors are corrected at the terminal by replacing incorrect lines with correct lines, and the job is resubmitted at the terminal. Ask your instructor about your system's editing capabilities, which greatly simplify program modifications.

FIGURE 3.9   *Illustration of Logic Errors*

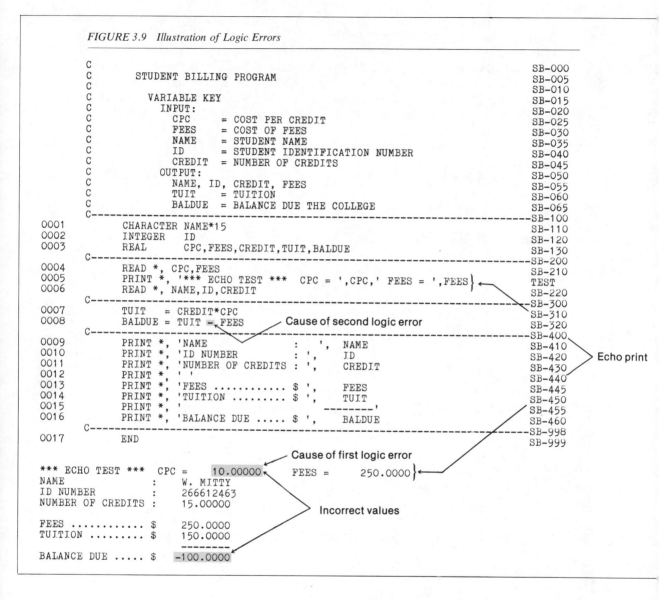

Figure 3.9 illustrates a run with no syntax or execution errors, but with two logic errors. Note that the output for BALDUE is −$100, instead of the expected $1750. The first logic error is easily uncovered by the echo print in line 5 for CPC and FEES. It appears that the value for FEES was input properly, but 10. instead of 100. was input for CPC, which can be further confirmed by examining the data card (not shown). The second logic error is identified by noting that FEES was subtracted rather than added to TUIT in the assignment statement for BALDUE. Correcting these two errors and removing the echo print results in the run illustrated by Figure 3.6 on page 76.

Follow-up Exercise

5. Duplicate our debugging illustration on your system, noting any differences.

Time-Sharing Environment

In this section we run the savings account program once more, with the exceptions that syntax, execution, and logic errors are purposely included.

1.

```
USER ID -SAG20
PASSWORD--
▮▮▮▮▮▮▮▮▮▮▮▮
```

As before.

2.

```
*OLD BANKE
```

Copy of program BANKE taken from library and placed in work area.

3.

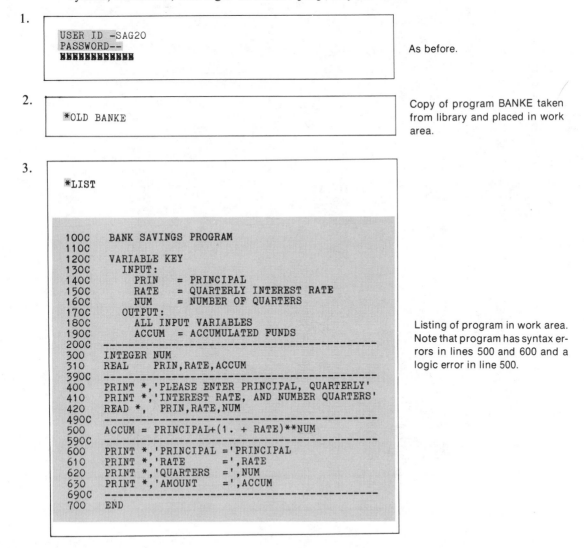

```
*LIST


100C     BANK SAVINGS PROGRAM
110C
120C     VARIABLE KEY
130C       INPUT:
140C         PRIN  = PRINCIPAL
150C         RATE  = QUARTERLY INTEREST RATE
160C         NUM   = NUMBER OF QUARTERS
170C       OUTPUT:
180C         ALL INPUT VARIABLES
190C         ACCUM = ACCUMULATED FUNDS
200C     ---------------------------------------------
300      INTEGER NUM
310      REAL    PRIN,RATE,ACCUM
390C     ---------------------------------------------
400      PRINT *,'PLEASE ENTER PRINCIPAL, QUARTERLY'
410      PRINT *,'INTEREST RATE, AND NUMBER QUARTERS'
420      READ *,   PRIN,RATE,NUM
490C     ---------------------------------------------
500      ACCUM = PRINCIPAL+(1. + RATE)**NUM
590C     ---------------------------------------------
600      PRINT *,'PRINCIPAL ='PRINCIPAL
610      PRINT *,'RATE      =',RATE
620      PRINT *,'QUARTERS  =',NUM
630      PRINT *,'AMOUNT    =',ACCUM
690C     ---------------------------------------------
700      END
```

Listing of program in work area. Note that program has syntax errors in lines 500 and 600 and a logic error in line 500.

4.

```
*FRN

SOURCE LINE    500
<F>1270 VARIABLE IN STATEMENT HAS >8 CHARACTERS
SOURCE LINE    600
<F>1287 P IS ILLEGAL AFTER A LOGICAL OR CHARACTER
  CONSTANT IN PRINT
STATEMENT
```

Execution aborted and lines (500 and 600) with syntax errors identified. We realize that PRINCIPAL exceeds six characters (note that this system enhances names to eight characters). A syntax error of this type generally causes an error message for each line containing this name. In this case, a second syntax error (missing comma after right apostrophe) in line 600 obscured the other syntax error in naming the variable.

5.

```
*500    ACCUM = PRIN+(1. + RATE)**NUM
*600    PRINT *,'PRINCIPAL =',PRIN
```

Syntax errors corrected by retyping incorrect lines. The new lines replace the old lines in the work area.

6.

```
*FRN

PLEASE ENTER PRINCIPAL, QUARTERLY
INTEREST RATE, AND NUMBER QUARTERS
=1000.,.015,R
```

The fact that the program now executes shows that syntax errors have been eliminated; however, note that we typed R instead of 4 in the data input.

7.

```
1000.,.015,R
    ^
FILE CODE 41 ILLEGAL CHAR. CORRECTION =4
```

We have committed an execution error in our data input. In this case the system identifies the offending value and requests a value that is type consistent. Systems differ in their responses here. Try yours.

8.

```
PRINCIPAL =   0.10000000E 04
RATE      =   0.15000000E-01
QUARTERS  =            4
AMOUNT    =   0.10010614E 04
```

Calculated by hand, the answer for ACCUM is $1061.36. The computer, however, prints $1001.06. Since data input is correct, it follows that a logic error must exist within the program.

9.

```
*500    ACCUM = PRIN*(1. + RATE)**NUM
```

Correction of logic error; new line 500 replaces old line 500 in work area.

10.

```
*LIST



100C   BANK SAVINGS PROGRAM
110C
120C   VARIABLE KEY
130C     INPUT:
140C        PRIN   = PRINCIPAL
150C        RATE   = QUARTERLY INTEREST RATE
160C        NUM    = NUMBER OF QUARTERS
170C     OUTPUT:
180C        ALL INPUT VARIABLES
190C        ACCUM  = ACCUMULATED FUNDS
200C   -----------------------------------------------
300    INTEGER NUM
310    REAL     PRIN,RATE,ACCUM
390C   -----------------------------------------------
400    PRINT *,'PLEASE ENTER PRINCIPAL, QUARTERLY'
410    PRINT *,'INTEREST RATE, AND NUMBER QUARTERS'
420    READ *,  PRIN,RATE,NUM
490C   -----------------------------------------------
500    ACCUM = PRIN*(1. + RATE)**NUM
590C   -----------------------------------------------
600    PRINT *,'PRINCIPAL =',PRIN
610    PRINT *,'RATE      =',RATE
620    PRINT *,'QUARTERS  =',NUM
630    PRINT *,'AMOUNT    =',ACCUM
690C   -----------------------------------------------
700    END
```

Confirmation that program stands corrected.

11.

```
*FRN



PLEASE ENTER PRINCIPAL, QUARTERLY
INTEREST RATE, AND NUMBER QUARTERS
=1000.,.015,4



PRINCIPAL =  0.10000000E 04
RATE      =  0.15000000E-01
QUARTERS  =           4
AMOUNT    =  0.10613636E 04
```

Correct output.

12.

```
*RESAVE BANKE


DATA SAVED-BANKE
```

Present copy of program in work area stored in the library. Old copy in the library gets replaced, but copy in the work area remains there.

13.

```
*BYE
```

Sign off.

Note that the compiler will identify syntax errors and the operating system will print execution error messages, but you must identify any logic errors by checking the correctness of the output. In this case, all errors are corrected by simply retyping the entire lines of instruction. All time-sharing systems, however, include specific system commands that greatly facilitate the process of editing programs. Ask your instructor about your system.

One final note: *Anytime you replace an old line with a new line, the replacement is made in the work area, not in your library.* So if you wish to use your corrected program at a later date, you must type the system command that stores or replaces the program in your library, as done in box 12.

Follow-up Exercise

6. Duplicate our debugging illustration on your system, noting any differences.

ADDITIONAL EXERCISES

7. Define or explain each of the following terms associated with batch environments.

punched card	computer printout
keypunch machine	listing
instruction cards	source program
comment cards	object program
control cards	rules for placing instructions,
data cards	data, and comments
card deck	on punched cards

8. Define or explain each of the following terms associated with time-sharing environments.

system commands	line numbers
work area	comment line
secondary storage area	conversational (interactive) programming
library	continuation line
data file	

9. Define or explain each of the following terms.

execution
compilation
use of the blank character
documentation
debugging
syntax error
execution error

logic error
initialization
roleplaying the computer
mirror printing
echo printing
diagnostic PRINT
trace statement

10. **Debugging Problem.** Run the program below on your system *exactly* as shown. On the first run let the compiler identify syntax errors and then make the necessary corrections. On the second run let the operating system identify execution errors and then make the necessary corrections. Finish with an error-free run. Use the following data input: First try 4.2 for X and 0. for Y; next try −4.2 for X and 0.1 for Y; finally, try 4.2 for X and 0.1 for Y.

PROGRAM WHICH ADDS, SUBTRACTS, MULTIPLIES, DIVIDES, AND EX-PONENTIATES TWO NUMBERS

```
READ      X,Y
SUMMATION = X + Y
SUB = X − Y
X*Y = MULT
DIV + X/Y
EXP = X**Y
PRINT,SUMMATION,SUB,MULT,DIV,EXP
```

11. **Precision.** Determine your system's precision by solving the exercises below.
   a. Write a simple program to determine how accurately you can express the value for pi (3.141592654 . . .) on your system. In the same program, store and output PI1 as a real variable and PI2 as a double-precision variable.
   b. Run the following program on your system using the following values for X: 50, 70, and 90; and for N: 15, 31, and 47.

```
READ *,X,N
PRINT *,10.**X,2**N − 1
END
```

What are your system's limits for real and integer values?
   c. Run the following program on your system:

```
INTEGER I,J,K
REAL A,B,C
DOUBLE PRECISION D,E,F
A = 500.6182
B = 500.618273
C = 9876543.26
PRINT *,A,B,C,B*C
D = 500.6182
E = 500.618273
F = 9876543.26
PRINT *,D,E,F,E*F
PRINT *,A*C,A*F
I = 1234567890
```

(Continued on next page.)

```
J = 9876543210
K = 1234567890123
PRINT *,I,J,K,I*J
END
```

Comment on the roundoff error associated with real arithmetic versus double-precision arithmetic. Did you get integer overflow on your system?

12. **Temperature Conversion.** Run the program of Exercise 32 in Chapter 2 on page 64. Determine the degree Celsius equivalents of −10, 0, 32, and 80 degrees Fahrenheit.

13. **Area Problem.** Run the program of Exercise 33 in Chapter 2 on page 64. What is the total cost of 500,000 container tops, where each top has a radius of 5 inches and costs $0.02 per square inch? What if the cost is $0.005 per square inch, all other things being the same?

14. **Microeconomics Problem.** Run the program of Exercise 34 in Chapter 2 on page 64. How many units should be produced to maximize profit? *Hint:* Try input values of 1, 2, 3, . . . , 10 for UNITS.

15. **Blood Bank Inventory Problem.** Run the program of Exercise 35 in Chapter 2 on page 65. How many units of blood should be ordered if it costs $50 to place an order, weekly demand averages 3000 pints, and it costs $0.20 per week per pint of blood to refrigerate? How much should be ordered if the refrigeration cost increases to $0.30? What is the expected cost per week for each of the above?

16. **Forecasting Population Growth.** Run the program of Exercise 36 in Chapter 2 on page 65. Predict the earth's population in the year 2000. The population in 1976 was approximately 4 billion.
    a. Assume a birth rate of 0.025 (2.5 percent) per year and a death rate of 0.009 (0.9 percent), both of which are expected to remain constant until the year 2000.
    b. How would your prediction change if the birth rate fell to 0.02? *Suggestion:* Input the 1976 population as a real constant having one digit (that is, as 4.). Why did we make this suggestion?
    c. How many years before the earth's population doubles? Use the birth and death rates given in part a. *Hint:* Try different input values for *n* and observe the output values for *p*.
    ** d. Go to your library and look up comparable current population level, birth rate, and death rate figures for a country or state. Make some predictions.

17. **Automobile Financing Problem.** Run the program of Exercise 37 in Chapter 2 on page 65 for a car costing $7200, with a down payment of $1000, a trade-in allowance of $1200, a financing life of 60 months, and an *annual* interest rate of 0.15. What are the effects if the down payment is increased to $2000? What if the life of the loan changes to 36 months, the interest rate drops one percentage point (0.01), and the down payment remains at $1000?

CHAPTER 4

Control Structures and the DO-Loop

Programmers often consider the programs they write their own creations without regard for others who have to modify them. The programs work but they may include confusing or tricky logic that may be understood only by the original programmer. This increases the costs and creates difficulties whenever it's necessary to modify the programs. In addition, without a standard method of solving a problem, a programmer may spend more time than necessary in determining the appropriate solution and developing the program. To counter these trends a concept known as structured programming has received widespread acceptance.

Structured programming is an approach to designing, coding, and testing programs which is based on a body of principles that promotes well-thought-out, readable code and reliable execution. The basic foundation of structured programming is that any program can be written using three logical structures.

1. Sequence structure
2. Decision structure
3. Loop structure

These so-called **control structures** can be used to describe the logic of any program completely, as we illustrate in the next four sections.

4.1
SEQUENCE STRUCTURE

The **sequence structure** consists of a sequence of instructions that occur one after the other *without* any transfer of control. When **transfer of control** or **branching** occurs the computer interrupts the normal sequential execution of a program and branches (jumps or transfers control) to some other *executable* statement in the program that is not necessarily the next instruction in the normal sequence.

Figure 4.1 illustrates the concept of the sequence structure for the student billing program. Up to now, the sequence structure is the only type of control structure we have presented.

99

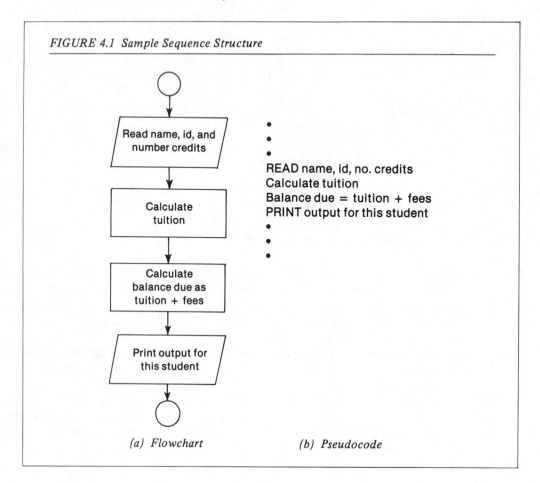

FIGURE 4.1 *Sample Sequence Structure*

READ name, id, no. credits
Calculate tuition
Balance due = tuition + fees
PRINT output for this student

(a) *Flowchart*   (b) *Pseudocode*

The connectors (circle symbols) in the flowchart allow us to focus on the structure of interest. *The first connector defines the beginning of or entry point to the structure; the second connector defines the end of or exit point from the structure.*

4.2
DECISION STRUCTURES

Decision structures consist of choices among alternatives based on the testing of *conditions*. In the two-alternative case, either a particular **block** (sequence of one or more statements) is to be executed if the condition is true, or an alternative block is to be executed if the condition is false. Figure 4.2a–b illustrates this two-choice structure or **IF-THEN-ELSE structure.** Note that the pseudocode version directly incorporates the terms IF, THEN, and ELSE; the flowchart version uses the *diamond symbol* to represent the test of a stated condition.

Sometimes we have a situation in which, if a condition is true, we execute a particular block; otherwise we continue in the program sequence. This is called the single-choice or **IF-THEN structure,** as illustrated in Figure 4.2c–d.

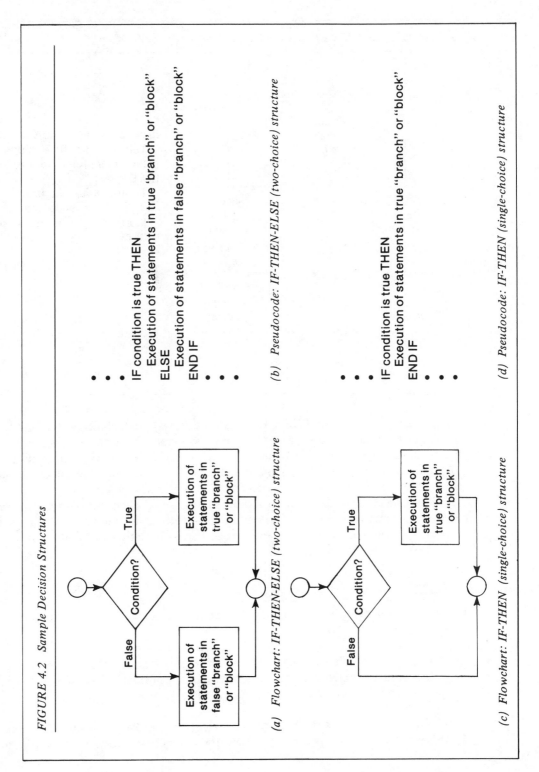

FIGURE 4.2 Sample Decision Structures

IF condition is true THEN
    Execution of statements in true 'branch" or "block"
ELSE
    Execution of statements in false "branch" or "block"
END IF

(b) Pseudocode: IF-THEN-ELSE (two-choice) structure

IF condition is true THEN
    Execution of statements in true "branch" or "block"
END IF

(d) Pseudocode: IF-THEN (single-choice) structure

True

Execution of statements in true "branch" or "block"

Condition?

False

Execution of statements in false "branch" or "block"

(a) Flowchart: IF-THEN-ELSE (two-choice) structure

True

Execution of statements in true "branch" or "block"

Condition?

False

(c) Flowchart: IF-THEN (single-choice) structure

FIGURE 4.3   *IF-THEN-ELSE Structure for Student Billing Problem*

IF no. credits ≥ cutoff THEN
   Tuition = full-time tuition
   Increment full-time counter
ELSE
   Tuition = no. credits ×
              cost per credit
   Increment part-time counter
END IF

(a) *Flowchart*   (b) *Pseudocode*

One example of the IF-THEN-ELSE structure is the calculation of tuition based on part-time (less than a cutoff of, say, 12 credits) versus full-time (12 credits or more) student status, as illustrated in Figure 4.3. The term *counter* refers to the fact that each block counts the number of students that are processed through that block. Note that the *pseudocode version indents the statements in each block to improve readability.*

More complicated decision structures are possible when more than two choices need to be made or more than one condition needs to be tested. We discuss these decision structures in the next chapter, together with methods of coding all decision structures in FORTRAN.

4.3
LOOP STRUCTURES

The **loop structure** refers to the repeated execution of a sequence of instructions. This structure consists of two parts.

1. A **loop body,** which represents the sequence of statements that are to be repeated
2. A **loop control,** which specifies either the number of times a loop must be executed or the condition under which the loop is to be terminated

Figure 4.4 represents the logic of the loop structure. Part a specifically represents the **DO-WHILE structure.** In this structure, the first action is to test whether or not the

FIGURE 4.4   Loop Structures

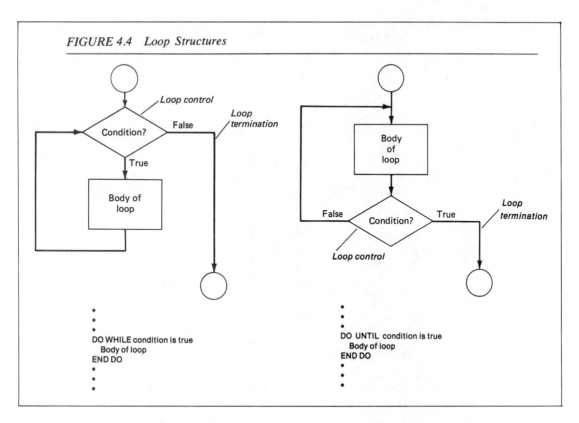

body of the loop is to be executed. If the condition is true, then control passes to the body of the loop. After the statements within the body have been executed, control goes back to the test statement preceding the loop body. When the test indicates a false condition, looping is finished and control passes to the next statement outside the loop. Thus *looping continues WHILE the condition is true.*

A variation of the loop structure is the **DO-UNTIL structure.** This structure ensures that the body of the loop is executed at least once. In this case, the test for the end of the loop is made after the loop body is executed. Thus *looping continues UNTIL the condition is true.*

The major difference between these two loop structures is that the test precedes the body in a DO-WHILE loop whereas the body precedes the test in a DO-UNTIL loop. A more subtle difference is that the former gives a loop exit when the condition is false, whereas the latter results in a loop exit when the condition is true.

Loop structures are powerful features of programming languages, as they enable the automatic processing of large amounts of similar data. For example, any realistic version of the student billing program must include a loop for processing all students at the college in one computer run, as illustrated in Figure 4.5. Note that *the pseudocode version indents the body of the loop for better readability.*

We present the FORTRAN coding of loop structures in Section 4.5 and continue the treatment of loops in Chapter 6.

FIGURE 4.5 *Loop Structures for Student Billing Problem*

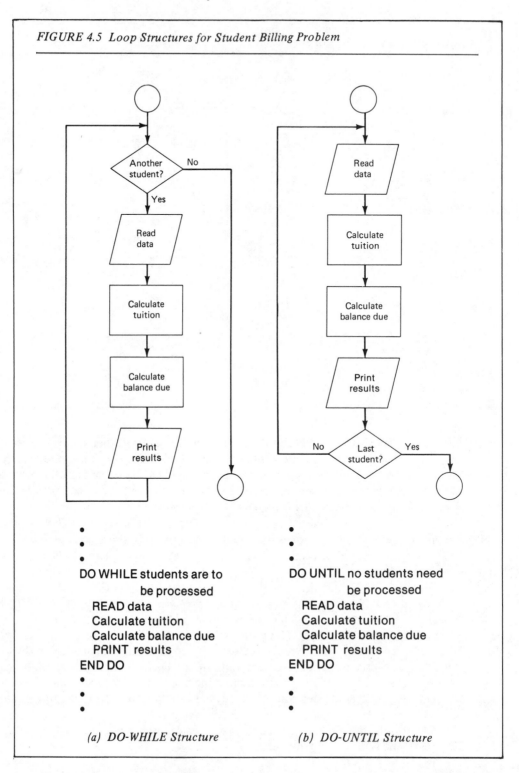

DO WHILE students are to
        be processed
   READ data
   Calculate tuition
   Calculate balance due
   PRINT results
END DO

(a) DO-WHILE Structure

DO UNTIL no students need
        be processed
   READ data
   Calculate tuition
   Calculate balance due
   PRINT results
END DO

(b) DO-UNTIL Structure

4.4
STRUCTURED PROGRAMMING

Let's define a **structured program** as one that is written strictly in terms of sequence, decision, and loop structures. The flowchart that corresponds to a structured program is defined as a **structured flowchart.** Pseudocode itself reflects a structured design when it is based strictly on sequence, decision (IF-THEN-ELSE, IF-THEN, or CASE[1]), and loop (DO-WHILE or DO-UNTIL) structures.

If you look back at Figures 4.1 to 4.5, you should realize that *each control structure has a single entry point and a single exit point,* as denoted by the ○ circle symbol. In effect, a structured program is simply a set of these control structures put together in some meaningful fashion. For example, the IF-THEN-ELSE structure in Figure 4.3 includes a sequence structure within each of its branches, and the loop structure in Figure 4.5 contains a sequence structure as its body. Are you ready for this? If we were to replace "Calculate tuition" in Figure 4.5 by the IF-THEN-ELSE structure in Figure 4.3, the revised Figure 4.5 would be a loop structure having a body made up of a sequence structure with an embedded IF-THEN-ELSE structure.

In essence, control structures can be viewed as *blocks* or *modules,* which together make up the whole. Thus, *structured programs inherently utilize a concept called "modular programming",* which encompasses a design philosophy that aims to improve the readability and reliability of programs.[2]

Moreover, the execution of structured programs proceeds from the top down to the bottom; that is, transfers of control to upper parts of the program are not acceptable (except for the loop structure, of course). This idea also facilitates readability and reliability, and is partially related to what is called "top-down design."[3]

Follow-up Exercise

1. Incorporate Figure 4.3 into Figure 4.5 by reworking the following.
   a. Flowchart version in Figure 4.5
   b. Pseudocode version in Figure 4.5

4.5
DO/CONTINUE STATEMENTS

In this section we present a common type of loop structure called the DO-loop. Looping by this method is used when we know beforehand the number of **loop iterations,** that is, the number of times the body of the loop is to be repeated. In this case, the DO and CONTINUE statements are used to handle automatically all details of looping.

---

[1] The CASE structure is presented in Chapter 6.

[2] Module F includes a detailed discussion of modular programming, which is best covered at the end of Chapter 9.

[3] Top-down design is fully discussed in Module E, which we recommend reading at the end of Chapter 5.

Loop Mechanics

A **DO-loop** is best defined by a DO statement at the beginning of the loop and by a CONTINUE statement at the end of the loop. For example, the statements

define a DO-loop that iterates three times.

The general form of the **DO statement** is

> **DO** *statement number* *DO-variable* = *initial expression,* *terminal expression,* *incrementation expression*

The **CONTINUE statement** that is paired with a DO statement has the following general form.

> *statement number* **CONTINUE**

In the DO statement you must

1. Indicate the range of the DO statement. The statements that are to be repeated as part of the loop are those *executable* statements beginning with the statement *immediately following* the DO and ending with the statement specified by the *statement number* in the DO. These statements are called the **body** or **range** of the DO-loop. Statement number 50 in the above example indicates that the last executable statement in the loop is the one labeled 50, the CONTINUE statement. A **statement number** is a sequence of one to five digits. When used as a statement label, as in

    ```
    50 CONTINUE
    ```

    it must precede the statement on the same line. If you are using punched cards, the statement number must be punched in columns 1–5, preferably right-justified (up against column 5). By the way, the CONTINUE statement need not end a DO-loop, but we recommend this practice as it visually facilitates DO-loop identification and neatly bypasses our having to remember what statements may *not* end a DO-loop.
2. Specify the **DO-variable,** which can be an integer, real, or double-precision variable. In the above example, J is the DO-variable.

3. Specify the initial value of the DO-variable through a numeric constant, numeric variable, or generally any arithmetic expression, called the *initial expression*. For example, J is first set to 1 in the sample DO statement, since 1 is the value of the initial expression. The initial expression can be any integer, real, or double-precision arithmetic expression.

4. Specify the terminal value of the DO-variable through a numeric constant, numeric variable, or generally any arithmetic expression, called the *terminal expression*. The value of the DO-variable must exceed (when the incrementation value is positive) or be less than (when the incrementation value is negative) the terminal value before the loop is terminated. In our example, when J first exceeds 3, looping terminates. The terminal expression can be any integer, real, or double-precision expression.

5. Specify the incrementation value through a numeric constant, numeric variable, or generally any arithmetic expression, called the *incrementation expression*. The value of the DO-variable changes by the incrementation value at each iteration of the DO-loop. Thus, each time our sample DO-loop iterates, the value of J increases by 1. The incrementation expression can be integer, real, or double precision. Also, *the incrementation expression can be omitted, in which case the computer assumes it has a value of 1*. For example,

```
DO 50 J = 1,3
```

is equivalent to our earlier version. Note the omission of the comma following the 3.

To illustrate better the mechanics of a DO-loop consider Figure 4.6, the loop structure

```
DO   100 KOUNT = 1,5
    .
    .  } Loop body
    .
100 CONTINUE
```

and Table 4.1.

TABLE 4.1 *DO-Loop Mechanics Based on Figure 4.6, Five Iterations*

VALUE OF DO-VARIABLE (KOUNT)	DO-VARIABLE ≤ TERMINAL VALUE OF 5? (EXECUTE BODY?)	ITERATION
1	Yes	1
2	Yes	2
3	Yes	3
4	Yes	4
5	Yes	5
6	No	Loop exit

When the DO statement is executed the DO-loop is *activated,* whereby KOUNT is set to 1 and the loop control test is performed. Since the current value of KOUNT (1) is less than or equal to its terminal value (5), the body of the loop is processed for the first time (iteration 1). Next, according to Figure 4.6, KOUNT is increased by its incrementation value (assumed to be 1) to a value of 2. The loop control test is performed again, the result is "yes," and the body gets processed a second time (iteration 2). This process continues until the DO-variable is incremented to 6. Now the loop control test yields a "no" response, which means that control is transferred to the next executable statement following the DO-loop. At this time the DO-loop is said to be *inactive.* Note that this loop iterates *5* times, which means that the body is sequentially processed five times.

In general, assuming integer expressions, the number of iterations for a DO-loop having initial and incrementation values of 1 is given by the terminal value. In this case the DO-variable is said to be a *counter* and the loop is called a *counter-controlled loop.*

FIGURE 4.6 *Logic of DO-Loop for Positive Incrementation Values (Change ≤ to ≥ When Incrementation Value is Negative)*

TABLE 4.2   *DO-Loop Mechanics Based on Figure 4.6, Four Iterations*

I	EXECUTE BODY?	ITERATION
3	Yes	1
5	Yes	2
7	Yes	3
9	Yes	4
11	No	Loop exit

To make sure you understand loop iterations, confirm Table 4.2 given the following DO-loop.

```
    DO 200 I = 3,10,2
        .
        .
        .
200 CONTINUE
```

Note that the DO-loop in FORTRAN 77 is a DO-WHILE structure, since the loop control test precedes the body and the body is processed *while* the condition is true.[4]

Follow-up Exercises

2. What values get printed for each of the loops below? How many times does each loop iterate?

   a.
   ```
       DO 75 K = 1,7
          PRINT *,K
    75 CONTINUE
   ```

---

[4] In reality, the loop control test is based on what is called an *iteration count*, as given either by the integer part of the expression

$$\left[\frac{\text{terminal value} - \text{initial value} + \text{incrementation value}}{\text{incrementation value}} \right]$$

or by zero, whichever is greater. For example, the number of iterations for the loop of Table 4.1 is

$$\left[\frac{5 - 1 + 1}{1} \right] = [5]$$

or five. The number of iterations for the loop of Table 4.2 is

$$\left[\frac{10 - 3 + 2}{2} \right] = [4.5]$$

or four. With respect to Figure 4.6, the iteration count is computed just after the DO-variable is set to its initial value, the loop control test is actually "Iteration count > 0?," and the iteration count is decremented (reduced) by 1 just after the value of the DO-variable is changed.

.b. Same as part a except
DO 75 K = 1,7,3

c.   DO 85 L = 2,5
PRINT *,L
85 CONTINUE

d. Same as part c except
DO 85 L = 5,5

e. Same as part c except
DO 85 L = 6,5

3. Modify Figure 4.6 and Tables 4.1 and 4.2 according to footnote 4.

Example 4.1   Student Billing with DO-Loop

Consider the following version of the student billing problem.

```
C     STUDENT BILLING PROGRAM
C
C     KEY:
C        CPC       = COST PER CREDIT
C        FEES      = COST OF FEES
C        N         = NUMBER OF STUDENTS
C        NAME      = STUDENT NAME
C        ID        = STUDENT IDENTIFICATION NUMBER
C        CREDIT    = NUMBER OF CREDITS
C        TUIT      = TUITION
C        BALDUE    = BALANCE DUE THE COLLEGE
C
      CHARACTER  NAME*15
      INTEGER    ID,N
      REAL       CPC,FEES,CREDIT,TUIT,BALDUE
C
      READ *,CPC,FEES
      READ *,N
C
      PRINT *,'STUDENT NAME    IDENTIFICATION    BALANCE DUE'
      PRINT *,'  '
C
      DO 50 J = 1,N
         READ *,NAME,ID,CREDIT
         TUIT      = CREDIT*CPC
         BALDUE    =TUIT+FEES
         PRINT *,NAME,ID,BALDUE
   50 CONTINUE
C
      END
```

These print table headings. — See output part A.

This prints table lines. See output part B.

Input data appear as follows:

    100.,250.
    3
    'W. MITTY', 266612463, 15.
    'X. MITTY', 266612464, 18.5
    'Y. MITTY', 266612465, 12.

Output from this program would appear as follows:

STUDENT NAME	IDENTIFICATION	BALANCE DUE
W. MITTY	266612463	1750.0
X. MITTY	266612464	2100.0
Y. MITTY	266612465	1450.0

STUDENT NAME · IDENTIFICATION · BALANCE DUE } Part A

W. MITTY 1750.0, X. MITTY 2100.0, Y. MITTY 1450.0 } Part B

Note the following points.

1. The number of students to be processed is read in under the variable N. Its value of 3 in the input data is consistent with the fact that three students are to be processed.

2. The terminal expression in the DO statement is given by N. Since this is effectively a counter-controlled loop, it follows that the value of 3 in N is the number of loop iterations, that is, the loop will process three students. Note that *the use of the variable N instead of the constant 3 in the DO statement promotes the generality of the program.* In other words, the program itself need not be changed to process a different number of students; only the input data need be changed. This design reduces the cost of programming, which is an important consideration in actual programming environments.

3. The DO and CONTINUE statements act as "visual brackets" for the loop, thereby improving the readability of the program. We also indent the body of the loop to make it stand out further. *We will follow the convention of indenting the body of loops to identify them better visually.* Although it is not necessary to do this, it is yet another programming practice that promotes good program design.

4. The body of the loop iterates three times, which gives the following successive values in memory as if a "snapshot" were taken just before the CONTINUE statement is executed (see Table 4.3).

TABLE 4.3   Successive Values in Memory

CPC	FEES	N	J	NAME	ID	CREDIT	TUIT	BALDUE
100.	250.	3	1	W. MITTY	266612463	15.	1500.	1750.
			2	X. MITTY	266612464	18.5	1850.	2100.
			3	Y. MITTY	266612465	12.	1200.	1450.

5. Finally, note that output values within the loop for NAME, ID, and BALDUE give the appearance of a "table," and that column headings for this table must be printed *before* the loop.

Follow-up Exercises

4. Suppose we have to process 4562 students. What changes need to be made in the program and data of Example 4.1?

5. What would the output look like if the statement

    PRINT *,'STUDENT NAME   IDENTIFICATION   BALANCE DUE'

    were placed between the DO and READ statements?

6. Anything wrong with the following loop? Explain.

```
    DO 50 J = 1,N
    READ *,NAME,ID,CREDIT
    TUIT = CREDIT*CPC
    BALDUE = TUIT + FEES
50  PRINT *,NAME,ID,BALDUE
```

Example 4.2   Bank Savings with DO-loop

The bank savings program first introduced in Chapter 2 (page 62) is now modified to include a DO-loop for processing the effects of changing the quarterly interest rate from 0.01 to 0.02 in steps of 0.002. The principal (amount we deposit in the account) is $1000 and the number of quarters over which interest is earned is 20.

```
C     BANK SAVINGS PROGRAM
C
C     KEY:
C        PRIN    = PRINCIPAL
C        RATE    = QUARTERLY INTEREST RATE
C        R1      = INITIAL RATE
C        R2      = TERMINAL RATE
C        R3      = INCREMENTATION RATE
C        NUM     = NUMBER OF QUARTERS
C        ACCUM   = ACCUMULATED FUNDS AFTER NUM QUARTERS
C
      INTEGER  NUM
      REAL     PRIN,RATE,ACCUM,R1,R2,R3
C
      READ *,PRIN,NUM
      READ *,R1,R2,R3
C
      PRINT *,'RATE          ACCUM. FUNDS'
C
      DO 100 RATE = R1,R2,R3
         ACCUM = PRIN*(1.+RATE)**NUM
         PRINT *,RATE,ACCUM
  100 CONTINUE
C
      END
```

Input data would appear as follows:

```
1000., 20
.01, .02, .002
```

and output as

RATE	ACCUM. FUNDS
0.01	1220.172
0.012	1269.412
0.014	1320.560
0.016	1373.638
0.018	1428.738
0.02	1485.932

Note that the expressions in the DO statement are real, the loop iterates 6 times, and the DO-variable is used in the body of the loop both in the assignment and PRINT statements.

Follow-up Exercises

7. Why is it inadvisable to use the statement

    DO 100 RATE = .01,.02,.002

in Example 4.2?

8. a. Roleplay computer by filling in a memory table for the run in Example 4.2, as done in Table 4.3 on page 111.
   b. Describe the output if your input data for R1,R2,R3 were .02,.01,.002.

* 9. What changes need to be made in the program of Example 4.2 if R1, R2, and R3 are defined as *annual* rates instead of quarterly rates? Note that RATE still must be defined on a quarterly basis; the input data now appear as

```
1000.,20
.04,.08,.008
```

The rate to be output should be on an annual basis.

The Fine Points

Try to keep in mind the following points when using DO-loops.

1. The initial, terminal, and incrementation expressions can be integer, real, or double precision, and can take on positive, zero, or negative values. *The incrementation value, however, may not be zero,* as this would imply an **infinite loop** (one that never terminates).

2. If the incrementation value is negative, then the initial value should be greater than the terminal value, and looping continues until the value of the DO-variable is less than the terminal value. For example, the loop on the left below iterates 8 times, but the loop on the right is *inactive* or does not iterate at all (after the DO statement is

FIGURE 4.7 *Flowchart/Pseudocode for Example 4.1*

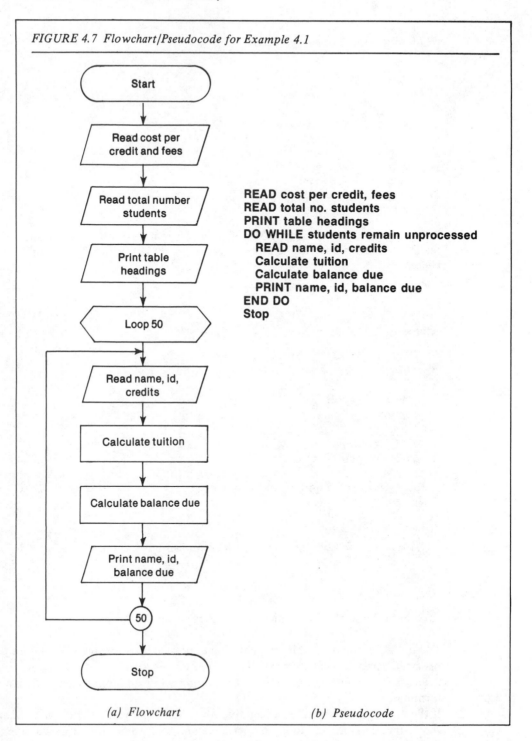

READ cost per credit, fees
READ total no. students
PRINT table headings
DO WHILE students remain unprocessed
   READ name, id, credits
   Calculate tuition
   Calculate balance due
   PRINT name, id, balance due
END DO
Stop

(a) Flowchart   *(b) Pseudocode*

executed, control passes to the next executable statement following the CON-TINUE statement).

DO 200 J = 8,1,−1   DO 300 X = .1,.5,−.1

.   .
.   .
.   .

200 CONTINUE   300 CONTINUE

3. The DO-variable can be utilized within the body of the loop, as illustrated in Example 4.2; however, *the value of the DO-variable may not be redefined within the body*. For example, the statement

RATE = RATE*4.

within DO-loop 100 in Example 4.2 would abort execution.

4. Branching within the body of a DO-loop is allowed, but not directly to the DO statement itself. Branching out of an active DO-loop is also allowed. This causes the DO-loop to become inactive and preserves the current value of the DO-variable. *Branching into the body of a DO-loop from outside the loop is not permissible*. At any rate, either branching into the body or branching out of the body of a DO-loop is not a good programming practice, since *it violates the single-entry single-exit philosophy of a control structure*. We come back to these issues later in the book, at a point when you are capable of making these errors.

5. There is no standard notation for specifying a DO-loop either in a flowchart or in pseudocode. One common flowcharting approach is to use the hexagon-shaped symbol to define the start of the loop (DO statement) and the circle symbol to define the end of the loop (CONTINUE statement). Figure 4.7 illustrates this approach for Example 4.1. Note that the loop returns to the first executable statement following the DO statement, not to the DO statement itself. Alternative approaches to flow-charting the DO-loop are illustrated in Figures 4.5a and 4.6.

Follow-up Exercises

10. Flowchart and pseudocode the program in Example 4.2.
11. What values get printed for each of the following loops and how many times does each loop iterate?

a.   DO 500 ITEM = 10,0,−1
                PRINT *,ITEM
          500 CONTINUE

b. Same as part a except that the incrementation value is −3.
c. Same as part a except that the terminal value is 20.

d.   DO 600 LAG = M,2*M − 1,M/4
                PRINT *,LAG
          600 CONTINUE
          where 10 is stored in M.

e.   DO 700 VOL = .25,.50,.05
              PRINT *,VOL
      700 CONTINUE

f. Same as part e except add
              PRINT *,VOL
      after the CONTINUE statement.

12. Why are the following DO-loops invalid?

a.   DO 50 X = 1.5,4.5,0.
              .
              .
              .
      50 CONTINUE

b.   DO J = 1,10
              .
              .
              .
      CONTINUE

c.   DO 100 K = 10,0
              .
              .
      100 CONTINUE

d.   DO 100 K = 10,0,−1
              K = N − 1
      100 CONTINUE

4.6
INITIALIZATIONS AND SUMS

In this section we illustrate the usual method of finding sums and introduce a new statement that initializes variables.

Accumulating a Sum

Accumulating and printing sums for one or more variables is a common computation in programming. For example, a payroll program computes gross pay, deductions, and net pay for each employee and also computes the total gross pay, total deductions, and total net pay paid for all employees. To illustrate how the computer can accumulate a sum, we return to our tuition and fee problem.

EXAMPLE 4.3   Student Billing Program with Sum

The Financial Vice-President of State College needs to know the total amount of money that State College will collect in tuition and fees. Conceptually, we set aside a memory location (that is, assign a variable) which represents the sum. Each time

---

FIGURE 4.8 *Incorporating a Sum in the Student Billing Loop*

```
                    READ cost per credit, fees
                    READ total no. students
                    PRINT table headings
                    Accumulator = 0
                    DO WHILE students remain unprocessed
                        READ name, id, credits
                        Calculate tuition
                        Calculate balance due
                        PRINT name, id, balance due
                        Accumulator = accumulator +
                                      balance due
                    END DO
                    PRINT accumulator
                    Stop
```

```
C
        CHARACTER    NAME * 15
        INTEGER      ID,N
        REAL         CPC,FEES,CREDIT,TUIT,BALDUE,SUM
C
        READ *,CPC,FEES
        READ *,N
C
        PRINT *,'STUDENT NAME    IDENTIFICATION    BALANCE DUE'
        PRINT *,' '
C
        SUM = 0.
C
        DO 50 J = 1,N
            READ *,NAME,ID,CREDIT
            TUIT      = CREDIT*CPC
            BALDUE = TUIT + FEES
            PRINT *,NAME,ID,BALDUE
            SUM       = SUM + BALDUE
     50 CONTINUE
C
        PRINT *,' '
        PRINT *,'TOTAL BALANCE DUE:     $',SUM
C
        END
```

Initialize SUM to zero to be sure zero and nothing else is stored in that memory location.

Each time the computer calculates the balance due for a student, the location for SUM is increased by the value stored in BALDUE.

SUM is printed following the loop.

the computer computes the amount owed by a student, the sum is increased by the amount the student owes. In effect the sum can be thought of as a running total whose final value is not known until all the student data are read in and processed. For our test data in Example 4.1, the amounts due from each student are $1750, $2100, and $1450. As the program is computing, the sum will be:

After the first student,	0 + 1750 = 1750
After the second student,	1750 + 2100 = 3850
After the third student,	3850 + 1450 = 5300

Thus a running total accumulates.

The shaded portions in the pseudocode of Figure 4.8 illustrate the incorporation of a sum in the version of Figure 4.7. Note that the only changes are the initialization of the accumulator (sum variable) to zero before the loop, the incorporation of the accumulator in the loop to compute the running total, and output of the accumulator following the loop.

In the program, SUM is the variable that stores the accumulated amount due from all students. Changes from the program in Example 4.1 are shaded.

First, we explicitly initialize SUM to zero for the reasons outlined on page 87 of Chapter 3. Even though some systems initialize all variables to zero, *it is a good programming practice to explicitly initialize variables that need zero initialization.* This makes programs more "portable," since they would also work on systems that don't initialize variables to zero. In other cases, as we illustrate later in this chapter, sums must be explicitly initialized to zero to avoid logic errors.

By placing the instruction

SUM = SUM + BALDUE

within the loop the value stored in BALDUE is added to the value stored in SUM, and the result of the addition is stored in SUM, replacing the value previously stored in SUM.

As the program is executed, the contents of memory locations for CREDIT, BALDUE, and SUM change in the following way.

After initialization:

After the first student is processed:

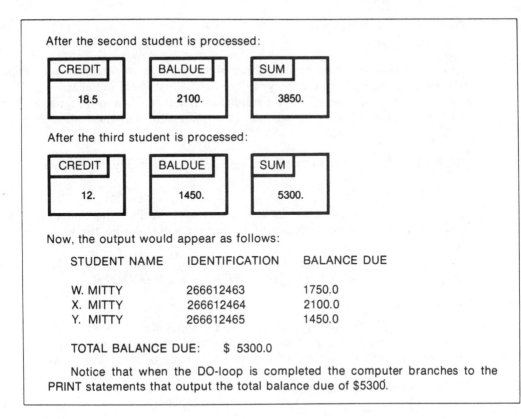

After the second student is processed:

CREDIT
18.5

BALDUE
2100.

SUM
3850.

After the third student is processed:

CREDIT
12.

BALDUE
1450.

SUM
5300.

Now, the output would appear as follows:

STUDENT NAME	IDENTIFICATION	BALANCE DUE
W. MITTY	266612463	1750.0
X. MITTY	266612464	2100.0
Y. MITTY	266612465	1450.0

TOTAL BALANCE DUE: $ 5300.0

Notice that when the DO-loop is completed the computer branches to the PRINT statements that output the total balance due of $5300.

DATA Statement

We have already introduced two ways to place values in memory cells: the assignment statement and the READ statement. Another method, the DATA statement, instructs the compiler to put initial values into specific memory locations.

A simple form of the DATA statement is given by

DATA *list of names / list of constants/*

For example,

DATA J,X,Y,ITEM/1,5.25,0.0,'TOY'/

is a *nonexecutable* statement that declares to the compiler that J is to store 1, X is to store 5.25, Y is to store 0.0, and ITEM is to store TOY. This statement has the same effect as

    J = 1
    X = 5.25
    Y = 0.0

and

ITEM = 'TOY'

Both approaches are termed initialization of variables; however, there is an important difference that should not escape you: The DATA statement initializes when the program is *compiled* and the assignment statements initialize when the program is *executed*.

If more than one variable needs to be initialized to the same value, as in

DATA S1,S2,S3/0.,0.,0./

then the list of three constants can be written in the form 3*0., as follows:

DATA S1,S2,S3/3*0./

We recommend using the DATA statement whenever the initialized variable does *not* need to be reinitialized to its former value during the execution of the program.

Finally, *the DATA statement may appear anywhere after PARAMETER statements and type statements such as INTEGER, REAL, and CHARACTER.*

Initialization of Parameters

In Example 4.3, CPC (cost per credit) and FEES (student fees) are called **parameters** because in reality they represent values that remain constant *while the program executes.* Parameters in programs are represented in any of the following ways.

1. As constants, for example,

```
                            ┌──────Cost per credit
     TUIT    = CREDIT*100.
     BALDUE = TUIT + 250.
                            └──────Student fees
```

2. As symbolic names of constants, for example,

```
     PARAMETER (CPC = 100., FEES = 250.)
     TUIT    = CREDIT*CPC
     BALDUE = TUIT + FEES
```

3. As variables initialized through assignment statements, for example,

```
     CPC     = 100.
     FEES    = 250.
     TUIT    = CREDIT*CPC
     BALDUE = TUIT + FEES
```

4. As variables initialized through READ statements, for example,

```
     READ *,CPC,FEES
     TUIT    = CREDIT*CPC
     BALDUE = TUIT + FEES
```

5. As variables initialized through DATA statements, for example,

```
     DATA CPC, FEES /100.,250./
     TUIT    = CREDIT*CPC
     BALDUE = TUIT + FEES
```

If parameters have descriptive meaning, as in the above examples, then it's a matter of good programming style to use names, as in options 2–5 above. This practice guarantees that parameters are unambiguous within the program, since names suggest contextual meaning and (presumably) are defined as part of the program's documentation.

More important, the use of names for parameters reduces software maintenance costs in environments where parameters are likely to change values over time. For example, if CPC and FEES change values each year, then option 4 requires a simple change in a single data input line whereas option 1 requires access to the program and changes in two lines of code. For simple programs like our student billing program, this consideration is insignificant (except in principle). However, in a commercial environment where programs are thousands of lines long, perhaps with parameters in hundreds of lines, we can begin to appreciate this design consideration.

Generally, we don't recommend option 1 for the reasons outlined earlier. Options 2 and 5 are essentially the same, except that option 2 directly emphasizes that CPC and FEES are indeed parameters not subject to changes in value within the same run. For instance, if we were inadvertently to assign a different value to CPC elsewhere in the program, the compiler would alert us to this error under option 2. Option 3 is cumbersome, and generally not preferred to options 2 and 5. Option 4 is desirable if the values of the parameters change often over time. If values don't change often, then we recommend option 2, with option 5 a close second.[5]

Follow-up Exercises

13. With respect to Example 4.3
    a. Would the output change if the instructions

    ```
    PRINT *,NAME,ID,BALDUE
    ```

    and

    ```
    SUM = SUM + BALDUE
    ```

    were reversed?
    b. Would the output change if the instruction

    ```
    SUM = SUM + BALDUE
    ```

    were placed before

    ```
    BALDUE = TUIT + FEES
    ```

14. Describe the output if the statement that prints SUM were placed just before the CONTINUE statement.
15. Modify the program of Example 4.3 to calculate and print the average balance due, AVE. Print AVE immediately after the output of SUM.

---

[5] Option 2 includes a further advantage when working with arrays (Chapters 7 and 8), as noted in Section G.5 in Module G.

*16. Modify the program in Example 4.3 to accumulate and print three sums: cumulative tuition, cumulative fees, and cumulative balance due. *Hint:* You need a separate variable to accumulate each total. Can you think of simplifications in the program that make use of the fact that once you have two of these sums you automatically have the third?

17. Specify a DATA statement for each of the following.
   a. To initialize SUM in Example 4.3
   b. To initialize PRIN and NUM in Example 4.2
   c. To initialize A, B, C, D, and E to 0.0, F to 100.0, and R1, R2, and R3 to YES

4.7
NESTED DO-LOOPS

As problems become more complex the solution may require the programmer to embed one loop inside another. For every iteration of an outside loop, the inside loop iterates through a complete cycle. The inside loop is said to be **nested** within the outside loop. DO-loops are nested when one DO-loop lies entirely within another DO-loop, as illustrated below.

Nested DO-loops must not cross over or overlap, as illustrated below.

To understand nested DO-loops you must pay careful attention to iterations and the values assigned to DO-variables. For example, in the program segment

```
DO 200 I = 1,2
    DO 100 J = 1,3
        PRINT *,I,J
100     CONTINUE
200 CONTINUE
```

the inner loop 100 gets "exhausted" for each value of the outer loop's DO-variable I; that is, J changes from 1 to 2 to 3 to 4 (at 4 the inner loop becomes inactive) before I is incremented to its next value. Thus the inner loop is said to "vary the fastest." Each time the inner loop is exhausted, its DO-variable J is reset to its initial value, since the statement

```
DO 100 J = 1,3
```

gets executed for each new value of I. For example, the output from the above segment would appear as follows:

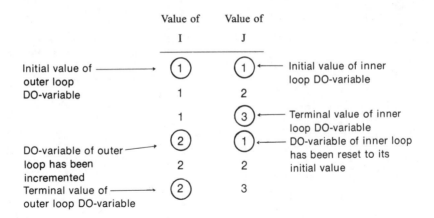

Notice that this double loop iterates a total of six times (2 × 3), or the product of the total iterations of the outer loop and the total iterations of the inner loop.

Example 4.4   Mean Exam Scores by Section

Consider Figure 4.9 for calculating the mean or average exam score for *each* section of a multisection academic course. Note the treatment of nested loops in the flowchart and pseudocode versions, particularly the indentation in the pseudocode version.

    In this example the inner loop processes the scores for a specific section and the outer loop processes sections. In particular note (1) that the sum is reinitialized each time the inner loop is reactivated or each time a new section is processed, (2)

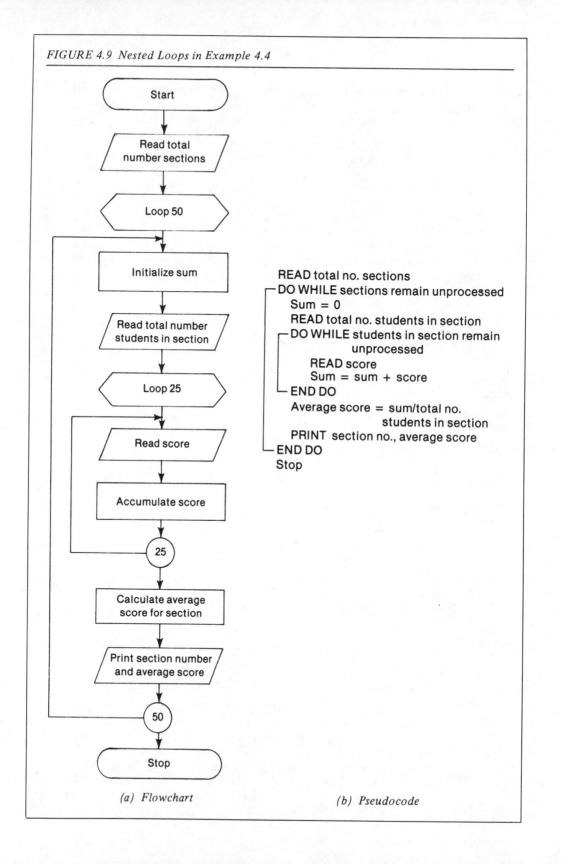

FIGURE 4.9 Nested Loops in Example 4.4

Flowchart nodes:

Start

Read total number sections

Loop 50

Initialize sum

Read total number students in section

Loop 25

Read score

Accumulate score

25

Calculate average score for section

Print section number and average score

50

Stop

Pseudocode:

```
READ total no. sections
DO WHILE sections remain unprocessed
    Sum = 0
    READ total no. students in section
    DO WHILE students in section remain
                    unprocessed
        READ score
        Sum = sum + score
    END DO
    Average score = sum/total no.
                       students in section
    PRINT  section no., average score
END DO
Stop
```

(a) Flowchart

(b) Pseudocode

that the scores for a section are summed within the inner loop, and (3) that the average score is calculated and printed immediately following the inner loop.
The program below reflects this design.

```
C    EXAM AVERAGING PROGRAM
C
C    KEY:
C      N       = NUMBER OF STUDENTS IN A SECTION
C      M       = NUMBER OF SECTIONS
C      SCORE   = EXAM SCORE FOR A STUDENT
C      SUM     = SUM OF SCORES IN SECTION
C      AVE     = MEAN EXAM SCORE FOR A SECTION
C
       INTEGER N,M
       REAL     SCORE,SUM,AVE
C
       READ *,M
C
       DO 50 I = 1,M
          SUM = 0.
          READ *,N
          DO 25 J = 1,N
             READ *,SCORE
             SUM = SUM + SCORE
25        CONTINUE
          AVE = SUM/N
          PRINT *,'MEAN SCORE FOR SECTION',I,'=',AVE
50     CONTINUE
C
       END
```

For example, given two sections with the scores

	Scores	
	Section 1	Section 2
	90	50
	70	90
	80	

input data would be prepared as

```
2   ←─────────────── Number of sections, M
3   ←─────────────── Number of scores in first section, N
90.⎫
70.⎬ ←────────────── Scores in first section
80.⎭
2   ←─────────────── Number of scores in second section, N
50.⎫
90.⎭ ←────────────── Scores in second section
```

and output would appear as

    MEAN SCORE FOR SECTION 1 = 80.0
    MEAN SCORE FOR SECTION 2 = 70.0

You should solve Exercise 18 to make sure you understand the mechanics of this program.

Follow-up Exercises

18. Roleplay computer for Example 4.4 by filling in values in the following memory locations, as if the snapshot of memory were taken just before execution of *each* CONTINUE statement.

M	N	I	J	SCORE	SUM	AVE

19. Modify the input/output data in Example 4.4 to process the scores 20, 90 for Section 1; 40, 100, 70, 80 for Section 2; and 60, 80, 70 for Section 3.

20. What would happen in Example 4.4 if

    DATA SUM/0./

were used instead of

    SUM = 0.

Be specific.

*21. Modify Figure 4.9 and the program in Example 4.4 to compute and print the average for all sections combined (COMAVE) in addition to the average for each section.

22. **Standard Deviation. Modify Figure 4.9 and the program in Example 4.4 to compute and print the standard deviation (a measure of variation about the mean) for each section, in addition to the average.

$$s = \sqrt{\frac{n \Sigma x^2 - (\Sigma x)^2}{n(n-1)}}$$

where

n = number of scores
x = score
Σx = sum of scores for a section
Σx^2 = sum of squared scores for a section

** Double-starred exercises are somewhat more difficult and/or tedious than other exercises. Answers to these exercises are not given in the back of the book.

** **23.** **Mean Absolute Deviation.** Modify Figure 4.9 and the program in Example 4.4 to compute and print the mean absolute deviation (MAD, a measure of variation about the mean) for each section, in addition to the average.

$$\text{MAD} = \frac{\Sigma |x - \bar{x}|}{n}$$

where

n = number of scores

x = score

$\bar{x}$ = mean score for section

$|x - \bar{x}|$ = absolute difference between x and $\bar{x}$

$\Sigma |x - \bar{x}|$ = sum of the absolute differences

24. Specify printed output and number of iterations for each of the following nested loops.

a.
```
      DO 500 J = 1,4
          DO 300 K = 1,2
              PRINT *,J,K
  300     CONTINUE
  500 CONTINUE
```

b. Same as part a except replace the second DO statement with

```
      DO 300 Q = 1.0,2.0,0.5
```

and replace K by Q in the PRINT statement.

c.
```
      DO 300 I = 1,2
          PRINT *,I
          DO 200 J = 1,3
              PRINT *,'b',J
              DO 100 K = 1,4
                  PRINT *,'b','b',K
  100         CONTINUE
  200     CONTINUE
  300 CONTINUE
```

d.
```
      M = 0
      DO 100 I = 1,10
          J = I
          DO 50 K = 1,5
              L = K
              M = M + 1
   50     CONTINUE
  100 CONTINUE
      PRINT *,J,L,M
      PRINT *,I,K
```

25. What is wrong, if anything, in each segment?

a.
```
        DO 100 X = 1.,P
            DO 200 Y = R,S
                PRINT *,'I LOVE NESTED LOOPS'
100     CONTINUE
200 CONTINUE
```

b.
```
        DO 300 I = 1,3
        DO 200 J = 1,4
        DO 100 K = 1,5
        PRINT *,'NOT ME'
100 CONTINUE
200 CONTINUE
300 CONTINUE
```

4.8
COMMON ERRORS

Beginning programmers are likely to make at least one of the following errors when applying the material in this chapter. Will you?

Statement Number Errors

Two types of syntax errors seem to occur often here: *multiple* statement numbers and *missing* statement numbers. In the first case, two or more statements have the same statement number. So, as you're writing your program, *make it a habit to scan your existing statement numbers prior to assigning a new statement number.* In the second case, a control statement references a statement number that does not exist. For example, if you have the statement DO 50 J = 1,N and no executable statement is labeled 50, then you have a missing-statement-number error.

DO-Loop Errors

1. *DO-variable redefined within loop.*

Syntax error occurs if you redefine DO-variable within loop.

DO 10 J = 1,N

$J = J + 1$

$N = 2*K$

On some systems a syntax error occurs if you redefine value of DO-expression within loop.

OK to use these variables following loop.

10 CONTINUE

$J = N + 5$

$N = 2*K$

2. *Improper values for DO expressions.*

DO 100 K = 1, (N) ⟵————————— Execution error or inactive loop
                                if N not explicitly assigned a
                                value and system stores zero in N

DO 200 J = J1,J2, (J3) ⟵————— Execution error or infinite
                                loop if J3 not explicitly
                                assigned a value and system
                                stores zero in J3

DO 300 L = (50,1) ⟵————————— Inactive loop since 50 > 1.
                                Incrementation value of −1
                                needs to be inserted

3. *Improper nesting.*   Watch out for crossovers like the following:

```
      ┌────DO 50 I = 1,L
      │ ┌──DO 40 K = 1,N
      │ │        .
      │ │        .
      │ │        .
      │ └─50 CONTINUE
      └───40 CONTINUE
```

and use of the same DO-variable for nested DO-loops:

DO 100 (I) = 1,M
      .
      .
      .   DO-variables for nested loops
                                     must be different to
      DO 50 (I) = 1,N   avoid error.
      .
      .
      .
50   CONTINUE
      .
      .
      .
100 CONTINUE   OK to use same DO-variable
    DO 200 (I) = 1,K   following its use elsewhere.
      .
      .
      .
200 CONTINUE

4. *Branching errors.*   A transfer of control to the DO statement is not permitted while the DO-loop defined by that DO statement is active; branching into the body of a DO-loop from outside the loop is not permitted. At this time it's not possible for you to commit these errors since we have not yet discussed other branching statements. We mention these errors for the sake of completeness.

Initialization Errors

If you forget to initialize S in the assignment statement

    S = S + X

and the system treats S as undefined, then an execution error results when this assignment statement is executed. It is good programming practice to initialize S through an assignment statement such as

    S = 0.

through a DATA statement such as

    DATA S/0./

or through a READ statement such as

    READ *,S

Caution: If S needs to be initialized more than once during the same computer run, then avoid use of the DATA statement, since this statement is nonexecutable (see Exercise 20).

** *Roundoff Errors*

As discussed in earlier chapters, roundoff error is a vexing computer problem. Not only does precision limit the representation of a value such as 1./3., but also the use of a binary computer to represent decimal (real) values automatically introduces roundoff error. Thus, a real value such as 1./10. cannot be represented *exactly* in a binary (0–1) system; it can only be *approximated*. For example, it's possible for a machine with seven-digit precision to compute the result 0.9999996 instead of 1.000000 when 1./10. is added 10 times.[6]

The roundoff problem is compounded if many *recursive calculations* are performed. (A recursive calculation is a calculation whose value is in part determined by a preceding calculation.) The use of DO-loops makes possible large numbers of recursive calculations, as illustrated by the following program.

```
      READ *,N
      S = 0.
      DO 100 J = 1,N
        S = S + 2./3.
100   CONTINUE
      PRINT *,S
      END
```

This program was run on an NAS/5 computer for various values of N, giving the results in Table 4.4. For example, when 2./3. is summed 12,000 times, the intended value is (12,000) · (2./3.), or 8,000; the printed value was 7983.813, which gives a roundoff error of 16.187, or 0.20 percent.

[6] Only fractional values given by $\frac{1}{2}$ to an integer power can be represented exactly, such as $\frac{1}{2}, \frac{1}{4}, \frac{1}{8}, \frac{1}{16}$, etc.

TABLE 4.4   *Roundoff Errors for Recursive Calculations with Seven-Digit Precision*

NUMBER OF LOOP ITERATIONS N	PRINTED VALUE OF S	INTENDED VALUE OF S	ABSOLUTE ROUNDOFF ERROR	PERCENT ABSOLUTE ROUNDOFF ERROR
3000	1999.571	2000.	0.429	0.02
12000	7983.813	8000.	16.187	0.20
48000	31890.06	32000.	109.94	0.34
192000	123869.2	128000.	4130.8	3.23

Note that the roundoff error increases as the number of iterations increases, *which clearly shows the magnification of roundoff error as the number of recursive calculations increases.* In some applications, particularly in engineering and the sciences, roundoff error of this magnitude can render the results useless. For such cases, special algorithmic procedures must be implemented that reduce the magnitudes of roundoff errors.[7]

The use of real expressions to evaluate initial, terminal, and incrementation values of DO-loops introduces other potential sources of roundoff error. For example, the DO-loop

```
DO 200 X = 1./6.,0.5,1./6.
     PRINT *,X
200 CONTINUE
```

may print either

```
0.1666666
0.3333332
0.4999998
```

for a system with seven-digit precision and truncation at the last digit or

```
0.1666667
0.3333334
```

for a system with seven-digit precision and rounding at the last digit.

First, note that *in the last case the loop iterates twice instead of the intended three times,* since the third value of the DO-variable is 0.5000001 (or 0.3333334 + 0.1666667), which exceeds the terminal value of 0.5. If the number of iterations is not large, then this problem can be corrected by adding a small value (less than the incrementation value) to the terminal value. For example, the terminal value 0.5 can be increased by, say, 0.01.

Second, note that roundoff error is affecting the value of the DO-variable itself. In effect, the computed values of the DO-variable will increasingly diverge from their

---

[7] These procedures are treated in a field of study called numerical analysis.

TABLE 4.5   *Roundoff Errors for Recursive Calculations with 16-Digit Precision*

NUMBER OF LOOP ITERATIONS N	PRINTED VALUE OF S (16 DIGITS)	PRINTED VALUE OF S (ROUNDED TO 7 DIGITS)	INTENDED VALUE OF S
3000	1999.999880790710	2000.000	2000.
12000	7999.999523162842	8000.000	8000.
48000	31999.99809265137	32000.00	32000.
192000	127999.9923706055	128000.0	128000.

intended values, since these values are determined recursively. As in our earlier illustration, this roundoff error will increase as the number of iterations increases.

A simple way of postponing roundoff error problems is to use double-precision variables. In this case, roundoff error is shifted to the extreme right set of digits, thereby having little effect on the first seven digits, unless the number of iterations is very large. For example, Table 4.5 is a modification of the run in Table 4.4, where S is declared as a double-precision variable.

Note that calculated values of S to 7 digits are identical to corresponding intended values. Double-precision arithmetic should be used sparingly, however, since it dramatically increases the computational burden on the computer.

For the most part, the effective treatment of roundoff error requires specialized knowledge not covered in this textbook. You should be aware of the problem, however, and recognize it when it occurs.[8]

ADDITIONAL EXERCISES

Please Note

End-of-chapter assignments in this and other chapters generally require you to prepare and submit the following

1. Flowchart and/or pseudocode
2. Listing of the program
3. Sample run showing test data and results

Ask your instructor to be sure.

---

26. Define or explain each of the following terms.

structured programming   structured program
control structures   structured flowchart

---

[8] One of the exercises at the end of this chapter (we won't say which) has potential roundoff error problems.

sequence structure
transfer of control
branching
decision structures
block
IF-THEN-ELSE structure
IF-THEN structure
loop structure
loop body
loop control
DO-WHILE structure
DO-UNTIL structure

loop iterations
DO-loop
DO statement
CONTINUE statement
body or range of DO-loop
statement number
DO-variable
infinite loop
DATA statement
parameters
nested DO-loops

27. Temperature Conversion. Modify the algorithm and program in Exercise 32 of Chapter 2 (page 64) as follows:

a. Convert degrees Fahrenheit to degrees Celsius by using a DO-loop that varies degrees Fahrenheit from its initial value (F1) to its terminal value (F2) in increments of F3. Run the program for the following sets of values.

F1	F2	F3
20	40	1
−30	120	5

For example, your output for the first run should look like this.

	DEGREES FAHRENHEIT	DEGREES CELSIUS
	20	−6.67
	21	−6.11
21 rows	22	−5.56
	:	:
	:	:
	40	4.44

b. Include an outer loop that processes as many sets of data as desired (two sets for the above data). Note that the loop of part a is completely within this outer loop.

28. Area Problem. Modify the algorithm and program in Exercise 33 of Chapter 2 (page 64) as follows.

a. Calculate and output total cost based on different values of cost per square inch (C). Use a DO-loop that varies C from its initial value (C1) to its terminal value (C2) in increments of C3. Run the program for the following three sets of values.

C1	C2	C3	RADIUS	X
0.005	0.100	0.005	5.0	500000
0.005	0.100	0.005	5.2	500000
0.010	0.150	0.010	5.2	650000

For example, your output for the first run should look like this.

	COST PER SQUARE INCH	TOTAL COST
	0.005	196349
	0.010	392699
	0.015	589048
20 rows	.	.
	.	.
	.	.
	0.100	3926991

b. Include an outer loop that processes as many sets of data as desired (three sets for the above data). Note that the loop of part a is completely within this outer loop.

29. **Microeconomics Problem.**   Modify the algorithm and program in Exercise 34 of Chapter 2 (page 64) as follows.

a. Calculate and print daily revenue, daily cost, and daily profit based on different values of UNITS. Use a DO-loop that varies UNITS from 1 to a maximum (MAX) in increments of 1. Input MAX for the following four sets of data.

MAX	Price
15	80
15	100
15	120
15	140

For example, your output for the first run should look like this.

UNITS PRODUCED	DAILY REVENUE	DAILY COST	DAILY PROFIT
1	80	245	−165
2	160	234	−74
3	240	223	17
.	.	.	.
.	.	.	.
.	.	.	.
15	1200	2275	−1075

b. Include an outer loop that varies price. In other words, the loop in part a is completely within this outer loop. Define initial (P1), terminal (P2), and incremental (P3) prices as input variables, along with MAX. The above input data now appear as follows.

P1	P2	P3	MAX
80	140	20	15

The computer now prints all four tables in one run. Note that the computer run terminates after the price variable reaches P2. Just before each table, print the price that corresponds to that table.

30. **Blood Bank Inventory Problem.** Modify the algorithm and program in Exercise 35 of Chapter 2 (page 65) as follows.

   a. Calculate and print the number of pints to order (Q) and the expected cost per week (E) based on different values of cost of refrigeration (H). Use a DO-loop to vary H from its initial value ($H1$) to its terminal value ($H2$) in increments of $H3$. Input $H1$, $H2$, $H3$, administrative and shipping costs (C), and average weekly demand (D) for the following three sets of values.

H1	H2	H3	C	D
0.20	0.30	0.01	50.	2500.
0.20	0.30	0.01	50.	3000.
0.20	0.30	0.01	50.	3500.

For example, your output for the first run should look like this.

	COST OF REFRIGERATION	ORDER QUANTITY	COST PER WEEK
	0.20	1118	223.61
	0.21	1091	229.13
11 rows	.	.	.
	.	.	.
	.	.	.
	0.30	913	273.86

Draw conclusions with respect to the behavior of Q and E as H and D change.

   b. Include an outer loop that varies D. In other words, the loop in part a is completely within this outer loop. Define initial ($D1$), terminal ($D2$), and incremental ($D3$) demands as input variables, along with $H1$, $H2$, $H3$, and C. The above input data now appear as follows:

H1	H2	H3	C	D1	D2	D3
0.20	0.30	0.01	50	2500	3500	500

The computer now prints all three tables in one run. Note that the computer run terminates after the demand variable reaches $D2$. Just before each table, print the demand that corresponds to that table.

31. **Automobile Financing.** Modify the algorithm and program in Exercise 37 of Chapter 2 (page 65) to include a DO-loop that processes as many sets of

input data as specified by the user. Run this program to process the three sets of data suggested in Exercise 17 of Chapter 3 (page 98).

32. Exponential Cumulative Distribution Function. The function

$$p = 1 - e^{-x/a}$$

describes the probability (p) that a random (chance) variable takes on a value less than or equal to x, where a is the expected (average) value of the random variable and e is the base of natural logarithms (see Module A). For example, if the random variable "number of hours an electronic component operates until failure (life)" is distributed exponentially and average life is known to be 8000 hours, then the probability this component lasts 5000 hours or less is

$$
\begin{aligned}
p &= 1 - e^{-5000/8000} \\
&= 1 - e^{-0.625} \\
&= 1 - 0.5352614 \\
&= 0.4647386
\end{aligned}
$$

that is, approximately 46 percent of these components will last 5000 hours or less.

a. Design a program that inputs average life (a), initial value for x, terminal value for x, and incremental value for x, and outputs a table of x-values and corresponding probabilities. For example, if we wish to run x from 1000 to 12,000 in increments of 1000, then output might appear as follows:

LIFE	PROBABILITY
1000	0.1175030
2000	0.2211992
3000	0.3127107
.	.
.	.
.	.
12000	0.7768698

Run your program for the above test data.

b. Include an outer loop that processes N different values for average life a. Now, the loop in part a is completely within this outer loop. Run this program for the following input data.

a	Initial x	Terminal x	Incremental x
8000	1000	12000	1000
10000	1000	15000	1000
11000	1000	25000	500

33. Form Letter. Write a program that prints the following personalized form letter.

APRIL 1, 1981

MS. JANE BUDWICK
10 NORTH ROAD
KINGSTON, RI 02881

DEAR MS. BUDWICK,
    YOU ARE INDEED ONE OF THE FORTUNATE FEW WHOM WE HAVE
SELECTED FOR OUR GALA PRIZE DRAWING. ALL YOU NEED TO DO, JANE,
IS FILL IN THE ENCLOSED HANDY MAGAZINE ORDER FORM, WHICH
MAKES YOU ELIGIBLE FOR ONE OF OUR MANY GALA PRIZES. INDEED, THE
BUDWICK RESIDENCE AT 10 NORTH ROAD MAY BE LUCKY ENOUGH TO
RECEIVE THE MOST GALA PRIZE, A FREE SET OF ENCYCLOPEDIAS AT A
MAINTENANCE COST OF ONLY 10 CENTS PER DAY FOR 30 YEARS.

GOOD LUCK!
HOODWINK G. FOX, MANAGER
DILL COMIC BOOK CO., INC.

In one computer run, print the letter for each of the following.

Name	Address	
MS. JANE BUDWICK	10 NORTH ROAD	KINGSTON, RI 02881
MR. AL BELLA BITTA	20 BIRCH ST.	CINCINNATI, OH 44451
DR. H. DOOLITTLE	10 DOWNING	LONDON, UK

Make sure that each letter fits nicely within an 8½-inch width and takes up 11
inches in length.

34. Bank Savings with Multiple Compounding.   Consider the formula

$$A = P \cdot (1 + R/M)^{N \cdot M}$$

where
A = accumulated funds
P = principal (amount we first invest)
R = annual interest rate
N = number of years
M = number of times per year the account is compounded (for example, if the
       account is compounded quarterly, then $M = 4$, or interest is added in four
       times a year)
To illustrate, if we start with \$1000 ($P = 1000$) at 6 percent per year ($R = 0.06$)
compounded once a year ($M = 1$), then after two years ($N = 2$) we end up with

$$A = 1000 \cdot (1 + 0.06/1)^{2 \cdot 1}$$
$$= \$1123.60$$

However, if we compound quarterly ($M = 4$), then in two years we end up with

$$A = 1000 \cdot (1 + 0.06/4)^{2 \cdot 4}$$
$$= \$1126.49$$

which is \$2.89 better than under annual compounding.

In recent years banks have competitively increased the number of compounding periods to attract customers. For example, under daily compounding (M = 365) your account earns interest daily, which is preferred to, say, monthly compounding (M = 12).

a. Design and run a program that processes the following input data in one run.

P	R	N	M
1000	0.06	10	1
1000	0.06	10	4
1000	0.06	10	12
1000	0.06	10	52
1000	0.06	10	365

As output, print the above table together with a new column for A. Comment on the behavior of A.

b. The "ultimate" account compounds continuously according to the formula

$$A = P \cdot e^{R \cdot N}$$

where e is the base of natural logarithms (see Module A). For example, if we start with $1000 and compound continuously at 6 percent per year, then after two years we end up with

$$A = 1000 \cdot e^{(0.06) \cdot (2)}$$
$$= 1000 \cdot e^{0 \cdot 12}$$
$$= (1000) \cdot (1.127496)$$
$$= \$1127.50$$

which is $1.01 better than under quarterly compounding. Wouldn't you rather earn money even as you read this? Modify the output in part a to include a last row in the table for continuous compounding. Comment on the behavior of A.

35. Retirement Contribution.   The personnel department of a large corporation is offering a new pension plan to its employees that works as follows. The employee contributes an amount C that is deducted from each biweekly paycheck. The company then matches this amount (also contributes C) and invests the money at an annual interest rate R. At the end of Y years, when it is time for the employee to retire, the employee can withdraw a tidy sum S. The necessary biweekly employee contribution to achieve S after Y years when the fund is compounded biweekly at rate R per year is given by

$$C = \left(\frac{S}{2}\right) \cdot \left(\frac{R/26}{(1 + R/26)^{26 Y} - 1}\right)$$

Thus, if the interest rate is 0.07 per year, 30 years remain toward retirement, and the employee desires $40,000 at retirement, then the employee must contribute

$$C = \left(\frac{40000}{2}\right) \cdot \left(\frac{.07/26}{(1 + .07/26)^{(26) \cdot (30)} - 1}\right)$$
$$= \$7.54$$

every two weeks.

a. Design and run a program that processes the input data

Name	Y	S
Tahiti Joe	30	$ 40,000
Jet-Set Sal	40	200,000
Too-Late Leroy	5	10,000

and prints the following output.

NAME	YEARS TO RETIREMENT	RETIREMENT SUM	BIWEEKLY CONTRIBUTION
XXXXXXXXXXX	XX	XXXXXX	XX.XX
.	.	.	.
.	.	.	.
.	.	.	.

What would be the effect of an increase in the interest rate to 9 percent per year?

b. Include an outer loop that processes interest rates from an initial value $R1$ to a terminal value $R2$ in increments of $R3$. Process the data in part a by varying the interest rate from 7 percent to 10 percent in increments of 1 percent. Thus, this run prints four output tables, or one table per interest rate. Precede the output of each table by printing the appropriate interest rate. Is the interest rate effect significant?

36. **Optimal Cost per Credit.** Suppose that the cost per credit charged by a college directly affects student enrollment according to the following *demand curve.*

$$S = D1 - D2 \cdot C$$

where
  S = number of students enrolled
  C = cost ($) per credit
  $D1$ = first parameter in demand curve
  $D2$ = second parameter in demand curve
For example, if the tuition charge is $80 per credit, $D1$ is 14,000, and $D2$ is 100, then the number of students that will enroll is estimated by

$$S = 14000 - (100) \cdot (80)$$
$$= 6000$$

If the cost per credit is increased to $90, then the estimated enrollment drops to

$$S = 14000 - (100) \cdot (90)$$
$$= 5000$$

The average balance due the college is given by

$$B = A \cdot C + F$$

where

B = average balance due the college
A = average number of credit hours for the college
C = cost per credit
F = average fee for the college

For example, if the average number of credit hours taken by students is 14, the cost per credit is $80, and average fees are $250, then the average bill per student is

$$B = (14) \cdot (80) + 250$$
$$= \$1370$$

Since projected enrollment is 6000 students when the per-credit charge is $80, it follows that the college would realize a projected revenue of ($1370 per student) · (6000 students), or $8,220,000.

a. Design and run a program that includes a DO-loop for varying C from $C1$ to $C2$ in increments of $C3$. Process the following input data.

D1	D2	A	F	C1	C2	C3
14000	100	14	250	50	80	1

Print an output table headed by four columns: Cost per Credit, Average Bill, Expected Enrollment, and Expected Revenue. On the basis of this output, what cost per credit maximizes expected revenue for the college?

b. Add an outer DO-loop that processes N colleges in a statewide system. Run the following test data through your program.

College Name	D1	D2	A	F	C1	C2	C3
Test 1	14000	100	14	250	50	80	1
Test 2	14000	25	14	250	200	300	5
Test 3	30000	250	13.5	500	10	60	1

Just before each output table print the name of the college, $D1, D2, A$, and F.

What tuition (cost per credit) should be charged at each college in order to maximize revenue? Would you say there's a flaw in the algorithmic logic if students freely change colleges within the system on the basis of tuition?

** c. Solve this problem by calculus. Do your analytic and computer results agree?

CHAPTER 5

The IF-THEN-ELSE Structure and Its Variants

The **decision structure** expresses the logic by which conditions are tested to determine the appropriate flow of execution among alternative paths. In this chapter we show how to implement variations of the IF-THEN-ELSE structure first discussed in the last chapter.

5.1 BLOCK IF, ELSE, AND END IF STATEMENTS

Each decision structure in this chapter begins with the block IF statement and ends with the END IF statement. These two statements enclose the body of the structure. In addition, two optional statements, the ELSE and ELSE IF, can be used to control the sequence of execution within the body.

IF-THEN-ELSE Structure

The two-choice or **IF-THEN-ELSE structure** is generally implemented as follows:

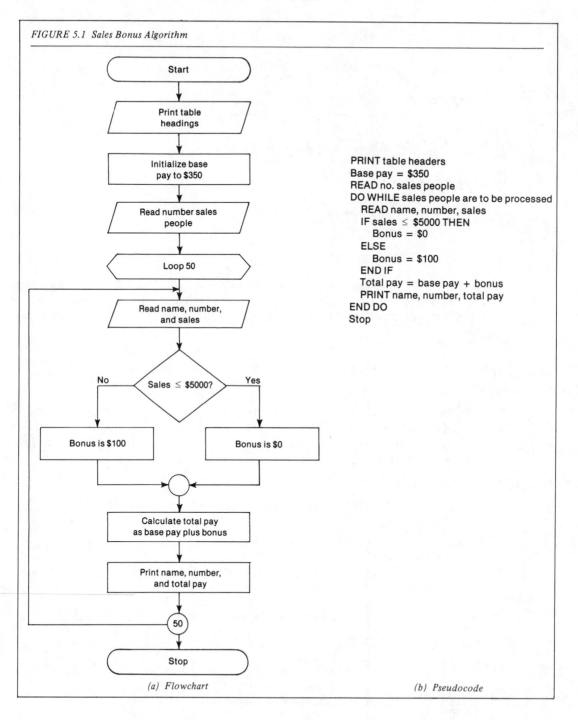

FIGURE 5.1 *Sales Bonus Algorithm*

(a) Flowchart

(b) Pseudocode

When the block IF statement is executed, the condition within parentheses is tested. If the result is true (the condition holds), then the *IF-block* (block of statements following the keyword THEN up to but not including the ELSE statement) is executed, after which control passes to the END IF statement (which has the same effect as passing control to the first executable statement following the END IF statement). If the condition is false (the condition does not hold), the *ELSE-block* (block of statements following the ELSE statement up to but not including the END IF statement) is executed, after which control passes to the END IF statement (that is, the first executable statement following the END IF statement).

EXAMPLE 5.1 Sales Bonus Problem

Suppose sales personnel earn a weekly base salary of $350 plus a $100 bonus if weekly sales are above $5000; otherwise no bonus is added to the base salary. Figure 5.1 illustrates the algorithm for the program below, where all data are expressed in whole dollars.

```
C     SALES BONUS PROGRAM
C
C     KEY:
C        BASE    = BASE SALARY
C        N       = NUMBER OF SALESPERSONS
C        NAME    = SALESPERSON'S NAME
C        SSN     = SOCIAL SECURITY NUMBER
C        SALES   = WEEKLY SALES
C        BONUS   = SALES BONUS
C        TOTPAY  = TOTAL PAY
C
      CHARACTER NAME*15
      INTEGER    BASE,N,SSN,SALES,BONUS,TOTPAY
C
      PRINT *,'EMPLOYEE NAME       SS NUMBER       TOTAL PAY'
      PRINT *,' '
C
      BASE = 350
      READ *,N
C
      DO 50 I = 1,N
         READ *,NAME,SSN,SALES
C
         IF (SALES .LE. 5000) THEN
            BONUS = 0
         ELSE
            BONUS = 100
         END IF
```

```
       C
                    TOTPAY = BASE + BONUS
                    PRINT *,NAME,SSN,TOTPAY
              50 CONTINUE
       C
                    END
```

A test run for three salespeople given the input data

```
3
'W. LOMAN',123456789,4500
'X. LOMAN',432198765,6500
'Y. LOMAN',987654321,5100
```

would result in the output

EMPLOYEE NAME	SS NUMBER	TOTAL PAY
W. LOMAN	123456789	350
X. LOMAN	432198765	450
Y. LOMAN	987654321	450

The salesperson's base salary of $350 is stored in a variable named BASE and the IF-THEN-ELSE structure determines whether or not the salesperson receives the $100 bonus.

The expression "SALES .LE. 5000" is called a "relational expression"; it represents the condition "sales less than or equal to $5000," where .LE. stands for "less than or equal to." When executed, the block IF statement tests this condition, giving one of two results: true or false. If the value in SALES is less than or equal to 5000, then the result of the test is true and the statements within the IF-block are executed. In other words, the computer executes

```
BONUS = 0
```

However, if the result of the test is false, control immediately goes to the ELSE-block. In this case the statement

```
BONUS = 100
```

is executed.

A simple condition in the block IF statement is expressed by a relational expression. Every **relational expression** takes the form of an (arithmetic or character) expression, then a relational operator, and then another arithmetic or character expression. A **relational operator** indicates a mathematical comparison such as less than, equal to, or greater than. FORTRAN uses six relational operators, as indicated in Table 5.1.

Notice that the periods that surround the letters are part of the relational operator. To test a condition, you use one of these relational operators "wedged" between the two arithmetic or character expressions, as follows.

Relational Expressions

arithmetic expression or character expression	relational operator	arithmetic expression or character expression

When evaluated, a relational expression will have either the value true or the value false.

As in Chapter 2, *arithmetic expressions* may consist of a single variable, a single constant, or a combination of variables, constants, parentheses, functions, and arithmetic operators. As in our previous work with arithmetic expressions, it is good programming practice not to mix type when coding a relational expression; that is, *the arithmetic expression to the left of the relational operator should be the same type as the arithmetic expression to the right.* A *character expression* usually includes either a character variable or a character constant.

TABLE 5.1   *Relational Operators in FORTRAN*

MATHEMATICAL COMPARISON	RELATIONAL OPERATOR	MEANING
=	.EQ.	Equal to
≠	.NE.	Not equal to
<	.LT.	Less than
≤	.LE.	Less than or equal to
>	.GT.	Greater than
≥	.GE.	Greater than or equal to

Notice in Figure 5.1 that the flowchart diamond symbol ◇ is used whenever a decision or test is made. The test is described within the diamond, and the arrows show the alternative paths that your program may take from that decision point. The circle symbol ○ indicates transfer of control points in the program.

Did you notice in the pseudocode and program of Example 5.1 that statements in the IF-block and ELSE-block are indented? *Although indentation is not required, it improves the readability of the IF-THEN-ELSE structure.*

Example 5.2 further illustrates the use of the IF-THEN-ELSE structure for testing conditions within programs.

EXAMPLE 5.2 Illustrations of IF-THEN-ELSE Structure

Flowchart	Pseudocode	FORTRAN	Explanation

a.

Pseudocode:
```
. . .
IF Hours Worked ≤ 40 THEN
    Regular pay = hours worked × rate of pay
    Overtime pay = 0
ELSE
    Regular pay = 40 × rate of pay
    Overtime pay = (hours − 40) ×
        rate of pay × 1.5
END IF
. . .
```

FORTRAN:
```
. . .
IF (HOURS.LE.40.) THEN
    REGPAY = HOURS * RATE
    OVRTM = 0.
ELSE
    REGPAY = 40. * RATE
    OVRTM = (HOURS − 40.)
        * RATE * 1.5
END IF
. . .
```

Explanation:
If the value stored in HOURS is less than or equal to 40. then the statements REGPAY = HOURS*RATE OVRTM = 0. are executed. If the value stored in HOURS exceeds 40, then the program executes the statements.
REGPAY = 40.*RATE OVRTM = (HOURS − 40.)* RATE*1.5

b.

Pseudocode:
```
. . .
IF distance/time > critical velocity THEN
    Acceleration = .9 × acceleration
ELSE
    Acceleration = 1.02 × acceleration
END IF
. . .
```

FORTRAN:
```
. . .
IF (DIST/TIME. GT. VELCRI) THEN
    ACCEL = .9 * ACCEL
ELSE
    ACCEL = 1.02 * ACCEL
END IF
. . .
```

Explanation:
If the value stored in DIST divided by the value stored in TIME is greater than the value stored in VELCRI, then execute ACCEL = .9*ACCEL otherwise execute ACCEL = 1.02*ACCEL

EXAMPLE 5.2 *(Continued)*

Flowchart	Pseudocode	*FORTRAN*	Explanation

c.

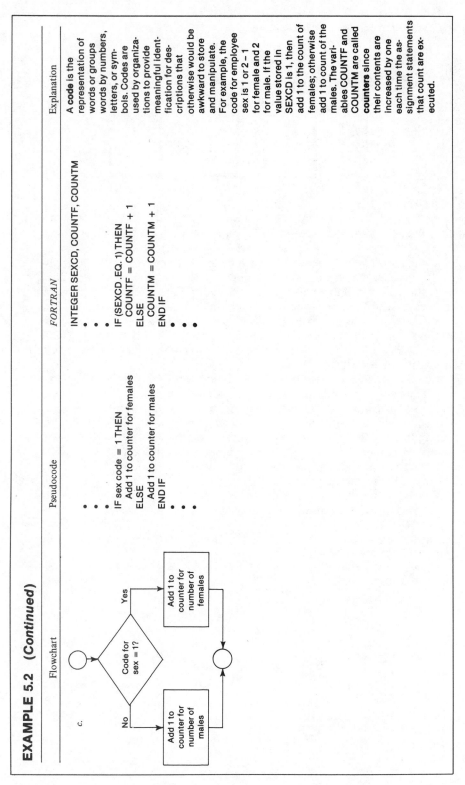

Yes

Code for sex = 1?

No

Add 1 to counter for number of females

Add 1 to counter for number of males

Pseudocode

• • •

IF sex code = 1 THEN
    Add 1 to counter for females
ELSE
    Add 1 to counter for males
END IF

• • •

FORTRAN

INTEGER SEXCD, COUNTF, COUNTM

• • • •

IF (SEXCD . EQ. 1) THEN
    COUNTF = COUNTF + 1
ELSE
    COUNTM = COUNTM + 1
END IF

• • •

Explanation

A **code** is the representation of words or groups words by numbers, letters, or symbols. Codes are used by organizations to provide meaningful identification for descriptions that otherwise would be awkward to store and manipulate. For example, the code for employee sex is 1 or 2 – 1 for female and 2 for male. If the value stored in SEXCD is 1, then add 1 to the count of females; otherwise add 1 to count of the males. The variables COUNTF and COUNTM are called **counters** since their contents are increased by one each time the assignment statements that count are executed.

Follow-up Exercises

1. Indicate whether a true or false condition exists for each relational expression.

a. K .LT. L
b. L .LE. N
c. M .GT. −58

d. N .EQ. 33
e. K + N .GE. L − M
f. L/K .NE. M + N

2. Modify Figure 5.1 and the program in Example 5.1 using the test "sales greater than 5000" instead of "sales less than or equal to 5000."

3. Modify the program of Example 5.1 to calculate and print the number of people who do not receive a bonus and the number of people who do receive a bonus.

* 4. Modify the program of Example 5.1 to incorporate the fact that base pay varies from salesperson to salesperson. Also assume that the current bonus of $100 and the cutoff of $5000 are likely to change often in the life of the program. As a result, we wish to treat these values under the names CURBON and CUTOFF.

5. Write IF-THEN-ELSE structures for each situation below. Include flowchart or pseudocode along with FORTRAN code.

   a. If credits taken are 12 or more, then tuition is $1200; otherwise tuition is $100 times the number of credits.

   b. If fixed costs plus variable costs are less than sales revenue, then compute profit as sales revenue minus (fixed costs plus variable costs) and output the message PROFIT = · · · ; otherwise, compute loss as fixed plus variable costs minus sales revenue and output the message LOSS = · · ·

   c. A department store has the following minimum payment policy for its customers. When the balance owed (BAL) is under $50, the customer pays (PAYS) the full balance owed. When the amount owed is $50 or more, the customer pays according to the formula $50 + 10 percent (balance owed − $50).

   d. If sex is male, then print the message "SEX = MALE"; otherwise print the message "SEX = FEMALE."

6. Code each flowchart into a segment of a FORTRAN program.

   a.

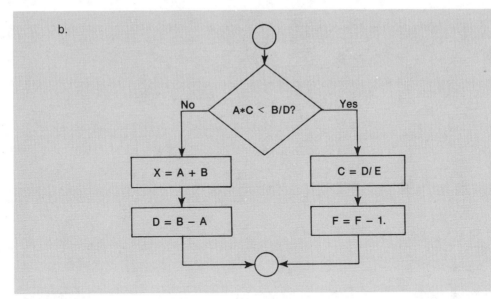

IF-THEN Structure

The block IF and END IF statements can be used to code the single-choice or **IF-THEN structure.** In this case the ELSE segment of the IF-THEN-ELSE structure is omitted, as the following variation indicates.

```
IF (condition) THEN
    ·⎫  true condition
    ·⎬  (IF-block)
    ·⎭
END IF
```

Thus, if the condition tested is true, the IF-block is executed, after which control passes to the first executable statement following the END IF statement. If the condition is false, control passes directly to the first executable statement following the END IF statement.

EXAMPLE 5.3   Condition Based on Character Expressions

In the following segment, if the name SMITH is found, the name and telephone number are printed; otherwise, execution continues. Note how this example illustrates the use of character data to express the condition that is to be tested. In this case, the relational expression consists of the relational operator .EQ. wedged between two character expressions.

EXAMPLE 5.3 *(Continued)*

Flowchart	Pseudocode	*FORTRAN*

Pseudocode:

```
. . .
READ name and phone number
IF name = 'Smith' THEN
    PRINT name and
        phone number
END IF
. . .
```

FORTRAN:

```
. . .
READ *, NAME, PHONE
IF (NAME .EQ. 'SMITH') THEN
    PRINT *, 'NAME :', NAME
    PRINT *, 'PHONE NUMBER :' PHONE
END IF
. . .
```

Flowchart:

Read name and telephone number → Name = Smith? → Yes → Print name and telephone number

No

EXAMPLE 5.4   Finding the Minimum Value

The Department of Health and Human Service has a data file that includes the per capita income (that is, total income divided by total number of people) for each standard metropolitan statistical area (SMSA) in the country. An administrator wishes to determine the SMSA code that has the smallest per capita income. The program below illustrates the determination of this minimum and its associated SMSA.

```
C   MINIMUM VALUE PROGRAM
C   KEY:
C     N        = TOTAL NUMBER OF SMSA'S
C     SMSA     = CODE ASSIGNED TO STANDARD METROPOLITAN
C                STATISTICAL AREA
C     PCI      = PER CAPITA INCOME OF SMSA
C     MINSMS = SMSA WITH MINIMUM PCI
C     MINPCI  = SMALLEST PCI
C
      INTEGER N,SMSA,MINSMS
      REAL    PCI,MINPCI
C
      MINPCI = 1E30
      READ *,N
C
      DO 100 I = 1,N
         READ *,SMSA,PCI
C
         IF (PCI .LT. MINPCI) THEN
            MINPCI  = PCI
            MINSMS = SMSA
         END IF
C
  100 CONTINUE
C
      PRINT *,'SMSA NUMBER',MINSMS
      PRINT *,'HAS MINIMUM PCI OF',MINPCI
C
      END
```

Test Data

```
5
147,5165.
 56,7860.
 75,6350.
 41,4293.
105,5415.
```

Output

SMSA NUMBER 41
HAS MINIMUM PCI OF 4293.0

Note that the variable that stores the minimum value (MINPCI) is initialized to a very large value (1E30). This assures that one of the data items for PCI will be the minimum value.

Follow-up Exercises

7. Draw a flowchart for the program of Example 5.4. Check the logic of the flowchart and program by roleplaying (with you as computer) through the provided test data. Indicate below the values stored successively, where the "snapshot" of memory is taken at each iteration just before the execution of the continue statement.

N	I	SMSA	PCI	MINPCI	MINSMS

8. Modify the program of Example 5.4 to find and output the largest per capita income (MAXPCI) and its associated SMSA (MAXSMS), in addition to MINPCI and MINSMS. First draw the flowchart.

9. Write IF-THEN structures for each situation below. Include flowchart or pseudocode along with FORTRAN code.
   a. If taxpayer's age (AGE) is 65 or over add 1 to number of dependents (NOD); otherwise go on to the next statement.
   b. If part name (PART) equals "WRENCH" output the quantity on hand (QOH); otherwise go on to the next statement.

10. Code this flowchart into a segment of a FORTRAN program.

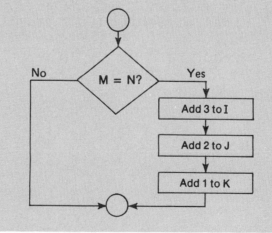

5.2
DECISION STRUCTURE VARIATIONS

The solutions to many problems require rather complicated sequences of decisions in order to determine what statements are to be executed. In this section we illustrate two popular variations of the IF-THEN-ELSE structure; in the next chapter we conclude the treatment of decision structures by presenting another variation called the CASE structure.

Nested Decision Structures

A **nested decision structure** is a structure that contains one or more decision structures within another decision structure. A nested decision structure constructed from block IF statements is often called **nested IF-blocks.** The example below illustrates how two related decisions can be programmed by nesting one IF-THEN-ELSE structure within another IF-THEN-ELSE structure.

EXAMPLE 5.5   Sales Bonus Problem with Nested IF-THEN-ELSE Structures

The illustration on page 154 shows how the decision structure in Example 5.1 on page 142 is modified to reflect the policy that a salesperson receives the $100 bonus if and only if weekly sales are above $500 *and* travel expenses are below $600.

  This program segment has two IF-THEN-ELSE structures, one nested within the other. The "inner" IF-THEN-ELSE structure in this case is within the IF-block of the "outer" IF-THEN-ELSE structure.

  If the condition "SALES .GT. 5000" is true, a second condition "TRAVEL .LT. 600" is tested. If travel cost is less than $600, the statement that sets BONUS to 100 is executed; otherwise BONUS is set equal to zero. If the condition "SALES .GT. 5000" is false, the second ELSE-block is executed and bonus is set equal to zero.

  Notice that there are two END IF statements in this program segment, *since each block IF statement requires its own END IF statement.* The first block IF statement is paired with the last END IF statement and the second block IF statement is paired with the next to last END IF statement. Thus the nesting scheme is similar to the nested DO-loop representation, as follows:

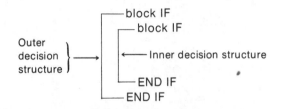

  You should also notice the indentation in the pseudocode and FORTRAN versions, which facilitates an understanding of the nesting logic.

EXAMPLE 5.5 *(Continued)*

Flowchart   Pseudocode   *FORTRAN*

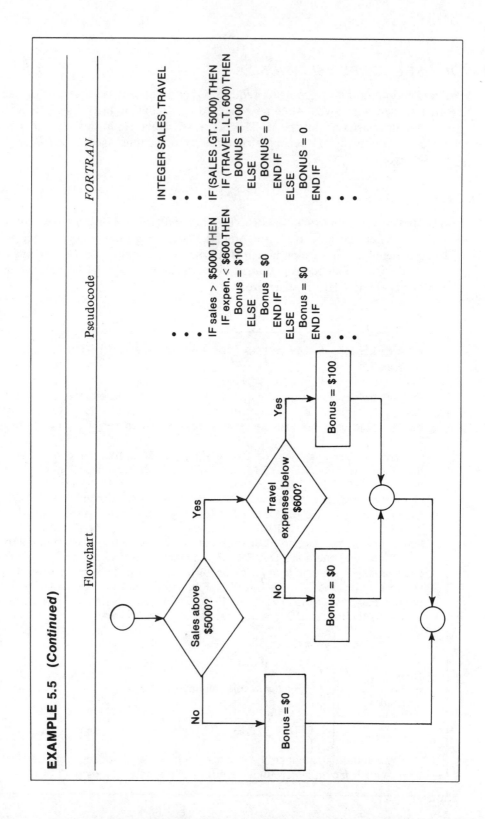

```
IF sales > $5000 THEN
    IF expen. < $600 THEN
        Bonus = $100
    ELSE
        Bonus = $0
    END IF
ELSE
    Bonus = $0
END IF
```

```
INTEGER SALES, TRAVEL
    . . . .
IF (SALES .GT. 5000) THEN
    IF (TRAVEL .LT. 600) THEN
        BONUS = 100
    ELSE
        BONUS = 0
    END IF
ELSE
    BONUS = 0
END IF
    . . . .
```

154

Follow-up Exercises

11. Modify the logic in Example 5.5 according to the following two versions.
    a. Replace the inner IF-THEN-ELSE structure by a sequence structure followed by an IF-THEN structure.
    b. Replace both IF-THEN-ELSE structures by a sequence structure followed by nested IF-THEN structures.

* 12. In Example 5.5, assume that the bonus is based on the following schedule, where travel expense does not play a role.

    Weekly sales under $4000   bonus is $0
    Weekly sales between $4000 and $5000   bonus is $50
    Weekly sales over $5000   bonus is $100

    Modify Example 5.5 to include this schedule.

** 13. Modify Example 5.5 to satisfy the following conditions.

    If sales > $5000 and travel cost < $300, bonus is $150.
    If sales > $5000 and travel cost ≥ $300 but < $600, bonus is $100.
    If sales ≤ $5000, bonus is $0.
    If travel cost ≥ $600, bonus is $0.

Multiple Alternative Decision Structures Using Block IF Statements

We now present a more general decision structure called the **multiple alternative decision structure,** as illustrated in Figure 5.2.

In this particular structure conditions are evaluated from top to bottom. Each diamond and its corresponding box in the flowchart represent an IF-THEN structure. Thus we have a sequence of block IF statements, IF-blocks, and END IF statements.

The last portion of the flowchart shows the logic if all conditions are false. In this case, if none of the conditions is true, an alternative block of statements is executed. This portion is optional, but is often used to include error routines. An **error routine** is a segment of the program that detects errors in either input data or computational results. Typically, an error routine prints a message that alerts the user to the problem and then continues with the normal execution sequence.

EXAMPLE 5.6   Postal Zone Fees Using Block IF Statements

The cost of mailing a package by priority mail is based on weight and destination of the package. The U.S. Post Office divides the country into eight postal zones, with the following fee schedule (page 157) for packages under one pound.

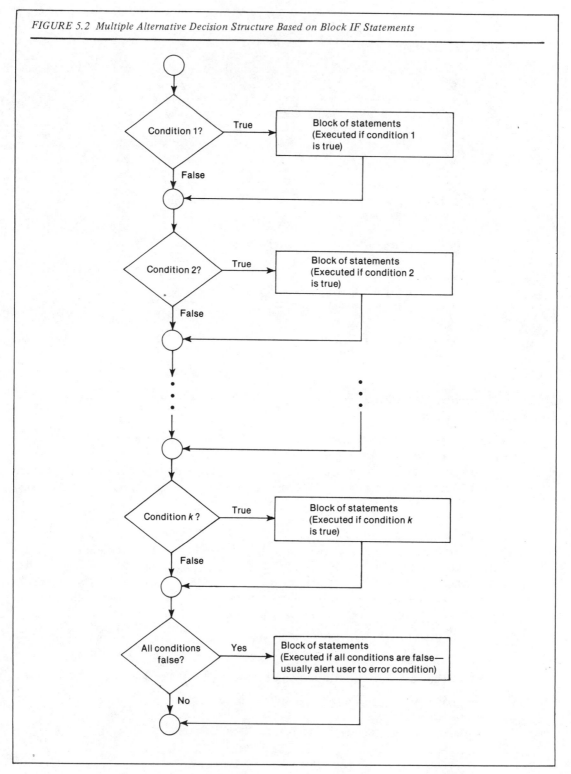

FIGURE 5.2 *Multiple Alternative Decision Structure Based on Block IF Statements*

	Zone 1, 2, 3	Zone 4	Zone 5	Zone 6	Zone 7	Zone 8
Fee for package under one pound	$1.71	$1.81	$1.88	$1.97	$2.06	$2.25

The flowchart, pseudocode, and FORTRAN code for this logic are illustrated next.

Flowchart	Pseudocode	FORTRAN

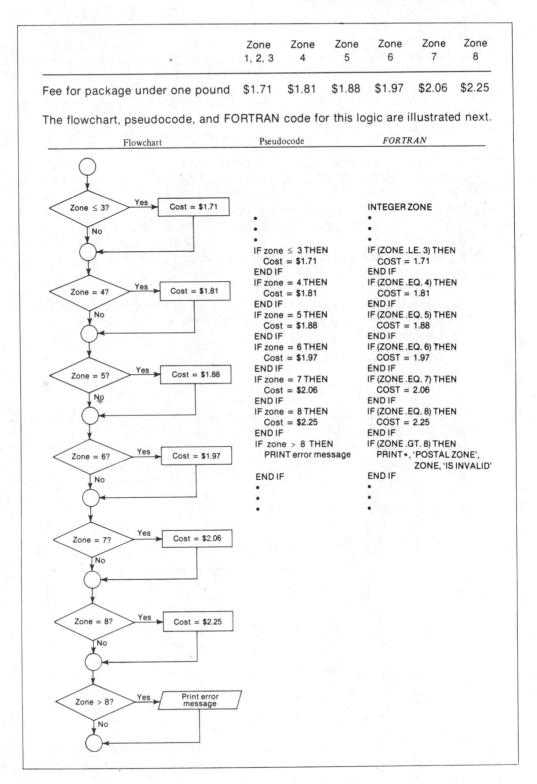

Pseudocode:

```
        •
        •
        •
IF zone ≤ 3 THEN
   Cost = $1.71
END IF
IF zone = 4 THEN
   Cost = $1.81
END IF
IF zone = 5 THEN
   Cost = $1.88
END IF
IF zone = 6 THEN
   Cost = $1.97
END IF
IF zone = 7 THEN
   Cost = $2.06
END IF
IF zone = 8 THEN
   Cost = $2.25
END IF
IF zone > 8 THEN
   PRINT error message

END IF
        •
        •
        •
```

FORTRAN:

```
      INTEGER ZONE
        •
        •
        •
IF (ZONE .LE. 3) THEN
   COST = 1.71
END IF
IF (ZONE .EQ. 4) THEN
   COST = 1.81
END IF
IF (ZONE .EQ. 5) THEN
   COST = 1.88
END IF
IF (ZONE .EQ. 6) THEN
   COST = 1.97
END IF
IF (ZONE .EQ. 7) THEN
   COST = 2.06
END IF
IF (ZONE .EQ. 8) THEN
   COST = 2.25
END IF
IF (ZONE .GT. 8) THEN
   PRINT *, 'POSTAL ZONE',
           ZONE, 'IS INVALID'
END IF
        •
        •
        •
```

For example, if ZONE stores a 5, then the first condition (Zone ≤ 3?) tests false, the second condition (Zone = 4?) tests false, and the third condition (Zone = 5?) tests true. Thus, the fee $1.88 is entered in COST, and execution continues with tests of the remaining four conditions (all false). At this point execution control exits the structure, with the proper fee stored in COST. Note that an error message is printed if the value in ZONE is above 8.

Multiple alternative decision structures based on block IF statements are inefficient with respect to CPU time because each condition is evaluated regardless of whether or not an earlier condition tested true. Typically, we design the structure so that only a single condition will test true in the sequence, which means that it is actually unnecessary to evaluate conditions that follow the one that tested true. This inefficiency can be corrected in one of two ways: either by nested IF-blocks or by use of a statement called the ELSE IF (as presented in the next subsection).

Although nested IF-blocks improve efficiency, we don't recommend their use in multiple alternative decision structures because readability diminishes drastically as the number of "nests" increases. In fact, some data processing organizations forbid nesting to depths beyond two or three to avoid potential logic errors. Try Exercise 14 to convince yourself.

Multiple Alternative Decision Structures Using ELSE IF Statements

An improved version of the multiple alternative decision structure is illustrated in Figure 5.3. Again, conditions are evaluated from top to bottom and the block of statements corresponding to the first true condition is executed. Now, however, *control passes to the end of the structure immediately after the execution of the block associated with the true condition. Thus, conditions following the first true condition are not evaluated, which eliminates the inefficiency of the block IF statement approach without sacrificing readability.* As before, if all conditions are false, the optional error routine is entered.

In FORTRAN 77 an **ELSE IF statement** is used to code the multiple alternative decision structure, where the general form is given by

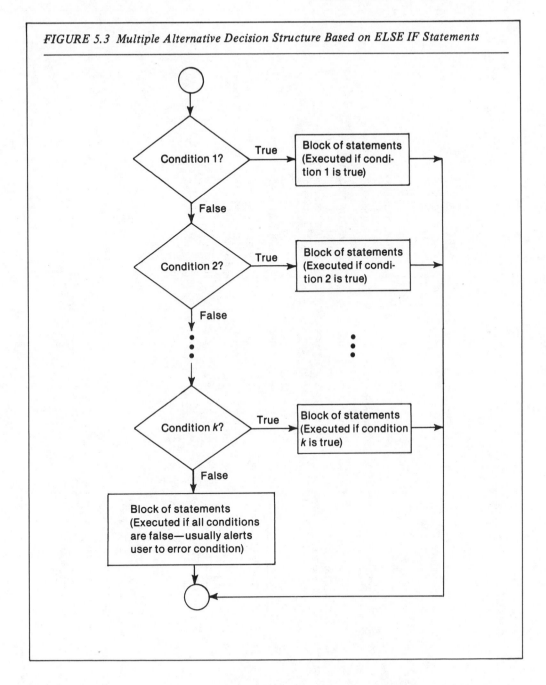

FIGURE 5.3 *Multiple Alternative Decision Structure Based on ELSE IF Statements*

The conditions are tested one by one until one is true, then the statements in that **ELSE-IF-block** are executed, after which control passes to the END IF statement. If all the conditions are false, the statements in the ELSE-block (optional) are executed, and control is then transferred to the END IF statement.

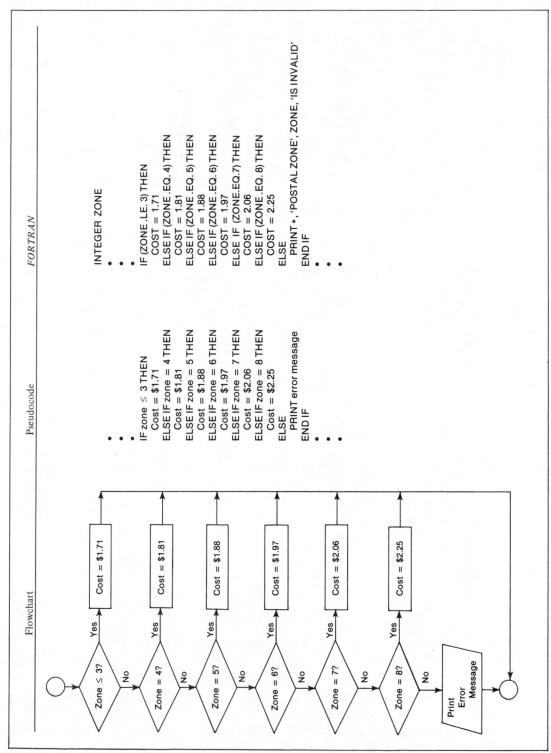

FORTRAN

```
INTEGER ZONE
. . . .
IF (ZONE .LE. 3) THEN
    COST = 1.71
ELSE IF (ZONE. EQ. 4) THEN
    COST = 1.81
ELSE IF (ZONE. EQ. 5) THEN
    COST = 1.88
ELSE IF (ZONE. EQ. 6) THEN
    COST = 1.97
ELSE IF (ZONE.EQ.7) THEN
    COST = 2.06
ELSE IF (ZONE. EQ. 8) THEN
    COST = 2.25
ELSE
    PRINT *, 'POSTAL ZONE', ZONE, 'IS INVALID'
ENDIF
. . . .
```

Pseudocode

```
. . .
IF zone ≤ 3 THEN
    Cost = $1.71
ELSE IF zone = 4 THEN
    Cost = $1.81
ELSE IF zone = 5 THEN
    Cost = $1.88
ELSE IF zone = 6 THEN
    Cost = $1.97
ELSE IF zone = 7 THEN
    Cost = $2.06
ELSE IF zone = 8 THEN
    Cost = $2.25
ELSE
    PRINT error message
END IF
. . .
```

Flowchart

EXAMPLE 5.7   Postal Zone Fees Using ELSE IF Statements

We now rewrite Example 5.6 using ELSE IF statements, as shown on page 160.

For example, assume 5 is stored in the integer variable ZONE. The first condition tested is "ZONE .LE. 3" which is false. Next the condition "ZONE .EQ. 4" is tested, which also is false. The third condition tested is "ZONE .EQ. 5" which is true; therefore, the statement

COST = 1.88

is executed, and control is transferred to the first executable statement following the END IF statement.

Notice that we do not indent each successive ELSE IF statement, since readability is not necessarily improved and statements toward the end of the structure would be shifted far too much to the right.

One last point: The interpretation of codes is common in programming. However, as the number of codes gets larger, multiple alternative decision structures become inefficient since each comparison (IF test) is executed until one succeeds (tests true). One suggestion is to arrange the IF tests on the basis of the frequency of occurrence of a particular code, placing codes occurring most often before codes that occur less frequently. Another solution, when codes are numeric, is to use the CASE structure, which is discussed in Chapter 6.

Follow-up Exercises

14. Rewrite the logic in Example 5.7 by using nested IF-THEN-ELSE structures. Discuss pros and cons of each approach.
15. What happens in Example 5.6 (or Example 5.7) if the value 9 is stored in ZONE? If the value 0 is stored in ZONE? Rewrite the logic to eliminate this bug in
     a. Example 5.6.
     b. Example 5.7.
16. Use the ELSE IF statement to solve
     *a. Exercise 12 on page 155.
     **b. Exercise 13 on page 155.
     Which approach do you prefer?
*17. Flowchart the following codes.

```
a.  M = 5                        b.  M = 5
    IF (J .LT. M) THEN               IF (J .LT. M) THEN
        J = J + 5                        J = J + 5
        M = M + 3                        M = M + 3
        IF (J .LT. 8) THEN           ELSE IF (J .LT. 8) THEN
            M = M + 10                   M = M + 10
        ELSE                         ELSE
            M = M + 20                   M = M + 20
        END IF                       END IF
    END IF
END IF
```

c.   What are the final values for J and M in parts a and b when initially J = 2? When initially J = 7? When initially J = 10?

*18.   A student is assigned a grade A, B, C, D, or F according to the following rule.

$$
\begin{aligned}
\text{test score} &\geq 90 &&\text{grade is A} \\
80 \leq \text{test score} &< 90 &&\text{grade is B} \\
70 \leq \text{test score} &< 80 &&\text{grade is C} \\
60 \leq \text{test score} &< 70 &&\text{grade is D} \\
\text{test score} &< 60 &&\text{grade is F}
\end{aligned}
$$

Write a program segment that prints the student's name (NAME) and grade (GRADE) based on the test score (SCORE).

19.   Code the following flowcharts.

a.

b.

* e.

20. With respect to Exercise 19, fill in the final value in R if R initially stores the characters NULL and the following values are stored in A, B, C, D, E.

	A	B	C	D	E	19a	19b	19c	19d	19e
a.	5	15	25	35	45					
b.	20	15	25	35	45					
c.	20	25	25	35	45					
*d.	20	20	35	50	45					

Final value in R based on Exercise

**21. Input Data Validation. Modify the program in Example 5.4 on page 151 to include an error routine that validates the input data. Specifically, following the input of SMSA and PCI values, test to make sure that SMSA is between 1 and 200 inclusive and PCI is greater than $1000 and less than $25,000. Program the following versions.

a. If an error is found, print the input data line number where the error is located, print the corresponding values in SMSA and PCI, and continue processing as if nothing is wrong.

b. Same as part a, except stop processing as soon as an error message is printed.

c. Same as part a, except once an error message is printed, bypass the IF-THEN structure that finds the minimum value and go on to process the next input line.

Include a flowchart or pseudocode for each version. Which approach do you prefer and why?

5.3
LOGICAL EXPRESSIONS

Up to now we have used a single relational expression made up of a relational operator (.EQ., .NE., .LT., .LE., .GE., .GT.) wedged between two arithmetic or character expressions to test one condition at a time. In many cases, nested and multiple alternative decision structures can be simplified by combining two or more relational expressions into a single logical expression. You can accomplish this by using the **logical operators** .AND., .OR., and .NOT. to connect relational expressions. The resulting expression is called a **logical expression.** For example, the relational expression B .GT. A can be combined with the relational expression B .LT. C using the logical operator .AND. as follows:

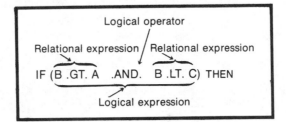

The entire expression within the parentheses is a logical expression which when tested will be either true or false. Note that the first relational expression is the first condition to be tested and the second relational expression is the second condition to be tested. Thus logical expressions can be used to test multiple conditions within one block IF or ELSE IF statement.[1]

---

[1] More generally, *simple* forms of logical expressions include a single logical constant (.TRUE. or .FALSE.), a single symbolic name of a logical constant (as defined in a PARAMETER statement), a single logical variable, or a single relational expression (besides other possibilities we don't discuss). More complicated logical expressions are formed using one or more of the five available logical operators (we only discuss three of these operators), where each logical operator is wedged between two simple logical expressions.

Logical Operator .AND.

When using the operator .AND., if *each* of the conditions (relational expressions) is true, then the logical expression is true, and the statements within the IF-block are executed. If, however, any condition is false, the statements within the IF-block are skipped, and control is transferred either to the ELSE-block (if used) or the END IF statement (if the ELSE-block is not used).

EXAMPLE 5.8   Sales Bonus Problem With Logical Expression

In Example 5.5 on page 154 a nested IF-THEN-ELSE structure was used to set the bonus at $100 if sales are above $5000 *and* travel expenses are below $600; otherwise, the bonus is set to $0. The alternative decision structure below eliminates nesting by using a logical expression.

```
    :
    :
IF (SALES .GT. 5000 .AND. TRAVEL .LT. 600) THEN
    BONUS = 100
ELSE
    BONUS = 0
END IF
    :
    :
```

Logical Operator .OR.

When using the operator .OR., if *any* relational expression is true, then the logical expression is true, and the statements within the IF-block are executed; however, if *all* the conditions are false, then the IF-block is skipped and control is transferred to either the ELSE-block (if used) or the END IF statement.

EXAMPLE 5.9   Use of .OR.

An employer is interested in interviewing students with an economics (ECN) or mathematics (MTH) major. A search routine to find such persons might include the following statement.

```
IF (MAJOR .EQ. 'ECN'  .OR.  MAJOR .EQ. 'MTH') THEN
    PRINT *,NAME,MAJOR
END IF
```

Logical Operator .NOT.

The logical operator .NOT. reverses the logical value to which it is applied. For example, if .NOT. is applied to a false relational expression, then .NOT. makes the logical expression true. If the relational expression is true, then .NOT. causes a false logical expression.

EXAMPLE 5.10 Use of .NOT.

To count the number of single people (marriage code = 1) who responded to a survey, the following statement can be used.

```
IF (.NOT. (MAR .NE. 1)) THEN
    SINGLE = SINGLE + 1
END IF
```

where we use the inner parentheses to improve style. This IF-THEN structure is equivalent to the following.

```
IF (MAR .EQ. 1) THEN
    SINGLE = SINGLE + 1
END IF
```

Do you find the second alternative simpler?[2]

Hierarchy

To represent more than two conditions you may use more than one logical operator within a logical expression. For logical expressions of this type there is a hierarchy among the logical operators that determines the order in which the operators are evaluated, unless the order is changed by using parentheses. Logical operators are evaluated according to the following hierarchy.

Operator	Order
.NOT.	Highest priority
.AND.	⇓
.OR.	Lowest priority

EXAMPLE 5.11 Hierarchy Rules and Use of Parentheses

If the following values are stored

then the logical expression in

```
IF (I .EQ. J  .OR.  I .GT. K  .AND.  AG .LE. 5.1) THEN
    SUM = SUM + AG
END IF
```

[2] There are more meaningful uses of .NOT., one of which we illustrate in Section 10.5.

is true and the IF-block

SUM = SUM + AG

is executed. This logical expression is evaluated in the following manner.

1. According to the hierarchy, .AND. is evaluated before .OR., which means that we should focus on the shaded portion below.

I .EQ. J   .OR.   I .GT. K   .AND.   AG .LE. 5.1
                  3 .GT. 5   .AND.   6.   .LE. 5.1
                  false   .AND.   false
                        false

2. We are now left with

I .EQ. J   .OR.   false
3 .EQ. 3   .OR.   false
  true   .OR.   false
        true

Thus the logical expression itself has the value true.

As in arithmetic expressions, parentheses can be used to modify the order of evaluation within logical expressions. For example, assuming the same values for I, J, K, and AG, the logical expression in

IF ((I .EQ. J   .OR.   I .GT. K)   .AND.   AG .LE. 5.1) THEN
    SUM = SUM + AG
END IF

is false and control goes directly to the END IF statement without executing the IF-block. Now the expression is evaluated in the following manner.

1. Expressions enclosed within parentheses are evaluated before expressions not enclosed within parentheses. Thus the shaded portion below is evaluated first as true.

(I .EQ. J   .OR.   I .GT. K) .AND.   AG .LE. 5.1
3 .EQ. 3   .OR.   3 .GT. 5
  true   .OR.   false
        true

2. We are now left with

The logical expression, therefore, is false.

Improving readability is an alternative use of parentheses within logical expressions, as it is in arithmetic expressions. For instance, the clarity of the original block IF statement in this example can be improved as follows.

IF ((I .EQ. J)   .OR.   (I .GT. K   .AND.   AG .LE. 5.1)) THEN

The value of this logical expression is true, as before; however, it is now quite clear that the operator .AND. is considered before the operator .OR., since .AND. is within parentheses.

Follow-up Exercises

22. Given the stored values

indicate whether or not the IF-block is executed for each of the following.

  a. IF (.NOT. (L .LT. M)) THEN
  b. IF (L .GT. M .AND. M .EQ. N .OR. L .LE. N .AND. M .LT. 4) THEN
  c. IF (L .GT. M .AND. (M .EQ. N .OR. L .LE. N) .AND. M .LT. 4) THEN
  d. IF ((L .GT. M .AND. M .EQ. N .OR. L .LE. N) .AND. M .LT. 4) THEN
 *e. IF ((L .GT. M .AND. (M .EQ. N .OR. L .LE. N)) .AND. M .LT. 4) THEN

23. Use logical operators to solve
   *a. Exercise 12 on page 155.
  **b. Exercise 13 on page 155.
*24. Solve Exercise 18 on page 162 using logical operators.
25. **Logical Variables and Assignment Statements.** As you might recall from Chapter 2, a logical variable is typed by using a LOGICAL statement, and stores either the value true or the value false. Moreover, logical variables can be assigned values as follows:

logical variable = logical expression

where the logical expression can be any of the forms described in footnote 1 on page 165.

Logical variables and assignment statements can be used to simplify the appearance of conditions in block IF or ELSE IF statements. For example, given that we use the statement

LOGICAL CON

then the statement

IF (A .LT. B) THEN

can be replaced by

CON = A .LT. B
IF (CON) THEN

Use this idea to rewrite

a. Example 5.8 based on the logical variable REQ.
b. Example 5.9 based on the logical variables COND1 and COND2.

26. Develop FORTRAN code for each flowchart. First use nested decision structures and relational expressions; then use logical expressions based on modified flowcharts. Which approach do you prefer?

a.

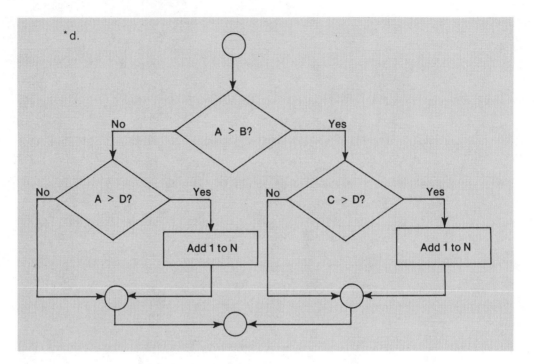

5.4
TOP-DOWN DESIGN

It would be best if you were to study Module E at this time. This not only would introduce you to an important topic called "top-down design," but also would further reinforce decision structures and the four-step procedure within the context of a new scenario. Before doing so, you should review the DO WHILE structure described in Section 4.3 on page 102 and the GO TO statement introduced in Section 6.1 on page 184. If you or your instructor choose not to cover Module E at this time, then you should study it by the end of Chapter 6.

5.5
COMMON ERRORS

Be alert for the following types of errors.

Errors in Logical Expressions

1. Don't forget that the periods are part of relational and logical operators. If we write

    IF (I .GT. J   AND   I .LT. K) THEN

    a syntax error has been committed: Having omitted the periods around AND causes the compiler to "think" that J AND I is the variable JANDI. This in itself does not cause a syntax error. The syntax error is provoked when the compiler next encounters the relational operator .LT. instead of a logical operator. This is illegal since the relational expression on the left must be connected by a logical operator to any relational expression on the right.

2. Remember to use the relational operators .LT., .LE., .GT., .GE., .EQ., and .NE. instead of algebraic symbol counterparts. For example, a common error is to use "=" instead of ".EQ.".

3. Do you see what's wrong with the following?

```
IF (I .GT. J .AND. .LT. K) THEN
```

The relational expression on the right is incomplete. We have a tendency to do this because of the way we would state this decision verbally: "If I is greater than J and less than K." To avoid a syntax error it must be written as follows.

```
IF (I .GT. J .AND. I .LT. K) THEN
```

4. Pay attention to hierarchy when using more than one logical operator. Reread Example 5.11 and make sure you understand the answers to Exercise 22.

5. If possible avoid using .EQ. when comparing real values, as *roundoff error* may guarantee a false result. For example, the relational expression in

```
IF (A/B .EQ. 0.1) THEN
```

may test false even if 1.0 is in A and 10.0 is in B. If the above real values must be tested for equality, we could allow for roundoff error up to ± 0.000001 by writing

```
IF ((A/B .GE. 0.999999) .AND. (A/B .LE. 1.000001)) THEN
```

END IF Statement Omissions

1. Remember that every block IF statement requires a corresponding END IF statement. For example, the following code will give a syntax error.

```
IF (J .EQ. 1) THEN
    K = K + 1
ELSE
    L = L + 1
              ←────────missing END IF
```

2. It's especially easy to forget an END IF statement when designing nested or multiple alternative decision structures. For example, the nested structure

```
IF (logical expression) THEN
    .
    .
    .
IF (logical expression) THEN
    .
    .
    .
ELSE
    .
    .
    .
END IF
```

would give a syntax error since the outer structure is missing an END IF, that is, the single END IF is paired with the inner block IF statement. This nested decision structure should be written as follows.

Note how indentation both helps to reduce the likelihood of forgetting an END IF statement and clarifies the nesting logic.

Logic Errors in Nested Decision Structures

You might construct a nested decision structure with a sequence of tests that you don't intend, thereby causing incorrect results. To avoid this, keep the following in mind: *Note the inner/outer nature of nested decision structures, take care in placing END IF statements, and indent accordingly,* as illustrated below.

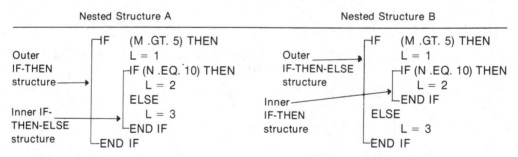

Nested structure A is an IF-THEN-ELSE structure nested within an IF-THEN structure, whereas version B is an IF-THEN structure nested within an IF-THEN-ELSE structure. Note that the placement of the first END IF statement is crucial in determining the nature of the nested structure. Also note how indentation helps to sort out the structure for us humans (it's irrelevant to the computer).

These two structures are quite different. In version A the IF-block for the outer structure includes the entire inner structure, as is the case in version B. The ELSE-block in version A, however, is part of the inner structure, which is not the case in version B. Thus the ELSE-block could be executed in version A when M .GT. 5 tests true (if N is unequal to 10), but could not possibly be executed in version B when M .GT. 5 tests true. To convince yourself, roleplay the following sets of values, where L initially stores a value of zero.

		Final value stored in L	
M	N	Version A	Version B
8	10	2	2
8	15	3	1
3	10	0	3
3	15	0	3

Make sure you understand the above results, as well as Exercises 17 and 19 on pages 161–162.

Many organizations avoid the nested decision structure when the number of levels exceeds three. They feel that the increasing complexity of the logic promotes the likelihood of coding error. Instead, they suggest using logical expressions, a series of block IF statements, or ELSE IF statements to simplify the logic.

Algorithmic Logic Errors

Now that you are designing more complicated algorithms, you need to validate your programs carefully and systematically during the debugging phase. *The key to this procedure is the deliberate selection of test data.*

Always select test input data that validate all blocks or branches in your program. For example, the following test input values ensure that each of the three branches in Example 5.5 on page 154 is tested.

SALES	TRAVEL
4000	500
6000	500
6000	700

The output from the program can be checked against a set of "hand" calculations. *The use of trace (diagnostic PRINT) statements in each branch further facilitates this process for programs with complicated decision and loop structures.*

Where appropriate, "extreme" data values should be selected to test potential problems. For example, "boundary" values in IF tests should be checked to ensure intended results. Boundary values for SALES and TRAVEL in the preceding example are 5000 and 600, respectively. In Example 5.6 on page 157 values outside the range of 1 through 8 for ZONE should be tested. Thus, 9 for ZONE prints an error message, but zero does not (see Exercise 15). Another example of an extreme data value is one that causes division by zero. A common cause of this type of error is incorrect input data, as when mistakes are made in keying in data. In general, these situations are corrected by error routines, as demonstrated in Example 5.6 and Exercise 15b.

The test data we give in exercises at the ends of chapters are designed to "push" you in this debugging direction. You should always check the test data for thoroughness, and add your own when warranted. To complete the validation, confirm the correctness of computer output by parallel hand calculations.

Data Input Errors

If you can't find fault with your algorithm, yet computer output does not validate your hand-calculated results, then (assuming that your hand-calculated results are correct) look for the possibility of faulty input data. For example, sometimes we inadvertently switch two or more values in the input sequence, or mistype values, or place values improperly on the input medium.

We can check any input data visually that are part of the output data to make sure correct values are stored. More generally, we can check for input data errors by inserting an *echo print* immediately after each READ statement, as follows:

```
READ *,list
PRINT *,list ← Same list as READ statement
```

Most commercial programs anticipate data input errors by using error routines that validate the input data. The error branch in the multiple alternative decision structure (see page 159) illustrates one approach, and the error routine described in Exercise 21 (see page 165) illustrates another.

In general, you should program "defensively" by testing all parts of your program and by training yourself to anticipate potential errors that can be overcome by good program design.

ADDITIONAL EXERCISES

27. Define or explain the following.

decision structure	counter
IF-THEN-ELSE structure	IF-THEN structure
block IF statement	nested decision structures
ELSE statement	nested IF-blocks
END IF statement	multiple alternative decision structures
IF-block	error routine
ELSE-block	ELSE IF statement
relational expression	ELSE-IF-block
relational operator	logical operators
code	logical expression

28. Property Tax Assessment. The property tax rate in a town is set at an increasing rate according to the following table.

Annual Property Tax Schedule

Value of Property	Tax Rate
Less than $10,000	3%
$10,000 and above	4%

a. Run a program to read in the value of the property, then determine and print the tax charge. Process the following test data.

Lot Number	Owner's Name	Property Value
613	A. Smith	$ 8,900
975	A. B. Smith	25,000
152	B. C. Smith	42,000
1642	C. B. Smith	37,000
1785	Deaf Smith	75,000

Sample Output

LOT NUMBER	OWNER	PROPERTY VALUE	TAX CHARGE
613	A. SMITH	8900	267
975	A. B. SMITH	25000	1000
152	B. C. SMITH	42000	2100
1642	C. B. SMITH	37000	1850
1785	DEAF SMITH	75000	3750

b. Modify the program in part a so that it prints the sum of property values, the total tax charge, the average property value, and the average tax charge.

**c. Instead of the tax schedule in part a use the following.

Value of Property	Tax Rate
Less than $10,000	3%
$10,000 or more but under $30,000	4%
$30,000 or more but under $60,000	5%
$60,000 and over	6%

**d. Check the input data for errors by ensuring that lot numbers are greater than zero and less than 5000 and property values are greater than $1 and less than $5 million. If an error is found, print an appropriate error message, bypass the tax charge calculation, and go on to the next property. Add new data to test each of these possible errors.

29. **Factorials.** The factorial of a number N (written $N!$) is a useful calculation in many problems in mathematics and statistics. By definition $N!$ is given by the product

$$N \cdot (N - 1) \cdot (N - 2) \cdot \ldots \cdot 2 \cdot 1$$

For example, if the value of N is 5, then

$$5! = 5 \cdot 4 \cdot 3 \cdot 2 \cdot 1 = 120$$

Note that 0! is defined to have a value of 1 and $N!$ is undefined if $N < 0$.

a. Run a program that inputs N and calculates and prints $N!$ What are the factorials of 1, 5, 10, 25, 50, and 100?

b. Did you get overflow in part a? By trial and error determine the maximum value of N whose factorial your computer can process. Then design your program to check each input of N to make sure it's within the allowable range of zero to the maximum value. If it's not, print a message to the user to this effect and then process the next input value.

c. Ensure that your program is capable of printing out the correct value of 0! should a user input zero for N.

d. Design an "outer" loop in your program for the purpose of processing K different values of N. For example, the data in part a would require six iterations of this loop.

e. Instead of the outer loop in part d, design an outer loop that processes values of N from some initial value ($N1$) to some terminal value ($N2$) in increments of $N3$. Print a table of N values and their factorials. Try two test runs: the first processes N from 1 to 10 in increments of 1; the second processes N from 10 to 50 in increments of 5.

30. **Quadratic Roots.**   A quadratic equation is defined by

$$y = ax^2 + bx + c$$

where a, b, and c are constants called parameters. Many mathematical applications require the "roots" of this equation. By definition, a root is a value of x that when substituted into the equation yields a value of zero for y. The following familiar *quadratic formula* determines the appropriate roots.

$$x = \frac{-b \pm (b^2 - 4ac)^{1/2}}{2a}$$

Run a program to calculate and print quadratic roots for the following input values of a, b, and c.

a	b	c
5	6	1.35
1	10	−1
1	2	1
7	4	2

Use a DO-loop to process these values. Your program should have three separate branches within the loop, depending on the value of the expression $b^2 - 4ac$. If this expression is negative, have the computer print "COMPLEX ROOTS"; if the expression equals zero exactly, evaluate the single root using $x = -b/(2a)$; if the expression is positive, use the above quadratic formula to calculate the two roots.

31. **Personnel Benefits Budget.**   A budget officer for the State Agency of Education is in the process of preparing the personnel budget for the next fiscal year. One phase of this process is to prepare a budget of personnel expenditures paid by the state in addition to salaries. The additional expenditures include the following.

1. *Social Security.*   The state contributes 6.13 percent of an employee's salary up to $22,900. No deduction is made for earnings above that amount.

2. *Retirement.*   The state contributes 9.6 percent of total salary if the employee belongs to the state retirement plan; 9 percent is contributed by the state if the employee elects a private plan; and nothing is contributed by

the state if the employee is not eligible for a retirement plan (for example, employees under 30 years of age are not eligible for a retirement plan).

3. *Group Life Insurance.* The state contributes $1.30 for every $1000 of salary paid to the employee. For purposes of calculation, round every salary to the next highest $1000. For example, a yearly salary of $11,150 results in a $15.60 contribution (12 × 1.30).

The input for each employee consists of

1. Name
2. Social Security number
3. Annual salary
4. Code for retirement: 1 = not eligible; 2 = state plan; 3 = private plan

Run a program that outputs each employee's name, Social Security number, salary, Social Security contribution, retirement contribution, group life contribution, and total contribution. After all employees have been processed, print the totals of each budget category (the four contribution columns) for all employees. Use the test data below to debug your program.

Name	Social Security Number	Salary ($)	Retirement Code
TEST 1	111-11-1111	17,000	2
TEST 2	222-22-2222	19,500	3
TEST 3	333-33-3333	21,300	2
TEST 4	444-44-4444	23,800	1
TEST 5	555-55-5555	22,900	2
TEST 6	666-66-6666	10,750	1
TEST 7	777-77-7777	24,375	2
TEST 8	888-88-8888	15,600	3

32. **Computerized Matching: A File Search.** The Placement Office on a college campus wants a program for the computerized matching of employers and graduating seniors looking for a job. Each student who registers with the Placement Office provides the following information.

Item

Name
Student ID
Address
Major (codes 1 to 10)
Grade point average (GPA)
Willing to relocate?
  (1 = no, 2 = yes)
Willing to travel?
  (1 = no, 2 = yes)

a. A firm is looking for a computer science major (code = 6) with a GPA of 3.25 or better who is willing to relocate and travel. Search the accompanying Placement Office file and print the name and address of each student who meets the criteria for this job.

Placement Office File

Name	ID	Address	Major	GPA	Relocate	Travel
Iris Abbot	2119	11 Estell Drive	6	3.45	1	2
Calvin Budnick	3112	Burnside Dorm	8	2.75	2	2
Susan Dent	4112	12 Upper College Rd.	3	2.50	2	2
Ken Driden	4819	RR3	4	2.85	1	1
Flo Further	5811	107 Ocean Rd.	1	3.00	1	2
Ben Lewis	6237	Heath Dorm	3	3.25	1	1
Bella Senate	6331	71 Boston Neck Rd.	6	3.75	1	2
Wally Tenure	6581	15 South Rd.	8	3.25	2	1
Alice Tillitson	8211	97 North Rd.	6	3.30	2	2
Martin Wiener	9112	10 Ballentine	6	3.70	2	1

**b. Generalize your program such that the Placement Office can output the name and address of each student who satisfies criteria which the firm specifies as part of the input. In other words, define variables in your program for (1) desired major, (2) desired minimum GPA, (3) relocation requirement, and (4) travel requirement. Thus, for the criteria in part a, the input for these variables would be 6, 3.25, 2, and 2, respectively. Assume that those students who are willing to relocate or travel would also be willing to accept a job that does not require relocation or travel. Test your program by running the following data for inquiries on the above four variables.

(1)	(2)	(3)	(4)
6	3.25	2	1
3	3.00	1	1
8	3.70	2	2

Are you capable of looping for these three inquiries? Or must you run the program again for each inquiry? Time-sharing users can accomplish the former by storing the Placement Office file on disk. Batch users, however, will have to wait until Chapter 8 to handle looping for this problem.

**c. Include an error routine to ensure that the major code is between 1 and 10 inclusive, GPA is 2.0 or above and 4.0 or less, relocate code is 1 or 2, and travel code is 1 or 2. If an error is found, print an appropriate error message and go on to the next student in the file. Add new data to test each of these possible errors.

33. **Credit Billing.** Design a flowchart or pseudocode and write a program that prints monthly bills (statements) for Muster Charge, an internationally renowned credit card company. Use the following input data for three customers.

Name	Address	Credit Limit	Previous Balance	Payments	New Purchases
Napoleon B.	19 Waterloo St. Paris, France	$ 800	$ 300.00	$ 100.00	$700.00
Duke Welly	1 Thames Ave. London, UK	1500	1350.70	1320.70	645.52
Betsy Ross	1776 Flag St. Boston, MA USA	2000	36.49	36.49	19.15

Printout for each person should take up exactly 12 lines in order to conform to the size of the billing statement. In other words, ideally the printout should appear exactly as illustrated.

Output for these three customers would appear as follows.

```
NAPOLEON B.        PREVIOUS               FINANCE   NEW           NEW
19 WATERLOO ST     BALANCE  - PAYMENTS +  CHARGE +  PURCHASES  =  BALANCE
PARIS FRANCE
                   300.00   - 100.00   +  3.00   +  700.00     =  903.00

                                          MINIMUM PAYMENT DUE =    183.00
**WARNING**
YOU HAVE EXCEEDED YOUR CREDIT LIMIT
CONTROL YOURSELF, OR ELSE...



DUKE WELLY         PREVIOUS               FINANCE   NEW           NEW
1 THAMES AVE       BALANCE  - PAYMENTS +  CHARGE +  PURCHASES  =  BALANCE
LONDON GB
                   1350.70  - 1320.70  +  .45    +  645.52     =  675.97

                                          MINIMUM PAYMENT DUE =    67.60






BETSY ROSS         PREVIOUS               FINANCE   NEW           NEW
1776 FLAG ST       BALANCE  - PAYMENTS +  CHARGE +  PURCHASES  =  BALANCE
BOSTON MA USA
                   36.49    - 36.49    +  0.     +  19.15      =  19.15

                                          MINIMUM PAYMENT DUE =    19.15
```

Certain conditions must be reflected by the program.

1. The finance charge is 1.5 percent of the difference between the previous month's balance and the payments made since the previous month.

2. The minimum payment due is determined according to one of four results.
    a. If the new balance exceeds the credit limit, then the minimum payment is the difference between the new balance and the credit limit plus 10 percent of the credit limit. Thus, for the first statement $(903 - 800) + 10$ percent (800) gives $183.
    b. If the new balance is $100 or more and does not exceed the credit limit, then the minimum payment is 10 percent of the new balance. Thus, for the second statement, 10 percent (675.97) gives $67.60.
    c. If the new balance is less than $100, then the minimum payment is set to the new balance (see the third statement).
    d. If the new balance is negative, then the minimum payment is zero.
3. A warning is printed if the credit limit is exceeded by the new balance (Muster Charge doesn't fool around).

34. **Police Car Replacement.** A police administrator would like to estimate the mileage at which a police cruiser should be replaced. Data analyses show that the *cost of operation* (gasoline, maintenance, and so on) is approximated by

$$c = f + v \cdot m + s \cdot m^2$$

where f, v, and s are called parameters, and m is the mileage reading (in thousands) on the odometer. For example, a cruiser that is driven for 30,000 miles and is characterized by $f = 1000, v = 200$, and $s = 2$ incurs an operating cost of approximately

$$c = 1000 + (200) \cdot (30) + (2) \cdot (30)^2$$
$$= \$8800.$$

The police department has an arrangement with the automaker for trade-ins of used police cruisers. The automaker has agreed to reduce the price of a new cruiser by the following amount.

$$r = pd^m$$

where r is the trade-in (salvage) value of a used cruiser, p is the original (new) car price, d is some depreciation factor, and m is defined as before. For example, if $p = \$10,000, d = 0.95$, and $m = 30$, then

$$r = (10,000) \cdot (0.95)^{30}$$
$$= \$2146.$$

This means that the police department pays $10,000 for a new cruiser, drives it for 30,000 miles, and gets $2146 on a trade-in. The *depreciation cost* in this case is $7854, or the difference between the new car price and the salvage price.

Thus, a cruiser driven for 30,000 miles costs $8800 to operate and $7854 in depreciation cost, for a total cost of $16,654. If this type of cruiser is replaced by a new cruiser of the same type at 30,000-mile intervals, then the total cost per 1000 miles is approximately $555 (that is, $16,654 ÷ 30).

a. Run a program that determines the mileage (to the nearest thousand) at which cruisers should be replaced. Input should include the following.

1. Number of analyses to be performed
2. f, v, s, p, d

Note that input of item 1 implies that you should have an outer loop in your program. Output should appear as follows:

m (1)	c (2)	$c \div m$ (3) = (2)/(1)	Depreciation Cost (4)	Depreciation Cost $\div m$ (5) = (4)/(1)	Total Cost per 1000 Miles (6) = (3) + (5)
1					
2					
3					
.					
.					
100					

Thus the best mileage at which to replace a cruiser is that which gives the smallest value in column (6). Note that 100,000 miles is the maximum replacement mileage that the police administrator is willing to consider. The police administrator is evaluating several types of cruisers, one of which must be selected. Their characteristics follow.

Cruiser Type	f	v	s	p	d
1	1000	200	2·0	10,000	0.95
2	800	300	2·5	8,000	0.93
3	1200	225	1·6	13,000	0.98

At what mileage should each type be replaced and what is the total cost per 1000 miles? Which cruiser is the cheapest on a total cost per 1000-mile basis?

**b. Design your program such that the program itself determines and outputs the best cruiser type and its associated total cost per 1000 miles.

**c. As you go down column (6) in this type of table, costs typically begin high, decrease to a minimum, and begin increasing again. Design your program to exit from the table loop once total cost begins to increase. Is this loop now a proper control structure? What is the advantage of this approach? Its disadvantage?

CHAPTER 6

Additional Control Statements and Structures

Chapter 4 presented an overview of control structures and focused on the loop structure defined by the DO statement, and Chapter 5 treated certain decision structures in detail. This chapter concludes the topic of control structures by presenting new control statements, a variation on multiple alternative decision structures called the CASE structure, implementations of DO-WHILE and DO-UNTIL structures, and a loop called the last-record-check loop.

6.1
GO TO STATEMENT

The GO TO statement causes the computer to interrupt the normal sequential execution of a program and branch (jump or transfer control) to some other executable instruction in the program that is not the next instruction in the normal sequence. This process of breaking the sequential flow of a program is referred to as **branching** or **transfer of control.**

The basic form of the GO TO statement is

> **GO TO** *statement number*

For example, when the statement

    GO TO 80

is executed, transfer of control goes to the statement labeled with number 80.

The problems caused by the excessive use of GO TO statements were one motivating factor in the development of structured programming concepts. Undisciplined use of this statement makes programs difficult to follow, hard to modify, and error prone.

can put continue statements anywhere
GO to (50,60,17,23), x
will goto one of the 4#'s depending on x value (12,3-74)

Logical IF Statement   185

EXAMPLE 6.1 GO TO's Go Wild

The following code is syntactically correct but you must admit it's confusing. Although the program serves no real purpose, it should give a feel for the "jumping around" that occurs if you don't harness the use of the GO TO statement.

```
        .
        .
        J = J + 1
        K = L*M
        IF (J .GT. K) THEN
            GO TO 100
        ELSE
            GO TO 115
        END IF
     85 PRINT *,L
        STOP
    100 L = J + K
        J = J + 1
        GO TO 85
    115 L = J - K
        J = J - 1
        GO TO 85
        END
```

There is no need for the undisciplined use of the GO TO statement when the basic control structures of structured programming are used correctly. In previous chapters we coded complex logic without the use of the GO TO statement. However, FORTRAN 77 does not provide some convenient control structures, so an occasional use of the GO TO statement may improve either efficiency or clarity in our programs.

Follow-up Exercises

1. What value gets printed in Example 6.1 if initially J stores 5, L stores 10, and M stores 2? What if J initially stores 50?
2. Flowchart the code in Example 6.1. Kind of a nightmare, isn't it?
3. Rewrite the code in Example 6.1 by entirely eliminating the GO TO statement.

6.2
LOGICAL IF STATEMENT

The **logical IF statement** is a FORTRAN instruction that requires the computer to test a condition and then, based on one of two possible results, to take a proper transfer of control action.

The general form of this instruction is

> **IF** *(logical expression) executable statement*

The logical expression is used to construct the condition that you want tested. The result of this test is either "true" or "false." If the result is true, the executable statement to the right of the parentheses is executed. If the result is false, however, then the next *executable* statement following the logical IF statement is executed. In general, the statement to the right of the parentheses can be any *executable* statement, except for another logical IF, block IF, ELSE IF, ELSE, END IF, END, or DO statement. In effect, *the logical IF statement is a convenient way of establishing an IF-THEN structure having a single statement in the IF-block.*

EXAMPLE 6.2   Sales Bonus Problem Revisited

The alternatives on the opposite page illustrate some decision structure variations based on logical IF and block IF statements.

In general, the logical IF statement is not as flexible as the block IF statement. There are situations, however, where it is convenient to use without sacrificing, or even improving, readability, as in version C of Example 6.2 and other examples later in this chapter.

Follow-up Exercises

4. Indicate what is wrong (if anything) for each of the following.
   a. IF (A .GT. B) END
   b. IF (SIZE .GE. 10. .AND. .LT. 20.)TP = 240.*(SIZE − 9.) + 2250.
   c. IF (A*C .EQ. 7.2 .OR. B .EQ. C) GO TO 10
   d. IF (IN .EQ. ON AND COST .LT. REV) PRINT *,NUM
   e. IF (MAJOR .EQ. 'ECN' .OR. 'MTH')PRINT *,NAME,GPA
5. Strictly use logical IF statements to rewrite
   a. Example 5.2 on page 146.
   b. Example 5.3 on page 150.
   c. Example 5.4 on page 151.
   d. Example 5.5 on page 154.
   e. Example 5.6 on page 157.
   * f. Exercise 18 on page 162.
   Use logical operators where appropriate. In each case, which version do you prefer and why?
6. **Counter-Controlled Loops.**   Rewrite the DO-loop in Example 4.1 on page 110 by eliminating DO and CONTINUE statements and using logical IF and GO TO statements. Which version do you prefer and why?

Version A

```
IF (SALES .LE. 5000) THEN
    BONUS = 0
ELSE
    BONUS = 100
END IF
```

This is the original version, which uses the IF-THEN-ELSE structure based on block IF, ELSE, and END IF statements.

Version B

```
IF (SALES .LE. 5000) THEN
    BONUS = 0
END IF
IF (SALES .GT. 5000) THEN
    BONUS = 100
END IF
```

This version uses two successive IF-THEN structures based on block IF and END IF statements. We prefer version A to this.

Version C

```
IF (SALES .LE. 5000) BONUS = 0
IF (SALES .GT. 5000) BONUS = 100
```

This version also uses two successive IF-THEN structures, but based on the logical IF statement. This version is preferable to version B because of its simplicity.

Version D

```
BONUS = 0
IF (SALES .GT. 5000) BONUS = 100
```

This version is somewhat less clear than version C, but effectively equivalent and slightly more CPU efficient. We prefer version C over this.

Version E

```
    IF (SALES .GT. 5000) GO TO 20
        BONUS = 0
        GO TO 30
20      BONUS = 100
30   . . .
```

This version is a good illustration of poor programming. It gives correct results, but combines logical IF and GO TO statements in a decision structure that is ill defined. Moreover, the GO TO statement requires labeling (statement numbers), which makes for another source of potential errors.

6.3
CASE STRUCTURE

The **CASE structure** is another variation of the multiple alternative decision structure first presented in Section 5.2. The need for this structure arises when the execution of one of many alternatives is selected on the basis of the value of a *numeric code*. For example, in a library circulation system we might have the following "cases": (1) books checked out logic, (2) books returned logic, (3) new book acquisitions logic, and (4) books withdrawn from circulation logic. Figure 6.1 illustrates the CASE structure for this example, where the numeric codes 1 through 4 represent the described four cases. Note in Figure 6.2 that the CASE structure can be described by nested IF-THEN-ELSE structures; however, as the number of cases gets large, the nested approach becomes unmanageable and inefficient.

This section discusses the FORTRAN 77 implementation of the CASE structure based on the computed GO TO statement.[1]

The **computed GO TO statement** is another transfer of control statement; it is a multiple transfer statement where control is passed to one of a group of statements on the basis of the value of an integer expression.

The general form of this statement is

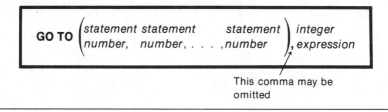

This comma may be
omitted

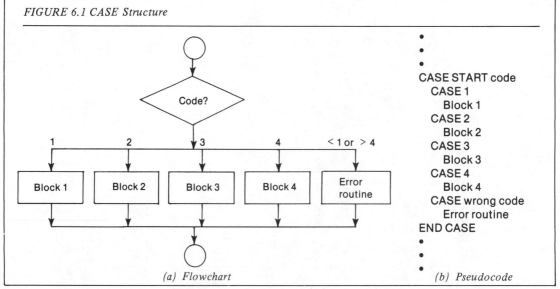

FIGURE 6.1 CASE Structure

CASE START code
  CASE 1
    Block 1
  CASE 2
    Block 2
  CASE 3
    Block 3
  CASE 4
    Block 4
  CASE wrong code
    Error routine
END CASE

(a) Flowchart   *(b) Pseudocode*

[1] Some FORTRAN dialects directly reflect the CASE structure by including statements that are similar to the pseudocode version in Figure 6.1b. If these statements are available to you, then see Exercise 11.

FIGURE 6.2 Nested IF-THEN-ELSE Structure Alternative to CASE Structure

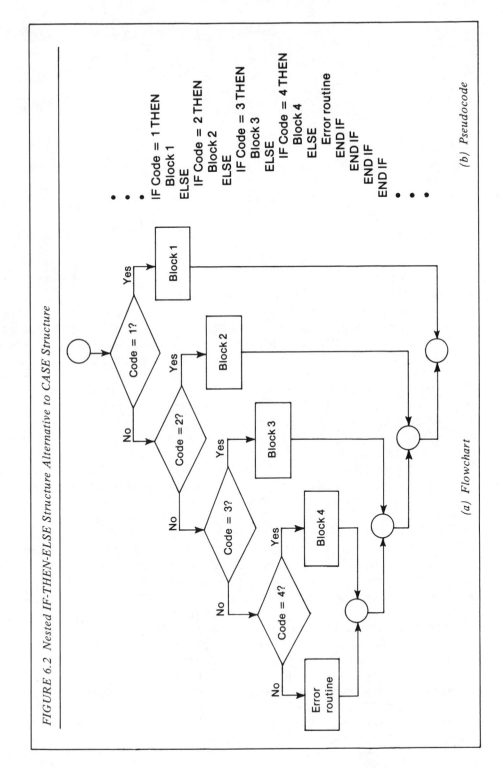

(a) Flowchart

```
. . .
IF Code = 1 THEN
    Block 1
ELSE
    IF Code = 2 THEN
        Block 2
    ELSE
        IF Code = 3 THEN
            Block 3
        ELSE
            IF Code = 4 THEN
                Block 4
            ELSE
                Error routine
            END IF
        END IF
    END IF
END IF
. . .
```

(b) Pseudocode

To illustrate this statement, consider the following program segments, which give the same results when L = 1 or 2.

Version A	Version B	Version C	Version D
IF (L .EQ. 1) THEN	IF (L .EQ. 1) THEN	IF (L .EQ. 1) THEN	GO TO(15,20) L
K1 = K1 + 1	K1 = K1 + 1	K1 = K1 + 1	15 K1 = K1 + 1
.	.	.	.
.	.	.	.
ELSE	END IF	ELSE IF (L .EQ. 2) THEN	GO TO 25
K2 = K2 + 1	IF (L .EQ. 2) THEN	K2 = K2 + 1	20 K2 = K2 + 1
.	K2 = K2 + 1	.	.
.	.	.	.
END IF	.	END IF	25 · · ·
	END IF		.

In all versions, K1 = K1 + 1 is executed when the value stored in L is 1, and K2 = K2 + 1 is executed when 2 is stored in L.

Now focus on version D. The integer expression (the variable L in this example) must store an integer value that falls within the range of 1 and the total number of statement numbers in the computed GO TO statement. In our example, L must be a 1 or 2 because there are only two statement numbers in the instruction. The program branches to the first statement number specified after GO TO if the value of the expression is 1; control passes to the second statement number if the value is 2, to the third statement number if the value is 3, and so on. In our example, if L stores a value of 1, then the program branches to the statement number in the first position, or statement 15; if L stores a 2, then the program branches to the statement number in the second position, or statement 20.

If the integer value of the expression is *out of range* (less than 1 or greater than the total number of statement numbers indicated in the instruction), execution continues at the next executable statement following the computed GO TO statement. For example, if L stores a 3 in version D, statement 15 will be executed, resulting in a logic error.

For only two code values, versions A, B, and C are preferred over version D, since the last requires the use of statement labels and GO TO statements. *As the number of branches increases, however, program length and CPU time efficiencies are realized by version D,* especially when compared with versions A and B. For example, assuming 100 cases (100 values for L), version D requires the same number of statements as version C, but 99 fewer statements than version B. In terms of CPU time, version D immediately transfers execution to the appropriate block of statements, whereas version C systematically tests all code values that precede the required block. For example, assuming 100 cases and a value of 95 for L, version D first executes the computed GO TO statement and then directly proceeds to the 95th block. Version C, however, has to perform 95 sequential IF tests before it gets to the correct block.

From the standpoint of programming style version C is strongly preferred to version D, regardless of the number of branches. For a large number of branches, however, version D is CPU efficient, which may prove attractive to an organization from a cost standpoint. *The enhancement mentioned in footnote 1 allows us to "have our cake (style) and eat it too (efficiency),"* but we restrict ourselves to illustrating the CASE structure in FORTRAN 77.

EXAMPLE 6.3 Traffic Court Fines

Each week the clerk in traffic court summarizes the fines collected for traffic violations by major categories: moving violation, standing violation, and warning. The data on each violation include traffic violation type (1 = moving violation; 2 = standing violation; 3 = warning) and amount of fine.

Figure 6.3 shows the algorithm that summarizes the traffic violations data. In our example, we wish to accumulate the dollar amount (total fines) collected for moving violations and count the number of moving violations; to accumulate the total fines collected and number of fines for standing violations; and to count the number of warnings (warnings do not involve a fine).

FIGURE 6.3   *Algorithm for Traffic Court Fines Problem*

```
Initialize summers and counters
READ no. tickets for week
DO WHILE tickets remain
    READ code, fine
    IF code <1 or >3 THEN
        Code = 4
    END IF
    CASE START code
        CASE 1
            Accumulate total fines for moving violations
            Count no. moving violations
        CASE 2
            Accumulate total fines for standing violations
            Count no. standing violations
        CASE 3
            Count no. warnings
        CASE 4 (wrong code)
            PRINT error message
    END CASE
END DO
PRINT summary report
Stop
```

(a) *Pseudocode*

FIGURE 6.3   (Continued)

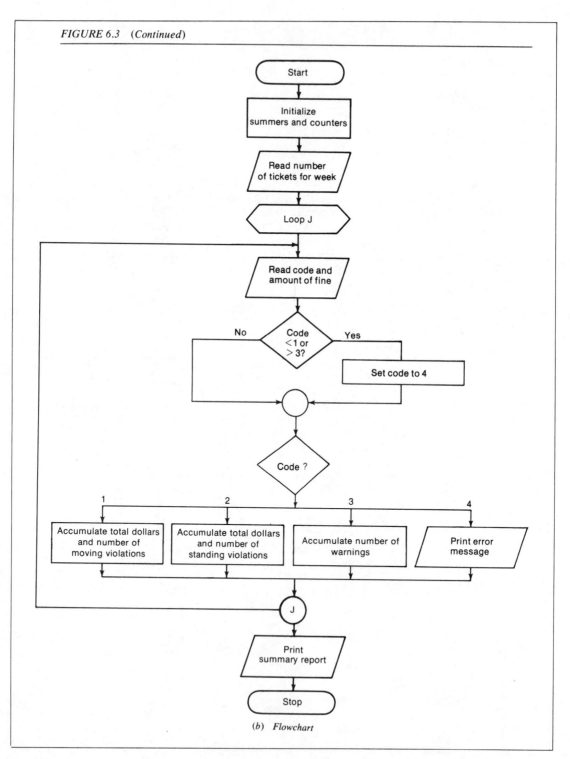

(b) Flowchart

```
C     TRAFFIC COURT FINES PROGRAM
C
C     KEY:
C        N        = NUMBER OF TICKETS PROCESSED
C        CODE     = CODE FOR TYPE OF VIOLATION
C                    (1 = MOVING, 2 = STANDING, 3 = WARNING)
C        FINE     = AMOUNT OF FINE
C        MOVFIN   = TOTAL FINES FOR MOVING VIOLATIONS
C        MOVNUM   = NUMBER OF MOVING VIOLATIONS
C        STDFIN   = TOTAL FINES FOR STANDING VIOLATIONS
C        STDNUM   = NUMBER OF STANDING VIOLATIONS
C        WARNUM   = NUMBER OF WARNINGS
C
      INTEGER  N,CODE,FINE,MOVFIN,MOVNUM,STDFIN,STDNUM,WARNUM
C
      DATA  MOVFIN,MOVNUM,STDFIN,STDNUM,WARNUM/5*0/
C
      READ *,N
      DO 500 I = 1,N
         READ *,CODE,FINE
         IF (CODE .LT. 1 .OR. CODE .GT. 3) CODE = 4
C
C        CASE START
C
         GO TO (100,200,300,400) CODE
C            CASE 1
  100          MOVFIN   = MOVFIN + FINE
               MOVNUM = MOVNUM + 1
               GO TO 500
C            CASE 2
  200          STDFIN   = STDFIN + FINE
               STDNUM = STDNUM + 1
               GO TO 500
C            CASE 3
  300          WARNUM = WARNUM + 1
               GO TO 500
C            CASE 4
  400          PRINT *,'ERROR IN CODE FOR TICKET',I
C
C        END CASE
C
  500 CONTINUE
C
      PRINT *,'  TYPE            NUMBER          AMOUNT'
      PRINT *,'  '
      PRINT *,'MOVING',MOVNUM,MOVFIN
      PRINT *,'STANDING',STDNUM,STDFIN
      PRINT *,'WARNING',WARNUM, 0
C
      END
```

Test Data	Sample Output		
7	TYPE	NUMBER	AMOUNT
1,50			
2,15	MOVING	2	125
2,20	STANDING	4	60
1,75	WARNING	1	0
3,0			
2,10			
2,15			

When CODE has the value 1, control branches to the statement labeled 100—based on the first statement number (100) from the list of statement numbers in the computed GO TO statement—thus increasing the counters for number and amount of fines for moving violations. When CODE has the value 2, control branches to statement 200—since the second statement number is 200 from the list of statement numbers in the computed GO TO statement—thus updating the counters for standing violations. Finally, when CODE has the value 3, control branches to statement 300, thereby updating a counter for number of warnings.

Most commercial programs include logic tests for errors in the input data. If an error is detected, the program branches to an error routine that indicates a problem. In our traffic court program the only valid values for CODE are 1, 2, or 3. If any other number is typed, an error exists in the data. Did you notice how we test the ticket code to assure it is within range before executing the computed GO TO statement? If the code is invalid, it is set to 4, which therefore puts us in the error branch of the CASE structure.

You should carefully note that this version of the CASE structure requires a GO TO statement at the end of each "CASE-block." Thus the statement

    GO TO 500

is placed in each CASE-block (except the last) in order to properly exit from the CASE structure.

Finally, notice the way we used comment statements for compatibility with the pseudocode version. Although it's not necessary to do so, it does improve the readability of the CASE structure.

Follow-up Exercises

7. What is wrong with each of the following?
   a. GO TO (25,20,15) IN
   b. GO TO (20,20,30), ON
   c. GO TO (4,6,8,10,12), K where 6 is stored for K

8. In Example 6.3 how would your output change if the test data included the line 5,75 instead of 1,75?

9. Rewrite Example 5.7 on page 160 using the computed GO TO statement. Which approach do you prefer and why?

*10. Rewrite Example 6.3 using
   a. Nested IF-blocks
   b. A series of block IF and END IF statements (consecutive IF-THEN structures)
   c. The multiple alternative decision structure based on block IF, ELSE IF, ELSE, and END IF statements.
   Which approach do you prefer and why?

*11. **CASE Structure Enhancement.** FORTRAN 77 dialects that include statements to reflect the CASE structure directly have certain advantages over our approach in this section: The structure is more readable, it has a built-in out-of-range test, and it reduces the likelihood of errors (since statement labels and explicit branching are avoided). If this enhancement is available to you, then rewrite
   a. Example 6.3
   b. Example 5.7 on page 160

6.4
DO-WHILE STRUCTURE

As you might recall from Chapter 4, the first action in a DO-WHILE structure (Figure 6.4) is to test whether or not the loop is to be executed. If the loop is to be executed, control passes to the body of the loop. After the statements within the body have been executed, control returns to the test statement preceding the loop body. When the test indicates that looping is finished, control passes to a statement outside the loop. Thus we are telling the computer to "DO" the loop "WHILE" the condition tests true.

In FORTRAN 77 the DO-loop is a special case of the DO-WHILE structure, where the condition tested is based on a comparison between the value of the DO-variable and its terminal value. This type of looping is called *counter-controlled looping* because the DO-variable is essentially a *counter* that gets incremented at each loop iteration.

Many iterative processes cannot be controlled by a counter variable, in which case the implementation of a general DO-WHILE structure may be warranted. In this section we illustrate how the DO-WHILE structure can be used to control loop repetition when the condition to be tested is based on a value computed within the loop body. Here the *loop variable* serves a dual function: It stores a computational result and controls loop repetition.

FIGURE 6.4 *Flowchart of DO-WHILE Structure*

EXAMPLE 6.4   The Inflation Curse

High rates of inflation in a "free" market economy can have devastating effects. For individuals, particularly those, such as retirees, who live on fixed incomes, purchasing power (the ability to buy goods and services) can erode dramatically over time. For the economy as a whole, it can lead to recession and unemployment as a result of such factors as uncertainty and high interest rates.

To illustrate, suppose an item currently costs $100 and increases in cost at a 10 percent rate of inflation per year. The future cost of this item one year from now would be $110, determined as follows:

$$100 + (100) \cdot (0.1)$$

or

$$100 \cdot (1 + 0.1)$$

Two years from now it would cost $110 plus an additional 10 percent for the price increase in the second year, or

$$110 \cdot (1 + 0.1)$$

which is $121. Thus if we define

C = current cost of item
R = rate of inflation

and

F = future cost of item one year from now

then we have

$$F = C \cdot (1 + R)$$

for the cost at the end of one year and

$$F = (\text{previous year's } F) \cdot (1 + R)$$

for future costs in subsequent years.

Figure 6.5 and the program below illustrate an algorithm that prints successive future costs by years until the future cost equals or exceeds double the current cost.

FIGURE 6.5 *Algorithm for Inflation Curse Problem*

```
READ current cost, inflation rate
PRINT input data and table headers
Future cost = current cost
Year = 0
DO WHILE future cost < 2 × current cost
   Year = year + 1
   Future cost = previous future cost ×
                    (1 + inflation rate)
    PRINT year, future cost
END DO
Stop
```

```
C     INFLATION CURSE PROGRAM
C
C     KEY:
C        YEAR  = YEARS INTO FUTURE
C        RATE  = RATE OF INFLATION
C        COSTC = CURRENT COST
C        COSTF = FUTURE COST
C
      INTEGER YEAR
      REAL    COSTC,COSTF,RATE
C
```

```
              READ *,COSTC,RATE
C
              PRINT *,'CURRENT COST: $',COSTC
              PRINT *,'INFLATION RATE:',RATE*100.,'%'
              PRINT *,'YEARS INTO FUTURE    FUTURE COST'
C
              COSTF = COSTC
              YEAR  = 0
C
           10 IF (COSTF .LT. 2.*COSTC) THEN
                 YEAR  = YEAR + 1
                 COSTF = COSTF*(1. + RATE)   ⎫ Loop body
                 PRINT *,YEAR,COSTF          ⎬
                 GO TO 10                    ⎭
              END IF
C
              END
```

When counter-controlled looping is inappropriate the DO-WHILE structure in FORTRAN 77 is implemented using an IF-THEN structure that contains a GO TO statement as the last statement in the IF-block. The condition "COSTF .LT. 2.*COSTC" is tested immediately before the body of the loop. As long as the condition is true, the body of the loop is executed. However, the first time the condition is false, the loop body is skipped and control is transferred to the first executable statement after the END IF statement.

To illustrate the program, suppose we wish to calculate and print the future cost of a house, which increases year by year at a constant rate of inflation. Assume a current cost of $60,000 and a 10 percent rate of inflation. The input/output appear as follows:

Input
    60000.,0.1

Output
    CURRENT COST: $ 60000.0
    INFLATION RATE: 10.0 %
    YEARS INTO FUTURE   FUTURE COST

YEARS INTO FUTURE	FUTURE COST
1	66000.0
2	72600.0
3	79860.0
4	87846.0
5	96630.6
6	106293.7
7	116923.1
8	128615.4

Thus, just to keep up with inflation, the house must sell at the indicated future costs. In the eighth year, the future cost exceeds double the initial cost, so execution terminates based on a false value for the relational expression in the block IF statement.

Follow-up Exercises

12. Confirm the output by roleplaying the computer. As you do this, fill in the contents of the indicated storage locations below as if a "snapshot" of memory were taken just before execution of the GO TO statement.

COSTC	RATE	YEAR	COSTF

13. In Example 6.4, what would happen if

    a. The statement

        COSTF = COSTC

    were omitted?

    b. The statement

        COSTF = COSTF*(1. + RATE)

    were changed to

        COSTF = COSTC*(1. + RATE)

    c. YEAR were initialized to 1? Modify the program to obtain the same output if the year is initialized to 1.

    Can you think of a way of improving the computational efficiency within the body of the loop?

14. Modify the program in Example 6.4 so the user specifies as input a multiplicative factor (M). In the example, M has a value of 2 (that is, the loop terminates when the future cost exceeds double the current cost).

15. Modify the program in Example 6.4 to terminate looping either when future cost equals or exceeds double the current cost or when ten years have passed.

16. In Example 6.4

    a. Modify the program to incorporate a second loop that processes N sets of data.

    b. Run the program for the following sets of values.

60000	0.05
60000	0.10
60000	0.15
100000	0.10

17. Modify the program in Example 6.4 by replacing the block IF statement with a logical IF statement. Technically, do we now have a DO-WHILE structure?

*18. What changes would you make in Example 6.3 on page 193 to replace the DO-loop with a counter-controlled DO-WHILE structure based on a block IF statement? Which approach do you prefer and why?

·19. DO-WHILE Structured Enhancements.   Some FORTRAN 77 dialects include statements that directly reproduce the DO-WHILE structure, unlike the ANSI Standard that requires the use of block IF and GO TO statements. Rewrite the program in Example 6.4 if this enhancement is available to you. Which approach do you prefer and why?

6.5
DO-UNTIL STRUCTURE

The DO-WHILE structure is a popular type of loop structure, but it is not necessarily preferred for all types of looping. Some problems are best served by the type of loop structure first discussed in Chapter 4 and illustrated in Figure 6.6. The DO-UNTIL structure first processes the body of the loop, after which a condition (logical expression) is tested to determine if the loop should be repeated. If the result of the test is false, control goes back to the beginning of the loop and the body is processed once more; if the result is true, control is transferred out of the loop. Thus we are telling the computer to "DO" the loop "UNTIL" the condition tests true. Note that, unlike the DO-WHILE structure, the DO-UNTIL structure ensures that the body is processed at least once.

FIGURE 6.6   DO-UNTIL Structure

EXAMPLE 6.5   Inflation Curse Using DO-UNTIL Structure

The inflation curse program using the DO-UNTIL structure is rewritten as follows.

Version A

```
C
        INTEGER YEAR
        REAL    COSTC,COSTF,RATE
C
        READ *,COSTC,RATE
C
        PRINT *,'CURRENT COST: $',COSTC
        PRINT *,'INFLATION RATE:' ,RATE*100.,'%'
        PRINT *,'YEARS INTO FUTURE     FUTURE COST'
C
        COSTF = COSTC
        YEAR  = 0
C
    10  YEAR  = YEAR + 1
        COSTF = COSTF*(1. + RATE)  } Loop body
        PRINT *,YEAR,COSTF
        IF (COSTF .GE. 2.*COSTC) STOP
        GO TO 10
C
        END
```

Implementation of the DO-UNTIL structure requires use of the logical IF and GO TO statements. Notice that the test to terminate the loop follows the loop body. Thus the loop body is processed at least once.

Now, suppose we wish to print the message "COST HAS AT LEAST DOUBLED xx YEARS FROM NOW" instead of printing the above output table. The loop is now revised as follows.

Version B

```
        .
        .
        .
    10  YEAR  = YEAR + 1
        COSTF = COSTF*(1. + RATE) } Loop body
        IF (COSTF .GE. 2.*COSTC) GO TO 20
        GO TO 10
C
    20 PRINT *,'COST HAS AT LEAST DOUBLED',YEAR,'YEARS FROM NOW'
C
        END
```

In this case the PRINT statement within the loop is omitted. Once cost has at least doubled, the IF test within the loop gives a true result and control passes to the PRINT statement labeled 20.

As we mentioned earlier in the chapter, it's best to minimize the use of GO TO statements, as they complicate the control logic and promote labeling errors. The following version is more consistent with this philosophy because it eliminates the use of one GO TO statement.

Version C

```
        .
        .
        .

   10    YEAR  = YEAR + 1
         COSTF = COSTF*(1. + RATE) } Loop body
         IF (.NOT. (COSTF .GE. 2.*COSTC)) GO TO 10
   C
         PRINT *,'COST HAS AT LEAST DOUBLED',YEAR,'YEARS FROM NOW'
   C
         END
```

Note that exit from the loop is still achieved when the condition "COSTF .GE. 2.*COSTC" tests true, which is consistent with the original version and with exits from DO-UNTIL loops when tested conditions are true. Use of the .NOT. operator, however, changes a true value to a false value, which appropriately drops us out of the loop to the PRINT statement. Conversely, when the condition is false, .NOT. changes it to true, the GO TO 10 is executed, and the loop iterates once more.

The .NOT. operator is bothersome to many programmers because it requires us to think in terms of opposites. It's probably simpler just to reverse the sense of the relational operator by using the following logical IF statement in place of the one used in version C.

```
   IF(COSTF .LT. 2.*COSTC) GO TO 10
```

Follow-up Exercises

20. For the program in version A of Example 6.5:
    a. Draw a flowchart.
    b. Write pseudocode.
21. Add an outer DO-loop to process N sets of data in Example 6.5.
22. Modify version A in Example 6.5 to use a block-IF statement in place of the logical IF statement. Which approach do you prefer and why?
*23. A $4000 bank deposit that is compounded quarterly at the rate 6 percent per year accumulates as follows:

Quarter	Amount
1	4060.00
2	4120.90
3	4182.71
4	4245.45
.	.
.	.
.	.

Note that the quarterly rate is 0.06 divided by 4. Write code in each of the three ways below to determine the balance at the end of the fourth quarter in 1990 if the $4000 is deposited at the beginning of the first quarter in 1980.
a. Use a DO-loop.
b. Use a DO-WHILE structure based on either the block IF statement or your system's enhancement.
c. Use a DO-UNTIL structure based on the logical IF statement.
Which approach do you prefer and why?

6.6
LAST-RECORD-CHECK (LRC) LOOPS

DO-loops are convenient when we know beforehand the number of desired loop iterations. If we do not wish to specify in advance (or do not know) the exact number of times the loop is to be repeated, the **Last-Record-Check (LRC) loop** may be appropriate.

Trailer Number Method

The construction of an LRC loop by the trailer number method requires a special data item that signals the end of the data. This special data item, sometimes called a **trailer number,** has a "unique" number (or string constant) assigned to one of the input variables. By a "unique" number we mean one that would never be part of normal input data. For example, in the sales bonus program of Chapter 5, a Social Security number (SSN) of -99 might serve as a trailer number since Social Security numbers are always positive. After a salesperson's data are read in, a test is made to determine whether or not the data just read in contain the trailer number. If the test determines that a particular value of SSN is the trailer number, control branches out of the loop; otherwise, looping continues. Figure 6.7 illustrates this method for the sales bonus problem and Example 6.6 presents the corresponding program.

EXAMPLE 6.6   Sales Bonus Problem with LRC Loop Based on Trailer Number

The following version replaces the DO-loop in Example 5.1 on page 143 with an LRC loop having a DO-WHILE structure.

```
C
      CHARACTER NAME*15
      INTEGER    BASE,SSN,SALES,BONUS,TOTPAY
C
      PRINT *,'EMPLOYEE NAME    SS NUMBER    TOTAL PAY'
      PRINT *,'  '
C
      BASE = 350
      READ *,NAME,SSN,SALES
```

This READ statement is used only for the first input line

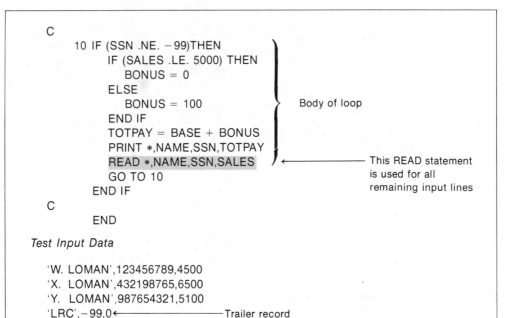

```
       C
          10 IF (SSN .NE. −99)THEN
                IF (SALES .LE. 5000) THEN
                   BONUS = 0
                ELSE
                   BONUS = 100
                END IF
                TOTPAY = BASE + BONUS
                PRINT *,NAME,SSN,TOTPAY
                READ *,NAME,SSN,SALES
                GO TO 10
             END IF
       C
             END
```

Body of loop

This READ statement is used for all remaining input lines

Test Input Data

```
   'W. LOMAN',123456789,4500
   'X. LOMAN',432198765,6500
   'Y. LOMAN',987654321,5100
   'LRC',−99,0 ←──────── Trailer record
```

The **trailer record** or last input line has the trailer number −99 assigned to the salesperson's Social Security number. This record does not represent another salesperson; it's simply placed at the end of the data to indicate no more data. When the computer reads this record, it has already processed data for all salespersons. The statement

IF (SSN .NE. −99) THEN

needs further explanation. Immediately after reading in the name, SS number, and sales for a given salesperson, the computer checks for the trailer number by testing the value of SSN against −99. After the data for the first salesperson are read in, the location SSN contains the value 123456789, which is not equal to −99. Thus the relational expression "SSN .NE. −99" is evaluated as true. As a result, the computer next computes and prints the total pay, reads in another line of data, and returns to the start of the loop to test for the trailer number. For the second and third salespeople the same process is repeated; that is, the loop body is executed. Finally, when the trailer record is processed, the contents of SSN test false against the value −99. As a result, control is transferred outside the loop and processing terminates.

Note that the loop structure in this example is a DO-WHILE structure, since the loop test precedes the body and looping continues "while" SSN is unequal to −99.

Output from a run of this program is identical to the earlier version in Chapter 5.

EMPLOYEE NAME	SS NUMBER	TOTAL PAY
W. LOMAN	123456789	350
X. LOMAN	432198765	450
Y. LOMAN	987654321	450

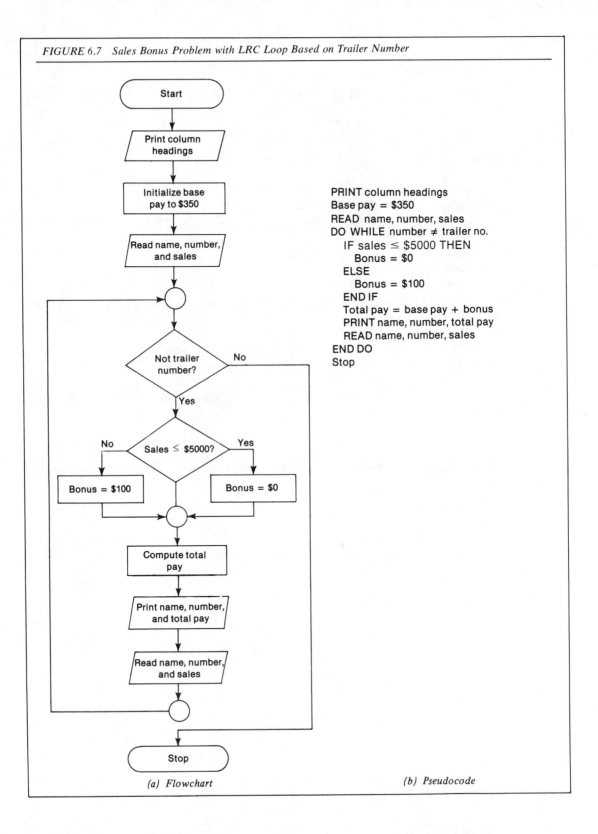

FIGURE 6.7   Sales Bonus Problem with LRC Loop Based on Trailer Number

Start

Print column
headings

Initialize base
pay to $350

Read name, number,
and sales

Not trailer
number?   No

Yes

Sales ≤ $5000?

No   Yes

Bonus = $100   Bonus = $0

Compute total
pay

Print name, number,
and total pay

Read name, number,
and sales

Stop

PRINT column headings
Base pay = $350
READ name, number, sales
DO WHILE number ≠ trailer no.
   IF sales ≤ $5000 THEN
      Bonus = $0
   ELSE
      Bonus = $100
   END IF
   Total pay = base pay + bonus
   PRINT name, number, total pay
   READ name, number, sales
END DO
Stop

(a) Flowchart   *(b) Pseudocode*

END = Specifier Method

The END = specifier is a second alternative for constructing LRC loops. This method requires the following variation of the READ statement.[2]

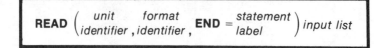

For example, the statement

    READ (5,*, END = 20) NAME, SSN, SALES

illustrates this form of the READ statement.

The *unit identifier* is usually an integer number that identifies the input unit to be used. On our computer system this number is "5" for a card reader or terminal. *Ask your instructor for the number on your system.* The *format identifier* is typically an asterisk (for list-directed input) or the number of a FORMAT statement (for format-directed input as described in Module C).

The **END = specifier** provides a statement label or number to which control is transferred when the end of the data is encountered. In our example, if the READ statement is executed and there's no more input data, then execution goes to the statement labeled 20. In effect, *the READ statement accomplishes both the input function and the loop control function,* as illustrated in the next example.

EXAMPLE 6.7   Sales Bonus Problem with LRC Loop Based on END = Specifier

We now rewrite the program in Example 6.6 to show an LRC loop that's constructed with an END = specifier.

---

[2] This form of the READ statement is explained in detail in Section 11.3, but you need not go to Chapter 11 to understand what follows here.

```
                    TOTPAY = BASE + BONUS
                    PRINT *,NAME,SSN,TOTPAY
                    GO TO 10
        C
        20 END              Exit from loop
```

What we have essentially is a DO-WHILE structure, whereby the body of the loop gets processed while a data line or card remains to be read. If we provide the input data,

```
'W. LOMAN',123456789,4500
'X. LOMAN',432198765,6500
'Y. LOMAN',987654321,5100
```

which we assume to be either on cards or in a disk data file, then the loop processes each line of data while data lines remain. When the READ statement is executed the *fourth* time, the end of the data is encountered and a loop exit is achieved by a transfer of control to statement 20.

The simplicity of this loop design is much preferred to that based on a trailer record, especially when using cards, disk, or tape as input media.

Follow-up Exercises

24. With respect to Example 6.6
    a. If we were to use zero as the trailer number, how would you change the input data and program in Example 6.6? Is there a danger in using zero?
    b. Do you need data entries for name and sales on the trailer record? Do these have to be "LRC" and zero? Explain.
    c. Change the program in Example 6.6 such that NAME is used to test the last line of data. Use the string constant "NO MORE DATA" as the trailer "number." How would the trailer record look in this situation?
25. Revise Figure 6.7 to reflect the END = method in Example 6.7.
26. What would happen in Example 6.7 if we were to use the input data from Example 6.6?
27. Does this version of Example 6.6 accomplish the same thing? Is it correct from a "structured" point of view? What is the advantage of this approach? In effect, is this version equivalent to that in Example 6.7?

```
              .
              .
              .
              BASE = 350
        10    READ *,NAME,SSN,SALES
              IF (SALES .EQ. −99) GO TO 20
              IF (SALES .LE. 5000) THEN
                  BONUS = 0
              ELSE
                  BONUS = 100
```

```
              END IF
              TOTPAY = BASE + BONUS
              PRINT *,NAME,SSN,TOTPAY
              GO TO 10
        20    END
```

* **28. DO-WHILE Structure Enhancement.** If your implementation includes a DO-WHILE structure enhancement, change either Example 6.6 or Example 6.7 accordingly.
* **29. Bank Savings Account Program.** Change the bank savings program of Section 2.7 on page 62 by inserting an LRC loop to process customers. Input customer name (20 characters) and use either an appropriate trailer "number" for customer name or an END = specifier. Include a flowchart or pseudocode.

**6.7
ROOT SEARCH ALGORITHM

In this section we illustrate the capability of an algebraic language such as FORTRAN to model intricate algorithmic logic.

Many mathematical applications, particularly in calculus, require values for the root(s) of a mathematical function. Given a general mathematical function where y is a function of x,

$$y = f(x)$$

a *root* of the function is a value of x that yields a value of zero for y. For example, the linear function

$$y = -1 + 2x$$

has a root at $x = 0.5$ since this value for x yields $y = 0$. The quadratic function

$$y = -2.25 - 4x + x^2$$

has two roots, one at $x = -0.5$ and another at $x = 4.5$. Figure 6.8 illustrates sketches of these functions. Note from the figure that real roots for the function

$$y = 2^x$$

are not defined, since this function approaches the x-axis asymptotically (gets closer and closer to it) but does not cross it.

A number of analytic procedures have been developed for finding the roots of functions. In this section we illustrate a trial-and-error search method for finding a real root (if it exists) of any function; Exercise 42 at the end of the chapter describes another procedure.

To illustrate the root search procedure for the linear function in Figure 6.8, consider Table 6.1.

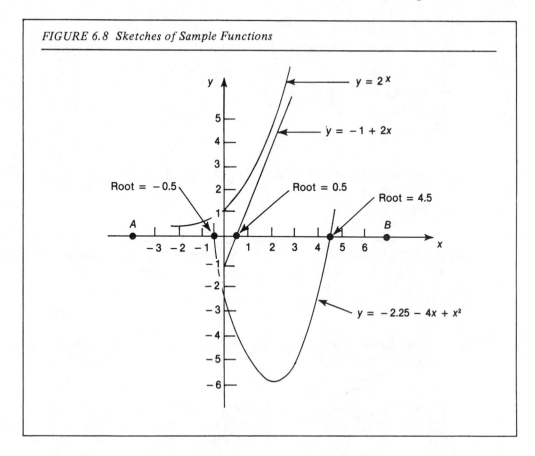

FIGURE 6.8 Sketches of Sample Functions

TABLE 6.1   Root Search for the Function $y = -1 + 2x$

TRIAL x	TRIAL y	INCREMENT IN x	COMMENT
3	5	1	Trial x and increment selected arbitrarily. Trial y calculated from function.
4	7	1	Trial x increased by increment. Since 7 (current trial y) is further from 0 than from 5 (most recent trial y), trial x must be reduced by increment.
3	5	1	Change in trial y is in direction toward 0; thus continue to reduce trial x by increment.
2	3	1	See preceding comment.
1	1	1	See preceding comment.
0	−1	0.5	Trial y has crossed over zero. Thus we know that the root is between $x = 1$ and $x = 0$. Increment reduced by 50 percent and trial x increased by new increment.
0.5	0	0.5	Root found at $x = 0.5$.

Step 1: *Statement*

Root search program that calculates a real root of a function, providing it exists.

- a. *Input data*
  Initial trial x
  Initial increment in x
- b. *Output data*
  A root (if it exists) or a message stating the root has not been found
- c. *Computations*
  Values of the function y given values of x (see Table 6.1)

Step 2: *Algorithm*

Figure 6.9 illustrates exploded pseudocode (as in Module E) for this algorithm. The block numbers and shaded portions in this figure tie together segments in the pseudocode, program, and discussion. First, you should trace the steps in Table 6.1 through Figure 6.9. Make sure you confirm that these steps trace a legitimate flow through Figure 6.9. Next, consider the following items.

1. Both the initial trial x and the initial increment in x can be set to any value. The initial increment in x, however, should be set to a relatively large value to ensure a rapid crossover when a real root exists.
2. The inner DO-WHILE loop moves the trial value of x in a direction that ensures a crossover, providing a real root exists and the algorithm does not enter a "leapfrog" cycle. A leapfrog cycle occurs when a large increment causes the algorithm to cycle back and forth between two points without detecting a crossover. For example, a leapfrog cycle is established for the quadratic function if we increment trial x from point A to point B in Figure 6.8. Without the procedure described in item 3, the algorithm would indefinitely cycle between points A and B. A maximum number of iterations must be specified for the inner loop, to avoid infinite looping either when real roots do not exist or when a leapfrog cycle is entered.
3. Looping terminates within the inner DO-WHILE loop when either a crossover or excessive looping is achieved. If the counter exceeds the cutoff, then either a real root may not exist (*block 3* in Figure 6.9) or the procedure may be in a leapfrog cycle (*block 4*). In the latter case the increment is successively reduced to discourage leapfrogging. If the counter does not exceed the cutoff, then either we have found a root (*block 5*) or we need to apply the crossover logic described in Table 6.1 (*block 6*).
4. The algorithm is not likely to find an exact root as in Table 6.1, for one of two reasons: roundoff error may prevent locating the exact value or the root may be an irrational number such as one-third (0.3333 . . .). For these reasons, we need to specify a certain error tolerance within which the precision of the computed root is acceptable. For example, we could terminate the algorithm and print the root whenever the increment in x is less than 0.00001. *Block 5* handles both situations— an exact root and an approximate root.

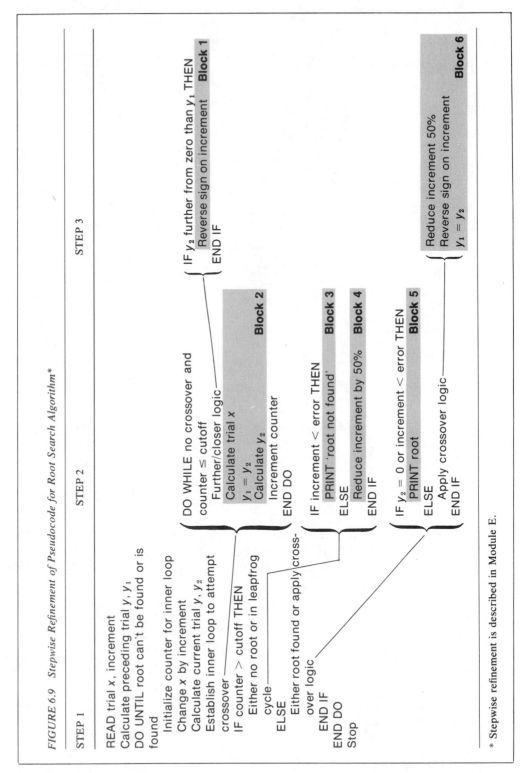

FIGURE 6.9 Stepwise Refinement of Pseudocode for Root Search Algorithm*

STEP 1	STEP 2	STEP 3

STEP 1

READ trial x, increment
Calculate preceding trial y, y_1
DO UNTIL root can't be found or is found
  Initialize counter for inner loop
  Change x by increment
  Calculate current trial y, y_2
  Establish inner loop to attempt crossover
  IF counter > cutoff THEN
    Either no root or in leapfrog cycle
  ELSE
    Either root found or apply crossover logic
  END IF
END DO
Stop

STEP 2

DO WHILE no crossover and counter ≤ cutoff
  Further/closer logic
  Calculate trial x   **Block 2**
  $y_1 = y_2$
  Calculate y_2
  Increment counter
END DO

IF increment < error THEN   **Block 3**
  PRINT 'root not found'
ELSE
  Reduce increment by 50%   **Block 4**
END IF

IF y_2 = 0 or increment < error THEN   **Block 5**
  PRINT root
ELSE
  Apply crossover logic
END IF

STEP 3

IF y_2 further from zero than y_1 THEN   **Block 1**
  Reverse sign on increment
END IF

Reduce increment 50%
Reverse sign on increment   **Block 6**
$y_1 = y_2$

* Stepwise refinement is described in Module E.

211

Step 3: Code

```
C   ROOT SEARCH PROGRAM
C
C   KEY:
C     X      = TRIAL VALUE OF X
C     Y1     = PRECEDING TRIAL VALUE OF Y
C     Y2     = CURRENT TRIAL VALUE OF Y
C     STEPX  = INCREMENT IN X
C     FLAG   = 0 TO STOP PROCESSING; 1 TO CONTINUE
C     SIGN   = +1 TO ADD INCREMENT; -1 TO SUBTRACT
C     MAX    = MAXIMUM NUMBER OF INNER LOOP ITERATIONS
C     J      = INNER LOOP ITERATIONS
C     ERROR  = ERROR TOLERANCE
C     F      = NAME OF STATEMENT FUNCTION
C
C   ---------------------------------------------------------
C
      INTEGER FLAG,MAX,J
      REAL    X,Y1,Y2,STEPX,SIGN,ERROR,F
C
C   ---------------------------------------------------------
C
      PARAMETER (MAX = 50000, ERROR = 0.00001)
C
C   ---------------------------------------------------------
C
      F(X) = -1. + 2.*X
C
C   ---------------------------------------------------------
C
      SIGN = +1.
      READ *, X,STEPX
      Y1 = F(X)
C
C   ---------------------------------------------------------
C
C     ****************** BEGIN OUTER LOOP ******************
C
50    J  = 1
      X  = X + SIGN*STEPX
      Y2 = F(X)
C
C     ****************** BEGIN INNER LOOP ******************
C
75    IF (Y1*Y2 .GT. 0.   .AND.  J .LE. MAX) THEN
         IF (ABS(Y2)-ABS(Y1) .GT. 0.) THEN
            SIGN = -1.*SIGN                              Block 1
         END IF
         X  = X + SIGN*STEPX
         Y1 = Y2                                          Block 2
         Y2 = F(X)
         J  = J + 1
         GO TO 75
      END IF
C
C     ****************** END INNER LOOP ******************
C
      IF (J .GT. MAX) THEN
         IF (STEPX .LT. ERROR) THEN
            PRINT *, 'ROOT NOT FOUND'                    Block 3
            FLAG = 0
         ELSE
            STEPX = .5*STEPX                             Block 4
            FLAG  = 1
         END IF
      END IF
```

```
      ELSE
        IF (Y2 .EQ. 0.    .OR.    STEPX .LT. ERROR) THEN
            PRINT *, 'ROOT =',X                                    Block 5
            FLAG  = 0
        ELSE
            STEPX = .5*STEPX
            SIGN  = -1.*SIGN                                       Block 6
            Y1    = Y2
            FLAG  = 1
        END IF
      END IF
C
        IF (FLAG .EQ. 1) GO TO 50
C
C       ******************** END OUTER LOOP ********************
C
C       ----------------------------------------------------------------
C
      END
```

Note the following logic in the program.

a. *Statement function.* The function $-1 + 2x$ is treated as a statement function named F. (Module A describes statement functions.) This simplifies the expression of the function to one line of code, rather than three lines without the use of the statement function.

b. *Crossover logic.* Detection of a crossover is found in statement 75. The program detects that a root has been crossed over (that is, trial y changes sign from positive to negative or from negative to positive) whenever the product Y1*Y2 is less than zero. If the product is zero, then a root has been found. *Block 6* applies the procedure in Table 6.1 when a crossover is accomplished.

c. *Further-closer logic.* The relational expression

"ABS(Y2)-ABS(Y1) .GT. 0."

always tests true whenever current trial y is further from zero than the immediately preceding trial y.[3] We must work with absolute values to get the correct signal when both Y1 and Y2 store negative values; that is, -10 is further away from zero than, say, -5.

d. *Sign logic.* We want to reverse the direction of change in trial x whenever we get further away from zero (see *block 1*) or whenever we cross over (see *block 6*).

Step 4: Debugging

The code in the preceding step was run for each function in Figure 6.8 under varying initial trial x and increment values. In our first several runs we had inadvertently omitted the sign and Y1 = Y2 logic in *block 6*, which tricked the algorithm into false crossovers, thereby giving us an infinite outer loop (statement 75 always tested false and *block 6* kept getting executed). We subsequently found the error by placing trace statements in each block that printed the block number and computational results.

---

[3] The ABS function is described in Module A.

Follow-up Exercises

30. With respect to the root search program:
    a. What type of loop structure is the outer loop?
    b. The inner loop?
    c. Are the true/false tests consistent with these loop structures? If not, how would you make them consistent?
    d. How would you modify the program to eliminate the use of FLAG? *Hint:* Use the STOP statement. Would the program remain a structured program? Why or why not?

31. Why would we not get into a leapfrog cycle from point *A* to point *B* for the linear function? Show what happens by hand calculation.

32. How many times does the inner loop iterate for the function $y = 2^x$? If the increment in *x* starts at 1, how many times will the outer loop iterate? What will be the total number of iterations to process this function?

** 33. Modify the root search program as follows.
    a. Reduce the maximum number of iterations to 10.
    b. Place a trace statement in each of blocks 2–6 to print block number J, trial *x*, increment in *x*, preceding trial *y*, and current trial *y*.
    c. Add a third loop for processing different sets of input values.
    d. Run the program repeatedly using each function in Figure 6.8 under various values for initial trial *x* and initial increment. Make sure in your test runs that execution enters each block.
    e. What happens if in block 6 you forget to include the statement

    SIGN = −1.*SIGN

    The statement

    Y1 = Y2

** 34. Modify the pseudocode and program to incorporate logic for finding multiple roots (if any). Use the test functions in Figure 6.8 to debug your program.

6.8
COMMON ERRORS

Here are some errors to watch for when using concepts from this chapter.

1. *Code value outside computed GO TO range.* Make sure the value of your code variable is always within the range given by 1,2, . . . , number of statement numbers in the computed GO TO statement.

    GO TO (100,200,300) CODE

    { If the value in CODE is less than 1 or greater than 3, then statement 100 is executed. }

    100 · · ·
    :
    :

To be safe, a range test should precede the use of any computed GO TO statement, as illustrated in Example 6.3 on page 193.

2. *Missing GO TO statements within logical branch.*   FORTRAN 77 implementations of the CASE structure based on the computed GO TO statement require the use of a GO TO statement between each case-block in order to avoid the inadvertent execution of statements in the next case-block. For example, a common error in the program of Example 6.3 on page 193 would be the following.

```
        :
        :
        GO TO (100,200,300,400) CODE
100     MOVFIN   = MOVFIN + FINE
        MOVNUM = MOVNUM + 1
200     STDFIN   = STDFIN + FINE                        Missing GO TO 500
        STDNUM = STDNUM + 1
300     WARNUM = WARNUM + 1
400     PRINT *,'ERROR IN CODE FOR TICKET',I
500  CONTINUE
        :
        :
```

As mentioned earlier, either block IF, ELSE IF, or enhanced CASE structure implementations are preferred to the computed GO TO implementation from the standpoint of style and error-free programs.

3. *Imprudent use of GO TO statements.*   The use of GO TO statements can cause all kinds of problems. For example, GO TO and computed GO TO statements require the numeric labeling of statements to which control is transferred. Subsequently, this "opens the door" to making mistakes with respect to mislabeling statements, forgetting labels, repeating labels as when two statements are numbered 50, and otherwise branching to the wrong statement. For these reasons, block IF statements are preferred to logical IF statements and ELSE IF statements are preferred to computed GO TO statements when designing CASE structures.

Programs that eliminate the use of GO TO statements and statement labels also greatly reduce the likelihood of certain execution errors, as when control is transferred from outside into the body of a DO-loop or into an IF-block, ELSE-block, or ELSE-IF-block. In short, use labeling and GO TO statements only when absolutely necessary, as in designing a loop structure that is better represented as a DO-UNTIL than as a DO-WHILE. Those of you using compilers with control structure enhancements can eliminate the need for GO TO statements altogether when implementing CASE, DO-WHILE, and other control structures.

4. *Unnecessary processing.*   When designing an LRC loop by the trailer number method, beginning programmers often use a DO-UNTIL structure by placing the IF test at the end of the loop rather than at the beginning of the loop. Thus the loop is processed unnecessarily one additional time. Although this does not provoke a syntax or execution error, it does promote programming inefficiency and may cause a logic error.

5. *Infinite loop.*   In designing the IF test for a DO-UNTIL structure take care that the condition tests true sometime during the processing of the loop. If the condition always tests false, then you have committed a logic error called an *infinite loop*. In this case, the body of the loop continues to be processed until execution is stopped

by outside intervention. *A common cause of infinite loops is testing for equality of real values.* If the test is based on a computational result, roundoff error may prevent the resulting value from *exactly* equaling the test value.

ADDITIONAL EXERCISES

35. Define or explain each of the following.

branching	DO-WHILE structure
transfer of control	DO-UNTIL structure
GO TO statement	LRC loop
logical IF statement	trailer number
CASE structure	trailer record
computed GO TO statement	END = specifier

36. **Forecasting Population Growth.** Modify the program and flowchart/pseudocode in Exercise 16 of Chapter 3 (page 98) as follows.

   a. Use an LRC loop to output predicted population based on the different sets of data.

   b. Let N be a counter in an "inner" DO-UNTIL loop that lies entirely within the "outer" loop in part a. This inner loop increments N by 1, calculates predicted population, and prints N, corresponding year, and predicted population. Initialize N by defining an input variable called N1. Exit from the loop when the ratio of predicted population to current population exceeds a desired ratio (R). Run the program for the following three sets of values.

Current Population	Base Year	B	D	N1	R
4	1976	0.025	0.009	10	2
4	1976	0.025	0.009	25	3
4	1976	0.020	0.009	30	3

For example, your output for the first run should look like this.

YEARS INTO FUTURE	CORRESPONDING YEAR	PREDICTED POPULATION
10	1986	4.688
11	1987	4.763
:	:	:
:	:	:
43	2019	7.915
44	2020	8.042

Note that the counter is initialized by N1 and that this loop terminates when the predicted population *exceeds* (not equals) double (R has a value of 2) the current population. Comment on the number of years it takes the current world population to double and triple relative to changes in the birth rate.

37. **Mailing List.** A professional group of computer specialists is planning a regional meeting in New Orleans. A subgroup of information system specialists within this professional group will have a well-known computer scientist as a guest speaker. The chairperson of this subgroup plans to send meeting notices to members in two regions—Southeast (code 3) and Southwest (code 5)—who have an interest in information systems (code 15) or computer science (code 18).

a. Design an algorithm and write a program that prepares mailing labels for members of the organization that satisfy the location and area of interest criteria.

   The organization maintains the following data on each member.
   (1) Last name
   (2) First name
   (3) Street address
   (4) City
   (5) State
   (6) Zip
   (7) Region code (one digit; there are nine regions overall)
   (8) Interest code (two digits; there are 20 interest areas overall)

Sample Data File

(1)	(2)	(3)	(4)	(5)	(6)	(7)	(8)
Fastcode	Frank	11 Flower	Dallas	TX	75215	5	15
Burden	Kathy	193 West St	Warwick	RI	02886	1	18
Peripheral	Leslie	18 Grande	Slidell	LA	70808	5	20
Crowley	M. I. S	1 Hope Rd	Atlanta	GA	30901	3	15
Deff	Doris	111 High St	Hartford	CT	06518	7	12
Aides	Clyde	963 Main St	Orlando	FL	32407	3	18
Frick	Ford	2 Rose Way	Boston	MA	01906	9	18

Sample Output (*The First Mailing Label*)

   FRANK FASTCODE
   11 FLOWER
   DALLAS, TX 75215

   Terminate input of the data file based on a last-record check.

b. Include error detection for region and interest codes. If an error is found, print an appropriate error message and go on to the next member. Add new data with incorrect codes to debug your error logic.

c. Generalize your program so mailing labels can be prepared for any region and/or area of interest criteria. Specifically, design your program to provide the following options.

Option Code	Criteria
1	Specific region only
2	Specific interest area only
3	Specific region or interest area
4	Specific region and interest area

This version is more general than part a, but requires more computer runs to print labels for multiple regions and interest areas. For example, the run in part a requires four separate runs for option 4: region 3 and interest area 15; region 3 and interest area 18; region 5 and interest area 15; and region 5 and interest area 18.

38. Poisson Probability Function. The function

$$p = \frac{a^x \cdot e^{-a}}{x!}$$

describes the probability (p) that a random or chance variable takes on a value equal to x, where a is the mean or average value of the random variable, e is the base of natural logarithms (see Module A), and $x!$ (x factorial) is the product $1 \cdot 2 \cdot 3 \cdot \ldots \cdot (x-1) \cdot x$. For example, if the random variable "number of electronic failures per year" is distributed according to the Poisson function above and the average number of failures is known to be 5.2 per year ($a = 5.2$), then the probability of zero failures ($x = 0$) in a one-year period is

$$p = \frac{(5 \cdot 2)^0 \cdot e^{-5.2}}{0!}$$
$$= \frac{(1) \cdot (0.005516564)}{(1)}$$
$$= 0.0055 \text{ (or } 0.55\%)$$

and the probability of five failures per year is

$$p = \frac{(5.2)^5 \cdot e^{-5.2}}{5!}$$
$$= \frac{(3802.040) \cdot (0.005516564)}{120}$$
$$= 0.1747850 \text{ (or } 17.5\%)$$

Note that 0! is defined as 1.

The Poisson function is widely used to describe phenomena; hence published tables of probabilities for this function are common.

a. Design and run a program that inputs the average a and outputs a table of probabilities as follows:

```
A = xxx.xxx
X          PROBABILITY
------------------
0          .xxxx
1          .xxxx
2          .xxxx
↓          ↓
```

Terminate this table when the probability drops below 0.0001.

b. Include an outer LRC loop that processes different values of a. Use the following input values: 2.0, 5.2, 6.0, 10.0, 20.0.

39. Telephone Company Billing. "Flat rate service" charges for telephone service is a method of billing that includes some fixed amount for the main station (main telephone, switchboard, and so on) plus a variable amount per extension phone in service. Distinctions also are made between residential and business customers according to the table below. Private Branch Exchange (PBX) service uses a switchboard for the main station, off which extensions can be wired. Centrex service is for large-scale business firms and governmental agencies, which require such a large number of extensions that the telephone switching equipment is located on the customer's premises.

Customer Type	Code	Type of Service	Monthly Flat Rates Main Station	Each Extension
Residential	1	Main phone/extensions	$ 13	$ 3
Business	2	Main phone/extensions	50	10
Business	3	PBX/extensions	150	5
Business	4	Centrex/extensions	500	3

In actual practice, PBX and Centrex include many special features. For example, options include fully automatic equipment versus partly manual equipment, facilities for data transmission, private lines that ring at specific locations when the receiver is picked up (PL's), facilities for foreign exchange (FX), and many others.

To illustrate a calculation, consider a business customer with PBX equipment and 50 extensions. In this case, the monthly flat rate is $400 (or $150 + 50 × 5) which, of course, excludes long distance charges, taxes, and charges due to special features.

a. Design and write a program that calculates flat rate service charges and outputs customer name, telephone number, and charge. Test your program with the following data.

Customer Name	Customer Phone Number	Code	Number of Extensions
Test 1	783-5123	2	5
Test 2	792-7541	4	400
Test 3	445-8162	4	550
Test 4	612-6148	3	75
Test 5	783-1235	1	0

Customer Name	Customer Phone Number	Code	Number of Extensions
Test 6	445-2164	1	3
Test 7	789-5849	2	7
Test 8	789-7812	4	730
Test 9	792-2674	1	1
Test 10	615-6513	3	50

Terminate customer read-in based on a last-record-check.

b. Modify the program in part a to include the calculation and output of the following.

1. Total number of customers by code category
2. Percent of customers by code category
3. Total charges by code category
4. Overall total charges

Try to design your output for easy readability.

c. Include error detection for code. If an error is found, print an appropriate error message and go on to the next customer. Do not include that customer's data in the output of part a or b. Add new data with incorrect codes to debug your error logic.

40. Checking Account Report. Prepare pseudocode and write a program that produces a monthly checking account report for each customer. Checking charges are calculated on the basis of the following information.

1. If the ending balance is less than $200, the following service charges are assessed: a monthly fee of 80 cents plus a charge of 10 cents per honored check (withdrawal). No charges are assessed for deposits.
2. If the ending balance is $200 or more, no service charges are assessed.
3. If a check "bounces" (that is, if the balance becomes negative when the bank attempts to honor a check), a charge of $5 is assessed, and the current balance is reduced by this amount. This charge is made for each check that bounces. Checks that bounce are not honored. In other words, a withdrawal is not made from the account, since the person to whom the check was made out does not get paid. Also, the $200 limit does not apply to this bounce charge; that is, if a check bounces, the $5 charge is assessed regardless of the ending balance.

For each bank customer

1. The first line of data contains four items:
   Item 1—the bank account number
   Item 2—name
   Item 3—number of transactions (N), or total number of withdrawals and deposits
   Item 4—beginning balance

2. N lines follow the first line, each line representing a single transaction. If the value is negative, the transaction is a withdrawal; if the value is positive, the transaction is a deposit.

Sample Input

```
614275,'WENDY BRANDON',3,741.62
50.75
−125
−260.50
216422,'RICHARD R. WEEKS',4,250.15
−115
−80.75
100
−236.80
```

Sample Output

BANK STATEMENT

WENDY BRANDON	614275
BEGINNING BALANCE	741.62
TOTAL DEPOSITS	50.75
TOTAL WITHDRAWALS	385.50
CHARGES	0.00
ENDING BALANCE	406.87

} 11 lines

} 6 blank lines and then next bank statement (if any)

BANK STATEMENT

RICHARD R. WEEKS	216422
BEGINNING BALANCE	250.15
TOTAL DEPOSITS	100.00
TOTAL WITHDRAWALS	195.75
CHARGES	6.00
ENDING BALANCE	148.40
TOTAL NOT HONORED	
	236.80

} 2 blank lines and then next bank statement (if any)

Debug your program using the above data and the following additional data.

Account Number	Name	N	Beginning Balance	Transactions
(Make these up)		4	240.00	−50.00
				−35.00
				−175.00
				+200.00
(Make these up)		7	450.00	−300.00
				−125.00
				+200.00
				−75.00
				−35.00
				+150.00
				−66.00

Before designing your program, make sure you understand the logic by solving these problems by hand. Note that each bank statement takes up exactly 17 lines of input in order to conform to a standardized form. By the way, this is a good program to use diagnostic PRINT statements (traces) for current balance and charges during the debugging phase.

41. **Crew Selection—A Combination Problem.** An oceanographic food firm is planning extensive underwater experiments in aquaculture (sea farming). These experiments require people to live together in an isolated underwater environment for extended periods of time. To avoid problems associated with incompatibility, the firm has decided to run isolation tests for the purpose of judging compatibility. These tests require individuals to live together for two weeks under monitored conditions in an above-ground capsule that is cut off from the outside world.

As an example, suppose that four people are available for the experiments, but only two are required to live together underwater. How many subgroups of two persons are possible from among four? If we let $P1$ represent the first person, $P2$ the second person, and so on, we have the following six distinct subgroups of two persons each: $(P1, P2)$, $(P1, P3)$, $(P1, P4)$, $(P2, P3)$, $(P2, P4)$, $(P3, P4)$. Right? This means that six separate isolation tests would have to be conducted in the capsule to select the most compatible two persons.

This approach of listing groups works fine when we are dealing with small numbers, but becomes impractical when the numbers get large. For instance, if ten people are available and we need four for the experiments, then we have 210 distinct groups of four each. If you have had a course in statistics, you probably recognize this as a so-called *combination problem*.

Given that n people are available and k are needed, then the number of combinations of n taken k at a time is given by the formula

$$C = \frac{(n) \cdot (n-1) \cdot (n-2) \cdot \ldots \cdot (2) \cdot (1)}{[(n-k) \cdot (n-k-1) \cdot \ldots \cdot (2) \cdot (1)] \cdot [(k) \cdot (k-1) \cdot \ldots \cdot (2) \cdot (1)]}$$

For the first example above, $n = 4$ and $k = 2$, so that

$$C = \frac{4 \cdot 3 \cdot 2 \cdot 1}{(2 \cdot 1) \cdot (2 \cdot 1)} = 6$$

For the second example, $n = 10$ and $k = 4$, so that

$$C = \frac{10 \cdot 9 \cdot 8 \cdot 7 \cdot 6 \cdot 5 \cdot 4 \cdot 3 \cdot 2 \cdot 1}{(6 \cdot 5 \cdot 4 \cdot 3 \cdot 2 \cdot 1) \cdot (4 \cdot 3 \cdot 2 \cdot 1)} = 210$$

a. Design and write a program that calculates C, given n and k. Output should include C, and the total number of days required for all isolation experiments given that each experiment takes 14 days. Run the following data through your program.

n	k
6	2
10	4
10	6
10	10
20	4
40	4
40	6
60	6

Design your program such that the above data are processed by an LRC loop.

** b. Did you have numeric overflow when $n = 60$ and $k = 6$? Certain efficiencies can be realized in the calculation of C by dividing terms in the numerator by terms in the denominator. For example, for $n = 60$ and $k = 6$, we can write

$$C = \frac{60 \cdot 59 \cdot 58 \cdot 57 \cdot 56 \cdot 55}{6 \cdot 5 \cdot 4 \cdot 3 \cdot 2 \cdot 1}$$

Design your program to take advantage of this efficiency.

42. Newton's Approximation Method. This method describes a procedure for approximating the root of a function. Consider Figure 6.10, which reproduces a blown-up portion of the quadratic function in Figure 6.8. If we arbitrarily select the first root approximation at $x = 6.00$, then the second approximation is at $x = 4.78$. Graphically, the second approximation is found by constructing a tangent line on the function at $x = 6.00$ and extending this line to the x-axis. The intersection of the tangent line with the x-axis gives the next root approximation, which is 4.78 approximately. Next we construct a tangent at $x = 4.78$, and it intersects the x-axis at roughly 4.51. This process continues until a desired precision is achieved. Note that each successive approximation gets closer and closer to the root at $x = 4.50$.

Analytically, a tangent line is determined as the first derivative of the function, which we label $y' \cdot (y$ prime). For the function

$$y = -2.25 - 4x + x^2$$

the first derivative is

$$y' = -4 + 2x$$

FIGURE 6.10 *Newton's Approximation Method (Exercise 42)*

The next root approximation is determined from the following formula.

$$\text{Next } x = \text{Current } x - \frac{y}{y'}$$

The table below illustrates three iterations of this procedure.

Current x	$y = -2.25 - 4x + x^2$	$y' = -4 + 2x$	Next x
6.000000	9.750000	8.000000	4.781250
4.781250	1.485351	5.562500	4.514220
4.514220	0.0713022	5.028440	4.500040
⋮	⋮	⋮	⋮

a. Design and run a program that approximates roots by this method. Terminate iterations when the difference between two successive x's is less than 0.00001. Use the following test data.

y	y'	Initial x values
$-2.25 - 4x + x^2$	$-4 + 2x$	6.0; 4.0; 4.5
$-1 + 2x$	2	3.0; -2.0
2^x	$(2^x) \cdot (\ln 2)^*$	10
$-20 + 108x^2 - 4x^3$	$216x - 12x^2$	Make up your own. Try to find multiple roots.

* In 2 stands for the natural (base-e) logarithm of 2 (see Module A).

**b. Incorporate logic for finding multiple roots (if any).

43. Numerical Integration. A continuous monotonic function

$$y = f(x)$$

plots as a smooth curve (no breaks) and either continually rises (monotonically increases) or continually falls (monotonically decreases). Figure 6.11 illustrates two such functions in the interval $x = a$ to $x = b$. *Numerical integration* is the process of computing areas under curves of functions, a process that has widespread applicability in engineering and the sciences.[4] The procedure described below applies only to continuous monotonic functions.

The rectangles of width d in Figure 6.11 suggest one method of estimating area under $f(x)$ in the interval a to b. Focusing on Figure 6.11a, note that the leftmost rectangle is divided into a lower area given by the hatched portion and a triangular shaded area. The hatched area is calculated by

$$\text{(width)} \cdot \text{(height)}$$

$$d \cdot f(a)$$

where $f(a)$ is the value of the function when $x = a$. The shaded area is the triangular lower half of the upper rectangle, or

$$(\tfrac{1}{2}) \cdot \text{(width of triangle)} \cdot \text{(height of triangle)}$$

$$(\tfrac{1}{2}) \cdot (d) \cdot [f(a + d) - f(a)]$$

The estimated area under the curve from $x = a$ to $x = a + d$ is the sum of these two areas, or

$$\text{Area from } a \text{ to } a + d = d \cdot f(a) + \tfrac{1}{2} \cdot d \cdot [f(a + d) - f(a)]$$
$$= d/2 \cdot [f(a) + f(a + d)]$$

which is equivalent to the area of a trapezoid. Since the interval from a to b contains three of these trapezoids, each of width d, it follows that

$$
\begin{aligned}
\text{Area from } a \text{ to } b = \quad & d/2 \cdot [f(a) + f(a + d)] \\
& + d/2 \cdot [f(a + d) + f(a + 2d)] \\
& + d/2 \cdot [f(a + 2d) + f(b)] \\
= \quad & d/2 \cdot [f(a) + 2f(a + d) + 2f(a + 2d) + f(b)]
\end{aligned}
$$

[4] Those who have had calculus should recognize this as equivalent to evaluating the definite integral

$$\int_a^b f(x)\,dx$$

FIGURE 6.11 Continuous Monotonic Functions (Exercise 43)

a. Monotonically Increasing Function

b. Monotonically Decreasing Function

is an approximation to the actual area under $f(x)$ from a to b. It should make sense to you that the greater the number of trapezoids between a and b (that is, the smaller the width d), the better is the approximation to the actual area.

a. Suppose we wish to find the area under

$$y = 2^x$$

from $x = 1$ to $x = 4$. By hand, estimate this area by using three trapezoids. Next, double the number of trapezoids to six and compare results. The actual area is 20.19773. Which approximation has the least error?

b. Design and write a program that inputs a, b, and number of trapezoids, and outputs an approximation to the area. Use the following test data.

Function*	a	b	Number of Trapezoids
2^x	1.0	4.0	3; 6; 100; 211; 1000
$-1 + 2x$	1.0	10.0	100
	0.5	10.0	2; 10
$1 - e^{-x/8000}$	0.0	5000.0	100

* The symbol e is the base of natural logarithms (see Module A).

c. The number of trapezoids needed for the approximation to be within a specified error (E) of the actual area is given by the formula

$$\text{Number of trapezoids} = \text{int}\left[\frac{(b-a) \cdot |f(a) - f(b)|}{2E}\right] + 1$$

where int stands for "integer part of" and $|f(a) - f(b)|$ is the absolute value of the difference. For example, if we want our estimated area for the first function in part b to be within 0.1 of the actual area, then we need 211 trapezoids.

$$\text{int}\left[\frac{(4-1) \cdot |2^1 - 2^4|}{2 \cdot (0.1)}\right] + 1 = 211$$

Was the estimated area within 0.1 of the actual area 20.19773 when you used 211 trapezoids in part b?

Modify your program to input E instead of number of trapezoids, and process the following data.

Function	a	b	E
$1 - e^{-x/8000}$	0.0	1000.0	0.001
	0.0	5000.0	0.001
	0.0	12000.0	0.001
	5000.0	12000.0	0.001

These data are consistent with the scenario outlined in Exercise 32 of Chapter 4 on page 136. What is the meaning of the area for the range 5000 to 12000?

CHAPTER 7

One-Dimensional Arrays

Most of the programs you've written or studied up to this point have had this structure.

1. Read in a set of data.
2. Process the data.
3. Print the results.
4. Return to Step 1 if more data are available.

In some problems you may want to read and store large quantities of related data before you begin any computations. This was not possible in many earlier programs because reading in a new set of data automatically erased the values stored from the previous set, thus preventing access to the stored data of the previous set.

7.1
MOTIVATION

An **array** is a group of consecutive memory locations that have the same name. The use of arrays

1. Permits access to any data item that has been read previously
2. Provides simple yet powerful capabilities to name and manipulate a large number of storage locations

To help you visualize this concept, the illustration below shows three storage locations for an array named DEPOS.

DEPOS

first storage location in DEPOS

second storage location in DEPOS

third storage location in DEPOS

Just how we specify and manipulate arrays will become clear in the next two sections. First, however, we motivate their use through the following example.

EXAMPLE 7.1 Analysis of Bank Deposits

The vice president of a small branch bank wants to compare the percent of deposits that each branch contributes to the bank's total deposits. The number of deposits for each of the three branches is given below.

Bank	Number of Deposits
1	3500
2	5000
3	4000

Let's first try to solve this problem using the approach used in previous chapters. A program such as the following might be written in this way.

Version A

```
INTEGER DEPOS, TOT
REAL    PER

TOT = 0

DO 10 I = 1,3
   READ *,DEPOS
   TOT = TOT + DEPOS
10 CONTINUE

DO 20 I = 1,3
   READ *,DEPOS
   PER = REAL(DEPOS)/REAL(TOT)*100.
   PRINT *,DEPOS,PER
20 CONTINUE

END
```

This program would not work if we use the following input data:

Test Input Data
3500
5000
4000

In the first loop, the three data items are read in and total deposits are accumulated for the bank; however, a problem occurs in the second loop when we try to *reenter* the data by executing the READ statement again, assuming we had only provided three input *records* or *lines*. The data already have been read in and an "OUT OF

DATA'' error message occurs when you attempt to reenter the data. This program would work only if we were to provide six input records, where the last three records are identical to the first three records.

Test Input Data		Output	
	3500	3500	28.0
	5000	5000	40.0
	4000	4000	32.0
repetition	3500		
of first	5000		
three records	4000		

This approach is not only conceptually unappealing but also inefficient, particularly if the program is used for a bank having many branches.

Now, consider the following program.

Version B

```
INTEGER DEPOS1,DEPOS2,DEPOS3,TOT
REAL     PER

READ *,DEPOS1
READ *,DEPOS2
READ *,DEPOS3

TOT = DEPOS1 + DEPOS2 + DEPOS3

PER = REAL (DEPOS1)/REAL(TOT)*100.
PRINT *,DEPOS1,PER

PER = REAL(DEPOS2)/REAL(TOT)*100.
PRINT *,DEPOS2,PER

PER = REAL(DEPOS3)/REAL(TOT)*100.
PRINT *,DEPOS3,PER

END
```

Test Input Data	Output	
3500	3500	28.0
5000	5000	40.0
4000	4000	32.0

This program works but . . . it's very rigid and inefficient. It works for three branches, but if you wish to add a fourth branch, the program will have to be rewritten. Worse yet, visualize this program written for the hundreds of Chase Manhattan branch banks in New York City. What a long and tedious program it would be for such a simple problem! A simpler solution to this problem is to use an array.

Version C

```
      INTEGER DEPOS(3),TOT
      REAL    PER

      TOT = 0

      DO 10 I = 1,3
         READ *,DEPOS(I)
         TOT = TOT + DEPOS(I)
   10 CONTINUE

      DO 20 I = 1,3
         PER = REAL(DEPOS(I))/REAL(TOT)*100.
         PRINT *,DEPOS(I),PER
   20 CONTINUE

      END
```

Test Input Data	Output	
3500	3500	28.0
5000	5000	40.0
4000	4000	32.0

In this program the first loop reads the number of deposits for each branch bank, storing them in an array called DEPOS, and accumulates the total deposits for all branches in TOT. The second loop references each element in the array DEPOS, divides the number of deposits for each branch by the total deposits, multiplies the fraction by 100 to give a percentage, and prints the number of deposits and the relative percent of total deposits for each branch bank. At this point, don't worry about the exact nature of the array. We discuss this topic next.

7.2 SUBSCRIPTS

An **array name** is the symbolic name of an array. A number of unique memory locations is associated with an array name; each memory location in the array is referred to as an **array element,** which can be referenced by its relative position in the array through the use of a *subscript*.

A **subscript** acts as an *index* or *pointer* to locate a specific array element. In FOR-TRAN, a subscript is a parenthetic expression following the array name, as follows:

For example, the first array element in our sample program can be identified as

Thus an **array element name** is an array name followed by a subscript. The subscript is a set of parentheses containing one or more subscript expressions.[1] A **subscript expression** is an *integer* expression which when evaluated has a *value*. In the above example, the array element name is DEPOS(1) and the subscript is (1); the subscript expression is the integer constant 1, which of course has a value of 1. The value of the subscript expression is used to identify an array element. In our example, the subscript value 1 identifies the first array element in the array named DEPOS. By the way, the same rules that apply to naming variable names (maximum of six characters, etc.) also apply to naming array names.

---

[1] Subscripts with more than one subscript expression are considered in the next chapter.

EXAMPLE 7.2

The use of subscripts in FORTRAN gives the language great ease and flexibility in naming and manipulating a large number of *related* variables. This feature is "borrowed" from algebra, as the following illustrates.

Stock Number	Price of Stock ($)	Subscripted Variables in Algebra	Array Element Names (Subscripted Variables) in FORTRAN
1	75	x_1	X(1)
2	42	x_2	X(2)
3	24	x_3	X(3)
.	.	.	.
.	.	.	.
.	.	.	.
500	105	x_{500}	X(500)

For example, if we are dealing with a series of 500 numbers, where each number represents the price of a stock at the end of a given day on the New York Stock Exchange, then the algebraic notation x_3 refers to the price of the third stock and x_{75} refers to the price of the 75th stock. Similarly, in FORTRAN, X(3) refers to the storage location for the price of the third stock and X(75) identifies the storage location for the price of the 75th stock. Naming so many related variables would be quite tedious and impractical without the use of subscripts. For example, you wouldn't recommend a scheme such as A, B, C, . . . to name 500 variables, would you? These names are cumbersome, are difficult to manipulate, cause inefficient coding, and do not in themselves suggest contextual meaning. As you will see, the use of arrays overcomes each of these difficulties.

You should keep in mind the following additional points when working with subscripts.

1. A subscript having a single subscript expression references what is called a **vector** or **one-dimensional array.**
2. Typically, subscript expressions are either *positive integer constants* or integer variables that store positive (nonzero) integer values. For example,

```
COST(K)
```

Integer variable as subscript expression

uses the *integer variable* K as a subscript expression. When you use a variable as a subscript expression you may reference any element in the array on the basis of the value you assign that variable. For example, the program segment

```
REAL SALE (20)
      .
      .
      .
K = 3
SALE(K) = 500.
```

results in the storage of 500. in the third location of the array SALE.

In Example 7.1, storage is accomplished as follows.

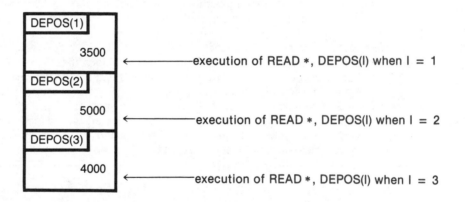

3. Generally the subscript expression can be any integer expression. For example, VALUE(K + 3) and LOAD(2*MUM + 1) are legitimate array element names.
4. Usually the value of a subscript expression is positive and nonzero, since this convention simplifies the relationship between this value and the array element. For example, if the value of the subscript expression is 3 in array SALE, then it simplifies our life if we can say that the array element name SALE(3) thus refers to the third array element (storage location) in the array, as in the above example. More generally, however, subscript expressions can take on negative and zero values. In this case an array element name such as SALE(-5), which has a subscript expression with a negative value, in itself does not imply the number of the storage location in the array. (How can you have a minus fifth storage location?) Here, SALE(-5) simply identifies a storage location named SALE(-5). More on this subtle point in the next section.
5. You can use the same variable name as a subscript expression to reference corresponding elements in different arrays. For example, the program segment

```
K = 2
PROFIT(K) = SALE(K) − COST(K)
```

subtracts the second array element in COST from the second array element in SALE and stores the result in the second array element of PROFIT.

6.   Subscripts are not part of the array name; thus TAB(J) and TAB(I) both reference the array TAB. In addition, if I and J are equal, then TAB(J) and TAB(I) reference the same element in TAB.

7.3
ARRAY DECLARATION

Arrays must be *declared* in order for the computer to reserve multiple memory locations. Type statements with which you are familiar (CHARACTER, INTEGER, REAL, DOUBLE PRECISION) are a convenient means to this end. The general form of these statements when used to declare *one-dimensional* arrays[2] is

```
type        array  (dimension )  array  (dimension )
keyword     name   (declarator ), name  (declarator ) . . .
```

where *type keyword* is usually one of the following: CHARACTER, INTEGER, REAL, or DOUBLE PRECISION. These statements declare to the compiler which names are array names, their type, and their sizes (total number of array elements). The **dimension declarator** provides information about the size of the array by specifying lower and upper bounds on the value of the subscript expression. In Example 7.1, the statement

```
                    ┌─────────── Dimension declarator
                    │            showing upper dimension bound
                    ↓
   INTEGER DEPOS(3),TOT
```

types DEPOS and TOT as integer and declares DEPOS a one-dimensional array with an *upper dimension bound* (on the value of the subscript expression) of 3. In this case a *lower dimension bound* of 1 is assumed since the lower dimension bound is not specified. Thus, array element names range from DEPOS(1) to DEPOS(3), which gives an array of *size* 3 in memory.

```
┌──────────────┐
│ DEPOS(1)     │
│              │
│              │
├──────────────┤
│ DEPOS(2)     │
│              │
│              │
├──────────────┤
│ DEPOS(3)     │
│              │
│              │
└──────────────┘
```

---

[2] These are generalized to multidimensional arrays in the next chapter.

Note that the contents (stored values) of these locations are left blank; they are filled in with the appropriate values when the READ statement is executed three times in DO-loop 10 on page 231. If we had used

    INTEGER DEPOS(5),TOT

then five memory locations would have been reserved for DEPOS.

Loops 10 and 20, however, still would utilize only the first three of these locations.

More than one array can be declared in a single type statement by using commas to separate each array specification. For example,

    REAL COST(80),REV(50),PROFIT(50)

reserves 80 locations for a real array named COST, another 50 locations for real array REV, and 50 more locations for real array PROFIT.

Here are some additional points to keep in mind when working with arrays.

1. A *lower dimension bound* can be indicated as part of the dimension declarator by placing a colon between the lower and upper dimension bounds. For example,

    INTEGER DEPOS(−2:3)

results in the following memory representation:

Note that the size of this array is six array elements, where the first array element is identified by the array element name DEPOS(−2) and the sixth array element is named DEPOS(3). In general, the size of an array is given by

$$size = \text{upper dimension bound} - \text{lower dimension bound} + 1$$

2. What size array should we declare? In general, the size of a declared array represents a trade-off between wasted storage costs and the software cost of updating the array declaration, taking into consideration actual and projected data needs. For example, if we currently have 75 branch banks and over the next 10 years expect at most 25 more branch banks, then it is reasonable to declare DEPOS as a 100-element array, since it is certain that the cost of updating the declaration in the program each time a branch bank is added far exceeds the cost of keeping at most 25 empty storage locations. However, if an array generally requires no more than 5000 elements, but once in a great while needs 100,000 elements, then it may be less costly to occasionally change the program itself by updating the array size from 5000 to 100,000 when needed.

3. Lower and upper dimension bounds must be integer constant expressions.[3] For example,

    REAL LENGTH(N)

    would yield a syntax error, since a variable is not permitted as a lower or upper dimension bound, except within subprograms (Chapter 9).
4. If during execution the value of a subscript expression falls outside the range given by the lower and upper dimension bounds, then either an execution or a logic error will occur.
5. The DIMENSION statement is an alternative to type statements for declaring arrays. The general form of this statement is

    $$\boxed{\textbf{DIMENSION} \; \begin{matrix} array \\ name \end{matrix} \begin{pmatrix} dimension \\ declarator \end{pmatrix}, \; \begin{matrix} array \\ name \end{matrix} \begin{pmatrix} dimension \\ declarator \end{pmatrix} \ldots}$$

    For example

    DIMENSION COST(80),REV(50),PROFIT(50)

    reserves 80 locations for the array COST, 50 locations for REV, and 50 locations for PROFIT. Note, however, that this statement does not type the arrays. Good programing style, therefore, would dictate an explicit declaration of type as follows:

    DIMENSION COST(80),REV(50),PROFIT(50)
    REAL   COST,REV,PROFIT

    Since both operations (array declaration and type) can be combined in a type statement, we recommend that you do not use DIMENSION statements.
6. The declaration of *character arrays* usually requires a length declaration for elements in the array. For example, suppose the array LINE is to store lines of text on a page (such as a letter, notice, or document). If we assume 60 lines per page and a maximum of 70 characters per line, then we can declare LINE as a 60-element one-dimensional array with a length of 70 characters per element as follows:

    CHARACTER LINE(60)*70

    Character arrays play an important role in what are called word-processing applications, a topic we take up in some detail in Chapter 10. In this chapter and the next we focus on *numeric arrays,* except for minor illustrations in Examples 7.9 and 7.12.

---

[3] A dimension declarator can be expressed generally by

$$\begin{matrix} \text{integer constant expression} \\ \text{for lower dimension bound} \end{matrix} : \begin{matrix} \text{integer constant expression} \\ \text{for upper dimension bound} \end{matrix}$$

where an integer constant expression is made up strictly of one or more integer constants and/or symbolic names for integer constants. Exceptions to this rule are discussed in Section 9.2.

Follow-up Exercises

1. How clear are you on the intricate terminology of the last two sections? For example, can you distinguish between
   a. An array and an array name?
   b. An array name and an array element name?
   c. An array element and an array element name?
   d. An array element and a storage location?
   e. A subscript and a subscript expression?
   f. The value of a subscript expression and the ith array element?

2. Can you reason why integer variables are not permitted in place of integer constants in dimension declarators?

3. Indicate what is wrong, if anything, with each of the following program segments.

   a. ```
      READ *,K,X(K)
      REAL X(K),T(4 + 3)
        .
        .
        .
      ```

   b. ```
      REAL A(50)
      DATA M,N/5,8/
      DATA A(0),A(15)/100.,500./
      A(M + 10*N) = M*N
        .
        .
        .
      ```

   c. ```
             DIMENSION D(10),E(10)
             INTEGER   D(10),E(10)
             DO 30 J = 1,20
                D(J) = J**2
      30 CONTINUE
             DO 40 J = 1,19
                E(J + 1) = D(J)*D(J + 1)
      40 CONTINUE
             .
             .
             .
      ```

   What would be stored in E(3) once the program is corrected?
      ```

4. Indicate the storage contents of specific array elements for the following, where a value of 4 is input for N.

```
        INTEGER R(5),S(5),T(5)
        READ *,N 4
        DO 10 J = 1,N
          R(J) = J
          L = N + 1 − J
          S(L) = L
     10 CONTINUE
        T(5) = 0
        DO 20 K = 1,N
          T(K) = R(K)*S(K)
          T(5) = T(5) + T(K)
     20 CONTINUE
```

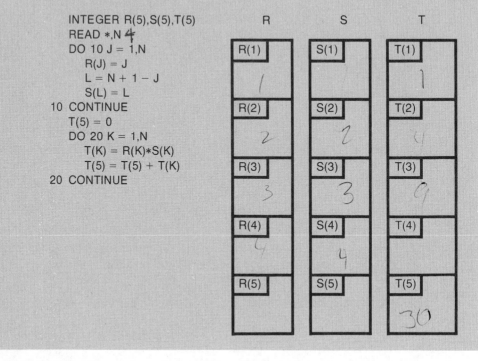

7.4
INPUT/OUTPUT

Essentially, we have three basic procedures for the efficient I/O of arrays. In the discussions that follow, assume that we wish to read or print every element in the array, beginning with the first element and moving sequentially through the array until the last element.

Using the DO Statement

The DO statement is a convenient device for performing I/O of arrays. In this case the DO-variable may be used as a subscript expression which takes on values that coincide with each element in the array.

EXAMPLE 7.3   I/O with the DO Statement

The program segment

```
      INTEGER DEPOS(3)
      DO 10 I = 1,3
         READ *,DEPOS(I)
   10 CONTINUE
      .
      .
      .
```

reads data found in three records and stores them in the array DEPOS, according to the following procedure. Initially, I is set equal to 1 (from the DO statement) and the first data item is read into DEPOS(1).

Then I is incremented to 2, the READ statement is executed a second time, the second input record is processed, and 5000 is stored in DEPOS(2).

Finally, I is incremented to 3, and the third memory location for DEPOS is filled.

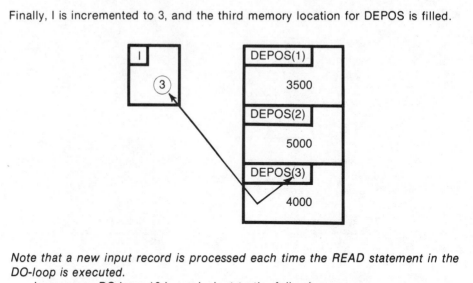

Note that a new input record is processed each time the READ statement in the DO-loop is executed.

In essence, DO-loop 10 is equivalent to the following.

```
READ *,DEPOS(1)
READ *,DEPOS(2)
READ *,DEPOS(3)
```

In other words, identical results would be obtained if loop 10 were replaced with the above three statements. If we were reading in deposits for 200 banks, then you should readily appreciate the power of the DO-loop approach.

This looping technique using the DO statement also can be used for output. For example, the following statements result in the printout of the contents of array DEPOS.

	Output
.	
.	
.	
DO 30 I = 1,3	3500
PRINT *,DEPOS(I)	5000
30 CONTINUE	4000
.	
.	
.	

Note that a new output line is written each time the PRINT statement is executed. In effect, DO-loop 30 is equivalent to the following.

```
PRINT *,DEPOS(1)
PRINT *,DEPOS(2)
PRINT *,DEPOS(3)
```

Follow-up Exercises

5. With respect to version C (the one using array DEPOS) in Example 7.1 on page 231:
    a. Change the program to process 100 branch banks. How many more statements would be needed in the version B program on page 230 to accomplish the same task? How about the length of the statement that calculates TOT? Do you now see why arrays give us a simple yet powerful means to name and manipulate a large number of storage locations?
    b. Generalize the program so it can handle any number of branch banks up to 500.
6. Consider the following program segment for reading 50 values into an array named LOAD.

```
REAL LOAD(50)  ⎫
READ *,LOAD(1)  ⎪
READ *,LOAD(2)  ⎬ 50 statements
    .           ⎪
    .           ⎪
READ *,LOAD(50) ⎭
```

Rewrite this segment using a DO-loop. Which approach is more code-efficient?
7. Describe output for the following.

	Input Data
REAL A(100),B(100),SUMA,SUMB,SUMDIF	
DATA SUMDIF,SUMA,SUMB/3*0./	
READ *,M	4
DO 50 J = 1,M	1,5
READ *,A(J),B(J)	10,4
SUMA = SUMA + A(J)	8,1
SUMB = SUMB + B(J)	2,10
SUMDIF = SUMDIF + (A(J) − B(J))	
50 CONTINUE	
DO 75 J = 1,M	
PRINT *,A(J),B(J),A(J) − B(J)	
75 CONTINUE	
PRINT *,SUMA SUMB,SUMDIF	
END	

8. Given the following data

Cost	Sales
40	100
20	125
75	95

write an efficient program segment to read these data into the 500-element integer arrays COST and SALES. How would you place your input data?

9. Formatted I/O. Answer the following regarding Example 7.1 on page 231 based on the material in Modules B, C, and D.

a. Describe input records if we were to use the following code:

```
2 FORMAT(I5)
     DO 10 I = 1,3
          READ 2,DEPOS(I)
  10 CONTINUE
```

b. Same as part a except

```
2 FORMAT(3I5)
```

c. Describe output if we were to use the following code:

```
4 FORMAT('0',I8,F7.1)
     DO 20 I = 1,3
          PER = REAL(DEPOS(I))/REAL(TOT)*100.
          PRINT 4,DEPOS(I),PER
  20 CONTINUE
```

d. Same as part c except

```
4 FORMAT('0',I8/'b',F8.1)
```

Using the Implied-DO List

The combination of the DO statement with the READ or PRINT statement causes the processing of a new record (line) with each execution of the READ or PRINT statement. Thus, only one data value per record can be stored or output whenever the list of the READ or PRINT statement contains only one item. Often we want to store several values on a record or print a number of values on a line of output. For example, if the bank deposit data were stored on a single record in the following manner:

```
3500,5000,4000
```

then the program segment

```
DO 10 I = 1,3
     READ *,DEPOS(I)
10 CONTINUE
```

would store the value 3500 in DEPOS(1), after which an "OUT OF DATA" error message would be printed.

The use of an **implied-DO list** *as an item within the list of a READ or PRINT statement* is a more flexible approach to reading and printing arrays. A general form of the implied-DO list is

$$\left(dlist, DO\text{-}variable = \begin{array}{ccc} initial & terminal & incrementation \\ expression, & expression, & expression \end{array}\right)$$

where *dlist* refers to constants, variable names, array element names, array names, and expressions used in READ and PRINT statements. The *DO-variable, initial, terminal, and incrementation expressions* are subject to the same rules as the DO statement (see Section 4.5).

Typically, the items within an implied-DO list are array element names followed by indexing information that specifies the specific array elements that are to be processed, as we illustrate in the next example.

EXAMPLE 7.4 Unformatted I/O Using an Implied-DO List

In the statement

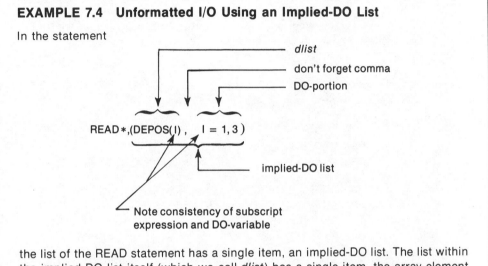

the list of the READ statement has a single item, an implied-DO list. The list within the implied-DO list itself (which we call *dlist*) has a single item, the array element name DEPOS(I). In this case the DO-variable I iterates from 1 to 3 in increments of 1 (the incrementation expression is given a value of 1 since it's omitted). The implied-DO list thus iterates three times, which means that DEPOS(I) is iterated three times with a different value in I each time. In other words, the array element name is repeated three times to yield an effect that is identical to the following.

    READ *,DEPOS(1),DEPOS(2),DEPOS(3)

Now we can place all three data items on the same input record

Input Data
_____

3500,5000,4000

since the list of the READ statement effectively has three separate items.

The implied-DO list also can be used to print data stored in arrays. For example,

    PRINT *,(DEPOS(I),I = 1,3)

prints three values from array DEPOS on one line.

Output
_____

3500   5000   4000

Moreover, we can label the output values as follows:

| PRINT *,(I,I = 1,3) | | Output | |
PRINT *,(DEPOS(I),I = 1,3)			
	1	2	3
	3500	5000	4000

Note that DO parameters (I, 1, and 3 in the above examples) must be type integer when they are utilized by subscript expressions (I in the above examples).

There are many variations in using the implied-DO list, as we further illustrate with the examples shown on the opposite page.

Follow-up Exercises

10. Code a more efficient way of handling each of the following statements.

    a. READ *,X(1),X(2),X(3),X(4),X(5),X(6),X(7),X(8)
    b. PRINT *,X(1),X(2),X(3),X(4),X(5),X(6),X(7),X(8)
    c. READ *,X(1),X(3),X(5),X(7),X(9),X(11)
    d. PRINT *,A(1),B(1),A(2),B(2),A(3),B(3)
    e. PRINT *,A(1),A(2),A(3),B(1),B(2),B(3),B(4),B(5)
    f. READ *,X(1),X(2),X(3),M,N
    g. PRINT *,A,X(1),X(2),X(3),B

11. Suppose the values 10, 20, 30, and 40 are stored in the four-element integer array YES and the values 5, 10, 15, and 20 are stored in the four-element integer array NO. Indicate output for each case, where N stores a 4.

    a. PRINT *,(YES(J),J = 1,N),(NO(J),J = 1,N)
    b. PRINT *,(YES(J),NO(J),J = 1,N)
    c. PRINT *(J,YES(J),NO(J),J = 1,N)
 *d.   DO 50 K = 1,2
          PRINT *,K,(YES(J),J = 1,N)
      50 CONTINUE

12. Specify READ statements with implied-DO lists for each case below.

    a. Input Lines

        100,125,95 ←—— Integer array SALES
        40,20,75 ←—— Integer array COST

    b. Input Lines

        100,40,125,20,95,75
        ↑ ↑ ↑ ↑ ↑ ↑———— Integer array SALES
                    ———— Integer array COST

EXAMPLE 7.4 (Continued)

Case	Implied-DO List Example	Equivalent to	Comment
a.	READ *,(A(I),I = 2,6,2)	READ *,A(2),A(4),A(6)	The DO-variable doesn't have to start at 1; it can start at any value. In addition, the increment can be any value.
b.	READ *,(A(I),I = 1,2),(B(I),I = 1,2)	READ *,A(1),A(2),B(1),B(2)	Read or print lists can contain more than one implied-DO list.
c.	READ *,(A(I),B(I),C(I),I = 1,2)	READ *,A(1),B(1),C(1),A(2),B(2),C(2)	The list section within the implied-DO list (dlist) can contain more than one array element name.
d.	PRINT *,X,Y,(A(I),I = 1,3),Z	PRINT *,X,Y,A(1),A(2),A(3),Z	The implied-DO list may appear along with other items in the print list.
e.	PRINT *,(I,A(I),I = 1,2)	PRINT *,1,A(1),2,A(2)	Nonarray items inside the implied-DO list are also repeated.
f.	READ *,N,(A(I),I = 1,N)	READ *,N,A(1),A(2),A(3)	If the first data value in the record is 3, the implied-DO list is equivalent to what is shown. This approach should be used with caution since an error in data could cause a difficult debugging session. It's better to read N through a separate statement.

13. Do you see anything wrong with the following? Explain.

   a. READ *,N,(X(J),J = 1,N)
   b. READ *,(J,X(J),J = 1,N)
   c. PRINT *,(X(P)**2,P = A,B,C/D)

EXAMPLE 7.5   Formatted I/O Using an Implied-DO List[4]

When we use the implied-DO list with format specifications, how the data are read or printed depends on how we code the format specification. For example,

```
    READ 1,(DEPOS(I), I = 1,3)
  1 FORMAT(3I6)
```

                                 Input Record

      1 2 3 4 5 6 7 8 9 10 11 12 13 14 15 16 17 18 . . .

      ──

        3 5 0 0   5 0 0 0   4 0 0 0

stores three values from one record; however, if we change the FORMAT statement to

```
  1 FORMAT(I6)
```

                            Input Records

               1 2 3 4 5 6 7 8 . . .

              ────────────────────

               3 5 0 0
               5 0 0 0
               4 0 0 0

then three values would be read into the array DEPOS, but from three records (one value per record). This occurs because of *imbalance* between list and descriptors; that is, the input list has more variables (three) than the FORMAT statement has repeatable descriptors (one). If you're fuzzy about the imbalance rules, review Section D.2 at the end of the text.
    The statements

```
    PRINT 3,(DEPOS(I),I = 1,3)
  3 FORMAT(1X,3I5)
```

---

[4] This example requires knowledge of topics in Modules B, C, and D.

print three values on one line as follows.

However, if we change the FORMAT statement to

    3 FORMAT (1X,I5)

then the imbalance rule causes the output to appear on three lines.

Follow-up Exercises

14. We wish to store the values 10, 20, 30, and 40 in the first four storage locations of the integer array MONEY. Indicate where you would place the data for each case.

Input Records

1 2 3 4 5 6 7 8 9 10 11 12 13 14 15 16 17 18 19 20 . . .

a.   READ 1, (MONEY(K), K = 1,4)
       1 FORMAT(4I3)
b.   READ 1, (MONEY(K), K = 1,4)
       1 FORMAT(I3)
c.   READ 1, (MONEY(K), K = 1,4)
       1 FORMAT(2I3)
d.   READ 1, (MONEY(K), K = 1,4)
       1 FORMAT(8I3)
e.   1 FORMAT(I3)
       DO 10 K = 1,4
          READ 1, MONEY(K)
    10 CONTINUE

15. Suppose we wish to output the contents of MONEY as defined in the preceding exercise. Indicate how output would appear for each case.

a.   PRINT 15, (MONEY(J), J = 1,4)
   15 FORMAT(1X,4I5)

b.   PRINT 15, (MONEY(J), J = 1,4)
   15 FORMAT(1X,I5)

c.   PRINT 15, (MONEY(J), J = 1,4)
   15 FORMAT(1X,2I5)

d.   15 FORMAT(1X,I1,I5)
      DO 20 J = 1,4
        PRINT 15, J,MONEY(J)
   20 CONTINUE

e.   PRINT 15, (J,MONEY(J), J = 1,4)
   15 FORMAT(1X,I1,I5)

*16. Consider real array SAG with 99 declared array elements. For a given run, N represents the number of elements to be used in SAG.

a. Write a complete program which inputs the single record given by

Input Record

1 2 3 4 5 6 7 8 9 10 11 12 13 14 15 16 17

3   2 5   5 5   6 5

N   SAG(1)   SAG(2)   SAG(3)

and outputs as follows:

b. Write a complete program which inputs the single record given in part a and outputs as follows:

Using the Short-List Technique

Entire arrays may be read or written by placing the array name without subscripts in the input or output command. This is sometimes referred to as the **short-list technique.** For example, in the program segment

    INTEGER DEPOS(3)

    READ *,DEPOS   ← Equivalent to READ *,(DEPOS(I), I = 1,3)

the computer reads in three values from *one* record, storing the first value in DEPOS(1), the second value in DEPOS(2), and the third value in DEPOS(3).

The presence of the array name without a subscript indicates that the values for *all the elements* in the array, *as specified in the type statement,* are to be read or written. Accordingly, this technique only can be used to read or write an *entire* array (as specified in the type statement); if only part of the array is to be processed, then the DO statement or implied DO must be used. To illustrate what we mean, the program segment

    REAL PRESS(10)
    READ *,PRESS
    PRINT *,PRESS

reads ten values on one record and prints ten values on one line. If we wish to input or output only five values of the array, but PRESS has been dimensioned to ten, then we can't use the short-list technique.

Follow-up Exercise

17. Describe I/O records for the following, where we wish to store 10 for N, the numbers 1, 2, . . . , 8 for the array KIN, and the fractions 0.1, 0.2, . . . , 1.5 for the array FRAC.

    a. INTEGER KIN(8)
        REAL   FRAC(15)
        READ *,N
        READ *,KIN
        READ *,FRAC

    b. Instead of the READ statements in part a use
        READ *,N,KIN,FRAC

    c.
        1 FORMAT(I2)
        2 FORMAT(8I1)
        3 FORMAT(15F4.1)
          READ 1,N
          READ 2,KIN
          READ 3,FRAC

    How would output appear for each of the following?

    d.   PRINT 4, KIN,(FRAC(J), J = 1,N)
            4 FORMAT(1X,8I2,15F5.2)
    e.   PRINT 4, KIN,(FRAC(J), J = 1,N)
            4 FORMAT(1X,8I2/1X,10F5.2)
    ** f.   PRINT 4, KIN,(FRAC(J), J = 1,N)
            4 FORMAT(1X,8(I2/1X)/(1X,F5.2))

7.5
MANIPULATING ARRAYS

This section presents four examples that illustrate techniques of manipulation for one-dimensional arrays.

EXAMPLE 7.6   Initialization

Often it is necessary to set each element in an array to some initial value. For example, to initialize all values in a 100-element real array to zero, we could write the following instructions.

        DO 10 I = 1,100
            SUM(I) = 0.
    10 CONTINUE

As the value of I changes from 1 to 100, each of the 100 locations in the array SUM is set to zero.

The above procedure initializes the array during execution of the program. Alternatively, we can initialize the array during compilation using the *DATA statement* first discussed in Section 4.6.

```
DATA SUM/100*0./ ◄─────────────── Using the short-list technique
DATA (SUM(I), I = 1,100)/100*0./ ◄──── Using an implied-DO list.
                                  Note: DO-variable and DO expressions
                                  must be integer and entirely
                                  defined within the implied-DO list.
```

Use of the DATA statement is efficient if we only need to initialize the array once. If the array needs to be reinitialized during execution, then we must use the DO-loop approach, since the DATA statement is nonexecutable.

EXAMPLE 7.7   Accumulation of a Sum

Quite often it is necessary to perform arithmetic operations on all the elements in an array. The following segment from Example 7.1 illustrates the accumulation of a sum.

```
      TOT = 0
      DO 10 I = 1,3
         READ *,DEPOS(I)
         TOT = TOT + DEPOS(I)
   10 CONTINUE
```

As the value of I changes from 1 to 3, each element of the array DEPOS is added to the accumulator TOT. When I = 1 we actually are executing

   TOT = TOT + DEPOS(1)   or   TOT = 0 + 3500;

when I = 2 we are executing

   TOT = TOT + DEPOS(2)   or   TOT = 3500 + 5000;

and when I = 3 we are executing

   TOT = TOT + DEPOS(3)   or   TOT = 8500 + 4000.

Thus, 12500 gets stored in TOT.

EXAMPLE 7.8   Correspondence Among Arrays

Sometimes we need to perform operations among corresponding elements of different arrays. For example, assume that a banking program has stored the current month's total dollar deposits in array DEPA and the total dollar withdrawals in array WITA. A third array can be used to accumulate the new balance (BAL), as follows.

```
      DO 30 I = 1,N
         BAL(I) = BAL(I) + DEPA(I) − WITA(I)
   30 CONTINUE
```

where N represents the number of customers to be processed. Note that the appearance of BAL(I) on the right side reflects the previous value of BAL(I), that is, last month's balance for the Ith account.

Sometimes we need not manipulate all elements in an array. For example, the following logic updates only specific accounts that are read in.

```
      INTEGER MAX
      PARAMETER (MAX = 1000)
      REAL  BAL(MAX),DEPA(MAX),WITA(MAX)
      READ *,J
30    IF (J .GT. O .AND. J .LE. MAX) THEN
         BAL(J) = BAL(J) + DEPA(J) − WITA(J)
         READ *,J
         GO TO 30
      END IF
```

If J has a value of 8 the eighth array element in BAL is updated by adding the value in the eighth location of DEPA and subtracting the value in the eighth location of WITA.

Did you notice the use of MAX, the symbolic name for a constant, as the upper dimension bound in the REAL statement? This approach simplifies subsequent updates of dimension bounds, thereby reducing software costs for programs that have many arrays.

EXAMPLE 7.9 Character Arrays

Character arrays are particularly useful when we need to store and manipulate a set of data with related character values, such as days of the week, months of the year, names of employees, and so on. Study the following program and then answer Exercise 23.

```
      CHARACTER DAY(7)*9
      DO 10 J = 1,7
         READ *,DAY(J)
10    CONTINUE
      READ *,K
20    IF (K .GE. 1 .AND. K .LE. 7) THEN
         PRINT *,DAY(K)
         READ *,K
         GOTO 20
      END IF
         PRINT *,'FINISHED'
      END
```

Sample Input	Sample Output
'MONDAY'	WEDNESDAY
'TUESDAY'	MONDAY
'WEDNESDAY'	SATURDAY
'THURSDAY'	FINISHED
'FRIDAY'	
'SATURDAY'	
'SUNDAY'	
3	
1	
6	
0	

Follow-up Exercises

18. With respect to Example 7.6, what would be wrong with the following?

    DATA (SUM(I),I = 1,N)/N*0./

19. A student, wishing to initialize an array with ten elements to zero, wrote the following.

    TOTAL (K) = 0.

On seeing this, his girlfriend (who also takes FORTRAN programming) says the above doesn't make sense because K is undefined. Perhaps, she reasons, we can try a short-list approach.

    TOTAL = 0.

Explain why each approach would provoke an error. Correct this segment of the program.

20. Sometimes, beginning programmers will try to use the implied-DO list for arithmetic operations. This is not possible. Correct the following attempt at summing the K elements in array REVEN.

    SUM = (SUM + REVEN(I), I = 1,K)

21. Suppose that before running the first program segment in Example 7.8, memory appears as follows:

What changes would occur for the first two customer accounts following execution of the first program segment in Example 7.8?

22. Modify the loop body in the second program segment in Example 7.8 to print the account number, ACCNO(J), and new balance whenever the new balance is less than zero.

23. With respect to Example 7.9:

a. What gets stored in DAY(1), DAY(2), . . . , DAY(7)?

b. Indicate output for the numeric input

    5
    4
    10

c. Can you think of a simpler alternative for defining values in array DAY?

* 24. Write a short program such that the sample numeric input

results in the output

    JULY 4, 1776

Terminate input if the year is zero or less. Print an error message if data input for either the month or the day is out of range.

* 25. DO-WHILE Statement. If your FORTRAN dialect has a DO-WHILE statement, use it to revise

a. The second segment in Example 7.8

b. Example 7.9

Which approach do you prefer?

26. Write code for the following manipulations of the 25-element integer array LIST.

a. Input N values in reverse order, that is, the first value gets stored in LIST(N), the second in LIST(N-1), and so on.

b. Find and print the largest value in the array.

c. Print locations of array elements (values of subscript expressions) that have values of zero.

*d. Create a second array, LIST2, consisting of all nonzero elements in LIST.

* e. Move all values in the array up one position, that is, the value in LIST(1) gets moved to LIST(0), LIST(2) to LIST(1), and so on. Insert −99 in the last array element.

7.6
APPLICATIONS

This section illustrates four common applications of one-dimensional arrays.

EXAMPLE 7.10   Direct Access to Array Element—SAT Scores

A more efficient method of utilizing arrays in some applications is to access or process values *directly* from one array location without moving sequentially through an entire array. To illustrate the direct access concept, consider the following problem.

Every year State College prints a Fact Book that includes average SAT scores of students categorized as freshman, sophomore, junior, and senior. Figure 7.1 and

FIGURE 7.1 *Algorithm for Direct Access Problem*

```
Initialize arrays
READ number students
DO WHILE student needs processing
   READ class code, SAT verbal, SAT math
   Combine SAT verbal and math
   Update class count by direct access
   Update class SAT sums by direct access
END DO
DO WHILE class needs processing
   PRINT class, count, average
END DO
Stop
```

the following program illustrate how an array can be used to accumulate these data.

```
C     SAT SCORES
C
C     KEY:
C        NOS     = NUMBER OF STUDENTS
C        CLASS   = CLASS CODE (1 = FRESHMAN, 2 = SOPHOMORE, ...)
C        SATVER  = SAT VERBAL SCORE
C        SATMTH  = SAT MATH SCORE
C        SATTOT  = SAT COMBINED VERBAL AND MATH SCORE
C        COUNT   = ARRAY CONTAINING COUNT OF STUDENTS BY CLASS
C        SUMSAT  = ARRAY CONTAINING SUM OF COMBINED SAT SCORES
C                   BY CLASS
C
      INTEGER NOS,CLASS,SATVER,SATMTH,SATTOT
      INTEGER COUNT(4),SUMSAT(4)
C
      DATA COUNT,SUMSAT/8*0/
C
      READ *,NOS
      DO 10 I = 1,NOS
         READ *,CLASS,SATVER,SATMTH
         SATTOT = SATVER + SATMTH
         COUNT (CLASS) = COUNT(CLASS)  + 1          } Direct access
         SUMSAT(CLASS) = SUMSAT(CLASS) + SATTOT     } logic
   10 CONTINUE
C
      DO 20 J = 1,4
         PRINT *,J,COUNT(J),SUMSAT(J)/COUNT(J)
   20 CONTINUE
C
      END
```

Sample Input	Sample Output
5	See Exercise 27b.
2,580,640	
3,720,680	
2,610,560	
1,560,590	
2,580,420	

Note 1. The variable CLASS stores coded values 1 through 4, which represent 1 for freshman, 2 for sophomore, 3 for junior, and 4 for senior. The array COUNT is used to store the accumulated count of students in each class. For example, COUNT(1) represents number of freshmen, COUNT(2) represents number of

sophomores, and so forth. The array SUMSAT stores the sum of combined SAT scores by class. For example, SUMSAT(1) will contain the sum of combined (math and verbal) SAT scores for all freshmen.

Note 2. If a student has a class standing of 2, then the statement

COUNT(CLASS) = COUNT(CLASS) + 1

increments by 1 the second storage location in COUNT. In other words, the equivalent statement given by

COUNT(2) = COUNT(2) + 1

is executed. Thus CLASS acts as a "pointer" (subscript expression) to the specific location in COUNT that is to be manipulated. The same approach is used to manipulate or update the array SUMSAT.

Note 3. Notice that both COUNT(J) and COUNT(CLASS) are used in this program to access specific elements in COUNT. Our use of J rather than CLASS as the subscript expression of COUNT in loop 20 illustrates the fact that one should focus on the *value* taken on by the subscript expression rather than the subscript expression itself. We have no need to use CLASS as a subscript outside of loop 10; hence we use the simpler J.

Note 4. In this particular example, the concept of "direct access" is illustrated by the fact that we need not loop through the entire array each time we wish to update (increment or sum) the contents of a specific location in COUNT or SUMSAT. The pointer CLASS conveniently serves to locate specific elements in COUNT and SUMSAT.

Follow-up Exercises

27. For the program in Example 7.10:
    a. Assuming a snapshot of memory is taken just before the execution of CONTINUE, indicate how the storage locations of COUNT and SUMSAT change as the program processes the sample input data in loop 10.

I	CLASS	SATVER	SATMTH	SATTOT	COUNT(1)	COUNT(2)	COUNT(3)	COUNT(4)	SUMSAT(1)	SUMSAT(2)	SUMSAT(3)	SUMSAT(4)
—	—				0	0	0	0	0	0	0	0
1												
2												
3												
4												
5												

    b. Indicate how the output would appear.
*28. Suppose we wish to process data for each of N years in the same run. Appropriately modify the program in Example 7.10.

EXAMPLE 7.11   Table Look-up: Life Insurance Premium

The term **table look-up** refers to procedures for accessing data that are stored in a table. These procedures satisfy a very common need across a wide variety of professional fields and occupational areas. In this example we work with one-dimensional "tables"; in the next chapter, we discuss two-dimensional tables.

Suppose that a life insurance company uses the following premium schedule to bill its customers. In this case, the annual premium is based on the age of the policyholder. For example, a policyholder who is 47 years old would pay a premium of $327 per year.

Premium Schedule

Upper Age Limit	Annual Premium ($)
25	277
35	287
45	307
55	327
65	357

When looking up information in a table, three basic elements are required. First, there is the "search key," which is the item of information that helps you to locate the right place within the table. In the case of the life insurance company, each policyholder's age is the search key.

The table that is to be searched usually makes up the other two sets of elements needed for the search: (1) the set of "keys" used to access the proper location, and (2) the set of "function values." In the premium schedule the set of keys is the limits on the various age classes, and the corresponding premiums are the function values.

Figures 7.2 and 7.3 describe the algorithm that processes policyholders. The stepwise refinement procedure in Figure 7.2 is fully described in Module E. Study these figures before going on to the program and discussion that follow.

```
C     LIFE INSURANCE PREMIUMS
C
C     KEY:
C       NAME    = NAME OF POLICYHOLDER
C       AGE     = AGE OF POLICYHOLDER
C       AGELIM  = ARRAY CONTAINING UPPER AGE LIMITS
C       PREM    = ARRAY CONTAINING PREMIUMS
C       N       = NUMBER OF POLICYHOLDERS
C
        CHARACTER NAME*20
        INTEGER    AGELIM(5),PREM(5),AGE
C
        DO 10 I = 1,5
          READ *,AGELIM(I),PREM(I)      } Premium schedule input
     10 CONTINUE
C
```

FIGURE 7.2 Stepwise Refinement of Pseudocode for Table Look-up Problem

STEP 1	STEP 2	STEP 3

READ premium schedule———

DO WHILE premium schedule incomplete
   READ age limit, premium
END DO

Housekeeping———

PRINT header
READ no. policyholders

Process policyholders———

DO WHILE policyholders need processing
   READ name, age
   Determine premium
   PRINT name, premium
END DO

Initialize subscript expression
DO WHILE age > age limit
   Increment subscript expression
END DO

Stop

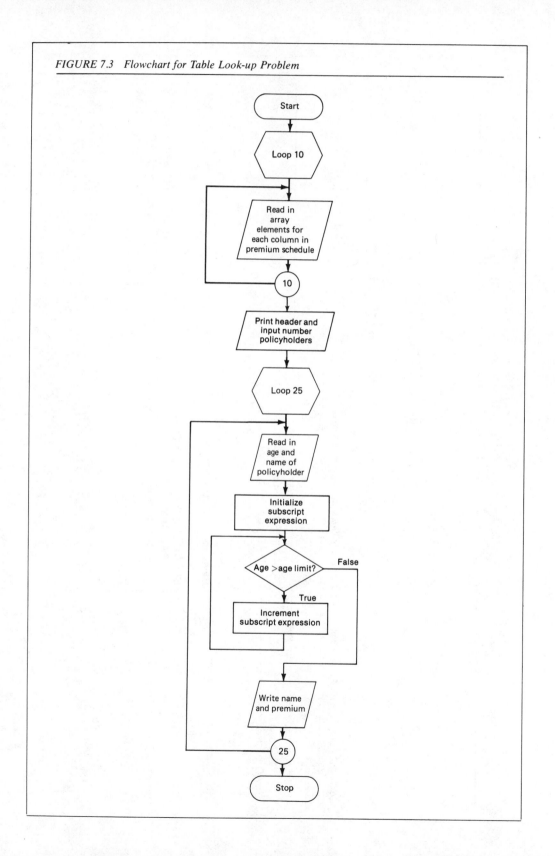

FIGURE 7.3   Flowchart for Table Look-up Problem

Start

Loop 10

Read in
array
elements for
each column in
premium schedule

10

Print header and
input number
policyholders

Loop 25

Read in
age and
name of
policyholder

Initialize
subscript
expression

Age >age limit?   False

True

Increment
subscript expression

Write name
and premium

25

Stop

```
        PRINT *,'NAME                    PREMIUM'
        READ *,N
        DO 25 J = 1,N
           READ *,NAME,AGE
C
           I = 1
   15   IF (AGE .GT. AGELIM(I)) THEN
           I = I + 1
              GO TO 15
        END IF
        PRINT *,NAME,PREM(I)
C
   25 CONTINUE
C
        END
```

⎫
⎬ Table look-up logic
⎠

Input data for the premium schedule and two customers are described below.

Input Records
─────────────

```
25,277
35,287
45,307
55,327
65,357
2
'CLARK S. KENT',42
'LOIS S. LANE',28
```

The premium schedule is read into two one-dimensional arrays: AGELIM and PREM. Memory locations for these arrays appear as follows *after* loop 10 is completed:

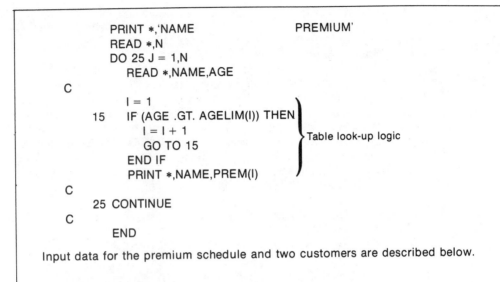

AGELIM(1)	25		PREM(1)	277
AGELIM(2)	35		PREM(2)	287
AGELIM(3)	45		PREM(3)	307
AGELIM(4)	55		PREM(4)	327
AGELIM(5)	65		PREM(5)	357

Next, the table header is printed and the number of policyholders that need to be processed (N) is read in, after which we enter DO-loop 25. The first statement in the loop reads in the policyholder's name and age.

The next segment contains the table look-up logic. In this case the "search key" is the value stored in AGE and the "set of keys" is the set of array elements in AGELIM. Starting with the first element (when I = 1), the loop test sequentially evaluates each element of AGELIM until the proper age class is found; that is, until the age of the policyholder (search key) is less than or equal to an age limit value in array AGELIM. When this condition is satisfied (the DO-WHILE-loop test gives a "false" result), the appropriate premium (function value) is identified as the array element of PREM that corresponds to the matching age class. For example, when 42 is stored in AGE, the DO-WHILE-loop operates as follows.

I	Is AGE Greater Than AGELIM(I)?	Result
1	True; 42 is greater than 25	Continue looping
2	True; 42 is greater than 35	Continue looping
3	False; 42 is not greater than 45	Exit from loop

Thus, when loop exit is achieved, the statement

    PRINT *,NAME,PREM(I)

is executed, and the correct value of 3 in I (age class) is used as the value of the subscript expression for PREM. In this case, the contents of PREM(3) are printed, which gives a premium of $307 for someone aged 42.

Sample output for the given input data is shown below.

NAME	PREMIUM
CLARK S. KENT	307
LOIS S. LANE	287

Follow-up Exercises

29. With respect to Example 7.11:
   a. What would the output look like if the last input record were as follows?

      'RIP VAN WINKLE', 99

   *b. Modify the program to print the message

       OVER 65--UNINSURABLE

   beginning in column 25 of the same line as the person's name for any person over 65 years of age.

30. Do you see anything wrong with the following table look-up logic?

       DO 15 I = 1,5
          IF (AGE .LE. AGELIM(I)) GO TO 20
       15 CONTINUE
       20 PRINT *,NAME,PREM(I)

* **31. DO-WHILE Statement.** If your FORTRAN dialect has a DO-WHILE statement, use it to revise the table look-up logic in Example 7.11. Which approach do you prefer?

EXAMPLE 7.12 Polynomial Plot

This example illustrates how we can use a one-dimensional array to plot the coordinates (x,y) of any polynomial function up to third degree,

$$y = b_0 + b_1x + b_2x^2 + b_3x^3$$

where the b_i are coefficients of the function and the values of x run from a lower limit to an upper limit in any desired increment.

Specifically, we plot the second-degree polynomial function

$$y = 21 - 2x - 3x^2$$

for values of x from -5 to $+5$ in increments of 0.5. In this case, $b_0 = 21$, $b_1 = -2$, $b_2 = -3$, and $b_3 = 0$; and y takes on values that range from -64.0 to 21.3.

Figure 7.4 illustrates the algorithm for the program on the next page.

The program plots the function by placing the desired symbol (in this case X according to data input) at the appropriate (x, y) coordinate. Values of x and y are printed along the left margin.

The graph appears with the horizontal axis as the y-axis and the vertical axis as the x-axis. Thus you should turn the page for conventional viewing.

Note how the 101-element character array LINE is used to print the function. First, the entire array is initialized to blanks through the DATA statement. Then, once the value of Y is determined, a corresponding location in the array LINE is set

FIGURE 7.4 *Algorithm for Polynomial Plot*

```
READ plot symbol
READ b₀, b₁, b₂, b₃, x-range
DO WHILE x-values remain
    Calculate y
    Place plot symbol in plot line vector
    PRINT x, y, plot line vector
    Eliminate plot symbol from plot line vector
END DO
Stop
```

```
C   POLYNOMIAL PLOT PROGRAM
C
C   KEY:
C    LINE   = PLOT LINE VECTOR
C    BLANK  = STORES BLANK CHARACTER
C    SYMBOL = STORES PLOT SYMBOL
C    X      = INDEPENDENT VARIABLE
C    Y      = DEPENDENT VARIABLE
C    B0,... = POLYNOMIAL COEFFICIENTS
C    LOWLIM = LOWER LIMIT ON X
C    UPLIM  = UPPER LIMIT ON X
C    INC    = INCREMENT IN X
C-----------------------------------------------------------------
      CHARACTER LINE(-70:30)*1,BLANK*1,SYMBOL*1
      REAL      X,Y,B0,B1,B2,B3,LOWLIM,UPLIM,INC
C-----------------------------------------------------------------
      DATA  LINE,BLANK /101*' ',' '/
C-----------------------------------------------------------------
      READ *,SYMBOL
      READ *,B0,B1,B2,B3
      READ *,LOWLIM,UPLIM,INC
C-----------------------------------------------------------------
      DO 10 X = LOWLIM,UPLIM,INC
         Y = B0 + B1*X + B2*X**2 + B3*X**3
         K = INT(Y)
         LINE(K) = SYMBOL
         PRINT 20,X,Y,LINE
         LINE(K) = BLANK
   10 CONTINUE
C-----------------------------------------------------------------
   20 FORMAT(1X,2F7.1,101A1)
C-----------------------------------------------------------------
      END
```

Sample Input

```
'X'
21.,-2.,-3.,0
-5,5,0.5
```

Sample Output

```
 -5.0  -44.0                             X
 -4.5  -30.3                                   X
 -4.0  -19.0                                      X
 -3.5   -8.3                                          X
 -3.0    0.0                                            X
 -2.5    7.3                                              X
 -2.0   13.0                                               X
 -1.5   17.5                                                 X
 -1.0   20.0                                                  X
 -0.5   21.5                                                   X
  0.0   21.0                                                   X
  0.5   19.5                                                   X
  1.0   16.0                                                  X
  1.5   11.5                                                X
  2.0    5.0                                             X
  2.5   -2.3                                          X
  3.0  -12.0                                     X
  3.5  -22.3                              X
  4.0  -35.0                        X
  4.5  -48.3                  X
  5.0  -64.0     X
```

equal to the plot symbol (all other elements in the array LINE remain blank). For example, at $x = -5.0$ we have $y = -44.0$ so that LINE would appear as follows:

LINE(-70)	LINE(-69)	. . .	LINE(-44)	. . .	LINE(29)	LINE(30)
ƀ	ƀ		X		ƀ	ƀ

Once a line of the graph is printed, the location containing the plot symbol is reinitialized to blank, to get ready for the next value of y.

Finally, note that this program is restricted to y values of at least -70 but less than 31 since the integer part of the y value is the subscript expression value for LINE, and these values are limited to the range -70 to 30 inclusive according to the dimension declarator in the CHARACTER statement. By the way, we could have omitted the length specification for character variable and array names as follows:

CHARACTER LINE $(-70:30)$,BLANK,SYMBOL

since a length of 1 is assumed when the length specification is omitted.

Follow-up Exercises

32. What change would you make to plot the asterisk symbol instead of X?

33. Modify the program to plot any mathematical function (not just polynomials) whereby the user provides the appropriate line of code that represents the function.

*   **34.** This program can be generalized to process any n-degree polynomial by storing the coefficients $b_0, b_1, \ldots, b_n$ in a one-dimensional array and using the subscript expression value to represent the exponent on x. Modify the program accordingly. *Hint:* Use a DO-loop to calculate values of y.

**   **35.** A shortcoming of the current program is restrictions of y values to -70 or above and less than 31.
    a.   Modify the program to handle any range of y values, so long as the integer difference between the minimum and maximum values doesn't exceed 100. *Hint:* Use limits of 0 and 100 for the dimension bounds on LINE.
    b.   Same as part a, except the range in y can exceed 100. *Hint:* LINE still has bounds of 0 and 100, but values of y are proportionally scaled to between 1 and 100.

EXAMPLE 7.13   Sorting

One of the most common operations performed in data processing, called **sorting,** is arranging data either numerically or alphabetically into sequential order according to some criterion. For example, a student file contains a number of records, one for each student. Each record contains student name and identification number in addition to other data. We could sort the file either by ID number in ascending or descending order or we could arrange the file alphabetically using the student names. In either case, the item in the record that is used to sort the file is known as the ''sort key.''

Let's assume we want a listing of students in ascending numeric order according to their ID numbers. For simplicity, let's further assume we have only four students. The one-dimensional array called LIST is used to store and sort ID numbers, as shown below.

For this problem, we use the **exchange method** of sorting. On each pass through the array, the first element is compared with the second: the smaller number is stored in the first position and the larger number is stored in the second position. Then the second element of the array is compared with the third: the smaller number is placed in the second position and the larger number is placed in the third position. This process of comparison and rearranging continues throughout the entire array. When this first pass through the array is complete, the array is processed again, from beginning to end. This procedure continues until no exchanges take place in a pass through the entire array. The exchange method is also called a **bubble sort** since items that are below their correct positions in the array tend to move upward to their proper places, like bubbles in a carbonated drink.

Figure 7.5 shows exploded pseudocode and Figure 7.6 illustrates the flowchart for the sorting program below.

FIGURE 7.5 *Stepwise Refinement of Pseudocode for Sorting Problem*

STEP 1

STEP 2

STEP 3

READ no. items, list

Sort list
{
DO WHILE sort incomplete
   DO WHILE items in list remain
      IF two items need exchanging THEN
         Exchange items
         END IF
   END DO
END DO
}
{
Temporary location = current array element
Current array element = previous array element
Previous array element = temporary location
}

PRINT sorted list
Stop

FIGURE 7.6   *Flowchart for Sorting Program*

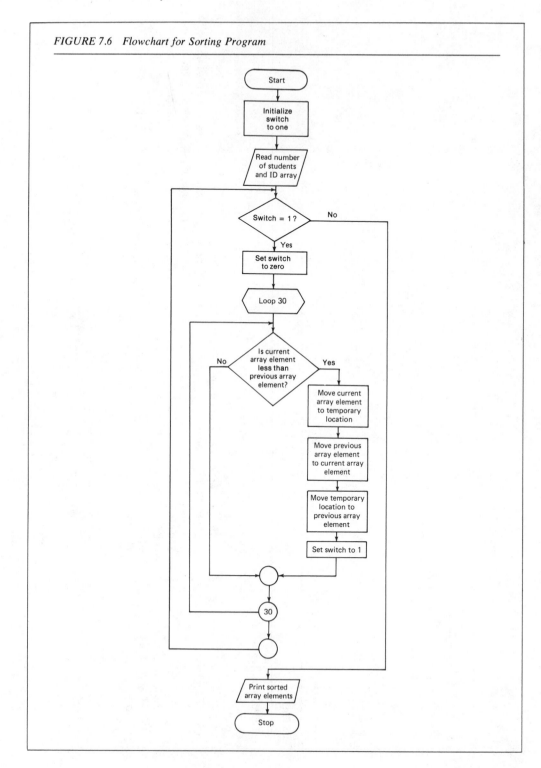

```
      C     SORT PROGRAM IN ASCENDING NUMERIC ORDER
      C
      C     KEY:
      C       N        = NUMBER OF ITEMS
      C       LIST     = INTEGER ARRAY TO BE SORTED
      C       SWITCH = 0 IF SORT COMPLETE; 1 IF NOT COMPLETE
      C       TEMP     = TEMPORARY STORAGE LOCATION
      C
              INTEGER N,LIST(100),SWITCH,TEMP
      C
              DATA SWITCH/1/
      C
              READ *,N
              READ *,(LIST(J),J = 1,N)
      C
          20 IF (SWITCH .EQ. 1) THEN
                SWITCH = 0
                DO 30 J = 2,N
                  IF (LIST(J) .LT. LIST(J − 1)) THEN
                    TEMP = LIST(J)
                    LIST(J) = LIST(J − 1)
                    LIST(J − 1) = TEMP
                    SWITCH = 1
                  END IF
          30    CONTINUE
                GO TO 20
              END IF
      C
              PRINT *,'SORT COMPLETED'
              PRINT *,(LIST(J),J = 1,N)
      C
              END
```

For the input line

```
4
8321,3076,2501,7771
```

we would get the following output.

```
SORT COMPLETED
   2501        3076        7771        8321
```

The logic within loop 30 illustrates the bubble sort. The subscript expressions J and $J − 1$ are used to compare values stored in adjacent array elements. When an exchange takes place between two adjacent elements, a separate memory location (TEMP) serves as a temporary location to hold one of the values while the exchange takes place. To understand exactly what's happening, follow the diagram and steps below for the case $J = 2$ in loop 30.

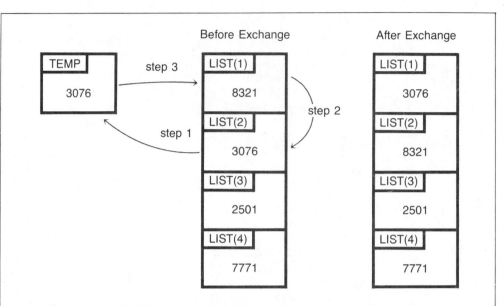

The variable SWITCH acts as a switch by storing either 0 or 1. If the value in SWITCH is 1 after a complete pass through the array LIST, then the sort is not complete and the entire array must be scanned again for the numbers out of sequence. If the value in SWITCH is 0 after a complete pass through the array LIST, then the sort is complete.

Follow-up Exercises

36. Fill in the following table based on the data in the example.

		Contents When Control Is at 30 CONTINUE				
J	TEMP	LIST(1)	LIST(2)	LIST(3)	LIST(4)	SWITCH
2	3076	3076	8321	2501	7771	1
3						
4						
2						
3						
4						
2						
3						
4						

How many passes through the entire array does it take to sort the array? How many passes does it take to terminate execution?

37. Make appropriate changes in the program for a numeric sort in descending order. Test your program by tracing through the given data.

38. Is it possible to sort alphabetic data using the program in Example 7.13? Make necessary modifications to the program and run it on your system to sort the following data: SMITH,JONES,DAVIS,KELLY.

*39. DO-WHILE statement.   If your FORTRAN dialect has a DO-WHILE statement, then use it to revise the switch logic. Which approach do you prefer?

7.7
COMMON ERRORS

Arrays are great for giving a lot of practice in debugging. Often one "small" error will result in an "avalanche" of error messages. Pay attention to the following and you might avoid apoplexy.

1. *Declaration of array.*   Don't forget to declare your array by using a type or DIMENSION statement. If you forget to dimension an array, then you will get a *syntax* error message for *each* line containing an array element name. So, if you get an error message such as "UNDEFINED ARRAY" or "UNDEFINED FUNCTION" for each line where the array element name appears, then check whether or not you dimensioned the array.

   Also, don't forget to declare arrays before their use in the program. To be safe, place your DIMENSION or type statement before all other executable statements in the program.

   Finally, you must use an integer constant to declare the size of your array. Don't try

   ```
   REAL X(N)
   ```

   if N is a variable name, unless you like to see syntax errors. A variable number of locations is not permitted, except for the material discussed in Chapter 9. You can, however, use symbolic names of constants as dimension bounds; which we illustrated on page 254.

2. *Subscripts.*   If you get an *execution* error message such as "SUBSCRIPT OUT OF BOUNDS" or "SUBSCRIPT OUT OF RANGE," then a subscript value violates the bounds in your dimension declaration. Two kinds of mistakes are possible here: either you reserved too few locations for your array or you made a logic error in assigning values to subscript expressions. In the latter case, you might want to diagnose the error by using a *trace* to print subscript expression values, as illustrated by the following example.

```
        REAL X(5)
          .
          .
          .
        DO 10 J = 1,5
          K = 5 - J
          PRINT *,J,K
          X(K) = J**3
     10 CONTINUE
          .
          .
          .
```

Output
_____

```
    1   4
    2   3
    3   2
    4   1
    5   0
SUBSCRIPT OUT OF BOUNDS
```

The error message is the result of a zero in the subscript K. If we wish K to take on the successive values 5, 4, 3, 2, 1, then the statement that defines K should read

$$K = 6 - J$$

Other common subscripting errors include using a real variable or constant for a subscript, and entirely forgetting the subscript for a variable that has been declared an array.

3. *Array names.* A common point of confusion among beginning programmers is exactly what represents the *array name*. For example, are B(J) and B(I) one and the same array? Yes. In this case, the array name is B, not B(J) or B(I). B(J) and B(I) are called *array element names,* which simply reference specific elements in array B.

A related problem is the following: Many students, thinking that the parentheses are part of the array name, believe it is all right also to use B as a *variable name* that is different from the array B. Not so. Once B is dimensioned, the variable B is treated as an array throughout the program, as the following illustrates.

B treated as array name by programmer; no syntax errors.

```
        REAL B(100)
        DATA B/100*0./
        DO 20 I = 1,100
          READ *,J
          B = J
          B(I) = B(I) + B
     20 CONTINUE
        PRINT *,B
          .
          .
```

B treated as variable name by programmer; syntax errors.

4. *Initialization.* If an array is to act as a summer or counter, then don't forget to initialize its contents to whatever values are required. (See Example 7.6.) Some compilers automatically initialize all storage locations to zero, but others don't. If yours does not, you will get an execution error the first time your program attempts to use an uninitialized counter or summer. Sometimes during the same computer run you need to reinitialize your array. If so, don't use a DATA statement, as illustrated below for a 500-element array.

Correct	Incorrect

DO 20 J = 1,N
  DO 10 I = 1,500
    SUM(I) = 0.
10   CONTINUE
   .
   .
   .
20 CONTINUE
	DO 20 J = 1,N
	  DATA SUM/500*0./
	   .
	   .
	   .
	20 CONTINUE

A DATA statement is nonexecutable, so it would not be possible to reinitialize an array by this method once the program begins executing.

5. *I/O.* Don't forget to coordinate the placement of data on the input record with the design of your input loop, as the following illustrates.

Input Record 1 2 3 4 5 6 7 8 9 . . .	Program Segment

1 0 2 5	1 FORMAT(3I2)
	  DO 10 I = 1,3
	    READ 1,LOAD(I)
	10 CONTINUE

An "OUT OF DATA" execution error message would occur here, since loop 10 attempts to read three records. Don't forget that a new input record is processed each time a READ statement is executed. Also, the list in the foregoing READ statement contains only one array element, so the fact that 3I2 appears in the FORMAT statement is irrelevant according to the imbalance rules. For the given input record, we need to use an implied-DO list.

Finally, unless you use the short-list technique, don't forget to use a loop to output an array. We often see the following approach in an attempt to output the entire contents of an array:

PRINT 15,ARR(I)

This statement either prints one element (if an integer value within the bounds of the array is stored for I) or results in an execution error.

ADDITIONAL EXERCISES

40. Define or explain each of the following.

array	vector	table look-up
array name	one-dimensional array	sorting
array element	dimension declarator	exchange method
array element name	DIMENSION statement	bubble sort
subscript	implied-DO list	
subscript expression	short-list technique	

41. Property Tax Assessment Revisited.   Solve Exercise 28 in Chapter 5 on page 176 as follows.
   a. Store the tax schedule, lot numbers, names, property values, and tax charges in one-dimensional arrays. Treat the number of rows in the rate schedule as an input variable. Nicely label your output. Following the output table print the sum of property values and the total tax charge. *Hint:* Let the numbers 10,000, 30,000, and 60,000 represent the "set of keys."
 **b. Following the output in part a, print a second table that shows tax charges (together with corresponding lot numbers, names, and property values) in descending order.

42. Crime Data Summary.   The data below represent the number of arrests for felony crimes in a state over a three-year period.

Arrest Data by Year

	1	2	3
Homicide	1,000	1,000	1,000
Robbery	10,000	9,000	11,000
Burglary	27,000	24,000	28,000
Assault	13,000	15,000	16,000
Theft	19,000	20,000	23,000
Forgery	10,000	9,000	10,000

   a. Design an algorithm and write a program to read the data into several one-dimensional arrays. Print out the data in a table format that includes a new row for total arrests in each year and a new column for average arrests for each crime over the past three years. No need to label rows and columns here.
   b. In the output of part a, label your columns 1, 2, 3, and AVERAGE. Label your rows according to the felony names in the above table, the last row being TOTALS. Preferably, the output of felony names should be handled through the use of arrays.
   c. Print a second table which gives the percent of arrests for each crime to the total number of arrests in that year.

43. Support Facility for Oil Drilling Platforms.   Consider the coordinate system below, where the plotted points 1 through 5 represent the coordinate locations of offshore oil drilling platforms and the plotted point labeled (x_0, y_0) is a

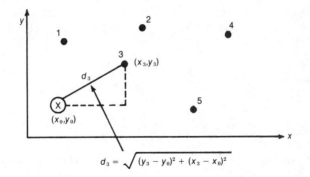

$$d_3 = \sqrt{(y_3 - y_0)^2 + (x_3 - x_0)^2}$$

possible location for a support facility. The figure also illustrates the distance d_3 between the support facility and platform 3. The formula for calculating d_3 is called the *Euclidian distance formula.* The coordinates in miles are given below.

Platform i	x_i	y_i
1	5	20
2	15	22
3	12	15
4	25	21
5	21	5

a. Design an algorithm and write a (preferably interactive) program that calculates and prints distance between each platform and the following proposed locations for the support facility.

x_0	y_0
4	6
20	14
20	18
23	20

Include the *total* distance $(d_1 + d_2 + \cdots + d_5)$ as part of your output.

b. Use your program interactively to determine the coordinate (to the nearest mile) for the support facility that minimizes total distance. In other words, by trial and error input a proposed location, and based on the output make a judgment regarding your next proposed coordinate. Repeat this procedure until you're satisfied you have converged on the coordinate that minimizes total distance.

**c. Instead of the trial-and-error search in part b, design your program systematically to vary x_0 and y_0 between chosen ranges. Include x_0, y_0, and total distance in your output. Also, have the program print the coordinate, of the ones considered, that minimizes total distance.

44. **Revenue Sharing.** Consider the allocation program whereby the federal government apportions certain federal funds to the states on the basis of a

ratio of each state's population to the total U.S. population. The table below provides population figures for all 50 states according to a recent census.

Population by State (in Thousands)

ME	1,059	NC	5,451
NH	808	SC	2,818
VT	468	GA	4,926
MA	5,199	FL	8,327
RI	938	KY	3,396
CT	3,080	TN	4,188
NY	18,101	AL	3,614
NJ	7,322	MS	2,364
PA	11,841	AR	2,068
OH	10,745	LA	3,762
IN	5,313	OK	2,681
IL	11,160	TX	12,017
MI	9,117	MT	748
WI	4,566	ID	820
MN	3,905	WY	374
IA	2,857	CO	2,534
MO	4,772	NM	1,147
ND	636	AZ	2,224
SD	681	UT	1,206
NB	1,541	NV	592
KS	2,266	WA	3,544
DE	577	OR	2,288
MD	4,089	CA	20,876
VA	4,967	AK	341
WV	1,803	HI	854

a. Write a program that uses one array for the names of the states and another array for the population figures. Read these arrays, calculate how much revenue should go to each state if $380 million is available for allocation, and output a table with appropriate labels that lists each state and its allocated amount. Include a flowchart or pseudocode.

b. Modify the preceding program to include a loop that processes more than one allocation. For example, if three allocation programs are to be run, then the output should appear as follows:

DOLLAR AMOUNTS ALLOCATED UNDER
EACH PROGRAM

STATE	1	2	3	TOTALS
ME	XXXXXXX	XXXXXXX	XXXXXXX	XXXXXXX
NH	XXXXXXX	XXXXXXX	XXXXXXX	XXXXXXX

The number of allocations to be made (three in the above example) should be a variable. Note that the total amount that is to be allocated to each state is given by row sums and output under the column labeled "TO-

TALS." Test your program by processing the following funds available for allocation under three programs: $380 million, $800 million, $500 million.

**c. Modify your output in either part a or part b such that the states are listed in alphabetical order. *Hint:* The bubble sort can be used for character data.

45. **Sales Forecasts.** Design a flowchart and write a program that calculates and prints sales forecasts by quarters for future years based on current sales and projected annual growth rate. For example, if currently we are at the end of the second quarter in the year 1981 and sales this quarter were $1.2 million with a projected growth rate of 2 percent per quarter, then forecasts through 1983 should appear as follows:

SALES FORECAST FOR OUIJA BOARD

CURRENT YEAR QUARTER SALES

1981   2 $ 1.2 M

YEAR	QUARTER	SALES
1981	3	1.224
1981	4	1.248
1982	1	1.273
1982	2	1.299
1982	3	1.325
1982	4	1.351
1983	1	1.378
1983	2	1.406
1983	3	1.434
1983	4	1.463

Note that the next forecast is always the last forecast increased by the growth rate.

a. Run your program for the following data.

Product Name	Current Sales	Growth Rate	Years Into Future
OUIJA BOARD	1.20	0.02	2
STAR TREK CHARM	0.85	0.05	4

Note that the sample output is based on the first set of data. Your program should allow input for a variable number of products.

b. *Graphical Output.* To the right of each sales forecast, print the asterisk character in a graph format. Do this as follows: Reserve columns 30 through 70 for graphical output. In this case, column 30 really represents 0 on a graph and column 70 represents 40 (that is, there are 40 print columns between 30 and 70). This means that all sales forecasts must be scaled to a range between 0 and 40.

$$\text{Scaled forecast} = \left(\frac{\text{forecast}}{\text{maximum forecast}}\right) \cdot 40$$

For example, the scaled forecast for the fourth quarter in 1982 is (1.351/ 1.463) · 40, or 36.9. This means that we wish an asterisk printed in column 66 (or 30 + 36) of the print line where 1.351 is printed for sales.

c. Print a table that summarizes total sales over the next four quarters by product. Entries in this table should be arranged in descending order of total sales.

d. Same as part c, except the table should list the results in alphabetical order by product name.

46. **Exam Grading.** Consider an N-question multiple choice exam, where only one answer is correct for each question.

a. Design an algorithm and write a program to grade the exam and print the student's name, the number right, the number wrong, and the final grade. The final grade is the percent number right. The data consist of
1. One line for N
2. One line containing N integers representing the N correct answers (answer key)
3. One line indicating the number of students in the class who took the exam (M)
4. M lines, one for each student, containing the student's name and N answers

Use two one-dimensional numeric arrays to store the answer key and a student's answers. Test your program with the following test data.

```
20
1,3,5,4,4,1,1,2,3,5,5,1,2,3,4,4,5,3,2,1
5
'PETROCELLI',1,3,4,4,4,1,1,2,3,3,5,1,2,3,4,4,5,1,1,1
'BAKER',1,3,5,4,3,2,1,2,3,4,3,2,2,3,3,3,5,1,2,1
'VALENTINO',1,3,5,4,4,1,1,2,3,5,5,1,2,3,4,4,4,3,2,1
'SIMPSON',1,2,5,4,4,2,2,3,3,1,2,1,3,3,3,5,5,3,1,1
'CARTER',2,3,5,4,4,1,1,3,3,5,4,1,5,4,4,4,5,2,1,3
```

b. Print the name and grade of the student with the highest grade.

c. Modify your output in part a such that the required output is in alphabetical order according to last name. *Hint:* The bubble sort can be used for character data.

**d. Print a frequency distribution of final grades for the exam, as follows:

90 or ABOVE	XX
80 BUT UNDER 90	XX
70 BUT UNDER 80	XX
60 BUT UNDER 70	XX
50 BUT UNDER 60	XX
BELOW 50	XX
	XX

AVERAGE GRADE FOR EXAM = XX.X

47. Stock Portfolio Valuation. Companies, universities, banks, pension funds, and other organizations routinely invest funds in the stock market. The set of stocks in which the organization invests its funds is called a *stock portfolio*. The table below illustrates a sample stock portfolio, including the number of shares owned of each stock, the purchase price per share, and the latest price per share quoted by the stock exchange.

Stock Portfolio

STOCK	NUMBER OF SHARES	PURCHASE PRICE ($/SHARE)	CURRENT PRICE ($/SHARE)
Allegh Airls	40,000	$5\frac{7}{8}$	$7\frac{1}{4}$
Boeing	5,000	$61\frac{1}{2}$	56
EastmKo	10,000	60	$64\frac{1}{2}$
Hewlett P	15,000	80	$100\frac{1}{8}$
IBM	2,500	$77\frac{1}{8}$	$80\frac{3}{4}$
Texaco	8,000	$23\frac{1}{2}$	19
Tex Inst	12,000	80	$85\frac{7}{8}$

a. Design and run a program to calculate the initial (purchase) value of the portfolio, the current value of the portfolio, and the net change in the value. Store number of shares, purchase prices, and current prices in separate vectors. *Hint:* The value of the portfolio is found by multiplying shares by corresponding prices and summing, which is equivalent to multiplication of two vectors.

b. Include a loop in the program for processing more than one portfolio. Find two copies of a newspaper, where one copy is at least two weeks apart from the other. Select a portfolio, make up shares owned, and use the two sets of prices for purchase and current prices. Process the given portfolio and the new portfolio in one run, and include the output of combined value of all portfolios.

CHAPTER 8

Multidimensional Arrays

In many situations it is convenient to store data in arrays with more than one dimension. FORTRAN 77 allows up to seven dimensions, but here we focus on the more common two-dimensional arrays.

8.1
MOTIVATION

Generally, it is desirable to use two-dimensional arrays whenever we wish to store and manipulate data that are characterized by two attributes, as the following examples illustrate.

Occupied beds in a hospital are tabulated by day of the week and by ward.
Deposits for a major bank are recorded for all branch banks on a quarterly or monthly basis.
Enrollments at a college are tabulated by major and class standing.
Exam scores for a course are recorded for all students.
Ten financial ratios from the Fortune 500 list of major U.S. corporations are recorded for all 500 corporations.

8.2
SUBSCRIPTS

You will more easily understand a **matrix** or **two-dimensional array** (an array with two subscript expressions) if you visualize a group of memory locations as a grid of boxes (table) arranged in rows and columns.

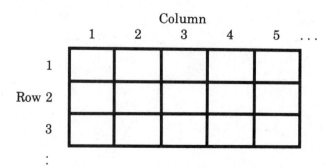

An array element within a two-dimensional array is referenced by specifying two subscript expressions: one for row number and one for column number. For example, in the three-row by four-column array below, the memory location that is marked with an X is found by looking at row 2, column 3; the memory location marked with XX is found in row 3, column 2.

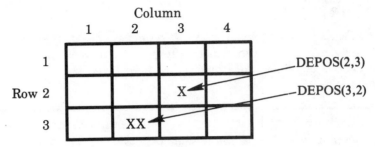

As you can see, two subscript expressions are needed when we use two-dimensional arrays. In FORTRAN, the *subscript* for a two-dimensional array has two *subscript expressions* separated by a comma within the parentheses following the array name. For example, if the above array is named DEPOS, then the location where the X is found is referenced as DEPOS(2,3) and the location where the XX is found is referenced as DEPOS(3,2). Notice that, in accordance with mathematical convention, the subscript expressions of the array element name are always given in the following order.

Except for the use of two-subscript expressions, according to the above convention, *subscripts for two-dimensional arrays are treated in the same manner as for one-dimensional arrays*. For example, subscript expressions must be integer arithmetic expressions.

Alternatively, the preceding table can be depicted by using array element names as follows:

	Column 1	Column 2	Column 3	Column 4
Row 1	DEPOS(1,1)	DEPOS(1,2)	DEPOS(1,3)	DEPOS(1,4)
Row 2	DEPOS(2,1)	DEPOS(2,2)	DEPOS(2,3)	DEPOS(2,4)
Row 3	DEPOS(3,1)	DEPOS(3,2)	DEPOS(3,3)	DEPOS(3,4)

In actual practice, storage locations for two-dimensional arrays don't "look" like a table in memory, but that need not concern us since the FORTRAN convention treats them like a table.

8.3
ARRAY DECLARATION

Just as with one-dimensional arrays, two-dimensional arrays must be declared in order to reserve memory locations that correspond to array elements. The same statements that declare one-dimensional arrays are used to declare multidimensional arrays, as follows:

where *type keyword* is usually CHARACTER, INTEGER, REAL, or DOUBLE PRE-CISION. *Dimension declarators* in the list are separated by commas. The number of dimension declarators corresponds to the number of dimensions in the array: one dimension declarator for a one-dimensional array, two dimension declarators for a two-dimensional array, and so on.[1]

For example, we might store the number of deposits for three branch banks in each of four quarters in a three-row by four-column two-dimensional integer array named DEPOS, where each row stores the quarterly data for one branch. The INTEGER statement would be specified as

    INTEGER DEPOS(3,4)

If we wanted DEPOS to store branch deposits for each month of the year, then we could set up an array with 3 rows and 12 columns. In this case, the INTEGER statement would be given by

    INTEGER DEPOS(3,12)

In the first case DEPOS has 12 elements in memory, whereas in the second case, 36 locations are reserved in memory.

Both one- and two-dimensional arrays can be dimensioned in a single type statement by using commas to separate each array specification. For example,

    REAL LOAD(5,10),EXP(10,8),TOT(5)

This results in the reservation of 50 locations for the two-dimensional real array LOAD, 80 locations for the two-dimensional real array EXP, and 5 locations for the one-dimensional real array TOT.

As with one-dimensional arrays, the dimension declarator can specify both *lower*

---

[1] The DIMENSION statement introduced in the last chapter is also used to declare arrays; however, we don't recommend its use over type statements since type is not explicitly specified.

and *upper dimension bounds*. For example,

```
                                    ┌──Lower dimension bound⎫ Second dimension
                                    │                       ⎬ declarator
                                    │  ┌Upper dimension bound⎭ (for columns)
             INTEGER DEPOS (0:3,-1:2)
                              ↑ ↑
   First dimension ⎧ Lower dimension bound─┘
   declarator      ⎨
   (for rows)      ⎩ Upper dimension bound──┘
```

results in the following memory representation.

DEPOS(0,−1)	DEPOS(0,0)	DEPOS(0,1)	DEPOS(0,2)
DEPOS(1,−1)	DEPOS(1,0)	DEPOS(1,1)	DEPOS(1,2)
DEPOS(2,−1)	DEPOS(2,0)	DEPOS(2,1)	DEPOS(2,2)
DEPOS(3,−1)	DEPOS(3,0)	DEPOS(3,1)	DEPOS(3,2)

It might make sense to declare these bounds if, for example, row 0 represents the home office and other rows represent branch 1, branch 2, and branch 3; column −1 might represent the immediately preceding quarter, column 0 the current quarter, column 1 the next quarter, and column 2 two quarters hence.

As with one-dimensional arrays, dimension bounds must be integer constant expressions, the value of a subscript expression must not fall outside the dimension bounds, and the declaration of character arrays usually requires a length declarator (see pages 233–238).

8.4
INPUT/OUTPUT

The same three methods for I/O that we illustrated for one-dimensional arrays can be used for two-dimensional arrays. For the examples that follow, we illustrate I/O for the two-dimensional integer array DEPOS, which is to store the following data on the number of deposits by branch and by quarter.

	Quarter			
Branch	1	2	3	4
1	1000	800	500	1200
2	500	2000	2000	500
3	1500	300	700	1500

Using DO Statements

I/O of two-dimensional arrays with DO statements requires the use of two DO statements, one "nested" within the other, as illustrated in the next example.

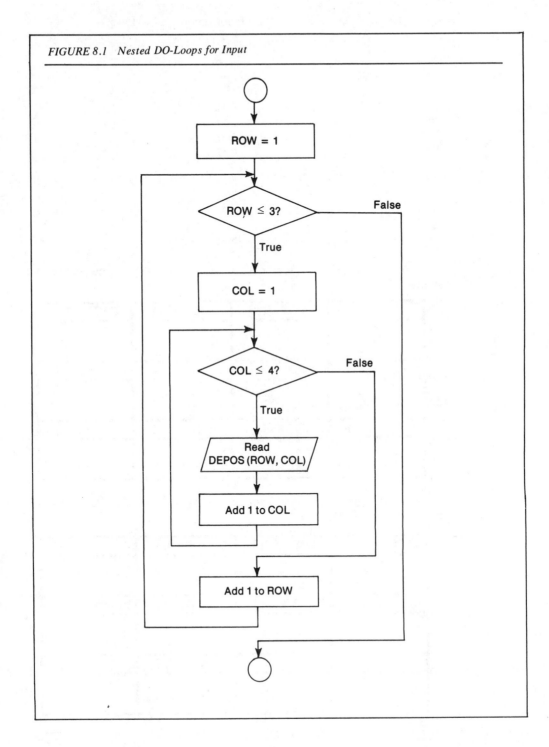

FIGURE 8.1   Nested DO-Loops for Input

Suppose we have placed our data on input records as follows:

Data Input
———

1000
800
500
1200
500
2000
2000
500
1500
300
700
1500

The first time through the loops, ROW = 1 and COL = 1, so the first data item is read into DEPOS(1,1).

DEPOS(1,1)	DEPOS(1,2)	DEPOS(1,3)	DEPOS(1,4)
1000			
DEPOS(2,1)	DEPOS(2,2)	DEPOS(2,3)	DEPOS(2,4)
DEPOS(3,1)	DEPOS(3,2)	DEPOS(3,3)	DEPOS(3,4)

The second time through the inner loop, ROW = 1 and COL = 2, so the second item is read into DEPOS(1,2).

DEPOS(1,1)	DEPOS(1,2)	DEPOS(1,3)	DEPOS(1,4)
1000	800		
DEPOS(2,1)	DEPOS(2,2)	DEPOS(2,3)	DEPOS(2,4)
DEPOS(3,1)	DEPOS(3,2)	DEPOS(3,3)	DEPOS(3,4)

The third time through the inner loop, ROW = 1 and COL = 3, so the third item is read into DEPOS(1,3).

DEPOS(1,1)	DEPOS(1,2)	DEPOS(1,3)	DEPOS(1,4)
1000	800	500	
DEPOS(2,1)	DEPOS(2,2)	DEPOS(2,3)	DEPOS(2,4)
DEPOS(3,1)	DEPOS(3,2)	DEPOS(3,3)	DEPOS(3,4)

The fourth time through the inner loop, ROW = 1 and COL = 4, so the fourth item is read into DEPOS(1,4).

DEPOS(1,1)	DEPOS(1,2)	DEPOS(1,3)	DEPOS(1,4)
1000	800	500	1200
DEPOS(2,1)	DEPOS(2,2)	DEPOS(2,3)	DEPOS(2,4)
DEPOS(3,1)	DEPOS(3,2)	DEPOS(3,3)	DEPOS(3,4)

At this point COL gets incremented to 5 and the inner loop tests false (see Figure 8.1). Then, ROW is incremented to 2 and again COL varies from 1 to 4 within the subscript. This results in the following sequence.

ROW	COL	
2	1	READ *,DEPOS(2,1)
2	2	READ *,DEPOS(2,2)
2	3	READ *,DEPOS(2,3)
2	4	READ *,DEPOS(2,4)

Now the array appears as follows in memory.

DEPOS(1,1)	DEPOS(1,2)	DEPOS(1,3)	DEPOS(1,4)
1000	800	500	1200
DEPOS(2,1)	DEPOS(2,2)	DEPOS(2,3)	DEPOS(2,4)
500	2000	2000	500
DEPOS(3,1)	DEPOS(3,2)	DEPOS(3,3)	DEPOS(3,4)

Finally, ROW is set equal to 3 and COL varies from 1 to 4. This results in the sequence:

ROW	COL	
3	1	READ *,DEPOS(3,1)
3	2	READ *,DEPOS(3,2)
3	3	READ *,DEPOS(3,3)
3	4	READ *,DEPOS(3,4)

At this point, read-in of the array is complete, yielding the following configuration in memory.

DEPOS(1,1)	DEPOS(1,2)	DEPOS(1,3)	DEPOS(1,4)
1000	800	500	1200
DEPOS(2,1)	DEPOS(2,2)	DEPOS(2,3)	DEPOS(2,4)
500	2000	2000	500
DEPOS(3,1)	DEPOS(3,2)	DEPOS(3,3)	DEPOS(3,4)
1500	300	700	1500

Note that the READ statement is executed exactly 12 times. *Since there is only one item in the list of the READ statement, this means that 12 input records are required, each with a single value.*

We might note that typically I is used in place of ROW as the subscript expression for rows, and J is used instead of COL, as these are consistent with mathematical convention.

Finally, we cannot overemphasize the need for you to concentrate on the manner in which the subscript expressions change values. Again, *the inner loop must be exhausted (the DO-variable must exceed its terminal value) for each iteration of the outer loop. Once the inner loop is exhausted, then the DO-variable of the outer loop is incremented and the DO-variable of the inner loop is reset to its initial value.*

Follow-up Exercises

1. Write a program segment that utilizes nested DO-loops to output the contents of DEPOS. Indicate how the printout would appear.
2. Suppose the following program segment were executed using the same input records as the example.

```
      DO 20  J = 1,4
          DO 10 I = 1,3
              READ *,DEPOS(I,J)
   10       CONTINUE
   20 CONTINUE
```

How would DEPOS appear in memory? Does the array in memory get filled in row by row or column by column? How should we place data on the input records so as to store the proper values in DEPOS using this program segment?

Using Nested Implied-DO Lists

Implied-DO lists are used with two-dimensional arrays for more flexible control of I/O than is possible with the nesting of DO-loops. A common form of the implied-DO list with two-dimensional arrays is given by

$$\left(\left(\begin{array}{c}\text{array}\\\text{name}\end{array}\left(\begin{array}{cc}\text{row}&\text{column}\\\text{subscript}&\text{subscript}\\\text{expression,}&\text{expression}\end{array}\right)\begin{array}{c},\text{inner}\\\text{DO-variable}\end{array}=\begin{array}{ccc}\text{initial}&\text{terminal}&\text{incrementation}\\\text{expression,}&\text{expression,}&\text{expression}\end{array}\right),\right.$$
$$\left.\begin{array}{c}\text{outer}\\\text{DO-variable}\end{array}=\begin{array}{ccc}\text{initial}&\text{terminal}&\text{incrementation}\\\text{expression,}&\text{expression,}&\text{expression}\end{array}\right)$$

In this case one implied-DO list is an item in the *dlist*[2] of another implied-DO list; that is, one implied-DO list is nested within another implied-DO list—hence the term **nested implied-DO lists.**

---

[2] You might want to review the terminology in Section 7.4, page 244.

Within the inner parentheses is the array name, followed by the two subscript expressions enclosed within parentheses, followed by a comma, followed by the DO portion of the inner implied-DO list, followed by a right parenthesis (which terminates the inner implied-DO list), followed by a comma, and finally followed by the DO portion of the outer implied-DO list and the closing parenthesis. As in the one-dimensional array case, the DO-variables also serve as subscript expressions.

EXAMPLE 8.2   Unformatted I/O with Nested Implied-DO Lists

To illustrate nested implied-DO lists, consider the following statement:

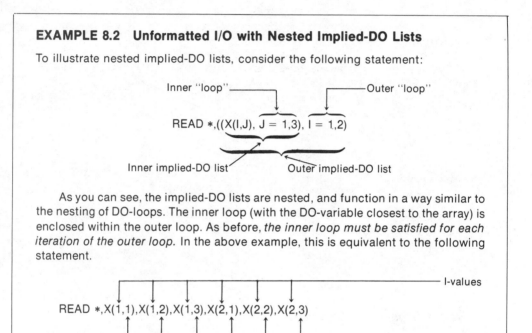

As you can see, the implied-DO lists are nested, and function in a way similar to the nesting of DO-loops. The inner loop (with the DO-variable closest to the array) is enclosed within the outer loop. As before, *the inner loop must be satisfied for each iteration of the outer loop.* In the above example, this is equivalent to the following statement.

As you can see, the implied-DO lists are nested, and function in a way similar to the nesting of DO-loops. The inner loop (with the DO-variable closest to the array) is enclosed within the outer loop. As before, *the inner loop must be satisfied for each iteration of the outer loop.* In the above example, this is equivalent to the following statement.

In effect, *the READ statement contains a list of six items, which allows us to input all six values for X on one input record.*

Did you pay attention to the manner in which subscript expression values (I and J) varied? The DO-variable of the inner loop (J subscript expression) varies from 1 to 3 while the DO-variable of the outer loop (I subscript) is held constant at 1. Then, expression I is incremented to 2 and the inner loop varies from 1 to 3 once more.

If we wish to store the following in real array X,

X(1,1)	X(1,2)	X(1,3)
10.1	8.2	6.3
X(2,1)	X(2,2)	X(2,3)
4.4	2.5	0.6

then the following input record can be used with the above READ statement.

    10.1, 8.2, 6.3, 4.4, 2.5, 0.6

However, suppose we wish to prepare row-by-row input records. In other words, the input records are to be set up in a manner which is conceptually compatible with the table nature of a two-dimensional array, as follows:

    10.1, 8.2, 6.3
     4.4, 2.5, 0.6

Then, the following *combination of the DO-loop and the implied-DO list* can be used to store these values into a two-dimensional array.

```
                                              Inner loop
                                            ⌐‾‾‾‾‾‾‾¬
                       ⎧    DO 10 I = 1,2
             Outer     ⎨        READ *,(X(I,J), J = 1,3)
             loop      ⎩    10 CONTINUE
```

In this case, *the implied-DO list is the inner loop and the DO/CONTINUE statements define the outer loop.* You should carefully note that the READ statement is executed twice, once for each value of I (two input records are provided). Also, note that the list of the READ statement contains three items (which is why we have three values for each line of input). This is equivalent to the following statements.

    READ *,X(1,1),X(1,2),X(1,3)
    READ *,X(2,1),X(2,2),X(2,3)

Similarly, the statement

    PRINT *,((X(I,J),J = 1,3),I = 1,2)

outputs all six values in X on one print line

    10.1   8.2   6.3   4.4   2.5   0.6

whereas the statements

```
        DO 20 I = 1,2
            PRINT *,(X(I,J),J = 1,3)
    20 CONTINUE
```

print X in a row-by-row manner:

    10.1   8.2   6.3
     4.4   2.5   0.6

This latter approach is more desirable since it's consistent with the two-dimensional conceptualization of X.

Follow-up Exercises

3. Modify the PRINT statement in the last example such that rows in X are numbered

   ```
   1    10.1  8.2  6.3
   2     4.4  2.5  0.6
   ```

   Can you figure out how to number the columns as well?

4. Write the appropriate statement(s) such that DEPOS of Example 8.1 is printed out without FORMATs as follows:
   a. The entire array is printed on one line.
   b. The first row of the array appears on one line, the second row on the next line, and so on.
   c. The first column of the array appears on one line, the second column on the next line, and so on.

EXAMPLE 8.3 Formatted I/O with Nested Implied-DO Lists

Getting back to the banking problem in Example 8.1, suppose that the data are recorded on three input records as follows:

```
1 2 3 4 5 6 7 8 9 10 11 12 13 14 15 16 17 18 19 20 21 22 23 24 25
   1000      8 0 0      5 0 0      1 2 0 0
    500     20 0 0      2 0 0 0      5 0 0
   1500      3 0 0      7 0 0      1 5 0 0
```

Then the execution of

```
    READ 1,(DEPOS(I,J), J = 1,4),I = 1,3)
  1 FORMAT(4I6)
```

results in the following storage for DEPOS.

DEPOS(1,1)	DEPOS(1,2)	DEPOS(1,3)	DEPOS(1,4)
1000	800	500	1200
DEPOS(2,1)	DEPOS(2,2)	DEPOS(2,3)	DEPOS(2,4)
500	2000	2000	500
DEPOS(3,1)	DEPOS(3,2)	DEPOS(3,3)	DEPOS(3,4)
1500	300	700	1500

Carefully note that there is *imbalance* between the number of items (12) in the list of the READ statement and the number of edit descriptors (4) in the FORMAT statement. Thus, according to the procedure outlined in Module D on page 487, *the computer resets to the beginning of this format specification (and reads a new input record) after reading in each group of four values.* Do you realize why we selected a repeat specification of 4 in the FORMAT statement? Because we wish to input four values per line, which is consistent with the number of values found in each row of this table.

This array can be printed in table form using

```
    PRINT 9, ((DEPOS(I,J), J = 1,4),I = 1,3)
9 FORMAT ('0', 4I6)
```

which gives the following output.

	1000	800	500	1200
	500	2000	2000	500
	1500	300	700	1500

If we were to change the FORMAT statement to

```
9 FORMAT(1X,I6)
```

the following would be printed.

Finally, if the FORMAT statement is given by

```
9 FORMAT(1X,12I6)
```

then we have

Follow-up Exercises

5. Specify the exact appearance of input records if DEPOS is read in using the nested implied-DO lists in the example and

   a. 1 FORMAT(I6)
   b. 1 FORMAT(16I5)

6. Consider the statements

   ```
   1 FORMAT(13I6)
      DO 30 I = 1,3
         READ 1, (DEPOS(I,J),J = 1,4)
   30 CONTINUE
   ```

   Would these statements properly process the input records in Example 8.3? What is the advantage of this combined DO-loop/implied-DO list approach to the nested implied-DO lists used in Example 8.3?

7. Write the appropriate READ and FORMAT statements if the data for DEPOS are recorded as follows:

   ```
   1 2 3 4 5 6 7 8 9 10 11 12 13 14 15 16
   1000    500    1 5 0 0
    800   2000    3 0 0
    500   2000    7 0 0
   1200    500    1 5 0 0
   ```

   Note that input records contain column entries rather than row entries in this case; however, we still wish to store the data as in Example 8.3.

8. Specify the exact appearance of output records for the program segment

   ```
      DO 70 I = 1,3
         PRINT 2, (DEPOS(I,J), J = 1,4)
   70 CONTINUE
   ```

   using each of the following FORMAT statements.

   a. 2 FORMAT(1X,I6)
   b. 2 FORMAT(1X,4I6)
   c. 2 FORMAT(1X,12I6)
   d. 2 FORMAT('0', 'BANK DEPOSITS'//'0', 4I6)
   * e. What must you do to the statement in part d such that the label BANK DEPOSITS is printed once rather than three times?

9. Specify the exact appearance of output records for the following.

```
        DATA M,N/3,4/

    2 FORMAT('1','BANK DEPOSITS'/'0',7X,16I7)
    4 FORMAT(1X,'BANK',I3,16I7)

        PRINT 2,(J,J = 1,N)

        DO 30 I = 1,M
            PRINT 4, I,(DEPOS(I,J),J = 1,N)
    30 CONTINUE
```

What is the advantage of this combined DO-loop/implied-DO list approach to the nested implied-DO lists used in Example 8.3?

*10. Consider the following memory.

M			LOT(1,1)	LOT(1,2)		LOT(1,20)
	3		10	50	. . .	
N			LOT(2,1)	LOT(2,2)		LOT(2,20)
	2		4	320	. . .	
			LOT(3,1)	LOT(3,2)		LOT(3,20)
			15	8	. . .	

Design code to output the following.

Note that your code should accommodate arrays up to 3 rows by 20 columns.

Using the Short-List Technique

The short-list technique can be used with two-dimensional arrays to input or output entire arrays. In other words, the array name without subscripts can appear in a READ or WRITE statement.

```
INTEGER DEPOS(3,4)
READ *,DEPOS
```

The number of elements read in is equal to the number of rows times the number of columns that have been specified in the dimension declarators. In this case, there are 12 items (3 × 4 array elements) in the list of the READ statement.[3]

One word of caution: *this technique requires that the data be arranged by column.* In other words, the above READ statement is equivalent to the following:

```
READ *,DEPOS(1,1),DEPOS(2,1),DEPOS(3,1),DEPOS(1,2),DEPOS(2,2),
       DEPOS(3,2), . . . , DEPOS(2,4),DEPOS(3,4)
```

The data would appear as follows on the input record.

```
1000 ,500 ,1500 ,800 ,2000 ,300 ,500 ,2000 ,700 ,1200 ,500 ,1500
```

Also, the short-list technique can be applied only if the entire array, as specified by the dimension declarators, is to be read or written. If only part of the array is to be used, then you must use DO-loops or implied-DO lists.

Follow-up Exercises

11. Specify the appearance of input records for each of the following.

```
       INTEGER DEPOS(3,4)
       READ 1, DEPOS
   a.  1 FORMAT(I5)
   b.  1 FORMAT(12I5)
   c.  1 FORMAT(3I5)
```

12. Are the following PRINT statements equivalent?

```
       REAL Y(5,8)
       PRINT *,Y
       PRINT *,((Y(I,J),J = 1,8),I = 1,5)
```

---

[3] More generally, the number of array elements is given by

$$n = (u_1 - l_1 + 1) \times (u_2 - l_2 + 1)$$

where

u_k = upper dimension bound for kth dimension
l_k = lower dimension bound for kth dimension

For example,

```
   INTEGER DEPOS(3,4)
```

declares that $u_1 = 3$, $l_1 = 1$, $u_2 = 4$, and $l_2 = 1$ so that

$$n = (3 - 1 + 1) \times (4 - 1 + 1) = 3 \times 4 = 12$$

13. Suppose we wish the following memory for arrays A and B.

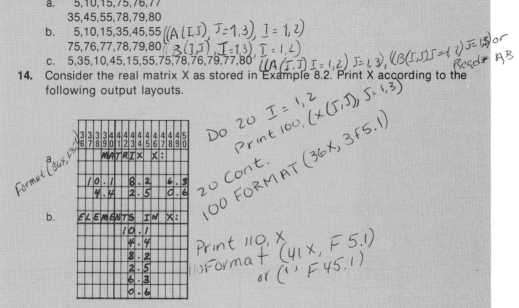

Specify input code if the data are to be input as follows.

a. 5,10,15,75,76,77
    35,45,55,78,79,80

b. 5,10,15,35,45,55 *((A(I,J), J=1,3), I=1,2)*
    75,76,77,78,79,80 *B(I,J), I=1,3), I=1,2)*

c. 5,35,10,45,15,55,75,78,76,79,77,80 *((A(I,J) I=1,2) J=1,3), (B(I,J)J=1,) J=1,3) or*
                                        Read A,B*

14. Consider the real matrix X as stored in Example 8.2. Print X according to the following output layouts.

a. *Format (36X, F5.1)*

```
                                    3 3 3 3 4 4 4 4 4 4 4 4 4 4 5
                                    6 7 8 9 0 1 2 3 4 5 6 7 8 9 0
                                        M A T R I X   X :

                                        1 0 . 1     8 . 2     6 . 3
                                        4 . 4     2 . 5     0 . 6
```

Do 20 I=1,2
Print 100, (X(I,J), J=1,3)
20 Cont.
100 FORMAT (36X, 3F5.1)

b.
```
                                    E L E M E N T S   I N   X :
                                                1 0 . 1
                                                4 . 4
                                                8 . 2
                                                2 . 5
                                                6 . 3
                                                0 . 6
```

Print 110, X
110 Format (41X, F 5.1)
or (', F 45.1)

*15. Given memory as on page 294, print the values stored in DEPOS so the output appears as follows:

	1 2 3 4 5 6 7 8 9 0 1 2 3 4 5 6 7 8 9 0 1 2 3 4 5 6 7 8 9 0 1 2 3 4 5
1	DEPOSITS AT BANK
2	1 2 3
3	
4	QUARTER 1 1000 500 1500
5	QUARTER 2 800 2000 300
6	QUARTER 3 500 2000 700
7	QUARTER 4 1200 500 1500
8	
9	
10	
11	
12	

8.5
MANIPULATING ARRAYS

Processing data stored in two-dimensional arrays normally involves nesting of DO-loops. The next example illustrates some common manipulations of two-dimensional arrays.

EXAMPLE 8.4   Row and Column Totals

One of the more common processing tasks is finding totals of each row or column in an array. The row or column totals can be stored either in one-dimensional arrays or in an extra row or column of the two-dimensional array. For example, to find the annual bank deposits in each branch for the data given on page 294, we need to sum the entries in each row. The following program segment would determine row sums.

```
        DO 30 I = 1,3
            SUM(I) = 0
            DO 25 J = 1,4
                SUM(I) = SUM(I) + DEPOS(I,J)
25          CONTINUE
30 CONTINUE
```

When I = 1, SUM(1) is initialized to zero; the inner loop 25 sums the values in the first row given by DEPOS(1,1), DEPOS(1,2), DEPOS(1,3), and DEPOS(1,4), and stores this sum in the first element of the array SUM.

SUM(1)	DEPOS(1,1)	DEPOS(1,2)	DEPOS(1,3)	DEPOS(1,4)
3500	1000	800	500	1200
SUM(2)	DEPOS(2,1)	DEPOS(2,2)	DEPOS(2,3)	DEPOS(2,4)
	500	2000	2000	500
SUM(3)	DEPOS(3,1)	DEPOS(3,2)	DEPOS(3,3)	DEPOS(3,4)
	1500	300	700	1500

After the DO-variable in the outer loop is incremented (I = 2), SUM(2) is initialized to zero, and the values in row 2 are accumulated and stored in the second element of array SUM.

SUM(1)	DEPOS(1,1)	DEPOS(1,2)	DEPOS(1,3)	DEPOS(1,4)
3500	1000	800	500	1200
SUM(2)	DEPOS(2,1)	DEPOS(2,2)	DEPOS(2,3)	DEPOS(2,4)
5000	500	2000	2000	500
SUM(3)	DEPOS(3,1)	DEPOS(3,2)	DEPOS(3,3)	DEPOS(3,4)
	1500	300	700	1500

Finally the outer loop iterates for the last time (I = 3) and the values of the third row are added to the third element in the array SUM.

SUM(1)	DEPOS(1,1)	DEPOS(1,2)	DEPOS(1,3)	DEPOS(1,4)
3500	1000	800	500	1200
SUM(2)	DEPOS(2,1)	DEPOS(2,2)	DEPOS(2,3)	DEPOS(2,4)
5000	500	2000	2000	500
SUM(3)	DEPOS(3,1)	DEPOS(3,2)	DEPOS(3,3)	DEPOS(3,4)
4000	1500	300	700	1500

Follow-up Exercises

16. Write a program segment that accumulates the bank's total deposits for each quarter. Store these totals in a one-dimensional array called TOT.

*17. Assume that DEPOS has been dimensioned to four rows and five columns. Instead of using SUM as in the example and TOT as in the preceding exercise, use the fourth row of DEPOS to store column totals and the fifth column to store row totals. Write program segments that accomplish this. Don't forget to initialize your summers to zero.

18. Write a program segment that calculates the percentage of each quarter's deposit to the annual number of deposits for each branch. Store these percentages in the two-dimensional array PER. After processing, PER should have the stored values shown on the next page. Can you fill in the third row? Note that, except for possible rounding error, rows of PER sum to 100.

PER(1,1)	PER(1,2)	PER(1,3)	PER(1,4)
28.57143	22.85714	14.28571	34.28571
PER(2,1)	PER(2,2)	PER(2,3)	PER(2,4)
10.00000	40.00000	40.00000	10.00000
PER(3,1)	PER(3,2)	PER(3,3)	PER(3,4)

19. Suppose the following array has been dimensioned as follows:

    REAL WEIGHT(100,50)

    Write a program segment that initializes each element in WEIGHT to 100 using
    a. Two nested DO-loops.
    b. A DATA statement.
    Under what circumstances should you not use the approach in part b?
    c. How would your answers change if weight were declared as follows?

    REAL WEIGHT (−20:20, 30:50)

20. Write a program segment to initialize every element in the (5 × 6) real array D to the value 100.

21. Write a program segment that initializes the (4 × 4) integer array X in the following manner.

    ```
    1   0   0   0
    0   1   0   0
    0   0   1   0
    0   0   0   1
    ```

*22. Suppose a 10 × 20 real array X already exists in memory. Write code to
    a. Interchange the values of corresponding array elements in column 3 and column 1.
    b. Print out the smallest value in X and its location (row and column).

*23. Given a 5 × 5 integer array A, write code to
    a. Print the lower triangle and main diagonal as shown below.

    b. Fill in the upper triangle symmetrically; that is, assuming only the lower triangle and main diagonal have been input as above, fill in the upper triangle to give the symmetric matrix shown on the next page.

A

	1	2	3	4	5
1	90	85	10	75	35
2	85	80	20	70	40
3	10	20	30	65	45
4	75	70	65	60	50
5	35	40	45	50	55

** 24. **Vector Representation of a Matrix.** A *symmetric matrix* is one whereby the triangle of elements above the main diagonal has values identical to the triangle of elements below the main diagonal (see the preceding exercise). Many applications, particularly in statistics, deal with very large symmetric matrices (which by definition have the same number of rows as columns). Often it's desirable to save storage by working with the lower triangle (including the main diagonal) and ignoring the upper triangle, since only one triangle is needed to represent all of the information. This is accomplished by using a vector (one-dimensional array) in place of the $N \times N$ matrix (two-dimensional array), with the following correspondences among subscript expression values.

Subscript Expression Values in 2-D Array (Main Diagonal and Lower Triangle)		Corresponding Subscript Expression Values in 1-D Array
I	J	K
1	1	1
2	1	2
2	2	3
3	1	4
3	2	5
3	3	6
.		.
.		.
.		.
N	1	
N	2	
.		
.		
.		
N	N	$\dfrac{N \cdot (N + 1)}{2}$

For example, the lower triangle and main diagonal of a 5×5 symmetric matrix (which requires a declaration of all 25 elements in the matrix) can be stored as a 15-element ($5 \times \frac{6}{2}$) vector, giving a saving of 10 storage locations (see the preceding exercise). A 500×500 symmetric array stored as a vector yields a substantial saving of 124,750 storage locations.

Write a complete program that (a) inputs N and a vector that stores the lower triangle/main diagonal of a symmetric matrix, (b) prints the lower triangle/main diagonal as shown in the preceding exercise, and (c) prints any two-dimensional A(I,J) element desired by the user. Use the matrix in the preceding exercise as test data. In part (c), use the following input:

Row Value	Column Value
3	2
2	2
5	1
1	5 ◄——— Note upper triangle element
0	0 ◄——— Terminate run

Hint: Given the scheme in the I-J-K table above, derive a formula that expresses K as a function of I and J.

8.6
INCOME TAX APPLICATION

After taking a tax course, you decide to earn some extra money (so that you can pay more taxes) by opening a computerized tax service for local accountants and individual taxpayers.

Given a taxpayer's wages (WAGES) from Form W-2, dividends (DIV), interest income (INTINC), income other than wages (OTHER), and adjustments (ADJ) such as moving expenses, the adjusted gross income (AGI) is given by

AGI = WAGES + DIV + INTINC + OTHER − ADJ

Taxable income (TI) is determined as adjusted gross income less excess itemized deductions (EXDED) less the product of number of exemptions (EXEM) and the allowance per exemption (APE).

TI = AGI − EXDED − EXEM*APE

EXDED is set equal to zero if a single taxpayer's itemized deductions (DED) are less than $2200; however, if DED is greater than $2200, then EXDED = DED − 2200. The income tax for single (unmarried) taxpayers is based on the taxable income according to the schedule below.

Tax Schedule for Single Taxpayers

		Column		
(1)	(2)	(3) (4)		(5)
	But not			of the amount
Over—	over—	Income Tax		over—
$ 0	$ 2,200	$ 0 + 0%		—
$ 2,200	$ 2,700	$ 0 + 14%		$ 2,200
$ 2,700	$ 3,200	$ 70 + 15%		$ 2,700
$ 3,200	$ 3,700	$ 145 + 16%		$ 3,200

Tax Schedule for Single Taxpayers (Continued)

		Column		
(1)	(2)	(3)	(4)	(5)
	But not			of the amount
Over—	over—	Income Tax		over—
$ 3,700	$ 4,200	$ 225 + 17%		$ 3,700
$ 4,200	$ 6,200	$ 310 + 19%		$ 4,200
$ 6,200	$ 8,200	$ 690 + 21%		$ 6,200
$ 8,200	$ 10,200	$ 1,110 + 24%		$ 8,200
$ 10,200	$ 12,200	$ 1,590 + 25%		$ 10,200
$ 12,200	$ 14,200	$ 2,090 + 27%		$ 12,200
$ 14,200	$ 16,200	$ 2,630 + 29%		$ 14,200
$ 16,200	$ 18,200	$ 3,210 + 31%		$ 16,200
$ 18,200	$ 20,200	$ 3,830 + 34%		$ 18,200
$ 20,200	$ 22,200	$ 4,510 + 36%		$ 20,200
$ 22,200	$ 24,200	$ 5,230 + 38%		$ 22,200
$ 24,200	$ 28,200	$ 5,990 + 40%		$ 24,200
$ 28,200	$ 34,200	$ 7,590 + 45%		$ 28,200
$ 34,200	$ 40,200	$10,290 + 50%		$ 34,200
$ 40,200	$ 46,200	$13,290 + 55%		$ 40,200
$ 46,200	$ 52,200	$16,590 + 60%		$ 46,200
$ 52,200	$ 62,200	$20,190 + 62%		$ 52,200
$ 62,200	$ 72,200	$26,390 + 64%		$ 62,200
$ 72,200	$ 82,200	$32,790 + 66%		$ 72,200
$ 82,200	$ 92,200	$39,390 + 68%		$ 82,200
$ 92,200	$102,200	$46,190 + 69%		$ 92,200
$102,200	—	$53,090 + 70%		$102,200

To illustrate the computations, consider an individual who declares $19,700 in wages, $225 in dividends, $305.20 in interest income, $3200 in income other than wages, and no adjustments. This gives an AGI of $23,430.20. If itemized deductions amount to $4230 and one exemption is claimed at a $1000 allowance per exemption, then EXDED is $2030 and TI is $20,400.20. From the above tax schedule, the income tax (TAX) is determined as $4510 + (.36) × (20,400.20 − 20,200), or $4582.07. If the taxpayer had paid taxes during the year that amounted to more than TAX, then the taxpayer would receive a welcome refund from the IRS; otherwise, a not-so-welcome balance due the IRS would have to be paid.

This is another example of a table look-up, this time using a two-dimensional array to store the table. To solve this problem the data in columns 2, 3, and 4 of the tax schedule are stored in a two-dimensional array named TAXTAB. The "search key" is the taxpayer's taxable income (TI); the "set of keys" is the upper limits of each income class (column 1 of TAXTAB, which is column 2 of the tax schedule) and the "function values" are in columns 3 and 4 of the tax schedule (columns 2 and 3 of TAXTAB).

Figure 8.2 shows exploded pseudocode for the income tax program that follows.

FIGURE 8.2 Stepwise Refinement of Pseudocode for Income Tax Program

STEP 1	STEP 2	STEP 3	STEP 4

Initial tasks
- Initialize constants
- READ tax schedule
- READ no. taxpayers

- Allowance per exemption = $1000
- Deductions parameter = $2200

Process taxpayer

```
DO WHILE taxpayers need
              processing
    READ input data
    Calculate adj. gross inc.
    Calculate excess item. ded.
    Calculate taxable income
    Determine tax
    PRINT name, adj. gross inc.,
          tax. inc., tax
    Refund/Balance due logic
END DO
```

Stop

```
IF deductions > $2200 THEN
    Excess item. ded. = ded. − $2200
ELSE
    Excess item. ded. = 0
END IF
```

```
Table look-up logic
Calculate tax
```

```
IF tax < tax withheld THEN
    Calculate refund
    PRINT refund
ELSE
    Calculate bal. due
    PRINT bal. due
END IF
```

```
Initialize row subscript
DO WHILE taxable inc. > table limit
    Increment row subscript
END DO
```

```
C   INCOME TAX PROGRAM
C
C   KEY:
C     NUM   = NUMBER OF TAXPAYERS
C     NAME  = TAXPAYER'S NAME
C     WAGES = WAGES
C     DIV   = DIVIDENDS
C     INTINC = INTEREST INCOME
C     OTHER = INCOME OTHER THAN WAGES
C     ADJ   = ADJUSTMENTS TO INCOME
C     DED   = ITEMIZED DEDUCTIONS
C     EXEM  = NUMBER OF EXEMPTIONS
C     TAXPAY = TOTAL TAX PAID (OR WITHHELD)
C     AGI   = ADJUSTED GROSS INCOME
C     APE   = ALLOWANCE PER EXEMPTION ($1000)
C     EXDED = EXCESS ITEMIZED DEDUCTIONS
C     TI    = TAXABLE INCOME
C     TAX   = INCOME TAX
C     BALDUE = BALANCE DUE IRS
C     REFUND = REFUND FROM IRS
C     DEDPAR = DEDUCTIONS PARAMETER ($2200)
C     TAXTAB = ARRAY WHERE COLUMNS 1,2,3 STORE
C              COLUMNS 2,3,4 OF TAX SCHEDULE
C
C------------------------------------------------------------
C
      CHARACTER NAME*20
      INTEGER   NUM,EXEM
      REAL      WAGES,DIV,INTINC,OTHER,ADJ,DED,TAXPAY,AGI,
     1          APE,EXDED,TI,TAX,BALDUE,REFUND,DEDPAR,
     2          TAXTAB(26,3)
C
C------------------------------------------------------------
C
      DATA APE,DEDPAR/1000.,2200./
C
C------------------------------------------------------------
C
      READ *,TAXTAB
      READ *,NUM
C
C------------------------------------------------------------


C
      DO 25 K=1,NUM
C
        READ *,NAME,WAGES,DIV,INTINC,OTHER,ADJ,DED,EXEM,TAXPAY
C
        AGI = WAGES + DIV + INTINC + OTHER - ADJ
C
C       EXCESS DEDUCTIONS LOGIC
C       --------------------------------------------
        IF (DED .GT. DEDPAR) THEN
          EXDED = DED - DEDPAR
        ELSE
          EXDED = 0.
        END IF
C       --------------------------------------------
C
        TI = AGI - EXDED - REAL(EXEM)*APE
C
```

```
C          TABLE LOOK-UP LOGIC
C          -----------------------------------------------
           I = 1
    10     IF (TI .GT. TAXTAB(I,1)) THEN
              I = I + 1
              GO TO 10
           END IF
C          -----------------------------------------------
C
           TAX = TAXTAB(I,2) + (TI - TAXTAB(I-1,1))*TAXTAB(I,3)/100.
C
           PRINT 90,NAME,AGI,TI,TAX
C
C          REFUND/BALANCE DUE LOGIC
C          -----------------------------------------------
           IF (TAX .LT. TAXPAY) THEN
              REFUND = TAXPAY - TAX
              PRINT 92,REFUND
           ELSE
              BALDUE = TAX - TAXPAY
              PRINT 94,BALDUE
           END IF
C          -----------------------------------------------
C
    25 CONTINUE
C
C-------------------------------------------------------------------
C
    90 FORMAT(' NAME                        :  ' ,A20/
      1        'OADJUSTED GROSS INCOME:  $',F11.2/
      2        ' TAXABLE INCOME        :  $',F11.2/
      3        ' INCOME TAX            :  $',F11.2)
    92 FORMAT('OREFUND FROM IRS        :  $',F11.2////)
    94 FORMAT('OBALANCE DUE IRS        :  $',F11.2////)
C
C-------------------------------------------------------------------
C
           END
```

Follow-up Exercises

25. Identify what the following array element names represent in the program.
   a. TAXTAB(I,1)
   b. TAXTAB(I,2)
   c. TAXTAB(I,3)
   d. TAXTAB(I −1,1)

26. Describe how the tax schedule is to be input. What entry would you use for the last item in column 1 of TAXTAB?

27. Given the following input records

    . . . input records for tax schedule (see preceding exercise) . . .
    2
    'TEST 1',19700.,225.,305.20,3200.,0.,4230.,1,4100.
    'TEST 2',12100.,0.,0.,0.,0.,1900.,1,2530.

   a. Describe stored contents of the following memory locations for the *second* taxpayer when the computer executes statement 25: WAGES,DIV,INTINC, OTHER,ADJ,DED,EXEM,TAXPAY,AGI,EXDED,TI,TAX,REFUND,BALDUE
   b. Describe printout for the entire run.

*28. As the program stands, it has a minor bug whenever income tax exactly equals the total tax paid. Can you identify the problem? Modify the program to eliminate this bug.

*29. As the program stands, it has a bug whenever TI is less than $2200. Can you identify the problem? Modify the program to eliminate this bug.

8.7
THREE OR MORE DIMENSIONS

FORTRAN allows arrays up to seven dimensions. In this section we focus mostly on the more common three-dimensional arrays.

If data are classified by three attributes, then three-dimensional arrays may be useful to store and manipulate these data. The following examples illustrate three-attribute data.

1. Ten financial ratios for each of the top 100 corporations on the Fortune 500 list for each of the last five years can be conceptualized as a 10 by 100 by 5 (10 × 100 × 5) array where the attributes (dimensions) are ratios, corporations, and years.

2. Enrollments at a college tabulated by 50 major subject areas, sex, and five class standings (first year, second year, . . . , graduate) imply a 50 × 2 × 5 array with dimensions representing major subject area, sex, and class standing.

3. Airline reservations classified by 200 flight numbers, day of month, and type of ticket (first class, tourist, standby) suggests a 200 × 31 × 3 array for the attributes flight number, day, and type of ticket.

Attributes beyond three simply add more dimensions. For example, if we further classify reservations by month in the airline example, we have a four-dimensional 200 × 31 × 12 × 3 array; if we additionally classify enrollments by residency (in-state,

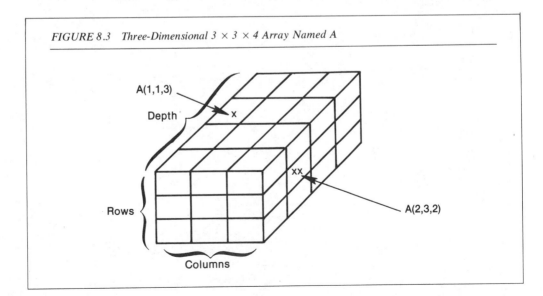

FIGURE 8.3   *Three-Dimensional 3 × 3 × 4 Array Named A*

out-of-state, foreign) and by ten ethnic origins, we have a five-dimensional 50 × 2 × 5 × 3 × 10 array.

Three-dimensional arrays are best visualized as a group of adjacent memory locations arranged in cube-like fashion by rows, columns, and depth, as illustrated in Figure 8.3.

An element within a three-dimensional array is referenced by specifying three subscript expressions: row number, column number, and depth number. For example, the memory location marked with an X in Figure 8.3 is referenced by A(1,1,3) since it is located in row 1, column 1, and depth 3; the XX locates A(2,3,2) in row 2, column 3, and depth 2.

You should carefully note the ordering of subscript expressions when using three-dimensional array element names.

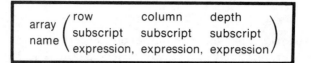

Otherwise, all the rules that name, declare, reference, input, output, and manipulate two-dimensional arrays apply to three- (and greater) dimensional arrays.

FIGURE 8.4   *Projected Enrollments*

EXAMPLE 8.5 Projected Enrollments

The administration of a small university has estimated enrollments for three years by college (Social Science, Physical Science, Humanities) and by level (lower, upper, graduate), as illustrated in Figure 8.4.

These data can be represented by a three-dimensional array named ENROLL, where the first dimension represents the colleges, the second dimension the levels, and the third dimension the years. Thus, ENROLL (I,J,K) references the enrollment in the Ith college, the Jth level, and the Kth year.

Looking at Figure 8.4, we can conceptualize ENROLL as a three-layered "sandwich" or "accordion," where the first layer is the first-year matrix, the middle layer is the second-year matrix, and the back layer is the third-year matrix. In other words, a three-dimensional array can be visualized as a cube with three layers, where each layer is a two-dimensional array. For example, ENROLL (3,1,1) references the value 600, ENROLL (1,3,1) references 100, and ENROLL (1,1,3) references 130.

The program below inputs the enrollment data, computes row and column totals, and prints the results.

```
C  PROJECTED ENROLLMENTS PROGRAM
C
C  KEY:
C    NOC    = NUMBER OF COLLEGES
C    NOL    = NUMBER OF LEVELS
C    NOY    = NUMBER OF YEARS
C    COL    = 1-D ARRAY STORING COLLEGE NAMES
C    LEVEL  = 1-D ARRAY STORING LEVEL NAMES
C    YEAR   = 1-D ARRAY STORING YEARS
C    ENROLL = 3-D ARRAY STORING ENROLLMENT DATA; ENROLL(I,J,K)
C             REFERENCES ITH COLLEGE, JTH LEVEL, KTH YEAR
C    COLTOT = 1-D ARRAY STORING TOTAL ENROLLMENT FOR EACH COLLEGE
C    LEVTOT = 1-D ARRAY STORING TOTAL ENROLLMENT FOR EACH LEVEL
C------------------------------------------------------------------
       CHARACTER *18 COL(6)
       CHARACTER *10 LEVEL(4)
       INTEGER NOC,NOL,NOY
       INTEGER YEAR(5),ENROLL(6,4,5),COLTOT(6),LEVTOT(4)
C------------------------------------------------------------------
       PARAMETER (NOC=3, NOL=3, NOY=3)
       DATA (COL(I),I=1,NOC) /'SOCIAL SCIENCE','PHYSICAL SCIENCE',
      *                       'HUMANITIES'/
       DATA (LEVEL(J),J=1,NOL) /'LOWER','UPPER','GRADUATE'/
C------------------------------------------------------------------
       DO 20 K=1,NOY
         READ *, YEAR(K)
         DO 10 I=1,NOC
           READ *, (ENROLL(I,J,K),J=1,NOL)
   10    CONTINUE
   20  CONTINUE
C------------------------------------------------------------------
       DO 100 K=1,NOY
C
         DO 40 I=1,NOC
           COLTOT(I) = 0
           DO 30 J=1,NOL
             COLTOT(I) = COLTOT(I) + ENROLL(I,J,K)
   30      CONTINUE
   40    CONTINUE
```

```
C
        DO 60 J=1,NOL
          LEVTOT(J) = 0
          DO 50 I=1,NOC
            LEVTOT(J) = LEVTOT(J) + ENROLL(I,J,K)
   50     CONTINUE
   60   CONTINUE
C
        PRINT *,'              ENROLLMENT DATA FOR',YEAR(K)
        PRINT *,' '
        PRINT *,'                          ',(LEVEL(J),J=1,NOL),
     *                                       '  TOTALS'
C
        DO 70 I=1,NOC
          PRINT *, COL(I),(ENROLL(I,J,K),J=1,NOL),COLTOT(I)
   70   CONTINUE
C
        PRINT *,'TOTALS         ',(LEVTOT(J),J=1,NOL)
        PRINT *,' '
        PRINT *,' '
C
  100 CONTINUE
C-------------------------------------------------------------------
      END
```

Sample Output

```
              ENROLLMENT DATA FOR         1981

                      LOWER        UPPER      GRADUATE       TOTALS
SOCIAL SCIENCE         150          100          100          350
PHYSICAL SCIENCE       250          250           50          550
HUMANITIES             600          200          300         1100
TOTALS                1000          550          450


              ENROLLMENT DATA FOR         1982

                      LOWER        UPPER      GRADUATE       TOTALS
SOCIAL SCIENCE         120          110           90          320
PHYSICAL SCIENCE       230          250           70          550
HUMANITIES             550          300          200         1050
TOTALS                 900          660          360


              ENROLLMENT DATA FOR         1983

                      LOWER        UPPER      GRADUATE       TOTALS
SOCIAL SCIENCE         130          100           90          320
PHYSICAL SCIENCE       220          245           90          555
HUMANITIES             500          350          150         1000
TOTALS                 850          695          330
```

Follow-up Exercises

30. Describe input data
    a. For the test run.
    b. If we declare three elements in YEAR, 3 × 3 × 3 elements in ENROLL, and replace DO-loops 10 and 20 with the short-list input

        READ *,YEAR
        READ *,ENROLL

31. With respect to the program:
    a. Up to how many years, levels, and colleges can it handle?
    b. What's stored in ENROLL (3,2,2), ENROLL (2,3,2), and ENROLL (3,3,4)?
    c. If a DATA statement is used to define NOC, NOL, and NOY, what other changes need to be made?

32. Modify the program to input data as follows:

        150, 100, 100, 1981
        120, 110, 90, 1982
        130, 100, 90, 1983
        250, 250, 50, 1981
              ⋮
              ⋮

33. Modify the program so that the total enrollment (TE) at the university is printed as the last item in the row labeled "TOTALS."

*34. Modify the program to print the following totals (TOTALS), once the other three matrices have been printed.

	1981	1982	1983
Social Science	350	320	320
Physical Science	550	550	555
Humanities	1100	1050	1000

*35. Can you think of a more efficient way of coding DO-loops 30, 40, 50, and 60, whereby the two totals vectors are summed within one nested DO-loop? What have you sacrificed by gaining some efficiency?

8.8
COMMON ERRORS

Errors associated with two-dimensional arrays are as likely to occur as errors associated with one-dimensional arrays. So review once more the common errors discussed on pages 273–275.

Errors associated with the I/O of two-dimensional arrays are perhaps the most common. If you use the short-list technique, then remember that I/O is column by column, not row by row. Otherwise, you must use nested loops for the I/O of two-dimensional arrays.

When using nested loops, keep in mind that the inner loop DO-variable varies faster than the outer loop DO-variable. Typically, we let the inner loop DO-variable represent the column subscript expression and the outer loop DO-variable the row subscript expression. This gives us row-by-row I/O, which is conceptually consistent with the usual way we treat tables.

If you want input records or printout to "look" like a table, then you must use an implied-DO list. In this case, the usual approach is to use the DO/CONTINUE pair for the outer loop (rows) and an implied-DO list for the inner loop (columns). Alternatively, a nested implied-DO list can be used, but this requires a FORMAT statement that sets the number of repeatable descriptors equal to the number of columns.

Case A

Input Record	Program Segment	Result
| 1 2 3 4 5 6 7 8 9 ...<br><br>10  20  30<br>40  50  60 | ```
1 FORMAT(3I3)
   DO 20 I = 1,2
      DO 10 J = 1,3
         READ 1,KAT(I,J)
10       CONTINUE
20 CONTINUE
``` | "OUT OF DATA ERROR" condition during execution. |
| | ```
1 FORMAT(3I3)
   DO 20 I = 1,2
      READ 1,(KAT(I,J), J = 1,3)
20 CONTINUE
```<br><br>*Note:* Repeat specification in the FORMAT statement must be 3 or greater. | KAT<br><br>| 10 | 20 | 30 |<br>| 40 | 50 | 60 | |
| | ```
1 FORMAT(3I3)
   READ 1,((KAT(I,J), J = 1,3),I = 1,2)
```<br><br>*Note:* Repeat specification in the FORMAT statement must be exactly 3. | KAT<br><br>| 10 | 20 | 30 |<br>| 40 | 50 | 60 | |
```

Case B

Column headers: Program Segment | Expected Output | Actual Output

Array KAT in Memory

10	20	30
40	50	60

Program Segment 1

```
2 FORMAT(1X,3I3)
  DO 40 I = 1,2
     DO 30 J = 1,3
        PRINT 2,KAT(I,J)
30   CONTINUE
40 CONTINUE
```

Expected Output (columns 1234567890):

	1 2 3 4 5 6 7 8 9 0
1	
2	10 20 30
3	40 50 60
4	

Actual Output:

	1 2 3 4 5 6 7 8 9 0
1	
2	10
3	20
4	30
5	40
6	50
7	60

Program Segment 2

```
2 FORMAT(1X,3I3)
  DO 40 I = 1,2
     PRINT 2,(KAT(I,J), J = 1,3)
40 CONTINUE
```

Note: Repeat specification in the FORMAT statement must be 3 or greater.

Actual Output:

	1 2 3 4 5 6 7 8 9 0
1	
2	10 20 30
3	40 50 60
4	

Program Segment 3

```
2 FORMAT(1X,3I3)
  PRINT 2,((KAT(I,J), J = 1,3),I = 1,2)
```

Note: Repeat specification in the FORMAT statement must be exactly 3.

Actual Output:

	1 2 3 4 5 6 7 8 9 0
1	
2	10 20 30
3	40 50 60
4	

315

ADDITIONAL EXERCISES

36. Mailing List Revisited. Rewrite the program in part c of Exercise 37 in Chapter 6 on page 217 by storing columns (7) and (8) of the data file in a two-dimensional array. Store columns (1) to (6) in six one-dimensional arrays. Design your program to include a loop for processing multiple regions and interest areas. Thus one run can handle the four separate runs required by the old version.

37. Computerized Matching Revisited. Rewrite the program in part b of Exercise 32 in Chapter 5 on page 179 by incorporating a loop to handle the different inquiries. Store the numeric portion of the placement office file in a two-dimensional array. Store name, ID, and address in three one-dimensional arrays.

38. Crime Data Summary Revisited. Solve Exercise 42 in Chapter 7 on page 276 using two-dimensional arrays for numeric data.

39. Interactive Airline Reservation System. All major airlines have automated their systems for handling seat reservations. A central computer keeps a record in storage of all relevant information describing the services being sold: flight numbers, flight schedules, seats available, prices, and other data.

A reservation clerk can request information on seat availability, can sell seats to passengers (providing they are available), can cancel reservations (which increases available seats), and, if a flight is full, can put individuals on a waiting list.

a. Develop an algorithm and an interactive program to incorporate the following options.

1. Update the flight information table shown on the opposite page. For example, if a customer requests one tourist reservation on flight number 4, the program should check for available tourist seats. Since one is available, it should then adjust the available tourist seats to zero and print a message such as RESERVATION ALLOWED. If the passenger had requested two seats, however, the program should print RESERVATION DISALLOWED. SORRY, OUR HIGH ETHICAL STANDARDS PREVENT OVERBOOKING.

2. Retrieve status on a particular flight by printing the appropriate row in the flight information table.

3. Print entire flight information table.

4. Terminate the run.

Remember to read the flight information data into arrays at the start of the program.

Current Table of Flight Information

Flight Number	Departing Airport	Arriving Airport	Time of Departure	Time of Arrival	Available Seats First Class	Available Seats Tourist	Seats Sold First Class	Seats Sold Tourist
1	BOS	CHI	0730	0855	20	8	10	75
2	BOS	CHI	1200	1357	20	20	10	50
3	BOS	TOR	0810	1111	30	10	0	120
4	ATL	SF	1145	1604	15	1	25	129
5	CHI	BOS	0645	0948	30	25	5	90
6	CHI	NY	0945	1237	30	8	0	120
7	CHI	LA	1530	1851	20	10	30	60
8	CHI	TOR	1955	2114	5	5	25	85
9	TOR	DEN	1025	1611	10	6	60	60
10	TOR	SF	1435	1556	20	10	10	89

Process the following requests in your computer run on an interactive basis.

Option Request	Flight Number	Seat Type	Number of Tickets	Reservation Request
1	4	Tourist	1	Reserve
1	6	Tourist	4	Reserve
2	3	—	—	—
1	9	Tourist	2	Cancel
1	9	1st Class	4·	Cancel
1	4	Tourist	2	Reserve
3	—	—	—	—

b. Besides the options in part a, give your program the capability to retrieve and print flight information on all flights between two specified airports. Test your program for flights from Boston to Chicago and from Chicago to Los Angeles. In the first case, you should get a printout of the first two rows; in the second case, the seventh row should be printed.

40. Poisson-Distributed Electronic Failures. The likelihoods (probabilities) of failures for many electronic processes can be described by the Poisson probability function

$$f(x) = \frac{\lambda^x \cdot e^{-\lambda}}{x!}$$

where

$f(x)$ = probability of x failures per time period
λ = average number of failures per time period (lambda)
e = base of natural logarithm (the irrational number 2.71828 $\cdots$)
x = number of failures per time period
$x!$ = x factorial, or the product $1 \cdot 2 \cdot 3 \cdots (x - 1) \cdot (x)$
(*Note:* 0! is defined as 1.)

For example, suppose that malfunctions of onboard navigation systems for a large squadron of aircraft are Poisson-distributed with a failure rate of 20 per month (that is, $\lambda = 20$). In this case, the probability of 15 failures (that is, $x = 15$) in a month is

$$f(15) = \frac{(20)^{15} \cdot e^{-20}}{15!} = 0.0516$$

or about 5.16 percent.

a. Print a table of Poisson probabilities where rows represent values of x from 0 to 40 in increments of 1 and columns represent values of λ from 10 to 20 in increments of 2. Use a two-dimensional array to store probabilities. *Note:* You might want to use the exponential function described in Module A.

b. Print a table of cumulative probabilities where again rows represent the same values of x and columns represent the same values of λ. The cumulative probability of x for a given λ is defined as the probability of x or less failures, or

$$F(x) = f(0) + f(1) + f(2) + \cdots + f(x)$$
$$= \sum_{i=0}^{x} f(i)$$

For example, the probability of three or *fewer* failures during a month when $\lambda = 10$ is

$$F(3) = f(0) + f(1) + f(2) + f(3)$$
$$= 0.0000 + 0.0005 + 0.0023 + 0.0076$$
$$= 0.0104$$

or just over 1 percent.

c. Use your tables to find the following probabilities.

1. The probability of exactly 20 failures given $\lambda = 20$
2. The probability of 20 or fewer failures given $\lambda = 20$
3. The probability of exactly 0 failures given $\lambda = 10$
4. The probability of exactly 10 failures given $\lambda = 10$
5. The probability of exactly 20 failures given $\lambda = 10$
6. The probability of 20 or fewer failures given $\lambda = 10$
7. The probability of 20 or fewer failures given $\lambda = 16$
8. The probability of more than 20 failures given $\lambda = 16$

41. **Personnel Salary Budget.** The personnel office for a state government agency is in the process of developing a salary budget for the next fiscal year. The personnel file contains the following information on each employee.

1. Employee name
2. Social Security number
3. Current annual salary
4. Union code (1 = clerical, 2 = teachers, 3 = electrical)
5. Current step in pay schedule (1 through 5)
6. Year hired

The state agency deals with three labor unions: clerical, teachers, and electrical. Each union has negotiated a separate salary schedule that entitles each employee to an annual step increase. The salary schedules are listed in the table below. Each employee is hired at the lowest step in the salary schedule for his or her union, and moves up one step each year. The field "current step in pay schedule" indicates the employee's step prior to the new salary for the coming year; that is, "current annual salary" is consistent with this step. The salary for the upcoming year is to be based on the next highest step. Employees who have reached step 5 are at the maximum salary level for that job. Thus next year's step salary is the same as their current annual salary.

In addition to the salary step increase, employees who have been employed by the state for ten years or more are entitled to a longevity increase. A longevity increase represents a 5 percent increment added to the employee's *new* step salary.

a. Design an algorithm and write a program that prints a budget report for the personnel office. Output from the report includes employee's name,

Salary Schedules

Step	Clerical	Teachers	Electrical
1	10176	9133	12170
2	10592	10433	14260
3	10956	11833	16668
4	11320	13333	19501
5	11921	14893	22801

Personnel File

SMYTHIE SMILE	032166789	10956	1	3	71
ALFRED ALFREDO	123454321	13333	2	4	68
MENDAL MICKEY	987654345	22801	3	5	67
FIELD FLORA	543297541	12170	3	1	76
CURRAN CURRENT	045811222	10176	1	1	76
HANDEL HALO	315791123	11320	1	4	70
UNKIND CORA	129834765	9133	2	1	75

current salary, increase in salary due to step, increase in salary due to longevity, and new salary. Following the output table, print totals for the four numeric columns. Treat the salary schedules as a two-dimensional (5 × 3) array that is to be read in. Data in the personnel file and in the output table need not be treated as arrays.

b. Print a table that summarizes the salary budgets as follows:

SALARY BUDGETS

CLERICAL	$ xxxxxx
TEACHERS	$ xxxxxx
ELECTRICAL	$ xxxxxx
	$ xxxxxx

**c. Print the table of part b *prior* to the output in part a. *Hint:* Unlike part a, now you must subscript both the variables in the personnel file and the output in the report of part a. Do you see why? Use two-dimensional arrays.

42. **Questionnaire Analysis.** A university is conducting a survey to determine its undergraduates' "attitudes toward and experiences with the consumption of alcoholic beverages." The following questionnaire has been designed for this survey.

_____1. What is your sex? 1. male_____ 2. female_____

_____2. Where do you live? 1. on campus_____ 2. off campus with parents _____ 3. off campus alone/with roommates_____

_____3. What is your class standing? 1. freshman_____ 2. sophomore_____ 3. junior_____ 4. senior_____ 5. other_____

_____4. How often on the average do you drink alcoholic beverages? 1. never_____ 2. less than once a week_____ 3. 1–3 times per week_____ 4. 4–5 times per week_____ 5. more than 5 times per week_____

_____5. Do you feel other people's drinking has any adverse effects on your life? 1. frequently_____ 2. occasionally_____ 3. rarely_____ 4. never_____

_____6. Do your drinking habits affect your academic life? 1. frequently_____ 2. occasionally_____ 3. rarely_____ 4. never_____

_____7. Do you ever feel guilty about your drinking? 1. frequently_____ 2. occasionally_____ 3. rarely_____ 4. never_____

_____8. Do you feel you drink primarily because of 1. boredom_____ 2. peer pressure_____ 3. tension_____ 4. other_____ (specify)

Before conducting the full survey, it has been decided to pretest the questionnaire on ten students. The results are shown in the table on page 321.

Student	Answer to Question Number							
	1	2	3	4	5	6	7	8
1	1	1	3	3	4	4	2	3
2	1	1	3	1	2	2	1	1
3	2	2	2	2	1	3	3	2
4	2	3	1	4	3	1	3	3
5	1	1	4	4	1	1	2	3
6	1	2	2	2	1	1	2	3
7	2	3	4	1	3	2	1	2
8	2	1	1	2	4	4	2	1
9	1	2	3	3	1	1	1	1
10	2	2	1	4	2	3	2	1

a. Design an algorithm and write a program that reads questionnaire data into a two-dimensional array and outputs a frequency distribution for each question. For example, the frequency distribution for the first question and the above data would be

	Responses	
Question	1	2
1	5	5

For the second question, we have

	Responses		
Question	1	2	3
2	4	4	2

Label your output and try to make it as efficient as possible.

**b. Modify your program to provide cross-tabulation of responses for any two questions that are specified by the user. For example, if we wish to assess differences between the drinking frequencies of men and women, then our output might appear as follows:

		QUESTION 1	
		1	2
	1—	1	1
QUESTION 4	2—	1	2
	3—	2	0
	4—	1	2
	5—	0	0

To make sure you understand this cross-tabulation, confirm the numbers based on the data.

43. **Matrix Multiplication.**   Let's define a matrix, **A**, as having dimensions (rows and columns) m_1 by n_1, or $(m_1 \times n_1)$. Another matrix, **B**, has dimensions $(m_2 \times n_2)$. Two matrices may be multiplied if and only if they are *compatible*, that is, the number of columns in the first matrix equals the number of rows in the second matrix. As an example, the multiplication of matrix **A** times matrix **B**, defined by **AB**, is possible if and only if $n_1 = m_2$. Similarly, the product **BA** is possible if and only if $n_2 = m_1$.

If two matrices are compatible, then the resulting matrix will have dimensions $(m \times n)$ where m equals the number of rows in the first matrix and n equals the number of columns in the second matrix. Referring to the matrices **A** and **B**, we see that if **AB** is possible and

$$AB = C$$

then the product matrix, **C**, will have dimensions $(m_1 \times n_2)$. Similarly, if **BA** is possible and

$$BA = D$$

then **D** will have dimensions $(m_2 \times n_1)$.

To compute the product matrix, consider the product

$$AB = C$$

Let c_{ij} be a generalized element that is located in row i and column j of the product matrix. To compute any c_{ij}, the elements in row i of matrix **A** are multiplied times the respective elements in column j of matrix **B** and are algebraically summed.

For example, if

$$A = \begin{pmatrix} 1 & 4 \\ 5 & -3 \end{pmatrix}$$

and

$$B = \begin{pmatrix} 1 \\ 4 \end{pmatrix}$$

then **A** is a (2×2) matrix and **B** is a (2×1) matrix. If we wish to find the product **AB**, then we must first examine the dimensions of the matrices. The product **AB** involves multiplying matrices with dimensions

Inner dimensions

(2×2) times (2×1)

Outer dimensions

This product is defined because the "inner" dimensions are equal; that is, the number of columns of **A** equals the number of rows of **B**. The product matrix **C** will have dimensions equal to the "outer" dimensions indicated above, that is, (2×1). Thus the product will be of the form

$$\mathbf{AB} = \mathbf{C}$$

or

$$\begin{pmatrix} 1 & 4 \\ 5 & -3 \end{pmatrix} \begin{pmatrix} 1 \\ 4 \end{pmatrix} = \begin{pmatrix} c_{11} \\ c_{21} \end{pmatrix}$$

To compute the elements of $\mathbf{C}$,

$$c_{11} = (1 \quad 4) \begin{pmatrix} 1 \\ 4 \end{pmatrix} = (1)(1) + (4)(4)$$
$$= 17$$

and

$$c_{21} = (5 \quad -3) \begin{pmatrix} 1 \\ 4 \end{pmatrix} = (5)(1) + (-3)(4)$$
$$= -7$$

or

$$\mathbf{C} = \begin{pmatrix} 17 \\ -7 \end{pmatrix}$$

The product **BA** is not defined because the inner dimensions do not match; that is, it involves multiplying a (2×1) matrix times a (2×2) matrix and the number of columns of **B** *does not equal* the number of rows of **A** ($1 \neq 2$).

Design an algorithm and write a program to input two matrices and print the two matrices together with their matrix product (if defined). Process the following to debug your program.
a. Find **AB** given **A** and **B** as in the example.
b. Find **BA** given **A** and **B** as in the example.
c. Find **AB** given

$$\mathbf{A} = \begin{pmatrix} 1 & 0 & 6 \\ 2 & -3 & 1 \end{pmatrix}$$

$$\mathbf{B} = \begin{pmatrix} 1 & 0 & 0 \\ 0 & 1 & 0 \\ 0 & 0 & 1 \end{pmatrix}$$

CHAPTER 9

Subprograms

A **subprogram** is an independent section of code that's used for a specialized purpose. Typically a subprogram is designed to solve a part of the overall problem, such as input, error detection, output, sorting, or specialized computations. It is a complete program in itself, but plays a "subrole" in the total solution to the problem. The program that controls the overall program is usually termed the **main program.** Subprograms are combined with the main program to form the entire program. This design effectively conceptualizes a program as a set of distinct and independently compiled **program units** or **program modules** (main program plus subprograms).

Subprograms are an important feature of the FORTRAN language. Strictly speaking, however, they are not essential to writing complex programs. Rather, subprogramming capability is a sophisticated refinement of the language that permits a unique 'building-block' or *modular* approach to programming. This in turn promotes programs that are easier to code, debug, and maintain.

This chapter presents two types of subprograms—*subroutine subprogram* and *function subprogram*—and discusses a style of programming called *modular programming.*[1]

9.1
SUBROUTINE SUBPROGRAMS

A **subroutine subprogram** (also called a **subroutine**) is a separate and complete program that accomplishes some particular task and may include such operations as input, output, computations, and logic.

In fact, any of the statements you have used up to this point can be included in a subroutine. The subroutine is placed immediately following the main program. If additional subroutines are required, they are placed one after another following the main program. This arrangement of main program and subroutine subprograms is shown next.

---

[1] A third type of subprogram called the block data subprogram is briefly presented in Section 9.2.

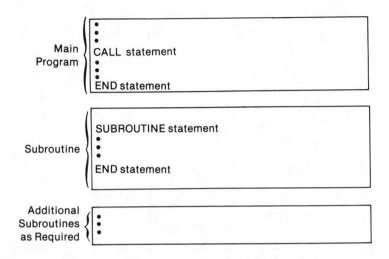

Note how this arrangement effectively subdivides a program into blocks or modules.

Subroutine subprograms represent the most powerful class of the subprograms. To illustrate their use, we first present a new problem.

EXAMPLE 9.1 Combinations

The number of combinations of n objects taken k at a time (where $n \geq k$) is a common calculation in many statistical and mathematical applications.[2] The formula is given by

$$C = \frac{n!}{(n - k)!k!}$$

where the exclamation point represents "factorial." For example, 5! reads "the factorial of 5" or "5 factorial," which is defined by the product $1 \cdot 2 \cdot 3 \cdot 4 \cdot 5$, or 120. The number of combinations of 5 taken 2 at a time ($n = 5$ and $k = 2$) is calculated from

$$C = \frac{5!}{(5 - 2)!2!} = \frac{5!}{3!2!} = \frac{1 \cdot 2 \cdot 3 \cdot 4 \cdot 5}{(1 \cdot 2 \cdot 3)(1 \cdot 2)} = \frac{120}{6 \cdot 2} = \frac{120}{12} = 10$$

Combinations are defined only if $n \geq k$, $n > 0$, and $k \geq 0$. Moreover, 0! is defined as 1.

The following program calculates and prints combinations given n and k.

---

[2] For example, see page 222.

```
******************* COMBINATIONS PROGRAM ***********************
*
******************* BEGIN MAIN PROGRAM ***********************
*
*   MAIN PROGRAM--CALCULATES AND PRINTS COMBINATIONS GIVEN N,K
*               BY REPEATEDLY CALLING SUBROUTINE FACTOR
*
*   KEY:
*    N      = AS IN FORMULA
*    K      = AS IN FORMULA
*    NFAC   = FACTORIAL OF N
*    NKFAC  = FACTORIAL OF N-K
*    KFAC   = FACTORIAL OF K
*    COMB   = COMBINATIONS
*
*-----------------------------------------------------------
*
      INTEGER N,K,NFAC,NKFAC,KFAC,COMB
*
*-----------------------------------------------------------
*
      READ *,N,K
   10 IF (N ,GE, K   ,AND,  N ,GT, 0   ,AND,  K ,GE, 0) THEN
        CALL FACTOR(N,NFAC)
        CALL FACTOR(N-K,NKFAC)
        CALL FACTOR(K,KFAC)
        COMB = NFAC/(NKFAC*KFAC)
        PRINT *,'N =',N,'K =',K,'COMBINATIONS =',COMB
        READ *,N,K
        GO TO 10
      END IF
*
*-----------------------------------------------------------
*
      END
*
******************* END MAIN PROGRAM ***********************
*
*
******************* BEGIN SUBROUTINE FACTOR ***********************
*
*
      SUBROUTINE FACTOR (NUMBER,FAC)
*
*
*   SUBROUTINE FACTOR--CALCULATES THE FACTORIAL OF A NUMBER
*                   GIVEN THE NUMBER
*
*   KEY:
*    NUMBER = NUMBER WHOSE FACTORIAL IS TO BE CALCULATED
*    FAC    = FACTORIAL OF NUMBER
*
*-----------------------------------------------------------
*
      INTEGER NUMBER,FAC
*
*-----------------------------------------------------------
*
      FAC = 1
      IF (NUMBER ,GE, 2) THEN
        DO 10 J=2,NUMBER
          FAC = FAC*J
   10   CONTINUE
      END IF
*
*-----------------------------------------------------------
*
      END
```

```
Sample Input

5,2
10,4
5,0
0,0

Sample Output


N =         5   K =        2   COMBINATIONS =         10
N =        10   K =        4   COMBINATIONS =        210
N =         5   K =        0   COMBINATIONS =          1
```

At this time don't worry about exactly how this program works, as we explain the new statements in what follows next.

Calling the Subroutine

The execution of a subroutine is invoked from another program unit (referred to as the **calling program**) by using the CALL statement. The general form of this statement is

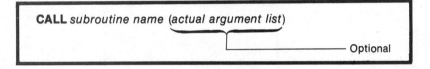

CALL *subroutine name (actual argument list)*
—————————————————— Optional

The *subroutine name* indicates the particular subroutine to be executed. Naming a subroutine follows the same rules as naming variables, for example, a subroutine name cannot have more than six characters.[3] The **actual argument list** passes values between the calling program and the subroutine. The list is made up of items (actual arguments) separated by commas. *Typical actual arguments include variable names, array names, array element names, constants, and expressions.*

For example, the statement

```
CALL FACTOR(N,NFAC)
```

in Example 9.1 is used to call subroutine FACTOR, and the contents of the variables N and NFAC are passed between the calling program and the subroutine. When this CALL statement is executed, control reverts to the subroutine, the subroutine utilizes the value in N to calculate its factorial, the value of the factorial is placed in NFAC, and control returns to the point of call in the calling program.

Now look at the main program on page 326. Next, the execution of

```
CALL FACTOR(N — K,NKFAC)
```

---

[3] However, the first letter of the subroutine name has no effect on type.

provides the value of the expression N − K to the subroutine, the subroutine calculates the factorial of this value, places the result in NKFAC, and returns control to the main program. The statement

    CALL FACTOR(K,KFAC)

is executed next, which after execution yields the factorial of the value in K as the contents in KFAC. Finally, the number of combinations is calculated and stored in COMB, results are printed, the next set of N,K values is read in, and we loop back to the test in the DO-WHILE loop.

The effect of calling the subroutine is similar to placing the set of statements in the subroutine at the point of call (sometimes referred to as the "point of invocation") in the calling program.

In general, the calling program can be the main program or another subprogram. Further, subroutines may include calls to other subprograms. However, a subroutine cannot call itself nor can two subroutines call each other.

Structure of the Subroutine

A subroutine has the following general structure.

The subroutine *always begins* with a subroutine statement having the following general form.

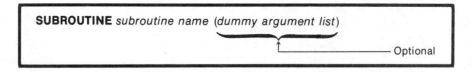

This statement identifies both the name of the subroutine and the variables in the argument list whose values are to be passed between the calling program and the subroutine. In Example 9.1 the subroutine statement is

    SUBROUTINE FACTOR(NUMBER,FAC)

In this case FACTOR is the name of the subroutine and NUMBER,FAC represents the **dummy argument list.** When the subroutine is called and control is transferred to the subroutine, *actual arguments are associated with corresponding dummy arguments,* as the following illustrates for the first call.

```
    .
    .
    .
    CALL FACTOR(N,NFAC)
    .
    .
    .
    SUBROUTINE FACTOR(NUMBER,FAC)
```

In effect, the value in N is associated with the value in NUMBER and the value in NFAC is associated with the value in FAC. Similarly, N − K is matched with NUMBER and NKFAC is matched with FAC during the second call; K is matched with NUMBER and KFAC with FAC during the third call. *Typical dummy arguments include variable names and array names.* Moreover, *dummy and actual argument lists must correspond with respect to number of arguments and their type.*

The "body" of the subroutine is sandwiched between the SUBROUTINE statement and the END statement. In general, the body can include any statement except a SUBROUTINE, FUNCTION (see Section 9.3), or BLOCK DATA (see Section 9.2) statement. In Example 9.1, the statements

```
        INTEGER NUMBER,FAC
        FAC = 1
        IF(NUMBER .GE. 2)THEN
            DO 10 J = 2,NUMBER
                FAC = FAC*J
10      CONTINUE
        END IF
```

represent the body of the subroutine.

Now carefully note the following procedure. During the first call, 5 is stored in the actual argument N according to the sample input data. Since the dummy argument NUMBER is paired with N *during this call,* NUMBER utilizes the value 5 during execution of the body in the subroutine. Thus DO-loop 10 is processed in the subroutine and FAC emerges with a value of 120.

After the body is processed, the END statement in the subroutine is executed, *at which time control returns to the calling program at the point of call.* Since the actual argument NFAC is paired with the dummy argument FAC, it follows that NFAC stores 120 at this time. Similarly, the value 3 for the expression N − K is utilized by NUMBER during the second call and the result 6 for FAC gets passed to NKFAC in the calling program; during the third call, 2 in K is used by NUMBER and 2 in FAC is returned to KFAC. We can represent this process as follows:

First Call	Second Call	Third Call

CALL FACTOR   (N,   NFAC)
    ↓5   ↑120
SUBROUTINE FACTOR(NUMBER, FAC)
	CALL FACTOR (N − K, NKFAC)
	    ↓3 ↑6
	SUBROUTINE FACTOR(NUMBER, FAC)
		CALL FACTOR (K, KFAC)
		    ↓2 ↑2
		SUBROUTINE FACTOR(NUMBER, FAC)

Thus *values in the calling program required by the subroutine are passed to the subroutine via the argument lists; similarly, computational results in the subroutine required by the calling program are returned to the calling program via the argument lists.*

Additional Considerations

1. A subroutine is compiled independently from the main program and all other subprograms. Thus identical variable names and statement labels can be used in different program units without concern for syntax errors. For example, the label 10 was used in both the main program and subroutine of Example 9.1.

2. The actual and dummy argument lists must agree with respect to number of arguments, type correspondence (integer with integer, real with real, character with character, etc.), and kind correspondence (for example, a constant, variable name, or expression as an actual argument is usually matched with a variable name as the dummy argument and an actual array name is matched with a dummy array name). Also, note that constants or expressions are not allowed as dummy arguments.

3. You should ensure length correspondence between character actual and dummy arguments by declaring the character dummy argument the same length as the character actual argument. For example,

Calling program
```
CHARACTER TOY*15
    .
    .
    .
CALL OUT (TOY)
    .
    .
    .
END
```

Subroutine
```
SUBROUTINE OUT (ITEM)
CHARACTER ITEM*15
    .
    .
    .
END
```

In this case, the character dummy argument ITEM has a declared length of 15 characters, the same as the character actual argument TOY. *For greater generality, it's best to use an asterisk in parentheses (*) as the length declarator for a character dummy argument in the subroutine,* as follows:

```
CHARACTER ITEM*(*)
```

In this case, the dummy argument ITEM assumes the same length as the associated actual argument. This means that there is length consistency regardless of the declared length in the calling program. For example, the subroutine would also be consistent with the following calling program, where the declared length is 30.

```
CHARACTER TV*30
    .
    .
    .
CALL OUT (TV)
    .
    .
    .
END
```

4. Symbolic names for variables and arrays in the dummy argument list need not have the same names as corresponding actual arguments. In Example 9.1 real arguments N and K were matched with the dummy argument NUMBER during separate calls; the dummy argument FAC was matched in turn with the real arguments NFAC, NKFAC, and KFAC. This feature generalizes the subprogram for greater flexibility; that is, the same subprogram can be used by CALL statements having different actual argument lists. More important, generalized subprograms can be designed for use by different programs altogether without the need to match identical symbolic names.

5. Example 9.1 illustrated a simple application whereby the argument lists effectively passed one value from the calling program to the subroutine and returned one value from the subroutine to the calling program. In general, multiple values may be passed in either direction, as illustrated below.

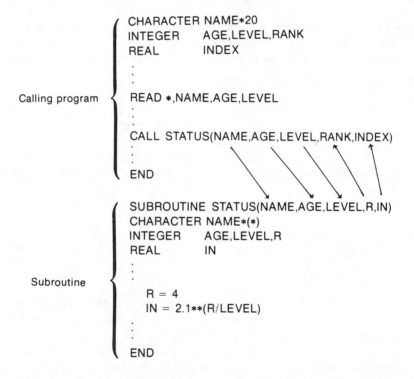

In this case, NAME, AGE, and LEVEL are passed to the subroutine and computational results for R and IN in the subroutine are returned to locations RANK and INDEX in the calling program. Note how the two argument lists match with respect to number, type, and kind. In particular, note the use of the parenthetical asterisk (*) as the length declarator for the dummy argument NAME, as discussed in item 3.

6. Argument lists may be omitted altogether, either when the design does not require data communication between the calling program and the subroutine or when COMMON statements (discussed in the next section) are used to pass values. For

example, a subroutine that simply prints extensive titles and table headings might be treated as follows:

7. Execution of the END statement in a subroutine returns control to the point of call in the calling program. Some designs may require a return to the calling program at points other than at the physical end of a subroutine. In this case, the statement

RETURN

may be used in the body of the subroutine. For example, the body of the subroutine in Example 9.1 can be rewritten by using logical IF and RETURN statements as follows.

```
      FAC = 1
      IF(NUMBER .LT. 2)RETURN
      DO 10 J = 2,NUMBER
         FAC = FAC*J
   10 CONTINUE
```

Convince yourself that this version is equivalent to the version on page 329, that is, control is immediately returned to the calling program whenever the number is zero or 1 (which gives a factorial of 1).

For reasons discussed in Section 9.4, *it's best to design a subroutine with one entry point and one exit point.* Consequently we prefer the original one-exit design in Example 9.1 to the two-exit design above.

** 8. In our earlier descriptions of argument association we were purposely vague about the actual mechanics of just how values are passed and returned between corresponding actual and dummy arguments. (We decided to spare you the agony at that point.) Now that your subroutine knowledge is maturing, consider the following statement. Argument association between two symbolic names is usually implemented either by *value/result* or by *location/address*.

To illustrate argument association by value/result, consider the following scheme for the first call in Example 9.1.

In this case dummy names have storage locations separate from corresponding actual names. When the CALL statement is executed, values in N and NFAC are copied into the storage locations for NUMBER and FAC. In the body of the subroutine, the value in NUMBER is used to calculate the factorial 120, which is then stored in FAC. When the END (or RETURN) statement in the subroutine is executed, we can visualize the following.

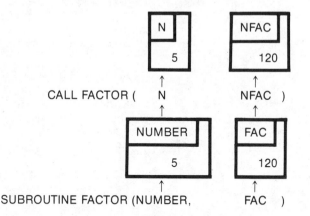

Now the flow is reversed as values in NUMBER and FAC are copied into N and NFAC, respectively.

Argument association between names by location/address does not assign separate storage locations for dummy names. In this case dummy names share the storage locations of corresponding actual names. Thus, rather than a flow of values or contents between separate memory locations, there is a transfer of addresses, so that the dummy name can utilize the same storage location as its "sister" actual name.

In either case, we have a word of caution: *If a dummy argument is assigned a new value in the subroutine, the value of the corresponding actual argument also is changed.* Make sure you don't inadvertently change the value in a dummy argument. In particular, never change the value in a dummy argument that corresponds to an expression or constant in the actual argument.

Follow-up Exercises

1. Roleplay the computer in Example 9.1 by processing the following data through the program (don't forget to specify the output).

   8,6
   4,4
   4,0
   4,1
   1,4

2. Would it be alright to initialize FAC in the subroutine of Example 9.1 by using a DATA statement? Would there be a problem if we had forgotten the INTEGER statement in the subroutine? Do you see any problem with using the name FACTOR in place of FAC in the subroutine?

3. Specify what's wrong, if anything, with each of the following.

Calling Program	Subroutine
a. INTEGER N,NFAC CALL FACTOR(N,NFAC)	SUBROUTINE FACTOR(N,NFAC) INTEGER N,NFAC
b. INTEGER N,NFAC CALL FACTOR(N,NFAC)	SUBROUTINE(NUMBER,FAC) INTEGER NUMBER,FAC
c. CALL ADD	SUBROUTINE ADD(A,B,C)
d. CHARACTER A*10 INTEGER B,C REAL D,E,F CALL SEARCH(A,B,C,D,E,F,100,'YES')	SUBROUTINE SEARCH(P,Q,R,S,T,U) CHARACTER Q*50 INTEGER P,T REAL R,S,U
e. REAL R,A CALL AREA(R,A)	SUBROUTINE AREA(RADIUS,AREA) REAL RADIUS,AREA,PI . . . AREA = PI*RADIUS**2

4. Specify output for the program below. Assume the following input: 1.1, 2.2, 3.3.

   ```
   REAL A,B,C,SUM
   CALL INPUT(A,B,C)
   CALL ADD(A,B,C,SUM)
   CALL OUTPUT(A,B,C,SUM)
   END

   SUBROUTINE INPUT(X,Y,Z)
   REAL X,Y,Z
   ```

```
        READ *,X,Y,Z
        END

        SUBROUTINE ADD(X,Y,Z,TOTAL)
        REAL X,Y,Z,TOTAL
        Y = X + Y
        Z = Y + Z
        X = Z + X
        TOTAL = X + Y + Z
        END

        SUBROUTINE OUTPUT(X,Y,Z,TOTAL)
        REAL X,Y,Z,TOTAL
        PRINT *,'VALUES:',X,Y,Z
        PRINT *,'TOTAL:',TOTAL
        END
```

Have the original contents in A, B, C changed?

5. Write a subroutine named HEAD that inputs a character value up to a length of 25 characters (stored in DATE) and prints the following heading.

    PERIODIC REPORT
    DECEMBER 15, 1982 ← Sample input/output value

No data need be passed to and from this subroutine.

9.2
ADDITIONAL TOPICS

In this section we cover some further topics on the use of subroutines: the design of flowcharts and pseudocode, the passing of arrays, an alternative method of passing values, and methods of sharing storage locations.

Flowcharts/Pseudocode

Figure 9.1 illustrates the flowcharts for the main program and subprogram of Example 9.1. Note the following.

1. Each subprogram has a separate flowchart. Thus a program with one main program and four subprograms would have five distinct flowcharts.
2. The **predefined process symbol** can be used to indicate the call of the subprogram, as illustrated in Figure 9.1a. The exact nature of the writing within the symbol is a matter of personal preference.
3. The Start-Stop symbol is used to indicate entry and exit points in the subprogram. The entry point is labeled with the name of the subprogram and the exit point is labeled with the word return. Between these two symbols, the logic of the subprogram is illustrated using any of the legitimate symbols for main programs.

Figure 9.2 illustrates pseudocode for Example 9.1. Note how each program module begins with a "start" and ends with an "end," to identify program modules clearly. Moreover, this identification is further enhanced by indenting the module itself. Finally,

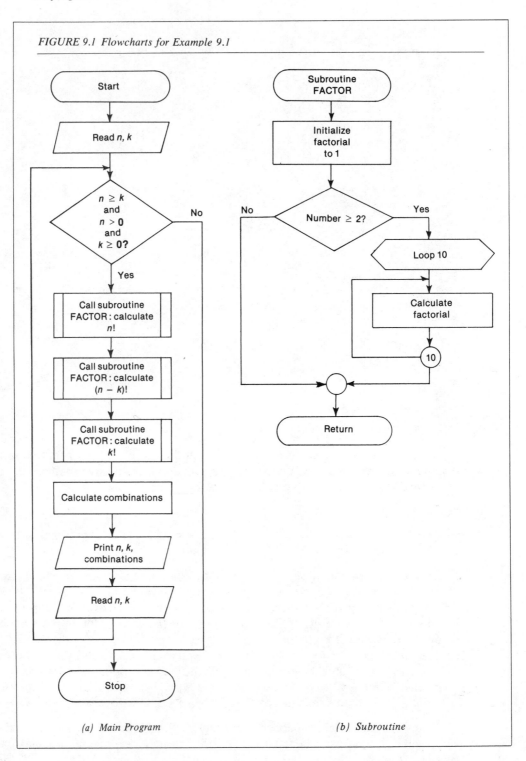

FIGURE 9.1 *Flowcharts for Example 9.1*

(a) *Main Program*   (b) *Subroutine*

FIGURE 9.2 *Pseudocode for Example 9.1*

```
              Start main program
                 READ n,k
                 DO WHILE n ≥ k,n > 0,k ≥ 0
                    CALL FACTOR to calculate n!
                    CALL FACTOR to calculate (n − k)!
                    CALL FACTOR to calculate k!
                    Combinations = n!/(n − k)!/k!
                    PRINT n,k, combinations
                    READ n,k
                 END DO
                 Stop
              End main program

              Start subroutine FACTOR
                 Factorial = 1
                 IF no. ≥ 2 THEN
                    DO WHILE factorial not calculated
                       Recursively update factorial
                    END DO
                 END IF
                 Return
              End subroutine FACTOR
```

note that the word "return" should be included in the subroutine to indicate the return point unambiguously (since return points can differ depending on the design).

Follow-up Exercises

6. Change the flowchart and pseudocode for subroutine FACTOR based on the subroutine body on page 332.
7. **Crew Selection Revisited.** Design flowchart or pseudocode and write a program to solve part a of Exercise 41 in Chapter 6 on page 222. Use the following modular design.

   Main program inputs all data, calls subroutine combinations, and outputs required results.
   Subroutine combinations calculates combinations by repeatedly calling subroutine factorial.
   Subroutine factorial calculates the factorial of a number.

* 8. **Crew Selection Re-Revisited.** Design flowchart or pseudocode and write a program to solve part b of Exercise 41 in Chapter 6 on page 222. Use the following modular design.

Main program inputs all data, calls subroutine combinations, and outputs required results.
Subroutine combinations calculates combinations based on the logic in part b of the original exercise in Chapter 6.

Passing Arrays

Up until now we have avoided the use of arrays in argument lists, in order for you to concentrate on the essentials of subroutines. Most analytical and statistical programming packages that are available commercially make use of subprograms that pass arrays, as the following example illustrates.

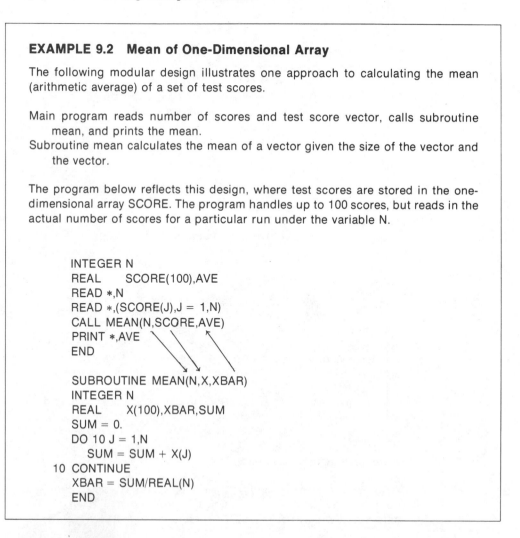

EXAMPLE 9.2   Mean of One-Dimensional Array

The following modular design illustrates one approach to calculating the mean (arithmetic average) of a set of test scores.

Main program reads number of scores and test score vector, calls subroutine mean, and prints the mean.
Subroutine mean calculates the mean of a vector given the size of the vector and the vector.

The program below reflects this design, where test scores are stored in the one-dimensional array SCORE. The program handles up to 100 scores, but reads in the actual number of scores for a particular run under the variable N.

```
      INTEGER N
      REAL    SCORE(100),AVE
      READ *,N
      READ *,(SCORE(J),J = 1,N)
      CALL MEAN(N,SCORE,AVE)
      PRINT *,AVE
      END

      SUBROUTINE MEAN(N,X,XBAR)
      INTEGER N
      REAL    X(100),XBAR,SUM
      SUM = 0.
      DO 10 J = 1,N
         SUM = SUM + X(J)
   10 CONTINUE
      XBAR = SUM/REAL(N)
      END
```

Note the following.

1. The actual argument list passes to the subprogram the number of storage locations (N, total number of exam scores) that are used in the array and the array itself (SCORE).

2. The dummy argument list pairs N with N, X with SCORE, and XBAR with AVE. The dummy array X merely utilizes the storage locations for the real array SCORE; however, X *must be dimensioned in the subprogram.* Otherwise the compiler has no way of knowing that X is an array.[4]

3. Many subprograms are commonly used as modules by different programs. A potential shortcoming of the above subroutine is its dependence on the explicit dimensioning of 100 elements in the main program. In other words, if this subprogram were to be used with a calling program having, say, 500 elements in the array, then it would seem reasonable to dimension X to 500 in the subroutine. We can overcome this shortcoming in consistency in the size of dummy arrays in two ways. First, an **assumed-size array declarator** can be used for the dummy array, as follows.

In this case the asterisk indicates that the size of the *numeric* dummy array is to be the same as the size of the associated *numeric* actual array. This element-by-element correspondence in size is also true for character arrays, provided the declared lengths of actual and dummy array elements are the same; otherwise a complicated rule applies for establishing the size of the character dummy array. In general, *assumed-size array declarators are specified by using an asterisk as the upper dimension bound of the last dimension.* Second, an **adjustable array declarator** can be used for the dummy array, as follows.

┌──────── Adjustable array declarator
│
REAL X(N),XBAR,SUM
        └──────── Adjustable dimension

In this case N is called an **adjustable dimension,** which means that the dummy array X is assumed to have a size given by the value in N. For example, if N stores 75, the dummy array X is assumed to have 75 elements, which is exactly consistent with the number of elements utilized in the main program for array SCORE. In general, *adjustable array declarators are specified by using integer variables in the expressions for lower and/or upper dimension bounds.* The use of either assumed-size

---

[4] Systems invariably use argument association by location/address for arrays, which means that X does not have its own separate storage locations. Association by value/result for arrays would be storage and time inefficient.

array declarators or adjustable array declarators allows us to pair the same general subprogram with calling programs having varying array sizes, without concern for the size of the dummy array. In doing so, however, we should keep the following in mind.

a. An adjustable dimension must be an integer expression, must be included in the dummy argument list,[5] and must take on values that are compatible with the dimension bounds that were declared for the corresponding actual array. In the example, N is an integer expression for the upper dimension bound of a one-dimensional dummy array X, it appears within the dummy argument list, and its value must not exceed 100 since this is the value of the upper dimension bound for the corresponding actual array SCORE.

b. When using adjustable dimensions for dummy arrays of two or more dimensions, the value of each *adjustable* dimension should equal exactly the corresponding *actual* dimension; otherwise the conceptual relations of array elements (for example, a table of numbers) would not be maintained. Thus the CALL statement in

```
        .
        .

    REAL A(10,5)
        .
        .

    CALL TABLE(10,5,A)
        .
        .

    END
    SUBROUTINE TABLE(M,N,T)
        .
        .

    REAL T(M,N)
        .
        .

    END
```

ensures that the arrays A and T are conceptually identical (that is, the first row of elements in T is the same as the first row in A, etc.). This is so because the number of rows and columns in T (given by M and N, respectively) is identical to the number of rows and columns reserved for A in the REAL statement (10 and 5, respectively); however, the statement

```
    CALL TABLE(4,3,A)
```

would not preserve this row-by-row conceptual relationship.

c. Remember that the asterisk in an assumed-size array declarator is only allowed for the *upper* dimension bound of the *last* dimension. For example, the following is conceptually identical to the above illustration.

---

[5] Alternatively, it can be included in the list of a COMMON statement (page 342).

```
      .
      .
      .
REAL A(10,5)
      .
      .
      .
CALL TABLE(10,A)
      .
      .
END

SUBROUTINE TABLE(M,T)
      .
      .
REAL T(M,*)
      .
      .
END
```

However, the use of

```
REAL T(*,*)
```

would provoke a syntax error.

Follow-up Exercises

9. Indicate errors, if any, in the following.

   a. SUBROUTINE X(X,M,N,T)
       REAL X(M),Y(M,2*K + 1),T(N)
             .
             .
       END

   b. INTEGER K,N,TOT(500),A(K,N)
             .
             .
       CALL SUM(K,N,TOT(3))
             .
             .
       END

       SUBROUTINE SUM(M,N,S)
       INTEGER M,N,S,POINT(M)
             .
             .
       END

```
      c.  INTEGER ROW,COL
          PARAMETER (ROW = 100,COL = 50)
          INTEGER DOT(ROW,COL),SUM(ROW)
          CALL MOD1(ROW,COL,DOT,SUM)
            .
            .
            .
          END

          SUBROUTINE MOD1(M,N,X,S)
          INTEGER M,N,X(200,50),S(*)
            .
            .
            .
          END
```

10. Modify Example 9.2 such that SUM, the sum of the scores, is output in the main program along with AVE.

11. Modify Example 9.2 such that N and the array are input and XBAR is output by the subroutine. Under what conditions can we input N through the subroutine?

* **12.** Add a second subroutine to Example 9.2 called SORT, which rearranges and outputs the scores in ascending order. Use a desirable array declarator. *Hint:* See Example 7.13 on page 267.

* **13.** **Data Editing.** Modify Example 9.2 by adding a new subroutine that edits scores for input errors right after the score array is read in by the main program. Specifically, if all scores are in the range 0 to 100, control is returned to the main program. Otherwise execution stops after printing all scores outside this range together with their positions in the array.

** **14.** Modify Example 9.2 as follows: Treat SCORE as a 100 × 10 array; treat AVE as a ten-element one-dimensional array which is to contain column averages from SCORE; declare SCORE and AVE using symbolic name constants; read in N (number of students or rows used in SCORE), M (number of tests or columns used in SCORE), and SCORE (row by row); modify the subroutine such that dummy arrays are properly declared and AVE stores column averages from X.

COMMON Statement: Blank Common Block

Up until now, the only means of communication between the calling program and the subprogram has been through their arguments. An alternative means of communication between program units is through a common storage area that can be referenced by two or more program units that use COMMON statements. There are two kinds of COMMON statements: blank (unlabeled) COMMON and named (labeled) COMMON. First we discuss the blank COMMON statement.

The **blank COMMON statement** has the general form

COMMON *list of names*
---

where the *list of names* refers to variable names, array names, and array declarators, all separated by commas. The blank COMMON statement causes the compiler to establish an area of storage that is to be "shared in common" by all program modules using blank COMMON statements.

EXAMPLE 9.3   Mean of One-Dimensional Array Using a Blank COMMON Statement

The following is a rewrite of Example 9.2 on page 338. Note that the only differences are the elimination of argument lists and the insertion of two COMMON statements.

```
      INTEGER N
      REAL      SCORE(100),AVE
      COMMON N,SCORE,AVE
      READ *,N
      READ *,(SCORE(J),J = 1,N)
      CALL MEAN                                    ← Note no argument list
      PRINT *,AVE
      END

      SUBROUTINE MEAN                              ← Note no argument list
      INTEGER N
      REAL      X(100),XBAR,SUM
      COMMON N,X,XBAR
      SUM = 0.
      DO 10 J = 1,N
         SUM = SUM + X(J)
   10 CONTINUE
      XBAR = SUM/REAL(N)
      END
```

Conceptually, the memory for this program can be visualized as illustrated in Figure 9.3. The COMMON statement allocates 102 cells to the **blank common block.** Each program unit that includes a blank COMMON statement can use or alter any of the values stored in this blank common block. Note that the storage location for J in the main program is *local* to the main program; the storage locations for J and SUM in the subroutine are local to the subroutine.

Here are some additional points concerning the use of blank COMMON statements.

1. The association in a common block is by storage rather than by name. This means that it is the order of names in COMMON statements that determines which variable names or array element names are associated among program units (as is the case with argument lists). In looking at the two COMMON statements in the exam-

FIGURE 9.3 Storage Allocations in Example 9.3

ple and at Figure 9.3, we see that N in the main program and N in the subroutine refer to the same storage location, as do SCORE(1) and X(1), SCORE(2) and X(2), and so on.

2. Corresponding names among COMMON statements should be consistent with respect to type; that is, you should pair integer with integer, real with real, character with character, and so on. *If a character variable or array is in a common block, then all names in that block must store character values.*

3. It should be noted that the COMMON statement is a nonexecutable statement that serves to declare certain information about storage, and hence must appear in the program before instructions that use common storage. *The COMMON statement must precede all DATA and executable statements in the program module.*

4. The list of names in the COMMON statement can include array declarations. For example, in the main program of Example 9.3 we could have written

```
REAL      SCORE,AVE
COMMON N,SCORE(100),AVE
```

——————— Array declarator here, not in REAL
statement

instead of

```
REAL      SCORE(100),AVE
COMMON N,SCORE,AVE
```

Similarly, in the subroutine we could have written

```
REAL      X,XBAR,SUM
COMMON N,X(100),XBAR
```

——————— Constant array declarator

instead of

```
REAL      X(100),XBAR,SUM
COMMON N,X,XBAR
```

You might note that assumed-size and adjustable array declarators are not permitted in COMMON statements. For example,

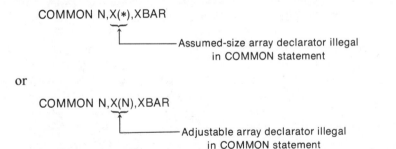

```
COMMON N,X(*),XBAR
```

——————— Assumed-size array declarator illegal
in COMMON statement

or

```
COMMON N,X(N),XBAR
```

——————— Adjustable array declarator illegal
in COMMON statement

would give a syntax error. These array declarators are permitted only in type or DIMENSION statements and only if the array is a *dummy* array, that is, it appears in a dummy argument list.

5. It's permissible to pass values among program modules by a mixture of argument lists and common blocks. For example, if other program modules were to be added to Example 9.3, each of which uses N and X (or SCORE) but not XBAR (or AVE), then it would make sense to place N and X (or SCORE) in a common block and to pass XBAR (or AVE) through an argument list. Thus in the main program of Example 9.3 we could write

```
COMMON N,SCORE
CALL MEAN(AVE)
```

and change the subroutine by writing

```
SUBROUTINE MEAN(XBAR)
COMMON N,X
```

A word of caution: Dummy arguments must not be part of a common block. For example, the following is illegal, since XBAR is both a dummy argument and in the common block.

```
SUBROUTINE MEAN(XBAR)
COMMON N,X,XBAR
```

6. For convenience and efficiency, many programmers prefer the use of COMMON statements to argument lists whenever many of the same names are to be passed among several program modules. Argument lists are thus simplified or entirely eliminated. Note, however, that the inclusion of an array name in a COMMON statement (rather than in a dummy argument list) precludes the declaration of that array through assumed-size or adjustable array declarators.

7. In certain applications, common blocks also can substantially reduce storage requirements. For example, suppose that three program modules within the same executable program each use a very large local array of 100,000 elements. Further assume that these modules do not communicate with one another, and that once a module finishes executing its results need not be used by another module. These arrays thus take up 300,000 locations of local storage (100,000 in each of three local storage areas). If we use COMMON statements to associate these arrays, we can reduce storage requirements by two thirds to 100,000 locations. Note, however, that in doing so we must make sure that the contents of a previously filled array are not needed once the next associated array starts utilizing the common block.

**8. Consider the following subtle point on how the use of a common block differs from the use of argument lists with respect to methods of storage and data "transfers." When using argument lists, the compiler must supply a special set of instructions in machine code that specifies the correspondence between actual and dummy argument lists. *Each time a subprogram is called, these instructions must be executed.* When using a common block, however, no special instructions are needed for "passing" values, since passing is eliminated due to the direct sharing of storage locations. To put it another way, the use of a common block results in the explicit sharing of storage locations whereas the use of argument lists results in implicit sharing. Thus the use of a common block promotes fewer machine code instructions (which is storage-efficient) and faster execution times (since there are fewer instructions to execute).

COMMON *Statement: Named*
Common Blocks

In some programs the common area may be treated as a single block; in other programs the programmer may wish to subdivide the common area into smaller blocks, where each block has a name. We can accomplish this by using the following form of the COMMON statement.

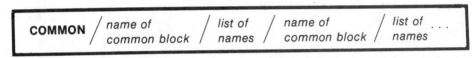

The block name is formed in the same way as a variable name; however no type is associated with the common name. For example, the statement

COMMON/BLOCK1/A,B,C /BLOCK2/D,E

sets up two **named common blocks,** as illustrated below.

The following program units

```
COMMON F,G,H          ⎫
COMMON/BLOCK1/A,B,C   ⎬  or COMMON F,G,H  /BLOCK1/A,B,C  /BLOCK2/D,E
COMMON/BLOCK2/D,E     ⎭
    .
    .
    .
END
```

```
SUBROUTINE ONE
COMMON F,G,H          ⎫
COMMON/BLOCK1/A,B,C   ⎬  or COMMON F,G,H  /BLOCK1/A,B,C
    .
    .
    .
END
```

```
SUBROUTINE TWO
COMMON F,G,H
COMMON/BLOCK2/D,E } or COMMON F,G,H   /BLOCK2/D,E
   .
   .
   .
END
```

create the following storage configuration.

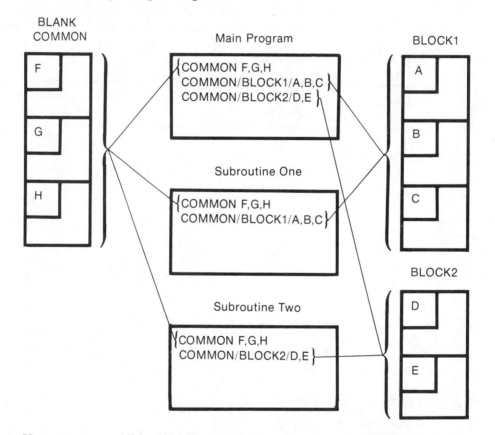

Here are some additional points to consider regarding named common blocks.

1. Named common blocks are preferred to a blank common block when there are several program units, a few of which have a need to share data that are of no concern to other program units. Another reason for using named common blocks is to store character data, since a common block cannot contain both character and noncharacter data. Thus it is necessary to set up one or more common blocks exclusively for character data and other common blocks exclusively for noncharacter data since a common block cannot contain both character and noncharacter data. Therefore, it may be necessary to set up one block for all common storage of character type and another block for noncharacter type.

2. Note the following differences between blank and named common blocks:
   a. References to the same named common block among different program modules must be consistent with respect to the size of the block, but references to a blank common block may imply different block sizes, as the following examples illustrate.

Main Program	Subprogram	Comment
COMMON /BLOCKA/A,B,C	COMMON /BLOCKA/D,E,F	Size consistency; three storage locations each
COMMON /BLOCKB/X,Y,Z	COMMON /BLOCKB/R,S	Not permitted, since first specifies three locations and second specifies two locations
COMMON M,N,A(500)	COMMON K,L,B(300)	Permitted in blank common; K with M, L with N, B(1) with A(1), . . ., B(300) with A(300); A(301) to A(500) are defined but not used by subprogram

   b. Arrays and variables in blank common cannot be initialized through DATA statements; however, in named common they can be initialized by using DATA statements in a **block data subprogram** with the following structure.

```
BLOCK DATA name of block data subprogram
      Statements such as PARAMETER, DIMENSION, COMMON,
:  }  EQUIVALENCE, DATA, and type; comment lines may be included
      also.
END
```

For example, the block data subprogram given by

```
BLOCK DATA SET1
   INTEGER N,A,B,C
   REAL    X
   COMMON /BLOCK1/A,B,C
   COMMON /BLOCK2/N,X(1000)
   DATA A,B,C/10,20,30/
   DATA X/1000*0./
END
```

specifies that A, B, and C are in named common BLOCK1, and these are to be initialized to 10, 20, and 30, respectively. BLOCK2 contains N and the 1000 elements in X. Of these, N is left undefined but each element in X is initialized to zero.

The block data subprogram is a *nonexecutable* program module which, like any other subprogram, can be placed anywhere following the main program. If desired the name of this subprogram may be omitted, but an executable program may not have more than one unnamed block data subprogram.

Follow-up Exercises

15. Is it feasible to eliminate argument lists in Example 9.1 on page 326 by using COMMON statements? Explain

16. Given the following program

```
INTEGER X,A
COMMON X(2),A
X(1) = 10
X(2) = 20
A = 5
CALL SUB
PRINT *,X(1),X(2),A
END

SUBROUTINE SUB
INTEGER Y,B
COMMON Y(2),B
B = Y(1) + Y(2) + B
END
```

    a. Schematically represent the blank common block and show how contents change as the program executes.

    b. Specify the output.

    c. Indicate what happens if we use

        COMMON B,Y(2)

    in the subroutine.

17. For each of the following, identify what is wrong, if anything (assume implicit typing).

Calling Program	Subprogram
a. COMMON M,N,Y(1),Q	COMMON R,J,P,K
b. COMMON L,S(50),T	COMMON K,R(30)A
c. COMMON A,B,C	COMMON D,E First subprogram (D,E,F are to be paired with A,B,C)
d. COMMON A,B,C,I,J	COMMON D,E,F COMMON M,N Second subprogram (M,N are to be paired with I,J)
e. COMMON M,N,A(500,20)	COMMON M,N,A(500,20)
f. COMMON /B2/X(1000)	COMMON /B2/A(800)

Calling Program	Subprogram
*g. COMMON A,B,C CALL SUB(A)	SUBROUTINE SUB(R) COMMON S,T,U

**h. CHARACTER C*50
        COMMON N,B(1000),C
        CALL SUB
	SUBROUTINE SUB
	CHARACTER C*20
	COMMON N,B(N),C
	DATA C/'TRUE'/

*18. Solve Exercise 12 using COMMON statements.
*19. Solve Exercise 13 using COMMON statements.
**20. Solve Exercise 14 using COMMON statements.

EQUIVALENCE Statement**

The COMMON statement specifies that storage locations are to be shared by items (variable names, array names, etc.) *in different program units.* If we wish items *within the same program unit* to share storage locations, then we can use

> **EQUIVALENCE** *(list of associated names),(list of associated names), . . .*

where each list of associated names (variables, arrays, etc.) enclosed within the same parentheses share the same memory locations.

For example, suppose that in a large program a programmer accidentally uses the variables LARGE and BIG for the same quantity. Instead of changing one of the names, the following EQUIVALENCE statement could be inserted.

    EQUIVALENCE(LARGE,BIG)

This results in the following storage configuration.

Whenever LARGE or BIG is referenced the same memory location is accessed. Note the following points.

1. The EQUIVALENCE statement specifies that the storage sequence of the associated names in the list is to have the same *first* storage location. For example, the statements

    REAL A(5),B(5),C(3), D(5),E(4),F(100000),G(100000)
    EQUIVALENCE (A(1),B(1)),(C(2),D,E(3)),(F,G))

result in the following storage configuration for the list (A(1),B(1)).

***

** Can be skipped without loss of continuity.

A(1) and B(1) share or reference the first storage location in the sequence. The relationships between A(2) and B(2), etc., are automatically equivalenced since array names imply a sequence of adjacent storage locations. Thus five locations instead of ten are needed.

For the list (C(2), D, E(3)) we have

E(2) and C(1) share; E(3), C(2), and D(1) share; E(4), C(3), and D(2) share. Seven instead of 12 locations used, so five locations saved.

For the list (F, G) we have

F and G totally share corresponding elements. One hundred thousand instead of 200,000 locations used, so 100,000 locations saved.

2. Arrays C, D, and E are said to be *partially associated* whereas arrays A and B, and F and H, are *totally associated*.

3. Names of type character can be equivalenced only with other names of type character. For example, the statements

    ```
    CHARACTER A*10,B*6
    EQUIVALENCE (A,B)
    ```

    equivalence the first six (of ten) *character storage units* in A with the six character storage units in B.

4. The EQUIVALENCE statement is nonexecutable, but must precede executable statements in the program unit.

5. Dummy arguments must not be equivalenced.

6. Two names in one common block or in two different common blocks must not be equivalenced.

7. Names having different numeric type may be equivalenced, but it's not suggested in practice as it may lead to unpredictable logic errors, depending on the hardware.

8. Associations in the list of an EQUIVALENCE statement apply only within the program unit where the EQUIVALENCE statement resides, unless one of the equivalenced names is part of a common block (see Exercise 21f).

The primary justification for using EQUIVALENCE statements is that they can substantially reduce storage requirements. This is particularly desirable when several large arrays are used in one program, as illustrated by the 100,000 storage locations saved by equivalencing arrays F and G in the above example. Assuming F and G have different meanings and purposes within the program unit, then the act of equivalencing them is feasible only if we're through with one of the arrays before we begin manipulating the other. Otherwise logic errors may result.

Unless storage is critical, we don't recommend the use of EQUIVALENCE statements, as they reduce program readability and increase the likelihood of syntax, execution, and logic errors.

Follow-up Exercise

21. Specify storage configurations for each part, given the following type statements.

```
CHARACTER A*4,B*4,C(2)*3
INTEGER    D,E(5),F(4),G(5)
REAL X(8),Y(6)
DOUBLE PRECISION Z (Note: A double-precision variable name
                          takes up two adjacent storage locations)
```

    a. EQUIVALENCE (E(1),G,F(4)),D,E)
    b. EQUIVALENCE (A,D)
    c. EQUIVALENCE (Y(5),Z)
    d. EQUIVALENCE (X(8),Y(6))
    e. EQUIVALENCE (A,C(1)),(B,C(2))
** f. COMMON /ONE/D,E(5)
       EQUIVALENCE (E(4),F)

9.3
FUNCTION SUBPROGRAMS*

A **function subprogram** is another type of subprogram that looks very much like a subroutine. Unlike a subroutine, however, it is called in the manner of an intrinsic function such as SQRT, and returns a single value to the calling program.

EXAMPLE 9.4 Combinations Using Function Subprogram

The following program is a rewrite of the program in Example 9.1 on page 326, with the subroutine replaced by a function subprogram. Key differences between this version and the original version are shaded in. Make note of these differences and then read on.

---

* This section may be skipped without loss of continuity.

```
********************* COMBINATIONS PROGRAM ***********************
*
*
********************* BEGIN MAIN PROGRAM ************************
*
*   MAIN PROGRAM--CALCULATES AND PRINTS COMBINATIONS GIVEN N,K
*                 BY REPEATEDLY CALLING FUNCTION FACTOR
*
*   KEY:
*    N       = AS IN FORMULA
*    K       = AS IN FORMULA
*    FACTOR  = FACTORIAL FUNCTION
*    COMB    = COMBINATIONS
*
*------------------------------------------------------
*
      INTEGER N,K,FACTOR,COMB          ⟵ Function name replaces
*                                        NFAC, NKFAC, KFAC
*------------------------------------------------------
*
      READ *,N,K
   10 IF (N .GE. K  .AND.  N .GT. 0  .AND.  K .GE. 0) THEN
*                                    ⟵ CALL statements
*                                       eliminated
*                                                        ⟵ Function
      COMB = FACTOR(N)/(FACTOR(N-K)*FACTOR(K))              references
      PRINT *,'N =',N,'K =',K,'COMBINATIONS =',COMB
      READ *,N,K
      GO TO 10
      END IF
*
*------------------------------------------------------
*
      END
*
********************* END MAIN PROGRAM ************************
*
*
********************* BEGIN FUNCTION FACTOR ******************
*
*                                    ⟵ Function statement
      FUNCTION FACTOR (NUMBER) ⟵          replaces
*                                          subroutine statement
*
*   FUNCTION FACTOR--CALCULATES THE FACTORIAL OF A NUMBER
*                    GIVEN THE NUMBER
*
*   KEY:
*    NUMBER = NUMBER WHOSE FACTORIAL IS TO BE CALCULATED
*    FACTOR = FACTORIAL OF NUMBER
*
*------------------------------------------------------
*
      INTEGER NUMBER,FACTOR
*
*------------------------------------------------------
*
      FACTOR = 1                    ⟵ Function name
      IF (NUMBER .GE. 2) THEN          replaces FAC
         DO 10 J=2,NUMBER
         FACTOR = FACTOR*J
   10    CONTINUE
      END IF
*
*------------------------------------------------------
*
      END
```

Sample Input

```
5,2
10,4
5,0
0,0
```

Sample Output

```
N =        5   K =        2   COMBINATIONS =         10
N =       10   K =        4   COMBINATIONS =        210
N =        5   K =        0   COMBINATIONS =          1
```

Calling the Function Subprogram

A function subprogram is executed by referencing the function through another program termed the **calling program.** Any reference to a function in a calling program transfers control to the function subprogram. The **function reference** (or **call**) consists of the *function name* followed by the actual argument list enclosed in parentheses. Functions are named and typed in the same manner as variables. **Actual arguments** are usually names and expressions whose values are transferred to the function subprogram from the calling program and are treated the same as in subroutine calls.

In all cases the function subprogram is called by using its name and actual arguments in an expression. In Example 9.4 the assignment statement

contains three function references to the function subprogram called FACTOR. The reference FACTOR(N) passes the value in N (5 for the first set of test data above) to the function subprogram. The subprogram then returns the value of the factorial (120 in this case) to the point of call. The other two references work in the same manner. In effect, COMB is evaluated as follows:

```
COMB = FACTOR(5)/(FACTOR(5 - 2)*FACTOR(2))
     = 120/(6*2)
     = 120/12
     = 10
```

Note that the function name FACTOR is typed integer in the main program. It's a good programming practice to type explicitly all function names by using type statements (REAL, CHARACTER, etc.) in the calling program.

You should further note the fact that the mechanics of function subprogram references are essentially the same as references to statement functions (Section A.4) or to intrinsic functions such as MAX and LOG. This type of reference is said to be *implicit,* as opposed to the *explicit* reference of a subroutine through a CALL statement.

In general, the calling program can be the main program, another function subprogram, or a subroutine. Also, a function subprogram can call other subprograms, but may not call itself.

Structure of the Function Subprogram

A function subprogram has the following general structure:

```
FUNCTION statement
: }  body of function subprogram (function name must be defined here)
END statement
```

The function subprogram always begins with a function statement having the following general form.

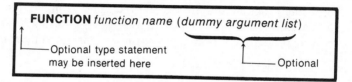

Naming the function subprogram follows the same rules as naming variables. This means that the first letter in the *function name* implicitly determines the type of the function (real or integer). As usual, however, we strongly recommend explicit typing by using a type statement such as CHARACTER, LOGICAL, INTEGER, REAL, or DOUBLE PRECISION. The **dummy argument list** is used in the same manner as subroutines, that is, when the function is called actual arguments are associated with corresponding dummy arguments. In Example 9.4 the statement

```
FUNCTION FACTOR(NUMBER)
```

identifies the beginning of a function subprogram called FACTOR and NUMBER is a dummy argument.

The body of the function subprogram follows the function statement and precedes the END statement. In general, the body can include any statement except a SUBROUTINE, FUNCTION, or BLOCK DATA statement.

When the function is called by the reference FACTOR(N), the dummy argument NUMBER assumes the value in the actual argument N (5 in the first line of input data) and the body is executed.

Within the body the name of the function must be defined (assigned a value), since the function name is the vehicle by which the result is transmitted back to the calling program. Normally this is accomplished by placing the function name on the left side of an assignment statement, as illustrated by

FACTOR = 1

and

FACTOR = FACTOR*J

in Example 9.4. The appearance of the name of the function, FACTOR, to the left of an equal sign ensures that the value of the function is returned to the calling program once a RETURN or END statement is executed. Thus, when the END statement is executed in the function subprogram of Example 9.4, the value 120 in FACTOR is returned as the function value for the reference FACTOR(N) in the calling program (when 5 is in N).

Additional Considerations

1. Note that a function subprogram returns a *single* result to the calling program through the name of the function itself, unlike a subroutine that returns one or more results through the argument list.
2. Don't forget to specify the type of the function, both in the calling program and in the subprogram. In the subprogram, you have a choice as to how you explicitly type the function. Either you can use a type statement in the body (as in Example 9.4) or you can insert the type statement in front of the keyword FUNCTION in the FUNCTION statement. For example, we could have written

   INTEGER FUNCTION FACTOR(NUMBER)
   INTEGER NUMBER

   in place of

   FUNCTION FACTOR(NUMBER)
   INTEGER NUMBER,FACTOR

   in Example 9.4.
3. Example 9.4 illustrates one argument, but as in the use of subroutines, multiple arguments are allowed in the argument lists. Moreover, the argument list can be eliminated (as when common blocks are used), but the parentheses following the function name must always be included.
4. If only a single result is needed from a subprogram, many programmers prefer to use a function subprogram rather than a subroutine. The program in Example 9.4, for example, is "cleaner" than the program in Example 9.1. If multiple results are needed, however, a subroutine is preferred to a function subprogram.
5. As in subroutines, a change in the value of a dummy argument within the body of the function subprogram has corresponding effects on actual arguments. As a matter of style, a function subprogram should never be designed to change the value of a dummy argument, as this obscures the intended effect of a function—namely, to return a single result through the function name.
6. The treatment of all other issues discussed under subroutines is the same in function subprograms as in subroutines. For example, there are no differences with respect to independent compilation, the treatment of actual and dummy arguments, use of RETURN statements, specification of flowcharts and pseudocode, the passing of arrays, or the use of common blocks.

Follow-up Exercises

22. Modify Figure 9.1 on page 336 and Figure 9.2 on page 337 to reflect the program in Example 9.4.
23. Solve the following using function subprograms in place of subroutines.
    a. Exercise 7 on page 337.
    *b. Exercise 8 on page 337.
24. Modify Example 9.2 on page 338 to use a function subprogram in place of the subroutine. Also, use adjustable dimensions in the function subprogram.
25. Is it possible to solve Exercise 10 on page 342 using a function subprogram? If so, is it recommended?
26. Modify Example 9.3 on page 343 to use a function subprogram in place of the subroutine. Can you use adjustable dimensions in this function subprogram?
27. Specify output for the program below, given the following input: 5,10,7,15,2,4.

```
INTEGER N,A(500),MAXVAL
READ *,N,(A(J),J = 1,N)
PRINT *,MAXVAL(N,A)
END


FUNCTION MAXVAL(N,A)
INTEGER N,A(N),MAXVAL
MAXVAL = −9999999
DO 50 J = 1,N
    MAXVAL = MAX(MAXVAL,A(J))
50 CONTINUE
END
```

*28. Design two versions of a real function called MINMAX that returns either the minimum or maximum value in an N-element one-dimensional array A, given that the calling program passes N,A, and either the character constant 'MIN' or 'MAX.'
    a. In the first version, use the type of logic illustrated in the preceding exercise.
    b. In the second version, use the function subprogram to call subroutine SORT (see Exercise 12 on page 342).

9.4
MODULAR PROGRAMMING

Subroutines and function subprograms are convenient vehicles for dividing programs into groups of related instructions called **modules.** This style of programming is called **modular programming,** and we fully discuss and illustrate it in Module F. If you have the stamina, it would be best that you study Module F at this time since the topic is strongly related to this chapter. Moreover, Module F describes a complete scenario that makes extensive use of subroutines and illustrates **nested subprograms** or the call of one subprogram by another.

9.5
COMMON ERRORS

Certain errors regarding subprograms seem to occur more commonly than others. Make note of these.

1. *Forgetting END.*   Don't forget the END statement following the main program and each subprogram or a syntax error may result. Many beginning programmers figure they only need one END statement at the very end of the last subprogram. Not so. Since the main program and each subprogram are treated as independent program units, the END statement at the end of each program unit signals the compiler that the current program unit is over.

2. *Type of a function.*   Logic and/or mixed type errors can result if you forget that the first letter of a function name implicitly determines the type of the value returned by that function. The best approach is to explicitly type the function name, as we have done with all other names. By the way, *don't forget to define the function name within the body of the function subprogram.*

3. *Mismatches in argument lists.*   Pay close attention to the number, order, and type of actual and dummy arguments lists. In many cases, mismatches may not result in syntax or execution error messages. Instead, you may get unpredictable results (wrong answers) that are system dependent, as the following chart illustrates. (Assume that type is determined implicitly.)

Actual Argument	Corresponding Dummy Argument	Comment
IN	ON	Inconsistent mode.
X	J	Inconsistent mode.
2	COST	Inconsistent mode.
2.	COST	OK, as long as the value of COST is not changed within the subprogram.
COST	2.	Not allowed. Dummy arguments must be names.
M	N	OK, but if the subprogram redefines the value of N, then M changes accordingly. If you're not aware of this, you've committed a logic error.
A(3)	B(1)	OK when A and B are declared arrays.
A(3)	C	OK when A is declared an array.
6*K + 3	JOB	OK, as long as the value in JOB is not changed within the subprogram.

4. *Dummy argument pitfalls.*   Take care in defining and using dummy arguments. For example, you get a syntax error if a dummy argument is used in a DATA, PARAM-ETER, EQUIVALENCE, or COMMON statement. More insiduously, you commit execution and/or logic errors if you *unintentionally* define a dummy argument within the body of a subprogram. In particular, results are unpredictable if the correspond-ing actual argument is a constant or expression. If the corresponding actual argu-

ment is a name, remember that its contents are changed whenever the dummy argument is assigned a value.

5. *Common block pitfalls.* Use COMMON statements consistently across program units to avoid readability and error problems. For example, match array names with array names and take care that their sizes correspond. If global names must be used, try to use the same names in each program unit *so that COMMON statements across program units are duplicates of one another.* This avoids difficult-to-detect errors, such as misspelling a name or violating positional correspondence. When changing a COMMON statement in one program unit, take care that corresponding changes are made in all program units using the same common block. Remember that character data must be in a common block by themselves (without numeric data). Named common is a good vehicle for this, but note item 2 on page 349.

6. *Mismatch in size between actual array and corresponding dummy array.* Reread item 3 on page 339. Consider the following program.

```
      REAL X(5)
      DO 10 J = 1,5
         X(J) = J
   10 CONTINUE
      CALL TRY(X)
      END

      SUBROUTINE TRY(A)
      REAL A(10)
      PRINT *,(A(J),J = 1,5)
      END
```

In this case the size of the dummy array A (ten elements) exceeds the size of the actual array X (five elements). We ran this program using the WATFIV compiler and got the following execution error message when subroutine TRY was called: DECLARED SIZE OF ARRAY A EXCEEDS SPACE PROVIDED BY CALLING ARGUMENT. However, when the manufacturer's ANSI compiler was used, the same program executed without error.

Next we changed the size of the dummy array to something less than the size of the actual array by using

```
      REAL A(1)
```

in the subroutine. As before, the program that had been translated by the ANSI compiler ran without error, but the program using the WATFIV compiler gave an execution error as soon as the subscript J equaled 2 in

```
      PRINT *,(A(J),J = 1,5)
```

Moral of the story? To be safe, specify the same sizes for actual and dummy arrays. Better yet, use either adjustable dimensions or assumed-size array declarators.

7. *Array declaration pitfalls.* Don't forget to type and declare arrays in both the calling program and the subprogram. Remember to match array sizes either (a) by using identical constant array declarators or (b) by using either assumed-size or

adjustable array declarators. In the latter case, remember that they apply only to *dummy* arrays within subprograms. This means that assumed-size and adjustable declarators can't be used either to declare *actual* arrays or to declare arrays through the COMMON statement. When working with adjustable dimensions, don't forget that the variables that make up the adjustable dimensions must be passed from the calling program to the subprogram through either argument lists or COMMON statements.

ADDITIONAL EXERCISES

29. Define or explain the following

subprogram	adjustable array declarator
main program	adjustable dimensions
program units	COMMON statement
program modules	blank common block
subroutine subprogram	named common block
subroutine	block data subprogram
calling program	BLOCK DATA statement
CALL statement	EQUIVALENCE statement
actual argument list	function subprogram
SUBROUTINE statement	function reference (call)
dummy argument list	FUNCTION statement
RETURN statement	modular programming
predefined process symbol	modules
assumed-size array declarator	nested subprograms

30. Revisit. Modify a program in a previous chapter by using modular programming concepts. You might design modules as follows:
   a. A main program calls all modules.
   b. One module reads and edits the input data.
   c. Another module performs calculations.
   d. Another module outputs results.

31. Electric Bill. Gotham City Electric Company wishes to redesign the computerized bills that it sends to commercial and residential customers. It has announced a city-wide contest to determine the best algorithm/FORTRAN program for this purpose.

   a. Provided data *include the following.*

   Initialization data

   1. Month (three letters) and day (two digits) for beginning date of monthly billing cycle
   2. Month and day for ending date of monthly billing cycle
   3. Year (two digits)
   4. Number of customers to be billed (up to four digits)

Customer data

5. Previous meter reading in kilowatthours (up to seven digits)
6. New meter reading in kilowatthours
7. Customer rate code (one digit)
8. Past due amount (dollars and cents)
9. Payment since last bill (dollars and cents)
10. Name of customer (up to 20 characters)
11. Street address of customer (up to 20 characters)
12. City, state, and ZIP (up to 24 characters)
13. Account number of customer (up to eight digits)
    Use the following sample data for the computer run.

| | Billing Cycle | | | Number of |
From	To	Year	customers
SEP 19	OCT 18	1981	5

Use the following sample data per customer.

Previous Reading	New Reading	Rate Code	Past Due Amount	Payment	Name	Street Address	City, State, Zip	Account Number
27648	28648	1	60.10	60.10	make these up		....	
42615	45115	2	45.20	0.00	make these up		....	
314625	354625	3	3110.00	3110.00	make these up		....	
615700	695700	3	8000.00	8000.00	make these up		....	
800500	1025500	3	3000.00	1000.00	make these up		....	

Rate codes and their corresponding rates per kilowatthour (kWh) are explained by the following table.

Rate Code	Rate Per kWh(cents)	Comment
1	5.25	Residential, partly electric home
2	4.85	Residential, all electric home
3	8.50	Commercial, usage under 50,000 kWh
3	7.50	Commercial, usage between 50,000 kWh and 100,000 kWh
3	6.50	Commercial, usage above 100,000 kWh

If past due amount less payment is above zero, then a 1 percent per month charge on this difference is added to the customer's bill. For example, the last customer in the input data is commercial and used 225,000 kWh (1,025,500 − 800,500). Thus the customer is charged at 6.5 cents per kWh, which amounts to a current bill of $14,625.00. This customer, however, has a $3000 past due account and payments of only $1000. At an interest rate of 1 percent per month, the interest charge is

$20, that is, $(3000 - 1000) \times 0.01$; hence the total now due from this customer is $16,645.00, that is, $2000 + 20 + 14,625$.

Output from your program should include the following.

1. Name of customer
2. Street address of customer
3. City, state, and ZIP
4. Account number
5. Billing cycle: from (month,day) to (month,day,year)
6. Kilowatthours
7. Current amount owed
8. Past due amount
9. Interest charge
10. Total amount due

Label your output and design it to fit within a 3- by 5-inch image, since these statements must fit in a standard size envelope.

b. Include error detection to ensure that the rate code is 1, 2, or 3 and the new meter reading is greater than the previous meter reading. If an error is encountered, print an appropriate error message that includes the customer's name, complete address, and account number; bypass the calculations and printout for this customer; space down to the next statement; and go on to the next customer. Add new data to test each of the possible input errors.

Use a modular design for your program. By the way, the winner of the contest gets to ride the Batmobile, which recently was retrofitted with an all-electric power plant.

32. **Statistical Analysis Program.** Large programs that give options for various statistical analyses are common in commercial applications. For example, IBM's STATPACK, UCLA's BMD, North Carolina State's SAS, and the University of Chicago's SPSS are all widely used packages for implementing a variety of statistical analyses across many disciplines.

a. *Measures of central tendency and dispersion.* Design and write a modular program that calculates and prints the statistics described below for analyzing a set of *n* data items given by $x_1, x_2, \ldots, x_n$. In the descriptions below, assume the following set of values for x: 7, 14, 10, 6, 3.

1. *Mean,* given by

$$\bar{x} = \frac{x_1 + x_2 + \cdots + x_n}{n} = \frac{\sum_{i=1}^{n} x_i}{n} = \frac{40}{5} = 8$$

2. *Median,* a value such that one-half of the values are above it and one-half of the values are below it. First sort the data in ascending order, and then find the *position* of the median using the formula $(n + 1)/2$. For example, if the sorted values of x are

3   6   7   10   14

↑————————————location of median

then the median is found in position $(5 + 1)/2$, or third position.

Thus the median is 7. If *n* is an even number, however, the median is defined as halfway between the two adjacent positions in the center. For example, in the six-item sequence

$$3 \quad 6 \quad 7 \quad 10 \quad 14 \quad 16 \qquad\qquad \frac{6+1}{2}$$

$$\text{location of median in position}$$

the median is in position 3.5, or midway between the third item (7) and the fourth item (10). Thus the median is 8.5.

3. Minimum value of *x*, or 3 for the given data.
4. Maximum value of *x*, or 14 for the given data.
5. *Range,* the difference between max *x* and min *x*, or 11 for the given data.
6. *Mean absolute deviation (MAD),* given by

$$MAD = \frac{\sum\limits_{i=1}^{n} |x_i - \bar{x}|}{n} = \frac{16}{5} = 3.2$$

7. *Variance,* given by

$$s^2 = \frac{\sum\limits_{i=1}^{n} (x_i - \bar{x})^2}{n - 1} = \frac{70}{4} = 17.5$$

8. *Standard deviation,* given by

$$s = \sqrt{s^2} = \sqrt{17.5} = 4.1833$$

b. *Frequency distribution.* Add a second option to the program to print a frequency distribution. Let the user specify two suboptions here: (1) enter number of classes and upper class limits, or (2) just enter number of classes and let the computer determine class limits. For example, in the first suboption we might want to group the data into four classes with upper limits 5, 10, and 15 for the first three classes.

In this case, the frequency distribution is given by

Class Limits	Frequency
under 5	1
5 but under 10	2
10 but under 15	2
15 or above	0
	5

Thus, of the five data items, one was under 5, two were at least 5 but under 10, two were in the range 10 but under 15, and none were 15 or above. In the second suboption, a four-class frequency distribution would be given by

min x.	Class Limits	Frequency
Width of each class	⟨3.00⟩but under 5.75	1
is 2.75, or range	5.75 but under 8.50	2
divided by number	8.50 but under 11.25	1
of classes	11.25 but under⟨14.01⟩	1
		5

max x + .01

c. *Bar chart.* Add a third option that prints a bar chart, as illustrated for the second frequency distribution in part b.

```
    CLASS +      FREQUENCIES
    ----------------------
        1 +* 1
        2 +** 2
        3 +* 1
        4 +* 1
```

**d. *Histogram.* Instead of the bar chart in part c, print a histogram as follows:

```
                 2
                 _
      1         ***      1        1
     ***        ***     ***      ***
     ------------------------------
     5.75      8.50    11.25    14.01
```

Operations on Character Data

In earlier chapters we liberally used character constants, variables, and arrays to store, test, and print character data such as names, addresses, and descriptions. Simple character processing of the type we have described is used routinely in practice, but is not suggestive of more sophisticated manipulative requirements in such applications as text editing, text analysis, linguistics analysis, and the encoding/decoding of secret messages. In this chapter, following a review of character-related terminology and statements, we describe features of FORTRAN 77 that allow operations on character data.

10.1 REVIEW

A **character datum** or **character string** or simply **string** is a sequence of characters, including any blank characters. The **length** of a string is the number of characters in the string.

The form of a **character constant** is an apostrophe followed by a nonempty string followed by an apostrophe. The *value* of the character constant is the string. Thus 'I LOVE FORTRAN.' is a character constant with a value given by the string I LOVE FORTRAN., which has a length of 15 characters. Remember that an apostrophe within a string is represented as two successive apostrophes within the character constant. Thus 'I DON''T LOVE FORTRAN.' is a character constant with value I DON'T LOVE FORTRAN., with length 21 characters. *The length of a character constant must be greater than zero.*

The **CHARACTER statement** is used to type symbolic names that are to store character values, and to declare the length of stored strings. Its general form is

```
CHARACTER [*dl[,]] item [*dl] [,item [*dl]] . . .
```

where we use brackets to denote optional portions and where

dl represents the **declared length** expressed as
    (1)   an unsigned, nonzero integer constant
    (2)   an integer constant expression *enclosed in parentheses* and with positive value
    (3)   an asterisk enclosed in parentheses (used when its corresponding item is a dummy argument, as described on page 330)

item is the symbolic name of a constant, or a variable name, or an array name, or an array declarator, or a function name.[1]

If the length is declared just after the keyword CHARACTER, then each item in the list without its own declared length assumes this length. If the length is not declared just after the keyword CHARACTER, then each item in the list without its own declared length assumes a length of 1. For example, the statements

```
CHARACTER A*10,B,C(100)*80
CHARACTER*20 D,E*10,F,G
```

specify that the names A, B, C, D, E, F, and G store character strings, where A and E store strings of length 10, B stores one character, each element in the 100-element vector C stores 80 characters, and D, F, and G each stores 20 characters.

The **symbolic name of a character constant** stores a character constant and is defined through a PARAMETER statement. For example, the statements

```
CHARACTER TITLE*20
PARAMETER TITLE = 'ENGINEERING REPORT'
```

define the following storage:

TITLE

Note that TITLE has a declared length of 20 characters and the character constant 'ENGINEERING REPORT' has a length of 18 characters. Thus the last two character positions in storage are "padded" with blanks. By definition, *symbolic names of character constants must not be redefined* (assigned another value) within the same program unit.

A **character variable name** stores a string that's replaceable during the same run, that is, *a character variable can be redefined.* Thus the segment

```
CHARACTER ITEM*15
     .
     .
     .
DO 50 J = 1,N
   READ *,ITEM
     .
     .
     .
50 CONTINUE
```

results in the following storage sequence for the given input records.

---

[1] This list also includes a dummy procedure name, that is, a dummy argument that corresponds to the name of a procedure such as a function subprogram.

J	Input Record		Value in ITEM

1   'BARBIEbDOLL'

1	2	3	4	5	6	7	8	9	10	11	12	13	14	15
B	A	R	B	I	E		D	O	L	L				

Declared
length in
CHARACTER
statement

2   'POCKETbMICROPROCESSOR'

1	2	3	4	5	6	7	8	9	10	11	12	13	14	15
P	O	C	K	E	T		M	I	C	R	O	P	R	O

In the above example, note the following.

1. Character strings on input records processed by *list-directed* input statements must be enclosed in apostrophes. Apostrophes are not used if processing is by *format-directed* input (as described in Modules B and C).

2. We have numbered the 15 *character positions* within the *storage location* identified by ITEM to get you to focus on individual characters within a string and to realize that these positions are numbered sequentially (are adjacent to one another).

3. If the length of the input string is less than the declared length of the character variable, then the rightmost unused character positions in storage are "padded" with blanks, as illustrated when J = 1.

4. If the length of the input string is greater than the declared length of the character variable, then the input string is "truncated" on the right before storage occurs, as illustrated when J = 2.

Character array names store a string for each array element, where each array element (location) stores the number of character positions defined by the declared length. For example, if the one-dimensional array DAY is to store the names of days in the week, then the statements

```
      CHARACTER DAY(7)*9
      DATA DAY/'MONDAY', 'TUESDAY', 'WEDNESDAY', 'THURSDAY',
     +          'FRIDAY', 'SATURDAY', 'SUNDAY'/
```

store as follows:

D A Y

	1	2	3	4	5	6	7	8	9
1	M	O	N	D	A	Y			
2	T	U	E	S	D	A	Y		
3	W	E	D	N	E	S	D	A	Y
4	T	H	U	R	S	D	A	Y	
5	F	R	I	D	A	Y			
6	S	A	T	U	R	D	A	Y	
7	S	U	N	D	A	Y			

Recall that DAY(3), for example, is called a **character array element name;** it references the third element in array DAY.

Character function names are symbolic names that store character values defined in either *statement functions* (Section A.4) or *function subprograms* (Section 9.3). Later in this chapter we describe function subprograms that return character values.

A **character expression** expresses a character string and has one of the following forms.

1. A character constant
2. A symbolic name of a character constant
3. A character variable name
4. A character array element name
5. A character function name
6. A character substring (Section 10.2)
7. A sequence of character operands together with character operators and parentheses (Section 10.3).

For example, if ANS is a variable typed character, then the block IF statement

    IF (ANS .EQ. 'YES') THEN

illustrates a logical expression that compares two simple character expressions. The character expression to the left of the relational operator is the character variable ANS; the character expression to the right is the character constant 'YES'. We illustrate more complicated character expressions in the next two sections.

A **character assignment statement** has the following general form

$$v = character\ expression$$

where v is the name of a character variable, character array element, or character substring (Section 10.2). For example, the following illustrates character assignment statements and the resulting storage.

CHARACTER*9 DAYOFF,DAY(7),ANS*5

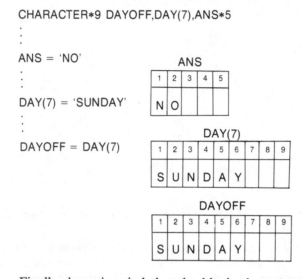

Finally, keep in mind that the blank character takes up a character position in the internal representation of a string. In particular, note how blank characters are placed into the rightmost unused positions in storage. For example, when the 11-character string BARBIE DOLL is input into the 15-character variable ITEM (page 368), the rightmost four positions within ITEM each stores a blank character; when the six-character string SUNDAY is assigned to the nine-character array element DAY(7), positions 7 through 9 store blanks. *The computer pads blanks into the string before the string is placed in the memory location. It accomplishes this by increasing the length of the string with as many blanks as necessary to make the length of the string equal to the declared length of the name.*

This blank-padding procedure also has implications when strings within logical expressions are being compared. For example, if ANS has a declared length of 5 and stores

ANS

1	2	3	4	5
Y	E	S		

then the logical expression

ANS .EQ. 'YES'

has the value true, since the character constant 'YES' is converted to 'YES bb' before the logical expression is evaluated.

That ends a somewhat lengthy, but reasonably complete, review of character-related topics scattered throughout the text. In the next several sections we show, among other things, FORTRAN 77's capability to replace or remove part of a string, insert a string within a string, search a string for the occurrence of another string, and compare strings.

10.2 SUBSTRINGS

Programs that perform editing functions must specify precise spots within strings that are to be tested, changed, or printed. Strings stored as values within symbolic names of constants, variables, and array elements have a defined length denoted by *dl* in the CHARACTER statement. As illustrated in our review, the first character in the string is in character position 1, the second character is in position 2, and so on to the last character in position *dl*. By specifying a starting (leftmost) position and an ending (rightmost) position within the string, we identify a portion of the string called a **substring.** For example, all possible substrings of the string LOVE are noted below.

Length of substrings	Substrings
1	L and O and V and E
2	LO and OV and VE
3	LOV and OVE
4	LOVE

Substrings can be given names, which in turn can be referenced and assigned values. A **substring name** has the following general form.

name of character variable or array element	(substring expression for leftmost position	: substring expression for rightmost position)

For example, the substring name ITEM(2:5) references characters in positions 2 through 5 of the string stored in the character variable ITEM; the substring name DAY(7)(1:3) references characters in positions 1 through 3 of the character array element DAY(7); and ITEM(L:L + 1) references the adjacent positions of ITEM given by position "value in L" and position "value in L plus 1."

Note that *substring expressions must be integer expressions and either substring expression can be omitted.* If the leftmost substring expression is omitted, character position 1 is implied; if the rightmost substring expression is omitted, character position *dl* is implied. Moreover, *substring expressions must have values between 1 and dl inclusive, and the value of the leftmost substring expression must not exceed the value of the rightmost substring expression.* If both substring expressions are omitted, then the entire string is referenced.

EXAMPLE 10.1 Substrings and Character Variables

Assume the following for the illustrations below.

```
CHARACTER  PHRASE*15,SUB*5
INTEGER    L,R
```

Substring Name	Substring	Sample Use	Result
a. PHRASE(3:6)	LOVE	SUB = PHRASE(3:6)	SUB — LOVE
b. PHRASE(7:11)	ƀFORT	SUB = PHRASE(7:11)	SUB — FORT
c. PHRASE(L:R)	ƀLOVEƀFOR	SUB = PHRASE(L:R)	SUB — LOVE
d. PHRASE(R + 1:R + 1)	T	PRINT *,PHRASE(R + 1:R + 1)	T
e. PHRASE(1:6)	IƀLOVE	PRINT *,PHRASE(1:6)	IƀLOVE
f. PHRASE(:6)	IƀLOVE	PRINT *,PHRASE(:6)	IƀLOVE
g. PHRASE(8:)	FORTRAN.	PRINT *,PHRASE(8:)	FORTRAN.
h. PHRASE(1:1)	I	IF (PHRASE(1:1) .EQ. 'ƀ') THEN	False; IF-block not executed
i. PHRASE(L:20)	Illegal; goes beyond end of string		

EXAMPLE 10.2 Substrings and Character Arrays

Assume the days of the week are stored in character vector DAY. The segment below prints the first three positions of an element as the abbreviation for the day.

```
CHARACTER DAY(7)*9
    .
    .
DO 10 J = 1,7
    PRINT *,'ABBREVIATION FORƀ',DAY(J),'ƀISƀ',DAY(J)(1:3)
10 CONTINUE
    .
    .
    END
```

Output

```
ABBREVIATION FOR MONDAY    IS MON
ABBREVIATION FOR TUESDAY   IS TUE
ABBREVIATION FOR WEDNESDAY IS WED
    .
    .
ABBREVIATION FOR SUNDAY    IS SUN
```

EXAMPLE 10.3   Printing Individual Characters in a String

Study the program below, and its input and output.

```
CHARACTER PHRASE*50
INTEGER    BLANKS
BLANKS = 0
READ *,PHRASE
DO 10 J = 1,50
   PRINT *,PHRASE(J:J)
   IF (PHRASE(J:J) .EQ. 'b') BLANKS = BLANKS + 1
10 CONTINUE
PRINT *,'END OF PHRASE. NUMBER OF BLANKS =',BLANKS
END
```

Input Record

'I''Mb BEGINNINGb TOb ENJOYb THIS.'

Output

```
I
'
M
b
B
E
G
I
N
N
I
N
G
b
T
O
b
E
N
J
O
Y
b
T
H
I
S
.
b  ⎫
b  ⎬  22 blank characters
:  ⎭
:
b
END OF PHRASE.  NUMBER OF BLANKS =        26
```

Note that a substring name with identical leftmost and rightmost substring expressions is a convenient way to extract individual characters in a string.

EXAMPLE 10.4 Simple Text Editing: Replacing a Substring

Suppose the character variable TEXT, having length 20, stores the following.

TEXT

1	2	3	4	5	6	7	8	9	10	11	12	13	14	15	16	17	18	19	20
I		L	O	V	E		F	O	R	T	R	A	N						

The text-editing program segment below illustrates how we can repeatedly change a specific substring in positions J to K to another substring *having the same length.*

```
      READ *,J,K
10 IF (J .GT. 0) THEN
         READ *,TEXT(J:K)
         READ *,J,K
         GO TO 10
      END IF
```

For example, the input

```
3,6
'HATE'
15,18
'ƀ77.'
0,0
```

would change the value in TEXT to the following.

1	2	3	4	5	6	7	8	9	10	11	12	13	14	15	16	17	18	19	20
I		H	A	T	E		F	O	R	T	R	A	N		7	7	.		

In Section 10.5 we illustrate techniques that are useful in replacing a substring by one of a different length. (See also Exercise 6, Example 10.9, and Exercise 47.)

Follow-up Exercises

1. Given that e_1 represents the value of the leftmost substring expression and e_2 the value of the rightmost substring expression, state an expression for the length of a character substring.
2. Is LVE a substring in LOVE? Explain.
3. Specify each result given the conditions in Example 10.1.

   a.   PRINT *,PHRASE(R:R)
   b.   PRINT *,PHRASE(:)
   c.   PRINT *,PHRASE(R:L)
   d.   SUB = PHRASE(L + 2:2*R − 8)

```
   e.        DO 10 J = 1,15
                 IF (PHRASE(J:J) .EQ. '.') THEN
                     PRINT *,J
                 END IF
             10 CONTINUE
```

4. Suppose we change the body in DO-loop 10 of Example 10.2 as follows.

```
   READ *,K,L
   PRINT *,DAY(J),'--',DAY(J)(K:K),DAY(J)(L:L)
```

Also, assume that the declared length is 10 rather than 9. Specify output given the following input records.

```
1,10
1,2
1,10
1,2
1,10
1,2
1,2
```

5. Modify Example 10.3 so that trailing blanks are not printed. Assume two blanks never appear together until after the last nonblank character.

6. In Example 10.4, specify memory if we insert just before 0,0 the input

```
   3,7
   'ADORE'
```

Do we have a problem here? If so, modify the input to correct it.

7. Given the character variable CODE with length 30, specify FORTRAN code to print the characters within CODE
   a. With a space between each character, all on one line.
   b. Backwards, all on one line.

*8. Design code to print the message NULL STRING if the character variable NOTE contains all blank characters. Assume a declared length of 70.

**9. Write programs that input the character variable WORD, having a declared length of 30, and print
   a. All substrings of length K, where K is input along with WORD.
   b. All possible substrings, beginning with length M and ending with length N, where M and N are input variables and the value in M is less than or equal to the value in N.

Roleplay the computer by processing substrings of length 3, 4, and 5 for the string MICRO.

10.3
CONCATENATION

Concatenation is the act of joining two or more strings to form one longer string. This is accomplished as follows.

> character expression // character expression . . .

where the double slash is called the **character operator.**

EXAMPLE 10.5   Character Expressions Involving Concatenation

Assume the following for the examples below.

FIRST	MIDDLE	LAST	INI
1 2 3 4 5 6 7 8	1 2 3 4 5 6 7 8	1 2 3 4 5 6 7 8 9 10 11 12	1 2 3
F R A N K	H A R R Y	N E W M A N	

Use/Expression   Result/Value

a.   PRINT *,'MRS.ƀ'//'CALABASH'   MRS. ƀCALABASH
b.   PRINT *,'DEARƀ'//'MRS.ƀ'//'CALABASH'   DEARƀMRS.ƀCALABASH
c.   PRINT *,FIRST//MIDDLE//LAST   FRANKƀƀƀHARRYƀƀƀNEWMANƀƀƀƀƀƀ
d.   PRINT *,LAST//FIRST//MIDDLE(:1)//'.'   NEWMANƀƀƀƀƀƀFRANKƀƀƀH.
e.   INI = FIRST(:1)//MIDDLE(:1)//LAST(:1) INI

1	2	3
F	H	N

10.4
CHARACTER INTRINSIC FUNCTIONS

By this time you have surely used some of the intrinsic functions presented in Module A, all of which relate to numeric data. FORTRAN 77 also includes eight intrinsic functions that specifically process character data, as presented next.

LEN Function

The intrinsic function LEN determines the length of a character string. Its general form is given by

> **LEN** (*character expression*)

The function returns an *integer* value equal to the number of characters in the string.

EXAMPLE 10.6   Sample Uses of LEN

Assume the following.

```
CHARACTER NAME*20
NAME = 'DOOLITTLE'
```

Use/Function	Result/Value
a. PRINT *,LEN('DOOLITTLE')	9
b. PRINT *,LEN(NAME)	20
c. PRINT *,LEN('DR. b//NAME)	24
d. PRINT *,LEN(NAME(4:9))	6
e. DO 10 J = 1,LEN(NAME)	J runs from 1 to 20

The LEN function has limited uses in main programs because the length of a string is generally known and fixed according to the declared length of a character variable. For instance, this example declares a length of 20 for the string in NAME. Thus 20 could simply be used for LEN(NAME) in part e. Still, we prefer to use LEN(NAME) rather than 20 in the DO statement because this generalizes the program better and reduces upkeep should there be a subsequent change in the declared length of NAME. Better yet, we prefer to declare DL as a symbolic name for an integer constant and therefore use DL instead of either 20 or LEN(NAME), as follows:

```
INTEGER    DL
PARAMETER (DL = 20)
CHARACTER NAME*DL
   .
   .
   .
DO 10 J = 1,DL
```

The LEN function comes into its own in the next example.

EXAMPLE 10.7   Function Subprogram TRIM

In the preceding example NAME stored the following.

NAME

1	2	3	4	5	6	7	8	9	10	11	12	13	14	15	16	17	18	19	20
D	O	O	L	I	T	T	L	E											

In many applications—for instance, names in form letters—we wish to consider the string only through its last nonblank character. To illustrate the motivation, consider the following.

```
CHARACTER NAME*20,SEX,TITLE*4
    .
    .
    .
READ *,SEX,NAME

IF (SEX .EQ. 'M') THEN
    TITLE = 'MR.ƀ'
ELSE IF (SEX .EQ. 'F') THEN
    TITLE = 'MS.ƀ'
ELSE
    PRINT *,'ERROR IN INPUT FOR SEX'
END IF

PRINT  *,'THANKƀYOUƀ'//TITLE//NAME//',ƀFORƀYOURƀCONCERN.'
    .
    .
    .
END
```

Given the input

    'M', 'DOOLITTLE'

this program segment prints the following output.

THANKƀYOUƀMR.ƀDOOLITTLEƀƀƀƀƀƀƀƀƀƀƀ,ƀFORƀYOURƀCONCERN.

⟵——— Eleven nonwanted
        blank characters

In reality we would prefer not to print the 11 unused (blank) positions in NAME, as follows.

THANKƀYOUƀMR.ƀDOOLITTLE,ƀFORƀYOURƀCONCERN.

⟵———Eleven blank
        characters suppressed

The function subprogram below "trims" or truncates the string in NAME by returning the length of a substring that runs from position 1 to the position containing the last nonblank character. If all characters are blank, the returned length is zero.

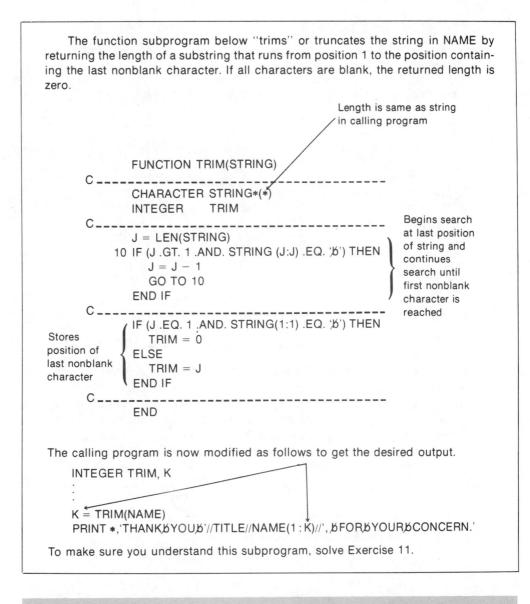

Length is same as string in calling program

```
      FUNCTION TRIM(STRING)
C ------------------------------------------------------
      CHARACTER STRING*(*)
      INTEGER    TRIM
C ------------------------------------------------------
      J = LEN(STRING)
   10 IF (J .GT. 1 .AND. STRING (J:J) .EQ. 'ᵬ') THEN
      J = J − 1
      GO TO 10
      END IF
C ------------------------------------------------------
      IF (J .EQ. 1 .AND. STRING(1:1) .EQ. 'ᵬ') THEN
      TRIM = 0
      ELSE
      TRIM = J
      END IF
C ------------------------------------------------------
      END
```

Begins search at last position of string and continues search until first nonblank character is reached

Stores position of last nonblank character

The calling program is now modified as follows to get the desired output.

```
      INTEGER TRIM, K
      :
      :
      K = TRIM(NAME)
      PRINT *,'THANKᵬYOUᵬ'//TITLE//NAME(1 : K)//', ᵬFORᵬYOURᵬCONCERN.'
```

To make sure you understand this subprogram, solve Exercise 11.

11. In Example 10.7:
    a. What alternative do we have to using function LEN?
    b. Roleplay the computer as the subprogram executes for the sample input data. What value gets stored in TRIM? What gets stored in TRIM if NAME stores the string ACE? If NAME stores all blanks?
    c. What's the problem with the following simplified logic? Roleplay the computer if you don't see it at once.

```
                    J = LEN(STRING)
        10 IF (J .GT. O .AND. STRING(J:J) .EQ. 'b') THEN
                    J = J − 1
                    GO TO 10
                 END IF
                 TRIM = J
                 END
```

    d. Why do we backtrack character positions in the loop rather than go forward from 1 to LEN(STRING)?

12. Put the function LEN to good use in Example 10.3 on page 373.

13. Utilize function TRIM in solving Exercise 5 on page 375.

*14. Utilize function TRIM in solving Exercise 9 on page 375 to avoid printing substrings with blank characters.

INDEX Function

The intrinsic function given by

$$\boxed{\textbf{INDEX } (string,substring)}$$

searches the specified *string* for the occurrence of the *substring*. If the string contains the substring, INDEX returns an integer value corresponding to the character position where the substring begins. If the substring is not found within the string, INDEX returns a value of zero. If the substring appears more than once, INDEX returns the starting position of the *leftmost* substring. This function, for example, can be used to find specific characters within words, specific words within sentences, and specific phrases within text.

EXAMPLE 10.8   Sample Uses of INDEX

Assume the following storage for the examples below.

PHRASE

1	2	3	4	5	6	7	8	9	10	11	12	13	14	15	16	17	18	19	20
I		L	O	V	E		F	O	R	T	R	A	N		7	7	.		

CODE

1	2	3	4	5	6	7	8	9
F	O	R	T	R	A	N		

Use/Function	Result/Value
a. PRINT *,INDEX('AGAIN', 'G')	2
b. PRINT *,INDEX('AGAIN', 'H')	0
c. PRINT *,INDEX('AGAIN', 'A')	1

d.	PRINT *,INDEX(PHRASE, '77')	16
e.	PRINT *,INDEX(PHRASE, '7')	16
f.	PRINT *,INDEX(CODE, 'b́')	8
g.	PRINT *,INDEX(PHRASE, 'FORTRAN')	8
h.	PRINT *,INDEX(PHRASE, CODE)	0
i.	PRINT *,INDEX(PHRASE, CODE(1:7))	8
j.	PRINT *,INDEX(PHRASE, CODE(1:INDEX(CODE, 'b́') − 1))	8

Make sure you understand the results given in parts g, h, and i.

EXAMPLE 10.9   Simple Text Editing: Replacing a Substring Again

In Example 10.4 on page 374 we replaced a substring by another of equal length, given the position range (J to K) and the new substring. This approach requires the user to know exactly what character positions need replacing, the determination of which is always tedious and often error prone.

A realistic text-editing routine, such as the one you might have used on your computer system, requires input of the substring to be replaced rather than input of the character positions where the replacement is to be made. The routine below edits TEXT as before, on the basis of the given input.

TEXT

1	2	3	4	5	6	7	8	9	10	11	12	13	14	15	16	17	18	19	20
I		L	O	V	E		F	O	R	T	R	A	N	.					

Input
'LOVE', 'HATE'
'.b́b́b́', 'b́77.'
'***', 'b́'

```
      CHARACTER*20   OLD,NEW,TEXT
      INTEGER        TL,FIRST,LAST,TRIM
        :
        :
      READ *,OLD,NEW
   10 IF (OLD .NE. '***') THEN
         TL    = TRIM(OLD)
         FIRST = INDEX(TEXT,OLD(:TL))
         LAST  = FIRST + MAX(TRIM(OLD),TRIM(NEW)) − 1
         TEXT(FIRST:LAST) = NEW
         READ *,OLD,NEW
         GO TO 10
      END IF
```

Note that TL stands for trim length, TRIM is the function subprogram in Example 10.7, FIRST represents the first character position in the string to be replaced, LAST represents the last position to be replaced, and MAX is an intrinsic function in Module A. You should confirm that, for the first input record, TL = 4, FIRST = 3, LAST = 6, and HATE gets placed in positions 3–6 of the string. For the second input record, TL = 1, FIRST = 15, LAST = 18, and b́77. gets placed in positions 15–18.

Follow-up Exercises

15. What value is returned in each case?

    a. INDEX('ABCDEF','X')
    b. INDEX('ABCDEF','D')
    c. INDEX('ABCDEF','DE')
    d. INDEX('MISSISSIPPI','S')

16. On the basis of what's given in Example 10.8, what gets printed by the code below?

    ```
    DO 10 J = 1,LEN(CODE)
        PRINT *,J,INDEX(PHRASE,CODE(J:J))
    10 CONTINUE
    ```

17. In Example 10.9:
    a. Why is the following wrong?

       FIRST = INDEX(TEXT,OLD)

    b. Why are the following wrong?

       LAST = FIRST + TRIM(OLD) − 1

       or

       LAST = FIRST + TRIM(NEW) − 1

    c. What values get stored for TL, FIRST, and LAST given the input below? (Assume I LOVE FORTRAN. is in TEXT.)

       'TRAN.ƀƀ','MULAS.ƀ'
       'MULAS.','TS. ƀƀƀ'
       '***',ƀ'

18. Modify Example 10.9 to account for the possibility that the user might input an "old" substring that's not present in the string. If this happens, print an error message and terminate processing.

*19. Suppose that input data for NAME, with a declared length of 30, are *always* in the following form.

    'last name,ƀfirst name'

    Write a program segment that separates the string in NAME into two parts, for storage of first name in FIRST (declared length of 12) and last name in LAST (declared length of 18).

LGE, LGT, LLE, and LLT Functions

As you know from Chapter 1, characters are encoded by the computer as patterns of *bits,* where a bit is a binary digit (0 or 1). For example, the letter "A" might be coded by the 8-bit binary number 01000001 and the digit "1" by the 8-bit binary number 11110001, depending on the encoding scheme.[2]

Given that each character is uniquely represented by a binary number, it follows that each character has an associated *integer* value. This means, for example, that the binary representation of the digit "1" has a value that's less than the binary representations of the digits "2" through "9." Similarly, we can say, regardless of the particular coding scheme, that "A" is less than "B" and "T" is greater than "K."

The arrangement of characters in ascending numeric order based on the integer values of their binary representations is called the **collating sequence.** For example, A, B, C, . . . , Z represents the collating sequence for capital letters and 0, 1, 2, . . . , 9 represents the collating sequence for digits. The collating sequence thus represents a *lexicographic* arrangement (dictionary-type alphabetic ordering) of characters, where characters that precede others in the sequence have a lower value.

When we make lexicographic comparisons by using character expressions within logical expressions, we necessarily utilize the collating sequence of the computer. For example, the logical expressions

```
        'A' .LT. 'K'
        'B' .NE. 'A'
      'ACE' .EQ. 'ACE'
   'JONES' .LT. 'SMITH'
        '2' .LT. '3'
    'THREE' .LT. 'TWO'
```

all test true, regardless of which method the computer uses to encode characters.

Note that each comparison above is a comparison of either all digits or all letters. Moreover, a string has a value that implies position in a sequence. For example, the value of THREE is lexically less than the value of TWO, since THREE alphabetically precedes TWO.

Problems arise, however, when we compare strings that include a mixture of letters, digits, and special characters. For example, the comparison

```
   '007DOLL' .GT. 'BARBIE/DOLL'
```

may be true or false, depending on which scheme the computer uses to collate letters, digits, and special characters.[3]

In general, all encoding schemes are consistent with respect to either "pure" string comparisons (all letters versus all letters and all digits versus all digits) or .EQ. and .NE. types of comparisons for "mixed" strings. If "less than" or "greater than" types of mixed-string comparisons are required, however, then it's best to use the intrinsic functions described in Table 10.1. Note that arguments (s_1 and s_2) are character expressions and the value returned is a logical value (true or false).

---

[2] The most used character encoding methods are American Standard Coding for Information Interchange (ASCII), which uses 7 bits to code each of 128 characters; Binary Coded Decimal (BCD), which uses 6 bits to code each of 64 characters; and Extended Binary Coded Decimal Interchange Code (EBCDIC), which uses 8 bits to code each of 256 characters.

[3] For example, ASCII uses a collating sequence based on the ordering: blank, subset of special characters, digits, remaining special characters, uppercase letters, lowercase letters; EBCDIC collates in the sequence: blank, all special characters, lowercase letters, uppercase letters, digits.

TABLE 10.1   *Lexical Intrinsic Functions*

FUNCTION	VALUE IS TRUE IF
LGE(s_1,s_2)	The string s_1 follows or equals (is lexically greater than or equal to) the string s_2 in the collating sequence.
LGT(s_1,s_2)	The string s_1 follows (is lexically greater than) the string s_2 in the collating sequence.
LLE(s_1,s_2)	The string s_1 precedes or equals (is lexically less than or equal to) the string s_2 in the collating sequence.
LLT(s_1,s_2)	The string s_1 precedes (is lexically less than) the string s_2 in the collating sequence.

In effect, it's as though these lexical functions convert the computer's collating sequence to a standard collating sequence so that programs that use these functions provide identical results regardless of the computer. For example, if we specify

    IF (LLE(NAMEA, NAMEB)) THEN

and we store

then the result is true. If we specify

    IF (LGT('007DOLL','BARBIE/DOLL')) THEN

the result is false.[4]

As a matter of good programming style, we recommend the use of lexical intrinsic functions for all greater than or equal to, greater than, less than or equal to, and less than types of string comparisons. These functions are especially useful for ordering or sorting character strings (see Exercise 22).

Follow-up Exercises

20. Could we have used

    IF (NAMEA .LE. NAMEB) THEN

in our first example above and guaranteed the same result regardless of the computer? Explain.

---

[4] The value is false because ANSI FORTRAN uses ASCII as the standard collating sequence, which places digits before letters in the collating sequence (as noted in footnote 3).

21. Specify the value returned for each of the following.
   a. LLT('ABC','ABD')
   b. LLT('ABD','ABC')
   c. LGE('ABC','123')
   d. LGT(' + $*:','NOT NICE')

* **22. Sorting Strings.** Design the sorting routine in Example 7.13 on page 271 as a subroutine named SORTCH that sorts character data in ascending order. Include N and LIST as dummy arguments. The sorted vector does not get printed; it's simply returned to the calling program. Assume that declared lengths in calling programs never exceed 200.

ICHAR and CHAR Functions

The intrinsic function

$$\boxed{\textbf{ICHAR}\ (\textit{character expression})}$$

converts a string of length 1 (a single character) to an integer value that corresponds to the *position* of the character in the processor's collating sequence.[5] The first character in the collating sequence corresponds to position 0 and the last character to position $n - 1$, where n is the number of characters represented by the processor. For example, if the blank character is the first character in the collating sequence (position 0),

PRINT *,ICHAR('b')

outputs a zero. If the character "A" is in position 29 of the collating sequence, ICHAR (WORD(5:5)) returns the value 29 if the character "A" is the fifth character in the string within WORD.

The intrinsic function

$$\boxed{\textbf{CHAR}\ (\textit{integer expression})}$$

is the inverse of function ICHAR; it returns the character in the ith position of the processor's collating sequence, where i is the value of the integer expression and i must be between zero and $n - 1$ inclusive ($0 \leq i \leq n - 1$).

For example,

PRINT *,CHAR(0)

would print the blank character and CHAR(3*K) would return the character "B" if K stores 10 and "B" is in position 30 of the collating sequence.

A practical use of these functions relates to the encoding and decoding of cryptograms (writings in code), which we illustrate in Exercise 45.

---

[5] The set of integer values produced by ICHAR is processor-dependent.

Follow-up Exercises

23. Specify what gets printed for the following.
    a. PRINT *,ICHAR(CHAR(10))
    b. PRINT *,CHAR(ICHAR('*'))

* 24. Design and run a program that
    a. Prints the collating sequence position for the digits 0 through 9, the capital letters A through Z, the lowercase letters a through z, and the special characters ⌷ + − * / = ( ) , ' $: .
    b. Prints the characters corresponding to positions 0, 1, 2, . . . , $n - 1$ in the collating sequence, where you should use the value for n that corresponds to your processor (if you can't find out, use 256).

10.5
SELECTED APPLICATIONS

In this section we illustrate limited applications within two important, broad areas of character processing: text analysis and text editing. Greater depth for these applications, together with other applications, are left to the end-of-chapter exercises.

Text Analysis: Finding and Printing Words

Certain applications in fields such as literature, linguistics, publishing, and office management require analyses of text content. For example, an assessment of keyboard skill in a publishing company might involve a timed keyboard input test in which a typist keys in text at a terminal for, say, 20 minutes. A text analysis program could then calculate statistics such as number of words typed, average word length, number of keyboard strokes, and so on.

Suppose that the text below

1	2	3	4	5	6	7	8	9	10	11	12	13	14	15	16	17	18	19	20	21	22	23	24	25	26	27	28	29	30		69	70
I		L	O	V	E		F	O	R	T	R	A	N			7	7	.			D	O		Y	O	U	?			...		.

is already stored in memory and we wish to design a subroutine that prints each word in the text individually, based on the following call.

CALL WORDS(TEXT)

First we must explicitly define what we mean by a "word." Let's define a word as a substring made up entirely of one or more letters, where the first letter in the word is immediately preceded by a character that's not a letter and the last letter in the word is immediately succeeded by a character that's not a letter. Let's also include contractions such as DON'T in our definition of a word, which means that the apostrophe is treated as a "letter." Based on this definition of a word, the subroutine below would print the following five words for the text given above.

```
I
LOVE
FORTRAN
DO
YOU
```

```
      SUBROUTINE WORDS (STRING)
*
*     -----------------------------------------------------------
*
*         PRINTS INDIVIDUAL WORDS IN A LINE OF TEXT
*
*         KEY:
*          STRING = LINE OF TEXT
*          LETTER = LETTERS OF ALPHABET PLUS APOSTROPHE
*          NEW    = .TRUE. IF NEXT CHARACTER IS CANDIDATE FOR
*                   START OF NEW WORD
*          IN     = VALUE OF INDEX FUNCTION
*          MARK   = POSITION THAT MARKS START OF NEW WORD
*
*     -----------------------------------------------------------
*
      CHARACTER STRING*(*),LETTER*27
      INTEGER   IN,MARK
      LOGICAL   NEW
*
*     -----------------------------------------------------------
*
      DATA LETTER /'ABCDEFGHIJKLMNOPQRSTUVWXYZ'''/
      NEW = .TRUE.
*
*     -----------------------------------------------------------
*
      DO 10 J=1,LEN(STRING)
*
        IN = INDEX (LETTER,STRING(J:J))
        IF (IN .EQ. 0 .AND. (.NOT. NEW)) THEN
*
*         ----- PRINT WORD AND RESET NEW --------
*
          PRINT *, STRING(MARK:J-1)
          NEW = .TRUE.
*
        ELSE IF (IN .NE. 0 .AND. NEW) THEN
*
*         ----- MARK NEW WORD AND RESET NEW -----
*
          MARK = J
          NEW  = .FALSE.
*
*         ----- ELSE GO ON TO NEXT CHARACTER -----
*
        END IF
*
   10 CONTINUE
*
*     -----------------------------------------------------------
*
      END
```

In studying the subroutine, note that a word is printed within the IF-block only when INDEX returns a zero (the present character is not a letter or apostrophe) *and* NEW stores .FALSE. (the preceding character was a letter or apostrophe). Execution enters the ELSE IF-block only when INDEX is not zero (the present character is a letter or apostrophe) *and* NEW stores .TRUE. (the preceding character was not a letter or apostrophe), in which case we mark the beginning of a new word. Execution enters neither block (goes on to the next character) whenever the present character is of the same type as the preceding character (for example, the present and preceding characters are both blanks). Solve Exercise 25 to make sure you understand this logic.

Finally, note that only *uppercase* letters are considered by the subroutine. Exercise 26 modifies the subroutine to include both uppercase and *lowercase* letters.

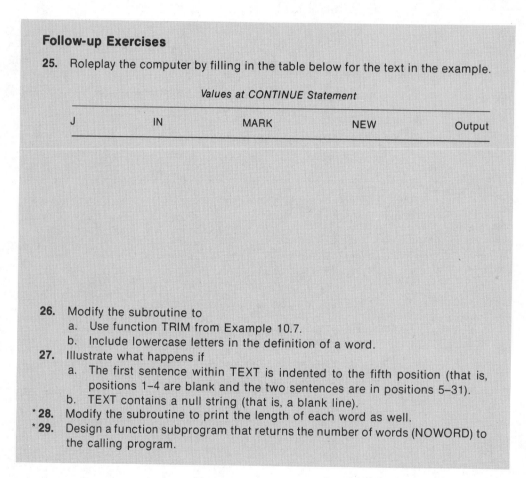

Follow-up Exercises

25. Roleplay the computer by filling in the table below for the text in the example.

Values at CONTINUE Statement

J	IN	MARK	NEW	Output

26. Modify the subroutine to
   a. Use function TRIM from Example 10.7.
   b. Include lowercase letters in the definition of a word.
27. Illustrate what happens if
   a. The first sentence within TEXT is indented to the fifth position (that is, positions 1–4 are blank and the two sentences are in positions 5–31).
   b. TEXT contains a null string (that is, a blank line).
*28. Modify the subroutine to print the length of each word as well.
*29. Design a function subprogram that returns the number of words (NOWORD) to the calling program.

Text Editing: Inserting a Substring

Text-editing programs are widely used to create, modify, and print textual material such as letters, notices, computer programs, articles, manuscripts, and books. Examples 10.4 and 10.9 illustrated rather simple text-editing functions. In this example we design a subroutine that generalizes the act of inserting a substring; in Exercise 47 at the end of the chapter we ask you to put together a complete (although relatively simple) text-editing package.

Suppose we currently store the string

TEXT

1	2	3	4	5	6	7	8	9	10	11	12	13	14	15	16	17	18	19	20	21	22	23	24	25		30
I	'	M		G	E	T	T	I	N	G		W	O	R	R	I	E	D	.						. . .	

and we wish to insert the substring ƀVERY by calling

TEXT

1	2	3	4	5	6	7	8	9	10	11	12	13	14	15	16	17	18	19	20	21	22	23	24	25		30
I	'	M		G	E	T	T	I	N	G		V	E	R	Y		W	O	R	R	I	E	D	.	. . .	

subroutine INSERT using

    CALL INSERT(TEXT,AFTER,NEW)

where AFTER stores GETTING and NEW stores ƀVERY. In other words, we wish the subroutine to insert ƀVERY immediately after GETTING, taking care first to shift the remaining text (ƀWORRIED.) to the right.

The pseudocode below describes the text-editing logic to accomplish this.

1. Calculate trim length—last nonblank character position—of string (20 in example) and trim length of new string to be inserted (5 in example).

2. IF no space for new substring THEN   (There's space in example,)
      PRINT error message   (since 20 + 5 doesn't)
      RETURN   (exceed declared length)
   END IF   (of 30 for string.)

3. Calculate first and last character positions of new substring to be inserted (12 and 16 in example).

4. IF substring insertion is in middle of string THEN
      Shift appropriate portion of string to right   (Yes, shift ƀWORRIED from positions)
   END IF   (12-20 to positions 17-25.)

5. Insert new substring within string. (Insert ƀVERY in positions 12–16).

Step 4 can be refined as follows.

IF first character position of new substring < trim length of string THEN

Determine last character position of shifted substring
Determine first character position of shifted substring

DO WHILE character needs shifting
    Shift rightmost remaining character to new position
END DO
END IF

FORTRAN code readily follows from the pseudocode. Note that function TRIM is given in Example 10.7. You should relate the code below to the pseudocode, and then solve the follow-up exercises.

```
      SUBROUTINE INSERT(STRING,AFTER,NEW)
*
*----------------------------------------------------------------
*
*      SUBSTRING INSERT ROUTINE
*
*      KEY:
*        STRING = STRING TO BE CHANGED
*        AFTER  = SUBSTRING AFTER WHICH INSERT IS PLACED
*        NEW    = NEW SUBSTRING TO BE INSERTED
*        TLA    = TRIM LENGTH OF AFTER
*        TLS    = TRIM LENGTH OF STRING
*        TLN    = TRIM LENGTH OF NEW SUBSTRING
*        FIRSTN = FIRST CHARACTER POSITION OF NEW SUBSTRING
*        LASTN  = LAST CHARACTER POSITION OF NEW SUBSTRING
*        FIRSTS = FIRST CHARACTER POSITION OF SHIFTED SUBSTRING
*        LASTS  = LAST CHARACTER POSITION OF SHIFTED SUBSTRING
*
*----------------------------------------------------------------
      CHARACTER*(*)   STRING,AFTER,NEW
      INTEGER         TLA,TLS,TLN,FIRSTN,LASTN,FIRSTS,LASTS,TRIM
*
*------------------------STEP 1----------------------------------
*
      TLS = TRIM(STRING)
      TLN = TRIM(NEW)
*
*------------------------STEP 2----------------------------------
*
      IF(TLS + TLN .GT. LEN(STRING)) THEN
        PRINT *,'DECLARED LENGTH OF STRING EXCEEDED'
        RETURN
      END IF
*
*------------------------STEP 3----------------------------------
*
      TLA = TRIM(AFTER)
      FIRSTN = INDEX(STRING,AFTER(:TLA)) + TLA
      LASTN = FIRSTN + TLN - 1
*
*------------------------STEP 4----------------------------------
*
      IF(FIRSTN .LT. TLS) THEN
        LASTS = TLS + TLN
        FIRSTS = FIRSTN + TLN
        DO 10 J = LASTS,FIRSTS,-1
          STRING(J:J) = STRING(J-TLN:J-TLN)
```

```
  10    CONTINUE
        END IF
*
*------------------------STEP 5-----------------------------------
*
        STRING(FIRSTN:LASTN) = NEW
*
*----------------------------------------------------------------
*
        END
```

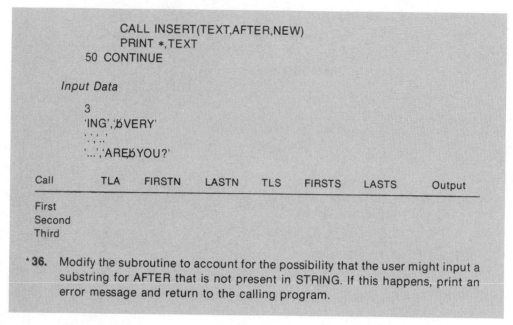

```
                CALL INSERT(TEXT,AFTER,NEW)
                PRINT *,TEXT
          50 CONTINUE
```

Input Data

```
       3
      'ING','ḃVERY'
      '.','.'
      '...','AREḃYOU?'
```

Call	TLA	FIRSTN	LASTN	TLS	FIRSTS	LASTS	Output
First							
Second							
Third							

*36. Modify the subroutine to account for the possibility that the user might input a substring for AFTER that is not present in STRING. If this happens, print an error message and return to the calling program.

10.6
COMMON ERRORS

Logic errors are the most common errors in string processing, so it pays to devote special attention to test data selection and output validation during the debugging phase. In particular, take care when using the INDEX function that you account for a returned value of zero. For example, it's best to design an error routine if we *always* expect to match substrings within strings (see Exercises 18 and 36).

If we expect to find a substring within a string and no match is found, then (assuming the string is correct) it could be due to any one of the following logic errors.

1. The wrong substring is used.
2. The string and substring are reversed in the INDEX function.
3. Declared length instead of trim length was used in the INDEX function for the name that contains the substring.

To illustrate all three errors, consider the following memory.

If the user inputs 'NEVAR' when

```
READ *,FIND
```

is executed, the first error is committed. If the programmer uses

    IND = INDEX(FIND,TEXT)

the second error is committed. *The function reference INDEX(s_1, s_2) returns a value of zero whenever LEN(s_1) < LEN(s_2)*, as in the above error (10 is less than 50). If the programmer uses

    IND = INDEX(TEXT,FIND)

instead of

    IND = INDEX(TEXT,FIND(:TRIM(FIND))

then possibly (depending on the system) the third error is committed. In this case the substring is taken to be NEVERɓɓɓɓɓ, which is not present in TEXT. However, using our TRIM function, the substring name FIND(:TRIM(FIND)), or FIND(:5), specifies NEVER as the substring, which is present in TEXT.

Finally, in an assignment statement, *don't use character positions to the left of an equal sign that are simultaneously referenced in the expression to the right of the equal sign.* For example, if we wish to insert ɓUSUALLY in positions 2–9 of TEXT and move ɓNEVERɓMAKEɓERRORS to positions 10–27, the following will result in either a logic or an execution error.

    TEXT(10:27) = TEXT(2:19)
    TEXT(2:9) = 'ɓUSUALLY'

In this case positions 10–19 are simultaneously referenced on both sides of the equal sign. (See the answer to Exercise 34 for the rationale and another example.)

ADDITIONAL EXERCISES

37. Define or explain the following.

character datum	character array element name
character string	character function name
string	character expression
length (of a string)	character assignment statement
character constant	substring
CHARACTER statement	substring name
declared length	concatenation
symbolic name of a character constant	character operator
character variable name	intrinsic functions for character data
character array name	collating sequence

38. Form Letter Revisited. Solve Exercise 33 in Chapter 4 on page 136 on the basis of the following additional considerations.
   a. Use the character operator where appropriate.
   b. Suppress trailing blanks following the output of names and addresses by using substring names.
   c. Appropriately use lowercase and uppercase letters.

**d. Preliminary to the loop that prints a form letter for each person, input the constant portions of the form letter into a vector that stores each line of the form letter. In this version, PRINT statements don't have character constants in their lists.

The following texts are used as test data by Exercises 39 to 42.

Column 1
↓

Text 1

Jack and Jill went up the hill
  To fetch a pail of water;
Jack fell down and broke his crown,
  And Jill came tumbling after.

Text 2

Among other duties, a regional office of the Environmental
Protection Agency (EPA) is charged with investigating complaints
regarding industrial pollution, when "warranted." A complaint is
investigated by sending a panel of three experts, collectively
called the "proboscis patrol," to the site of the alleged offender.
By consensus, the proboscis patrol then renders one of three opin-
ions: low level, medium level, or high level of pollution. (We
might note that the human nose has yet to find an electronic "equal"
in detecting offending odors.) Following an opinion, the regional
director of the EPA then has the option of issuing or not issuing a
citation to the offender. Alternatively, the EPA may choose not to
investigate the complaint and then make a decision regarding issuance
of a citation.

---

39. **Character Frequency Text Analysis I.** Write a program that processes *any number* of separate texts and prints the following for *each* text.
    a. Number of characters
    b. Number of letters and proportion of characters that are letters
    c. Number of vowels and proportion of letters that are vowels
    **d. Number of lowercase letters and proportion of letters that are lowercase
    Process each text one line at a time (maximum line length is 80 characters) and ignore trailing blanks in a line. Process the two given texts in your run.

40. **Character Frequency Text Analysis II.** Write a program that processes *any number* of separate texts and prints the number and proportion of *each* letter in the alphabet for each text. Make no distinction between lowercase and uppercase letters for purposes of the count. Process each text one line at a time, where the maximum line length is 80 characters. Process the two given texts in your run.

41. **Word Frequency Text Analysis.** Write a program that processes *any number* of separate texts and prints the following for *each* text.

a. Number of words

b. Number and proportion of words specified by the user (use "the" or "The" and "and" or "And" as test input)

c. Number and proportion of words that end in a substring specified by the user (use "ing" as test input)

d. Number and proportion of words that begin with a letter (or more generally any substring) specified by the user (use the letters "a" or "A" and "e" or "E" as test input)

Process each text one line at a time, where the maximum line length is 80 characters. Process the two given texts in your run.

42. **Keyboard Text Analysis.** A typing textbook contains numerous exercises consisting of paragraphs for students to type. These exercises vary in their level of difficulty according to the following criteria.

1. *Number of strokes* in the exercise. A stroke is any keyboard act, such as typing a letter, typing a space, and returning the carriage to the next line (except for the last line in the exercise), and so on.

2. *Number of words* in the exercise. Words can include a single letter. For example, the phrase "I love computers" has three words.

3. *Average word length* in the exercise. This is defined as the number of strokes divided by the number of words.

The usual approach to developing these exercises is for someone manually to count strokes, words, and word length for each proposed exercise, to ensure that exercises having various levels of difficulty are selected—a tedious task. This is where you come in. You are to computerize this task.

Write a program that processes *any number* of separate exercises and outputs each line of the exercise followed by a count of the number of strokes and words for that line. For example, the first two lines of Exercise 1 (Text 1) might be printed as follows:

	STROKES	WORDS
Jack and Jill went up the hill	31	7
To fetch a pail of water;	28	6

At the end of each exercise print summary values for the three criteria discussed earlier. Process each exercise one line at a time, where the maximum line length is 70. Use the two given texts as test data.

43. **Text Processing.** Write a program that inputs and stores lines of text (80 characters per line) as a vector, one array element per line, and then processes this text as follows.

a. Prints *n* copies of the text, where each copy begins on a new page (*n* is input by the user).

b. Prints no more than *m* lines on a page. If the text exceeds *m* lines, continue printing lines on subsequent pages. Subsequent pages should be numbered at the bottom center. (*m* is input by the user.)

c. Starts text at line *k* of each page, where *k* is input by the user.

**d. Right-justifies text to *max* print characters per line, where *max* is the character position of the line that has the rightmost nonblank character. The program determines *max* by processing each line of text, and then right-justifies text by appropriately placing blank characters in all lines of text whose rightmost nonblank characters are less than *max*. For example, if *max* = 70, a line having its last nonblank character at position 65 needs to have five blanks inserted. The program should select five reasonably spaced words in this line (never the *first* word) and insert a *single* blank in *front* of each. Make sure you don't right-justify the last line in a paragraph. The first line of each paragraph is indented. (Programs that set computerized type for books must handle this feature.) Use the first five paragraphs of the Preface in this text (ignoring headings) as test data. Use $n = 3, m = 10$, and $k = 20$.

44. Cryptography I. Cryptography is the encoding and decoding of messages in secret code, a task well suited for the character processing capabilities of computers. To illustrate a straightforward procedure called "increment coding" consider the following coding scheme for letters.

$$|\leftarrow \text{Increment} = 10 \longrightarrow|$$

Actual letter: A B C D E F G H I J K L M N O P Q R S T U V W X Y Z
Encoded letter: K L M N O P Q R S T U V W X Y Z A B C D E F G H I J

In this case the encoded letter is obtained by displacing the actual letter by an increment of 10; that is, K is the tenth letter from A, L is the tenth letter from B, and so on. Once an encoded letter reaches the end of the alphabet, the next encoded letter starts at the beginning of the alphabet.

It follows that messages are encoded by using encoded letters in place of actual letters, as illustrated below.

Actual message: HELP IS ON THE WAY
Encoded message: ROVZ SC YX DRO GKI

a. Write an encoding program that inputs an actual message and an increment and prints the actual message together with an encoded message.
b. Write a decoding program that inputs an encoded message and outputs the encoded message together with a decoded message. Include the option of not knowing the increment, in which case the program outputs 25 "decoded" messages, or one for each possible increment. In your test runs include the message encoded in part a and the following additional encoded message: A DGNW XGJLJSF.
c. Include the blank character and the ten digits 0 through 9 as part of the character set. Place these 11 additional characters just after the actual letter Z.

45. Cryptography II. An alternative method of increment coding, in addition to that discussed in the preceding exercise, is to apply the increment to the position of the character in the computer's collating sequence. In this case we don't use a letter table as in the preceding exercise; instead we first convert the actual letter to its corresponding position in the collating sequence, change this position value by the increment (making sure we stay within the inclusive range 0 to $n - 1$), and finally use this incremented position value to generate the encoded letter based on the computer's collating sequence. Note that all characters used by the particular computer are now part of the character set.

   a. Write an encoding program that inputs an actual message and an increment, and prints the actual message together with an encoded message. In your test runs, use HELP IS ON THE WAY as the actual message and increments of 1, 50, and 100.

   b. Write a decoding program that inputs an encoded message and increment, and outputs the encoded message together with the decoded message.

46. Cryptography III. Another, more cunning, variation on the increment coding described in Exercise 44 is "keyword" coding, whereby letters in a keyword are used to establish variable increments, as illustrated below.

Keyword: IBM

     First increment = 9 since I is 9th letter in alphabet

     Second increment = 2 since B is 2nd letter in alphabet

     Third increment = 13 since M is 13th letter in alphabet

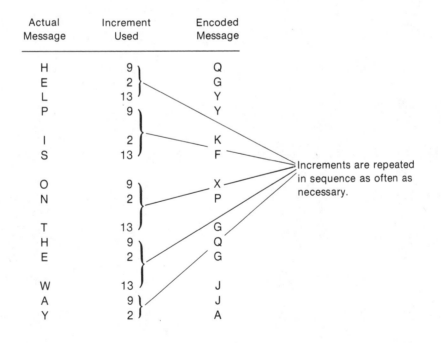

Actual Message	Increment Used	Encoded Message
H	9	Q
E	2	G
L	13	Y
P	9	Y
I	2	K
S	13	F
O	9	X
N	2	P
T	13	G
H	9	Q
E	2	G
W	13	J
A	9	J
Y	2	A

Increments are repeated in sequence as often as necessary.

   a. Write an encoding program that inputs a keyword of up to ten characters and an actual message and outputs the actual message together with an encoded message. In your test runs, use the above message and the keywords IBM and DIGITAL.

   b. Write a decoding program that inputs an encoded message and keyword and outputs the encoded message together with the decoded message.

**47. Text Editing.   Write a reasonably comprehensive text editing package that contains the following user-selected options:

a.   Input new text.
b.   Display text.
c.   Insert line(s).
d.   Delete line(s).
e.   Insert substring.
f.   Delete substring.
g.   Replace substring by another of either equal or unequal length.
h.   Stop.

Use a character vector to store one line of text per element. In your design, you should consider features and issues such as: Is the change to be made within a specified line, a set of specified lines, or all lines? Can the user delete or insert groups of lines at a time (such as a paragraph) or must the user repeatedly specify one line at a time? What should be done if a substring insert is too large for a line? Should it be rejected, or should the package automatically modify the current and immediately succeeding lines until the change is accommodated? . . . Have fun!

CHAPTER 11

External Files

Up until now, we have processed small amounts of input data, either from punched cards or from the terminal, and have printed output data at either the printer or a terminal. Moreover, we physically have represented a file (as described in Module C) by either a set of data cards or a set of data input lines at the terminal.

Many applications, particularly those with large amounts of data, require the processing of files that reside in external or secondary storage on media other than punched cards. For example, customer files for a telephone company are placed on either magnetic disk or magnetic tape for processing by either disk drives or tape drives that are online to the CPU.

This chapter is an introduction to the processing of external files on media such as magnetic tape or magnetic disk.

11.1
FIELDS, RECORDS, AND FILES

Let's first define what we mean by a field, record, and file within our present context.

Field. A data item (fact or attribute) about some entity such as a person, place, thing, or event. For example, an employer might maintain data on employees' name, Social Security number, rate of pay, number of deductions, and other items. Each of these attributes is considered a field.

Record. A collection of related fields grouped together and retrievable as a unit. For example, all of the data items relating to a single employee represent a record.

File. A collection of related records. Each record is a logical part of the file because it contains the same data items as all the other records in the file. For example, an "employee file" contains the data on each employee.

Figure 11.1 illustrates this relationship among fields, records, and a file. In this case, the file is made up of three records, and each record contains four fields.

FIGURE 11.1   *Relationship Among Fields, Records, and File*

		Name	SS Number	Salary	Sex
			Fields		
	Record 1	ABATAR JANE A.	099-34-2101	20000	F
File	Record 2	BOMBERG BO B.	881-12-1113	15800	M
	Record 3	DRURY DAVID D.	125-71-8112	18000	M

11.2
FILES IN FORTRAN

Any file that is used in a FORTRAN program has the following characteristics.

1. The file is either external or internal.
2. Access to the file is either sequential or direct.
3. The file is either formatted or unformatted.

External versus Internal Files

An **external file** is a collection of records written on an I/O medium such as paper tape, punched cards, cassette, magnetic tape, or magnetic disk. The data are stored on a storage medium external to primary memory, and so the file is called an "external" file.

Punched cards technically can store external files. However, the use of punched cards for large external files is costly, unwieldy, and functionally limited compared with media such as tape and disk. In this chapter we implicitly assume the use of tape or disk as the relevant external storage media.

An **internal file** is a collection of records stored within an area of main memory. Internal files allow the transfer of data among different portions of primary memory for specialized uses that are not considered in this text.

Unformatted versus Formatted Files

An **unformatted file** consists strictly of unformatted records. An **unformatted record** contains data in a form that's identical to the machine's internal representation of data (in binary form). Unformatted records are read or written only by *unformatted* input/output statements, as defined in the next section.

A **formatted file** is made up entirely of formatted records. A **formatted record** contains data in "external" form as characters (numeric, alphabetic, or special). Formatted records are read or written only by *formatted* input/output statements, as defined in the next section.

Unformatted files are processed more rapidly than formatted files because it's not necessary to convert internal/external representations. When the computer inputs a formatted record from an external file into primary memory, it first must convert data from external representation (as stored in the file) to internal representation (as stored within primary memory). Similarly, when the computer writes a formatted record onto an external file, it first must convert data from internal representation to external representation. If the external file is unformatted, however, then there's no need for time-consuming conversion operations, since all data are represented using the "internal" form.

Unformatted files are useful when secondary storage media such as tape and disk are used as extensions of primary memory. This type of memory extension is desirable, for example, when a particular application has data storage requirements that exceed the available size of primary memory. Unformatted files, however, are processor-dependent. Thus, if a particular file is likely to be used by more than one type of computer, it is then necessary to use formatted files.

Sequential Access versus Direct Access

We can process a file in either of two ways—by sequential access or by direct access. File processing by **sequential access** writes or reads records one after the other in serial or "sequential" fashion. For example, if a personnel file contains 1000 records (employees), sequential processing means that we can read the 900th record if and only if we first read or process the first 899 records.

Figure 11.2a illustrates the file in Figure 11.1 as a file set up for sequential access. The last record in this file is called an **endfile record.** It signals the processor that the physical end of this file has been reached. An endfile record is permitted only as the *last* record in a *sequential-access file*. Sequential-access files, however, need not have endfile records. For example, if the first record in a sequential-access file contains a value for the total number of records that follow next in the file, there is no need for an endfile record.

We might note that

1. *All* records in a sequential-access file must be either formatted or unformatted, except for the endfile record.
2. Sequential-access files are processed only by *sequential-access* input/output statements, as described in Section 11.3.

File processing by **direct access** writes or reads a record without the need to process any other record in the file. For example, if there are 1000 records in a direct-access personnel file, we can "directly" read the 900th record without having to read the previous 899 records.

Figure 11.2b depicts our sample file as a file that is compatible with direct access. Each record in the file is uniquely identified by a positive integer called a **record number.** You should keep the following points in mind with regard to *direct-access files*.

1. All records must be either formatted or unformatted.
2. All records have the same *length.* For example, all records in a formatted, direct-access file have the same number of characters.
3. Reading and writing of records are accomplished only by *direct-access* input/output statements, as described in Section 11.3.

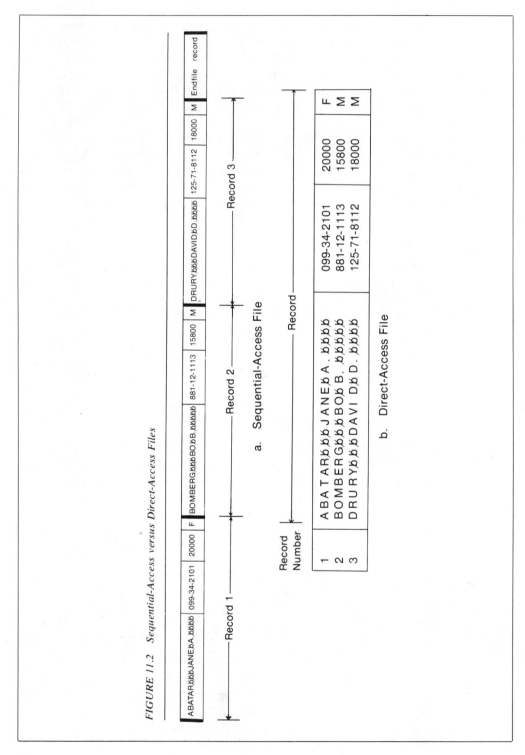

FIGURE 11.2 Sequential-Access versus Direct-Access Files

ABATAR bbbJANE b A. bbbb	099-34-2101	20000	F	BOMBERG bbb Bo b B. bbbbb	881-12-1113	15800	M	DRURY bbb DAVID b D. bbbb	125-71-8112	18000	M	Endfile record

Record 1 ⟵————————⟶ Record 2 ⟵————————⟶ Record 3 ⟵————————⟶

a. Sequential-Access File

Record Number	⟵——————— Record ———————⟶		
1	A B A T A R b b b J A N E b A . bbbb	099-34-2101	20000	F
2	B O M B E R G b b b B O b B . bbbbb	881-12-1113	15800	M
3	D R U R Y b b b D A V I D b D . bbbb	125-71-8112	18000	M

b. Direct-Access File

4. Record numbers are placed on a file only when records are written. Once established, a record number cannot be changed. In fact, records in an existing direct-access file cannot be deleted—they can only be read or rewritten.
5. The order of the records is the order of their record numbers; however, records may be read or written in any order. For example, it's permissible to write record 5 without having written records 1 through 4.
6. *List-directed* input/output statements are not permissible for processing direct-access files. (More on this in the next section.)

By the way, files stored on magnetic tape can be processed only by sequential access whereas files stored on magnetic disk can be processed by either sequential access or direct access. In general, the access method allowed depends on both the file medium and the processor. Issues regarding which medium to use and which access method to implement relate to factors such as speed, cost, application, and processing environment. For example, time-shared processing invariably uses magnetic disk and airline reservation inquiry systems process direct-access files.

Follow-up Exercises

1. Briefly describe the possible makeup of records in a "student grade" file for your course. Would you expect this file to be processed by sequential access or by direct access? Would you expect it to be formatted or unformatted?
2. Can you think of a change in Figure 11.2a that would eliminate the need for an endfile record?
3. Is it possible to process a direct-access file sequentially? Why or why not? Is it possible to process a sequential-access file by direct access? Why or why not?

11.3
SELECTED FILE-RELATED STATEMENTS

In this section we define and illustrate commonly used statements for processing external files.

OPEN Statement

The OPEN statement is an executable statement that defines properties and establishes links among the input/output unit (for example, tape drive or disk drive), the file (stored on tape or disk), and the FORTRAN program.[1] Its general form is given by

> **OPEN** (*list of specifiers*)

---

[1] Systems also require the use of file-related control cards for batch processing and file-related system commands for time-shared processing. Either ask your instructor or consult your system's manual.

where *specifiers* within the list are separated by commas. The following list of selected **specifiers** apply to this statement, where *all specifiers are optional except for the first.*

UNIT $= u$ The *unit identifier u* for an external file identifies the specific I/O unit that is to be used (such as tape drive). It must be either an integer expression with a nonnegative value or an asterisk.[2] The portion UNIT $=$ can be omitted, but u must be present. A value of, say, 10 for u might refer to a specific tape drive. The relationship of specific values for u to specific I/O units is system-dependent, so ask your instructor.

FILE $= name$ *name* is a character expression whose value (after the removal of trailing blanks) identifies the name of the file to be connected with the specified I/O unit. If this specifier is omitted and the I/O unit is not connected to a file, the I/O unit becomes connected to a system-determined file.

STATUS $= sta$ *sta* is a character expression whose value (after the removal of trailing blanks) is OLD, NEW, SCRATCH, or UNKNOWN. OLD is specified when the file already exists on the I/O unit, NEW when the file does not exist, SCRATCH when the file is used temporarily and deleted (''scratched'') either following the run or following the execution of a CLOSE statement (page 410), and UNKNOWN when we wish the status to be system-dependent. If OLD or NEW is specified, the specifier FILE $=$ must be given. If SCRATCH is specified, don't use the specifier FILE $=$. If the specifier STATUS $=$ is omitted, UNKNOWN is assumed.

ACCESS $= acc$ *acc* is a character expression whose value (after the removal of trailing blanks) is SEQUENTIAL or DIRECT. This specifier establishes the access method. If omitted, sequential is assumed.

FORM $= fm$ *fm* is a character expression whose value (after the removal of trailing blanks) is FORMATTED or UNFORMATTED. It specifies whether we have a formatted or an unformatted file. If this specifier is omitted, FORMATTED is assumed for sequential-access files and UNFORMATTED is assumed for direct-access files.

RECL $= length$ *length* is an integer expression with positive value that specifies the record length in a direct-access file. *Length* is expressed in number of characters for formatted records and number of processor-dependent units for unformatted records. This specifier *must* be given for direct-access files; otherwise it *must* be omitted.

EXAMPLE 11.1

The statements below illustrate the OPEN statement under varying conditions.

   a. To connect an existing formatted sequential-access file named PERSONNEL to unit 1:

```
OPEN (UNIT = 1,FILE = 'PERSONNEL',STATUS = 'OLD',
+       ACCESS = 'SEQUENTIAL',FORM = 'FORMATTED')
```

---

[2] The asterisk identifies a particular system-determined unit (for example, disk drive) that's preconnected for formatted sequential access.

b. To create an updated (new) version of the personnel file, name it UPDATE, and connect it to unit 2:

```
OPEN (UNIT = 2,FILE = 'UPDATE',STATUS = 'NEW',
+       ACCESS = 'SEQUENTIAL',FORM = 'FORMATTED')
```

c. To connect an existing formatted direct-access file (30 characters per record) named INVENTORY to unit 10:

```
OPEN (FORM = 'FORMATTED',ACCESS = 'DIRECT',RECL = 30,
+       FILE = 'INVENTORY',UNIT = 10,STATUS = 'OLD')
```

Note that specifiers need not appear in the order described, as illustrated by the last example. Also note that record length must be specified if the file is for direct access.

READ/WRITE Statements

Once the file is defined through the execution of an OPEN statement, it can be processed with READ and WRITE statements. The READ statement transfers (copies) a record from a file to primary memory. The WRITE statement transfers data stored in primary memory to a file.

The general forms of these statements are given by

> **READ** (*control list*) *input list*
> **WRITE** (*control list*) *output list*

Each item in the *input list* must be one of the following.

1. Variable name
2. Array element name
3. Array name
4. Implied-DO list
5. Character substring name

Each item in the *output list* must be one of the following.

1–5.   As in the input list
  6.   Expression

The *control list* is a list of any of the following selected *specifiers*.

UNIT = *u*   See page 404. If the portion UNIT = is omitted, *u* must be the first item in the list. This specifier *must* be present.

FMT = *f*   *f* is a *format identifier* that identifies the *format specification* to be used. It can be an integer constant that's the same as the statement label of the FORMAT statement, or an integer variable storing a value that's the same as the statement label of the FORMAT statement, or a character array name that stores the format specification, or a character expression whose value is the format specification, or an asterisk for list-directed formatting. (See Section D.3 if you're "fuzzy" on these terms.) If the portion FMT = is omitted, *f* must be the second item in the control list, where the first item *must* be *u*.

REC = *rn*   *rn* is an integer expression whose value is positive. It represents the record number to be processed in a direct-access file. This specifier must be present to process a direct-access file.

ERR = *s*   *s* is the statement label of an executable statement that appears in the same program unit as this *error specifier*. Control is transferred to statement *s* whenever an error condition is encountered during the execution of this READ or WRITE statement.[3]

END = *s*   *s* is the statement label of an executable statement that appears in the same program unit as this *end-of-file specifier*. Execution of the READ statement terminates, and control is transferred to statement *s* whenever the processor encounters an endfile record. This specifier is used only when reading a sequential-access file; it cannot be used either with a direct-access file or within a WRITE statement.

EXAMPLE 11.2

The following READ/WRITE statements are consistent with the files "opened" in Example 11.1.

    a. To read a record into primary memory from the formatted sequential-access file named PERSONNEL:

                 ┌─Note that unit identifier is consistent with first OPEN statement.
                 ↓

```
      READ (UNIT = 1,FMT = 900)NAME,SSN,ADDRES
  900 FORMAT(A20,A11,A60)
```

---

[3] This error specifier also is a legitimate specifier within the OPEN statement.

b. The following statement is a modification of the first READ statement to include end-of-file and error specifiers.

READ (UNIT = 1,FMT = 900,END = 999,ERR = 800)NAME,SSN,ADDRES

c. To write a record from primary memory to the formatted sequential-access file named UPDATE:

————Consistent with second OPEN statement

WRITE (UNIT = 2,FMT = 900)NAME,SSN,ADDRES

————Same FORMAT statement as used by READ statement, since records have same format structure in this example. Note that "carriage control" is not relevant for file output.

d. To read record number 500 into primary memory from the formatted direct-access file named INVENTORY, as opened by the third OPEN statement:

————Consistent with third OPEN statement

READ (UNIT = 10,FMT = 3,REC = 500)NAME,LEVEL
3 FORMAT (A20,I10)

Consider the following points.

1. The control list must contain exactly one *unit specifier* (UNIT = u), and none or one of any of the other specifiers. Moreover, these specifiers can be in any order (unless UNIT = and FMT = portions are omitted).
2. If the control list contains a *format specifier* (FMT = f), the statement is a **formatted input/output statement;** otherwise it's an **unformatted input/output statement.** If the format identifier f is an asterisk, the statement is a **list-directed input/output statement.**
3. If the control list contains a *record specifier* (REC = rn), the statement is a **direct-access input/output statement;** otherwise it's a **sequential-access input/output statement.**
4. Record specifiers are not allowed in list-directed input/output statements since such statements are not permitted to process direct-access files.
5. A control list must not contain both a record specifier and an end-of-file specifier.
6. These READ/WRITE statements are perfectly general for all input/output. For example, if the line printer is unit 6,

PRINT *,A

is equivalent to

WRITE (6,*)A

The WRITE statement also can be used to punch output onto cards. For example, if the card punch is unit 7 and we wish to punch the values within M and N in five-column fields on a card, we can use

```
    WRITE (7,90)M,N
90 FORMAT(2I5)
```

Follow-up Exercises

8. Can you reason out the logic behind item 5?

9. In Example 11.2 what happens in each of the first two READ statements if the processor encounters
   a. An error condition?
   b. An endfile record?

10. Describe the nature of this statement:

```
    WRITE (15)A
```

Specify an appropriate OPEN statement such that unit 15 is linked to an existing file called STRESS.

11. Write code to

Create a new formatted direct-access file named GRADES that gets connected to unit 20 and has record lengths of 31 characters.

Read from a card reader or terminal the integer variable student identification (ID), the character variable student name (NAME), and the character variable final letter grade (GRADE).

Write to the file student name and final grade, using ID as the record number and a FORMAT statement labeled 90.

*12. Consider the flowchart below for a segment of a program that uses the same file described by the third OPEN statement in Example 11.1 and the third READ statement in Example 11.2.

> Write FORTRAN code for this segment. Treat all specifiers as variables whose values are read in from the card reader/terminal just before this segment. Also, use a variable (execution-time) format specification.
>
> *13. Modify the preceding exercise such that part number and new level are read in from an unformatted sequential tape file (named TRANSACTION) on unit 9. Exit from the DO-WHILE structure when the endfile record is encountered. Get the part name from file INVENTORY by reading the appropriate record. Then combine the part name with the new level and rewrite the record in the inventory file.

ENDFILE Statement

Execution of an ENDFILE statement places an endfile record as the next record in a *sequential*-access file. The general forms of this statement are

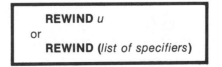

```
        ENDFILE u
    or
        ENDFILE (list of specifiers)
```

where the *list of specifiers* includes (of those we have described) only the unit specifier (UNIT $= u$) and the error specifier (ERR $= s$).

To illustrate, suppose we have just finished writing an entire sequential file on unit 2. If we wish an endfile record, we should next use

    ENDFILE(UNIT = 2)

or more simply

    ENDFILE 2

REWIND Statement

If we need to process the same *sequential* file more than once during a run, we must start over at the beginning of the file—that is, the file must be rewound. Execution of the REWIND statement repositions the file at its initial point (the first record).

The general forms of this statement are

```
        REWIND u
    or
        REWIND (list of specifiers)
```

where the *list of specifiers* includes (of those we have described) only the unit specifier (UNIT $= u$) and the error specifier (ERR $= s$).

On magnetic tape the REWIND statement activates the tape drive to rewind the tape physically. On magnetic disk the REWIND statement repositions the read/write arms of the disk drive to the first record of the file.

To illustrate, suppose we have just finished writing a complete sequential file on unit 10. If we next wish to read all records in the file for the purpose of printing (displaying) its contents, we must first specify that the file is to be rewound by using the statement

    REWIND(UNIT = 10)

or more simply

    REWIND 10

Many programmers also prefer to use REWIND statements at the beginning of programs to ensure that sequential files are properly positioned and at the end of programs to ensure that sequential files are properly repositioned for subsequent use in other runs.

CLOSE Statement

After a file is processed and before execution terminates, it's best properly to disconnect the file from the input/output unit. This is accomplished by execution of a CLOSE statement having the following general form

CLOSE (*list of specifiers*)

where the list of specifiers includes the following selected items:

UNIT $= u$ See page 404. This specifier is required.
ERR $= s$ See page 406. This specifier is optional.
STATUS $= sta$ sta is a character expression whose value (after the removal of trailing blanks) is KEEP or DELETE. We should specify KEEP to retain the data on the file for later use and DELETE to "wipe out" the data on file. KEEP must not be used if SCRATCH was specified in the OPEN statement. This specifier is optional. If omitted, KEEP is assumed—unless SCRATCH was specified earlier, in which case DELETE is assumed.

To illustrate, we can close and keep the file on unit 2 by using either

    CLOSE(UNIT = 2,STATUS = 'KEEP')

or simply

    CLOSE(2)

assuming this file is not a "scratch" file.

Keep in mind the following points regarding the closing of files.

1. A unit, having been disconnected by the execution of a CLOSE statement, can be reconnected within the same run either to the same file or to a different file.
2. A file, having been disconnected by the execution of a CLOSE statement, can be reconnected within the same run either to the same unit or to a different unit, provided that the file was not deleted.

3. Systems implicitly close all files at the termination of execution if CLOSE statements are not used. The effect is as though a CLOSE statement without a STATUS = specifier were executed on each connected unit. As a matter of programming style, however, we recommend the explicit closing of all units.

Follow-up Exercise

14. Suppose we wish to rewind and keep old files on units 1 and 2. Is anything wrong with the following? If so, make corrections.

```
REWIND 1,2
CLOSE(1,2)
```

11.4
SEQUENTIAL-ACCESS PERSONNEL FILE—AN EXAMPLE

Now that we have the necessary "tools," let's illustrate the creation and display of the formatted sequential-access personnel file in Figure 11.2a on page 402, based on the following record layout.

Field Description	Symbolic Name	Type	Columns
Employee name	NAME	Character	1–20
Social Security number	SSN	Character	21–31
Salary (nearest dollar)	SAL	Integer	32–36
Sex code (M or F)	SEX	Character	37

The pseudocode below describes the algorithm.

```
              READ unit, file name, status specifiers from card/terminal
              OPEN file/unit
             ⎧READ record from card/terminal
             ⎪DO WHILE record remains
             ⎪   WRITE record on file
File-creation logic⎨   READ record from card/terminal
             ⎪END DO
             ⎩Create endfile record
              REWIND file
              PRINT header at printer/terminal
             ⎧Initialize record count
             ⎪DO WHILE record remains
             ⎪   READ record from file
File-display logic⎨   Increment record count
             ⎪   PRINT record count, record at printer/terminal
             ⎩END DO
              PRINT "end of file" at printer/terminal
              CLOSE file/unit
              Stop
```

The file-creation logic first inputs a record into primary memory from the card reader or terminal; then the record is transferred from primary memory to the file medium (tape or disk). Finally, after all records have been written to the file, an endfile record is written.

The file-display logic first reads a record from the file and stores this record in primary memory; then this record is transferred from primary memory to printer paper or terminal paper/screen.

Figure 11.3 illustrates the data flows for both file creation and display. Make sure

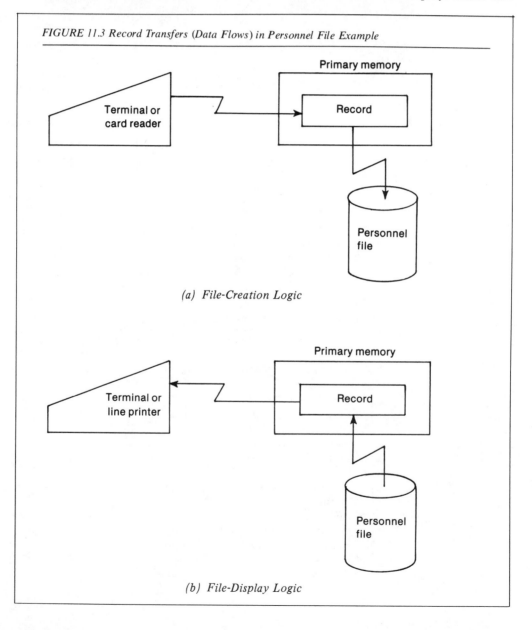

FIGURE 11.3 Record Transfers (Data Flows) in Personnel File Example

Primary memory

Terminal or card reader

Record

Personnel file

(a) File-Creation Logic

Primary memory

Terminal or line printer

Record

Personnel file

(b) File-Display Logic

you understand these record transfers. The program below reflects this pseudocode design. You should note the following.

1. The inputting of values for unit, file name, and status specifiers (as used in the OPEN statement) from a card or terminal, for greater generality
2. The necessary use of SEQUENTIAL as the value for the ACCESS = specifier in the OPEN statement, to establish sequential-access processing
3. Use of the ENDFILE statement to place an endfile record on the file
4. Use of the REWIND statement before the file is displayed, to reinitialize the file to the first record
5. Use of the END = specifier in the READ statement (in loop 60), a convenient device for establishing a last-record-check loop as a DO-WHILE structure

```
C    FORMATTED SEQUENTIAL-ACCESS PERSONNEL FILE CREATION/DISPLAY PROGRAM
C
C    KEY:
C      NAME    = EMPLOYEE NAME
C      SSN     = SOCIAL SECURITY NUMBER
C      SAL     = SALARY
C      SEX     = SEX CODE (M OR F)
C      U       = UNIT IDENTIFIER
C      FNAME   = FILE NAME
C      STA     = STATUS OF FILE (OLD, NEW, SCRATCH, OR UNKNOWN)
C
C    RECORD DESIGN:
C      NAME       TYPE CHARACTER      COLUMNS   1-20
C      SSN        TYPE CHARACTER      COLUMNS  21-31
C      SAL        TYPE INTEGER        COLUMNS  32-36
C      SEX        TYPE CHARACTER      COLUMN   37
C-------------------------------------------------------------------------
      CHARACTER NAME*20,SSN*11,SEX,FNAME*10,STA*7
      INTEGER   SAL,U
C-------------------------------------------------------------------------
   10 FORMAT (2A,I5,A)
   20 FORMAT ('1','RECORD',T18,'NAME',T31,'SS NUMBER',T44,
      +          'SALARY',T53,'SEX'/1X,54('-')/)
   30 FORMAT (1X,I5,T10,A,T30,A,T45,I5,T54,A)
C-------------------------------------------------------------------------
      READ *,U,FNAME,STA
      OPEN (UNIT = U,FILE = FNAME,STATUS = STA,
      +      ACCESS = 'SEQUENTIAL',FORM = 'FORMATTED')
C-------------------------------------------------------------------------
      READ *,NAME,SSN,SAL,SEX
   50 IF (NAME .NE. 'EOF') THEN
         WRITE (UNIT = U,FMT = 10) NAME,SSN,SAL,SEX
         READ *,NAME,SSN,SAL,SEX
         GO TO 50
      END IF
C-------------------------------------------------------------------------
      ENDFILE U
      REWIND  U
C-------------------------------------------------------------------------
      PRINT 20
      J = 0
   60 READ (UNIT = U,FMT = 10, END = 70) NAME,SSN,SAL,SEX
      J = J + 1
      PRINT 30,J,NAME,SSN,SAL,SEX
      GO TO 60
C-------------------------------------------------------------------------
   70 PRINT *,'END OF FILE'
      CLOSE (UNIT = U,STATUS = 'KEEP')
C-------------------------------------------------------------------------
      END
```

Follow-up Exercises

15. With respect to the example:
    a. Specify the exact layout of input data that would give the file in Figure 11.2a. Assume we wish to use unit 15, PERSONNEL as the file name, and NEW as the status.
    b. Specify the exact printed output.
    c. Exactly how does the program terminate execution?
16. Suppose we were to modify the program as follows.

```
        :
        :
60      READ (UNIT = U,FMT = 90,ERR = 65,END = 70)NAME,SSN,SAL,SEX
        :
        :
        GO TO 60
65 PRINT *,'ERROR IN FILE READ IN'
   CLOSE (U)
   STOP
70 PRINT *,'END OF FILE'
   CLOSE (U)
   END
```

What's the advantage of this approach? Can you think of a disadvantage?
17. Modify the program to give the option of creating either a formatted file or an unformatted file. Use FM as a character variable of length 11 to store either FORMATTED or UNFORMATTED.
*18. Modify the program to eliminate the need for an endfile record. Assume we know beforehand the number of records, which is input as the variable N in the first READ statement. Write the value in N as the first record in the file, using an I5 edit descriptor. Would you recommend this approach as good programming practice?
*19. Write a program that reads the personnel file and performs an analysis to print the number of females and their average salary and the number of males and their average salary.

11.5
DIRECT-ACCESS PERSONNEL FILE—AN
EXAMPLE

In many cases it's desirable to create direct-access rather than sequential-access files. For example, direct-access files are normally used by inquiry systems, such as those implemented by airlines to provide flight information.

To illustrate the creation and display of a direct-access file, let's return to our personnel example. The file design below is a variation of the formatted direct-access file shown in Figure 11.2b.

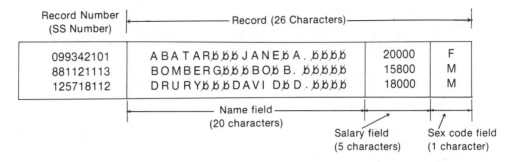

Note that Social Security number is now treated as an integer value rather than as a character value. We use it here to represent the record number, which serves as a convenient "key" for writing and reading specific records. That is, to access any record in the file directly, we need only specify the SS number of that employee.

The pseudocode below describes the algorithm.

```
                        READ unit, file name, status specifiers from card/terminal
                        OPEN file/unit
                       ⎧READ SS no. (record no.), record from card/terminal
                       ⎪DO WHILE SS no.>0
File-creation logic⎨      WRITE record on file
                       ⎪   READ SS no., record from card/terminal
                       ⎩END DO
                        PRINT header at printer/terminal
                       ⎧READ SS no. from card/terminal
                       ⎪DO WHILE SS no.>0
File-display logic ⎨     READ record from file
                       ⎪   PRINT SS no., record at printer/terminal
                       ⎪   READ SS no. from card/terminal
                       ⎩END DO
                        PRINT "file display terminated"
                        CLOSE file/unit
                        Stop
```

The file-creation logic first inputs the SS number (record number) and record into primary memory from the card reader or terminal; then the record is transferred from primary memory to the file medium (magnetic disk).

The file-display logic first inputs the SS number into primary memory from the card reader or terminal. The SS number is then used as the record number to locate the appropriate record on the file. Next the record is read from the file and stored in primary memory. Finally, the SS number and record are transferred from primary memory to printer paper or terminal paper/screen. This type of file-display logic is the basis of computerized direct-access inquiry systems.

The program below reflects the pseudocode design. You should carefully note the following.

1. The necessary use of DIRECT as the value for the ACCESS = specifier in the OPEN statement, to establish direct-access processing

2. The necessary use of the RECL = specifier in the OPEN statement, and its assigned length of exactly 26 characters
3. The necessary use of the REC = specifier in direct-access READ/WRITE statements
4. The integer typing of SSN and its use as the record number in the REC = specifier

```
C     FORMATTED DIRECT-ACCESS PERSONNEL FILE CREATION/DISPLAY PROGRAM
C
C     KEY:
C       NAME      = EMPLOYEE NAME
C       SSN       = SOCIAL SECURITY NUMBER/RECORD NUMBER
C       SAL       = SALARY
C       SEX       = SEX CODE (M OR F)
C       U         = UNIT IDENTIFIER
C       FNAME     = FILE NAME
C       STA       = STATUS OF FILE (OLD, NEW, SCRATCH, OR UNKNOWN)
C
C     RECORD DESIGN:
C       NAME        TYPE CHARACTER        COLUMNS  1-20
C       SAL         TYPE INTEGER          COLUMNS 21-25
C       SEX         TYPE CHARACTER        COLUMN  26
C-------------------------------------------------------------------
      CHARACTER NAME*20,SEX,FNAME*10,STA*7
      INTEGER   SAL,U,SSN
C-------------------------------------------------------------------
   10 FORMAT (A,I5,A)
   20 FORMAT ('1','RECORD/SS NUMBER',T27,'NAME',T40,
     +          'SALARY',T49,'SEX'/1X,50('-')/)
   30 FORMAT (4X,I9,T19,A,T41,I5,T50,A)
C-------------------------------------------------------------------
      READ *,U,FNAME,STA
      OPEN (UNIT = U,FILE = FNAME,STATUS = STA,
     +      ACCESS = 'DIRECT',FORM = 'FORMATTED',RECL = 26)
C-------------------------------------------------------------------
      READ *,SSN,NAME,SAL,SEX
   50 IF (SSN .GT. 0) THEN
         WRITE (UNIT = U,FMT = 10,REC = SSN) NAME,SAL,SEX
         READ *,SSN,NAME,SAL,SEX
         GO TO 50
      END IF
C-------------------------------------------------------------------
      PRINT 20
      READ *,SSN
   60 IF (SSN .GT. 0) THEN
         READ (UNIT = U,FMT = 10,REC = SSN) NAME,SAL,SEX
         PRINT 30,SSN,NAME,SAL,SEX
         READ *,SSN
         GO TO 60
      END IF
C-------------------------------------------------------------------
      PRINT *,'FILE DISPLAY TERMINATED'
      CLOSE (U)
C-------------------------------------------------------------------
      END
```

Follow-up Exercises

20. With respect to the example:
    a. Specify the exact input that would give the sample file. Assume we wish to use unit 15, PERSONNEL as the file name, and NEW as the status.
    b. Specify the exact printed output.

21. What can be done if a mistake is made in entering an employee's Social Security number and the record already has been written on the direct-access file?

*22. Solve Exercise 19 on the basis of the direct-access file. Supply record numbers as card/terminal input. Which file is more convenient for this type of processing?

**23. Assuming that a direct-access personnel file already has been created (as in the example), write a complete program to update the file according to the following options.

(i) Display a record.

(ii) Add a new record to the file.

(iii) Change an existing record in the file.

(iv) "Delete" a record from the file by replacing character fields with blanks and numeric fields with zeros.

(v) "Delete" records from the file by creating a complete new direct-access file given the new set of record numbers as card/terminal input. The new set of record numbers would not include those records we wish deleted. Records in the new file are identical to records that we wish to keep from the old file. The old file is to be deleted. Stop processing after this option is executed.

(vi) No more options (stop processing).

Design your program such that after an option is carried out, control returns to the statement that requests the next option.

11.6
DATA PROCESSING APPLICATIONS

Data processing applications such as payroll, inventory control, and accounts receivable routinely use external files to process large amounts of data. In these types of applications it's useful to make a distinction between two file types called master files and transaction files.

A **master file** contains data items that are central to continued operation of the organization. These files are relatively permanent collections of records containing informational, historical, and current-status items. For example, the master file for bank checking accounts might contain a record for each customer account that includes the customer's name, account number, address, telephone, and last month's ending balance.

A **transaction file** is a relatively temporary collection of records containing data about transactions that have occurred during the most recent operating period of time. This type of file is used to process data against the master file. For example, a transaction file for bank checking accounts might contain data on all checks processed during the current month. At the end of the current month, data from both the transaction file and the master file are processed into a new master file that updates the current status of ending balance for each account.

EXAMPLE 11.3   Computerized Inventory Control System

Controlling inventory is a very important function for most organizations. Poor inventory control can lead to unnecessarily high levels of inventory, resulting in high rates of spoilage and obsolescence, and high costs for storing, maintaining, and insuring goods. At the other extreme, poor inventory control can lead to frequent shortages, resulting in customer's ill will and lost sales. Good inventory control means that management is able to provide a desired level of service to its customers (by delivering goods from inventory) at the least expense to the organization. For most organizations, good inventory control generally dictates a computerized inventory control system.

In a computerized inventory control system every addition and deletion in stock is recorded in a transaction file. Periodically, data in the transaction file are used to update (change) an inventory master file that maintains, among other things, the current balance of each inventory item.

To illustrate an inventory control system, consider the "blood bank" (inventory of blood) at a hospital. To simplify the discussion, suppose that only two types of blood are carried in inventory, A-negative (ANEG) and A-positive (APOS), and three actions against inventory are possible: action code 1 means that inventory has been depleted by some amount (number of units) for use by a patient; action code 2 means that inventory has been depleted by the number of units in storage that have exceeded the maximum legal life of blood (21 days); and action code 3 means that inventory has been augmented by new blood.

The process of updating inventory is illustrated by the system flowchart in Figure 11.4. A **system flowchart** presents a general overview of an entire system, the sequence of major processing operations, and the data flow to and from files. The type of flowchart you have been drawing is technically called a **program flowchart.**

In our blood bank illustration, each inventory transaction (type of blood, action code, and number of units of blood) is entered at the terminal interactively under the control of an EDIT/SORT program. For example, at the end of a given day the following transactions might be entered.

Blood Type	Action Code	Amount (pints)	
APOS	1	3	
APOS	1	4	
ANEG	2	15	
APOS	3	50	
ANEG	1	5	
APOS	75	2	←——Incorrect entry
END	0	0	←——End-of-file record

The EDIT/SORT program in Figure 11.4 checks the validity of action codes (note the mistake in the last entry), sorts the data alphabetically according to blood type, and places the data on the transaction file as follows.

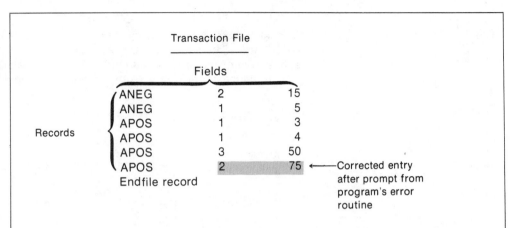

Transaction File

Fields

Records			
	ANEG	2	15
	ANEG	1	5
	APOS	1	3
	APOS	1	4
	APOS	3	50
	APOS	2	75
	Endfile record		

← Corrected entry after prompt from program's error routine

FIGURE 11.4   *System Flowchart for Inventory Control System (All Files Sequential-Access)*

The UPDATE program next utilizes the transaction file and the master file to create an updated master file. Additionally, the UPDATE program prints a report showing the date and a table of blood type and current inventory balance (as described in Exercise 30). If the master file contains the data shown below,

Master Inventory File

Blood type in alphabetical order   ⟶   ANEG   60

APOS   90 ⟵ Number of pints in inventory

Endfile record

the processing of the transaction file against the master file would result in the following updated master file.

Updated (New) Master Inventory File

ANEG	40
APOS	58
Endfile record	

A program flowchart for the UPDATE program is illustrated in Figure 11.5. The "transaction key" is the blood type (ANEG or APOS) read from a record of the transaction file and the "master key" is the blood type read from a record of the master file. In the discussion that follows keep in mind that records in both the transaction and master files are in alphabetical order according to blood type. Also, we assume that both files are processed by sequential access.

The update program compares the key of the transaction record with the corresponding data item (key) in the master record. If a match occurs (keys of both files are equal) the transaction data are used to update the number of pints in inventory for that master record (the inventory would increase or decrease based on the transaction amount), as illustrated by the middle branch in Figure 11.5.

When the transaction key tests greater than the master key, it follows that processing of the current blood type on the master file has been completed. Thus, the updated record for this blood type now can be written onto the new master file. For example, when the third record in the transaction file on page 419 is processed, the transaction key will test greater than the master key (APOS > ANEG). At this time the updated record for ANEG on the new master file can be written, as depicted in the third branch of Figure 11.5.

A transaction key greater than the master key may also indicate that no transaction (activity) occurred for that record. This is particularly common when master files have many records. In such cases, the master record is copied unchanged onto the new master file. Depending on the situation, however, an error may be indicated by the mismatch of keys. In this case, an error message is printed, as illustrated by the first branch in Figure 11.5.

FIGURE 11.5   *Program Flowchart for Inventory Update Program*

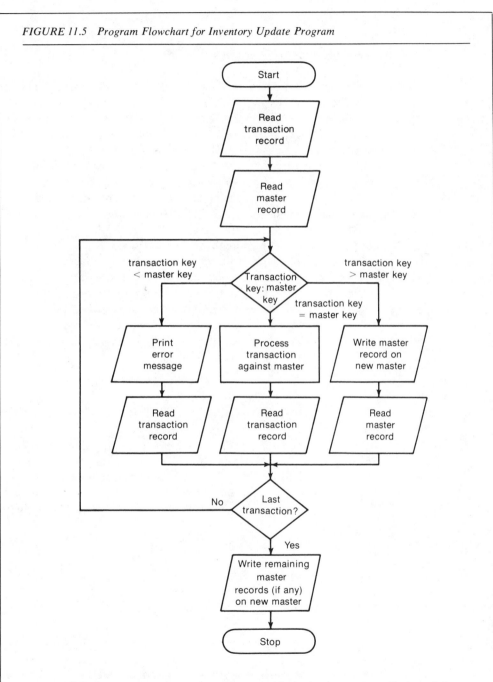

Alternatively, and more simply, we could design a system that updates a direct-access master inventory file as transactions are keyed in (see Exercise 28 on page 423).

11.7
COMMON ERRORS

Don't forget the following when working with files.

1. Use the necessary file-related control cards (batch processing) or system commands (time-shared processing) for your system. Mistakes in preparing these non-FORTRAN instructions are frequent (and very frustrating). Pay careful attention to your instructor, or carefully read the system's manual, or befriend a file expert at the computer center.
2. Open the file. If you forget this statement the computer may print an execution error message when it attempts to read from or write to the file.
3. Double-check the program for consistency in file/unit characteristics. For example, direct-access processing must have DIRECT for *acc* and a RECL = specifier in the OPEN statement, and a REC = specifier in READ/WRITE statements.
4. Double-check the logic that terminates the processing of sequential-access files. For example, a common error is attempting to read-in beyond the last record in the file. This execution error is possible when an endfile record is missing from the file. A possible logic error is forgetting to use the END = specifier in a sequential-access READ statement. In this case processing simply stops when the endfile record is encountered, which means that execution never enters any postprocessing logic to which control might have been transferred.

ADDITIONAL EXERCISES

24. Define or explain the following:

field	READ statement
record	WRITE statement
file	formatted input/output statement
external file	unformatted input/output statement
internal file	list-directed input/output statement
unformatted file	direct-access input/output statement
unformatted record	sequential-access input/output statement
formatted file	ENDFILE statement
formatted record	REWIND statement
sequential access	CLOSE statement
endfile record	master file
direct access	transaction file
record number	system flowchart
OPEN statement	program flowchart
specifiers	

25. Computerized Matching: A File Search Revisited. Design the program of Exercise 32 in Chapter 5 on page 179 or Exercise 37 in Chapter 8 on page 316 so that input of the placement office file is from an external sequential-access file.

26. Mailing List Revisited. Design the program of Exercise 37 in Chapter 6 on page 217 so that input of the data file is from an external sequential-access file.

27. **Revenue-Sharing Revisited.** Design the program of Exercise 44 in Chapter 7 on page 277 so that input of the state population file is from an external sequential-access file.

28. **Blood Bank Inventory System I.** Redesign the system in Figure 11.4 so that the master inventory file is a direct-access file. Inventory transactions are entered from a terminal or card reader and processed by an EDIT/UPDATE program that edits the input data for valid action codes and updates records in the master file. If input is by terminal, prompt the user for a correct entry whenever the action code is invalid. If input is by card reader, ignore updates for invalid action codes but include a printout of invalid input records as part of the inventory report. Use the blood types A$^+$, A$^-$, B$^+$, B$^-$, AB$^+$, AB$^-$, O$^+$, and O$^-$, and select appropriate blood type codes as record numbers. Include a table of new inventory balances for all blood types as part of the inventory report. Start by drawing a system flowchart. Note that the "transaction file" either is entered at the keyboard for terminals or is placed on cards for card input.

29. **Blood Bank Inventory System II.** As in the preceding exercise, except that the transaction file is a sequential-access file on a medium such as tape.

30. **Blood Bank Inventory System III.** Write and run the following programs for the system described in Example 11.3:
    a. EDIT/SORT. Don't forget to design the error routine for action codes.
    b. UPDATE. Modify Figure 11.5 and the program to read the current date and output an inventory report that includes the current date and a table of new inventory balances for each blood type. Include the eight blood types: A$^+$, A$^-$, B$^+$, B$^-$, AB$^+$, AB$^-$, O$^+$, and O$^-$.
    ** c. Add other useful features. For example, UPDATE could include an option to echo print all records in the transaction and master files, an option to provide summaries following the inventory table, etc.

31. **Interactive Airline Reservation System Revisited.** Modify Exercise 39 of Chapter 8 on page 316 as follows.
    a. Use a direct-access file instead of an array for the current table of flight information. Each table (file) of flight information is based on a specific week for the coming year. These files are named WEEK1, WEEK2, . . . , WEEK52. Use flight number as the record number.
    b. Instead of the record numbers in part a, use a record number based on the sum of flight number and day code. Assuming the ten flights in the table are numbered 240, 250, 260, 810, 100, 110, 120, 130, 950, and 960, and days in the week (Monday, Tuesday, . . . , Sunday) are coded 1, 2, . . . , 7, a request for flight 950 on Wednesday would access record number 953 whereas the same flight on Sunday would access record number 957.
    ** c. Add other useful features. For example, you might want to allow 1 percent overbooking of seats (a common practice); create a file that stores reservations information such as customer's name, address, telephone number, etc.; create a waiting list file that periodically gets processed against the flight table (master) file.

32. **Credit Billing Revisited.** Design the program of Exercise 33 in Chapter 5 on page 180 so that master and transaction files are used. The master file contains name, address, credit limit, and last billing period's ending (previous) balance for each customer. The transaction file contains name, payments, and new purchases.

a. Run your program for the data given in the problem such that bills are printed and the master file is updated.

**b. Include the following action codes in the transaction file and program logic.

1. Change in address
2. Change in credit limit
3. Delete customer from master file
4. Add customer to master file

Make up data to test each of these action codes.

33. Electric Bill Revisited. Design the program of Exercise 31 in Chapter 9 on page 361 so that master and transaction files are used. The master file contains previous reading, rate code, past due amount, name, street address, city, state, zip code, and account number for each customer. In addition to dates, the transaction file contains account number, name, new meter reading, and payments since last bill.

a. Run your program for the data given in the problem such that bills are printed and the master file is updated.

**b. Include the following action codes in the transaction file and program logic.

1. Change of address
2. Delete customer from master file
3. Add customer to master file

Make up data to test each of these action codes.

34. Payroll. Each week a small firm processes its weekly payroll for hourly employees. The following input is necessary to process the payroll.

Master Employee File
_____

Employee ID
Name
Hourly rate of pay
Number of dependents
Cumulative gross pay thus far this year
Cumulative FICA tax thus far this year
Cumulative withholding (income) tax thus far this year
Cumulative group health contribution thus far this year

Transaction File
_____

Date
Employee ID
Number of hours worked

Develop a program that

a. Generates a "wage summary report" consisting of a line for each employee; the line contains employee name, employee number, hourly rate, hours worked, gross pay, FICA, income tax, group health, and net pay. After individual figures are printed, the program is to print totals for gross pay, each deduction, and net pay. Include appropriate report and column headings.

b. Updates cumulative gross pay, cumulative FICA tax, cumulative withholding tax, and cumulative group health contribution for each employee in the master file.

To determine the pay for each employee, the following facts must be included in your program:

1. Gross pay is defined as pay for regular time plus pay for overtime. Overtime pay is 1.5 times the regular rate for each hour above 40.

2. Social Security tax (FICA) is 6.65 percent of gross pay. The deduction is made until the employee's cumulative earnings are above $29,700 after which there is no deduction.

3. Deduction for withholding tax and group health plan are tied to the number of dependents as follows.

Dependents	Income Tax (% of gross pay)	Group Health ($ per week)
1	22	2.50
2	20	3.60
3	18	5.10
4	16	6.00
5 or more	13	6.50

4. Net pay is defined as gross pay less FICA deduction less income tax deduction less group health deduction. Use the data below to test your program.

Master File

1940	Bella Bitta, Al	2.50	4	1500.00	99.75	240.00	180.00
1942	Budget, Frank	8.25	5	30000.00	1975.05	3900.00	195.00
2001	Manicotti, Diane	6.00	1	12300.00	817.95	2706.00	75.00
2542	Saintvi, Arun	8.00	3	29600.00	1968.40	5328.00	153.00

Transaction file for (date which you supply)

1940	60
1942	40
2001	45
2542	35

c. Run parts a and b again for the next week using the data below.

Transaction file for (date one week after preceding transaction file)

1940	32
1942	45
2001	35
2542	42

d. Design a routine that edits the input data for errors. Specifically it ensures that

1. Number of dependents is greater than zero and less than 15.
2. Rate of pay is greater than $2.30 and less than $10.00.
3. Number of hours worked is greater than zero and less than 65.
4. Total earnings thus far this year is zero or greater and less than $40,000.

If an error is detected, print an appropriate error message that includes the employee's name and number, bypass the calculations and printout for this employee, and go on to the next employee. Add new input data to test each of these four possible input errors.

**e. Design your program to include the processing of the following action codes in the transaction file.

1. Change in hourly rate of pay
2. Change in number of dependents
3. Delete employee from master file
4. Add employee to master file

Make up data to test each of these action codes.

35. **Student Grades. Design a comprehensive program that maintains and processes student grades for an academic course. You might include features such as file creation, file modifications (e.g., change a grade, add a grade, delete a grade, delete a record, add a record, etc.), file display, calculation of final numeric grade based on weights for individual grades (including the assignment of a letter grade if applicable), ... If a student is added to the file, make sure this student is placed in the correct alphabetic position. Once your program is debugged, hire yourself a marketing major and pedal your program to faculty members for an exorbitant software fee.

Modules

MODULE A*

Intrinsic and Statement Functions

This module defines intrinsic and statement functions and illustrates their use.

A.1
DEFINITIONS AND USES OF INTRINSIC FUNCTIONS

Suppose we wish to determine the square root of the arithmetic expression

$$b^2 - 4 \cdot a \cdot c$$

and to store it in the address labeled Y. As you know, we simply could use the assignment statement

    Y = (B**2 − 4.*A*C)**0.5

An alternative approach in this case is to use the following.

    Y = SQRT(B**2 − 4.*A*C)

The right-hand side of this statement is called an **intrinsic function,** which is of the following general type.

> function name (argument list)

The *argument list* is either a single expression or a list of expressions separated by commas. Expressions in the argument list are either arithmetic (integer, real, double precision, or complex), character, or logical, depending on the function. Each expression in the argument list is called an *argument*. The *function name* is identified according to the list of names given in the next section.

In the foregoing example, SQRT is the function name and the real arithmetic expression B**2 − 4.*A*C is the single argument. The purpose of this function, of course, is to determine the square root of the argument.

* Can be assigned anytime after Chapter 2.

The SQRT function is one of 85 intrinsic functions available in FORTRAN 77. These functions are commonly used to improve readability by simplifying code, to increase computational efficiency, and to obtain accurate values.

A.2
SELECTED INTRINSIC FUNCTIONS
HAVING GENERIC NAMES

Table A.1 illustrates a subset of frequently used intrinsic functions. Briefly study the examples in the table, note the following points, and then solve the follow-up exercises.

1. The function is *referenced* by using its name, followed by an open parenthesis, followed by the argument list, followed by a closed parenthesis. An intrinsic function is referenced or used in an expression; it supplies a value to the expression that references the function, this value being the value of the function. For example, the SQRT function in Table A.1 is referenced by its use in the expression

   (− B + SQRT(B**2 − 4.*A*C))/(2.*A)

   Thus, if 10.0 is in B, 1.0 is in A, and 9.0 is in C, the value of the argument is 64.0 and the value of the function is 8.0. In effect, the expression that references the function becomes

   (− B + 8.0)/(2.*A)

2. The function names used in Table A.1 are technically called **generic names.** This means that the type of the argument(s) determines the type of the value supplied by the function. Thus an argument list of *real* values in a MAX function means that the function supplies a *real* value; a *double-precision* argument in the EXP function yields a *double-precision* value for the function. Exceptions are INT, REAL, and NINT, which necessarily supply integer, real, and integer values, respectively, and ABS as footnoted in Table A.1.

3. FORTRAN 77 also includes **specific names** for functions. These are intrinsic functions whose names depend on the type of the argument(s). For example, AMAX0 is an intrinsic function with a specific name that selects the largest *integer* from its argument list and returns it as a *real* value. The fact that its name begins with the letter A (and not I through N) implicitly types its value as real. Thus AMAX0(10, J) supplies the real value 10.0 if, say, 7 is stored in J. Specific names for functions complicate their use since we must either remember or look up the specific relationship between the name and argument type. To illustrate, AMIN1 requires real arguments and returns a real value, whereas MIN0 requires integer arguments and returns an integer value. See what we mean? The use of generic names, which is new in the full version of FORTRAN 77, simplifies our life since the type of the argument list determines the type returned by the function (with the exceptions noted earlier). We do not use specific names for functions in this text.

4. Note that intrinsic functions can be used virtually anywhere expressions themselves can be used—for example, in the list of a PRINT statement as in

   PRINT *,A,B,LOG(A),LOG(B),LOG(A/B),LOG(A) − LOG(B)

TABLE A.1 *Selected Intrinsic Functions in FORTRAN 77*

FUNCTION NAME	PURPOSE	NUMBER OF ARGUMENTS	ALGEBRAIC EXAMPLES*	FORTRAN EXAMPLES
INT	Converts value of argument (which can be integer, real, double precision, or complex) to type integer by truncation	1	$m = k \cdot [x/y]$	M = K*INT(X/Y)
REAL	Converts value of argument (integer, real, double precision, or complex) to type real	1	$\bar{x} = \dfrac{\Sigma x}{n}$	XBAR = SUMX/REAL(N)
NINT	Rounds value of argument (integer, real, or double precision) to nearest integer	1	$m = [x + 0.5], \; x \geq 0$ $n = [x - 0.5], \; x < 0$	M = NINT(X) N = NINT(X)
ABS	Changes value of argument (integer, real, double precision, or complex) to absolute value of same type as argument†	1	$z = |x - y|$	Z = ABS(X − Y)
MAX	Selects largest value in argument list. All arguments in list must be of same type (all integer, or all real, or all double precision)	≥2	$p = \max(a, b, c)$	P = MAX(A,B,C)
MIN	Selects smallest value in argument list. All arguments in list must be of same type (all integer, or all real, or all double precision)	≥2	$n = \min(j, k, l, m)$	N = MIN(J,K,L,M)
SQRT	Takes square root of value in argument. Argument must be *positive* real value, *positive* double-precision value, or complex value	1	$r_1 = \dfrac{-b + \sqrt{b^2 - 4a \cdot c}}{2a}$	ROOT1 = (−B + SQRT (B**2 − 4.*A*C))/(2.*A)

(Continued on next page.)

431

TABLE A.1 (Continued)

FUNCTION NAME	PURPOSE	NUMBER OF ARGUMENTS*	ALGEBRAIC EXAMPLES*	FORTRAN EXAMPLES
EXP	Performs exponentiation. Base of natural logarithms, $e = 2.718 \ldots$, raised to power given by value of real, double-precision, or complex argument	1	$y = a \cdot e^{-2 \cdot t}$	$Y = A*EXP(-2.*T)$
LOG	Takes natural (base-e) logarithm of *positive* real, *positive* double-precision, or complex argument	1	$p = q \cdot \ln 5$	$P = Q*LOG(5.)$
LOG10	Takes common (base-10) logarithm of *positive* real, *positive* double-precision, or complex argument	1	$r = \log(a + 2b)$	$R = LOG10(A + 2.*B)$
SIN	Takes sine of real, double-precision, or complex argument	1	$y = \sin x$	$Y = SIN(X)$
COS	Takes cosine of real, double-precision, or complex argument	1	$y = \cos \dfrac{\pi}{3}$	$Y = COS(PI/3.)$
TAN	Takes tangent of real or double-precision argument	1	$z = \tan (x - y)$	$Z = TAN(X - Y)$
ASIN	Takes arcsine of real or double-precision argument	1	$x = \sin^{-1} y$	$X = ASIN(Y)$
ACOS	Takes arccosine of real or double-precision argument	1	$x = \cos^{-1} (0.5*p)$	$X = ACOS(.5*P)$
ATAN	Takes arctangent of real or double-precision argument	1	$x = y + \tan^{-1} z$	$X = Y + ATAN(Z)$

* Square brackets denote integer part of.
† Complex arguments, which are not discussed in this book, are changed to absolute values of type real.

or to the right of an equal sign in an assignment statement, or in relational and logical expressions (Chapter 5).

Follow-up Exercises

1. In Table A.1, look at the column headed "FORTRAN EXAMPLES" and answer the following.
   a. INT example. What is stored in M if 10 is in K, 4.0 is in X, and 3.0 is in Y? If 1.0 is in X and 3.0 is in Y? If 5.0 is in X and 3.0 is in Y? If −5.0 is in X and 3.0 is in Y?
   b. NINT example. What is stored in M if 5.1 is in X? If 5.9 is in X? What is stored in N if −1.8 is in X? If −1.2 is in X?
   c. ABS example. What is stored in Z if 10.0 is in X and 5.0 is in Y? If 5.0 is in X and 10.0 is in Y?
   d. MIN example. What is stored in N if 5 is in J, −2 is in K, 10 is in L, and 0 is in M?
   e. SQRT example. What is stored in ROOT1 if 10.0 is in B, 1.0 is in A, and 9.0 is in C?
   f. EXP example. What value is stored in Y if 50.1 is in A and 4.0 is in T?
   g. LOG10 example. What value is stored in R if −2.0 is in A and 6.0 is in B? If −2.0 is in A and −6.0 is in B?
   h. COS example. What value is stored in Y if 3.14159 is in PI?
2. Suppose the variable COST stores 375.4563. Specify code to round the value in COST to
   a. Two decimal places (dollars and cents).
   b. The nearest whole number (nearest dollar).
   c. The nearest hundred (nearest hundred dollars).
3. Define or explain the following.

   intrinsic functions
   generic names
   specific names

A.3
STATEMENT FUNCTIONS

A statement function is similar to an intrinsic function with respect to how it is referenced or used, but differs in that this function is provided by the programmer whereas intrinsic functions are provided by the compiler.

To illustrate the use of statement functions, consider the following program segments.

REAL POLY,XLEFT,XRIGHT,A,B,C,X

$\left.\vphantom{\begin{matrix}.\\.\end{matrix}}\right\}$ Type and PARAMETER statements

Statement function⟶ POLY(B0,B1,B2,B3,X) = B0 + B1*X + B2*X**2 + B3*X**3
statement

$\left.\vphantom{\begin{matrix}.\\.\end{matrix}}\right\}$ Executable and other statements

Function reference⟶ Y = POLY(10.5,0.2,0.,0.,XLEFT)

Function reference⟶ F = Q*POLY(10.5,0.2,0.,0.,(XLEFT + XRIGHT)/2.)

Function reference⟶ PRINT *,A,B,C,X,POLY(A,B,C,0.,X)

END

This example illustrates a **statement function statement** of the general form

> *function name (dummy argument list)* = *expression*

where the *function name* is a symbolic name in FORTRAN, the **dummy argument list** is a list of variable names that are used in the expression to the right of the equal sign, and the *expression* is a legitimate FORTRAN expression (integer, real, character, etc.).

In our illustration, POLY is the function name, B0,B1,B2,B3,X is the dummy argument list, and B0 + B1*X + B2*X**2 + B3*X**3 is the expression. POLY is typed real and represents a polynomial function up to third degree, as given by the following algebraic representation.

$$f(x) = b_0 + b_1x + b_2x^2 + b_3x^3$$

The statement function statement thus defines a function that is to be used or referenced at various points in the program. In our example, POLY is referenced at three different points in the program. In general, a function is referenced by using its **function reference** given by

> *function name (actual argument list)*

in an expression. For example, the first function reference above is

POLY(10.5,0.2,0.,0.,XLEFT)

When this function reference is executed, the following actions are taken.

a. The **actual argument list** is associated with the dummy argument list according to

```
B0,  B1,  B2,  B3,    X      ←Dummy argument list
 ↑    ↑    ↑    ↑      ↑
10.5, 0.2, 0.,  0.,  XLEFT   ←Actual argument list
```

b. The expression B0 + B1*X + B2*X**2 + B3*X**3 is evaluated using 10.5 for B0, 0.2 for B1, 0.0 for B2, 0.0 for B3, and the value in XLEFT for X.
c. The value of the expression is returned to the point where the function was referenced. For example, if 2.0 is stored in XLEFT, then the value returned for POLY at the first function reference is 10.9, which is then stored in Y.

The same procedure applies for any other function reference, except that expressions as actual arguments are first evaluated before dummy and actual arguments are associated. Thus, in the second function reference, the actual argument (XLEFT + XRIGHT)/2. is evaluated first.

When using statement functions, keep the following points in mind.

1. The statement function statement must follow type and PARAMETER statements and precede executable statements.
2. It's a good idea to type the name of a statement function, as done in our example.
3. Dummy arguments are *local* to the statement function statement (that is, have no meaning or effect anywhere else in the program) whereas actual arguments must be defined (have values) at points in the program that precede the function reference. For example, XLEFT must be defined before the first function reference; XLEFT and XRIGHT must be defined before the second reference; and A, B, C, and X must be defined before the third reference.
4. Actual arguments must agree in order, number, and type with corresponding dummy arguments. For example, if the dummy argument list has five integer variables, then the actual argument list must have five integer arguments; if the dummy argument list consists of an integer variable followed by a real variable, then the actual argument list must have an integer argument followed by a real argument. *Note that dummy arguments must be variables but actual arguments can include expressions.*
5. Statement functions are useful or convenient when a particular function would otherwise recur at several different points in the program. Under these circumstances, their use can save code and improve the style of programs.

Follow-up Exercises

4. With respect to our example:
   a. What gets stored in F if 10.0 is in XLEFT and 20.0 is in XRIGHT?
   b. What gets printed if 1.0 is in A, −2.0 is in B, 3.0 is in C, and 10.0 is in X?
5. Specify a statement function statement for the exponential function

$$a \cdot b^t$$

Name this function EXPO, type it real, and use dummy arguments A, B, and T. Specify a PRINT statement that prints this function, where 2.0 is used for *a*, 0.5 is used for *b*, and 10.0 is used for *t*. Specify a second PRINT statement where FIXED is used for *a*, DECAY is used for *b*, and TIME is used for *t*.

6. Define or explain the following.

statement function
statement function statement
function reference
dummy argument list
actual argument list

MODULE B*

Output with Formats

Up to now you have used **list-directed output.** This is convenient for beginning programmers and for problems requiring simple output. You may, however, have felt frustrated over your inability to control the exact positioning of output, over the untidiness of E-notation for numeric output, and over excessive time spent trying to align appropriate values under column headings.

Frustrations aside, many applications require rather extensive and precisely positioned output. For example, an elaborate report with many labels, column headings, and extensive character and numeric data requires careful output design to enhance communication with the reader. In other cases precise output is required, as in the printing of invoices and bills on standardized preprinted forms.

In this module you'll learn how to arrange data precisely on a printed page, called **format-directed output,** thereby (in theory) becoming master of your output. First, however, we motivate your interest by presenting a familiar example using format-directed output.

EXAMPLE B.1 Student Billing Program with Format-Directed Output

Consider the following version of the student billing program.

```
C    STUDENT BILLING PROGRAM WITH OUTPUT FORMATS
C
C    KEY:
C       CPC    = COST PER CREDIT
C       FEES   = STUDENT FEES
C       NAME   = STUDENT NAME
C       ID     = STUDENT ID NUMBER
C       CREDIT = NUMBER OF CREDITS
C       TUIT   = TUITION
C       BALDUE = AMOUNT OWED BY STUDENT
C       CUMBAL = AMOUNT OWED TO INSTITUTION
C       N      = NUMBER OF STUDENTS
C-------------------------------------------------------------
       CHARACTER NAME*15
       INTEGER   ID,N
       REAL      CPC,FEES,CREDIT,TUIT,BALDUE,CUMBAL
```

---

* Can be assigned anytime after Chapter 4.

```
C-----------------------------------------------------------------
        CUMBAL = 0.
C-----------------------------------------------------------------
        READ *,CPC,FEES
        READ *,N
C-----------------------------------------------------------------
        PRINT 30
   A    PRINT 40
        PRINT 50
C-----------------------------------------------------------------
        DO 5 J = 1,N
          READ *,NAME,ID,CREDIT
          TUIT   = CREDIT*CPC
          BALDUE = TUIT + FEES
          CUMBAL = CUMBAL + BALDUE
   B      PRINT 60,NAME,ID,BALDUE
      5 CONTINUE
C-----------------------------------------------------------------
        PRINT 70
   C    PRINT 80,CUMBAL
        PRINT 70
        PRINT 70
C-----------------------------------------------------------------
     30 FORMAT('1',/                    **TUITION REPORT**')
     40 FORMAT('0',/          NAME         SS NUMBER    BALANCE DUE')
   D 50 FORMAT(' ')
     60 FORMAT(' ',A15,I12,F14.2)
     70 FORMAT(' ',31X,'--------------')
     80 FORMAT(18X,'**TOTALS**    $',F10.2)
C-----------------------------------------------------------------
        END
```

For the input data

```
100.,250.
3
'W. MITTY',266612463,15.
'X. MITTY',266612464,18.5
'Y. MITTY',266612465,12.
```

the program would print the following output.

```
              **TUITION REPORT**

        NAME         SS NUMBER    BALANCE DUE

    W. MITTY         266612463      1750.00
    X. MITTY         266612464      2100.00
    Y. MITTY         266612465      1450.00
                                  --------------
                     **TOTALS**  $   5300.00
                                  --------------
                                  --------------
```

Labels that precede body of table. Printed by statements in box A, which reference statements 30, 40, and 50 in box D.

Body of table. Printed by repeated execution of PRINT statement in box B, which references statement 60 in box D.

Labels and summary that follow body of table. Printed by statements in box C, which reference statements 70 and 80 in box D.

At this point, don't worry about understanding the mechanics of the above output. Just look at the "big picture," realizing that we are now controlling exactly how and where data are to appear on the printed lines.

B.1
PRINT AND FORMAT STATEMENTS

Output from the computer often requires precise column-by-column and line-by-line control. The precise control of printing usually is accomplished by pairing the PRINT statement with a FORMAT statement.

The general form of the PRINT statement is

> **PRINT** *format identifier*, *list*

In previous programs the *format identifier* was an asterisk, which meant we desired list-directed output. For format-directed output the format identifier is usually a statement label (number) that identifies the FORMAT statement which is to be used by the PRINT statement.[1] As before, the *list* is a sequence of variable names, constants, or expressions separated by commas.[2]

To illustrate, the statement

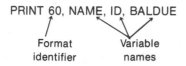

PRINT 60, NAME, ID, BALDUE

Format
identifier

Variable
names

in box B of Example B.1 specifies the variables whose values are to be printed (NAME, ID, and BALDUE) and identifies the FORMAT statement to use (statement number 60) for positioning these values on the print page.

The **FORMAT statement** for output is used to describe exactly how printed matter is to appear on the output medium. A general form of the FORMAT statement is given by

> *format
> statement* **FORMAT** *(list of edit descriptors)*
> *label*

where the *format statement label* is any unsigned, nonzero integer constant up to five digits that uniquely identifies the FORMAT statement and *edit descriptors* are codes that

---

[1] A format identifier also can be expressed as an integer variable whose value is assigned by an ASSIGN statement (see Exercise 3), as a character expression (see Exercise 2), or as a character variable name (see Module D, Section D.3).

[2] The output list may also include an array element name (Chapters 7 and 8), an array name (Chapters 7 and 8), a character substring name (Chapter 10), and implied-DO lists (Chapters 7 and 8).

specify the editing necessary to print the desired output (or read the desired input as described in Module C). These edit descriptors indicate the position, type (integer, real, etc.), size, and decimal point location (if applicable) of the values to be output.[3]

For example, the statement

ƅ is our symbol to denote the blank space character. We use it when necessary to avoid confusion

60 FORMAT ('ƅ', A15, I12, F14.2)

Format statement label   Edit descriptors

in box D of Example B.1 is utilized by the PRINT statement

        PRINT 60,NAME,ID,BALDUE

to print the body of the output table on page 438. Note how the format identifier 60 in the PRINT statement corresponds to the format statement label in the FORMAT statement.

The following points are worth remembering as you use format-directed output.

1.   A new line is printed each time a PRINT statement is executed. For example, the PRINT statement that outputs NAME, ID, and BALDUE in Example B.1 is executed three times within the loop; hence the body of the table on page 438 has three printed lines of new output. Note that the repeated execution of a PRINT statement within a loop, as illustrated by box B in the program, results in a "table-like" appearance of printed output.

2.   Look once more at the output on page 438. Note that PRINT statements that are to print table headings must precede the loop that creates the body of the table, as illustrated by box A in the program. Similarly, PRINT statements that summarize data in a table must follow the loop that prints the body of the table, as illustrated by box C in the program.

3.   The maximum length of a printed line varies. Typical sizes for printers are 121 and 133 characters. Terminals usually have maximum print line lengths of 72 to 135 characters. Make a note of the maximum print line length on your system.

4.   The FORMAT statement is a *nonexecutable statement* that serves as a reference for a PRINT statement. Since the FORMAT statement is nonexecutable, it can be placed virtually anywhere in the program prior to the END statement. In fact, many programmers prefer to place all FORMAT statements in a group, either at the beginning or the end of a program. This improves the readability of programs by "getting them out of the way" of the execution logic.[4]

---

[3] Technically, the portion (list of edit descriptors) following the key word FORMAT is called the *format specification*. More complicated format specifications include nested sets of parentheses, as discussed in Module D. Format specifications also can be provided without the use of a FORMAT statement, as illustrated in Exercise 2 of this section and Section D.3.

[4] FORMAT statements cannot precede the PROGRAM statement (not discussed in this book) and statements that identify the beginning of a subprogram (BLOCK DATA, FUNCTION, and SUBROUTINE in Chapter 9) when used within subprograms.

5. A FORMAT statement may be referenced by more than one PRINT statement. For example, the FORMAT statement labeled 70 on page 438 is referenced by three PRINT statements in Box C.

Follow-up Exercises

1. **WRITE Statement.** An alternative statement for processing format-directed output is

The *output unit number* is an integer variable or constant that specifies the output unit which is to be used. In many systems this number is "6" for either the line printer in batch processing or the terminal in time-shared processing, although it varies depending on what computer you're using. The *format statement label* identifies the FORMAT statement which is to be used by this WRITE statement. As before, the typical *list* is a sequence of variable names separated by commas.

The WRITE statement is more versatile that the PRINT statement since, among other things, it allows us to specify specific output units such as printer, disk drive, tape drive, and card punch (as described in Chapter 11).

Replace PRINT statements in Example B.1 with appropriate WRITE statements.

2. **Format Identifiers as Character Expressions.** FORTRAN 77 allows character expressions as legitimate format identifiers. For example, the two statements

```
    PRINT 900,J,X
900 FORMAT('0',I10,F15.4)
```

could be replaced by the single statement

```
    PRINT '("0",I10,F15.4)',J,X
```

Note that single apostrophes around '0' are replaced by double apostrophes, "0", to signal the compiler that embedded apostrophes are present.

Rewrite the PRINT statement in box B in Example B.1 to incorporate a character expression as a format identifier in the following ways.

a. By using a character constant in the PRINT statement
b. By using a character variable in the PRINT statement
Of the three approaches, which do you prefer and why?

3. **ASSIGN Statement.** In FORTRAN 77 statement labels can be assigned to integer variables by using the executable statement

ASSIGN *statement label* **TO** *integer variable name*

Thus the statements

    ASSIGN 900 TO INTLAB
    PRINT INTLAB,J,X

are equivalent to

    PRINT 900,J,X

In Example B.1 replace all PRINT statements in box C with PRINT statements that use integer variables as format identifiers. Do you see any advantages to this approach?

B.2
SELECTED EDIT DESCRIPTORS

The full version of FORTRAN 77 includes 25 distinct edit descriptors for input/output editing. In this section we discuss the most commonly used edit descriptors; additional edit descriptors and options are presented in Module D.

Apostrophe Edit Descriptor

The apostrophe edit descriptor is a character constant that is used either for carriage control or for textual matter.

Carriage Control.   If you are using a line printer or a terminal, carriage control is the first item or information that you need to communicate through your FORMAT statement. To illustrate what we mean, consider what happens when you're typing a term paper. Suppose you have just finished typing the last character on some line. You need to make a decision as to what to do next. In other words, should the carriage stay on the present line (as when you underscore words)? Should the carriage go down the page one line before typing (single space) or two lines (double space)? Should you go to the top of a new page? Just as you must make these simple decisions when you type, so too must you inform the printer how the vertical spacing is to appear.

In FORTRAN we control the carriage or line by using the **carriage control characters** indicated in Table B.1. You communicate your carriage control desires to the

TABLE B.1   *Control of Carriage**

CARRIAGE CONTROL CHARACTER	EFFECT ON CARRIAGE
+	Do not advance before printing (hold the line).
Blank space	Advance one line before printing (single space).
0	Advance two lines before printing (double space).
1	Go to the top of a new page.

* Some time-sharing systems may not utilize all of these characters; others may use different characters. Ask your instructor.

computer by enclosing one of these characters within apostrophes as the first edit descriptor of each FORMAT statement (just after the left parenthesis).[5]

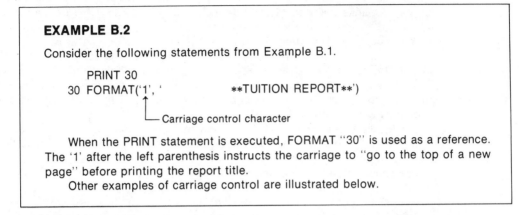

EXAMPLE B.2

Consider the following statements from Example B.1.

```
    PRINT 30
 30 FORMAT('1', '           **TUITION REPORT**')
```
Carriage control character

When the PRINT statement is executed, FORMAT "30" is used as a reference. The '1' after the left parenthesis instructs the carriage to "go to the top of a new page" before printing the report title.
Other examples of carriage control are illustrated below.

Textual Matter.   Textual matter such as report titles, column headings, and messages can be output by using the apostrophe edit descriptor. The character constant is printed exactly as it appears in the FORMAT statement.

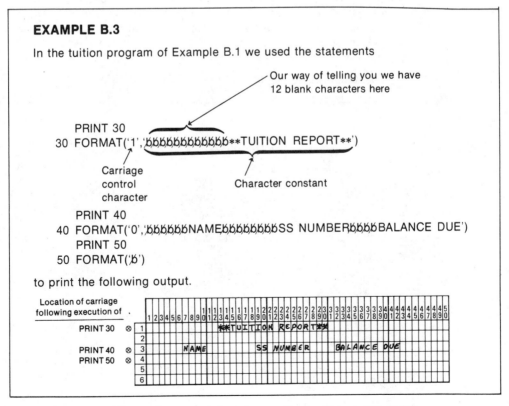

EXAMPLE B.3

In the tuition program of Example B.1 we used the statements

Our way of telling you we have 12 blank characters here

```
    PRINT 30
 30 FORMAT('1','ƀƀƀƀƀƀƀƀƀƀƀƀ**TUITION  REPORT**')
```
Carriage control character   Character constant

```
    PRINT 40
 40 FORMAT('0','ƀƀƀƀƀƀNAMEƀƀƀƀƀƀƀƀSS NUMBERƀƀƀƀBALANCE DUE')
    PRINT 50
 50 FORMAT('ƀ')
```

to print the following output.

[carriage control print positions grid showing:]
PRINT 30 — line 1: **TUITION REPORT**
PRINT 40 — line 3: NAME   SS NUMBER   BALANCE DUE
PRINT 50 — line 4

---

[5] Other means of providing carriage control characters are discussed later in this module.

The execution of PRINT 30 according to FORMAT "30" causes the carriage to go to the beginning of *print line* 1 at the top of a new page, after which the printer outputs 12 blanks followed by the title **TUITION REPORT**. *The carriage now returns to the beginning of the current print line* (that is, print line 1), awaiting the next carriage control instruction.

Next the statement PRINT 40 is executed. The '0' carriage control in FORMAT "40" tells the carriage to advance two lines (from print line 1, its current location, to print line 3) before printing the character constant exactly as shown by the second edit descriptor in FORMAT "40." After printing the word DUE the carriage returns to the beginning of print line 3.

Finally, the execution of PRINT 50 simply tells the carriage to advance one line to print line 4 before printing nothing. In effect we have "printed" a blank line following the column headings in print line 3.[6]

You should note the following points regarding this example.

1. The list of a PRINT statement can be left empty. In this case we're simply printing a report title and column headings, without the need to print contents within storage locations.
2. Use a comma to separate adjacent edit descriptors in the list within parentheses.
3. The apostrophe edit descriptor that controls the carriage at the beginning of each FORMAT statement is itself a character constant, since it's enclosed in apostrophes. If a carriage control apostrophe edit descriptor is followed by another apostrophe edit descriptor, both apostrophe edit descriptors can be combined into one. For example, FORMAT "30" could be written as

30 FORMAT ('1ƀƀƀƀƀƀƀƀƀƀƀƀ**TUITION REPORT**')

Follow-up Exercises

4. On the basis of your work in Chapter 3, how else could you print a blank line following the table headings in Example B.3? Can you think of a simple way of printing, say, 15 blank lines?
5. Suppose that the printer has just finished printing line 20 and that the statement

    PRINT 15

    is to be executed next. Write the appropriate FORMAT statement to print the label HAL SPEAKS
    a. At the beginning of line 20.
    b. At the beginning of line 21.
    c. At the beginning of line 22.
    d. Starting in the fifth print position (column) of line 22.
    e. Starting at the beginning of the first line on the next page.

---

[6] See Exercise 4 in this section and the slash edit descriptor in Module D for other methods of printing blank lines.

6. Indicate exactly how the output would appear when the following is executed while the carriage is at the beginning of line 1.

```
 9 FORMAT('ᵬSTUDENT')
10 FORMAT('ᵬID')
11 FORMAT('+ᵬᵬᵬNUMBER')
   PRINT 9
   PRINT 10
   PRINT 11
```

7. Write the necessary statements in such a way that, at the beginning of a line that is double-spaced from the preceding line of output, the computer prints

THE ANSWER =

Minus character

A Edit Descriptor

The output of character values based on character expressions is accomplished by using the A edit descriptor. The general form is either

A	or	Aw

where *w* is the *field width* or number of characters to be output for the corresponding character value. The portion of the print line allocated to the output value is called a **field**.

EXAMPLE B.4

In Example B.1 we used the statements

```
PRINT 60,NAME,ID,BALDUE

60 FORMAT('ᵬ',A15,I12,F14.2)
```

to produce the following portion of the output.

Field for NAME is 15 columns wide according to A15 descriptor

---

For now, ignore the variables ID and BALDUE and the descriptors I12 and F14.2. When this PRINT statement is executed, the carriage of the printer first goes down the page one line from its current position (from print line 4 to print line 5), as specified by 'b'. Then the character value stored in NAME is printed, *left-justified,* in the field given by columns 1 to 15. Thus NAME in the print list is paired with A15 in the list of edit descriptors.

Note that, in Example B.1, the statement

CHARACTER NAME*15

identifies NAME as a character variable with a *declared length* of 15 characters. Thus, during the first iteration of the loop, the first value stored in NAME is internally represented as follows based on the input data.

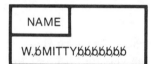

Seven blanks are padded in after the name because the input value was represented by the eight characters in 'W. MITTY'. The use of A15 to output the character value in NAME specifies a *field width* of 15, the same as the declared length in NAME. Conveniently, the output of NAME in print line 5 exactly corresponds to its internal representation. In effect, *the output of a character value is identical to its internal representation when the field width w equals the declared length l.*

Thus, under most circumstances, we suggest that you set the field width *w* in A edit descriptors equal to the declared length *l* of the character value to be printed. Alternatively, exactly the same is accomplished by omitting the field width *w* altogether. That is, *the descriptor A instead of Aw gives output identical to the internal representation.* For example, we could replace A15 by A in FORMAT "60" to get the same output as before.

In general, the field width w may differ from the declared length l of the character variable. In some instances (for example, right-justifying character output) you might find it convenient to select a field width w different from the declared length l, in which cases the following rules apply.

Rule 1: If the field width w is less than or equal to the declared length l of the character variable ($w \le l$), then the *leftmost w* characters in storage are output.

Rule 2: If the field width w exceeds the declared length l of the character variable ($w > l$), then all l characters in storage are printed *right-justified* within the field.

EXAMPLE B.5
Study the two examples below and relate them to the two rules above.

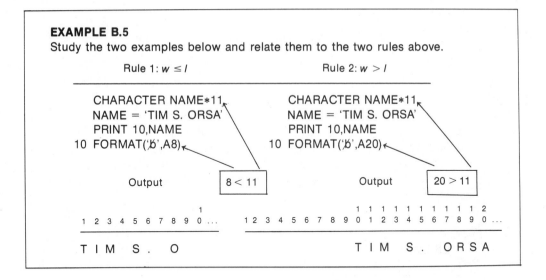

Rule 1: $w \leq l$

```
     CHARACTER NAME*11
     NAME = 'TIM S. ORSA'
     PRINT 10,NAME
10   FORMAT('ƀ',A8)
```

Output | 8 < 11 |

```
                    1
1 2 3 4 5 6 7 8 9 0 ...
```

T I M   S .   O

Rule 2: $w > l$

```
     CHARACTER NAME*11
     NAME = 'TIM S. ORSA'
     PRINT 10,NAME
10   FORMAT('ƀ',A20)
```

Output | 20 > 11 |

```
                    1 1 1 1 1 1 1 1 1 1 2
1 2 3 4 5 6 7 8 9 0 1 2 3 4 5 6 7 8 9 0 ...
```

T I M   S .   O R S A

Follow-up Exercises

8. Assume the character constant 'RHODE ISLAND' is stored in the character variable STATE as follows:

```
CHARACTER STATE*20
STATE = 'RHODE ISLAND'
```

How would the output appear in each of the following situations?

a.   PRINT 50,STATE
50 FORMAT('ƀƀƀƀƀ',A20)

b.   PRINT 50,STATE
50 FORMAT('ƀTHE OCEAN STATE IS ƀ',A20)

c.   PRINT 50,STATE
50 FORMAT('ƀ',A10)

d.   PRINT 50,STATE
50 FORMAT('ƀ',A25)

e.   PRINT 50,STATE
50 FORMAT('ƀ',A20,'IS THE SMALLEST STATE')

f.   PRINT 50,STATE,'IS THE SMALLEST STATE'
50 FORMAT('ƀ',A20,A21)

g.   PRINT 50,STATE,'IS THE SMALLEST STATE'
50 FORMAT('ƀ',A,A)

9. Rewrite the statements in Example B.3 on page 443 such that apostrophe edit descriptors in the FORMAT statements are replaced by A edit descriptors, except for carriage control.

I Edit Descriptor

Integer values can be output using the descriptor

$$\boxed{\text{I } w}$$

where w is the width of the field. The integer output is automatically *right-justified* when it appears on the line. If the value to be output does not fill the field, the left position of the field is padded with blanks. Also, you should note that the output of a negative integer requires a print position for the negative sign, which means that you should take this into consideration in specifying the field width. The plus sign for a positive integer is not printed, however.

EXAMPLE B.6

Continuing Example B.4, the statements

        PRINT 60,NAME,ID,BALDUE

    60 FORMAT('ƀ',A15,I12,F14.2)

yield the following output.

—Field for NAME
takes up columns
1 – 15

—Field for ID is 12 columns wide
according to I12 descriptor

Note that I12 is paired with ID, since A15 is paired with NAME and, of course, 'ƀ' is used for carriage control. Following the output of NAME in the field given by columns 1 through 15, the integer value in ID is printed *right-justified* in the *next* 12 columns according to *w* in I12. Thus columns 16–27 are reserved as the field for the value in ID. Note that these values are printed to the extreme right of this field (columns 19–27), with blanks in the unused portion of the field (columns 16–18).

EXAMPLE B.7

Study the following program and its output.

```
      INTEGER DAY,YEAR
      DAY = 24
      YEAR = 1942
      PRINT 10,DAY,YEAR
   10 FORMAT('ƀMY BIRTHDAY IS MARCH',I3,',',I5,'.')
      END
```

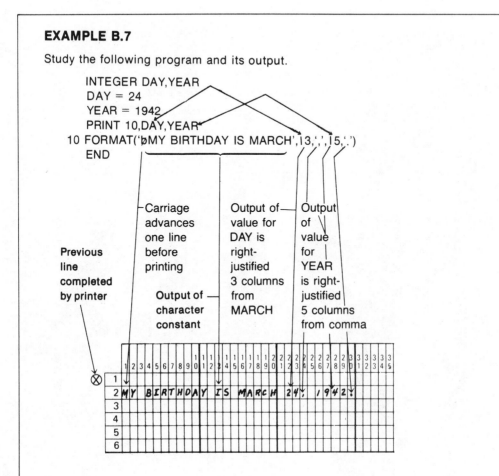

EXAMPLE B.8

Consider the statements

```
      PRINT 3,K
    3 FORMAT(' ',I4)
```

and the following variations.

	Output Columns
Contents of K	1 2 3 4 5 ...
705	7 0 5
−705	− 7 0 5
7050	7 0 5 0
−7050	* * * *
215305	* * * *

The last two cases each indicate that **format overflow** has occurred; that is, the field I4 is of insufficient width to handle the five characters in −7050 and the six characters in 215305. If K is not expected to exceed six characters, including a negative sign, then I6 should be used here.

In the above examples of format overflow, asterisks (∗) were printed in the field that overflowed. Not all systems, however, print asterisks when overflow occurs. Some systems simply print the rightmost characters that fit in the field (7050 and 5305 in the above illustrations), whereas other systems print some other character to indicate overflow.

Follow-up Exercises

10. Test out how format overflow occurs in your system by writing a short program that causes the overflow conditions illustrated in Example B.8.

11. Indicate the exact output for the following program.

```
      INTEGER L,M,N
        ⋮
        ⋮
      PRINT 15,M,N
      PRINT 20,L
   15 FORMAT ('1','M=',I4,'bN=',I5)
   20 FORMAT ('0','bbbbL=',I3)
      END
```

*12. Indicate the appropriate PRINT and FORMAT statements for the following desired output.

F Edit Descriptor

Real values can be output in decimal form using F edit descriptor. The general form is

$$\boxed{\mathbf{F}w.d}$$

where w is the width of the field and d is the number of digits in the fractional part of the value (the number of digits to the right of the decimal point). For example, F10.2 means *round* the real value to two decimal places and output the contents of the real variable right-justified within the ten-column field.

To reduce the likelihood of format overflow, care must be taken in specifying widths of sufficient size. A rule of thumb to keep in mind is that the width of the field to be used for printing the contents of a real variable must be large enough to include positions for the decimal point and the sign (only the minus sign is printed), in addition to the digits. For example, if -52.1 is stored in ANS, then the field specification F5.1 is the smallest field width that will avoid format overflow. We illustrate these situations by the examples that follow.

EXAMPLE B.9

To conclude Examples B.4 and B.6, consider once more the statements

    PRINT 60,NAME,ID,BALDUE

    60 FORMAT('b',A15,I12,F14.2)

and the resulting output when PRINT 60 is executed three times within the loop illustrated in Example B.1 on page 438.

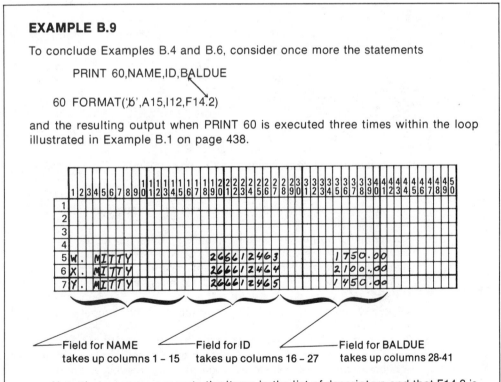

Field for NAME
takes up columns 1 – 15

Field for ID
takes up columns 16 – 27

Field for BALDUE
takes up columns 28-41

Note that commas separate the items in the list of descriptors and that F14.2 is paired with BALDUE. According to the F14.2 descriptor the value in BALDUE is printed to two decimal places right-justified in a 14-column field immediately to the right of the field for ID, as illustrated.

EXAMPLE B.10

Consider the variations shown below for output of various values for the real variable B using different F edit descriptors and the statements

    PRINT 8,B
    8 FORMAT('0',Fw.d)

Case	Contents in Memory for B	Fw.d	Printed Output 1 2 3 4 5 6 7 8 9 ...
a	735.	F6.0	7 3 5 .
b	735.	F6.2	7 3 5 . 0 0
c	735.	F5.2	* * * * *
d	−735.	F6.0	− 7 3 5 .
e	66.318	F8.3	6 6 . 3 1 8
f	66.318	F8.2	6 6 . 3 2
g	66.318	F8.1	6 6 . 3
h	.14	F7.2	0 . 1 4
i	.14	F4.2	0 . 1 4
j	.14	F3.2	* * *
k	−.14	F4.2	* * * *
l	−.14	F5.2	− 0 . 1 4
m	−.14	F5.3	* * * * *
n	−.14	F6.3	− 0 . 1 4 0
o	0.	F7.2	0 .

These cases illustrate some points worth remembering.

1. If the number is negative, the negative sign appears immediately to the left of the number (cases d and l); however, positive numbers usually do not appear with a plus sign.
2. For fractional numbers less than 1, most computers print a leading zero, as in cases i and l. If the value is exactly zero, however, many computers will print blanks to the right of the decimal point (case o).
3. Format overflow occurs when the field width is of insufficient size; see cases c, j, k, and m. These conditions are respectively corrected by cases b, i, l, and n. Overflow would not occur for cases k and m if the computer suppresses the leading zero.
4. The computer *rounds the output* to the specified number of decimal positions when the number of decimal positions in the F descriptor is less than the actual number of decimal digits stored in the variable. See cases f and g.
5. When the number of decimal positions specified in F*w.d* is greater than the decimal digits stored in the variable, the trailing positions are filled with zeros. See cases b and n.

Follow-up Exercise

13. Fill in the following table for the output of a real variable.

Case	Contents	F*w.d*	Printed Output 1 2 3 4 5 6 7 8 9
a	3.105		3 . 1
b	3.105		3 . 1 0 5 0
c	−.1074	F6.4	
d	−.1074	F7.4	
e	−.1074	F9.4	
f	.1074	F6.4	
g	3764.	F9.1	
h	3764.16	F9.1	
i	3764.16	F9.0	
j	3764.16	F9.3	
k	3764.16	F6.3	

E Edit Descriptor

The E edit descriptor allows the output of real values in exponential form. A general form of the E descriptor is given by

$$\boxed{E w.d}$$

where w is the field width and d represents the number of significant digits to be output. The usual exponential form of the output field is

In other words, values are printed as a number between 0.1 and 1.0 or −0.1 and −1.0 followed by the appropriate exponent ($E \pm z_1 z_2$).

EXAMPLE B.11

If 3.14159 is stored in PI, then the statements

        PRINT 5,PI
     5 FORMAT('ᵬᵬPIᵬ=',E15.5)

generally would print the following.

The computer thus rounds the value to five digits (since $d = 5$) and right-justifies the value in the 15-column field (since $w = 15$) given by columns 6–20.

To avoid format overflow, field width w should be at least seven more than significant digits d ($w \geq d + 7$) since we have to allow four columns for the exponent ($E \pm z_1 z_2$) and three columns for the sign, leading zero, and decimal point ($\pm 0.$).[7]

In the example for PI, if we wish d to be 5, then we should specify $w \geq 12$ to avoid format overflow. For example, if we had used E9.5, the field width would have been insufficient to output the value in PI.[8]

---

[7] The rule of thumb is $w \geq d + 6$ for systems that suppress the leading zero.

[8] The FORTRAN 77 standard allows the exponent from $\pm 0 z_1 z_2$ in addition to $E \pm z_1 z_2$ for exponents having absolute values less than 100 and the exponent form $\pm z_1 z_2 z_3$ for exponents having absolute values between 100 and 999 inclusive.

EXAMPLE B.12

Consider the variations below.

Case	Contents in Memory	Ew.d	Printed Output (columns 1–15)
a	38.716	E15.5	0 . 3 8 7 1 6 E + 0 2
b	38.716	E15.4	0 . 3 8 7 2 E + 0 2
c	38.716	E15.3	0 . 3 8 7 E + 0 2
d	38.716	E15.0	0 . E + 0 2
e	−38.716	E15.5	− 0 . 3 8 7 1 6 E + 0 2
f	0.000617	E12.5	0 . 6 1 7 0 0 E − 0 3
g	0.000617	E12.3	0 . 6 1 7 E − 0 3
h	0.000617	E12.2	0 . 6 2 E − 0 3
i	0.268	E12.4	0 . 2 6 8 0 E + 0 0
j	3.268	E9.4	* * * * * * * * *
k	3.268	E12.4	0 . 3 2 6 8 E + 0 1

The following points may be worth remembering.

1. If the number is negative, the negative sign appears immediately to the left of the number (case e); however, positive numbers usually do not appear with a plus sign.
2. We show a leading zero for each output value, but its inclusion depends on the system.
3. Format overflow occurs when the field width is of insufficient size; see case j. This condition is corrected by case k.
4. The computer rounds the output to the specified number of decimal positions given by d when d is less than the actual number of digits stored in the variable. See cases b, c, and h.
5. When d in E$w.d$ is greater than the digits stored in the variable, the trailing positions are filled with zeros. See cases f and i.
6. The d portion of the descriptor E$w.d$ must be greater than zero if any value is to be written (case d).

Follow-up Exercise

14. Fill in the following table for the output of a real variable.

Case	Contents	Ew.d	Printed Output 1 2 3 4 5 6 7 8 9 10 11 12 13 14 15
a	3.105		0 . 3 1 0 5 E + 0 1
b	3.105		0 . 3 1 E + 0 1
c	−.1074	E15.5	
d	−.1074	E15.4	
e	−.1074	E15.2	
f	−.1074	E15.9	
g	3764.	E14.5	
h	3764.16	E14.5	
i	3764.16	E14.6	
j	3764.16	E10.4	
k	3764.16	E12.3	

D Edit Descriptor

The D edit descriptor is used to output double-precision values. Its general form is

$$Dw.d$$

where w is the field width and d is the number of significant digits to be output. The D descriptor is treated identically to the way the E descriptor is treated, except that E is replaced by D.

EXAMPLE B.13

If 3.1415926536 is stored in the double-precision variable PI, the statements

    PRINT 5,PI
  5 FORMAT('bbPIb=',D20.11)

generally would print

which you should compare with the output in Example B.11 on page 454.

Follow-up Exercise

15. Describe the output of PI in Example B.13 based on the cases below.

		Printed Output
Case	FORMAT Statement	1111111111222222 1234567890123456789012345
a	5 FORMAT('ƀ',D20.11)	
b	5 FORMAT('ƀ',D15.8)	
c	5 FORMAT('ƀ',D15.11)	

X Edit Descriptor

The X edit descriptor is used to insert blanks in the printed line. The general form is

$$n\,X$$

where n represents the number of blanks to be inserted. For example, 5X means to print five blank spaces. This descriptor also can be used to single-space the carriage.

EXAMPLE B.14

The statements

        PRINT 70
    70 FORMAT('ƀ',31X,' ————————————')

are used in Example B.1 to "dress up" the output shown on page 438. In this case the carriage advances one line according to 'ƀ', prints 31 blank characters according to 31X, and prints 14 minus signs in columns 32–45 according to the apostrophe edit descriptor.

Alternatively, carriage control can be incorporated into the X descriptor as

    70 FORMAT(32X,' ————————————')

where it is understood that the first X transmits a blank for carriage control and the remaining 31 X's are used to print 31 blanks.

You should appreciate that use of the X edit descriptor represents a more efficient and less painful approach than the "brute force" approach given by

32 blank characters instead of 32X

    70 FORMAT('ƀƀƀƀƀƀƀƀƀƀƀƀƀƀƀƀƀƀƀƀƀƀƀƀƀƀƀƀƀƀƀƀ ————————————')

Follow-up Exercises

16. Rewrite FORMATs "30" and "40" in Example B.1 on page 438 to use the X edit descriptor. Which approach do you prefer and why?

*17. Indicate the appropriate PRINT and FORMAT statements for the following desired output. Use the X descriptor for four or more consecutive blanks.

T Edit Descriptor

The T edit descriptor controls horizontal spacing, as does the X edit descriptor. Its general form is given by

$$T_n$$

where n is the output column where the next output character is to be printed. Whereas the nX descriptor is used to skip the next n output columns, the Tn descriptor is used to "tab" to the nth output column. *Caution:* The first output column is taken to be carriage control; hence Tn actually tabs to the $(n-1)$th *print* column.

EXAMPLE B.15

Convince yourself that the following two FORMAT statements are equivalent.

    10 FORMAT('0',19X,'ITEM',16X,'RESULT')
    10 FORMAT('0',T21,'ITEM',T41,'RESULT')

In each case ITEM is in print columns 20–23 and RESULT is in print columns 40–45. Which approach to use is simply a matter of preference. Which do you prefer?

Follow-up Exercises

18. Use the T descriptor in FORMAT "80" of Example B.1 on page 438.

19. Rework the following exercises using the T descriptor.
   a. Exercise 16 above.
   * b. Exercise 17 above.

B.3
COMMON ERRORS

In our years of teaching FORTRAN, and in our own early efforts in learning FORTRAN "long" ago, we have witnessed time and again certain output errors that occur commonly.

1. *Unaligned output.*   Output that is other than trivial involves careful planning. For example, if you have to output table headings and values for several variables, then *before writing your FORMAT statements you can save yourself some grief by outlining your output on a sheet of plain paper, quadrille paper, or print chart.* To illustrate, consider the following layout:

This layout was done *before* the following PRINT/FORMAT statements were written.

```
35 FORMAT('0PRINCIPAL:$',F6.0)
40 FORMAT('0',5X,'RATE:',F8.4)
   PRINT 35,P
   PRINT 40,R
```

You should confirm that these two FORMATs exactly correspond to this output plan.

2. *Forgetting about carriage control in output FORMATs.*   If your output is to either a line printer or a terminal, the computer expects a carriage control character whether you like it or not. If you remember to specify carriage control in your output FORMAT, then you are in charge. Otherwise the printer will "rip off" a column from your first edit descriptor. For example, the statements

```
   PRINT 3
 3 FORMAT('RESULT')
   PRINT 4,J
 4 FORMAT(I3)
```

where 23 is stored for J in memory would yield the following output.

	1	2	3	4	5	6	7	8	9	10	11	12	13	14	15	16	17	18	19	20
1																				
2	E	S	U	L	T															
3	2	3																		
4																				
5																				
6																				

(ⓧ)

Carriage control was not specified before the character constant 'RESULT'; hence the printer uses the R for carriage control and prints out "ESULT." Again, carriage control is omitted in the second FORMAT. So the printer takes the first column of the descriptor I3 and prints the 23 right-justified in column 2 instead of column 3.

3. *Inconsistency of type between variables in the print list and edit descriptors in the format list.* Do you see anything wrong with the following?

```
      REAL Q
      INTEGER K
      PRINT 7,K,Q
    7 FORMAT(1X,F5.0,I10)
```

In this case the integer variable K is type mismatched with the real descriptor F5.0. Also, the real variable Q is mismatched with the integer descriptor I10. This type of error is insidious, as many compilers will not identify the error. Instead of getting either a syntax error or an execution error, you get a "junk" number printed; that is, the number that is printed will be in the proper form according to the specification, but its value will be incorrect.

Try writing and submitting a short program that assigns, say, 15 to K and 6.5 to Q, and use the PRINT and FORMAT statements above. What happens on your system?

4. *Insufficient field width for numeric output.* Some students misinterpret the way in which the F descriptor determines the width of a field. For example, a beginning student may use F5.2 to output a value such as 1059.25. The student adds the width of the field (5) and the number of decimal digits (2) and concludes, erroneously, that seven characters can be printed. Not so. Only five characters can be printed. Thus 99.99 is the largest value and -9.99 the smallest value that can be printed with a F5.2 descriptor. Values larger than this would cause format overflow (see Examples B.10 and B.12). What does your computer print when format overflow occurs?

5. *Memory lapses in using the F and E descriptors.* The only form of the F descriptor is Fw.d. When students use a real variable to store values with no decimal digits, they sometimes incorrectly use Fw instead of Fw.0 to output these values. Another error occurs when the field width (w) and decimal digits (d) in E and F descriptors are reversed. For example, E15.6 and F9.3 are written incorrectly as E6.15 and F3.9.

6. *Incorrect character output.* Pay careful attention to Rules 1 and 2 on page 446 when the field width w in your A descriptor differs from the declared length l of your character variable. The example for Rule 1 shows a common error.

7. *"Falling off" the print line.*   Check the maximum number of characters that can be printed on a print line of your terminal or printer. Make sure the format specification does not exceed that amount. When it does, the next print line is used to complete the current print line, which plays havoc with your (presumably) carefully designed output.

Follow-up Exercise

20. Define or explain the following.

list-directed output	A edit descriptor
format-directed output	I edit descriptor
general form of PRINT statement	F edit descriptor
FORMAT statement	E edit descriptor
apostrophe edit descriptor	D edit descriptor
carriage control	X edit descriptor
carriage control characters	T edit descriptor
field	format overflow

MODULE C*

Input with Formats

Up until this point you have used **list-directed input,** which is free of FORMAT statements. You probably found this method of data entry easy and felt little motivation to change. Many situations, however, require the precise arrangement of input data whereby each value is placed in certain columns of an input medium such as punched card or disk. To read in such values we must use **format-directed input** statements, which we explain in this module.

EXAMPLE C.1 Student Billing Program with Format-Directed Input/Output

To illustrate the use of formatted input, we have revised the student billing program once again, this time substituting format-directed input statements for list-directed input statements. The shaded segments indicate the changes introduced in this version from the version on page 438.

Review the program briefly now, and as you read this module the details will become clear.

```
C   STUDENT BILLING PROGRAM WITH INPUT/OUTPUT FORMATS
C
C   KEY:
C     CPC    = COST PER CREDIT
C     FEES   = STUDENT FEES
C     NAME   = STUDENT NAME
C     ID     = STUDENT ID NUMBER
C     CREDIT = NUMBER OF CREDITS
C     TUIT   = TUITION
C     BALDUE = AMOUNT OWED BY STUDENT
C     CUMBAL = AMOUNT OWED TO INSTITUTION
C     N      = NUMBER OF STUDENTS
C-------------------------------------------------------------------
      CHARACTER NAME*15
      INTEGER   ID,N
      REAL      CPC,FEES,CREDIT,TUIT,BALDUE,CUMBAL
C-------------------------------------------------------------------
      CUMBAL = 0.
```

---

* Can be assigned anytime after Chapter 4 and Module B.

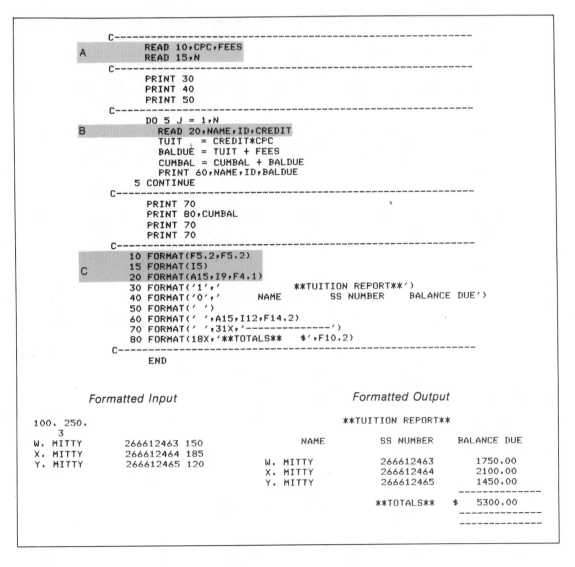

```
        C--------------------------------------------------------------
        A       READ 10,CPC,FEES
                READ 15,N
        C--------------------------------------------------------------
                PRINT 30
                PRINT 40
                PRINT 50
        C--------------------------------------------------------------
                DO 5 J = 1,N
        B         READ 20,NAME,ID,CREDIT
                  TUIT   = CREDIT*CPC
                  BALDUE = TUIT + FEES
                  CUMBAL = CUMBAL + BALDUE
                  PRINT 60,NAME,ID,BALDUE
              5 CONTINUE
        C--------------------------------------------------------------
                PRINT 70
                PRINT 80,CUMBAL
                PRINT 70
                PRINT 70
        C--------------------------------------------------------------
             10 FORMAT(F5.2,F5.2)
        C    15 FORMAT(I5)
             20 FORMAT(A15,I9,F4.1)
             30 FORMAT('1',/         **TUITION REPORT**')
             40 FORMAT('0',/     NAME        SS NUMBER    BALANCE DUE')
             50 FORMAT(' ')
             60 FORMAT(' ',A15,I12,F14.2)
             70 FORMAT(' ',31X,'---------------')
             80 FORMAT(18X,'**TOTALS**    $',F10.2)
        C--------------------------------------------------------------
                END
```

Formatted Input

Formatted Output

```
100. 250.                              **TUITION REPORT**
    3
W. MITTY      266612463 150      NAME         SS NUMBER    BALANCE DUE
X. MITTY      266612464 185
Y. MITTY      266612465 120      W. MITTY     266612463      1750.00
                                 X. MITTY     266612464      2100.00
                                 Y. MITTY     266612465      1450.00

                                 **TOTALS**   $    5300.00
                                              ---------------

                                              ---------------
```

C.1
ON FIELDS, RECORDS, AND FILES

You may find the following classification scheme useful in helping you understand the mechanics of input with FORMATs.

Field. A data item. For example, an employer might maintain data on the employee's name, Social Security number, rate of pay, number of deductions, and other items. Each of these data is considered a field. In the input data for the student billing example, name is a field, ID number is a field, and number of credits is another field. In the printed output, name is a field, ID number is a field, and the balance due is another field.

Record.   A collection of related fields. For example, all of the data items relating to a single employee represent a single record. In the student billing example, the data items pertaining to a single student make up a record. Typically, a single data card or a single line of printed output represents a record.

File.   A collection of related records. For example, a "payroll file" contains all the employee pay records; a "student file" contains data on all students.

Figure C.1A illustrates the relationship among fields, records, and files for the student billing data. Notice that these records are processed by the READ statement in box B of the program, which is associated with FORMAT "20" in box C.

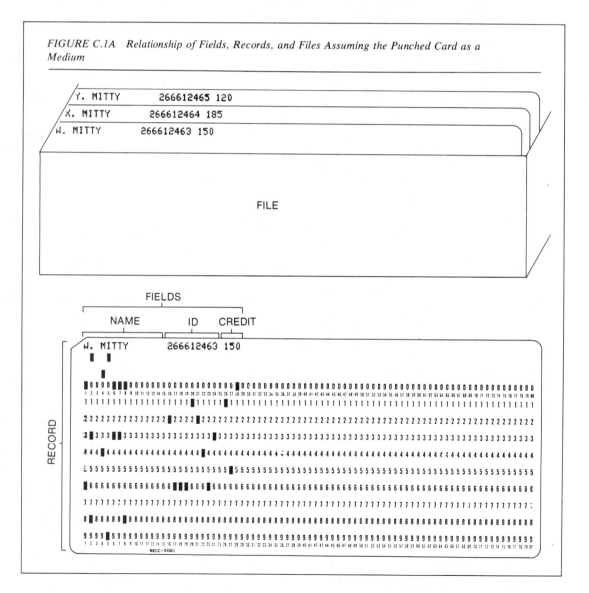

FIGURE C.1A   *Relationship of Fields, Records, and Files Assuming the Punched Card as a Medium*

FIGURE C.1B   Record Layout

Field Description	Variable Name	Type of Data	Columns	Edit Descriptor
Student name	NAME	Character	1–15	A15
Social Security no.	ID	Integer	16–24	I9
Credit hours	CREDIT	Real	25–28	F4.1

When designing the placement of input data, it's best first to design a layout similar to that in Figure C.1B. The **record layout** is a drawing and/or narrative that indicates the arrangement of data on an I/O record. In this type of documentation you might find some or all of the following.

Description of the field
Variable name assigned to the field
Type of data in the field
Location of the field on the record
Edit descriptor associated with the field

Notice that the record layout is consistent with both Figure C.1A and the input data in Example C.1.

C.2
READ AND FORMAT STATEMENTS

The input of data from specific columns of an input record requires format-directed input for precise control. This usually is accomplished by pairing the READ statement with a FORMAT statement.

The general form of the READ statement is

> **READ** *format identifier*, *list*

In earlier programs the *format identifier* was an asterisk, which meant list-directed input. For format-directed input the format identifier is usually a statement label (number) that identifies the FORMAT statement that is to be used by the READ statement.[1] As before, the *list* is a sequence of variable names.[2]

---

[1] A format identifier also can be expressed as an integer variable whose value is assigned by an ASSIGN statement (see Exercise 3), as a character expression (see Exercise 2), or as a character variable name (see Module D, Section D.3).

[2] The input list may also include an array element name (Chapters 7 and 8), an array name (Chapters 7 and 8), a character substring name (Chapter 10), and implied-DO lists (Chapters 7 and 8).

To illustrate, the statement

in box B of Example C.1 specifies the variables whose values are to be input (NAME, ID, and CREDIT) and identifies the FORMAT statement to use (statement 20) for selecting these values from the input record.

The FORMAT statement for input is used to describe the location of data on the input record. A general form of the FORMAT statement is given by

> *format*
> *statement* **FORMAT** (*list of edit descriptors*)
> *label*

where the *format statement label* is any unsigned, nonzero integer constant up to five digits that uniquely identifies the FORMAT statement and *edit descriptors* are codes that specify the editing necessary to process the I/O records. These edit descriptors indicate the position, type (integer, real, etc.), size, and decimal point location (if applicable) of the values to be input.[3]

For example, the statement

in box C of Example C.1 is utilized by the READ statement

READ 20,NAME,ID,CREDIT

to convert data values in the input record for storage in the variables NAME, ID, and CREDIT. Note how the format identifier 20 in the READ statement corresponds to the format statement label in the FORMAT statement.

The following points are worth remembering.

1. The READ statement directs the reading of a new record from the data file each time the READ statement is executed. For example, the READ statement in box B of Example C.1 is executed three times. Thus three new records are processed from the student file in Figure C.1A.
2. Since FORMAT statements are nonexecutable, the input FORMATs are often placed in a group out of the way of the execution logic, as was done with output FORMATs to improve readability.

---

[3] As also mentioned in Module B, the portion (list of edit descriptors) following the key word FORMAT is called the *format specification*. More complicated format specifications include nested sets of parentheses, as discussed in Module D. Format specifications also can be provided without the use of a FORMAT statement, as illustrated in Exercise 2 of this section and Section D.3.

3. The maximum length of an input record may depend on the processor and/or the input medium. For example, if a punched card is considered a complete input record, then 80 characters is the maximum length of this input record.

Follow-up Exercises

1. An alternative READ statement for processing format-directed input is

$$\text{READ} \left(\begin{array}{l} input \\ unit \\ number, \end{array} \begin{array}{l} format \\ statement \\ label \end{array} \right) list$$

The *input unit number* is an integer variable or constant that specifies the type of input unit that is to be used to read in your data, such as a card reader or a terminal. In our system we use the number "5" to identify either the card reader or the terminal, although this number varies depending on which computer system your institution is using. The *format statement label* references the FORMAT statement that is to be used by this READ statement. As before, the typical *list* is a sequence of variable names separated by commas.

This READ statement is more versatile than the other since, among other things, it allows us to specify specific input units such as card reader, disk drive, and tape drive.

Replace the READ statements in Example C.1 with this version.

2. **Format Identifiers as Character Expressions.** Apply Exercise 2 on page 441 to the first READ/FORMAT statements in Example C.1.

3. **ASSIGN Statement.** Apply Exercise 3 on page 441 to the READ statements in Example C.1.

C.3
SELECTED EDIT DESCRIPTORS

The same edit descriptors discussed in Module B, except for the apostrophe edit descriptor, are applied in the current section to format-directed input. Note that carriage control and textual matter (as discussed in pages 442–444) are not relevant to input data.

A Edit Descriptor

The input of a character value that is to be stored in a character variable is accomplished by using the A edit descriptor. The general form is either

where *w* is the width of the field used to input the character value.

EXAMPLE C.2

In Example C.1 the following statements were used to read in a student's record.

    READ 20,NAME,ID,CREDIT

    20 FORMAT(A15,I9,F4.1)

For now, ignore the variables ID and CREDIT and the descriptors I9 and F4.1. In effect, the READ statement tells the computer "to read the value of NAME according to the statement labeled 20." Format "20" tells the computer "the input value for NAME is to be found in a character field which is 15 columns wide." In other words, the first descriptor, A15, has been paired with the first variable in the list, NAME.

In the program of Example C.1, NAME is declared a character variable with a length of 15 characters according to the statement

    CHARACTER NAME*15

Thus, to simplify the rules associated with character input, we used A15 to edit the input value for NAME. In other words, we selected the *field width w* equal to the *declared length l,* or 15 characters.

Now look at the first input record that's processed by this READ/FORMAT pair.

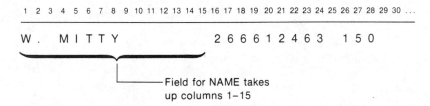

Field for NAME takes
up columns 1–15

The character value to be stored in NAME is found in columns 1–15 since A15 is the first edit descriptor in FORMAT "20." After this input record is processed, the first value stored in NAME is internally represented as follows:

Note that seven blank characters are stored as the last seven characters in NAME, since columns 9–15 of the input record are blank and NAME has a declared length of 15 characters. Also note that apostrophes are not placed around character data in formatted input records. In fact, if we were to use the formatted input record

    1 2 3 4 5 6 7 8 9 10 11 12 13 14 15 ...

    ' W .   M I T T Y '

NAME would appear incorrectly as

As we advised regarding format-directed output, we suggest that under most circumstances you set the field width *w* in A edit descriptors equal to the declared length *l* of the character variable. Alternatively, exactly the same is accomplished by omitting the field width *w* altogether. That is, *the descriptor A instead of Aw automatically gives a field width identical to the declared length l.* For example, we could replace A15 by A in FORMAT "20" and achieve the same results as before.

In general, the field width *w* may differ from the declared length *l*. In some instances you might find it convenient to select *w* unequal to *l*, in which case the following rules would apply.

Rule 1: *If $w \leq l$, the internal representation will be w characters left-justified followed by $l - w$ trailing blanks.*

Rule 2: If $w > l$, the internal representation will consist of the *rightmost l* characters in the input field.

EXAMPLE C.3

Study the two examples below and relate them to the two rules above, given the input record:

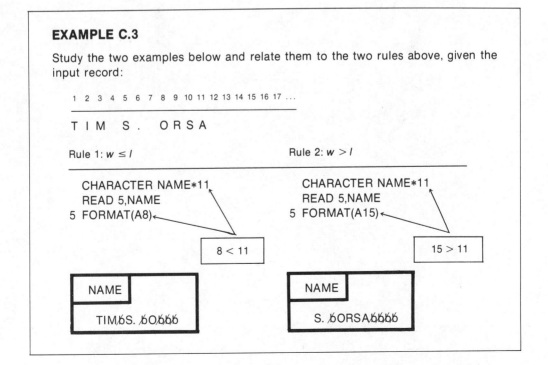

Follow-up Exercises

4. Suppose an input record contains an employee's first name in columns 1–8, second name in columns 9–16, and last name in columns 17–28. Using

CHARACTER FIRST*8,MIDDLE*8,LAST*12

a. Specify READ/FORMAT statements to enter these data.
b. Specify PRINT/FORMAT statements to give an output line at the top of a new page having last name in columns 50–61 followed by a comma, blank space, first name in columns 64–71, blank space, and middle name in columns 73–80.

5. Given the input record

1 2 3 4 5 6 7 8 9 10 11 12 13 14 15 16 17 ...

C A P T A I N   N E M O   D O L L

and the statements

```
                        ┌── l
                        ↓
        CHARACTER TOY*20
        READ 100,TOY
   100  FORMAT(A20)
             ↑
             └────── w
```

specify storage contents for each variation below.

Part	Declared Length, *l*	Field Width, *w*	Contents in TOY
a	20	20	
b	20	10	
c	20	25	
d	15	20	
e	15	10	

I Edit Descriptor

The input of integer values for storage within integer variables requires the descriptor

I*w*

where *w* is the field width.

EXAMPLE C.4

Consider the following statements from Example C.1

        READ 15,N
    15 FORMAT(I5)

and the associated input record

        1 2 3 4 5 6 7 8 9 ...
        ─────────────────
            3

The descriptor I5 in FORMAT "15" tells the computer "the value for N is type integer in a field 5 columns wide." Note that N is an integer variable; hence the I edit descriptor must be used.

Now look at the input record. The value that is to be stored in N is found in the first five columns of the record—specifically in column 5. In general, *leading blanks for numeric input are ignored;* hence the integer value 3 is stored in the integer variable N.

Embedded and trailing blanks in format-directed numeric input are either ignored or treated as zeros, depending on your system's implementation. For example, a 3 in column 1 of the above input record would be stored as either 3 or 30000. To be safe, it's best to *right-justify* numeric input in the field, as shown above.

Have you wondered why we chose a field width of 5 to input number of students (N)? We assumed that this program is to be used by universities with student enrollments up to 99,999. In general, *select a field width that's compatible with the width of the largest foreseeable input value.*

Finally, consider the following statements in Examples C.1 and C.2.

        READ 20,NAME,ID,CREDIT
    20 FORMAT(A15,I9,F4.1)

Note that A15 is paired with the character variable NAME and I9 is paired with the integer variable ID. The first input record in the student file is edited as follows:

Field for NAME in columns 1–15 according to A15

Field for ID in columns 16–24 according to I9

Thus the "9" in I9 tells the computer that the input field for ID is the next nine positions following the field for NAME. Since the first field takes up columns 1–15, it follows that the second field is in columns 16–24.

EXAMPLE C.5

Consider the statements

READ 805 J,K,L

805 FORMAT(I5,I8,I2)

and the input record

```
1  2  3  4  5  6  7  8  9  10 11 12 13 14 15 ...
```
```
   - 7 6 5                    8 0
```

⌣Field for   ⌣Field for   ⌐Field for
J based   K based   L based
on I5   on I8   on I2

In this case −765 is stored in J, zero is stored in K, and 80 is stored in L. *Note that a numeric null field, one containing all blanks, is edited as having a value of zero.*

Follow-up Exercises

6. For the statements

    INTEGER JACK,JILL,UP,HILL
    READ 3,JACK,JILL,UP,HILL

    and the input record

    ```
    1  2  3  4  5  6  7  8  9 10 11 12 13 14 ...
    ```
    ```
    5      6 2 4 1 9 8 4   7 5
    ```

    determine the stored values for each case below.
    a. 3 FORMAT(I1,I3,I4,I2)
    b. 3 FORMAT(I1,I8,I2,I3)

7. Given the input record

    ```
    1  2  3  4  5  6  7  8  9 ...
    ```
    ```
    6 1 3 0 4 2   1
    ```

    write the appropriate statements that result in the storage of 613 for K, 42 for M, and 1 for N.

8. Appropriately fill in the input record below if 35 for J, 600 for K, and −3 for L are to be stored using

    READ 25,J,K,L
    25 FORMAT(I4,I4,I4)

    ```
    1  2  3  4  5  6  7  8  9 10 11 12 13 14 ...
    ```

F Edit Descriptor

The F edit descriptor is used to input values for either real or double-precision variables. The general form is

$$Fw.d$$

where w is the field width and d is the number of digits in the fractional part of the value. The corresponding input field in the input record typically consists of an optional sign followed by a string of digits optionally containing a decimal point.[4] If the decimal point is omitted, the rightmost d digits of the string represent the fractional part of the value. If the decimal point is included in the input field, d has no effect on the value stored.

EXAMPLE C.6

Consider the following once more.

Statements in Example C.1	First input record in student file

READ 20,NAME,ID,CREDIT

20 FORMAT(A15,I9,F4.1)

1 2 3 4 5 6 7 8 9 10 11 12 13 14 15 16 17 18 19 20 21 22 23 24 25 26 27 28 29

W . M I T T Y   2 6 6 6 1 2 4 6 3   1 5 0

Field for NAME in columns 1–15 according to A15

Field for ID in columns 16–24 according to I9

Field for CREDIT in columns 25–28 according to F4.1

The value in CREDIT is read in from the third input field. The "4" in F4.1 tells the computer that the input field for CREDIT is the next four positions in columns following the second input field. Since the second input field is columns 16–24, it follows that the third input field is columns 25–28. The digits 150 appear in this field of the input record. The "1" in F4.1 specifies that the fractional part of the value contains one digit; hence 15.0 is stored in CREDIT. Note that the digits 150 were right-justified in the field, to be safe regarding the treatment of blanks.

Alternatively, we could have included the decimal point as part of the input field, in which case the "1" in F4.1 is ignored. For example, we could place the value in any of the following ways.

...25 26 27 28 ...

1 5 . 0
1 5 .
  1 5 .

In other words, by directly using the decimal point ourselves, the computer does not need to "figure out" where the decimal point is to be placed.

Finally, note that CREDIT and the F descriptor agree with respect to type; that is, CREDIT is a real variable and the F descriptor edits real values.

---

[4] The string of digits can be followed by an optional exponent, which we illustrate in the next subsection.

EXAMPLE C.7

Make sure you understand the variations below based on the statements

```
REAL HEIGHT,WEIGHT
READ 7,HEIGHT,WEIGHT
```

and the input record

```
1 2  3  4  5  6  7  8  9 10 11 12 13 14 15 16 17 18 19 ...
```

```
7 5 5 3        1 3 4 6
```

Case	FORMAT Statement	Values Stored in HEIGHT	WEIGHT
a	7 FORMAT(F6.2,F9.1)	75.53	134.6
b	7 FORMAT(F6.3,F9.1)	7.553	134.6
c	7 FORMAT(F6.4,F9.3)	0.7553	1.346
d	7 FORMAT(F6.5,F9.3)	0.07553	1.346

Follow-up Exercises

9. In Example C.1, page 463, what gets stored in CPC and FEES? What are the maximum values that can be stored in these variables?

10. For the statements

```
REAL JACK,JILL,UP,HILL
READ 3,JACK,JILL,UP,HILL
```

and the input record

```
1  2  3  4  5  6  7  8  9 10 11 12 13 14 ...
```

```
5      6 2 4 1 9 8 4   7 5
```

determine the stored values for each case below.
a. 3 FORMAT(F1.0,F3.0,F4.1,F2.2)
b. 3 FORMAT(F1.0,F8.3,F2.0,F3.3)

11. Consider Example C.6.
a. What's the maximum number of credits that a student can take assuming no decimal point is used in the input field? Assuming a decimal point is used?

b. Suppose fractional credits are not allowed by the university. Why would it be wrong to use the following?

>   READ 20,NAME,ID,CREDIT
>   20 FORMAT(A15,I9,I4)

12. Given the input record

>   1 2 3 4 5 6 7 8 9 . . .
>   ─────────────────
>   6 1 3 0 4 2   1

write appropriate statements that result in the storage of 6.13 for X, 42.0 for Y, and 0.1 for Z.

13. Appropriately fill in the input records below for storage of the indicated values using

>   READ 1,COST,NUM,QUANT
>   1 FORMAT(F5.2,I5,F5.0)

	Values Stored in			Columns in Input Record
Part	COST	NUM	QUANT	1 2 3 4 5 6 7 8 9 10 11 12 13 14 15 16 17 18 19 20
a	15.25	45	507.	
b	152.50	450	5070.	
c	1525.00	50	507.4	
d	105.	5	−300.	

14. Consider the following statements, which replace those in Example C.6.

>   19 FORMAT(A15)
>   20 FORMAT(I9)
>   21 FORMAT(F4.1)
>   READ 19,NAME
>   READ 20,ID
>   READ 21,CREDIT

Describe input records for the first student. How many input records are needed for each student?

15. More than one READ statement can reference a single FORMAT statement, since the latter is a nonexecutable statement that simply provides information to the control unit. To illustrate, consider the following.

>   10 FORMAT(F5.1,I5)
>   READ 10,X,J
>   READ 10,R,K

Indicate how the values 73.4 for X, 100 for J, 607. for R, and 3 for K should be placed on input records.

16. Consider the following layout for an input record.

Column	Variable	Type	Contents
1–11	SSN	Character	Social Security number (for example, 267-61-9814)
12–31	NAME	Character	Name
32–33	AGE	Integer	Age (for example, 37)
34	MS	Character	Marital status (M = married, S = single, O = other)
35	SEX	Character	Sex (M = male, F = female)
36–42	SAL	Real	Salary (to two decimal places; for example, 1534275 would be a salary of $15,342.75)
43–80	Blank		

Develop READ and FORMAT statements to enter these data. Include type statements for these variables.

E Edit Descriptor

Real values in exponential form are usually input using the E edit descriptor

$$\boxed{\text{E}w.d}$$

where w is the field width and d is the number of digits in the fractional part of the value. The corresponding input field in the input record consists of (1) an optional sign, (2) a string of digits optionally containing a decimal point, and (3) an exponent. The exponent can be denoted by either (a) a signed integer constant or (b) E followed by zero or more blanks, followed by an optionally signed integer constant. If the decimal point is included in the input field, d has no effect on the value stored. If the exponent is omitted from the input field, the E descriptor is equivalent to the F descriptor. In fact, *there is no distinction between E and F descriptors for input fields,* since exponents also can be used for input fields edited by F descriptors (see footnote 4 on page 473).

EXAMPLE C.8

Suppose we wish to input the value 6.6254×10^{-27} using the statement

    READ 9,PLANCK

where PLANCK is typed real. Study the following variations.

Case	FORMAT Statement	Input Record 1 2 3 4 5 6 7 8 9 10 11 12 13 14 15 16 17 18 19 . . .
a	9 FORMAT(E10.4)	6 6 2 5 4 E − 2 7
b		6 6 2 5 4 − 2 7
c		6 . 6 2 5 4 E − 2 7
d		6 . 6 2 5 4 − 2 7
e		. 6 6 2 5 4 E − 2 6
f	9 FORMAT(E15.1)	6 6 2 5 4 E − 3 0
g		6 6 2 5 4 − 3 0
h		6 . 6 2 5 4 E − 2 7
i		6 . 6 2 5 4 − 2 7
j		. 6 6 2 5 4 E − 2 6

Note that inclusion of the decimal point (cases c, d, e, h, i, and j) overrides the
d portion of the descriptor. Also, make sure that your field width is large enough to
accommodate the exponent. For example, E8.4 would be sufficient only for case b,
since cases a and d take up nine columns and cases c and e take up ten columns.
Finally, we could have used F10.4 in place of E10.4 and F15.1 in place of E15.1,
since E and F descriptors are equivalent for input fields.

Follow-up Exercise

17. Given the statements

        READ 5,V1,V2,V3
      5 FORMAT(E10.2,E10.3,E9.2)
    What values are stored in V1, V2, and V3 for each input record below?

	1 2 3 4 5 6 7 8 9 10 11 12 13 14 15 16 17 18 19 20 21 22 23 24 25 26 27 28 29 . . . .
a	− 1 2 . 1 E + 2 5 . 5 5 5 E + 3 . 3 3 E 0 4
b	− 1 2 E + 2 5 5 5 5 . E 3 3 3 E − 0 4
c	− 1 2 + 2 5 5 5 . 3 3

D Edit Descriptor

Double-precision values are usually input using the D edit descriptor

$$\boxed{\mathbf{D}w.d}$$

where w is the field width and d is the number of digits in the fractional part of the value.
Alternatively, the F descriptor can be used to input double-precision values. The D
descriptor is treated identically to the E descriptor, except that E is replaced by D.

EXAMPLE C.9

If we wish to input the value 3.1415926536 using the statements

```
      READ 7,PI
    7 FORMAT(D15.11)
```

where PI is typed double precision, any of the following input field variations will serve the purpose.

```
1  2  3  4  5  6  7  8  9  10 11 12 13 14 15  .  .  .
```
```
         3 . 1 4 1 5 9 2 6 5 3 6
   3 1 4 1 5 9 2 6 5 3 6 D + 0 1
     3 1 4 1 5 9 2 6 5 3 6 + 1
```

Follow-up Exercise

18. Make any necessary changes in the input records of Example C.9 when the descriptor D15.11 in FORMAT "7" is replaced by the following.
   a. D20.11
   b. D15.5
   c. D10.5
   d. F15.11

X Edit Descriptor

The X descriptor is used to skip columns in an input record. Its general form is

$$\boxed{n\,\mathbf{X}}$$

where n is the number of columns to skip.

EXAMPLE C.10

Suppose that FORMAT "20" in Example C.1 is changed as follows:

```
      READ 20,NAME,ID,CREDIT
   20 FORMAT(A15,5X,I9,1X,F4.1)
```

The input unit finds the value of NAME in columns 1–15 of the input record, skips the next five columns (16–20), finds the value for ID in columns 21–29, skips column

30, and finds the value for CREDIT in columns 31–34. The input record would look like this.

```
1  2  3  4  5  6  7  8  9 10 11 12 13 14 15 16 17 18 19 20 21 22 23 24 25 26 27 28 29 30 31 32 33 34 . . .
```

W .   M I T T Y   2 6 6 6 1 2 4 6 3   1 5 0

You might ask why columns 16–20 would contain blanks in the first place. Why not begin the next field in column 16? If you have room on an input record such as a card, then spacing between fields (or alternatively using wide fields) improves readability (for us humans). Otherwise blank fields in input records represent wasted space and effort. You should design input records efficiently. Generally, the X descriptor is used within input format specifications to skip fields that contain data not needed in the current analysis, as the following exercises illustrate.

Follow-up Exercises

19. In Example C.10 suppose that the input record contains ID in columns 1–9, the student's name in a field given by columns 10–24, the home address in columns 25–71, and the value of CREDIT in columns 72–75. We wish to read in only ID and CREDIT. Appropriately change the READ and FORMAT statements.

*20. You're given an input record with the following layout.

Column	Contents	Variable Name	Type
1–9	Social Security number	SSN	Integer
22–45	Name	NAME	Character
46–47	Age	AGE	Integer
48	Marital status	MAR	Character
49	Sex	SEX	Character
50–57	Salary (to two decimal places)	SALARY	Real
58–80	Blank	—	

Construct the READ and FORMAT statements necessary to read AGE, SEX, and SALARY.

T Edit Descriptor

The T edit descriptor indicates the location of the first position of the next field to be read in. The general form of this specification is

where *n* indicates the starting position of the next input field.

EXAMPLE C.11

In Example C.10 the field for NAME is in columns 1–15, for ID in columns 21–29, and for CREDIT in columns 31–34. Alternatively, the following statements can be used to enter the data.

```
    READ 20,NAME,ID,CREDIT
20  FORMAT(A15,T21,I9,T31,F4.1)
```

This is equivalent to

```
20  FORMAT(A15,5X,I9,1X,F4.1)
```

which was used in the previous example.

Notice that the T descriptor indicates the starting position of the next input field and the X descriptor indicates the number of spaces to skip to reach the next input field.

EXAMPLE C.12

The first three digits of the five-digit ZIP code are used to determine to which of eight postal zones in the United States a package is to be sent. This postal zone also determines the cost of mailing a package. Suppose that ZIP code is stored in columns 10–14. First we'll read the entire ZIP code into an integer variable called ZIP and then we'll read the first three digits into an integer variable called ZONE.

```
1 2 3 4 5 6 7 8 9 10 11 12 13 14 . . .
```
_____

```
              0 2 8 8 2
```

```
    READ 5,ZIP,ZONE
5  FORMAT(T10,I5,T10,I3)
```

Thus 02882 is stored in ZIP and 028 is stored in ZONE.

Interesting feature, isn't it? The T descriptor allows us to rescan data on the current record.

Follow-up Exercises

21. Rework Exercise 19 using the T descriptor instead of the X descriptor.
*22. Reword Exercise 20 using the T descriptor instead of the X descriptor.

C.4
COMMON ERRORS

Take care to avoid the following input errors.

1. *Type inconsistency.*   This error is perhaps the most common. Make sure that the variable type in the list of the READ statement matches the descriptor in the format specification and that both in turn match the value in the input field. Thus we require three-way agreement with respect to type. For example, use an F or E descriptor for a real variable and an input field containing a value in real form; use an I descriptor for an integer variable and an input field having an integer value; and use the A descriptor for a character variable and an input field containing a character value without enclosing apostrophes.

2. *Incorrect character input.*   Pay careful attention to Rules 1 and 2 on page 469 when your field width *w* in the A descriptor differs from your declared length *l* for the character variable. Also remember that, unlike list-directed input, format-directed input character fields do not include enclosing apostrophes, as illustrated on page 468.

Follow-up Exercise

23.   Define or explain the following.

list-directed input	A edit descriptor
format-directed input	I edit descriptor
field	F edit descriptor
record	E edit descriptor
file	D edit descriptor
record layout	X edit descriptor
general form of READ statement	T edit descriptor
FORMAT statement	

Additional Formatted I/O

This module completes your introduction to format-directed input/output by discussing the following features: additional options within FORMAT statements, situations where the number of items in the PRINT or READ list is different from the number of corresponding edit descriptors, and format specifications without the use of FORMAT statements.

D.1
OTHER FORMAT SPECIFICATIONS

The **format specification** is the portion of the FORMAT statement that follows the key word FORMAT, that is,

> statement label **FORMAT** *format specification*

In Modules B and C we simplified the format specification by omitting certain features that are useful. In this section we illustrate the repeat specification, the slash edit descriptor, and embedded format specifications.

Repeat Specification

A **repeat specification** is a nonzero, unsigned integer constant that appears immediately in front of a repeatable edit descriptor. A **repeatable edit descriptor** (are you ready for this?) is an edit descriptor that can be repeated. In practice, repeatable edit descriptors are those that edit input/output fields that correspond to items in READ/PRINT lists. Of the descriptors we have discussed, A, I, F, E, and D are repeatable edit descriptors; the apostrophe, X, and T descriptors, for example, are called **nonrepeatable edit descriptors.**

---

* Can be assigned anytime after Chapter 4 and Module C.

EXAMPLE D.1

Given the statements

```
      INTEGER JAY,KAY
      REAL     A,B,C
      PRINT 10,A,B,C,JAY,KAY
   10 FORMAT('0',F10.2,F10.2,F10.2,I5,I5)
```

it follows that A, B, and C are to be output with each using the repeatable descriptor F10.2, and JAY and KAY each using the repeatable descriptor I5. This FORMAT statement can be simplified by using repeat specifications, as follows:

```
   10 FORMAT('0',3F10.2,2I5)
```

Repeat
specifications

Slash Edit Descriptor

The **slash edit descriptor** is a nonrepeatable descriptor that terminates a record. For example, it terminates a line of printed output when using a line printer and terminates the reading of a data card when using a card reader.

A series of consecutive slashes within format specifications used for output has the effect of producing blank lines on the page. The number of blank lines will be one less than the number of consecutive slashes if the slashes are in the middle of the format specification, but will be equal to the number of slashes appearing at the very beginning or end of the format specification.

EXAMPLE D.2

Suppose we wish to output the contents in memory given by

using the statement

```
   PRINT 10.N.A.B
```

Study each FORMAT statement and its corresponding output on page 484. Note that a comma need not separate a slash from other edit descriptors.

Case	FORMAT Statement	Output	Comment
a	10 FORMAT('b',I5/'0',2F8.1)	Line 2: `613` (cols 2–4); Line 4: `72.4` `115.0`	The 'b' brings carriage to line 2 for printing of N. The slash terminates line 2, *which brings carriage back to beginning of line 2*. The '0' brings carriage to line 4 to print A and B.
b	10 FORMAT('b',I5//'b',2F8.1)	Line 2: `613`; Line 4: `72.4` `115.0`	The first slash terminates line 2 and the second slash terminates line 3. The 'b' brings the carriage to line 4. Result identical to case a.
c	10 FORMAT('b',I5////'b',2F8.1)	Line 2: `613`; Line 6: `72.4` `115.0`	Compared with case b, the two additional slashes cause lines 4 and 5 to be terminated as well.

d	10 FORMAT('b',I5/'b',F8.1/'b',F8.1)	Line 2: `613`; Line 3: `72.4`; Line 4: `115.0`	This case is identical to but more efficient than
			
			    PRINT 10,N
			10 FORMAT('b',I5)
			    PRINT 11,A
			    PRINT 11,B
			11 FORMAT('b',F8.1)

e	10 FORMAT(//5X,'PAYROLL REPORT'/'b', 'IDENTIFICATIONbbPAY'/)	Line 4: `PAYROLL REPORT`; Line 5: `IDENTIFICATION PAY`	The first slash brings carriage to line 2 and the second slash to line 3. The first X out of 5X brings carriage to line 4. The last slash brings carriage to beginning of line 5. *The right parenthesis brings carriage to line 6.*

To summarize the use of slashes for output: *n* slashes between two other edit descriptors cause *n* − 1 blank lines to be printed, where *the first slash is used to return the carriage to the beginning of the current line*. When *n* slashes are used at the beginning or the end of the format specification, however, *n* blank lines are printed. In the case where slashes appear at the end, the first slash is again used to return to the beginning of the current line, after which *n* − 1 blank lines by the remaining slashes plus one additional blank line by the right parenthesis are printed. Note that, in general, *the right outer parenthesis causes the identical behavior of a slash*. The same conclusions can be drawn about records on input. Note, however, that *on output the control unit looks for carriage control following the last slash in a sequence of slashes at the beginning or middle of the format specification*.

Embedded Format Specifications

A format specification may be *embedded* within another format specification for greater efficiency. This is equivalent to saying that inner parentheses may be used within the outer parentheses. The inner parentheses and their items make up what we call a *group*. The combination of pairing repeat specifications with groups is a powerful feature in output formats, which we illustrate next.

EXAMPLE D.3

In part d of Example D.2 the statement

    10 FORMAT ('b́',I5/'b́',F8.1/'b́',F8.1)

could have been written as

    10 FORMAT('b́',I5,2(/'b́',F8.1))

If the repeat factor had been 15, for example, then you should really appreciate the efficiency of this approach.

To illustrate another convenience due to grouping, try to determine what the following statements accomplish before reading on:

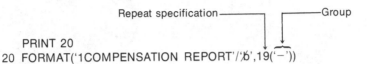

        PRINT 20
    20 FORMAT('1COMPENSATION REPORT'/'b́',19('−'))

First, the carriage goes to the top of a new page. Next, the heading, COMPENSATION REPORT is printed in columns 1–19 of line 1. The slash then instructs the carriage to return to the beginning of line 1. The 'b́' causes the carriage to go to line 2, after which 19 underscore (dash or minus sign) characters are printed immediately under the heading. Do you realize what would be required without the use of the repeat specification and inner parentheses? An apostrophe edit descriptor with 19 underscore characters.

Follow-up Exercises

1. Improve the program of Example B.1 on page 438 as follows.
   a. Eliminate PRINT 50 and FORMAT "50" by appropriately modifying FORMAT "40."
   b. Make FORMAT "70" more efficient.
2. Can you think of two reasonably efficient ways of printing, say, 15 blank lines?
* 3. Rework Exercise 17 in Module B on page 458 using options in this section.
* 4. Rework Exercise 12 in Module B on page 450 using options in this section. Underscore the heading BLOOD TYPE A+.
5. Indicate an appropriate FORMAT statement for

    READ 25,A,B,C,D,E

   where three input fields for A, B, and C of ten columns each are on the first input record and two input fields for D and E of five columns each are on the next input record. Each value is to be entered to two decimal places.
6. Determine the FORMAT statement for

    PRINT 30,A,I,B,J,C,K,D,L

   which results in output of 12-column field widths all on one print line at the top of a new page. Output real variables to one decimal place and insert a percent sign (%) immediately after the output of each real variable. Use inner parentheses.
7. Describe output for each of the following.

    PRINT 3,M,N

   In each case the carriage is currently on line 20.

   a. 3 FORMAT(1X,I5,10(/)1X,I5)
   b. 3 FORMAT(10(/)1X,2I5)
   c. 3 FORMAT(1X,2I5,10(/))
   d. 3 FORMAT(1X,6('*'),2I5,2X,6('*'))
   **e.   PRINT 3,K,L,M,N
        3 FORMAT(1X,2(/1X,2(10X,I5)))

    where the contents of M and N are given above and

8. Indicate what is wrong with each of the following.
   a.   3 FORMAT(1X,I5//I5)
   b.   3 FORMAT(///2I5)
   c.   3 FORMAT(1X,I523X,I5)

D.2
IMBALANCE BETWEEN LIST AND DESCRIPTORS

In our work thus far, the number of items in the list of a READ or PRINT statement has equaled (balanced) the number of repeatable edit descriptors in the format specification. FORTRAN allows imbalance between these two numbers for greater flexibility.

Fewer Items in List Than Repeatable Descriptors

In this case the following procedure is adopted by the processor. Each item in the list is processed according to its corresponding repeatable edit descriptor. Format control then terminates at the *first repeatable* descriptor not having a corresponding item in the list.

EXAMPLE D.4

Given the statements

    READ 8,A,B
  8 FORMAT(F5.1,F10.2,I5)

F5.1 is used to read in A, F10.2 is used to read in B, and I5 is simply ignored. Then why have I5 in the first place? Perhaps because some other READ statement such as

    READ 8,X,Y,J

also is used in the program, which allows us to get by with one FORMAT statement.

More Items in List Than Repeatable Descriptors

For this situation the procedure states: Items in the list are processed until the descriptors in the format specification are exhausted, after which the record is terminated; the scan of the format specification is repeated as many times as needed until all items in the list are processed. If inner parentheses are present, repeat scans begin with the *rightmost* group, including the repeat specification that may be present.

EXAMPLE D.5

Suppose we wish to output the contents in memory given by

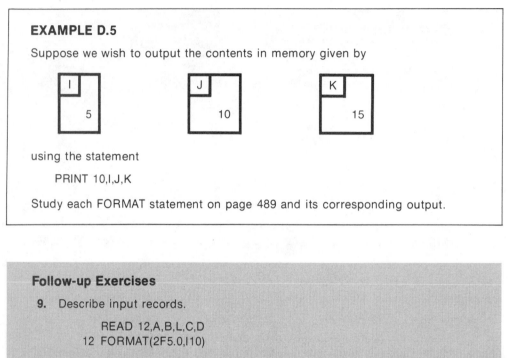

using the statement

    PRINT 10,I,J,K

Study each FORMAT statement on page 489 and its corresponding output.

Follow-up Exercises

9. Describe input records.

        READ 12,A,B,L,C,D
    12 FORMAT(2F5.0,I10)

10. Fill in the output.

    PRINT 20,A,B,C,D

Case	FORMAT Statement	Output
a.	20 FORMAT('0',2F5.1)	
b.	20 FORMAT(1X,F5.1)	

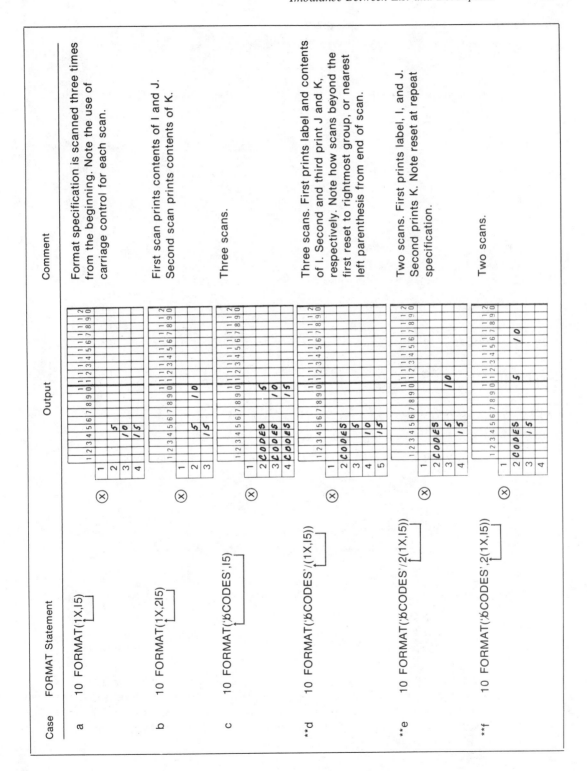

Case	FORMAT Statement	Output	Comment
a	10 FORMAT(1X,I5)	5 / 10 / 15	Format specification is scanned three times from the beginning. Note the use of carriage control for each scan.
b	10 FORMAT(1X,2I5)	5 10 / 15	First scan prints contents of I and J. Second scan prints contents of K.
c	10 FORMAT('ƀCODES',I5)	ƀCODES 5 / ƀCODES 10 / ƀCODES 15	Three scans.
**d	10 FORMAT('ƀCODES'/(1X,I5))	ƀCODES 5 / 10 / 15	Three scans. First prints label and contents of I. Second and third print J and K, respectively. Note how scans beyond the first reset to rightmost group, or nearest left parenthesis from end of scan.
**e	10 FORMAT('ƀCODES'/2(1X,I5))	ƀCODES 5 5 / 10	Two scans. First prints label, I, and J. Second prints K. Note reset at repeat specification.
**f	10 FORMAT('ƀCODES',2(1X,I5))	ƀCODES 5 5 / 10	Two scans.

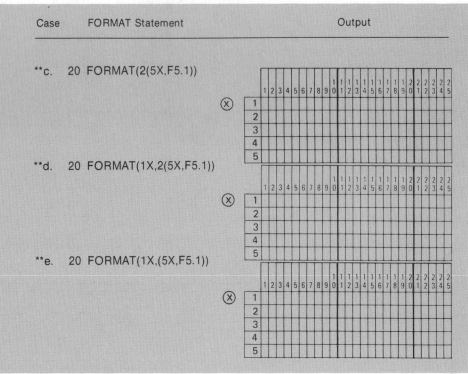

D.3
EXECUTION-TIME FORMAT SPECIFICATIONS

Any given format specification can be provided in one of three ways.

1. Through a FORMAT statement, for example,

```
      PRINT 75,X
   75 FORMAT(10X,F11.4)
```

2. Through a character expression as a format identifier, for example,

```
   PRINT '(10X,F11.4)',X
```

3. Through a character variable as a format identifier, for example,

```
   CHARACTER FM*80
   FM = '(10X,F11.4)'
   PRINT FM,X
```

The third approach actually stores the format specification within the character variable FM *during execution of the program,* rather than during compilation. For this reason, the third alternative is called **execution-time** (or **variable**) **format specifications.**

In actual practice variable format specifications are almost always implemented by reading in the character values, as the following illustrates.

```
        CHARACTER FM*80
        READ 2,FM
      2 FORMAT(A80)
        PRINT FM,X
```

In this case the format specification (10X, F11.4) is provided as data input during execution.

This flexibility of providing format specifications as part of the input data is quite important in certain commercial applications, as it allows complete independence between the programmer and the user with respect to specific formatting requirements. The following example illustrates this advantage.

EXAMPLE D.6

Statistical packages widely available in the software libraries of computer installations often make use of execution-time format specifications. Motivations for doing so include flexibility, convenience, and lower costs in preparing large amounts of data input.

In many commercial and research environments, input data are often in formatted form on cards, tape, or disk for use by a variety of different programs. Without the variable formatting feature, either each program would have to have identical input formats consistent with the input data file or the data file would have to be modified for consistency with each program. Either approach would be costly, which is why FORTRAN has the option of using variable format specifications.

To illustrate, suppose that the program below is designed for a software library available to many different users.

```
C                 PROGRAM THAT CALCULATES THE ARITHMETIC
C                 MEAN OF N REAL VALUES
C
C                 FM      = VARIABLE FORMAT SPEC.
C                 N       = NUMBER OF VALUES
C                 VALUE = REAL VALUE
C                 MEAN  = ARITHMETIC MEAN (AVERAGE)
C
        CHARACTER FM*80
        INTEGER    N
        REAL        VALUE,SUM,MEAN
C

        READ 1,FM

        READ 3,N
C
        SUM = 0.
```

```
C
          DO 50 I = 1,N

          READ FM,VALUE

          SUM = SUM + VALUE
    50 CONTINUE
C
          MEAN = SUM/N
C
          PRINT 5,MEAN
C


     1 FORMAT(A80)

     3 FORMAT(I5)
     5 FORMAT(T10,'MEAN = ',F15.4)
C
          END
```

First User's Input Data File

123456789101112131415...

──────────

(F5.1) } Format specification
 900   } Value of N
75.
60.2
97.8   } 900 input records
:
:
32.1

Second User's Input Data File

123456789101112131415...

──────────

(10X,F2.0)   } Format specification
 1500   } Value of N
RED   80
BLUE   50
GREEN   20   } 1500 input records
:
:
BLUE   75

Note that the shaded portions of the program identify the variable format specification logic, and that the single program accommodates two (or any number of) users with differently formatted input files. However, each set of data is run separately.

Follow-up Exercise

11. Answer the following with respect to Example D.6.
    a. Why do you think we declared the length of FM as 80?
    b. Specify the input file for a user that has 115 numbers to two decimal places, one each in columns 16 to 25.
    c. Suppose that a user's 98 values are placed five at a time on an input record, where each value is to three decimal places in a field 15 columns wide. The 98 values are thus placed on 20 input records. Explain why the program can't handle this data file.
    **d. Modify the program so that it also handles files of the type described in part c. *Hint:* You need to store values in an array (Chapter 7).

D.4
COMMON ERRORS

Pay close attention to the effect of slashes in format specifications. Remember that n slashes at the beginning or the end cause the printing of n blank lines; however, n slashes between two other descriptors cause the printing of $n - 1$ blank lines. Moreover, n slashes by themselves in a format specification result in $n + 1$ blank lines (see the answer to Exercise 2 in this module).

Also, *don't forget to specify carriage control following the last slash in a sequence that appears at the beginning or the middle of output FORMATs.* For example, suppose 3 is stored in J and 500 is stored in K and we use the following statements.

```
    PRINT 1,J,K
  1 FORMAT(1X,I1//I3)
```

We would get the following output.

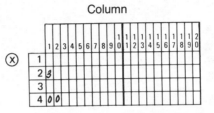

Column

In this case carriage control was not specified following the second slash, so the printer "rips off" the first position in the field for carriage control, effectively leaving 00 for the output of 500. The statement

```
  1 FORMAT(1X,I1//1X,I3)
```

would give the desired output.

Column

	1	2	3	4	5	6	7	8	9	10	11	12	13	14	15	16	17	18	19	20
1																				
2	3																			
3																				
4	5	0	0																	

(X)

Follow-up Exercise

12. Define or explain the following.

format specification
repeat specification
repeatable edit descriptor
nonrepeatable edit descriptor
slash edit descriptor
embedded format specifications
imbalance between list and descriptors (two rules)
execution-time format specifications
variable format specifications

Top-Down Design and Stepwise Refinement

Recent programming trends indicate a growing use of certain design techniques collectively called top-down design. This module motivates and illustrates the top-down philosophy.

E.1 MOTIVATION

The term **top-down design** refers to a process for simplifying and systematizing the design and development of complex programs. Strictly speaking, it is not a specific technique, but rather a philosophy that translates into a personalized process for writing programs. As such, the manner of implementing top-down design will vary from programmer to programmer or organization to organization.

Top-down design starts with an overall "look" at the entire problem, that is, a look from the "top." Subsequently the problem is refined further by working "down" through successive levels of greater detail. To illustrate what we mean, consider the process of writing a textbook. First we decide the topic of the book. This is the least level of detail and the highest level of abstraction. Next we write down the titles of chapters, which gives us the next level of detail. Next we specify the main headings within each chapter, which represents a further refinement in the level of detail. Next we state the subheadings within each main heading. Finally, we provide the greatest level of detail: each word in the body of the text.

The *implementation* of top-down design at the programming stage is often carried out by a process called **stepwise refinement,** which is an iterative (stepwise) procedure that successively refines the problem at each step. In other words, stepwise refinement is a step-by-step process that continually expands or refines the flowchart, pseudocode, or program, starting at a low level of detail and working toward a high level of detail.

In addition to the guidelines and techniques illustrated in Chapters 2 through 9 and in Module F, top-down design is an effort to control exploding software costs by pro-

* This module is best assigned at Section 5.4, but can be assigned anytime after Chapter 5.

moting better organization and development of complex programs. In effect, top-down techniques promote lower costs with respect to program development, debugging, reliability, and maintenance.

E.2
ILLUSTRATION: GOVERNMENT PRINTING OFFICE ORDERS

Let's design a simplified program that prints billing information for publications produced by the Government Printing Office. Stepwise refinement is illustrated under "Algorithm," following the statement of the problem.

Statement

This program determines the charge for an order of publications, prints the charge together with other data regarding the order, and finally prints summary statistics once all orders are processed. The basic charge is the unit price of the publication multiplied by the quantity ordered. This basic charge is then modified to include a 10 percent discount for orders between 50 and 100 copies of a single publication; a 25 percent discount is given if more than 100 copies are ordered. In addition, a surcharge of 25 percent is added to any order mailed to a non-U.S. address.

The data obtained from the order blank include (1) customer name, (2) customer address, (3) whether or not from a foreign country, (4) title of publication, (5) unit price of publication, and (6) quantity ordered.

At the end of each day a report is printed that lists the individual orders. In addition, a summary of the day's activities is printed that includes (1) number of orders for the day, (2) average order size, and (3) total amount billed for the day.

a. *Input data*
1. Customer name
2. Customer address
3. Foreign country, yes or no
4. Title of publication
5. Unit price of publication
6. Quantity ordered
b. *Output data*
For each customer:
1. Customer name
2. Title of publication
3. Quantity ordered
4. Charge
Summary:
5. Number of orders
6. Average order size
7. Total amount billed
c. *Computations*
1. Charge = unit price × quantity ordered
2. Discount according to the following schedule:

Size of order	Percent Discount
49 or less	0
50–99	10
100 or more	25

3. Surcharge of 25 percent if mailed to foreign address, after any discount

Algorithm

We now illustrate stepwise refinement, first through flowcharts and then through pseudocode. Figure E.1 is an example of stepwise refinement through the "explosion" of flowcharts. Step 1, the first level of detail, describes the nature of the program. Step 2, the next level of refinement, divides the program's tasks into three segments: initial tasks, order processing, and concluding tasks. Step 3 provides a greater level of detail for each segment in Step 2. Note that the task "process order" is actually a DO-WHILE structure.[1] Step 4 further elaborates Step 3 by specifying the nature of the charge and identifying the specific variables to be accumulated. Finally, Step 5 gives the "nitty gritty" of the discount and surcharge logic, based on decision structures in Chapter 5.

Figure E.2 illustrates the same procedure by exploding the pseudocode. The flow-chart and pseudocode approaches are essentially equivalent, although the use of flowcharts is more tedious and more difficult to modify than the use of pseudocode. In practice only one of the two is needed, according to the preference of the programmer or the organization.

Regardless of which approach you might prefer, you should note that each iteration in stepwise refinement describes the logic of the problem in greater detail. Moreover, this very process of starting with the "big picture" followed by progressive "fine tuning" is conceptually appealing and consistent with the way the human mind most effectively solves complex problems.

You should also remember that the specifics for each step in stepwise refinement are apt to vary from programmer to programmer. We ask you to consider variations of Figures E.1 and E.2 in Exercises 1 and 2.

As your algorithms have become more elaborate, particularly beginning with some of the problems at the end of Chapter 5, we advise that you practice stepwise refinement as a means of programming more effectively.[2]

Code

FORTRAN code readily follows from either the flowchart or pseudocode version in Figures E.1 and E.2, as illustrated in Figure E.3. You should confirm that the code is consistent with the flowchart/pseudocode versions, except for the fact that discount and surcharge parameters in the program have been generalized and initialized through DATA statements.

---

[1] The DO-WHILE structure is defined in Section 4.3. This particular example of the DO-WHILE structure is called a last-record-check loop, as described in Section 6.6.

[2] The explosion process takes up a lot of room, so we suggest you use printer paper. Try using the back of discarded paper, which then gives you claim to being an ecologically conscious programmer.

FIGURE E.1 Stepwise Refinement by Exploding Flowcharts

FIGURE E.2 *Stepwise Refinement by Exploding the Pseudocode*

STEP 1   STEP 2   STEP 3   STEP 4

Initial ──┐ Declare variables   IF quantity < 50 THEN
tasks   │ No. orders = 0   Charge = quantity × unit price
          │ Cumulative quant. = 0   END IF
          │ Cumulative charge = 0   IF 50 ≤ quantity ≤ 99 THEN
          └ READ customer data   Charge = 0.90 × quantity × unit price
                                                                                 END IF
                                              ┌ Compute charge based on discount IF quantity ≥ 100 THEN
                                              │ Compute charge based on surcharge   Charge = 0.75 × quantity × unit price
                                              └   END IF

Process ──┐ DO WHILE more orders   IF foreign country THEN
order   │   Compute charge ─────   Charge = 1.25 × charge
          │   Accumulate totals ──┐ ┌ Add 1 to no. orders   END IF
          │   PRINT customer data │ │ Add quant. to cum. quant.
          │   READ customer data │ └ Add charge to cum. charge
          └ END DO

Concluding ┐ Ave. order size =
tasks   │   cumulative quant. ÷ no.
           │   orders
           └ PRINT summary data

Stop

FIGURE E.3   FORTRAN Code for Government Printing Office Problem

---

```
C   GOVERNMENT PRINTING OFFICE PROGRAM
C
C   VERSION:  GOP.1     DATE:  JANUARY, 1981
C
C   PROGRAMMERS:  R. AGELOFF/R. MOJENA
C                 UNIVERSITY OF RHODE ISLAND
C
C--------------------------------------------------------------------
C   STATEMENT
C-------------
C     THIS PROGRAM PROCESSES ORDERS FOR PUBLICATIONS.
C     IT INPUTS ORDER DATA, CALCULATES THE CHARGE, PRINTS
C     SELECTED ORDER INFORMATION, AND PRINTS SUMMARIES
C     ONCE ALL ORDERS ARE PROCESSED.
C--------------------------------------------------------------------
C   INPUT VARIABLES
C-------------------
C     NAME    = CUSTOMER'S NAME
C     ADDRES  = CUSTOMER'S ADDRESS
C     FOR     = YES IF FOREIGN; OTHERWISE DOMESTIC
C     TITLE   = TITLE OF PUBLICATION
C     PRICE   = UNIT PRICE OF PUBLICATION
C     QUANT   = QUANTITY ORDERED
C
C     NOTE:   TERMINATE RUN BY USING 'END' FOR NAME
C             ALL INPUT LIST-DIRECTED
C--------------------------------------------------------------------
C   OUTPUT DATA
C-------------
C   PER ORDER:
C     NAME, TITLE, QUANT
C     CHARGE = CHARGE IN DOLLARS
C
C   PER RUN:
C     NUMORD = NUMBER OF ORDERS
C     AVERAGE ORDER SIZE, CUMQTY/NUMORD WHERE CUMQTY
C        IS CUMULATIVE QUANTITY
C     TOTBIL = TOTAL AMOUNT BILLED
C--------------------------------------------------------------------
C   OTHER VARIABLES (AS CONSTANTS)
C----------------------------------
C     BREAK1 = FIRST BREAK IN DISCOUNT SCHEDULE (=50)
C     BREAK2 = SECOND BREAK IN DISCOUNT SCHEDULE (=100)
C     DISC1  = DISCOUNT FOR FIRST BREAK (=0.10)
C     DISC2  = DISCOUNT FOR SECOND BREAK (=0.25)
C     SURC   = SURCHAGE (=0.25)
C--------------------------------------------------------------------
C   DECLARATIONS
C--------------
      CHARACTER NAME*15, ADDRES*20, FOR*3, TITLE*20
      INTEGER   NUMORD, CUMQTY, QUANT, BREAK1, BREAK2
      REAL      PRICE, CHARGE, TOTBIL, DISC1, DISC2, SURC
C--------------------------------------------------------------------
C   INITIALIZATIONS
C-------------------
      DATA BREAK1,BREAK2/50,100/
      DATA DISC1,DISC2,SURC/0.10,0.25,0.25/
      DATA NUMORD,CUMQTY,TOTBIL/2*0,0./
C--------------------------------------------------------------------
C   INITIAL ORDER READ IN
C-------------------------
      READ *,NAME,ADDRES,FOR,TITLE,PRICE,QUANT
C--------------------------------------------------------------------
```

```
C      DO WHILE MORE ORDERS
C----------------------------
   10 IF (NAME .NE. 'END') THEN
C
C      PROCESS NEXT ORDER
C      -----------------
C         DISCOUNT LOGIC
C         --------------
C
         IF (QUANT .LT. BREAK1) THEN
            CHARGE = QUANT*PRICE
         END IF
         IF (QUANT .GE. BREAK1 .AND. QUANT .LT. BREAK2) THEN
            CHARGE = (1. - DISC1)*QUANT*PRICE
         END IF
         IF (QUANT .GE. BREAK2) THEN
            CHARGE = (1. - DISC2)*QUANT*PRICE
         END IF
C
C         SURCHARGE LOGIC
C         ---------------
         IF (FOR .EQ. 'YES') THEN
            CHARGE = (1. + SURC)*CHARGE
         END IF
C
C         ACCUMULATE TOTALS
C         -----------------
         NUMORD = NUMORD + 1
         CUMQTY = CUMQTY + QUANT
         TOTBIL = TOTBIL + CHARGE
C
C         PRINT ORDER DATA
C         ----------------
         PRINT *,' '
         PRINT *,'NAME     :',NAME
         PRINT *,'TITLE    :',TITLE
         PRINT *,'QUANTITY :',QUANT
         PRINT *,'CHARGE   :',CHARGE
C
C         READ ORDER DATA
C         ---------------
         READ *,NAME,ADDRES,FOR,TITLE,PRICE,QUANT
C
C         LOOP BACK
C         ---------
         GO TO 10
C
C      END DO
C      ------
      END IF
C------------------------------------------------------------
C     CONCLUDING TASKS
C     ----------------
      PRINT *,'------------------------------'
      PRINT *,' '
      PRINT *,'SUMMARY'
      PRINT *,'-------'
      PRINT *,' '
      PRINT *,'NUMBER OF ORDERS   :',NUMORD
      PRINT *,'AVERAGE ORDER SIZE :',REAL(CUMQTY)/REAL(NUMORD)
      PRINT *,'TOTAL AMOUNT BILLED :',TOTBIL
C------------------------------------------------------------
C
      END
```

FIGURE E.4   Test Output for Government Printing Office Problem

```
NAME       :NAME1
TITLE      :T1
QUANTITY :                40
CHARGE   :   0.40000000E 03

NAME       :NAME2
TITLE      :T2
QUANTITY :                40
CHARGE   :   0.50000000E 03

NAME       :NAME3
TITLE      :T3
QUANTITY :                80
CHARGE   :   0.57600000E 03

NAME       :NAME4
TITLE      :T4
QUANTITY :               500
CHARGE   :   0.37500000E 03
-------------------------------------

SUMMARY
--------

NUMBER OF ORDERS      :                4
AVERAGE ORDER SIZE  :   0.16500000E 03
TOTAL AMOUNT BILLED :   0.18510000E 04
```

Debugging

Processing the test data in Table E.1 through the program in Figure E.3 gave the results in Figure E.4. You should confirm that the output is correct by roleplaying the computer. Note that the loop terminates when statement 10 in the program tests false, that is, when NAME contains the string value END, which is the name used as the last input line in Table E.1.

TABLE E.1   Test Data for Government Printing Office Problem

NAME	ADDRESS	FOREIGN COUNTRY?	TITLE	UNIT PRICE ($)	QUANTITY
NAME1	ADD.1	No	T1	10.00	40
NAME2	ADD.2	Yes	T2	10.00	40
NAME3	ADD.3	No	T3	8.00	80
NAME4	ADD.4	No	T4	1.00	500
END	—	—	—	0.00	0

E.3
LOOSE ENDS

In this section we tie up some loose ends by relating top-down design to structured programming, our four-step procedure, and modular programming.

Top-Down Structured Programming

You should realize that *structured programming is related to the stepwise refinement process in top-down design.* The billing problem illustrated in Figure E.2 on page 499 begins with a sequence structure and successively builds into the design additional sequence, loop, and decision structures. This approach to designing programs is often called **top-down structured programming.** Moreover, the execution of structured programs proceeds from the top down to the bottom; that is, transfers of control to upper parts of the program are not possible (except for the loop structure, of course).

Also note that execution enters each control structure from the top and exits from the bottom, which is clearly evident from the diagrams in Sections 4.1 to 4.3, pages 100–103.

Top-Down Design and the Four-Step Procedure

The four-step procedure first introduced in Chapter 2 and used as the subheadings in Section E.2 of this module also utilizes top-down design ideas. The problem statement in Step 1 is the first level of detail. Once the nature of the problem is fully defined in words, the process can be refined further by working "down" through successive levels of greater detail. The specification of the algorithm through exploded flowcharts or pseudocode in Step 2 is the next level of detail. Step 3, specification of code, is a further refinement of the flowchart/pseudocode versions. Finally, the debugging process in Step 4 is the final level of detail.[3]

Top-Down Testing[4]

Another aspect of top-down design relates to the method of testing or debugging a modular program of the type described in Figure F.1 on page 507. One popular way of implementing **top-down testing** is first to code and test the control module before coding the other modules. In this case "dummy" modules (also called program stubs) are used in place of modules 1–5. For example, these dummy modules might be nothing more than a PRINT statement for tracing execution and an END statement. Once the control module is debugged, we proceed to the next level of detail (modules 1, 2, and 3) and repeat the coding and testing procedure. Now modules 4 and 5 are the dummy modules. Finally, we code and test modules 4 and 5.

Variations on this modular, top-down procedure are common, depending on the programmer and the problem. For example, we could: first, code and test the control module and module 2, with modules 1, 3, 4, and 5 as dummies; second, code and test modules 4 and 5, with modules 1 and 3 remaining as dummies; and third, code and test modules 1 and 3.

---

[3] The description of modules in modular programming (Chapter 9 and Module F) can be incorporated under Step 2.

[4] This subsection requires knowledge of concepts in Chapter 9 and Module F.

Follow-up Exercises

1. Discuss how the process in Figures E.1 and E.2 might explode differently. In other words, can you think of legitimate variations in these explosions that still would be consistent with the program in Figure E.3?

2. An alternative to the explosion scheme in Figure E.2 is to label each task in the first step as 1, 2, . . . , n, where n is the number of tasks in the first step (4 in Figure E.2); thus, in place of Figure E.2 we would write:

   1. Initial tasks
   2. Process order
   3. Concluding tasks
   4. Stop

   Successive refinements then build on this numbering scheme by adding further digits. For example, item 3 is further refined by

   3.1 Ave. order size = cumulative quant. ÷ no. orders
   3.2 PRINT summary data

   Complete this stepwise refinement scheme for the problem illustrated in Figure E.2. Which approach do you prefer?

3. Modify Figure E.3 by using either
   a. three logical IF statements (Section 6.2) or
   b. block IF, ELSE IF, and ELSE statements (Chapter 5) to represent the multiple alternative decision structure for the discount logic. Which approach seems clearest to you?

*4. If your system supports a DO-WHILE statement, modify the program in Figure E.3 accordingly. Which version is preferable and why?

*5. Modify Figure E.3 to include the fact that a given order can include more than one publication. For example, one order might include a quantity of 10 for a first title, 700 for a second title, and 200 for a third title.

6. Define or explain the following.

   top-down design
   stepwise refinement
   top-down structured programming
   top-down testing

Modular
Programming

Another approach to the organization and development of complex programs is modular programming. This approach divides a program into groups of related instructions called modules. Each module within a program typically performs one function related to the overall purpose of the program. For example, in a telephone billing program separate modules might be developed for the following purposes.

1. Data input and error routine
2. Calculation of bills
3. Printing of bills
4. Management report, which includes statistical summaries of billing information—for example, sums, averages, frequency distributions (Exercise 32 in Chapter 9)
5. Bills sorted by ZIP codes (for the purpose of simplifying mailings)

F.1
FUNDAMENTALS

Before presenting an illustration, we first discuss the properties, implementation, and advantages of modular programming.

Properties

In theory there is no general agreement on either the exact meaning of modular programming or the exact definition of a module. For our purposes let's say that **modular programming** decomposes a program into distinct modules, and then let's focus on certain properties of modules. A growing concensus in the field defines the following properties of a **module.**

* This module is best assigned at Section 9.4.

1. *A module has a single entry point and a single exit point.*   In essence a module is like a "black box" that is uniquely activated (entered at a specific point), performs some assigned function, and is uniquely deactivated (exited at a specific point).
2. *A module is "independent" from other modules.*   Essentially this means that we should be able to change or modify a module without affecting other modules. In reality absolute independence may not be achievable in many cases; however, modules should at least exhibit the type of functional independence described in the five modules of the telephone billing example. Independence is further enhanced by certain design considerations. For example, data overlap among modules should be minimized. A module should access memory only to achieve its designated function. In the context of subprograms this means that we should try to minimize the use of common blocks. Independence is also promoted by carefully designing the hierarchical relationships among modules, which we illustrate in the next subsection.
3. *A module is "not too large."*   The industry rule of thumb says that a module should not exceed 50 to 100 lines of code, which is one or two pages of listing. The basic idea here is that the size of a module should not become so unwieldy that the programmer loses "intimacy" (understanding in depth) with this portion of the code. Needless to say, this property is subjective but well-meaning.

Implementation

How can we represent modules within a program? A *control structure* (sequence, decision, or loop) is a good candidate for a module because it can come close to the three properties described earlier. In this case the independence property is the most easily violated whereas the single entry/exit property is exactly adhered to. In effect, a structured program can be decomposed into its separate control structures (building blocks or modules). On the basis of this perspective, control structures are not unlike modules that together make up the whole. Structured programs thus utilize modular programming concepts.

Subprograms are also obvious candidates for modules. In this case the main program, called the **control module,** directs the entire program by calling modules (subprograms) as required.

A **hierarchy chart** is a useful way to express the relationships among modules. This chart is similar in appearance to an organization chart, with each box representing a module. For example, the telephone billing modules might be related as shown in Figure F.1. In this case the control module (main program) not only calls modules (subroutines) 1, 2, and 3 as required but also might perform certain "housekeeping" chores such as documentation (features of programs, definition of variables, and so forth) and initializations.

Notice that module 2 successively calls modules 4 and 5 in Figure F.1. This illustrates **nested subprograms,** where modules 4 and 5 are said to be separately nested within module 2. In the spirit of promoting independence among modules, *no module should call another module at the same or higher level in the hierarchy chart.* Otherwise, the top-down look of the hierarchy chart is compromised, which degrades readability and complicates debugging.

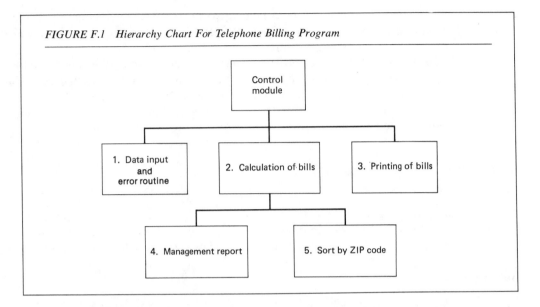

FIGURE F.1   *Hierarchy Chart For Telephone Billing Program*

A hierarchy chart, together with a description of each module, is an early step in good program design. In effect, the hierarchy chart allows the programmer to focus on defining *what* needs to be done before deciding *how* it is to be done.

Advantages

The use of modular programming concepts results in several well-established advantages in the writing of long, complicated programs.

1. *Facilitates design, coding, and debugging process.*   The design process is simplified because a large problem is decomposed into simpler, more manageable tasks. For example, the hierarchy chart gives the "big picture" and shows interrelationships among programming tasks. Moreover, a modular design is consistent with *top-down programming principles* (as described in Module E). As we design pseudocode or main code, we need not refine the subprogram at the point of call. In addition execution of a module proceeds from the top down to the bottom. Debugging is facilitated by the fact that experience now shows that structured, modular, top-down programs are coded with fewer errors than programs that don't utilize these principles. *Top-down testing* (see Section E.3, page 503) also simplifies the debugging process, and the independence of modules better isolates bugs for their diagnosis and correction.

2. *Provides flexibility in a dynamic environment.*   Most applications programs evolve over time, which means that they are changed either to reflect new conditions or to incorporate improvements. The use of modules simplifies this evolutionary process by minimizing the effort required in making changes: that is, modules can be changed, added, or deleted with greater independence and ease. Additionally, **general-purpose** or **utility modules** (for example, statistical and sort routines) can be written for use in more than one program, thereby reducing overall programming

effort. The importance of this advantage is underscored by the fact that as much as 50 percent of entire data processing budgets is allocated to maintaining, modifying, and improving existing programs.[1]

3. *Allows specialization and division of labor.*   Specific modules can be assigned to specific programmers, which can promote greater productivity and more effective programs. For example, programmer A might be better at designing I/O features than programmer B, but the latter is better at designing efficient calculating procedures. The assignment of modules should reflect these specializations.

F.2
AUTOMOBILE RENTAL DECISION PROGRAM

In our next program we illustrate how subroutines can be used to structure a program into modules, whereby each module accomplishes a set of related tasks. Additionally, we illustrate *nested subroutines,* that is, the call of one subroutine by another subroutine.

Statement

Hartz Rent-Some-Wheels, the largest and most progressive car rental company, has decided to improve customer service by designing a computer program that would be used by its agents to quote projected rental fees. Basically, the program computes projected total cost for each of its two rental plans: the daily plan and the weekly plan. A customer who rents a car under the daily plan pays a fixed cost per day plus a charge per mile but does not pay for gasoline expenses. Under the weekly plan, the customer pays both a fixed cost per week and buys gasoline, but does not pay a mileage charge. Which plan is cheaper for a customer depends on factors such as the various costs for the specific type of automobile, the projected number of miles to be driven, the number of days that the car is to be rented, the price of gasoline, the efficiency of the automobile, and (of course) the driving habits of the customer.

Table F.1 defines the required variables and illustrates sample data.

Thus, for the first request the best plan is the weekly plan, since the total cost of the daily plan ($364.00) is greater than the total cost of the weekly plan ($330.00); however, for the second request the daily plan is best ($175.00 versus $224.50).

Before going on, you should confirm these cost calculations. Note that the fixed cost under the weekly plan is incurred for any part of a week; that is, the fixed cost in car group 1 for 12 days is the same as for two weeks, or $290.00 ($2 \times 145$); the fixed cost in car group 2 for five days is the same as for one week, or $199.00.

Note that the first request specifies a car from group 1 (the "compact" group) and the second request specifies a car from group 2 (the "luxury" group). At this time, the company offers cars in only two groups, but plans to add a "superluxury" group in the future. Other rental plans are also under consideration. Finally, the number of days in a

---

[1] Edward Yourdon, *Techniques of Program Structure and Design,* Englewood Cliffs, N.J.: Prentice-Hall, 1975, page 97.

TABLE F.1 *Variable Descriptions and Computations*

			TEST VALUES	
VARIABLE DESCRIPTION	NAME		REQUEST 1	REQUEST 2
a. *Run input*				
Number of customer requests	NUM			
b. *Customer request input*				
Name of customer	NAMEC		TEST 1	TEST 2
Car group	GROUP		1	2
Projected miles of driving	MILES		800	300
Number of days in rental	DAYS		12	5
c. *Car group initializations*				
Daily fixed cost ($/day)	DFC		17.00	20.00
Charge per mile ($/mile)	CPM		0.20	0.25
Weekly fixed cost ($/week)	WFC		145.00	199.00
Price of gasoline ($/gallon)	PRICE		1.50	1.70
Miles per gallon (EPA rating)	MPG		30	20
d. *Output per customer request*				
Total cost of daily plan ($)	COST(1)		364.00	175.00
Total cost of weekly plan ($)	COST(2)		330.00	224.50
Best plan	BEST		WEEKLY	DAILY
e. *Computations*				

$$COST(1) = DFC \cdot DAYS + CPM \cdot MILES$$

$$COST(2) = WFC \cdot \left(int \left[\frac{DAYS - 1}{7} \right] + 1 \right) + \frac{MILES \cdot PRICE}{MPG}$$

$$Minimum\ cost = \min_{i} COST\ (i)$$

rental is limited to 90. Rentals for more than 90 days are treated as leases under a leasing plan not considered by this program.

Algorithm

The primary programming tasks are divided into the eight modules described in Table F.2. The hierarchy chart in Figure F.2 clearly shows the relationships described in Table F.2. Note that subroutines DAILY, WEEKLY, and MINVAL are each nested within subroutine PLANS.

Figure F.3 illustrates the pseudocode for these eight modules. Note how the design is upward-compatible for (easily accommodates) new car groups within subroutine CARDAT: Each new car group simply represents a new case in the CASE structure. The design of the algorithm also facilitates the subsequent addition of new rental plans: We simply nest new modules within module 4 (PLANS).

TABLE F.2   *Description of Modules*

MODULE	DESCRIPTION
1	Main program inputs number of customer requests and processes these requests by iteratively calling modules 2, 3, 4, and 5.
2	Subroutine INPUT reads the data for a specific customer request (see part b in Table F.1) and tests for maximum limit on days in rental.
3	Subroutine CARDAT initializes data for the given car group (group 1 or group 2 as in part c of Table F.1).
4	Subroutine PLANS calls modules 6 and 7, stores results in the vector COST, calls module 8, and determines the name of the best rental plan.
5	Subroutine OUTPUT prints the name of the customer, the name and cost of each rental plan, and the name of the best rental plan.
6	Subroutine DAILY calculates the total cost of the daily plan.
7	Subroutine WEEKLY calculates the total cost of the weekly plan.
8	Subroutine MINVAL determines the minimum total cost plan by finding the smallest element in COST.

Code

The program beginning on page 512 reflects the algorithm in Figure F.3. As you read through the program and relate it to the algorithm, you should note the following.

1. The design of any module requires decisions regarding its
   a. *Purpose within the overall program.* What activities is this module to perform?
   b. *Specific needs or requirements.* Exactly what data are to be input by the module and/or passed to the module from some other module?
   c. *Specific results.* Exactly what data are to be output by the module and/or returned to the calling program?

FIGURE F.2   *Hierarchy Chart for Automobile Rental Decision Program*

```
Start main program
   READ NUM
   DO WHILE requests need processing
      CALL INPUT
      CALL CARDAT
      CALL PLANS
      CALL OUTPUT
   END DO
   Stop
End main program
```
a. Module 1

```
Start subroutine CARDAT
   IF group no. < 1 or > max THEN
      Set group no. to error code
   END IF
   CASE START group no.
      CASE 1
         Initialize car group 1 data
      CASE 2
         Initialize car group 2 data
      CASE wrong group
         PRINT error message
         STOP
   END CASE
   Return
End subroutine CARDAT
```
c. Module 3

```
Start subroutine OUTPUT
   PRINT NAMEC
   DO WHILE plans need processing
      PRINT element in NAMEP,COST
   END DO
   PRINT name of best plan
   Return
End subroutine OUTPUT
```
e. Module 5

```
Start subroutine WEEKLY
   Calculate no. weeks in rental
   Calculate total cost weekly plan
   Return
End subroutine WEEKLY
```

g. Module 7

```
Start subroutine INPUT
   READ customer request data
   IF no. days > limit THEN
      PRINT error message
      STOP
   END IF
   Return
End subroutine INPUT
```
b. Module 2

```
Start subroutine PLANS
   Initialize NOP
   Initialize NAMEP
   CALL DAILY
   CALL WEEKLY
   CALL MINVAL
   Assign name of best plan
   Return
End subroutine PLANS
```

d. Module 4

```
Start subroutine DAILY
   Calculate total cost daily plan
   Return
End subroutine DAILY
```

f. Module 6

```
Start subroutine MINVAL
   Initialize min. value
   DO WHILE plans need processing
      IF element < min. value THEN
         Update min. value
         Update associated subscript
            expression value

      END IF
   END DO
   Return
End subroutine MINVAL
```
h. Module 8

2. Pay attention to style, particularly documentation, as programs become more complex. Look at the car rental program and note that
   a. Modules are identified and summarized at the beginning of the program.
   b. The beginning and end of each module are clearly visible.
   c. Within each module we document its purpose, needs, and results, and describe the names relevant to this module (if not described previously).
   d. As a matter of style in the argument lists, we first list items that are to be passed and then list items that are to be returned. For example, in the argument list of subroutine PLANS, the items MILES, DAYS, DFC, CPM, WFC, PRICE, and MPG are "passed" to the module (which coincide with its described "needs") and the items NOP, NAMEP, COST, and BEST are "returned" from the module (which coincide with its described "results").

3. It pays to double-check actual and dummy argument lists for agreement with respect to number, type, and kind, as mismatches here are common sources of error. Don't forget to type explicitly names in argument lists and COMMON statement lists.

4. Module 8 (MINVAL) illustrates the use of a general-purpose (utility) module for finding the location and value of the minimum-valued element in a vector. This same module can be used exactly as is by any other program or module that has the same need for a minimum value.

```
*************** AUTOMOBILE RENTAL DECISION PROGRAM ***************
*
*
*             PROGRAM COMPUTES AND PRINTS THE TOTAL COST OF ALTERNA-
*             TIVE RENTAL PLANS AND PRINTS THE NAME OF THE LOWEST
*             COST PLAN
*
*             MODULES IN PROGRAM:
*                 1.  MAIN PROGRAM---------ESTABLISHES PROCESSING LOOP AND
*                                          REPEATEDLY CALLS MODULES 2,3,4,5
*                 2.  SUBROUTINE INPUT----READS CUSTOMER REQUEST DATA AND
*                                          PERFORMS ERROR CHECK
*                 3.  SUBROUTINE CARDAT---INITIALIZES CAR-GROUP DATA AND
*                                          PERFORMS ERROR CHECK
*                 4.  SUBROUTINE PLANS----DETERMINES NAME OF BEST RENTAL
*                                          PLAN BY CALLING MODULES 6,7,8
*                 5.  SUBROUTINE OUTPUT---PRINTS CUSTOMER NAME, NAME AND
*                                          COST OF EACH PLAN, AND NAME OF
*                                          BEST PLAN
*                 6.  SUBROUTINE DAILY----CALCULATES COST OF DAILY PLAN
*                 7.  SUBROUTINE WEEKLY---CALCULATES COST OF WEEKLY PLAN
*                 8.  SUBROUTINE MINVAL---UTILITY TO FIND MINIMUM-VALUED
*                                          ELEMENT IN VECTOR
*
*
*************** BEGIN MODULE 1:   CONTROL MODULE ****************
*
*             PURPOSE--PROCESSES CUSTOMER REQUESTS BY ITERATIVELY
*                       CALLING MODULES 2,3,4,5
*             NEEDS-----INPUTS NUM
*             RESULTS--NONE
```

```
*             KEY--------NUM    = NUMBER OF CUSTOMER REQUESTS
*                        NAMEC  = NAME OF CUSTOMER
*                        GROUP  = CAR GROUP NUMBER
*                        MILES  = PROJECTED MILES OF DRIVING
*                        DAYS   = NUMBER OF DAYS IN RENTAL
*                        DFC    = DAILY FIXED COST ($/DAY)
*                        CPM    = CHARGE PER MILE ($/MILE)
*                        WFC    = WEEKLY FIXED COST ($/WEEK)
*                        PRICE  = PRICE OF GASOLINE ($/GALLON)
*                        MPG    = MILES PER GALLON (EPA RATING)
*                        NOP    = NUMBER OF RENTAL PLANS (=2)
*                        NAMEP  = VECTOR THAT STORES NAME OF EACH
*                                 PLAN:  1=DAILY, 2=WEEKLY
*                        COST   = VECTOR THAT STORES TOTAL COST OF
*                                 EACH PLAN:  1=DAILY, 2=WEEKLY
*                        BEST   = NAME OF BEST PLAN
*
*----------------------------------------------------------------
*
      CHARACTER NAMEC*20,NAMEP(6)*10,BEST*10
      INTEGER   NUM,GROUP,MILES,DAYS,NOP
      REAL      DFC,CPM,WFC,PRICE,MPG,COST(6)
*
*----------------------------------------------------------------
*
      READ *,NUM
*
*----------------------------------------------------------------
*
      DO 50 J=1,NUM
        CALL INPUT (NAMEC,GROUP,MILES,DAYS)
        CALL CARDAT(GROUP,DFC,CPM,WFC,PRICE,MPG)
        CALL PLANS (MILES,DAYS,DFC,CPM,WFC,PRICE,MPG,
     1              NOP,NAMEP,COST,BEST)
        CALL OUTPUT(NAMEC,NOP,NAMEP,COST,BEST)
   50 CONTINUE
*
*----------------------------------------------------------------
*
      END
*
********************** END MODULE 1 ***********************
*
*
********************** BEGIN MODULE 2 *********************
*
      SUBROUTINE INPUT (NAMEC,GROUP,MILES,DAYS)
*
*         PURPOSE---READS CUSTOMER REQUEST DATA AND TESTS INPUT
*                   LIMIT ON DAYS.  ERROR MESSAGE PRINTED AND
*                   PROCESSING STOPS IF LIMIT EXCEEDED
*         NEEDS-----INPUTS NAMEC, GROUP, MILES, DAYS
*         RESULTS---RETURNS NAMEC, GROUP, MILES, DAYS TO MODULE 1
*         KEY-------DLIMIT = LIMIT ON DAYS (=90)
*                   SEE MODULE 1 FOR OTHER NAMES
*
*----------------------------------------------------------------
*
      CHARACTER NAMEC*(*)
      INTEGER   GROUP,MILES,DAYS,DLIMIT
*
*----------------------------------------------------------------
*
```

```
        DATA DLIMIT /90/
*
*-------------------------------------------------------------------
*
        READ *,NAMEC,GROUP,MILES,DAYS
*
*-------------------------------------------------------------------
*
        IF (DAYS .GT. DLIMIT) THEN
          PRINT *, NAMEC
          PRINT *,'NUMBER OF DAYS IN RENTAL EXCEEDS',DLIMIT
          PRINT *,'TRY OUR LEASING PLAN...'
          PRINT *,'IT''S AN OFFER YOU CAN''T REFUSE.'
          STOP
        END IF
*
*-------------------------------------------------------------------
*
        END
*
************************* END MODULE 2 ************************
*
*
************************* BEGIN MODULE 3 ************************
*
        SUBROUTINE CARDAT (GROUP,DFC,CPM,WFC,PRICE,MPG)
*
*          PURPOSE--INITIALIZES CAR-GROUP DATA;  IF WRONG GROUP,
*                   ERROR MESSAGE PRINTED AND PROCESSING STOPS
*          NEEDS-----RECEIVES GROUP FROM MODULE 1
*          RESULTS--RETURNS DFC, CPM, WFC, PRICE, MPG TO MODULE 1
*          KEY-------NOG   = NUMBER OF CAR-GROUP CATEGORIES (=2)
*                    SEE MODULE 1 FOR OTHER NAMES
*
*-------------------------------------------------------------------
*
        INTEGER GROUP,NOG
        REAL    DFC,CPM,WFC,PRICE,MPG
*
*-------------------------------------------------------------------
*
        DATA NOG /2/
*
*-------------------------------------------------------------------
*
        IF (GROUP .LT. 1 .OR.  GROUP .GT. NOG) GROUP = NOG + 1
*
*-------------------------------------------------------------------
*
*       BEGIN CASE
*
          GO TO (100,200,300) GROUP
*
*         CASE 1
*
  100     DFC   =  17.00
          CPM   =   0.20
          WFC   = 145.00
```

```
              PRICE  =    1.50
              MPG    =   30.00
              GO TO 400
*
*         CASE 2
*
  200       DFC    =   20.00
              CPM    =    0.25
              WFC    =  199.00
              PRICE  =    1.70
              MPG    =   20.00
              GO TO 400
*
*         CASE WRONG GROUP
*
  300       PRINT *,'GROUP NUMBER INCORRECT.'
              STOP
*
*       END CASE
*
  400 CONTINUE
*
*----------------------------------------------------------------
*
       END
*
************************** END MODULE 3 **************************
*
*
*
************************** BEGIN MODULE 4 **************************
*
       SUBROUTINE PLANS (MILES,DAYS,DFC,CPM,WFC,PRICE,MPG,
      1                  NOP,NAMEP,COST,BEST)
*
*          PURPOSE---INITIALIZES NOP AND NAMEP, CALLS MODULES 6
*                    AND 7, STORES RESULTS IN VECTOR COST, CALLS
*                    MODULE 8, AND DETERMINES NAME OF BEST PLAN
*          NEEDS-----RECEIVES MILES, DAYS, DFC, CPM, WFC, PRICE,
*                    MPG FROM MODULE 1
*          RESULTS---RETURNS NOP, NAMEP, COST, BEST TO MODULE 1
*          KEY-------MINJ  = ELEMENT IN COST STORING MIN VALUE
*                    MINX  = MINIMUM VALUE IN COST
*                    SEE MODULE 1 FOR OTHER NAMES
*
*----------------------------------------------------------------
*
       CHARACTER BEST*(*),NAMEP(*)*(*)
       INTEGER   MILES,DAYS,NOP,MINJ
       REAL      DFC,CPM,WFC,PRICE,MPG,COST(*),MINX
*
*----------------------------------------------------------------
*
       NOP = 2
       NAMEP(1) = 'DAILY'
       NAMEP(2) = 'WEEKLY'
*
*----------------------------------------------------------------
*
       CALL DAILY (MILES,DAYS,DFC,CPM,COST(1))
       CALL WEEKLY(MILES,DAYS,WFC,PRICE,MPG,COST(2))
       CALL MINVAL(NOP,COST,MINJ,MINX)
```

```
*
*----------------------------------------------------------------------
*
      BEST = NAMEP(MINJ)
*
*----------------------------------------------------------------------
*
      END
*
*************************** END MODULE 4 ***************************
*
*
*************************** BEGIN MODULE 5 ***************************
*
      SUBROUTINE OUTPUT (NAMEC,NOP,NAMEP,COST,BEST)
*
*         PURPOSE--PRINTS ALL OUTPUT, EXCEPT ERROR MESSAGES
*         NEEDS----RECEIVES NAMEC, NOP, NAMEP, COST, BEST FROM
*                    MODULE 1
*         RESULTS--PRINTS NAMEC, NAMEP, COST, BEST
*         KEY------SEE MODULE 1
*
*----------------------------------------------------------------------
*
      INTEGER   NOP
      REAL      COST(NOP)
      CHARACTER NAMEC*(*),NAMEP(NOP)*(*),BEST*(*)
*
*----------------------------------------------------------------------
*
      PRINT 10,NAMEC
      DO 5 J=1,NOP
        PRINT 20,NAMEP(J),COST(J)
    5 CONTINUE
      PRINT 30,BEST
      RETURN
*
*----------------------------------------------------------------------
*
   10 FORMAT(////'0','RENTAL COSTS FOR ',A/
     1          '0','RENTAL PLAN   PROJECTED COST'/
     2          ' ',28('-')/)
   20 FORMAT(' ',A,7X,'$',F8.2)
   30 FORMAT(' ',28('-')/
     1       '0','THE BEST PLAN IS ',A//)
*
*----------------------------------------------------------------------
*
      END
*
*************************** END MODULE 5 ***************************
*
*
```

```
*
*********************** BEGIN MODULE 6 ***********************
*
      SUBROUTINE DAILY (MILES,DAYS,DFC,CPM,TCDP)
*
*          PURPOSE---CALCULATES TOTAL COST OF DAILY PLAN
*          NEEDS------RECEIVES MILES, DAYS, DFC, CPM FROM MODULE 4
*          RESULTS---RETURNS TCDP TO MODULE 4
*          KEY--------TCDP  = TOTAL COST OF DAILY PLAN
*                     SEE MODULE 1 FOR OTHER NAMES
*
*----------------------------------------------------------------
*
      INTEGER MILES,DAYS
      REAL    DFC,CPM,TCDP
*
*----------------------------------------------------------------
*
      TCDP = DFC*REAL(DAYS) + CPM*REAL(MILES)
*
*----------------------------------------------------------------
*
      END
*
*********************** END MODULE 6 ***********************
*
*
*********************** BEGIN MODULE 7 ***********************
*
      SUBROUTINE WEEKLY (MILES,DAYS,WFC,PRICE,MPG,TCWP)
*
*          PURPOSE---CALCULATES TOTAL COST OF WEEKLY PLAN
*          NEEDS------RECEIVES MILES, DAYS, WFC, PRICE, MPG FROM
*                     MODULE 4
*          RESULTS---RETURNS TCWP TO MODULE 4
*          KEY--------TCWP  = TOTAL COST OF WEEKLY PLAN
*                     WEEKS = NUMBER OF WEEKS IN RENTAL
*                     SEE MODULE 1 FOR OTHER NAMES
*
*----------------------------------------------------------------
*
      INTEGER MILES,DAYS,WEEKS
      REAL    WFC,PRICE,MPG,TCWP
*
*----------------------------------------------------------------
*
      WEEKS = (DAYS - 1)/7 + 1
      TCWP  = WFC*REAL(WEEKS) + REAL(MILES)*PRICE/MPG
*
*----------------------------------------------------------------
*
      END
*
*********************** END MODULE 7 ***********************
*
*
*********************** BEGIN MODULE 8 ***********************
*
      SUBROUTINE MINVAL (N,X,MINJ,MINX)
*
*          PURPOSE---UTILITY THAT FINDS MIN VALUE IN VECTOR AND
*                    CORRESPONDING SUBSCRIPT EXPRESSION VALUE
```

```
*              NEEDS----RECEIVES N, X FROM CALLING PROGRAM
*              RESULTS--RETURNS MINJ AND MINX TO CALLING PROGRAM
*              KEY-------N     = NUMBER OF ELEMENTS IN VECTOR
*                        X     = VECTOR
*                        MINJ  = SUBSCRIPT EXPRESSION VALUE CORRES
*                                PONDING TO ELEMENT WITH MIN VALUE
*                        MINX  = MINIMUM VALUE IN X
*
*----------------------------------------------------------------
*
      INTEGER N,MINJ
      REAL    X(N),MINX
*
*----------------------------------------------------------------
*
      MINX = 1.E30
      DO 10 J=1,N
        IF (X(J) .LT. MINX) THEN
          MINX = X(J)
          MINJ = J
        END IF
   10 CONTINUE
*
*----------------------------------------------------------------
*
      END
```

Debugging

Sample Input

```
3
'TEST1',1,800,12
'TEST2',2,300,5
'TEST3',1,1200,91
```

Sample Output

```
RENTAL COSTS FOR TEST1

RENTAL PLAN    PROJECTED COST
-----------------------------------

DAILY            $   364.00
WEEKLY           $   330.00
-----------------------------------

THE BEST PLAN IS WEEKLY



RENTAL COSTS FOR TEST2

RENTAL PLAN    PROJECTED COST
-----------------------------------

DAILY            $   175.00
WEEKLY           $   224.50
-----------------------------------

THE BEST PLAN IS DAILY



TEST3
NUMBER OF DAYS IN RENTAL EXCEEDS         90
TRY OUR LEASING PLAN...
IT'S AN OFFER YOU CAN'T REFUSE.
```

Follow-up Exercises

1. Answer the following with respect to the algorithm/program.
   a. What happens if 100 is input for DAYS?
   b. What happens if 4 is input for GROUP?
   c. Why do you think we use a RETURN statement in subroutine OUTPUT?
   d. In module 7 why do we subtract the constant 1 in the calculation for WEEKS? Could we subtract some other value?
   e. In module 4, among others, why do we use a parenthetical asterisk in the CHARACTER and REAL statements?
   f. Roleplay the computer and indicate the exact output for the following input data.

       ```
       3
       'B. HOLLY',2,1000,21
       'R. VALENS',0,500,7
       'F. DOMINO',1,5000,100
       ```

2. Modify the program to print the following.

   ⋮

   THE BEST PLAN IS cccccccccc WITH A PROJECTED COST OF $xxxxx.xx
                                 Character field   Real field

3. Modify the program to print the following at the end of the run.

   ⋮

   THE SUM OF COST MINIMA IS $xxxxxxx.xx
                                        Real field

4. Describe the changes needed in the program to add a "superluxury" car group.

5. Modify the program to make all relevant names global through common blocks. Discuss pros and cons of this approach.

*6. **CASE Statements Enhancement.** If your implementation supports the CASE structure, modify the program accordingly.

7. Eliminate modules DAILY and WEEKLY and include the cost calculations in PLANS. Discuss pros and cons of this design.

8. Which subroutines are naturally covertible to function subprograms? Make the necessary changes to do so. Which approach do you prefer in this case?

9. Modify subroutine CARDAT as follows.
   a. Declare a 7×5 real array PAR that stores the five car-group parameters for up to seven car-group categories. Input this array at the beginning of the run just before the input of NUM. CARDAT is called as before, checks the group number, and assigns values to DFC, CPM, WFC, PRICE, and MPG by using PAR. What's the advantage of this approach with respect to car-group parameter updates?
   *b. Use array PAR as in part a but eliminate the use of module CARDAT altogether. Incorporate the error check on GROUP in module INPUT. Which version do you prefer and why?

10. Modify the program as follows.
     a. If the limit on DAYS is exceeded, print the error message and go on to the next customer's request.
     b. If the input item for GROUP is in error, print the error message and go on to the next customer's request.
     Roleplay the data in Exercise 1.

*11. Modify the program to add module SORT, so that the output shows the plans in ascending order of cost. Eliminate the use of module MINVAL.

*12. Modify the program to include subroutine HYBRID, which calculates the total cost of the following new plan: The customer pays an extra $1.95 over the daily fixed cost ($18.95 per day for car group 1 data), pays for gasoline expenses, and pays a charge of 35 cents for each mile over an allotment given by 100 times the number of days in the rental.

13. Modify the program as follows.
     *a. Eliminate subroutine OUTPUT. Modify subroutine PLANS to print the customer's name, table headings, and best plan. Modify subroutines DAILY and WEEKLY to print their respective plan names and costs.
     **b. *Sensitivity analysis.* Elaborate the output in subroutines DAILY and WEEKLY as follows: Each subroutine has a nested DO-loop, where MILES1 (projected miles of driving) is the DO-variable of the outer loop and MPG1 (miles per gallon) is the DO-variable of the inner loop. Use the same data as in the example, except let MILES1 run from 50 to 150 percent of MILES in steps of 10 percent of MILES (all expressed as integers) and let MPG1 run from MPG − 4 to MPG + 4 in steps of 1. (*Note:* DAILY need not have a loop for MPG1.) The purpose of each nested loop is to print a cost table, where rows represent projected miles of driving and columns represent miles per gallon. Do a nice job of labeling your output. Conduct four runs so as to vary the number of days in the rental as follows: 2, 5, 12, 23. What factors favor each plan?

14. Define or explain the following.

     modular programming
     module
     control module
     hierarchy chart
     nested subprograms
     general purpose or utility modules

On Designing Better Programs

By now you have studied and put into practice the key features of the FORTRAN language. As you probably realize, the act of writing good programs for solving specific problems requires not only knowledge of FORTRAN and an understanding of the problem, but also practice, skill, judgment, thought, and art. This module reviews principles and techniques *used throughout this text* to improve the design of programs.

G.1
MOTIVATION

Most computer applications in business, government, education, and other organizations require complex programs. For instance, an application such as a company's payroll may include dozens of programs with hundreds of instructions within each program.

A programmer's ability to organize and develop a program becomes considerably more important as the complexity of the task increases. Unfortunately, many applications programs have been planned inadequately, which makes them difficult to follow, hard to debug, and time consuming to modify. The result is low software productivity and higher costs. In fact, *industry estimates now place the total cost of software above the total cost of hardware.*

In an effort to control software costs, guidelines and new techniques have evolved for improving the design of programs. In all cases their aim is to produce readable, well-organized, easy-to-debug, reliable, easy-to-update programs. The remainder of this module summarizes a number of these guidelines and techniques, many of which you will recognize. The page references within boxes in the margin indicate earlier discussions of these issues.

* This module can be assigned anytime after Chapter 9 and Modules E and F. Except for some material in Sections G.2 and G.7, this module could be assigned as early as Chapter 6.

G.2
STRUCTURED, TOP-DOWN, MODULAR PROGRAMMING

See pages 99–105

We should strictly use *control structures—sequence structure, decision structure* (IF-THEN, IF-THEN-ELSE, nested, multiple alternative, CASE), *loop structure* (DO WHILE, DO UNTIL)—to enhance the readability and reliability of programs.

See pages 184–185

We should *use GO TO statements sparingly,* to reduce the likelihoods of inadvertently writing *un*structured programs and of transferring control to wrong statements. Ideally, it would be best to eliminate the use of the GO TO statement altogether by having statements that directly reflect all control structures. For example, the block IF, ELSE, and END IF statements exactly reproduce the IF-THEN-ELSE structure. Perhaps the next revision of the ANSI FORTRAN standard will include specific statements for CASE, DO-WHILE, and DO-UNTIL structures.

See pages 495–504

When designing complex programs, we can reduce development and maintenance costs by incorporating *top-down* principles. *Stepwise refinement* at the pseudocode/flowchart stage facilitates development of the algorithm. Remember that structured and top-down programming are related. Each control structure has a single entry point at the top and a single exit point at the bottom. Thus structured programs execute from the top down to the bottom.

See pages 505–520

We should break elaborate programs down into *modules* to enhance program development, improve readability, facilitate subsequent modifications, and allow specialization and division of labor. Also note that structured programming utilizes modular programming principles, since control structures can be viewed as modules which together make up the whole. Moreover, modular programming is consistent with top-down design, since the process of designing a hierarchy chart, followed by a simplified main program, followed by more refined modules all suggest a top-down process.

G.3
DOCUMENTATION

Programs that are *actually* used for scientific and data processing should be carefully documented. Documentation can be subdivided into two broad categories, depending on the intended reading audience: documentation to be read by programming staff, and documentation to be read by users of the program.

Staff Documentation

Staff documentation is to be read by other programming staff for the purpose of updating the program either to incorporate improvements and new circumstances or to debug newly found errors. Staff documentation is found in two places: within the program and in a manual separate from the program. **Program documentation** appears within the program as comment lines. Generally, it includes

See pages 500, 512

1. A block of comments at the beginning of the program that usually includes the title of the program, version and/or date of the program, name of programmer, a short narrative summary describing the scope and purpose of the program, a description

of input/output, the names and definitions of key variables, and other useful information such as subprograms used and specific system-dependent features.

See pages 501, 513

2. A liberal use of comment lines within the program that identify major tasks, explain logic, describe modules, and otherwise improve the appearance and facilitate the readability of the program.

A **program manual** is a piece of documentation separate from the program itself, but meant for use by maintainers of programs within the programing staff. This piece of documentation is essentially an elaboration of problem statement, algorithm, and debugging (Steps 1, 2, and 4 in our four-step procedure). It often includes a description of the problem, input/output, definitions of key variables, descriptions of modules, the calling sequence of modules and/or a *hierarchy chart,* a *system flowchart* (see Figure 11.4), a *program flowchart* or *pseudocode* (ideally showing *stepwise refinement*), test data used to debug the program together with sample runs of the program, and other useful features such as system-dependent peculiarities and suggestions for incorporating additional tasks.

See pages 419, 510

User Documentation

User documentation is to be read by users of the program. It is typically called a **user's manual** or **user's guide,** and is meant to acquaint users with the features and implementation of a specific program. A user's manual typically includes a description of the program's features, ways to implement these features, instructions on the preparation of input data, sample computer runs showing input/output, actions to take in the event of program error messages, and other useful features such as formulas, references, and (particularly in scientific, mathematical, and statistical applications) descriptions, assumptions, and limitations of underlying theory.[1]

G.4
OTHER STYLE CONSIDERATIONS

Readability is further enhanced by incorporating the following familiar features.

1. *Indentation.*   Indentation of loop bodies and decision blocks clearly identifies loop and decision logic.
2. *Selecting names.*   The effective selection of symbolic names requires paying attention to meaning and data structure. If names reflect what they represent, a programmer can follow programming logic without constantly referring to a key that defines names. For example, the variable COST has more meaning than the variable X if we wish to represent the cost of an item. The data structure that the variable is to represent also should be considered. For example, a table of numbers is better represented by a two-dimensional array name than by a series of one-dimensional array names or by an ''army'' of unsubscripted variable names. In other situations, the use of array names promotes shorter programs.

---

[1] Next time you're at the computer center look up a user's manual for any of the widely available statistical computer packages such as BMD, SPSS, and SAS.

3. *Type statements.*   Use type statements to declare the type of all key symbolic names in your program, particularly since we recommend suppression of the I-N typing convention when it interferes with the selection of meaningful names. For example, if we wish to store the mean of a set of numbers as a real value, then we prefer the variable name MEAN together with the explicit typing

    REAL MEAN

    to the implicitly typed XMEAN. Minor variables in the program such as I and J can be typed implicitly according to the I-N convention.

4. *Statement numbers.*   Select statement numbers with care, in a manner that promotes readability and reduces the likelihood of error. For example, a round number such as 100 is more readable than a number such as 57. Use sequential numbering by consistently increasing the magnitude of numbers as you go down the program, since we tend to associate higher numbers with statements further down in the listing. Finally, associate groups of numbers with logical segments in the program. For example, FORMAT statements might be numbered sequentially in the 900s. By the way, the use of statement numbers is a source of bugs that it is best to avoid. Statements in FORTRAN that directly reflect control structures altogether eliminate the use of direct transfers to labeled statements.

See pages 438, 501

5. *Nonexecutable statements.*   Enhance the readability of executable code by placing nonexecutable statements "out of harm's way." For example, place all FORMAT statements in a group either at the beginning or end of a program. And design comment lines to make them easily distinguishable from executable code—by liberal vertical spacing, underlining, or indenting to the right of executable code.

See page 438

6. *Output formats.*   Take care in designing output formats. Keep the user in mind by providing labeled, unambiguous, attractive, concise, informative output.

7. *Block programming.*   Break programs down into identifiable *blocks* of code, where each program block performs a set of related tasks. For example, the program in Module E is broken down into the following *program blocks.*

See pages 71, 500–501

Declarations
Initializations
Initial order read-in
Order processing
Concluding tasks

In effect, *block programming* is a simple implementation of *modular programming.*

G.5
GENERAL VERSUS SPECIFIC PROGRAMS

A general program requires less upkeep than a specific program for applications where certain data items may change. To illustrate what we mean, consider a program that calculates the mean (average) of a set of numbers or items. A general program would treat the number of items as an input variable (say, N), whereas a specific program would calculate the mean for, say, 100 items. Thus the general program can calculate the mean for any number of items whereas the specific program is restricted to 100 items. If the number of items is likely to change from one application to the next, then the general program is best since the specific program would require frequent changes.

Some estimates now place the cost of designing and maintaining software above the cost of purchasing or leasing hardware. Thus *it is good programming practice to treat all required data as either variables or symbolic names of constants rather than as constants.* This practice reduces the cost of updating programs in situations where data may change.

See page 500
For example, the program in Section E.2 generalizes the discount and surcharge parameters (constants) by specifying the variables BREAK1, BREAK2, DISC1, DISC2, and SURC and initializing them through DATA statements. Should these values change in the future, it would be easier to update DATA statements than to update statements in the discount and surcharge decision structures. Alternatively, we could have input the values through a READ statement, or assigned values through assignment statements, or used a PARAMETER statement.

See pages 38, 311
The PARAMETER statement defines symbolic names of constants rather than variable names. From a style point of view, this approach is preferred to the use of a DATA statement, as it directly treats parameters as constants. Moreover, the use of symbolic names of constants has the added advantage of reducing upkeep when updating many array declarations.

See pages 120–121
If parameters change often in a program (for example, weekly or daily as in international currency exchange rates), then rather than initializing through assignment, DATA, or PARAMETER statements, it might be best to read in parameters as input data.

G.6
TRANSPORTABILITY

A **transportable program** is one that can be used by different installations with little or no modification. If a particular program either is to be run on different computer systems or the system on which it is to be used is likely to change in the future (a virtual certainty), then software costs will be reduced if the program is designed with transportability in mind. Thus, as much as possible, transportable programs maximize the use of statements in the ANSI standard and simultaneously minimize the use of statements based on local enhancements.

G.7
EFFICIENCY

A good program, in addition to being readable, is one that accomplishes its objective efficiently with respect to computer time and storage. Here are a few suggestions to help you write more efficient programs.

1. *Integer arithmetic is faster than real arithmetic.* On some machines 25 or more integer computations can be performed in the time it takes to execute one real computation. Thus use integer expressions in place of real expressions whenever the expected value of the expression is a whole number. Moreover, if a numeric

variable is to store strictly whole numbers and is not used in real arithmetic expressions (except as an exponent), it should be typed as an integer variable. For example, the variable TIME should be typed integer in the expression RATE**TIME if TIME is to store whole-number values, since this avoids time-consuming logarithmic routines for evaluating real expressions raised to real powers. Finally, avoid the indiscriminate use of mixed-type arithmetic expressions, since the required type conversions are costly.

2. *Intrinsic functions are usually faster and more accurate than using alternative codes.* For example,

```
B = SQRT(A)
```

is preferred to

```
B = A**.5
```

and

```
C = ABS(X − Ẏ)
```

is preferred to

```
C = X − Y
IF(C .LT. 0.)THEN
    C = − C
END IF
```

3. *When possible avoid unnecessary loops since time is spent in incrementing and testing loop termination.* For example, the segment

```
SUM = 0.
DO 100 I = 1,N
    READ *,VOLUME(I)
    SUM = SUM + VOLUME(I)
100 CONTINUE
```

is more efficient than

```
DO 100 I = 1,N
    READ *,VOLUME(I)
100 CONTINUE
    SUM = 0.
    DO 150 I = 1,N
    SUM = SUM + VOLUME(I)
150 CONTINUE
```

4. *Constant computations should be removed from within a loop.* For example, the segment

```
DO 200 J = 1,M
    READ *,X(J)
    Y(J) = (A + B**2/C)*X(J)
200 CONTINUE
```

unnecessarily recomputes the expression (A + B**2/C) a total of M − 1 times more than needed. A more efficient design is

```
D = A + B**2/C
DO 200 J = 1,M
    READ *,X(J)
    Y(J) = D*X(J)
200 CONTINUE
```

5. *Use ELSE IF statements for extensive multiple alternative decision structures* rather than a sequence of block IF statements, since the former avoids the unnecessary testing of conditions once the "true" condition is found. Similarly, use the CASE structure in place of nested IF-THEN-ELSE structures where appropriate.

See pages 158–161, 188

6. *To save space in primary memory,* avoid unnecessarily large arrays and use COMMON and EQUIVALENCE statements to share space among large arrays. These statements, however, must be applied with care as their use increases the likelihood of errors.

See pages 343–353

7. *A poorly designed algorithm is a primary factor that contributes to excessive computer time.* This factor is so important in certain applications that professionals in applied mathematics, statistics, and computer science have devoted extensive research efforts to improving the time efficiency of many algorithms. More often than not, this involves the development of an entirely new algorithm that achieves the same end result. For example, sorting algorithms have been developed that significantly reduce the cost of sorting by traditional methods such as the bubble sort described in Chapter 7.

In general programmers should *look for economies that make a significant difference, but without degrading the readability of the program.* In commercial applications, an esoteric, obscure code that saves CPU time is generally not preferred to a less efficient version that is readable, understandable, and easy to change.

G.8
DEBUGGING

The process of testing and correcting programs for errors is time-consuming and costly. In fact, an industry rule of thumb states that *debugging consumes on the average between one-third and one-half of the total project time.* The incorporation of good design principles as discussed in this module, the use of classic debugging techniques as discussed in Section 3.3, and familiarity with common programming errors as discussed at the end of Chapters 3 through 11 all serve to promote an efficient debugging phase. In particular, great care must be exercised in designing test data to ensure that all branches, combinations of branches, and boundary values of data are tested, as discussed in Section 5.5.

See page 88

See page 175

If you're working with lengthy modules, then top-down testing as discussed in Section E.3 is a good aid for breaking a large debugging job down into smaller components.

See page 503

G.9
RELIABILITY

A program should reliably operate as intended once it is implemented on an ongoing basis. A process called **defensive programming** means that the design of a program should anticipate "unforeseen circumstances" as much as feasible. For example, good commercial programs anticipate errors in the input data through programmed error routines, as emphasized in Chapters 5, 6, and 9. Generally, programmers should anticipate what might go wrong operationally, thereby designing their programs to react accordingly. At the same time the temptation to make programs "overreliable" must be tempered by judgments regarding the benefits versus the costs. In other words, reliable program design requires assessments regarding the nature of potential difficulties, their likelihood of occurrence, the costs of incorporating programmed reactions to these difficulties, and the benefits (or cost savings) realized when these difficulties are avoided through program design.

See pages 160, 165, 193, 513–515

G.10
MANAGEMENT PRACTICES

It can be argued that "all the tools, techniques, and subprograms (utilities) needed to properly develop the successful advanced commercial applications in the 1980s are already here today—everything except the discipline, the training, and the understanding." Generally, there "is a combination of poor technical training, lack of leadership at the top management level, strong resistance to change, and short-term fire fighting instead of long-term planning."[2]

In effect, problems regarding poor productivity (that is, costly software development, implementation, and maintenance) are attributable to personnel and their management, not to the state of the art in the technology. Among the solutions are the following.

1. Massive training and retraining of programming personnel with respect to improving the design of programs
2. Recognition that programming is more a science than an art by requiring, for example, the use of top-down design, structured programming, and modular programming
3. Encouragement of group processes in programming, which brings individuals together as a group for specific tasks such as evaluating program design and code[3]
4. Improvement in the organizational structure of a data processing department (a) by unambiguously specifying relationships among managers, chief programmers, programmers, project directors, and group leaders, and (b) by clarifying the relationships that relate personnel to projects and functions[4]

---

[2] Martin A. Goetz, "Advanced Commercial Applications in the '80s," *DATAMATION*, Vol. 25, No. 13, November 1979, pp. 104–108.
[3] See, for example, Ben Shneiderman, *Software Psychology: Human Factors in Computer and Information Systems*, Cambridge, Mass.: Winthrop Publishers, 1980.
[4] See, for example, Edward B. Daly, "Organizing for Successful Software Development," *DATAMATION*, Vol. 25, No. 14, December 1979, pp. 106–120.

Follow-up Exercises

1. Define or explain the following.

   staff documentation
   program documentation
   program manual
   user documentation
   user's manual (guide)
   transportable program
   defensive programming

2. What are the three key characteristics of modules? Do control structures have the same characteristics?
3. How is modular programming related to top-down design?
4. How is modular programming related to structured programming?
5. How is top-down design related to structured programming?
*6. Select one of the programs that you have completed and perform and answer the following.
   a. Improve its program documentation.
   b. Improve its style both in ways discussed in Sections G.2 and G.4 and through possible ideas of your own.
   c. Improve its generality.
   d. Can you improve its efficiency without degrading its readability?
   e. Incorporate defensive programming, specify modules, and draw a hierarchy chart. Include the description of modules within the program documentation. In describing a module, state its data needs, its purpose, and its results. Explode the pseudocode before writing code.
   f. Select a thorough set of test data to debug your program.
7. **Electric Bill Revisited. The following poorly written program is a technically correct solution to Exercise 31 in Chapter 9 on page 361.

```
       K = 0
     2 K = K + 1
       IF (K.GT.5)GO TO 38
       READ *,A,B,C,D,E,F,G,H,I,J,K,L
       IF(C.NE.1)GO TO 13
       M1 = B*.0525 - A*.0525
       N1 = 1.01*D - 1.01*E + M1
       PRINT *,F,G,H,I
       PRINT *,J,K,L
       PRINT *,'FROM SEP 19 TO OCT 18, 1981'
       PRINT *,B - A,M1,D - E,(D - E)*0.1,D - E + (D - E)*0.01 + M1
       GO TO 2
    13 IF(C.NE.2) GO TO 10
       M2 = B*0.0485 - A*0.0485
       N2 = 1.01*D - 1.01*E + M2
       PRINT *,F,G,H,I
       PRINT *,J,K,L
       PRINT *,'FROM SEP 19 TO OCT 18, 1981'
```

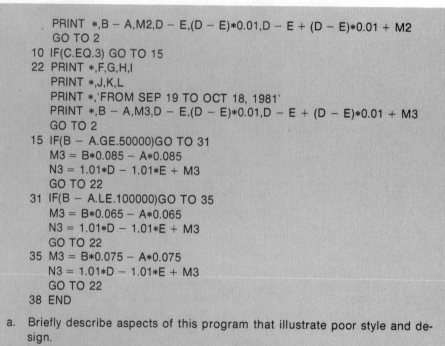

```
      PRINT *,B - A,M2,D - E,(D - E)*0.01,D - E + (D - E)*0.01 + M2
      GO TO 2
   10 IF(C.EQ.3) GO TO 15
   22 PRINT *,F,G,H,I
      PRINT *,J,K,L
      PRINT *,'FROM SEP 19 TO OCT 18, 1981'
      PRINT *,B - A,M3,D - E,(D - E)*0.01,D - E + (D - E)*0.01 + M3
      GO TO 2
   15 IF(B - A.GE.50000)GO TO 31
      M3 = B*0.085 - A*0.085
      N3 = 1.01*D - 1.01*E + M3
      GO TO 22
   31 IF(B - A.LE.100000)GO TO 35
      M3 = B*0.065 - A*0.065
      N3 = 1.01*D - 1.01*E + M3
      GO TO 22
   35 M3 = B*0.075 - A*0.075
      N3 = 1.01*D - 1.01*E + M3
      GO TO 22
   38 END
```

a. Briefly describe aspects of this program that illustrate poor style and design.

b. Flowchart this program. Kind of a nightmare, isn't it?

c. Redesign the program (from scratch) by following the steps described in Exercise 6.

d. Incorporate part b of Exercise 31 in Chapter 9.

Answers to Selected Follow-up Exercises

1. (a) Acceptable. (b) Acceptable. (c) Unacceptable; begins with number. (d) Acceptable. (e) Unacceptable; special character. (f) Acceptable. (g) Unacceptable; special character. (h) Unacceptable; more than six characters. (i) Acceptable. (j) Unacceptable; special character, more than six characters. (k) Acceptable. (l) Acceptable.

2. (a) Unacceptable constant; comma. (b) Integer constant. (c) Real constant. (d) Real constant. (e) Real constant. (f) Real constant. (g) Real constant. (h) Unacceptable; comma. (i) Integer constant.

3. (a) Real variable. (b) Integer variable. (c) Integer variable. (d) Real variable. (e) Real variable. (f) Integer variable. (g) Unacceptable variable. (h) Real variable.

4. (a) $-6.142E15$ or $-0.6142E16$ etc. (b) $-6142E12$ or $-0.6142E16$ etc. (c) $0.7E-9$ or $7E-10$ etc. (d) $7E-10$ etc. (e) $0.167E125$ *Note:* May exceed maximum value of the machine.

5. (a) 123×10^4 (b) 0.123×10^7 or 123×10^4
   (c) 456×10^{-8} (d) 0.456×10^{-5} or 456×10^{-8}

6. (a) Missing right apostrophe.
   (b) Quotation marks not part of the ANSI standard; use apostrophes.
   (c) Use double apostrophes for apostrophes embedded within outer apostrophes: 'YOU''RE OK, I''M OK'. Otherwise the computer can't distinguish between legitimate apostrophes within the character constant and the outer apostrophes that enclose the character constant. The double apostrophe is internally represented (stored) correctly as a single apostrophe.

7. LATHE and PRESS must be typed explicitly before the PARAMETER statement; the INTEGER statement must precede executable statements; the length specification on FOIL cannot precede FOIL as shown. The following is correct.

   ```
   CHARACTER FOIL*15,LEVEL*5
   INTEGER   I,PRESS
   REAL      LATHE,COST,X
   PARAMETER (LATHE = 4.178,PRESS = 7042)
   .
   .
   .
   END
   ```

(Continued on the next page.)

Note: We could also write the CHARACTER statement as

    CHARACTER*15 FOIL,LEVEL*5

In this case the length specification immediately following the key word CHARACTER specifies the length of each variable in the list not having its own length specification.

8. CHARACTER NAME*20
   NAME = 'CLARK S. KENT'

If we had used

    CHARACTER NAME*15

there would be only two trailing blanks in storage instead of seven. If the length specification had been ten, storage would appear as follows.

9. **(a)** Variable must appear to left of the equal sign.

   A = B + C

   (b) Two operation symbols next to each other.
   (c) Variable must appear to left of the equal sign.

   AGE = 5.

   (d) Incorrect two assignments. Change to

   X = 5.3
   Y = 5.3

   (e) Not permissible to raise a negative value to a decimal (real) power since the computer attempts to take the logarithm of a negative number.
   (f) OK to raise a negative integer value to an integer power since integer arithmetic in this example is performed as follows.

   J*J*J

10.

11.

12.

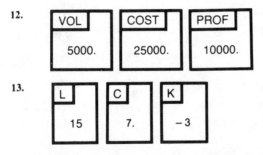

13.

14. **(a)** STRESS − 100. **(b)** 5*K − 1 **(c)** 7.**Q **(d)** Undefined; execution error because base is negative. See Example 2.5. **(e)** OK. Not considered mixed type. Y**2 computes faster than Y**2., since the latter uses logs.

15. **(a)** Integer result; 0 **(b)** Real result; 0.4 **(c)** Integer result; will cause integer overflow. **(d)** Real result; 8E120 (May cause real overflow.) **(e)** Double-precision result; 8D120 (Note that the expression here is mixed type, since A is double precision and B is real; the pairwise computation upgrades the result to double precision, although the magnitude of the result may cause overflow.)

16. No, since expressions appear only to the right of the equal sign. The computer stores 15. in CREDIT and copies the integer value in MONEY for storage in COST as a real value.

17. 85.77778

18. **(a)** 116.   **(d)** 8.5   **(g)** 10.5   **(j)** 2.
    (b) 28.   **(e)** 4.   **(h)** 4.   **(k)** 5.4
    (c) 28.   **(f)** 4.   **(i)** 4.

19. **(a)** X**(I + 1)   **(e)** SQRT(7. − X)
    (b) X**I + 1   **(f)** (Y − 5./(X*T) + 2.)*(−4.)
    (c) (X − A)**2/(S + 4.)   **(g)** (Y − 3.**(X − 1.) + 2.)**5
    (d) SQRT((X − A)**2/(S + 4.))   **(h)** INT((X − Y)/100.)*(1./(A + B))

20. **(a)** 1.875 **(b)** 0.2625 **(c)** 16 **(d)** 24

21.
```
    INTEGER ID,CREDIT,TUIT,BALDUE
     :
     :

    CREDIT = 15
    TUIT = CREDIT*100
    BALDUE = TUIT + 250
     :
     :

    END
```

Output values for these variables now expressed as integers.
Advantages: Improves visual look of output; integer arithmetic faster, more precise.
Disadvantages: Can't process fractional credits; financial data can't be expressed to the nearest cent.

24. **(a)** PRINT *,(−6.5 + SQRT(6.5**2 − 4.*(−3.4)*50.))/(2.*(−3.4))
    (b) PRINT *,100.56**2,100.56**3,SQRT(100.56),100.56**(1./3.)
    (c) PRINT *,LOG10(100.),10.**LOG(100.)
    (d) PRINT *,EXP(6.21461),LOG(50.),LOG(EXP(6.21461))

25. For an IBM 370 system,

WRITE(6,*)CREDIT,TUIT,BALDUE

27. For an IBM 370 system,

READ(5,*)NAME,ID,CREDIT

28. Otherwise the program has to be changed each time we wish to process different values.

29.
```
PRINCIPAL = 1000.0
RATE      = 0.015
QUARTERS = 2
AMOUNT    = 1030.225
```

Note: Systems will differ with respect to the exact form and placement of numeric values.

30.
```
CHARACTER NAME*20,STREET*20,CSZ*30

INTEGER    NUM
REAL       PRIN,RATE,ACCUM

READ *,NAME,STREET,CSZ

READ *,PRIN,RATE,NUM
ACCUM = PRIN*(1. + RATE)**NUM

PRINT *,NAME
PRINT *,STREET
PRINT *,CSZ
PRINT *,' '
PRINT *,' '
   .
   .
   .
END
```

CHAPTER 3

1. (a) Confirmed by student.

(b)
```
CHARACTER NAME*15,ID*11
INTEGER    CPC,FEES,CREDIT,TUIT,BALDUE
   .
   .
   .
END
```

See answer to Exercise 21 in Chapter 2 for advantages and disadvantages of typing integer.

2. Confirmed by student.

3. (a) $1061.36 (b) $1346.82

4. (a) Confirmed by student.
    (b) Expected output:

PRIN	RATE	NUM	ACCUM
1000.	.015	4	1061.36
1000.	.015	8	1126.49
1000.	.015	12	1195.60
1000.	.015	16	1268.96
1000.	.015	20	1346.82
1000.	.015	40	1813.95

5. System dependent.
6. System dependent.

CHAPTER 4

1. (a)

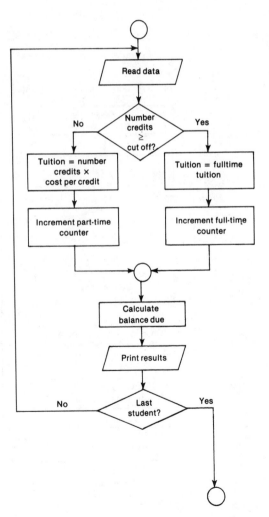

(b) DO WHILE students are to be processed
    READ data
    IF no. credits ≥ cut off THEN
        Tuition = full-time tuition
        Increment full-time counter
    ELSE
        Tuition = no. credits × cost per credit
        Increment part-time counter
    END IF
    Calculate balance due
    PRINT results
    END DO

DO UNTIL no students need be processed
    READ data
    ⋮ } Same body as DO WHILE

    Calculate balance due
    PRINT results
    END DO

2. **(a)** 1
      2
      3
      4 } 7 iterations
      5
      6
      7

(b) 1
    4 } 3 iterations
    7

(c) 2
    3
    4 } 4 iterations
    5

(d) 5} 1 iteration

(e) Inactive loop. Nothing gets printed.

3.

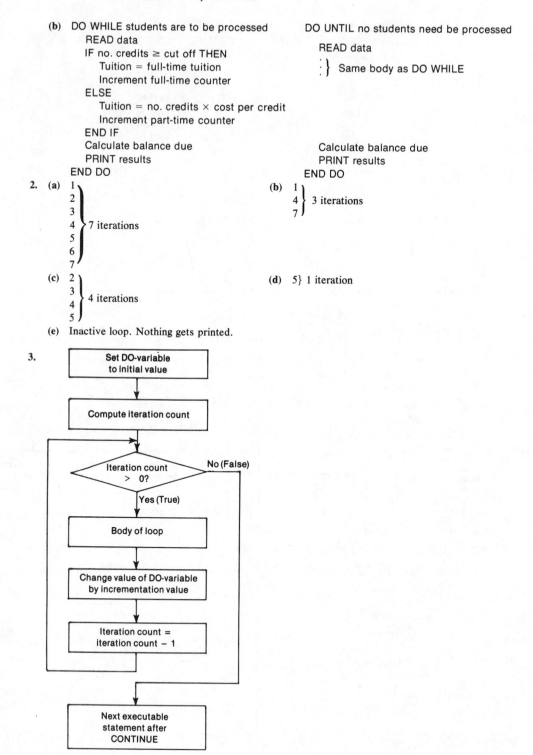

TABLE 4.1

VALUE OF DO-VARIABLE (KOUNT)	ITERATION COUNT	ITERATION COUNT > 0? (EXECUTE BODY?)	ITERATION
1	5	Yes	1
2	4	Yes	2
3	3	Yes	3
4	2	Yes	4
5	1	Yes	5
6	0	No	Loop exit

TABLE 4.2

VALUE OF DO-VARIABLE (KOUNT)	ITERATION COUNT	ITERATION COUNT > 0? (EXECUTE BODY?)	ITERATION
3	4	Yes	1
5	3	Yes	2
7	2	Yes	3
9	1	Yes	4
11	0	No	Loop exit

4. No changes in program. In the input data replace the 3 by 4562 and add the remaining data lines for all students.

5. These column headings would be printed just before each output line in the table, which would be a logic error.

```
STUDENT NAME    IDENTIFICATION    BALANCE DUE
W. MITTY        266612463         1750.0
STUDENT NAME    IDENTIFICATION    BALANCE DUE
X. MITTY        266612464         2100.0
etc.
```

6. Syntactically no, but it's not good programming style to align the body left and to place the statement number at the last statement in the body.

7. The use of constants instead of variables as DO parameters makes the program inflexible with respect to changing the interest rates. It's preferable (cheaper) to make changes in the input data than to make changes in the program itself.

8. (a)

PRIN	NUM	R1	R2	R3	RATE	ACCUM
1000.	20	0.010	0.02	0.002	0.010	1220.172
					0.012	1269.412
					0.014	1320.560
					0.016	1373.638
					0.018	1428.738
					0.020	1485.932

(b) Only the table heading

RATE   ACCUM. FUNDS

would be printed. The loop remains inactive, since $R1 > R2$ and $R3 > 0$. If we make this line of input

$$0.02,\ 0.01,\ -0.002$$

then the output table shows rates in decreasing order of magnitude.

10.

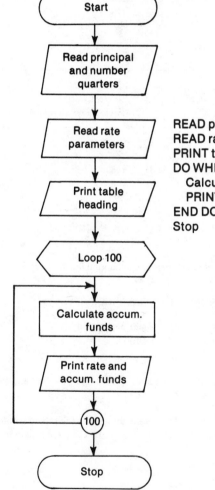

READ principal, no. quarters
READ rate parameters
PRINT table heading
DO WHILE rate remains
    Calculate accum. funds
    PRINT rate, accum. funds
END DO
Stop

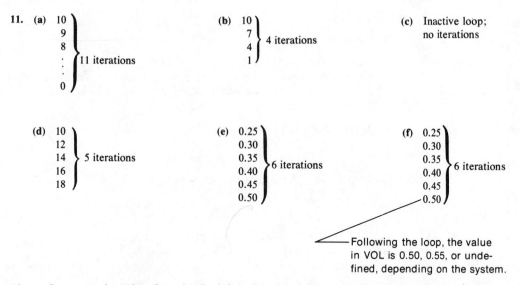

11. **(a)** 10
9
8
·
·
·
0
} 11 iterations

(b) 10
7
4
1
} 4 iterations

(c) Inactive loop;
no iterations

(d) 10
12
14
16
18
} 5 iterations

(e) 0.25
0.30
0.35
0.40
0.45
0.50
} 6 iterations

(f) 0.25
0.30
0.35
0.40
0.45
0.50
} 6 iterations

Following the loop, the value in VOL is 0.50, 0.55, or unde-fined, depending on the system.

12. **(a)** Incrementation value of zero implies infinite loop, i.e., infinite iteration count according to footnote 4. **(b)** Missing statement number in both DO and CONTINUE statements. **(c)** Must have negative incrementation value; otherwise an inactive loop. **(d)** DO-variable redefined within loop.

13. **(a)** No. **(b)** Yes. First time through BALDUE is undefined, which can result in an execution error, depending on the system. If the system initializes BALDUE to zero, then SUM would not include the last student's balance owed.

14.

STUDENT NAME	IDENTIFICATION	BALANCE DUE
W. MITTY	266612463	1750.0
TOTAL BALANCE DUE: $ 1750.0		
X. MITTY	266612464	2100.0
TOTAL BALANCE DUE: $ 3850.0		
Y. MITTY	266612465	1450.0
TOTAL BALANCE DUE: $ 5300.0		

15. ·
·
·

```
REAL CPC,FEES,CREDIT,TUIT,BALDUE,SUM,AVE
```
·
·
·

```
PRINT *,'TOTAL BALANCE DUE: $',SUM
AVE = SUM/N
PRINT *,'AVERAGE BALANCE DUE:$',AVE
END
```

17. **(a)** Eliminate SUM = 0. and place the following just after the REAL statement.

```
DATA SUM/0./
```

Note: Caution must be exercised when using DATA statements to initialize sums. (We're getting ahead of ourselves, but see Exercise 20.)

(b) Replace the statement

```
READ *,PRIN,NUM
```

with the statement

    DATA PRIN,NUM/1000.,20/

and eliminate the first line of input data.

Note: Using a DATA statement is probably not a good idea here, since different values in PRIN and NUM are likely to be used for different runs. It's easier to change input data than DATA statements.

(c) DATA A,B,C,D,E,F,R1,R2,R3 /5*0.0,100.0,3*'YES'/

or

DATA A,B,C,D,E /5*0.0/, F/100.0/, R1,R2,R3 /3*'YES'/
etc.

18.

M	N	I	J	SCORE	SUM	AVE
2	3	1	1	90.	90.	—
			2	70.	160.	—
			3	80.	240.	—
			—	80.	240.	80.0
	2	2	1	50.	50.	80.0
			2	90.	140.	80.0
			—	90.	140.	70.0

Note 1: The placement of the snapshot does not record the fact that SUM gets initialized to zero before it contains 90.0 and again gets initialized to zero between values of 240.0 and 50.0.

Note 2: AVE is undefined in the first three rows of the table; J may become undefined after the J-loop gets exhausted, depending on the system.

19.

Input	Output
3	
2	
20.	MEAN SCORE FOR SECTION 1 = 55.0
90.	
4	MEAN SCORE FOR SECTION 2 = 72.5
40.	
100.	MEAN SCORE FOR SECTION 3 = 70.0
70.	
80.	
3	
60.	
80.	
70.	

20. SUM would not get reinitialized to zero before each new section is to be processed, since the DATA statement is nonexecutable. The mean for the second section would be calculated incorrectly as 190.0. In general, we don't recommend using a DATA statement to initialize sums, unless you're sure that the sums need not be reinitialized.

24.

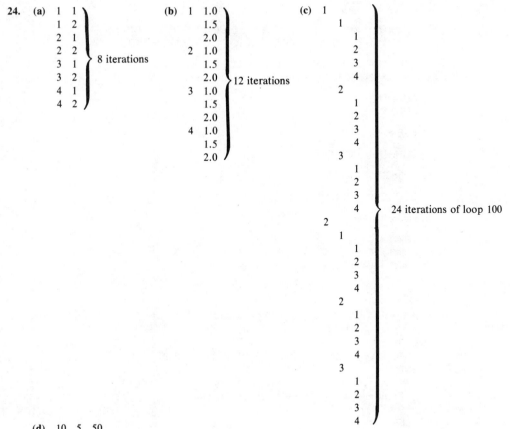

(a)
```
1  1
1  2
2  1
2  2      } 8 iterations
3  1
3  2
4  1
4  2
```

(b)
```
1  1.0
   1.5
   2.0
2  1.0
   1.5
   2.0      } 12 iterations
3  1.0
   1.5
   2.0
4  1.0
   1.5
   2.0
```

(c) — 24 iterations of loop 100

(d)   10   5   50
       11   6

Note: The DO-variables I and K may be undefined following the loop, depending on the system.

25.   (a) DO-loops overlap. (b) Syntactically OK, but best to indent loop bodies.

CHAPTER 5

1.   (a) True. (b) False. (c) True. (d) True. (e) False. (f) True.

2.

```
IF sales > $5000 THEN
    Bonus = $100
ELSE
    Bonus = $0
END IF
```

```
IF (SALES .GT. 5000) THEN
    BONUS = 100
ELSE
    BONUS = 0
END IF
```

3. Define

>   COUNTN = NO. SALES PEOPLE WHO DON'T RECEIVE BONUS
>   COUNTY = NO. SALES PEOPLE WHO DO RECEIVE BONUS

Add COUNTN and COUNTY to list of INTEGER statement.
Between the INTEGER statement and loop 50 insert

>   COUNTN = 0
>   COUNTY = 0

In the IF-block insert

>   COUNTN = COUNTN + 1

and in the ELSE-block insert

>   COUNTY = COUNTY + 1

After loop 50 insert

>   PRINT *,'b'
>   PRINT *,'NON-BONUS COUNT = ',COUNTN
>   PRINT *,'BONUS COUNT   = ',COUNTY

5. (a)

```
IF credits ≥ 12 THEN          IF (CREDIT .GE. 12.) THEN
     Tuition = $1200               TUIT = 1200.
ELSE                          ELSE
     Tuition = $100 × credits      TUIT = 100.*CREDIT
END IF                        END IF
```

(b)

```
IF fixed cost + var. cost < revenue THEN         IF (FIXED + VAR .LT. REV) THEN
     Profit = revenue − (fixed + variable costs)      PROF = REV − FIXED − VAR
     PRINT profit                                     PRINT *, 'PROFIT = ',PROF
ELSE                                             ELSE
     Loss = fixed cost + variable cost − revenue      LOSS = FIXED + VAR − REV
     PRINT loss                                       PRINT *, 'LOSS = ',LOSS
END IF                                           END IF
```

(c)

```
IF balance < $50 THEN               IF (BAL .LT. 50.) THEN
     Payment = balance                   PAYS = BAL
ELSE                                ELSE
     Payment = $50 + 10% (balance − $50)     PAYS = 50. + .10*(BAL − 50.)
END IF                              END IF
```

(d)

```
IF sex = male THEN            IF (SEX .EQ. 'MALE') THEN
     PRINT "sex = male"            PRINT *, 'SEX = MALE'
ELSE                         ELSE
     PRINT "sex = female"         PRINT *, 'SEX = FEMALE'
END IF                       END IF
```

6. (a)

```
IF (CUME .GT. 25900.) THEN
     FICA = 0.
ELSE
     FICA = .0613*SAL
END IF
```

(b)

```
IF (A*C .LT. B/D) THEN
     C = D/E
     F = F − 1.
ELSE
     X = A + B
     D = B − A
END IF
```

7.

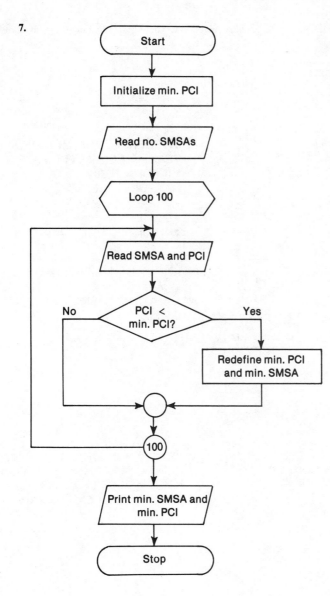

N	I	SMSA	PCI	MINPCI	MINSMS
5	1	147	5165.	5165.	147
	2	56	7860.	5165.	147
	3	75	6350.	5165.	147
	4	41	4293.	4293.	41
	5	105	5415.	4293.	41

8. Modify the flowchart in the preceding exercise as follows, where corresponding program segments are shown to the right.

```
INTEGER N, SMSA, MINSMS, MAXSMS
REAL     PCI, MINPCI, MAXPCI
MINPCI = 1E30
MAXPCI = -1E30
   ·
   ·
   ·
```

```
IF (PCI .GT. MAXPCI) THEN
    MAXPCI  = PCI
    MAXSMS = SMSA
END IF
   ·
   ·
   ·
```

```
PRINT *, 'MIN SMSA = ', MINSMS
PRINT *, 'MAX SMSA = ', MAXSMS
PRINT *, 'MIN PCI = ', MINPCI
PRINT *, 'MAX PCI = ', MAXPCI
```

9. (a)
```
IF age ≥ 65 THEN
    No. dependents = no. dependents + 1
END IF
```
```
IF (AGE .GE. 65) THEN
    NOD = NOD + 1
END IF
```

(b)
```
IF part name = wrench THEN
    PRINT quantity on hand
END IF
```
```
IF (PART .EQ. 'WRENCH') THEN
    PRINT *,QOH
END IF
```

10.
```
IF (M .EQ. N) THEN
    I =  I + 3
    J =  J + 2
    K = K + 1
END IF
```

11. (a)

```
IF (SALES .GT. 5000) THEN
    BONUS = 100
    IF (TRAVEL .GE. 600) THEN
        BONUS = 0
    END IF
ELSE
    BONUS = 0
END IF
```

(b)

```
BONUS = 0
IF (SALES .GT. 5000) THEN
    IF (TRAVEL .LT. 600) THEN
        BONUS = 100
    END IF
END IF
```

The original version has the "cleanest" logic but the longest code. The logic in part (b) is reasonably clear, and it has the shortest code. We prefer the original version.

14.
```
IF (ZONE .LE. 3) THEN
    COST = 1.71
ELSE
  IF (ZONE .EQ. 4) THEN
      COST = 1.81
  ELSE
    IF (ZONE .EQ. 5) THEN
        COST = 1.88
    ELSE
      IF (ZONE .EQ. 6) THEN
          COST = 1.97
      ELSE
        IF (ZONE .EQ. 7) THEN
            COST = 2.06
        ELSE
          IF (ZONE .EQ. 8) THEN
              COST = 2.25
          ELSE
              PRINT *,'POSTAL ZONE',ZONE,'IS INVALID'
          END IF
        END IF
      END IF
    END IF
  END IF
END IF
```

As in Example 5.7, this approach is CPU time efficient, since we exit from the structure as soon as a true condition is found. Unlike Example 5.7, it's a visual nightmare. Example 5.7 is preferred to other approaches by all criteria: clarity, code efficiency, CPU time efficiency. *Note:* The code in this exercise exactly reproduces the structure in Figure 5.3. Thus the structure in Figure 5.3 is a proper control structure, since it's equivalent to k nested IF-THEN-ELSE structures.

15. If 9 is in ZONE, then the error message for an invalid code is printed, as it should be. If 0 is in ZONE, then 1.71 is stored in COST; however, in reality, codes less than 1 are also invalid.

(a) Replace the first IF-THEN structure by

```
IF (ZONE .EQ. 1) THEN
    COST = 1.71
END IF
IF (ZONE .EQ. 2) THEN
    COST = 1.71
END IF
IF (ZONE .EQ. 3) THEN
    COST = 1.71
END IF
```

(b) Replace the first two lines by

```
IF (ZONE .EQ. 1) THEN
    COST = 1.71
ELSE IF (ZONE .EQ. 2) THEN
    COST = 1.71
ELSE IF (ZONE .EQ. 3) THEN
    COST = 1.71
```

19. **(a)**
```
IF (A .GT. 10) THEN
    IF (B .GT. 20) THEN
        R = 'T2'
    END IF
ELSE
    R = 'F1'
END IF
```

(b)
```
IF (A .GT. 10) THEN
    IF (B .GT. 20) THEN
        R = 'T2'
    ELSE
        R = 'F2'
    END IF
END IF
```

(c)
```
IF (A .GT. 10) THEN
    R = 'T1'
    IF (B .GT. 20) THEN
        R = 'T2'
    ELSE
        R = 'F2'
    END IF
ELSE
    R = 'F1'
END IF
```

(d)
```
IF (A .GT. 10) THEN
    IF (B .GT. 20) THEN
        R = 'T2'
    ELSE
        R = 'F2'
    END IF
ELSE
    IF (C .GT. 30) THEN
        R = 'T3'
    ELSE
        R = 'F3'
    END IF
END IF
```

20.

	EXERCISE				
PART	19a	19b	19c	19d	19e
a	F1	NULL	F1	F3	NULL
b	NULL	F2	F2	F2	F2
c	T2	T2	T2	T2	F3

22. (a) No. (b) Yes, since (false).OR.(true) gives true. (c) No, since (false).AND.(true).AND.(true) is followed by (false).AND.(true), which is false. (d) Yes, since (true).AND.(true) gives true.

25. **(a)**
```
LOGICAL REQ
    :
    :
REQ = SALES .GT. 5000 .AND. TRAVEL .LT. 600
IF (REQ) THEN
    BONUS = 100
ELSE
    BONUS = 0
END IF
    :
    :
```

(b)
```
LOGICAL COND1,COND2
    :
    :
COND1 = MAJOR .EQ. 'ECN'
COND2 = MAJOR .EQ. 'MTH'
IF (COND1 .OR. COND2) THEN
    PRINT *,NAME,MAJOR
END IF
```

26. **(a)**

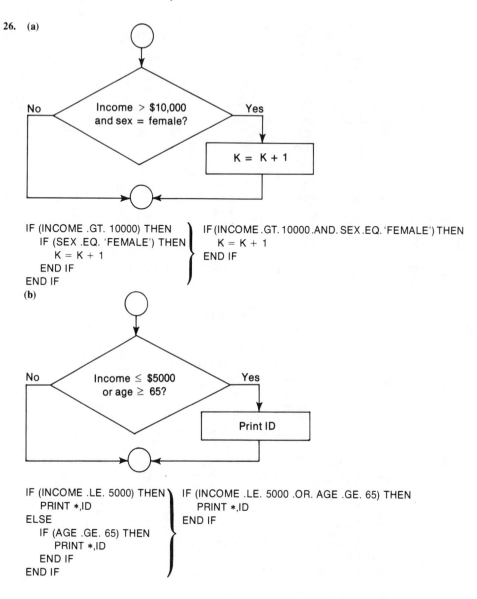

IF (INCOME .GT. 10000) THEN   IF (INCOME .GT. 10000 .AND. SEX .EQ. 'FEMALE') THEN
   IF (SEX .EQ. 'FEMALE') THEN   K = K + 1
      K = K + 1   END IF
   END IF
END IF

(b)

IF (INCOME .LE. 5000) THEN   IF (INCOME .LE. 5000 .OR. AGE .GE. 65) THEN
   PRINT *,ID   PRINT *,ID
ELSE   END IF
   IF (AGE .GE. 65) THEN
      PRINT *,ID
   END IF
END IF

(c)

IF (K .EQ. 1) THEN
  IF (J .EQ. 2) THEN
    IF (L .EQ. 1) THEN
      TUIT = 2000
    ELSE
      TUIT = 3000
    END IF
  END IF
END IF

IF (K .EQ. 1 .AND. J .EQ. 2 .AND. L .EQ. 1) THEN
  TUIT = 2000
END IF
IF (K .EQ. 1 .AND. J .EQ. 2 .AND. L .NE. 1) THEN
  TUIT = 3000
END IF

Alternatively:

IF (K .EQ. 1 .AND. J .EQ. 2) THEN
  IF (L .EQ. 1) THEN
    TUIT = 2000
  ELSE
    TUIT = 3000
  END IF
END IF

CHAPTER 6

1. $-14; 71$

2.

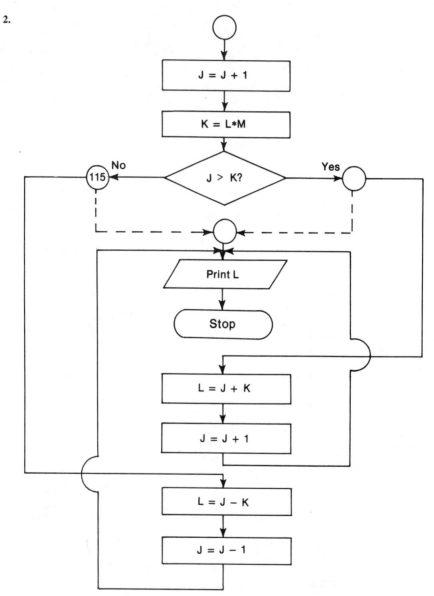

Note how control structures are obscured (is that really an IF-THEN-ELSE structure?) and how "top-down" execution of a program is violated (going back to statement 85 doesn't establish a loop, which is the only legitimate flow reversal).

3.  ```
    J = J + 1
    K = L*M
    IF (J .GT. K) THEN
        L = J + K
        J = J + 1
    ELSE
        L = J - K
        J = J - 1
    END IF
    PRINT *,L
    END
    ```

4. (a) END statement not legitimate here, since it must be the last statement in the program. Could use STOP. (b) Insert SIZE between .AND. and .LT. (c) OK, but take care in using the GO TO statement. (d) Need dots around AND; possible type inconsistency when comparing IN (integer?) and ON (real?). (e) After .OR. must use MAJOR .EQ. 'MTH'

5. In general, logical IF statements are desirable for reflecting IF-THEN structures with only one statement in the IF-block; otherwise GO TO statements must be used, which is undesirable.

    (a)   *Part a*
    ```
            IF (HOURS .GT. 40.) GO TO 20
                REGPAY = HOURS*RATE
                OVRTM = 0.
            GO TO 30
    20      REGPAY = 40.*RATE
            OVRTM = (HOURS - 40.)*RATE*1.5
    30  . . .
        .
        .
    ```

    Part b
    ```
            IF (DIST/TIME .GT. VELCRI) ACCEL = 0.9*ACCEL
            IF (DIST/TIME .LE. VELCRI) ACCEL = 1.02*ACCEL
    ```

    Part c
    ```
            IF (SEXCD .EQ. 1) COUNTF = COUNTF + 1
            IF (SEXCD .NE. 1) COUNTM = COUNTM + 1
    ```
    (b)
    ```
            IF (NAME .NE. 'SMITH') GO TO 50
                PRINT *,'NAME:',NAME
                PRINT *,'PHONE NUMBER:',PHONE
    50  . . .
        .
        .
    ```

    (c)
    ```
            IF (PCI .GE. MINPCI) GO TO 100
                MINPCI = PCI
                MINSMS = SMSA
    100 CONTINUE
    ```

    (d)
    ```
            BONUS = 0
            IF (SALES .GT. 5000 .AND. TRAVEL .LT. 600) BONUS = 100
    ```
    (e)
    ```
            IF (ZONE .LE. 3) COST = 1.71
            IF (ZONE .EQ. 4) COST = 1.81
        .
        .
        .
            IF (ZONE .GT. 8) PRINT *,'POSTAL ZONE',ZONE,'IS INVALID'
    ```
    ```

```
 6.    J = 1
    30 IF (J .GT. N) GO TO 60
          READ *,NAME,ID,CREDIT
          .
          .
          .
          PRINT *,NAME,ID,BALDUE
          J = J + 1
          GO TO 30
    60 END
```

Note that this is exactly what the DO/CONTINUE statements accomplish (except for the reversal of the true/false condition).

7. (a) OK, since it's alright to omit the comma following the right parenthesis in FORTRAN 77. (b) OK, so long as ON is declared integer. (c) Value in **K** is out of range, since it must be between 1 and 5.

8. The error message

    ERROR IN CODE FOR TICKET   4

    gets printed and the output results for moving violations would read as follows:

    MOVING   1   50

```
 9.    IF (ZONE .GT. 8) ZONE = 9
       GO TO (10,10,10,20,30,40,50,60,70) ZONE
    10    COST = 1.71
       GO TO 80
    20    COST = 1.81
       GO TO 80
       .
       .
       .
    70    PRINT *,'POSTAL ZONE',ZONE,'IS INVALID'
    80    . . .
       .
       .
       .
```

This approach is slightly more CPU time efficient, but messy with respect to style and subject to errors because of the use of statement numbers.

12.

COSTC	RATE	YEAR	COSTF
60000.	0.1	1	66000.
		2	72600.
		.	
		.	
		8	128615.4

13. (a) If the system initializes COSTF to zero, we have an infinite loop since zero remains in COSTF; otherwise we get an execution error at statement 10.
    (b) COSTF would always store 66000.0, which gives us an infinite loop.
    (c) The output for YEAR would be one year too high. To initialize YEAR to 1, place the counter for YEAR just before the GO TO statement.

(d) Just before statement 10 use

RATE = 1. + RATE

Then replace the assignment statement for COSTF with

COSTF = COSTF*RATE

Since 1. + RATE remains constant within the loop, we need only calculate it once before the loop instead of repeatedly within the loop.

14.
.
.
.

REAL COSTC,COSTF,RATE,M
READ *,COSTC,RATE,M
.
.
.

10 IF (COSTF .LT. M*COSTC) THEN
.
.
.

15. 10 IF (COSTF .LT. 2.*COSTC .OR. YEAR .LE. 9) THEN

16. **(a)** Insert

READ *,N
DO 20 J = 1,N

just after the REAL statement and

20 CONTINUE

just after the END IF statement.

(b)

Data set	Year when doubling achieved
1	15
2	8
3	5
4	8

Note that the original cost makes no difference as to when there's a doubling. Only the inflation rate makes a difference.

17.
.
.
.

10 IF (COSTF .GE. 2.*COSTC) GO TO 20
.
.
.

    GO TO 10
20 END

Not in the sense that the loop body is executed whenever the condition tests true. The original version is preferable both because the body is executed when the condition is true and because we avoid an extra GO TO statement.

20.

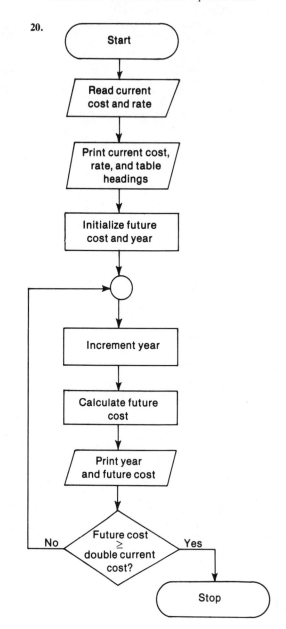

READ current cost, rate
PRINT current cost, rate,
        table headings
Future cost = current cost
Year = 0
DO UNTIL future cost ≥
        twice current cost
  Year = Year + 1
  Future cost = future cost ×
        (1 + rate)
  PRINT year, future cost
END DO
Stop

21. Just after the REAL statement insert

```
READ *,N
DO 50 J = 1,N
```

Just before the END statement insert

```
50  CONTINUE
```

22.   Replace the logical IF and GO TO statements with

```
IF (COSTF .GE. 2.*COSTC) THEN
   STOP
ELSE
   GO TO 10
```

The original approach is simpler.

24.   **(a)**   The trailer record becomes

```
'LRC',0,0
```

Change statement 10 to

```
10 IF (SSN .NE. 0) THEN
```

There should be no danger in using zero as a trailer number since Social Security numbers are never zero.

(b)   Yes, otherwise we get an "out of data" execution error when the READ statement is executed. No, they can be any string value and integer value, respectively, since they're not utilized following the READ statement.

(c)   Statement 10 changes to

```
10 IF (NAME .NE. 'NO MORE DATA') THEN
```

and the trailer record changes to

```
'NO MORE DATA',0,0
```

25.   In the flowchart eliminate the READ at the end of the loop body, return the loop to the READ above the diamond, and change the diamond to "Not end of file?" In the pseudocode, place the first READ just after the DO WHILE, change the DO WHILE to

```
DO WHILE data line remains
```

and eliminate the READ at the end of the loop body.

26.   We would end up processing the trailer record as if it were a salesperson.

27.   Yes, this version processes the data the same way as the original version does. No, strictly speaking, this is not a DO-WHILE or DO-UNTIL structure, since the loop control test is *within* the body of the loop (rather than preceding or succeeding the body). This approach saves an extra READ statement, since the original version in Example 6.6 requires a READ statement before the loop structure and another READ statement as the last statement in the body. We prefer either the original version because it preserves a DO-WHILE structure, or better yet the version in Example 6.7, which gives us one READ statement and a "clean" loop body.

30.   **(a)**   DO-UNTIL.   **(b)**   DO-WHILE.

(c)   Yes for the inner (DO-WHILE) loop, since the body is processed "while" the test is true. No for the outer (DO-UNTIL) loop, since here the body is processed "until" the condition is false rather than true. To make the latter strictly consistent we could replace the last logical IF with

```
IF (FLAG .EQ. 1) STOP
GO TO 50
```

(d)   Eliminate FLAG from the INTEGER statement, eliminate the statement

```
FLAG = 1
```

from blocks 4 and 6, replace

```
FLAG = 0
```

with

STOP

in blocks 3 and 5, and replace the last logical IF with

GO TO 50

The outer loop is not a proper control structure in this case since it does not have an explicit loop control.

31. Because the linear function has opposite signs at points A and B. At point A, X = −4 and to leap to point B we must have STEPX = 11. This gives Y1 = −9 at point A and Y2 = 13 at point B. Statement 75 then tests false (a crossover has been detected), which subsequently puts us in block 6, then back to statement 50. If we were in a leapfrog cycle, we would cycle within the inner loop until J exceeded MAX. To convince yourself, trace through what happens for the function

$$y = -2.25 - 4x + x^2$$

You should confirm that we iterate through the inner loop until J exceeds MAX (we keep cycling between the points $x = -4$ to $x = 7$ to $x = 18$ to $x = 7$ to $x = -4$ to $x = 7$, etc.). Subsequently we enter block 4, which reduces STEPX enough to prevent leapfrogging for the next go around.

32. 50,000 times, as x keeps getting more and more negative and y approaches zero asymptotically. Block 4 successively reduces the value in STEPX by 50 percent. Thus STEPX takes on the values 1, 0.5, 0.25, 0.125, 0.0625, 0.03125, 0.015625, 0.0078125, 0.00390625, 0.001953125, 0.0009765625, 0.0004882812, 0.0002441406, 0.0001220703, 0.0000610351, 0.0000305175, 0.0000152587, and 0.0000076293. When we enter block 3 the outer loop has iterated 18 items, which gives 900,000 iterations (50,000 × 18) to process this function.

CHAPTER 7

1. (a) The array is conceptualized as the (physical) group of memory locations whereas the array name identifies this group by name. In mathematics, the array is the list of items or values.
   (b) The array name depicts or implies the entire array whereas the array element name (i.e., the array name with attached subscript) identifies a specific element of the array.
   (c) The array element suggests a specific (physical) storage location (the box) whereas the array element name gives a name to this storage location (identifies the box by name).
   (d) No distinction in our terminology.
   (e) The subscript is a subscript expression enclosed in parentheses. The subscript expression takes on a value, not the subscript. In mathematics, no distinction is made between these two.
   (f) These are identical when the lower dimension bound is 1 and the upper dimension bound is greater than zero. The general correspondence is given by

   array element i = 1 + value of subscript expression − lower dimension bound

   For example, when the lower dimension bound on DEPOS is −2, a value of 1 for the subscript expression corresponds to array element 4 (fourth storage location) as given by

   $$i = 1 + 1 - (-2) = 4$$

   See the depiction on page 237 to confirm that DEPOS(1) is indeed the fourth storage location. By the way, the ANSI standard calls i the *subscript value*, which further escalates the terminology war (we mercifully avoided this term in the text).

2. Arrays are allocated memory during compilation, not during execution. Values in variables are not available until the execution phase. Note that symbolic names of constants can be used within dimension declarators, provided that the PARAMETER statement precedes the array declarator. For example, the following logic simplifies subsequent changes in array declarations:

```
INTEGER      ITEMS
PARAMETER  (ITEMS = 500)
REAL         A(ITEMS),B(ITEMS + 1),C(− ITEMS:2∗ITEMS)
```

If in the future ITEMS is to take on a value of 2000, then we need only make the one change in the PARAMETER statement.

3. **(a)** Array declarations must precede use of the arrays, so the REAL statement must precede the READ statement. In general, type statements must precede executable statements. K cannot be used as an upper dimension bound in declaring the array X (see Exercise 2). If we wish 50 elements in X, we write

       REAL X(50),T(4 + 3)

(b) M + 10∗N evaluates as 85. Thus the value of the subscript expression in A(85) exceeds the upper dimension bound in the array declarator A(50). We must declare at least 85 elements in A.

(c) Arrays D and E have only ten elements. As soon as J reaches 11, an execution error occurs. Also, we cannot dimension D and E twice, so either eliminate the DIMENSION statement or change the INTEGER statement to INTEGER D, E. E(3) would store 36.

4.

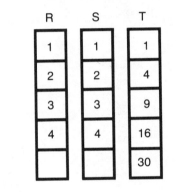

R   S   T

R	S	T
1	1	1
2	2	4
3	3	9
4	4	16
		30

5. **(a)**   INTEGER DEPOS (100), TOT

       .
       .
       .

       DO 10 I = 1,100

       .
       .
       .

       DO 20 I = 1,100

The second program would require 291 new statements. One hundred variables would appear to the right of the equal sign in the calculation of TOT.

(b)   INTEGER DEPOS (500), TOT
       READ ∗,N

       .
       .
       .

       DO 10 I = 1,N

       .
       .
       .

       DO 20 I = 1,N

       .
       .

6.
```
      REAL LOAD (50)
      DO 10 J = 1,50
          READ *,LOAD(J)
   10 CONTINUE
```

7.

1	5	-4
10	4	6
8	1	7
2	10	-8
21	20	1

8.
```
      INTEGER COST(500),SALES(500)      Input Data
      READ *,N                          3
      DO 50 J = 1,N                     40,100
          READ *,COST(J),SALES(J)       20,125
   50 CONTINUE                          75,95
```

9. (a)   1 2 3 4 5 6 7 8 9 ...

——————————
```
   3500
   5000
   4000
```

(b)   Same as part (a).

(c)

(d)

10. (a)   READ *,(X(J),J = 1,8)

(b)   PRINT *,(X(J),J = 1,8)

(c)   READ *,(X(J),J = 1,11,2)

(d)   PRINT *,(A(J),B(J),J = 1,3)

(e)   PRINT *,(A(J),J = 1,3),(B(J),J = 1,5)

(f)   READ *,(X(J),J = 1,3),M,N

(g)   PRINT *,A,(X(J),J = 1,3),B

11. (a)
```
10  20  30  40   5  10  15  20
```
(b)
```
10   5  20  10  30  15  40  20
```
(c)
```
 1  10   5   2  20  10   3  30  15   4  40  20
```

12. (a)   READ *,(SALES(J),J = 1,3)   **(b)**   READ *,(SALES(J),COST(J),J = 1,3)
      READ *,(COST(J),J = 1,3)

13. (a) OK. **(b)** J can't be an input item and a DO-variable, since values of the DO-variable would be redefined. **(c)** OK, as long as P, A, B, C, and D are declared type integer. Generally, DO parameters need not be integer. They must be in this case because they are associated with the subscript expression for array X.

14.
```
             1 2 3 4  5 6 7  8  9 10 11 12 13 14 15 16 17 18 19 20 . . .
```
(a) and (d)   1 0   2 0   3 0   4 0

(b) and (e)   1 0
             2 0
             3 0
             4 0

(c)   1 0   2 0
          3 0   4 0

15. (a)

(b)

(c)

(d) and (e)

17. (a) 10
  1,2,3,4,5,6,7,8
  .1,.2,.3,.4,.5,.6,.7,.8,.9,1.,1.1,1.2,1.3,1.4,1.5

(b) 10,1,2,3,4,5,6,7,8,.1,.2,.3,.4,.5,.6,.7,.8,.9,1.,1.1,1.2,1.3,1.4,1.5

(c)

(d)

(e)

18. Can't use variables as either DO expressions or repeat factors in DATA statements. This would work only if N were the symbolic name of a constant, as defined in a PARAMETER statement.

19. The first approach either gives an execution error, if K is undefined, or stores zero in location TOTAL(0), if the system initializes K to zero. The second approach simply sets the variable (not the array) TOTAL to zero.
  Use either

```
    DO 10 K = 1,10
        TOTAL(K) = 0.
    10 CONTINUE
```

or

```
    DATA TOTAL/10*0./
```

or

```
    DATA (TOTAL(K),K = 1,10)/10*0./
```

20.
```
    SUM = 0.
    DO 10 I = 1,K
        SUM = SUM + REVEN(I)
    10 CONTINUE
```

21.

22. Immediately after the assignment statement for BAL(J) insert:

Or use a
logical IF
statement
{
```
IF (BAL(J) .LT. 0.) THEN
    PRINT *,'ACCT. ,NO. = ',ACCNO(J),'BALANCE = ',BAL(J)
END IF
```

23. **(a)** MONDAY,TUESDAY, . . . , SUNDAY

(b) FRIDAY
THURSDAY
FINISHED

(c) DATA DAY/'MONDAY','TUESDAY','WEDNESDAY','THURSDAY',
*   'FRIDAY','SATURDAY','SUNDAY'/

26. **(a)**
```
      INTEGER LIST(25)
      READ *,N
      DO 10 J = N,1, − 1
         READ *,LIST(J)
   10 CONTINUE
```
(b)
```
      MAXI = −999999
      DO 20 J = 1,N
         IF (LIST(J) .GT. MAXI) THEN
            MAXI = LIST(J)
         END IF
   20 CONTINUE
      PRINT *,MAXI
```
Or use logical IF statement

(c)
```
      DO 30 J = 1,N
         IF (LIST(J) .EQ. 0) THEN
            PRINT *,J
         END IF
   30 CONTINUE
```
Or use logical IF statement

27. **(a)**

SATTOT	COUNT(1)	COUNT(2)	COUNT(3)	COUNT(4)	SUMSAT(1)	SUMSAT(2)	SUMSAT(3)	SUMSAT(4)
—	0	0	0	0	0	0	0	0
1220	0	1	0	0	0	1220	0	0
1400	0	1	1	0	0	1220	1400	0
1170	0	2	1	0	0	2390	1400	0
1150	1	2	1	0	1150	2390	1400	0
1000	1	3	1	0	1150	3390	1400	0

(b) 1 1 1150
2 3 1130
3 1 1400
4 0 **** ←

Execution error in loop 20 when we attempt to
divide by COUNT(4) = 0. Some systems allow
processing to continue, giving format overflow
in the output of SUMSAT(4)/COUNT(4).

29. **(a)** At the sixth iteration of the table look-up loop, the computer attempts to evaluate the following logical expression:

    AGE .GT. AGELIM(6)

    Since the upper dimension bound is 5, we would have an execution error and processing would terminate.

30. This traditional approach works in the sense that it gives correct results; however, it's an illustration of undesirable and ambiguous structure, since there are two possible exits from this loop structure:

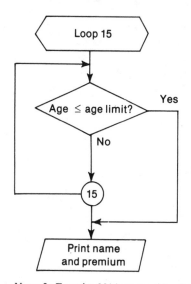

    Note: In Exercise 29(a) we would exit through statement 15, which would give an incorrect premium of $357 for Rip.

32. Change the first input record to '*'.

33. Eliminate the second READ statement and the variables B0, B1, B2, and B3 from the REAL statement. In loop 10, the user must insert the appropriate assignment statement for Y.

36.

J	TEMP	LIST(1)	LIST(2)	LIST(3)	LIST(4)	SWITCH
2	3076	3076	8321	2501	7771	1
3	2501	3076	2501	8321	7771	1
4	7771	3076	2501	7771	8321	1
2	2501	2501	3076	7771	8321	1
3	2501	2501	3076	7771	8321	1
4	2501	2501	3076	7771	8321	1
2	2501	2501	3076	7771	8321	0
3	2501	2501	3076	7771	8321	0
4	2501	2501	3076	7771	8321	0

Two passes; three passes.

37. Change the block IF statement to

    IF (LIST(J) .GT. LIST(J − 1)) THEN

38. Yes, since the internal computer coding of alphabetic data is expressed in numeric code. This means, for example, that the alphabetic character A is represented by a coded value that is "numerically" less than the code for the alphabetic character B.

CHAPTER 8

1.

Program segment	Output

```
    DO 40 I = 1,3
        DO 30 J = 1,4
            PRINT *,DEPOS(I,J)
30      CONTINUE
40  CONTINUE
```

Output:

1000
800
500
1200
500
2000
2000
500
1500
300
700
1500

2.   DEPOS

1000	1200	2000	300
800	500	500	700
500	2000	1500	1500

Array is filled column by column. Input data should be in the following order.

1000
500
1500
800
2000
300
500
2000
700
1200
500
1500

3. To number rows:

PRINT *,I,(X(I,J),J = 1,3)

To number columns place the following before loop 20.

PRINT *,(J,J = 0,3)

4.   **(a)**   PRINT *,((DEPOS(I,J),J = 1,4),I = 1,3)

(b)   DO 30 I = 1,3
             PRINT *,(DEPOS(I,J),J = 1,4)
        30 CONTINUE

(c)   DO 40 J = 1,4
             PRINT *,(DEPOS(I,J),I = 1,3)
        40 CONTINUE

5. (a) 1 2 3 4 5 6 . . .   (b) 1 2 3 4 5 6 7 8 9 10 11 12 . . . 56 57 58 59 60

    1000   1 0 0 0   8 0 0   . . .   1 5 0 0
    800
    500
     .
     .
     .
    700
    1500

6. Yes. The advantage here is that the repeat specification in the new FORMAT statement (13) allows up to 13 columns of input versus exactly 4 in the earlier version. Moreover, the fact that each row of input begins on a new input record is now explicit since DO-loop 30 processes rows (that is, the READ statement is reexecuted for each new value of I). In the earlier version it was necessary to use a repeat specification of *exactly* 4 to accomplish the same desirable "table" appearance of input data.

7.   READ 1,((DEPOS(I,J),I = 1,3),J = 1,4)
        1 FORMAT(3I5)

    In this case the array in memory gets filled in column by column, ending up the same as in Example 8.3.

8. (a)

(b) and (c)

(d)

```
        1111111111222222222233
  123456789012345678901234567890
1
2
3 BANK DEPOSITS
4
5
6    1000    800    500   1200
7
8 BANK DEPOSITS
9
10
11   500   2000  2000    500
12
13 BANK DEPOSITS
14
15
16   1500    300    700   1500
17
18
```

9.

```
          1111111111222222222233333333334
  1234567890123456789012345678901234567890
BANK DEPOSITS
              1        2        3       4
BANK 1     1000     800     500    1200
BANK 2      500    2000    2000     500
BANK 3     1500     300     700    1500
```

Two advantages: greater flexibility and clearer design. The new repeat specification (16) allows up to 16 columns of output versus exactly 4 in the earlier version, which reduces program maintenance should the number of columns change. Moreover, the fact that each row of the matrix is printed on a new output record is now explicit since DO-loop 30 processes rows (that is, the PRINT statement is reexecuted for each new value of I). In the earlier version it was necessary to use a repeat specification of *exactly* 4 to accomplish the same desirable "table" appearance of output data. Additionally, the labeling of rows and columns improves the appearance of output. Finally, the use of variables M and N to generalize the loop iterations simplifies subsequent program maintenance should these values change.

11. (a) 12 records, each with one item within the first 5 columns.
     (b) 12 items on one record, with fields of 5 columns.
     (c) 4 records, each with 3 items, with fields of 5 columns.

Remember: Data are read column by column in the sequence 1000,500, 1500, . . . ,500,1500.

12. No. The first prints column by column and the second prints in the usual row-by-row manner.

13. (a)
```
       DO 10 I = 1,2
          READ *,(A(I,J),J = 1,3),(B(I,J),J = 1,3)
    10 CONTINUE
```

(b)   READ *,((A(I,J),J = 1,3),I = 1,2)
                 READ *,((B(I,J),J = 1,3),I = 1,2)

(c)   READ *,A,B   (provided A and B have been dimensioned as 2 × 3 arrays)

14. (a)   PRINT 90
                 DO 50 I = 1,2
                     PRINT 92,(X(I,J),J = 1,3)
            50 CONTINUE
            90 FORMAT ('1',38X,'MATRIX X:'/)
            92 FORMAT (36X,3F5.1)

  (b)   PRINT 2,X   (provided X is dimensioned as a 2 × 3 array)
             2 FORMAT ('0',35X,'ELEMENTS IN X:'/(1X,F45.1))

16.   DO 40 J = 1,4
                 TOT(J) = 0
                 DO 35 I = 1,3
                     TOT(J) = TOT(J) + DEPOS(I,J)
            35   CONTINUE
            40 CONTINUE

18.   REAL PER(3,4)
                 .
                 .
                 .
                 DO 80 I = 1,3
                     DO 75 J = 1,4
                         PER(I,J) = DEPOS(I,J)/SUM(I)*100.
            75   CONTINUE
            80 CONTINUE

        Third row in PER: 37.5   7.5   17.5   37.5

19. (a)   DO 10 I = 1,100
                     DO 5 J = 1,50
                         WEIGHT(I,J) = 100.
             5   CONTINUE
            10 CONTINUE

  (b)   DATA WEIGHT /5000*0./

        The alternative in (b) should not be used if there's a need to reinitialize to zero during execution.
  (c) In part (a) change the following.

                 DO 10 I = −20,20
                     DO 5 J = 30,50

        In part (b) change as follows:

                 DATA WEIGHT /3321*0./

20.   DATA D /30*100./

21.   DO 10 I = 1,4
                     DO 5 J = 1,4
                         IF (I .EQ. J)X(I,J) = 1
                         IF (I .NE. J)X(I,J) = 0
             5 CONTINUE
            10 CONTINUE

Or more simply:

```
      DATA X /16*0/
      DO 10 K = 1,4
        X(K,K) = 1
   10 CONTINUE
```

25. TAXTAB(I,1) = Upper limit of taxable income (column 2 in Tax Schedule)
TAXTAB(I,2) = Fixed amount of tax within a class (column 3 in Tax Schedule)
TAXTAB(I,3) = Variable percent amount of tax within a class (column 4 in Tax Schedule)
TAXTAB(I − 1,1) = Upper limit of taxable income for previous class, which is the same as lower limit in class I (column 1 in Tax Schedule)

26. Column by column: 2200,2700, . . . , 1E30,0,0,70, . . . , 53090,0,14,15, . . . , 70 The last entry in column 2 of the Tax Schedule theoretically is infinity. In practice, any large value would do, so long as it would never be exceeded by the value in TI. We used 1E30.

27. (a)

WAGES = 12100.	DED = 1900.	TI = 11100.
DIV = 0.	EXEM = 1	TAX = 1815.
INTINC = 0.	TAXPAY = 2530.	REFUND = 715.
OTHER = 0.	AGI = 12100.	BALDUE = 482.07
ADJ = 0.	EXDED = 0.	

(b)

```
1
2 NAME                        :  TEST 1
3
4 ADJUSTED GROSS INCOME       :  $     23430.20
5 TAXABLE INCOME              :  $     20400.20
6 INCOME TAX                  :  $      4582.07
7
8 BALANCE DUE IRS             :  $       482.07
9
10
11
12
13 NAME                       :  TEST 2
14
15 ADJUSTED GROSS INCOME      :  $     12100.00
16 TAXABLE INCOME             :  $     11100.00
17 INCOME TAX                 :  $      1815.00
18
19 REFUND FROM IRS            :  $       715.00
20
21
22
23
24
```

30. (a) 1981
150, 100, 100
250, 250, 50
600, 200, 300
1982
120, 110, 90
230, 250, 70
550, 300, 200
1983
130, 100, 90
220, 245, 90
500, 350, 150

(b) 1981, 1982, 1983
150, 250, 600, 100, . . . , 300, 120, 230, . . . , 200, 130, 220, . . . , 150

                    1981   1982   1983

Thus ENROLL gets input column by column from lowest to highest depth level. This is equivalent to

READ *,(((ENROLL(I,J,K),I = 1,NOC),J = 1,NOL),K = 1,NOY)

31. (a) Five years, four levels, and six colleges according to the array declarations. Note that changes up to these limits must be reflected in the PARAMETER statement. **(b)** 300, 70, and undefined (unless the compiler initializes all numeric memory locations to zero). **(c)** Changes NOC to 3 and NOL to 3 within the implied-DO lists in the DATA statements that define COL and LEVEL. NOC and NOL were valid originally because they were symbolic names for constants rather than variables.

32. Replace DO-loops 10 and 20 with

```
    DO 20 I = 1,NOC
      DO 10 K = 1,NOY
        READ *,(ENROLL(I,J,K),J = 1,NOL),YEAR(K)
10      CONTINUE
20    CONTINUE
```

33. To describe one alternative among several: Add TE to the list in the INTEGER statement, insert

TE = 0

just before DO-loop 70, insert

TE = TE + COLTOT(I)

within DO-loop 70, and place TE as the last item in the list of the PRINT statement following DO-loop 70.

CHAPTER 9

1. Assume snapshot just before execution of GO TO 10, and argument association by value/result.

N	K	NFAC	NKFAC	KFAC	COMB	NUMBER	FAC
8	6	40320	2	720	28	6	720
4	4	24	1	24	1	4	24
4	0	24	24	1	1	0	1
4	1	24	6	1	4	1	1

Execution terminates when 1 and 4 are read in for N and K, respectively.

Output

N =	8 K =	6 COMBINATIONS =	28
N =	4 K =	4 COMBINATIONS =	1
N =	4 K =	0 COMBINATIONS =	1
N =	4 K =	1 COMBINATIONS =	4

2. No, since FAC needs to be reinitialized to 1 for each new call. Yes, there would be a type mismatch between real FAC and integers NFAC, NKFAC, and KFAC. Yes, FACTOR is the name of the subroutine and FAC is the name of a variable local to that subroutine. We can't use the same name for both purposes.

3. (a) OK. (b) SUBROUTINE statement is missing the name of the subroutine, FACTOR. (c) Either add (A,B,C) to the CALL statement or delete it from the SUBROUTINE statement.

   (d) Incorrectly matched argument lists by number and type. There are eight actual arguments and only six dummy arguments. Moreover, character A is paired with integer P, integer B is paired with character Q, integer C is paired with real R, and real E is paired with integer T. Rewrite the dummy arguments as (Q,P,T,R,S,U,V,W) and declare as follows:

   ```
   CHARACTER Q*(*),W*3
   INTEGER    P,T,V
   REAL       R,S,U
   ```

   (e) The name AREA has two meanings in the subroutine. Either change the name of the subroutine in both the CALL and SUBROUTINE statements or change the dummy variable AREA to, say, A in the subroutine.

4. VALUES: 7.7 3.3 6.6
   TOTAL: 17.6

   Yes, the original contents in A, B, and C have changed. Often this is an unintended effect (logic error).

5.
   ```
   SUBROUTINE HEAD
   CHARACTER DATE*25        or use (*) in place of 25
   READ *,DATE
   PRINT *,'PERIODIC REPORT'
   PRINT *,DATE
   END
   ```

6.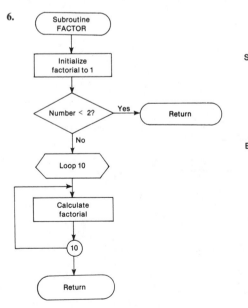

   Start subroutine FACTOR
     Factorial = 1
     IF no. < 2 THEN
       Return
     END IF
     DO WHILE factorial not calculated
       Recursively update factorial
     END DO
     Return
   End subroutine FACTOR

We generally don't recommend multiple returns (as discussed in Section 9.4).

7.

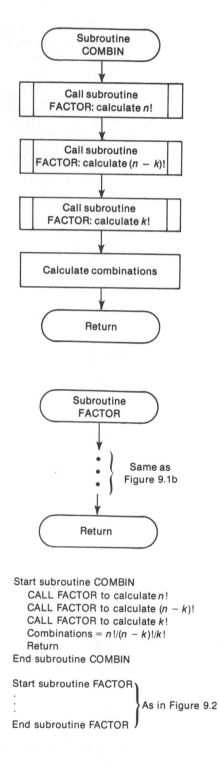

Start main program
  READ n,k
  DO WHILE $n \geq k, n \geq 0, k \geq 0$
    CALL COMBIN to calculate C
    No. days = $14 \times C$
    PRINT n,k,C, no. days
    READ n,k
  END DO
  Stop
End main program

Start subroutine COMBIN
  CALL FACTOR to calculate $n!$
  CALL FACTOR to calculate $(n - k)!$
  CALL FACTOR to calculate $k!$
  Combinations = $n!/(n - k)!/k!$
  Return
End subroutine COMBIN

Start subroutine FACTOR ⎫
  .   ⎬ As in Figure 9.2
  .
End subroutine FACTOR ⎭

```
      INTEGER N,K,C,DAYS,DAYPER
      PARAMETER (DAYPER = 14)
      READ *,N,K
   10 IF (N .GE. K .AND. N .GT. 0 .AND. K .GE. 0) THEN
         CALL COMBIN (N,K,C)
         DAYS = DAYPER*C
         PRINT *,'N = ',N,'K = ',K,'C = ',C,'DAYS = ',DAYS
         READ *,N,K
         GO TO 10
      END IF
      END


      SUBROUTINE COMBIN(N,K,C)
      INTEGER N,K,C,NFAC,NKFAC,KFAC
      CALL FACTOR(N,NFAC)
      CALL FACTOR(N - K,NKFAC)
      CALL FACTOR(K,KFAC)
      C = NFAC/(NKFAC*KFAC)
      END


      SUBROUTINE FACTOR (NUMBER,FAC)  ⎫
        .                             ⎬  As in Example 9.1
        .                             ⎪
        .                             ⎪
      END                             ⎭
```

Note: Subroutine FACTOR is said to be *nested* within subroutine COMBIN, since COMBIN calls FACTOR. Also, note the generality of subroutine FACTOR as a module that simply calculates factorials. This means it can be used unchanged in different programs, as done here and in Example 9.1.

9. **(a)** X can't be both a subroutine name and an array name. K must appear in the dummy argument list since it's an adjustable dimension.
   (b) Adjustable dimensions for array A are not allowed in the calling program, unless K and N are symbolic names for constants, in which case we need a PARAMETER statement. In the subroutine, POINT is not a *dummy* array, which means we can't give it an adjustable dimension. If POINT is local to the subroutine, use a *constant* dimension; otherwise place POINT in the dummy argument list and give it a corresponding actual argument.
   (c) In the dummy array declarator X(200,50), the size of the dummy array ($200 \times 50 = 10,000$) exceeds the size of the corresponding actual array ($100 \times 50 = 5000$). Use either X(M,N) or X(M,*). Also, we could use S(M) instead of S(*).

10. Make the following changes in the main program.

```
      REAL SCORE(100),AVE,SUM
      CALL MEAN(N,SCORE,AVE,SUM)
      PRINT *,AVE,SUM
```

Make the following change in the subroutine.

```
      SUBROUTINE MEAN(N,X,XBAR,SUM)
```

11.
```
      CALL MEAN
      END
      SUBROUTINE MEAN
      INTEGER N
      REAL X(100),XBAR,SUM
      READ *,N
      READ *,(X(J),J = 1,N)
```

(Continued on the next page.)

```
      SUM = 0.
      DO 10 J = 1,N
         SUM = SUM + X(J)
   10 CONTINUE
      XBAR = SUM/N        ← Same as SUM/REAL(N)
      PRINT *,XBAR
      END
```

Note that the main program has no function other than to call the subroutine. N can be input through the subroutine only if it's not used as an adjustable dimension. If N is to be an adjustable dimension for X, it will be necessary to input N in the main program and to have argument lists that contain both N and X.

15. No, since the unique identities of N, K, NFAC, NKFAC, and KFAC could not be preserved.

16. (a)

X(1)   X(2)   A

```
+-------+-------+-------+
|       |       |       |
+-------+-------+-------+
```

Y(1)   Y(2)   B

| X(1) | X(2) | A |
Y(1)	Y(2)	B
10	20	5
		35

(b) 10 20 35

(c) The common block changes to

X(1)   X(2)   A

```
+-------+-------+-------+
|       |       |       |
+-------+-------+-------+
```

B   Y(1)   Y(2)

Contents change as follows:

| X(1) | X(2) | A |
B	Y(1)	Y(2)
10	20	5
35		

The output changes to

35 20 5

17. (a) N and J, Y(1) and P matchups OK, but integer M must not be paired with real R; real Q must not be paired with integer K.

(b) Missing comma after R(30); dimension of S should coincide with dimension on R. Either change the 50 to 30 or the 30 to 50. If this dimension change is not made, then A will share storage with S(31).

(c) OK. D shares with A, and E shares with B.

(d) COMMON D,E,F, is OK, but COMMON for the second subprogram should be changed to:

```
COMMON A,B,C,M,N
```

in order to align M with I and N with J.

(e) OK.

(f) Named common must be size-consistent. Use A(1000).

21. (a)

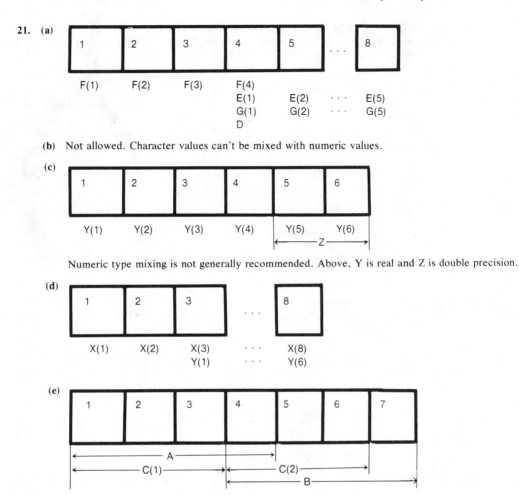

(b) Not allowed. Character values can't be mixed with numeric values.

(c)

Numeric type mixing is not generally recommended. Above, Y is real and Z is double precision.

(d)

(e)

22. In Figure 9.1a, eliminate the three CALL boxes and rewrite the next box as follows:

Calculate combinations
using function FACTOR

In Figure 9.1b, replace the start symbol with

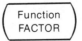

Function
FACTOR

In Figure 9.2, eliminate the three CALL lines in the main program and replace the combinations line with

Combinations = function FACTOR(n)/(function FACTOR($n - k$)*function FACTOR(k))

and replace the word "subroutine" with the word "function."

23. **(a)** Make the following changes to the answer beginning on page 570. In the flowcharts, eliminate all "call" boxes and replace the word "subroutine" with the word "function" in the start symbols. Replace corresponding boxes with the following.

<table>
<tr>
<td>Calculate number of
days for all experiments
using function COMBIN</td>
<td>Calculate combinations
using function FACTOR</td>
</tr>
</table>

In the pseudocode, eliminate the four CALL lines and use

No. days = 14 × function COMBIN(n,k)

and

Combinations = function FACTOR(n)/(function FACTOR($n - k$)* function FACTOR(k))

and replace the word "subroutine" with the word "function." In the main program, eliminate the CALL statement, use

DAYS = DAYPER*COMBIN(N,K)

and replace "C" with "COMBIN" in the INTEGER statement and "C" with "COMBIN(N,K)" in the PRINT statement.
In the first subprogram, replace the SUBROUTINE statement with

FUNCTION COMBIN(N,K)

replace "C" with "COMBIN" in the INTEGER statement, eliminate the three CALL statements, and use

COMBIN = FACTOR(N)/(FACTOR(N − K)*FACTOR(K))

In the second subprogram, replace the SUBROUTINE statement with

FUNCTION FACTOR(NUMBER)

and replace "FAC" with "FACTOR."

24. In the main program, eliminate the CALL statement and use the following in place of the originals.

REAL SCORE(100),MEAN
PRINT *,MEAN(N,SCORE)

In the subprogram, replace the SUBROUTINE statement with

FUNCTION MEAN(N,X)

replace the REAL statement with

REAL X(N),MEAN,SUM

and replace the assignment statement for XBAR with

MEAN = SUM/REAL(N)

25. Yes, we could make SUM a dummy argument by using

FUNCTION MEAN(N,X,SUM)

However, as a matter of style, we don't recommend doing this, since functions are expected to return a single value (not the two values in SUM and MEAN as would be the case here).

26. In the main program, eliminate the CALL statement and use the following in place of the originals.

```
REAL SCORE(100),MEAN
COMMON N,SCORE
PRINT *,MEAN( )
```

In the subprogram, replace the subroutine statement with

```
FUNCTION MEAN( )
```

the REAL statement with

```
REAL X(100),MEAN,SUM
```

the COMMON statement with

```
COMMON N,X
```

and the assignment statement for XBAR with

```
MEAN = SUM/REAL(N)
```

We can't use the adjustable dimension N for X in this subprogram because X is not part of a dummy argument list.

27. The value 15 gets printed.

CHAPTER 10

1. Substring length $= e_2 - e_1 + 1$

2. No. A substring consists of successive (adjacent) characters within the string.

3. (a) R (b) I LOVE FORTRAN. (c) Execution error. Value of leftmost substring expression cannot exceed value of rightmost substring expression. This would imply a substring length that's zero or negative (see Exercise 1).

(d)

SUB

1	2	3	4	5
O	V	E		F

(e) 15

4.
```
MONDAYɓɓɓɓ- - Mɓ
TUESDAYɓɓɓ- - TU
WEDNESDAYɓ- - Wɓ
THURSDAYɓɓ- - TH
FRIDAYɓɓɓɓ- - Fɓ
SATURDAYɓɓ- - SA
SUNDAYɓɓɓɓ- - SU
```

5. Replace the PRINT statement with

Prints nonblank characters ⟶
```
IF (PHRASE(J:J) .NE. 'ɓ') THEN
   PRINT *,PHRASE(J:J)
ELSE IF (J .LT. 50) THEN
```
Prints blank between two non-blank characters ⟶
```
   IF (PHRASE(J + 1:J + 1) .NE. 'ɓ') PRINT *,PHRASE(J:J)
END IF
```

6.

1	2	3	4	5	6	7	8	9	10	11	12	13	14	15	16	17	18	19	20
I		A	D	O	R	E		F	O	R	T	R	A	N		7	7		

Yes, the replacement substring ADORE is a different length from the replaced substring HATE; we need a space between ADORE and FORTRAN. We would have to input

    3,19
    'ADOREɓFORTRANɓ77.'

This approach is especially tedious and self-defeating for long strings requiring changes near the beginning. Ideally, the program should replace HATE with ADORE and shift the remaining part of the string one position to the right. The program in Section 10.5 illustrates techniques for accomplishing this.

7. **(a)** PRINT *,(CODE(J:J),'ɓ',J = 1,30)

　　(b) PRINT *,(CODE(J:J),J = 30,1,−1)

10. SEEɓɓJANEɓRUNɓɓ
　　RUNɓɓJANEɓRUNɓɓ
　　RUNɓɓRUNɓɓRUNɓɓ
　　JACKɓSEESɓJANE.

11. **(a)** None, as the function stands, since the declared length of 20 in the calling program is neither within the argument lists nor used to declare the length of STRING. We could have used the more restrictive

CHARACTER STRING*20

.
.

J = 20

but then the subprogram is not generalized, that is, it's incompatible with strings other than length 20 in calling programs. The current subprogram can be used without change with *any* calling program needing a trim length. In fact, function TRIM is so useful that we use it many times later in the chapter.

　　(b) 9; 3; 0.

　　(c) This works fine as long as STRING stores at least one nonblank character; otherwise J gets decremented to zero and we get an execution error in statement 10 when the computer attempts to evaluate STRING(0:0).

　　(d) If we were to test for the first blank character starting from character position 1, then we would exit from the loop prematurely whenever STRING stores one or more blank characters embedded between two nonblank characters. For example, if STRING stores BILLYɓTHEɓKID, we will get an incorrect trim length of 5 instead of 13.

12. DO 10 J = 1,LEN(PHRASE)

13. Replace the DO statement with

DO 10 J = 1,TRIM(PHRASE)

Within loop 10, BLANKS only counts blanks between words; to include the blanks that were trimmed, add the following just after the CONTINUE statement.

BLANKS = BLANKS + (50 − TRIM(PHRASE))

15. **(a)** 0　**(b)** 4　**(c)** 4　**(d)** 3.

16.

1	8
2	4
3	10
4	11
5	10
6	13
7	14
8	2
9	2

17. **(a)** A substring match would not be found since OLD stores 20 characters. For the first input record, OLD would store LOVE followed by 16 blanks. The substring LOVE followed by 16 blanks is not found in TEXT. First we must "trim" the 16 blanks using the utility TRIM; then we can find the LOVE match (pun intended).

  (b) In the first case we would get a wrong value for LAST whenever the input item for OLD contains trailing blanks. (See the second input record in the example, which would incorrectly give 15 instead of 18 for LAST.) In the second case the value for LAST would be incorrect whenever the input item for NEW has trailing blanks. [See the second input record in part (c).] If both input items have trailing blanks [as in the first record in part (c)], the unnecessary blanks are simply ignored [we could have used 'TRAN. b','MULAS.' in part (c)].

  (c) 5,11,16; 6,11,16.

18.
```
10 IF (OLD .NE. '***') THEN
       TL    = TRIM(OLD)
       FIRST = INDEX(TEXT,OLD(:TL))
       IF (FIRST .EQ. 0) THEN
          PRINT *,OLD(:TL)//'bNOTbFOUND.'
          STOP
       END IF
          .
          .
          .
       GO TO 10
    END IF
```

20. Yes, since both strings are pure letters and the relational operator .LE. is analoguous to the lexical function LLE.

21. **(a)** True. **(b)** False. **(c)** True, based on the ASCII collating sequence in footnote 2. **(d)** False, based on the ASCII collating sequence in footnote 2.

23. **(a)** 10 **(b)** Asterisk

25.

J	IN	MARK	NEW	Output
1	9	1	.FALSE.	
2	0	1	.TRUE.	I
3	12	3	.FALSE.	
4	15			
5	22			
6	5			
7	0		.TRUE.	LOVE
8	6	8	.FALSE.	
9	15			
10	18			
11	20			

J	IN	MARK	NEW	Output
12	18			
13	1			
14	14			
15	0		.TRUE.	FORTRAN
16				
17				
18				
19				
20				
21	4	21	.FALSE.	
22	15			
23	0		.TRUE.	DO
24	25	24	.FALSE.	
25	15			
26	23			
27	0		.TRUE.	YOU
28				
.				
.				
.				
70				

26. (a) DO 10 J = 1,TRIM(STRING)
    (b) Use *53 instead of *27 in the CHARACTER statement and add the 26 lowercase letters to the character constant in the DATA statement.

27. (a) For J = 1 – 4, we have IN = 0 and NEW = .TRUE., so neither the IF-block nor the ELSE IF-block is entered. At J = 5, IN gets set to 9, execution enters the ELSE IF-block, and we have MARK = 5 and NEW = .FALSE. . Thereafter, results are the same as before, except for values in MARK. Thus the subroutine handles sentence indentation, as when a new paragraph is started.
    (b) Execution never enters the IF-block or ELSE IF-block, so no words get printed.

30.

TLA = 7	J	STRING(J : J)
FIRSTN = 12	25	.
LASTN = 16	24	D
TLS = 20	23	E
FIRSTS = 17	22	I
LASTS = 25	21	R
TLN = 5	20	R
	19	O
	18	W
	17	b̸

STRING(12 : 16)   =   b̸VERY

31. We need not use TLA and TLS since, for example, we could replace TLA by TRIM(AFTER) in the calculation of FIRSTN; however, specifying TLA and TLS improves readability and processing efficiency (we need not call the function as often).

32. TLN = LEN(STRING(FIRSTN:LASTN))

33. **(a)** Not if the processor uses padded rightmost blanks in AFTER to locate the substring in STRING. For example, if AFTER has a declared length of 10, it will store GETTINGƀƀƀ in the example. If the processor does not automatically trim these constants, GETTINGƀƀƀ will not be found within STRING (or TEXT). By using our TRIM function we trim the three blanks that follow GETTING, thus ensuring a match. **(b)** No. FIRSTN and LASTN would be calculated incorrectly as 12 and 16, instead of the required 13 and 17. The problem lies in the fact that TRIM truncates trailing blanks from the input values of AFTER and NEW, which gives an incorrect length for the new substring whenever trailing blanks are part of the input. In effect, we can't use trailing blanks in the input for AFTER and NEW when using this subroutine.

34. **(a)** No. ƀWORRƀWOR would get placed in positions 17–25.
    (b) No. This is an unfair question since an obscure rule states that *none of the character positions being defined to the left of the equal sign may be referenced in the expression to the right of the equal sign* (ANSI X3.9-1978, page 10-3, lines 5–6). In this case, the seemingly plausible (and convenient)

    STRING(17:25) = STRING(12:20)

    may yield an execution or logic error since character positions 17, 18, 19, and 20 appear on both sides of the equal sign. Note that these are the very characters that caused the problem in part (a) above! In other words, when assigning new characters to positions 22–25, the computer uses the *new* characters ƀWOR in positions 17–20 (instead of the "erased" old characters IED. formerly in positions 17–20). What happens on your system? Execution error, logic error, or correct results?

CHAPTER 11

1. The record might have fields such as name of student, identification number, grade on assignment 1, . . . , grade on assignment *n*, grade on exam 1, . . . , grade on exam *m*. Most likely it would be a sequential-access file, since this type of file is generally processed in its entirety for the purpose of calculating final grades. It's likely to be an unformatted file since this reduces processing time and there's not likely to be a change in processor during the school term.

2. Specify a first record with a single field that stores the value 3. This indicates the number of records (employees) that follow in the file.

3. Yes, by sequentially specifying all record numbers. No, since the file doesn't have record numbers.

4. OPEN (1,FILE = 'PERSONNEL',STATUS = 'OLD')

   Elimination of the ACCESS = specifier defaults to SEQUENTIAL and elimination of the FORM = specifier defaults to FORMATTED when the file is sequential. Note that we can also omit the UNIT = portion of the UNIT = specifier. *The original version is best for style, since all characteristics are "up front."*

5. Open unit 20 for a sequential-access formatted file of unknown status and unspecified name.

6. Change 'FORMATTED' to 'UNFORMATTED'. Also, in the third example, the record length will change.

7. ```
CHARACTER *10,NAME,STA,ACC,FM
INTEGER U
   :
   :
READ *,U,NAME,STA,ACC,FM
   :
   :
OPEN (UNIT = U,FILE = NAME,STATUS = STA,ACCESS = ACC,FORM = FM)
```
```

The input record for the above READ statement is

    2, 'UPDATE','NEW','SEQUENTIAL','FORMATTED'

This approach is often desirable because it reduces program maintenance whenever these characteristics change.

8.   If a control list has a record specifier, then by definition the statement is a direct-access I/O statement, which is used for processing direct-access files. If simultaneously it has an end-of-file specifier, then this implies a sequential-access file, an inconsistency.

9.   **(a)**   In the first case execution terminates; in the second case control goes to the statement labeled 800.

      (b)   In the first case execution terminates; in the second case control goes to the statement labeled 999.

10.   It's an unformatted (no format specifier) output statement that transfers the value in A to a sequential-access (no record specifier) file.

```
    OPEN (UNIT = 15,FILE = 'STRESS',STATUS = 'OLD',
   +         ACCESS = 'SEQUENTIAL',FORM = 'UNFORMATTED')
```

11.
```
    CHARACTER NAME* 30 ,GRADE* 1
    INTEGER  ID
     .
     .
     .
    OPEN (UNIT = 20,FILE = 'GRADES',STATUS = 'NEW',
   +         ACCESS = 'DIRECT',FORM = 'FORMATTED',RECL = 31 )
     .
     .
    READ *,  ID ,NAME,GRADE
    WRITE (UNIT = 20,FMT = 90,REC = ID ) NAME,GRADE
     .
     .
 90 FORMAT (2A)
     .
     .
    END
```
Note

Note

14.   Can't have two UNIT = specifiers in the list. Use

    REWIND 1
    REWIND 2
    CLOSE(1)
    CLOSE(2)

15.   **(a)**   15, 'PERSONNEL','NEW'
          'ABATARƀƀƀJANEƀA.','099-34-2101',20000,'F'
          'BOMBERGƀƀƀBOƀB.','881-12-1113',15800,'M'
          'DRURYƀƀƀDAVIDƀD.','125-71-8112',18000,'M'
          'EOF',ƀ,0,ƀ'

(b)

		NAME	SS NUMBER	SALARY	SEX
1	RECORD	NAME	SS NUMBER	SALARY	SEX
2	—				
3					
4	1	ABATAR JANE A.	099-34-2101	20000	F
5	2	BOMBERG BOB B.	881-12-1113	15800	M
6	3	DRURY DAVID D.	125-71-8112	18000	M
7	END OF FILE				
8					
9					
10					

(c) When statement 60 encounters the endfile record, control is transferred to statement 70.

16. If an error is encountered during file read-in, the program prints an explicit error message and execution terminates; otherwise the system terminates execution and prints a system error message. The approach in this exercise is more explicit, however, it has the disadvantage of "murky" structure. The loop now has two possible exit points, so it's not really a DO-WHILE structure. Try flowcharting the logic.

17. Add FM*11 to the CHARACTER statement.
Add FM to the first READ statement.
Replace 'FORMATTED' with FM in the OPEN statement.
Replace the WRITE statement just after statement 50 with

```
        IF (FM .EQ. 'FORMATTED') WRITE (U,10)NAME,SSN,SAL,SEX
        IF (FM .EQ. 'UNFORMATTED') WRITE (U)NAME,SSN,SAL,SEX
```

Replace statement 60 with

```
    60 IF (FM .EQ. 'FORMATTED') READ (U,10,END = 70)NAME,SSN,SAL,SEX
        IF (FM .EQ. 'UNFORMATTED') READ (U,END = 70)NAME,SSN,SAL,SEX
```

20. **(a)**
```
    15,'PERSONNEL','NEW'
    099342101,'ABATARↃↃↃJANEↃA.',20000,'F'
    881121113,'BOMBERGↃↃↃBOB B.Ↄ',15800,'M'
    125718112,'DRURYↃↃↃDAVIDↃD.',18000,'M'
    0,'Ↄ',0,'Ↄ'
    099342101
    881121113
    125718112
    0
```

(b)

		SS NUMBER	NAME	SALARY	SEX
1	RECORD/SS NUMBER		NAME	SALARY	SEX
2	—				
3					
4		993421011	ABATAR JANE A.	20000	F
5		881121113	BOMBERG BOB B.	15800	M
6		125718112	DRURY DAVID D.	18000	M
7	FILE DISPLAY TERMINATED				
8					
9					
10					

21. We can neither change a record number nor delete a record once a direct-access file is created. We could, however, proceed as described in items (iv) and (v) of Exercise 23.

MODULE A

1. (a) 10; 0; 10; -10 (b) 5; 6; -2; -1 (c) 5.0; 5.0 (d) -2. (e) -1.0 (f) 0.01680668 (g) 1.0; undefined, since argument must be positive. (h) 0.5

2. (a) COST = NINT(100.*COST)/100.   (c) COST = NINT(COST/100.)*100.
(b) COST = NINT(COST)

3. Reread Section A.1.

4. (a) 13.5 (b) 281.0

5.
```
REAL EXPO,FIXED,DECAY,TIME
EXPO(A,B,T) = A*B**T
    .
    .

PRINT *,EXPO(2.0,0.5,10.0)
    .
    .

PRINT *,EXPO(FIXED,DECAY,TIME)
    .
    .
END
```

6. Reread Section A.3.

MODULE B

1. First you should find out the appropriate "output unit number" for your system. We use 6.

```
WRITE (6,30)
WRITE (6,40)
WRITE (6,50)
WRITE (6,60)NAME,ID,BALDUE
WRITE (6,70)
WRITE (6,80)CUMBAL
WRITE (6,70)
WRITE (6,70)
```

2. (a)   PRINT '("b",A15,I12,F14.2)',NAME,ID,BALDUE

(b)   CHARACTER F60*80 ————— Allows a maximum of 80 characters for the format specification
```
    .
    .

F60 = '("b",A15,I12,F14.2)'
PRINT F60,NAME,ID,BALDUE
```

3.   INTEGER FE,FF
.
.
.
ASSIGN 70 to FE
ASSIGN 80 TO FF
.
.
.
PRINT FE
PRINT FF,CUMBAL
PRINT FE
PRINT FE
.
.
.
70 FORMAT . . .
80 FORMAT . . .
       END

This approach requires more code, but slightly simplifies any future changes in numeric statement labels since these numbers appear as a group in ASSIGN and FORMAT statements. Moreover, in some applications, the ASSIGN statement is useful if alternative FORMAT statements are to be used by a single PRINT statement, as illustrated below.

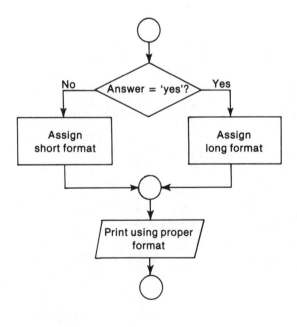

```
INTEGER FOUT
•
•
•
IF (ANS .EQ. 'YES') THEN
    ASSIGN 90 TO FOUT
ELSE
    ASSIGN 95 TO FOUT
END IF
PRINT FOUT, A, B, C
•
•
•
90 FORMAT . . .
95 FORMAT . . .
•
•
•
```

4. From Chapters 2 and 3 we could simply use

     PRINT *,'b'

instead of

     PRINT 50
     50 FORMAT('b')

(Continued on the next page.)

From Exercise 2 we could also use

    PRINT '(''ⱡ'')'

From Chapter 4 we can easily print 15 blank lines using a DO-loop.

```
      DO 3 K = 1,15
        PRINT *,'ⱡ'
    3 CONTINUE
```

5. (a) 15 FORMAT('+','HAL SPEAKS')   (d) 15 FORMAT('0','ⱡⱡⱡHAL SPEAKS')

    (b) 15 FORMAT('ⱡ','HAL SPEAKS')   (e) 15 FORMAT('1','HAL SPEAKS')

    (c) 15 FORMAT('0','HAL SPEAKS')

6.

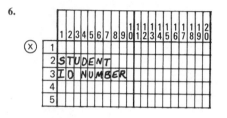

7.
```
    PRINT 90
    PRINT 95
      .
      .
      .
 90 FORMAT('0THE ANSWER = ')
 95 FORMAT('ⱡ _____ ')
```

8.

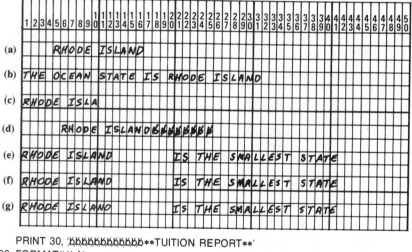

9.
```
    PRINT 30, 'ⱡⱡⱡⱡⱡⱡⱡⱡⱡⱡⱡⱡ**TUITION REPORT**'
 30 FORMAT('1',A)
```
    ⌐──── or A30

```
    PRINT 40, 'ⱡⱡⱡⱡⱡⱡNAMEⱡⱡⱡⱡⱡⱡⱡⱡⱡSS NUMBERⱡⱡⱡⱡBALANCE DUE'
 40 FORMAT('0',A)
```
    ⌐──── or A42

10. System dependent.

11.

	1	2	3	4	5	6	7	8	9	10	11	12	13	14	15	16	17	18	19	20
1	M	=		7	5	6		N	=			-4	0	1						
2																				
3			L	=		1	0													
4																				
5																				
6																				

13. **(a)** F5.1 **(b)** F8.4

		1	2	3	4	5	6	7	8	9	10
(c)	1	-	.	1	0	7	4					(Overflow if computer inserts leading zero.)
(d)	2	-	0	.	1	0	7	4			
(e)	3			-	0	.	1	0	7	4	
(f)	4	0	.	1	0	7	4				
(g)	5				3	7	6	4	.	0	
(h)	6				3	7	6	4	.	2	
(i)	7					3	7	6	4	.	
(j)	8			3	7	6	4	.	1	6	0
(k)	9	*	*	*	*	*	*				

14.

```
                        1 1 1 1 1 1
        1 2 3 4 5 6 7 8 9 0 1 2 3 4 5
(a) E12.4
(b) E12.2
(c)                 - 0 . 1 0 7 4 0 E + 0 0
(d)                 - 0 . 1 0 7 4 E + 0 0
(e)                     - 0 . 1 1 E + 0 0
(f)         * * * * * * * * * * * * * * *   ←—— If system doesn't suppress leading zero
(g)                   0 . 3 7 6 4 0 E + 0 4
(h)                   0 . 3 7 6 4 2 E + 0 4
(i)                 0 . 3 7 6 4 1 6 E + 0 4
(j)               0 . 3 7 6 4 E + 0 4
(k)                 0 . 3 7 6 E + 0 4
```

15.

```
                        1 1 1 1 1 1 1 1 1 1 2 2 2 2 2 2
        1 2 3 4 5 6 7 8 9 0 1 2 3 4 5 6 7 8 9 0 1 2 3 4 5
(a)             0 . 3 1 4 1 5 9 2 6 5 3 6 D + 0 1
(b)         0 . 3 1 4 1 5 9 2 6 D + 0 1
(c)         * * * * * * * * * * * * * *
```

16. 30 FORMAT('1',12X,'**TUITION REPORT**')
40 FORMAT('0',6X,'NAME',8X,'SS NUMBER',4X,'BALANCE DUE')

The advantage of the X edit descriptor is questionable here, since we lose alignment by sight as in the original version.

18. 80 FORMAT(T19,'**TOTALS**',T32,'$',F10.2)

19. **(a)**   30 FORMAT('1',T14,'∗∗TUITION REPORT∗∗')
            40 FORMAT('0',T8,'NAME',T20,'SS NUMBER',T33,'BALANCE DUE')

20.   Look up those you're not sure of.

MODULE C

1.   First you should find out the appropriate "input unit number" for your system. We use 5.

```
READ (5,10)CPC,FEES
READ (5,15)N
READ (5,20)NAME, ID,CREDIT
```

2. **(a)**   READ '(F5.2,F5.2)',CPC,FEES
   (b)   CHARACTER F10∗50 ⟵ Allows a maximum of 50 characters for the format specification
      .
      .
      .

```
F10 = '(F5.2,F5.2)'
READ F10,CPC,FEES
```

3.   INTEGER FA,FB,FC
         .
         .

```
ASSIGN 10 TO FA
ASSIGN 15 TO FB
ASSIGN 20 TO FC
```
         .
         .
         .

```
READ FA,CPC,FEES
READ FB,N
```
         .
         .

```
READ FC,NAME,ID,CREDIT
```
         .
         .

```
10 FORMAT . . .
15 FORMAT . . .
20 FORMAT . . .
```
         .
         .

```
END
```

See the answer to Exercise 3 on page 583 to reiterate motivations for using the ASSIGN statement.

4. **(a)**   READ 900,FIRST,MIDDLE,LAST
            900 FORMAT(A,A,A)
                  or   (A8,A8,A12)

   (b)   PRINT 950,LAST,FIRST,MIDDLE
            950 FORMAT('1',49X,A,',',b',A,'b',A)
                  or   A12 A8   A8

5. Part   TOY

  (a)   CAPTAIN NEMO DOLLƀƀƀ
  (b)   CAPTAIN NEƀƀƀƀƀƀƀƀƀ
  (c)   IN NEMO DOLLƀƀƀƀƀƀƀ
  (d)   IN NEMO DOLLƀƀƀ
  (e)   CAPTAIN NEƀƀƀƀƀ

6.

	JACK	JILL	UP	HILL
(a)	5	0	6241	98
(b)	5	62419	84	75

7.
```
    READ 1,K,M,N
  1 FORMAT(I3,I3,I2)
       or   (I3,I4,I1)
```

8.
```
1 2 3 4 5 6 7 8 9 10 11 12 13 14 ...
```

```
  3 5   6 0 0   − 3
```

9. 100. and 250.; 9999. and 9999.

10.

	JACK	JILL	UP	HILL
(a)	5.	0.	624.1	0.98
(b)	5.	62.419	84.	0.075

11. **(a)** 999.9; 999. **(b)** A real variable (CREDIT) is paired with an integer edit descriptor (I4). Retype CREDIT as integer.

12.
```
    READ 1,X,Y,Z
  1 FORMAT(F3.2,F3.0,F2.1)
       or   (F4.3,F2.0,F2.1)
```

13.
```
1 2 3 4 5 6 7 8 9 10 11 12 13 14 15 ...
```

  (a)
```
1 5 . 2 5    4 5   5 0 7 .
  1 5 2 5    4 5     5 0 7
```

  (b)
```
1 5 2 . 5    4 5 0 5 0 7 0 .
1 5 2 5 0    4 5 0   5 0 7 0
```

  (c)
```
1 5 2 5 .        5 0 5 0 7 . 4
```
Need field width of 6 to input COST without decimal point.

  (d)
```
1 0 5 .        5 − 3 0 0 .
1 0 5 0 0      5   − 3 0 0
```

14. 1 2 3 4 5 6 7 8 9 10 11 12 13 14 15 ...

W .   M I T T Y
2 6 6 6 1 2 4 6 3
  1 5 0

Three input records are needed per student.

15. 1 2 3 4 5 6 7 8 9 10 ...

---

   7 3 4   1 0 0
  6 0 7 0   3

17.

	V1	V2	V3
(a)	-12.1×10^2	5.555×10^3	0.33×10^4
(b)	-0.12×10^2	$5555. \times 10^3$	0.33×10^{-4}
(c)	-0.12×10^2	0.555	0.33

18. **(a)** No changes, when blanks ignored; right-justify in column 20 otherwise.
   (b) Use D-05 in the second record and -5 in the third record. **(c)** Insufficient field width for this edit descriptor. **(d)** No changes.

19.   READ 20,ID,CREDIT
   20 FORMAT(I9,62X,F4.1)

Also see Exercise 21.

21. 20 FORMAT(I9,T72,F4.1)

23. Look up those you're not sure of.

MODULE D

1. **(a)** Insert a slash edit descriptor just before the right parenthesis in FORMAT ''40.''
   (b) 70 FORMAT(32X,14('−'))

2.   DO 50 J = 1,15
      PRINT *,'b'
   50 CONTINUE
      PRINT 10
   10 FORMAT(14(/))
   Note: n slashes alone in a format specification print $n + 1$ blank lines.

5. 25 FORMAT(3F10.2/2F5.2)

6. 30 FORMAT('1',4(F12.1,'%',I12))

7. (a)

(b)

(c)

(d)

8. (a) No explicit carriage control after //. **(b)** No explicit carriage control after ///. **(c)** Do we mean I52,3X or I5,23X?

9.

	Columns	Variable
First record	1–5	A
	6–10	B
	11–20	L
Second record	1–5	C
	6–10	D

10. (a)

(b)

11. **(a)** Assuming card input, it allows use of the entire card for entering the format specification.

(b)   1 2 3 4 5 6 7 8 9 10 11 12 13 14 15 16 17 18 19 20 21 22 23 24 25

```
( 1 5 X , F 1 0 . 2 )
    1 1 5
```

x x x x x x x x x x⎫
        ↓   ⎬ 115 input records
x x x x x x x x x x⎭

(c) The statement

READ FM,VALUE

only reads a single value per input record. We would need to store values in an array (Chapter 7), as done in part (d).

12. Look up those you're not sure of.

MODULE E

1. For example, in Figure E.2 we could have placed within Step 2 the two lines regarding the change in Step 3. The tasks in Step 4 then could have been placed in Step 3. There are many such permutations for long, complicated programs.

2.
```
1.1   Declare variables
1.2   No. orders = 0
1.3   Cumulative quant. = 0
1.4   Cumulative charge = 0
1.5   READ customer data
```
```
2.1        DO WHILE more orders
    2.1.1        Compute charge
    2.1.2˙       Accumulate totals
    2.1.3        PRINT customer data
    2.1.4        READ customer data
2.2        END DO
```
```
2.1.1.1   Compute charge based on discount
2.1.1.2   Compute charge based on surcharge
```
```
2.1.2.1   Add 1 to no. orders
2.1.2.2   Add quant. to cum. quant.
2.1.2.3   Add charge to cum. charge
```
```
2.1.1.1.1     IF quant. < 50 THEN
    2.1.1.1.1.1   Charge = quant. × unit price
2.1.1.1.2     END IF
2.1.1.1.3     IF 50 ≤ quant. ≤ 99 THEN
    2.1.1.1.3.1   Charge = 0.9 × quant. × unit price
2.1.1.1.4     END IF
2.1.1.1.5     IF quant. ≥ 100 THEN
    2.1.1.1.5.1   Charge = 0.75 × quant. × unit price
2.1.1.1.6     END IF
```
```
2.1.1.2.1     IF foreign country THEN
    2.1.1.2.1.1   Charge = 1.25 × charge
2.1.1.2.2     END IF
```

The numbering scheme gets a bit tedious, don't you think?

3. **(a)**   IF (QUANT .LT. BREAK1) CHARGE = QUANT*PRICE
       IF (QUANT .GE. BREAK1 .AND. QUANT .LT. BREAK2) CHARGE =
       +   (1. − DISC1)*QUANT*PRICE
       IF (QUANT .GE. BREAK2) CHARGE = (1. − DISC2)*QUANT*PRICE

   (b) IF (QUANT .LT. BREAK1) THEN
           CHARGE = QUANT*PRICE
       ELSE IF (QUANT .GE. BREAK1 .AND. QUANT .LT. BREAK2) THEN
           CHARGE = (1. − DISC1)*QUANT*PRICE
       ELSE
           CHARGE = (1. − DISC2)*QUANT*PRICE

6. Look up those you're not sure of.

MODULE F

1. **(a)** Module 2 prints a default message, since 100 > 90, and execution stops. See TEST3 output.
   (b) Module 3 prints an error message, since 4 > 2, and execution stops.
   (c) As a matter of style, in order to emphasize that control returns to the calling program just after PRINT 30 is executed. Otherwise this fact is slightly obscured visually by the group of FORMAT statements. A minor point really.
   (d) To obtain the correct number of weeks when any of the values 7, 14, 21, . . . is stored in DAYS. Otherwise, for example, 7 in DAYS would give 2 in WEEKS. We could subtract any real constant between 0 and 1, but then the entire expression to the right of the equal sign would be evaluated using real arithmetic and the resulting value would be truncated to integer for storage in WEEKS. We would get correct results but with inefficient processing.
   (e) It makes this module more independent from module 1 should we need to change the lengths of the character names BEST and NAMEP or the sizes of the vectors NAMEP and COST. For example, if we wish to change the character lengths from 10 to 15, we use NAMEP(6)*15,BEST*15 in place of NAMEP(6)*10,BEST*10 within module 1—and we need not make any changes in module 4. This design thus reduces subsequent software maintenance costs.

   (f)

	1	2	3	4	5	6	7	8	9	10	11	12	13	14	15	16	17	18	19	20	21	22	23	24	25	26	27	28	29	30
ⓧ 27																														
28																														
29																														
30																														
31																														
32	R	E	N	T	A	L			C	O	S	T	S		F	O	R		B	.		H	O	L	L	Y				
33																														
34	R	E	N	T	A	L		P	L	A	N			P	R	O	J	E	C	T	E	D		C	O	S	T			
35	-	-	-	-	-	-	-	-	-	-	-	-	-	-	-	-	-	-	-	-	-	-	-	-	-	-	-	-		
36																														
37	D	A	I	L	Y								$			6	7	0	.	0	0									
38	W	E	E	K	L	Y							$			6	8	2	.	0	0									
39	-	-	-	-	-	-	-	-	-	-	-	-	-	-	-	-	-	-	-	-	-	-	-	-	-	-	-			
40																														
41	T	H	E		B	E	S	T		P	L	A	N		I	S		D	A	I	L	Y								
42																														
43																														
44	G	R	O	U	P		N	U	M	B	E	R		I	N	C	O	R	R	E	C	T								
45																														
46																														
47																														
48																														

2. Add MINX to the dummy argument lists in modules 4 and 5, to the actual argument lists in CALL PLANS and CALL OUTPUT in module 1, and to the REAL statements in modules 1 and 5. In module 5 use

    ```
    PRINT 30,BEST,MINX
    ```

    and in format 30 replace A// with

    ```
    A,'WITH A PROJECTED COST OF $',F8.2//
    ```

3. Add MINX to the dummy argument list in module 4, to the actual argument list in CALL PLANS in module 1, and to the REAL statement in module 1. Add MINSUM to the REAL statement in module 1. Just after the REAL statement in module 1 insert

    ```
    MINSUM = 0.
    ```

    Just before the CONTINUE statement in module 1 insert

    ```
    MINSUM = MINSUM + MINX
    ```

    Just before the END statement in module 1 insert

    ```
        PRINT 40,MINSUM
    40  FORMAT(///'0THE SUM OF COST MINIMA IS $',F10.2)
    ```

4. Only changes in module 3 are required. Initialize NOG to 3; use (1,2,3,6) as the list in the computed GO TO statement (this new list facilitates the addition of subsequent changes up to five car groups); change 100, 200, and 300 to 1, 2, and 6, respectively; and add a new third case, accessed by statement number 3, to initialize data for the new group.

5. Module 8 remains unchanged. In *each* of modules 1–7 use the following statements for *global* names.

    ```
    CHARACTER   NAMEC*20,NAMEP(6)*10,BEST*10
    INTEGER     GROUP,MILES,DAYS,NOP
    REAL        DFC,CPM,WFC,PRICE,MPG,COST(6)
    COMMON      /NAMES/NAMEC,NAMEP,BEST
    COMMON      GROUP,MILES,DAYS,NOP,DFC,CPM,WFC,PRICE,MPG,COST
    ```

    Note that all character data reside in a named common block.
    In modules 6 and 7 replace TCDP and TCWP by COST(1) and COST(2), respectively.
    In each of the modules below, add the indicated type statements for local variables.

Module	Type Statement	
1	INTEGER NUM	
2	INTEGER DLIMIT	
3	INTEGER NOG	
4	INTEGER MINJ	} Actually, MINJ and MINX are
	REAL MINX	} localized to modules 4 and 8
7	INTEGER WEEKS	

    Remove all argument lists in modules 1–7, except for the actual argument list that calls MINVAL in module 4.

    This approach is slightly more efficient, perhaps more convenient, and forces us to think in terms of global and local names. However, it deemphasizes the needs/results of (or which variables get passed to and from) modules. Since we can't use assumed-size and adjustable array declarators, this approach is slightly less convenient for array size and character length updates. It's basically a matter of the programmer's preferences.

7. Replace the first two CALL statements in module 4 with

```
COST(1) = DFC*DAYS + CPM*MILES
WEEKS  = (DAYS − 1)/7 + 1
COST(2) = WFC*WEEKS + MILES*PRICE/MPG
```

This design is more code efficient but less explicitly modular from the standpoint of adding and/or deleting car plans. Those who prefer the approach in this exercise can claim with good reason that the small size of modules 6 and 7 is a case of *overmodularization*. Exercises 12 and 13 better justify plans as separate modules.

8. Modules 6 and 7 are naturals for function subprograms, since they each return a single value to the calling program.

Module 4 changes
Add DAILY and WEEKLY to the REAL statement
Replace the first two CALL statements with

```
COST(1) = DAILY(MILES,DAYS,DFC,CPM)
COST(2) = WEEKLY(MILES,DAYS,WFC,PRICE,MPG)
```

Module 6 changes
Replace the SUBROUTINE statement with

```
FUNCTION DAILY(MILES,DAYS,DFC,CPM)
```

Replace TCDP with DAILY in the REAL and assignment statements.

Module 7 changes
Replace the SUBROUTINE statement with

```
FUNCTION WEEKLY(MILES,DAYS,WFC,PRICE,MPG)
```

Replace TCWP with WEEKLY in the REAL and assignment statements.
We have a slight preference for the approach in this exercise, as it's more direct with respect to defining elements in COST.

9. (a)
```
        SUBROUTINE CARDAT(GROUP,PAR,DFC,CPM,WFC,PRICE,MPG)
        .
        .
        .
        REAL PAR(7,5)
        .
        .
        .
100     DFC := PAR(1,1)
        CPM = PAR(1,2)
        WFC = PAR(1,3)
        .
        .
200     DFC = PAR(2,1)
        CPM = PAR(2,2)
        WFC = PAR(2,3)
        .
        .
        .

        .
        .
        END
```

Module 1 must be changed by adding NOG to the INTEGER statement, PAR(7,5) to the REAL statement, and

    READ *,NOG,((PAR(I,J),J = 1,5),I = 1,NOG)

just before the READ statement.

    This approach simplifies data updates for the five car-group parameters. It's worthwhile if these values change often. How obsolete is our price per gallon of gasoline?

10. **(a)** *Module 1 changes*
    Add the type statement

        LOGICAL FLAG

    Change DO-loop 50 as follows:

```
      DO 50 J = 1,NUM
         FLAG = .TRUE.
         CALL INPUT (add FLAG to this list)
         IF (FLAG) THEN
            CALL CARDAT (as before)
            CALL PLANS (as before)
            CALL OUTPUT (as before)
         END IF
   50 CONTINUE
```

Module 2 changes
Add FLAG to the dummy argument list.
Add the type statement

        LOGICAL FLAG

Replace the STOP statement with

        FLAG = .FALSE.

  (b) Here we assume that the changes in part (a) have been made.

Module 1 changes
Same changes as part (a).
Modify the DO-loop body in part (a) as follows:

```
         IF (FLAG) THEN
            CALL CARDAT (add FLAG to this list)
            IF (FLAG) THEN
               CALL PLANS (as before)
               CALL OUTPUT (as before)
            END IF
         END IF
   50 CONTINUE
```

Module 3 changes
Same changes that were made in module 2.
Given the input data in Exercise 1(f), processing now continues through the third customer, rather than stopping after the second customer. Besides the output shown in the answer to Exercise 1(f), we get the following output for the third customer.

```
      F. DOMINO
      NUMBER OF DAYS IN RENTAL EXCEEDS   90
      TRY OUR LEASING PLAN . . .
      IT'S AN OFFER YOU CAN'T REFUSE
```

MODULE G

1. Look up those you're not sure of.

2. (a) Single entry and single exit point. (b) Independence. (c) Not too large. Control structures exactly satisfy (a), usually satisfy (c), and often satisfy (b).

3. Reference to a module represents an unrefined level of detail, whereas the module itself is a more refined level of detail. Also, modules such as subroutines facilitate top-down testing.

4. Structured programming exclusively utilizes the three basic control structures; each control structure, in turn, can be viewed as a module based on the three main characteristics of modules (as summarized in Exercise 2).

5. Execution of control structures is from top to bottom, except for the loop structure, which *cycles* from top to bottom.

Index